THE INTERNATIONAL MONETARY FUND
1945-1965

Volume III: Documents

THE INTERNATIONAL MONETARY FUND
1945-1965

Twenty Years of International Monetary Cooperation

VOLUME III: DOCUMENTS

Edited by
J. Keith Horsefield

INTERNATIONAL MONETARY FUND
WASHINGTON, D. C.
1969

PREFATORY NOTE

This volume comprises documents relating to the history of the International Monetary Fund, including some which preceded the drafting of the Articles of Agreement. Among the latter are early versions of the plans for a Clearing Union (the Keynes Plan) and a Stabilization Fund (the White Plan) which have not hitherto been published.

The published documents of the Fund here reproduced include all those which are cited in Volumes I and II of this history, except for publications issued at regular intervals.

J.K.H.

CONTENTS

PART I: BEFORE BRETTON WOODS

Page

THE KEYNES PLAN

(A) Proposals for an International Currency (or Clearing) Union [February 11, 1942] 3

(B) Proposals for an International Clearing Union (April 1943) 19

THE WHITE PLAN

(A) Preliminary Draft Proposal for a United Nations Stabilization Fund and a Bank for Reconstruction and Development of the United and Associated Nations (April 1942) 37

(B) Preliminary Draft Outline of a Proposal for an International Stabilization Fund of the United and Associated Nations (Revised July 10, 1943) 83

THE FRENCH PLAN

Suggestions Regarding International Monetary Relations (May 1943) 97

THE CANADIAN PLAN

Tentative Draft Proposals of Canadian Experts for an International Exchange Union (July 12, 1943) 103

PROFESSOR WILLIAMS' KEY-CURRENCY PLAN

(A) Extract from a Paper on "The Adequacy of Existing Currency Mechanisms Under Varying Circumstances" (December 28, 1936) 119

(B) Extract from "Currency Stabilization: The Keynes and White Plans" (July 1943) 124

THE JOINT STATEMENT

Joint Statement by Experts on the Establishment of an International Monetary Fund (April 1944) 128

U.S. COMMENTARY

Questions and Answers on the International Monetary Fund (June 10, 1944) .. 136

PART II: BASIC DOCUMENTS

Page

ARTICLES OF AGREEMENT

Articles of Agreement of the International Monetary Fund (July 22, 1944) 185

AGREEMENT WITH THE UNITED NATIONS

Agreement Between the United Nations and the International Monetary Fund (November 15, 1947) 215

SELECTED DECISIONS

Selected Decisions of the Executive Directors (As at December 31, 1965) 219

BY-LAWS AND RULES AND REGULATIONS

By-Laws of the International Monetary Fund (As at December 31, 1965) 278

Rules and Regulations of the International Monetary Fund (As at December 31, 1965) 287

PART III: FUND PRONOUNCEMENTS

USE OF THE FUND'S RESOURCES

Circular Letter to All Members (June 7, 1947) 307

Memorandum (June 7, 1947) 308

TRANSACTIONS IN GOLD AT PREMIUM PRICES

Statement Communicated to All Members (June 18, 1947) 310

ADEQUACY OF MONETARY RESERVES

The Adequacy of Monetary Reserves (October 1953) 311

INTERNATIONAL RESERVES AND LIQUIDITY

International Reserves and Liquidity: A Study by the Staff of the International Monetary Fund (September 16, 1958) 349

Page

ENLARGEMENT OF FUND RESOURCES THROUGH INCREASES IN QUOTAS

Enlargement of Fund Resources Through Increases in Quotas: Report by the Executive Directors to the Board of Governors of the International Monetary Fund (December 1958) 421

COMPENSATORY FINANCING: FIRST REPORT

Compensatory Financing of Export Fluctuations: A Report by the International Monetary Fund on Compensatory Financing of the Fluctuations in Exports of Primary Exporting Countries (February 1963) 442

INCREASES IN QUOTAS: FOURTH QUINQUENNIAL REVIEW

Increases in Quotas of Members—Fourth Quinquennial Review: Report of the Executive Directors to the Board of Governors (February 26, 1965) 458

PART IV: AFTER 1965

COMPENSATORY FINANCING: SECOND REPORT

Compensatory Financing of Export Fluctuations—Developments in the Fund's Facility: A Second Report by the International Monetary Fund on Compensatory Financing of the Fluctuations in Exports of Primary Producing Countries (September 1966) 469

PROPOSED AMENDMENT OF THE ARTICLES OF AGREEMENT

Establishment of a Facility Based on Special Drawing Rights in the International Monetary Fund and Modifications in the Rules and Practices of the Fund: A Report by the Executive Directors to the Board of Governors Proposing Amendment of the Articles of Agreement (April 1968) 497

PART V: PUBLICATIONS

PUBLICATIONS OF THE FUND 545

PART I

Before Bretton Woods

The Keynes Plan

The first draft of Lord Keynes' plan for a Clearing Union was circulated within the British Treasury on September 8, 1941. A fourth draft was given to Ministers on February 11, 1942, and this is reproduced in (A) below.

The final draft was issued by the British Government in April 1943 as a White Paper (Cmd. 6437); it is reproduced in (B) below.

(A) Proposals for an International Currency (or Clearing) Union
[February 11, 1942]

1. The proposal is to establish a Currency Union, here designated an *International Clearing Union*, based on international bank-money, called (let us say) bancor, fixed (but not unalterably) in terms of gold and accepted as the equivalent of gold by the British Commonwealth and the United States and all members of the Union for the purpose of settling international balances. The Central Banks of all member-States (and also of non-members) would keep accounts with the International Clearing Union through which they would be entitled to settle their exchange balances with one another at their par value as defined in terms of bancor. Countries having a favourable balance of payments with the rest of the world as a whole would find themselves in possession of a credit account with the Clearing Union, and those having an unfavourable balance would have a debit account. Measures would be necessary (see below) to prevent the piling up of credit and debit balances without limit, and the system would have failed in the long run if it did not possess sufficient capacity for self-equilibrium to prevent this.

2. The idea underlying such a Currency Union is simple, namely, to generalise the essential principle of banking, as it is exhibited within any closed system. This principle is the necessary equality of credits and debits, of assets and liabilities. If no credits can be removed outside the clearing system but only transferred within it, the Union *itself* can never be in difficulties. It can with safety make what advances it wishes to any of its members with the assurance that the proceeds can only be transferred to the clearing account of another member. Its problem is solely to see to it that its members keep the rules and that the advances made to each of them are prudent and advisable for the Union as a whole.

3. It is proposed that the Currency Union should be founded by the United States and the United Kingdom, which would be designated founder-States and given a special position. Their representatives, and those of other members, on the Governing Board of the Clearing Bank would be appointed by the Governments of the several member-States; the daily business and technical arrangements being carried out, as at present, by their Central Banks.

❖ ❖ ❖

4. The plan aims at the substitution of an expansionist, in place of a contractionist, pressure on world trade.

5. It would effect this by allowing to each member-State overdraft facilities of a defined amount, proportionate to the importance of its foreign trade and subject to certain regulative provisions. That is to say, each country is allowed a certain margin of resources and a certain interval of time within which to effect a balance in its economic relations with the rest of the world. These facilities are made possible by the nature of the system itself and do not involve particular indebtedness between one member-State and another. A country is in credit or debit with the Clearing Union as a whole. This means that the overdraft facilities, whilst a relief to some, are not a real burden to others. For credit balances, just like the importation of actual gold, represent those resources which a country voluntarily chooses to leave idle. They represent a potentiality of purchasing power, which it is entitled to use at any time. Meanwhile, the fact that the creditor country is not choosing to employ this purchasing power would not necessarily mean, as it does at present, that it is withdrawn from circulation and exerting a deflationary and contractionist pressure on the whole world including the creditor country itself. No country need be in possession of a credit balance unless it deliberately prefers to sell more than it buys (or lends); no country loses its liquidity or is prevented from employing its credit balance whenever it chooses to do so; and no country suffers injury (but on the contrary) by the fact that the balance, which it does not choose to employ for the time being, is not withdrawn from circulation. In short, the analogy with a national banking system is complete. No depositor in a local bank suffers because the balances, which he leaves idle, are employed to finance the business of someone else. Just as the development of national banking systems served to offset a deflationary pressure which would have prevented otherwise the development of modern industry, so by extending the same principle into the international field we may hope to offset the contractionist pressure which might otherwise overwhelm in social disorder and disappointment the good hopes of our modern world.

6. These facilities will be of particular importance as soon as the initial shortages of supply have been overcome. Many countries, including ourselves, will find a difficulty in paying for their imports, and will need time and resources before they can establish a readjustment. The efforts of each of these debtor countries to preserve its own equilibrium, by forcing its exports and by cutting off all imports which are not strictly necessary, will aggravate the problem of all the others. On the other hand, if each feels free from undue pressure, the volume of international exchange will be increased and everyone will find it easier to re-establish equilibrium without injury to the standard of life anywhere. The creditor countries will benefit, hardly less than the debtors, by being given an interval of *time* in which to adjust their economies, during which they can safely move at their own pace without the result of exercising deflationary pressure on the rest of the world, and, by repercussion, on themselves.

7. Now this can only be accomplished by the countries whoever they may turn out to be, which are for the time being in the creditor position, showing themselves ready to remain so without exercising a pressure towards contraction, pending the establishment of a new equilibrium. The fact that this costs them nothing deserves emphasising. The accumulation of a bancor credit, as compared with an accumulation of gold, does not curtail in the least their capacity or their inducement either to produce or to consume. The substitution of a credit mechanism for hoarding would have repeated

in the international field the same miracle already performed in the domestic field of turning a stone into bread.

8. There might be one or two other ways of effecting this temporarily or in part. For example, U.S.A. might redistribute her gold. Or there might be a number of bilateral arrangements having the effect of providing international overdrafts, as for example an agreement by the Federal Reserve Board to accumulate, if necessary, a large sterling balance at the Bank of England.

9. The objection to particular arrangements of this kind is that they are likely to be influenced by extraneous, political reasons and put individual countries into a position of particular obligation towards others; and also that the distribution of the assistance between different countries may not correspond to need and to the actual requirements as they ultimately develop. Moreover, for reasons already given, we are not likely to be specially eligible applicants for bounty of this kind. If, for example, the problem were to be met by a redistribution of America's gold, it is unlikely that we should get any of it, partly because we should have so lately received assistance under Lend-Lease, partly because the British Commonwealth are the largest producers of gold, which output would be regarded, rightly or wrongly, as ours at one remove.

10. It should be much easier, and surely more satisfactory both for them and for us, to persuade the United States to enter into a general and collective responsibility, applying to all countries alike, that a country finding itself in a creditor position *against the rest of the world as a whole* should enter into an arrangement not to allow this credit balance so long as it chooses to hold it, to exercise a contractionist pressure against world economy and, by repercussion, against the economy of the creditor country itself. This would give us, and all others, the great assistance of multilateral clearing, whereby (for example) we could offset favourable balances arising out of our exports to Europe against unfavourable balances due to the United States or South America or elsewhere. How, indeed, can we hope to afford to start up trade with Europe (which will be of vast importance to us) during the relief and reconstruction period on any other terms?

11. These advantages of the proposed International Clearing Union are so great that they surely overshadow most reasons of objection on lesser grounds.

12. If, indeed, we lack the productive capacity to maintain our standard of life, then a reduction in this standard is not avoidable. If our wage and price-levels are hopelessly wrong, a change in the rate of exchange is inevitable. But if we possess the productive capacity and the difficulty is the lack of markets as a result of restrictive policies throughout the world, then the remedy lies in expanding opportunities for export by removal of restrictive pressure. There is great force in the contention that, if active employment and ample purchasing power can be sustained in the main centres of world trade, the problem of surpluses and unwanted exports will largely disappear, even though under the most prosperous conditions there may remain some disturbances of trade and unforeseen situations requiring special remedies.

13. There is no obvious means of offering a right measure of inducement to the general expansion of international trade except by a broadly based international organisation.

❖ ❖ ❖

14. The arrangement by which the members of the Clearing Union start with substantial overdraft facilities in hand will be mainly useful, just as the possession of

any kind of reserve is useful, to allow time and method for necessary adjustments and a comfortable safeguard behind which the unforeseen and the unexpected can be faced with equanimity. Obviously, it does not by itself provide any long-term solution against a continuing disequilibrium, for in due course the more improvident and the more impecunious, left to themselves, would have run through their resources. But, if the purpose of the overdraft facilities is mainly to give time for adjustments, we have to make sure, so far as possible, that they *will* be made. We must have, therefore, some rules and some machinery to provide that equilibrium is restored.

15. Perhaps the most difficult question to determine is how much to decide by rule and how much to leave to discretion. If rule prevails, the liabilities attaching to membership of the system are definite, whilst the responsibilities of central management are reduced to a minimum. On the other hand, liabilities which would require the surrender by legislation of too much of the discretion, normally inherent in a Government, will not be readily undertaken by ourselves or by the United States. If discretion prevails, how far can the ultimate decision be left to the individual members and how far to the central management? If the individual members are too free, indiscipline may result and unwarrantable liberties be taken. But if it is to the central management that the discretions are given, too heavy a weight of responsibility may rest on it, and it may be assuming the exercise of powers which it has not the strength to implement. If rule prevails, the scheme can be made more water-tight theoretically. But if discretion prevails, it may work better in practice. All this is the typical problem of any supernational authority. An earlier draft of this proposal was criticised for leaning too much to the side of rule. In the provisions below the bias is in the other direction. For it may be better not to attempt to settle too much beforehand and to provide that the plan shall be reconsidered after an initial experimental period of (say) five years. Only by collective wisdom and discussion can the right compromise be reached between law and licence.

16. The proposal put forward below differs in one important respect from the pre-war system because it aims at putting some part of the responsibility for adjustment on the creditor country as well as on the debtor. This is an attempt to recover the advantages which were enjoyed in the nineteenth century when a favourable balance in favour of London and Paris, which were the main creditor centres, immediately produced an expansionist pressure in those markets, but which have been lost since New York succeeded to the position of main creditor, the effect of this change being aggravated by the breakdown of international borrowing credit and by the flight of loose funds from one depository to another. The object is that the creditor should not be allowed to remain entirely passive. For if he is, an intolerably heavy task may be laid on the debtor country, which is already for that very reason in the weaker position.

17. The detailed provisions proposed (the particular proportions, &c., suggested being merely tentative as a basis of discussion) are the following:—

(1) The two founder States will agree between themselves the initial values of their own currencies in terms of bancor and the value of bancor in terms of gold; and the initial values of the currencies of other members will be fixed on their joining the system in agreement with them. A member-State may not subsequently alter the value of its currency in terms of bancor without the permission of the Governing Board except under the conditions dealt with below; but during the first five years after the inception of the system the Governing Board shall give special consideration to appeals

for adjustments in the exchange-value of a national currency on the ground of unforeseen circumstances.

(2) The amount of the maximum debit balance allowed to any member-State shall be determined by reference to the amount of its foreign trade, and shall be designated its *quota*. There need be no limit to the amount of a credit balance.

The initial quotas might be fixed by reference to the sum of each country's exports and imports on the average of (say) the three pre-war years, being either equal or in a determined *lesser* proportion to this amount, a special assessment being substituted in cases where this formula would be, for any reason, inappropriate. Subsequently, after the elapse of the transitional period, the quotas might be revised annually in accordance with the actual volume of trade in the three preceding years.

(3) A charge of 1 per cent. per annum will be payable to the Reserve Fund of the Clearing Union on the average balance of a member-State, whether credit or debit, in excess of a quarter of its quota; and a further charge of 1 per cent. on the average balance, whether credit or debit, in excess of half its quota. Thus only a country which keeps as nearly as possible in a state of international balance on the average of the year will escape this contribution. These particular charges are, clearly, not essential to the scheme. But if they are found acceptable, they would be valuable inducements towards keeping a level balance, and a significant indication that the System looks on excessive credit balances with as critical an eye as on excessive debit balances, each being, indeed, the inevitable concomitant of the other. Any member-State in debit may, however, borrow from the balances of any member-State in credit on such terms as may be mutually agreed, by which means each would avoid these contributions.

(4)—(*a*) A member-State may not increase its debit balance by more than a *quarter* of its quota within a year without the permission of the Governing Board. If its debit balance has exceeded a quarter of its quota on the average of at least a year, it shall be entitled to reduce the value of its currency in terms of bancor, provided that the reduction shall not exceed 5 per cent. within a year without the permission of the Governing Board.

(*b*) As a condition of allowing a member-State to increase its debit balance in excess of a *half* of its quota, the Governing Board may require (i) a stated reduction in the value of the member's currency, if it deems that to be the suitable remedy, (ii) the control of outward capital transactions if not already in force, and (iii) the surrender of a suitable proportion of any separate gold reserve it may hold in reduction of its debit balance.

(*c*) If a member-State's debit balance has exceeded *three-quarters* of its quota on the average of at least a year [or is excessive, as measured by some formula laid down by the Governing Board, in relation to the total debit balances outstanding on the books of the Clearing Union], it may be asked by the Governing Board to take measures to improve its position and, in the event of its failing to reduce its debit balance below the figure in question within two years, the Governing Board may declare that it is in default and no longer entitled to draw against its account except with the permission of the Governing Board. Each member-State, on joining the system, shall agree to pay to the Clearing Union any payments due from it to a country in default towards the discharge of the latter's debit balance and to accept this arrangement in the event of falling into default itself. A member-State which resigns from the Clearing Union without making approved arrangements for the discharge of any debit balance shall also be treated as in default.

(5) A member-State whose credit balance has exceeded a *half* of its quota on the average of at least a year shall discuss with the Governing Board (but shall retain the ultimate decision in its own hands) what measures would be appropriate to restore the equilibrium of its international balances, including—

(*a*) measures for the expansion of domestic credit and domestic demand;

(*b*) the appreciation of its local currency in terms of bancor, or, alternatively, an increase in money-wages;

(*c*) the reduction of excessive tariffs and other discouragements against imports;

(*d*) international loans for the development of backward countries.

❖ ❖ ❖

18. The special protective expedients which were developed between the two wars were sometimes due to political, social or industrial reasons. But frequently they were nothing more than forced and undesired dodges to protect an unbalanced position of a country's overseas payments. The new system, by providing an automatic register of the size and whereabouts of the aggregate debtor and creditor positions respectively, will give a clear indication whether it is reasonable for a particular country to adopt special expedients as a temporary measure to assist in regaining equilibrium in its balance of payments, in spite of a general rule *not* to adopt them.

19. It is not proposed to incorporate any specific arrangements for such relaxations in the constitution of the Clearing Union itself. But the existence of the Clearing Union would make it possible for member States contracting Commercial Treaties to use their respective debit and credit positions with the Clearing Union as a test. Thus, the contracting parties, whilst agreeing to clauses in a Commercial Treaty forbidding, in general, the use of certain measures or expedients in their mutual trade relations, might make this agreement subject to special relaxations if the state of their respective clearing accounts satisfied an agreed criterion. For example, a Treaty might provide that, in the event of one of the contracting States having a debit balance with the Clearing Union exceeding a specified proportion of its quota on the average of a period and the other having a credit balance of a specified amount, the former should be free to resort to import quotas or to barter trade agreements or to higher import duties of a type which was not permitted under the Treaty in normal circumstances. It might even provide that such exceptions should only be allowed subject to the approval of the governing Board of the Clearing Union, and in that case the possible grounds for exceptional action might cover a wider field and other contingencies.

20. Apart from such temporary indulgence, the members of the Clearing Union should feel sufficiently free from anxiety to contemplate the ultimate removal of the more dislocating forms of protection and discrimination and expect the prohibition of some of the worst of them from the outset. In any case, members of the Currency Union would not allow or suffer among themselves any restrictions on the disposal of receipts arising out of current trade or "invisible" income. It might also be possible to obtain recognition of the general principle that commercial treaties between members of the Union should, subject to any necessary safeguards and exceptions, exclude—

(i) import restrictions, whether quantitative or in the form of "duty-quotas" (excluding, however, prohibitions genuinely designed to safeguard, *e.g.*, public health or morale or revenue collection);

(ii) barter arrangements;

(iii) export quotas and discriminatory export taxes;

(iv) export subsidies either furnished directly by the State or indirectly under schemes supported or encouraged by the State; and

(v) excessive tariffs.

21. Subsidies in favour of domestic producers for domestic consumption, with a countervailing levy when such subsidised goods are exported, would not be excluded. This is a necessary safety-valve which provides for protective expedients called for on political, social and industrial grounds. Such subsidies and tariffs would be a permitted way of giving purely domestic protection to an industry which for special reasons ought to be maintained for domestic purposes only. The question of preferences and of other relaxations from most-favoured-nation treatment, which would be of a normal and continuing character, does not fall within the scope of this paper, and must be settled on principles outside the sphere of the Clearing Union.

22. The above provisions might enable us to give some satisfaction to Mr. Cordell Hull over a wide field, since we should be accepting a non-discriminatory international system as the normal and desirable régime.

❖ ❖ ❖

23. It is a great advantage of the proposed Currency Union that it restores unfettered multilateral clearing between its members; so that no action is necessary, except where a country is out of balance with the system as a whole.

24. Compare this with the difficulties and complications of a large number of bilateral agreements. Compare, above all, the provisions by which a country, taking improper advantage of a payments agreement (for the system is, in fact, a *generalised* payments agreement) as Germany did before the war, is dealt with not by a single country (which may not be strong enough to act effectively in isolation or cannot afford to incur the diplomatic odium of isolated action) but by the system as a whole. If the argument is used that the Currency Union may have difficulty in disciplining a misbehaving country and in avoiding consequential loss, with what much greater force can we urge this objection against a multiplicity of separate bilateral payments agreements.

25. Thus we should not only return to the advantages of an international gold currency, but we might enjoy them more widely than was ever possible in practice with the old system under which at any given time only a minority of countries were actually working with free exchanges.

26. The advantages of multilateral clearing are of particular importance to London. It is not too much to say that this is an essential condition of the continued maintenance of London as the banking centre of the Sterling Area. Under a system of bilateral agreements it would seem inevitable that the sterling area, in the form in which it has been historically developed and as it has been understood and accepted by the Dominions and India, must fall to pieces.

27. In conditions of multilateral clearing everything would go on exactly as before without our having to ask anyone to accept special or onerous conditions. We should, in this respect, be back again in the best days of the gold standard. The traditional advantages of banking in London would be retained, precisely because London has

been built up on the basis of an international currency having universal validity. But if we try to make of the sterling area a compact currency union as against the rest of the world, we shall be putting a greater strain on arrangements, which have been essentially (even in time of war) *informal,* than they can be expected to bear.

28. It is possible to combine countries, some of which will be in a debtor and some in a creditor position, into a Currency Union which, substantially, covers the world. But, surely, it is impossible, unless they have a common banking and economic system also, to combine them into a Currency Union not with, but against, the world as a whole. If other members of the sterling area have a favourable balance against the world as a whole, they will lose nothing by keeping them in sterling, which will be interchangeable with bancor and hence with any other currency, until they have occasion to use them. But if the sterling area is turned into a Currency Union, the members in credit would have to make a forced and *non-liquid* loan of their favourable balances to the members in debit. Incidentally, they might find themselves involved in making between them an involuntary loan to London at the rate, perhaps, of £100,000,000 a year cumulative. They would have to impose import regulations and restraints on capital movements according as the area as a whole was in debit or credit, irrespective of their own positions. They would have to be bound by numerous bilateral agreements negotiated primarily (at least so they would believe) in the interests of London. The sterling resources of creditor Dominions might come to be represented by nothing but blocked balances in a number of doubtfully solvent countries with whom it suited *us* to trade. Moreover, it is difficult to see how the system could work without a pooling of gold reserves.

29. It is improbable that South Africa or India would accept such arrangements even if other Dominions were more complying. We should soon find ourselves, therefore, linked up only with those constituents which were running at a debit, apart from the Crown Colonies, which, perhaps, we could insist on keeping.

30. Is it not a delusion to suppose that the *de facto,* but somewhat flimsy and unsatisfactory, arrangements, which are carrying us through the war, on the basis that we do our best to find the other members of the area a limited amount of dollars provided that they lend us a very much larger sum in sterling, can be carried over into the peace and formalised into a working system based on a series of bilateral agreements with the rest of the world, accompanied by a strict control of capital movements outside the Area?

31. The sterling area, if we mean by this the system under which the members of the British Commonwealth do their international banking through London, grew up under conditions of freedom. It lives and breathes by being a voluntary system. It is only in that same atmosphere of the City of London as Liberty Hall dealing in a currency of general acceptability that we can expect to preserve it. The notion that a multilateral plan, based on an international standard, jeopardises the position of the Sterling Area must be based on a rigid and (one would think) politically impracticable version of the Sterling Area concept and not on its historical and actual significance. A multilateral plan would, therefore, be of great assistance in maintaining the position of London in relation both to the British Commonwealth and to many other countries which like our way of doing business and would give up most reluctantly the facilities we have given them.

❖ ❖ ❖

32. It may be convenient at this point to note in more detail the position contemplated for centres of international banking such as London, New York or Paris, and for currency groups within the membership of the Clearing Union covering more than one country, such as the existing sterling area or groups, like the Latin Union of former days, which may come into existence covering, for example, the countries of North America or those of South America or the groups now under active discussion covering Poland and Czechoslovakia or certain of the Balkan States.

33. The governing principles should be: first, that the Clearing Union is set up, not for the transaction of daily business between individual traders or banks, but for the clearing and settlement of the ultimate outstanding balances between Central Banks (and certain other super-national Institutions), such as would have been settled under the old gold standard by the shipment or the earmarking of gold, and should not trespass unnecessarily beyond this field; and, secondly, that its purpose is to increase *freedom* in international commerce and not to multiply interferences or compulsions.

34. Thus the fabric of international banking organisation, built up by long experience to satisfy practical needs, should be left as undisturbed as possible. Except as regards a provision, explained below, concerning the balances of Central Banks themselves, there should be no obstacle in the way of the existing practices of international banking except those which necessarily arise through measures which individual Central Banks may choose to adopt for the control of movements of capital.

35. Nor should it be necessary to interfere with the discretion of Central Banks which desire to maintain a special intimacy within a particular group of countries associated by geographical or political ties. There is no reason why such Central Banks should not be allowed a double position, both as members of the Clearing Union in their own right with their proper quota, and also as making use of another financial centre along traditional lines, as for example, Australia and India with London or certain American countries with New York. In this case their accounts with the Clearing Union would be in exactly the same position as the independent gold reserves which they now maintain, and they would have no occasion to modify in any way their present practices in the conduct of daily business.

36. There would be other cases, however, in which a dependency or a member of a federal union would merge its currency identity in that of a mother Central Bank, with a quota appropriate to the merged currency unit as a whole, and *not* enjoy a separate individual membership of the Clearing Union, as, for example, the French colonies, the Federated States of the American Union or of Australia, and possibly the British Crown Colonies.

37. At the same time there should be a general encouragement to Central Banks, which do not belong to a special geographical or political group, to keep their reserve balances with the Clearing Union and not with one another, except in the case of a specific loan from a member-State in credit with the Clearing Union to a member-State in debit. It should, therefore, be laid down that overseas balances may not be held in another country except with the approval of the Central Bank of that country; and, in order that sterling and dollars might not appear to compete with bancor for the purpose of Central Bank reserve balances, the Founder States might agree together that they would not accept the reserve balances of other Central Banks in excess of normal working balances except in the case of Banks definitely belonging to a Sterling Area or Dollar Area group.

❖ ❖ ❖

38. The position of gold would be left substantially unchanged. What, in the long run, the world may decide to do with gold is another matter. The establishment of an International Clearing Union does not require any significant or immediate change. Indeed, by providing an automatic means by which some part of the favourable balances of the creditor countries can be settled, the current gold production of the world and the remnant of gold reserves held outside the United States may yet have a useful part to play. Moreover, gold still possesses great psychological value which will not have been diminished by recent events; for the desire to possess a gold reserve against unforeseen contingencies is likely to remain. Gold also has the merit of providing, in point of form whatever the underlying realities may be, an uncontroversial standard of value for international purposes, for which it would not yet be easy to find a serviceable substitute.

39. It is conceived, therefore, that the international bank-money which we have designated *bancor* would be defined in terms of a weight of gold. Since the national currencies of the member-States would also be given a defined exchange value in terms of bancor, it follows that they would have a defined gold content which would also be their official buying price for gold above which they must not pay. Any Central Bank would be entitled to obtain a credit in terms of bancor by paying actual gold to the credit of its Clearing Account, thus securing a steady and ascertained purchaser for the output of the gold-producing countries and for countries holding a large reserve of gold.

40. Central Banks would be entitled to retain their separate gold reserves and ship gold to one another against a clearance between them in the books of the Clearing Union, provided they did not pay a price above parity; they could coin gold and put it into circulation, and, generally speaking, do what they liked with it.

41. One restriction only would be, for obvious reasons, essential. No Central Bank would be entitled to demand gold from the Clearing Union against its balance of bancor; for bancor would be available only for transfer to the Clearing Account of another Central Bank. Thus between gold and bancor itself there would be a one-way convertibility only, such as ruled frequently before the war with national currencies which were on what was usually called a "gold-exchange standard." This need not mean that the Clearing Union would only receive gold and never pay it out. If the Clearing Union found itself in possession of a stock of gold, the Governors of the Bank should have the discretion to distribute the surplus between all Central Banks possessing a credit balance with it, proportionately to such balances, in reduction of their amount.

42. The question has been raised whether these arrangements are compatible with the retention by individual member-States of a full gold standard with two-way convertibility, so that, for example, any foreign bank acquiring dollars through the Clearing Union could use them to obtain gold for export. It is not evident that a good purpose would be served by this. But if any member-State should prefer to maintain full convertibility for internal purposes, it could protect itself from any abuse of the system or inconvenient consequences by providing that gold could only be exported under licence.

43. The value of bancor in terms of gold should be fixed but not unalterably. The two founder States, the United States and the United Kingdom, acting in agreement, should have the power to change it. Clearly, they should exercise this power if the stocks of gold tendered to the bank were to be super-abundant for their legitimate

purposes. No object would be served by attempting further to peer into the future or to prophesy the ultimate policy of the founder States in this regard.

44. Changes in the value of the national currencies of member-States stand in a different category. For the real significance of such changes is to be found not in relation to gold itself but in relation to the values of national currencies amongst themselves. The general principles by which such changes should be governed have been discussed in a previous section. It would be undesirable, if it can be avoided, to lay down more precise rules in advance, since it is difficult to distinguish by means of a rigid formula the cases, in which a change in the rate of exchange will assist the restoration of equilibrium and is the right remedy, from those cases where some other type of measure is more appropriate.

45. It is widely held that control of capital movements, both inward and outward, should be a permanent feature of the post-war system—at least so far as we are concerned. If control is to be effective, it probably involves the *machinery* of exchange control for *all* transactions, even though a general open licence is given to all remittances in respect of current trade. But such control will be more difficult to work, especially in the absence of a postal censorship, by unilateral action than if movements of capital can be controlled *at both ends*. It would therefore be of great advantage if the United States and all other members of the Currency Union would adopt machinery similar to that which we have now gone a long way towards perfecting in this country; though this cannot be regarded as *essential* to the proposed Union.

46. This does not mean that the era of international investment should be brought to an end. On the contrary, the system contemplated should greatly facilitate the restoration of international credit for loan purposes in ways to be discussed below. The object, and it is a vital object, is to have a means of distinguishing—

(a) Between movements of floating funds and genuine new investment for developing the world's resources; and

(b) Between movements, which will help to maintain equilibrium, from surplus countries to deficiency countries and speculative movements or flights out of deficiency countries or from one surplus country to another.

47. There is no country which can, in future, safely allow the flight of funds for political reasons or to evade domestic taxation or in anticipation of the owner turning refugee. Equally, there is no country that can safely receive fugitive funds which cannot safely be used for fixed investment and might turn it into a surplus country against its will and contrary to the real facts.

48. The general principles of the control of capital movements need not be discussed here. It is evident that the existence of an International Clearing Union would make such control easier.

49. It has been suggested that so ambitious a proposal is open to criticism on the ground that it requires from the members of the Currency Union a greater surrender of their sovereign rights than they will readily concede.

50. But, in the present version of the plan, no greater surrender is required than in any commercial treaty—certainly not greater than in the binding undertakings

against discrimination which the United States is inviting us to make. The obligations will be entered into voluntarily and can be terminated on certain conditions by giving notice.

51. In the second place a greater readiness to accept super-national arrangements must be required in the post-war world than hitherto. The arrangements proposed could be described as a measure of Financial Disarmament. They are very mild in comparison with the measures of Military Disarmament, which it is to be hoped the world may be asked to accept.

52. Surely it is an advantage, rather than a disadvantage, of the scheme that it invites the member States and groups to abandon that licence to promote indiscipline, disorder and bad-neighbourliness which, to the general disadvantage, they have been free to exercise hitherto.

53. There is nothing here which we need be reluctant to accept ourselves or to ask of others. Or if there be anything such, let it be amended.

54. An International Currency Union might become the instrument and the support of international policies apart from those which it is its primary purpose to promote. The following suggestions are not a necessary part of the plan. But they are illustrations of the additional purposes of high importance and value which the Union, once established, might be able to serve:—

(1) The Union might set up a clearing account in favour of the international body charged with post-war Relief and Reconstruction. If necessary, it might supplement contributions received from other sources by granting overdraft facilities in favour of this body, this overdraft being discharged over a period of years out of the Reserve Fund of the Union, or, if necessary, out of a levy on credit clearing balances. By this means it is possible to avoid asking any country to assume a burdensome commitment for relief and reconstruction, since the resources would be provided in the first instance by those countries having credit Clearing Accounts for which they have no immediate use and are voluntarily leaving idle, and in the long run by those countries which have a chronic international surplus for which they have no beneficial employment.

(2) If the United States were to wish to effect a redistribution of gold reserves, the Clearing Union would provide a suitable channel for the purpose, the gold so re-distributed being credited (*e.g.*) to the account of the Relief and Reconstruction Authority.

(3) The Union might set up an account in favour of the Super-national policing body charged with the duty of preserving the peace and maintaining international order. If any country were to infringe its properly authorised orders, the policing body might be entitled to request the Governors of the Clearing Union to hold the Clearing Account of the Central Bank of the delinquent country to its order and permit no further transactions on the account except by its authority. This would provide an excellent machinery for enforcing a financial blockade.

(4) The Union might set up an account in favour of international bodies charged with the management of a Commodity Control, and might finance stocks of commodities held by such bodies, allowing them overdraft facilities on their accounts up to an

agreed maximum. By this means the financial problem of holding pools and "ever-normal granaries" would be satisfactorily solved.

(5) The Union might be closely linked up with the Board for International Investment. It might act on behalf of this Board and collect for them the annual service of their loans by automatically debiting the Clearing Account of the country concerned. The statistics of the Clearing Accounts of the Member States would give a reliable indication as to which countries were in a position to finance the Investment Board, with the advantage of shifting the whole system of clearing credits and debits nearer to equilibrium. This important question is the subject of a separate paper.

(6) There are various methods by which the Clearing Union could use its influence and its powers to maintain stability of prices and to control the Trade Cycle. If an International Economic Board is established, this Board and the Clearing Union might be expected to work in close collaboration to their mutual great advantage. If an International Investment or Development Corporation is also set up together with a scheme of Commodity Boards for the control of stocks of the staple raw materials, we might come to possess in these four Institutions a powerful means of combating the evils of the Trade Cycle, by exercising contractionist or expansionist influence on the system as a whole or on particular sections. This, again, is a large and important question which cannot be discussed adequately in this paper; and need not be examined at length in this place because it does not raise any important issues affecting the fundamental constitution of the proposed Union. It is mentioned here to complete the picture of the large purposes which the foundation of the Currency Union might be made to serve.

55. Our post-war currency and exchange system should be one which is capable of wide, indeed of universal, extension as further countries become ready for it. Nevertheless it would be an advantage if the proposed Union could be brought into existence by the United States and the United Kingdom as joint founder-States, covering the United States and its possessions and the members of the British Commonwealth. The position of Russia, which might be a third founder, if she can be a party to so capitalist-looking an institution, would need special consideration. Other members would then be brought in—some from the outset, some as soon as they had established an internal organisation capable of sustaining the obligations of membership. This approach would have the great advantage that the United States and the United Kingdom (the former in consultation with the Pan-American countries and the latter with the other members of the British Commonwealth) could settle the charter and the main details of the new body without being subjected to the delays and confused counsels of an international conference. It would also mean that considerable progress could be made irrespective of the nature of the European political settlement and before the conditions of adherence of the European members could be finally determined. Moreover, membership would be thus established as a privilege only open to those who conformed to certain general principles and standards of international economic conduct. The management and the effective voting power might inhere permanently in the founder-States.

56. In view of our experience and of our geographical and political position in relation to Europe, the United States and the British Commonwealth, we could justifiably ask that the head office should be situated in London with the Board of Managers meeting alternately here and in Washington.

57. Members of the Board would be appointed by the Governments of the member-States, each of which would have a vote in proportion to its quota. But there might be a provision, at any rate for the first five years, by which the British and American members when acting in agreement could outvote the rest of the Board.

58. There is no reason why the Central Banks of non-member States should not keep Credit Clearing Accounts with the Union; and indeed it would be advisable for them to do so for the conduct of their trade with member-States. But they would have no say in the management.

59. Members should be entitled to withdraw from the Union on a year's notice, subject to their making satisfactory arrangements to discharge any debit balance. They would not, of course, be able to employ any credit balance except by making transfers from it, either before or after their withdrawal, to the Clearing Accounts of other Central Banks. Similarly it should be within the power of the Governing Board to require the withdrawal of a member subject to the same notice.

60. The principles and governing rules of the Union should be the subject of general reconsideration after five years' experience, if a majority of the Governing Board desire it.

61. It would be of great advantage if the general principles of the International Clearing Union could be agreed beforehand, with a view to bringing it into operation at an early date after the termination of hostilities. Such a proposal presents, however, something of a dilemma. On the one hand, many countries, ourselves not least, will be in particular need of reserves of overseas resources in the period immediately after the war. On the other hand, goods will be in short supply and the prevention of inflationary international conditions of the first importance. The expansionist tendency of the proposed system, which is a leading recommendation of it as soon as peace-time output is restored and the productive capacity of the world is in running order, might easily be a danger in the early days of a sellers' market and a superabundance of demand over supply.

62. A reconciliation in detail of these divergent purposes is not easily found until we know more than is known at present about the means to be adopted to finance post-war relief and reconstruction and particularly as to the intentions of the United States regarding a temporary continuance of Lease-Lend arrangements for food and raw materials after the termination of hostilities. If these intentions are on liberal and comprehensive lines, it might be better for relief and Lend-Lease arrangements to take the place of the proposed quotas during the "relief" period of (say) two years. The immediate establishment of the Clearing Union would be compatible with provisional arrangements regarding the overdraft quotas which could take alternative forms according to the character of the other "relief" arrangements.

63. If the finance of relief is actually furnished through the Clearing Union, which has been suggested above as one possibility, and if that, combined with some continuance of lend-leasing by the United States, appears likely to provide the world with as much purchasing power as is desirable in the early days, the coming into force of the overdraft quotas might be postponed until the Founder Members are agreed that the need for them is impending. In this case credit clearing balances would be limited to the amount of gold delivered to the Union, and the overdraft facilities created by the Union in favour of the Relief Council, the International Investment Board or the Commodity Controls. Alternatively overdraft quotas might be allowed on a reduced

scale during the transitional period. At any rate, it might be proper to provide that countries in receipt of relief or Lend-Lease assistance should not have access at the same time to overdraft facilities, and that the latter should only become available when the former had come to an end.

64. If, on the other hand, relief and Lend-Lease facilities look like being inadequate from the outset, the overdraft quotas may be even more necessary at the outset than later on.

65. We must not be over-cautious. A rapid economic restoration may lighten the tasks of the diplomatists and the politicians in the resettlement of the world and the restoration of social order. In our case the possibility of exports sufficiently expanded to sustain our standard of life and our solvency is bound up with good and expanding markets. We cannot afford to wait too long for this and we must not allow excessive caution to condemn us to perdition. Unless the Union is a going concern, the problem of proper "timing" will be almost insoluble. It is sufficient at this stage to point out that the problem of timing must not be overlooked, but that the Union is capable of being used so as to aid rather than impede its solution.

❖ ❖ ❖

66. In most of its objectives and in many of its methods this paper is in fundamental accord with alternative proposals which have been or could be put forward. The special merits claimed for this particular version include the following:—

For ourselves.

(1) Our British problem of gaining enough receipts overseas to balance our import requirements is so acute that we can scarcely hope to solve it except through a scheme which—

(a) by a strong expansionist stimulus throughout the world provides willing markets for a largely expanded volume of our exports;

(b) offers facilities for the multilateral clearing of international payments, since we cannot afford to have any of the credit balances, which we may acquire overseas, to be blocked and unavailable as a set-off against our debit balances elsewhere;

(c) provides us with a margin, during the period before we can re-establish equilibrium, by an international scheme which does not require us to ask particular favours or accommodations from the United States but merely gives to us, and requires of us, the same facilities for the expansion of international trade and the maintenance of international equilibrium which all the countries will be asked to receive and to allow;

(d) affords us the possibility of subsequent rectifications of the rate of exchange against the rest of the world without the risk of competitive depreciations or of complaints by other countries in the event of the initial value of sterling proving to be higher than the level at which we can balance our overseas trade.

(2) A multilateral system preserves, to the full extent compatible with the control of capital movements, the traditional freedom of London as a financial centre. Above all it allows the historical continuity of the sterling area in the same form and with the same absence of restraint as heretofore. For it is evident that any system of

numerous bilateral agreements would put in great jeopardy not only the sterling area but the whole position of London as an international centre.

For the United States and the World at large.

(1) It provides a general framework by the aid of which *all* countries can hope to rehabilitate their currencies.

(2) It offers a criterion by the help of which we can satisfy American aspirations, which we ourselves share with Mr. Hull and Mr. Sumner Welles, for the greater freedom of international trade supported by firm undertakings.

(3) It is a plan which can be used to further such general world purposes as—

(*a*) post-war relief and reconstruction;

(*b*) international T.V.A.;

(*c*) the finance of commodity agreements;

(*d*) the preservation of peace;

(*e*) the control of the Trade Cycle and the stabilisation of prices; and, generally,

(*f*) the maintenance of active employment everywhere.

(4) It is capable of arousing enthusiasm because it makes a beginning at the future economic ordering of the world between nations and "the winning of the peace," and might help to create the conditions and the atmosphere in which much else would be made easier.

(B) Proposals for an International Clearing Union [1]
(April 1943)

PREFACE

Immediately after the war all countries who have been engaged will be concerned with the pressure of relief and urgent reconstruction. The transition out of this into the normal world of the future cannot be wisely effected unless we know into what we are moving. It is therefore not too soon to consider what is to come after. In the field of national activity occupied by production, trade and finance, both the nature of the problem and the experience of the period between the wars suggest four main lines of approach:

1. The mechanism of currency and exchange;

2. The framework of a commercial policy regulating the conditions for the exchange of goods, tariffs, preferences, subsidies, import regulations and the like;

3. The orderly conduct of production, distribution and price of primary products so as to protect both producers and consumers from the loss and risk for which the extravagant fluctuations of market conditions have been responsible in recent times;

4. Investment aid, both medium and long term, for the countries whose economic development needs assistance from outside.

If the principles of these measures and the form of the institutions to give effect to them can be settled in advance, in order that they may be in operation when the need arises, it is possible that taken together they may help the world to control the ebb and flow of the tides of economic activity which have, in the past, destroyed security of livelihood and endangered international peace.

All these matters will need to be handled in due course. The proposal that follows relates only to the mechanism of currency and exchange in international trading. It appears on the whole convenient to give it priority, because some general conclusions have to be reached under this head before much progress can be made with the other topics.

In preparing these proposals care has been taken to regard certain conditions, which the groundwork of an international economic system to be set up after the war should satisfy, if it is to prove durable:

(i) There should be the least possible interference with internal national policies, and the plan should not wander from the international *terrain*. Since such policies may have important repercussions on international relations, they cannot be left out of account. Nevertheless in the realm of internal policy the authority of the Governing Board of the proposed Institution should be limited to recommendations, or at the most to imposing conditions for the more extended enjoyment of the facilities which the Institution offers.

(ii) The technique of the plan must be capable of application, irrespective of the type and principle of government and economic policy existing in the prospective member States.

---

[1] Reproduced by permission of the Controller, Her Britannic Majesty's Stationery Office.

(iii) The management of the Institution must be genuinely international without preponderant power of veto or enforcement to any country or group; and the rights and privileges of the smaller countries must be safeguarded.

(iv) Some qualification of the right to act at pleasure is required by any agreement or treaty between nations. But in order that such arrangements may be fully voluntary so long as they last and terminable when they have become irksome, provision must be made for voiding the obligation at due notice. If many member States were to take advantage of this, the plan would have broken down. But if they are free to escape from its provisions if necessary they may be the more willing to go on accepting them.

(v) The plan must operate not only to the general advantage but also to the individual advantage of each of the participants, and must not require a special economic or financial sacrifice from certain countries. No participant must be asked to do or offer anything which is not to his own true long-term interest.

It must be emphasised that it is not for the Clearing Union to assume the burden of long term lending which is the proper task of some other institution. It is also necessary for it to have means of restraining improvident borrowers. But the Clearing Union must also seek to discourage creditor countries from leaving unused large liquid balances which ought to be devoted to some positive purpose. For excessive credit balances necessarily create excessive debit balances for some other party. In recognising that the creditor as well as the debtor may be responsible for a want of balance, the proposed institution would be breaking new ground.

I.—THE OBJECTS OF THE PLAN

About the primary objects of an improved system of International Currency there is, to-day, a wide measure of agreement:—

(*a*) We need an instrument of international currency having general acceptability between nations, so that blocked balances and bilateral clearings are unnecessary; that is to say, an instrument of currency used by each nation in its transactions with other nations, operating through whatever national organ, such as a Treasury or a Central Bank, is most appropriate, private individuals, businesses and banks other than Central Banks, each continuing to use their own national currency as heretofore.

(*b*) We need an orderly and agreed method of determining the relative exchange values of national currency units, so that unilateral action and competitive exchange depreciations are prevented.

(*c*) We need a *quantum* of international currency, which is neither determined in an unpredictable and irrelevant manner as, for example, by the technical progress of the gold industry, nor subject to large variations depending on the gold reserve policies of individual countries; but is governed by the actual current requirements of world commerce, and is also capable of deliberate expansion and contraction to offset deflationary and inflationary tendencies in effective world demand.

(*d*) We need a system possessed of an internal stabilising mechanism, by which pressure is exercised on any country whose balance of payments with the rest of the world is departing from equilibrium *in either direction,* so as to prevent movements which must create for its neighbours an equal but opposite want of balance.

(*e*) We need an agreed plan for starting off every country after the war with a stock of reserves appropriate to its importance in world commerce, so that without due anxiety it can set its house in order during the transitional period to full peacetime conditions.

(f) We need a central institution, of a purely technical and non-political character, to aid and support other international institutions concerned with the planning and regulation of the world's economic life.

(g) More generally, we need a means of reassurance to a troubled world, by which any country whose own affairs are conducted with due prudence is relieved of anxiety for causes which are not of its own making, concerning its ability to meet its international liabilities; and which will, therefore, make unnecessary those methods of restriction and discrimination which countries have adopted hitherto, not on their merits, but as measures of self-protection from disruptive outside forces.

2. There is also a growing measure of agreement about the general character of any solution of the problem likely to be successful. The particular proposals set forth below lay no claim to originality. They are an attempt to reduce to practical shape certain general ideas belonging to the contemporary climate of economic opinion, which have been given publicity in recent months by writers of several different nationalities. It is difficult to see how any plan can be successful which does not use these general ideas, which are born of the spirit of the age. The actual details put forward below are offered, with no dogmatic intention, as the basis of discussion for criticism and improvement. For we cannot make progress without embodying the general underlying idea in a frame of actual working, which will bring out the practical and political difficulties to be faced and met if the breath of life is to inform it.

3. In one respect this particular plan will be found to be more ambitious and yet, at the same time, perhaps more workable than some of the variant versions of the same basic idea, in that it is fully international, being based on one general agreement and not on a multiplicity of bilateral arrangements. Doubtless proposals might be made by which bilateral arrangements could be fitted together so as to obtain some of the advantages of a multilateral scheme. But there will be many difficulties attendant on such adjustments. It may be doubted whether a comprehensive scheme will ever in fact be worked out, unless it can come into existence through a single act of creation made possible by the unity of purpose and energy of hope for better things to come, springing from the victory of the United Nations, when they have attained it, over immediate evil. That these proposals are ambitious is claimed, therefore to be not a drawback but an advantage.

4. The proposal is to establish a Currency Union, here designated an *International Clearing Union*, based on international bank-money, called (let us say) *bancor*, fixed (but not unalterably) in terms of gold and accepted as the equivalent of gold by the British Commonwealth and the United States and all the other members of the Union for the purpose of settling international balances. The Central Banks of all member States (and also of non-members) would keep accounts with the International Clearing Union through which they would be entitled to settle their exchange balances with one another at their par value as defined in terms of bancor. Countries having a favourable balance of payments with the rest of the world as a whole would find themselves in possession of a credit account with the Clearing Union, and those having an unfavourable balance would have a debit account. Measures would be necessary (see below) to prevent the piling up of credit and debit balances without limit, and the system would have failed in the long run if it did not possess sufficient capacity for self-equilibrium to secure this.

5. The idea underlying such a Union is simple, namely, to generalise the essential principle of banking as it is exhibited within any closed system. This principle is the necessary equality of credits and debits. If no credits can be removed outside the clearing system, but only transferred within it, the Union can never be in any difficulty as regards the honouring of cheques drawn upon it. It can make what advances it wishes to any of its members with the assurance that the proceeds can only be transferred to the clearing account of another member. Its sole task is to see to it that its members keep the rules and that the advances made to each of them are prudent and advisable for the Union as a whole.

II.—THE PROVISIONS OF THE PLAN

6. The provisions proposed (the particular proportions and other details suggested being tentative as a basis of discussion) are the following:—

(1) All the United Nations will be invited to become original members of the International Clearing Union. Other States may be invited to join subsequently. If ex-enemy States are invited to join, special conditions may be applied to them.

(2) The Governing Board of the Clearing Union shall be appointed by the Governments of the several member States (as provided in (12) below); the daily business with the Union and the technical arrangements being carried out through their Central Banks or other appropriate authorities.

(3) The member States will agree between themselves the initial values of their own currencies in terms of bancor. A member State may not subsequently alter the value of its currency in terms of bancor without the permission of the Governing Board except under the conditions stated below; but during the first five years after the inception of the system the Governing Board shall give special consideration to appeals for an adjustment in the exchange value of a national currency unit on the ground of unforeseen circumstances.

(4) The value of bancor in terms of gold shall be fixed by the Governing Board. Member States shall not purchase or acquire gold, directly or indirectly, at a price in terms of their national currencies in excess of the parity which corresponds to the value of their currency in terms of bancor and to the value of bancor in terms of gold. Their sales and purchases of gold shall not be otherwise restricted.

(5) Each member State shall have assigned to it a *quota*, which shall determine the measure of its responsibility in the management of the Union and of its right to enjoy the credit facilities provided by the Union. The initial quotas might be fixed by reference to the sum of each country's exports and imports on the average of (say) the three pre-war years, and might be (say) 75 per cent. of this amount, a special assessment being substituted in cases (of which there might be several) where this formula would be, for any reason, inappropriate. Subsequently, after the elapse of the transitional period, the quotas should be revised annually in accordance with the running average of each country's actual volume of trade in the three preceding years, rising to a five-year average when figures for five post-war years are available. The determination of a country's quota primarily by reference to the value of its foreign trade seems to offer the criterion most relevant to a plan which is chiefly concerned with the regulation of the foreign exchanges and of a country's international trade balance. It is, however, a matter for discussion whether the formula for fixing quotas should also take account of other factors.

(6) Member States shall agree to accept payment of currency balances, due to them from other members, by a transfer of bancor to their credit in the books of the Clearing Union. They shall be entitled, subject to the conditions set forth below, to make transfers of bancor to other members which have the effect of overdrawing their own accounts with the Union, provided that the maximum debit balances thus created do not exceed their quota. The Clearing Union may, at its discretion, charge a small commission or transfer fee in respect of transactions in its books for the purpose of meeting its current expenses or any other outgoings approved by the Governing Board.

(7) A member State shall pay to the Reserve Fund of the Clearing Union a charge of 1 per cent. per annum on the amount of its average balance in bancor, whether it is a credit or a debit balance, in excess of a quarter of its quota; and a further charge of 1 per cent. on its average balance, whether credit or debit, in excess of a half of its quota. Thus, only a country which keeps as nearly as possible in a state of international balance on the average of the year will escape this contribution. These charges are not absolutely essential to the scheme. But if they are found acceptable, they would be valuable and important inducements towards keeping a level balance, and a significant indication that the system looks on excessive credit balances with as critical an eye as on excessive debit balances, each being, indeed, the inevitable concomitant of the other. Any member State in debit may, after consultation with the Governing Board, borrow bancor from the balances of any member State in credit on such terms as may be mutually agreed, by which means each would avoid these contributions. The Governing Board may, at its discretion, remit the charges on credit balances, and increase correspondingly those on debit balances, if in its opinion unduly expansionist conditions are impending in the world economy.

(8)—(a) A member State may not increase its debit balance by more than a *quarter* of its quota within a year without the permission of the Governing Board. If its debit balance has exceeded a quarter of its quota on the average of at least two years, it shall be entitled to reduce the value of its currency in terms of bancor provided that the reduction shall not exceed 5 per cent. without the consent of the Governing Board; but it shall not be entitled to repeat this procedure unless the Board is satisfied that this procedure is appropriate.

(b) The Governing Board may require from a member State having a debit balance reaching a *half* of its quota the deposit of suitable collateral against its debit balance. Such collateral shall, at the discretion of the Governing Board, take the form of gold, foreign or domestic currency or Government bonds, within the capacity of the member State. As a condition of allowing a member State to increase its debit balance to a figure in excess of a half of its quota, the Governing Board may require all or any of the following measures:—

(i) a stated reduction in the value of the member's currency, if it deems that to be the suitable remedy;

(ii) the control of outward capital transactions if not already in force; and

(iii) the outright surrender of a suitable proportion of any separate gold or other liquid reserve in reduction of its debit balance.

Furthermore, the Governing Board may recommend to the Government of the member State any internal measures affecting its domestic economy which may appear to be appropriate to restore the equilibrium of its international balance.

(c) If a member State's debit balance has exceeded *three-quarters* of its quota on the average of at least a year and is excessive in the opinion of the Governing Board in relation to the total debit balances outstanding on the books of the Clearing Union, or is increasing at an excessive rate, it may, in addition, be asked by the Governing Board to take measures to improve its position, and, in the event of its failing to reduce its debit balance accordingly within two years, the Governing Board may declare that it is in default and no longer entitled to draw against its account except with the permission of the Governing Board.

(d) Each member State, on joining the system, shall agree to pay to the Clearing Union any payments due from it to a country in default towards the discharge of the latter's debit balance and to accept this arrangement in the event of falling into default itself. A member State which resigns from the Clearing Union without making approved arrangements for the discharge of any debit balance shall also be treated as in default.

(9) A member State whose credit balance has exceeded a *half* of its quota on the average of at least a year shall discuss with the Governing Board (but shall retain the ultimate decision in its own hands) what measures would be appropriate to restore the equilibrium of its international balances, including—

(a) Measures for the expansion of domestic credit and domestic demand.

(b) The appreciation of its local currency in terms of bancor, or, alternatively, the encouragement of an increase in money rates of earnings;

(c) The reduction of tariffs and other discouragements against imports.

(d) International development loans.

(10) A member State shall be entitled to obtain a credit balance in terms of bancor by paying in gold to the Clearing Union for the credit of its clearing account. But no one is entitled to demand gold from the Union against a balance of bancor, since such balance is available only for transfer to another clearing account. The Governing Board of the Union shall, however, have the discretion to distribute any gold in the possession of the Union between the members possessing credit balances in excess of a specified proportion of their quotas, proportionately to such balances, in reduction of their amount in excess of that proportion.

(11) The monetary reserves of a member State, viz., the Central Bank or other bank or Treasury deposits in excess of a working balance, shall not be held in another country except with the approval of the monetary authorities of that country.

(12) The Governing Board shall be appointed by the Governments of the member States, those with the larger quotas being entitled to appoint a member individually, and those with smaller quotas appointing in convenient political or geographical groups, so that the members would not exceed (say) 12 or 15 in number. Each representative on the Governing Board shall have a vote in proportion to the quotas of the State (or States) appointing him, except that on a proposal to increase a particular quota, a representative's voting power shall be measured by the quotas of the member States appointing him, increased by their credit balance or decreased by their debit balance, averaged in each case over the past two years. Each member State, which is not individually represented on the Governing Board, shall be entitled to appoint a permanent delegate to the Union to maintain contact with the Board and to act as *liaison* for daily business and for the exchange of information with the Executive of the Union. Such delegate shall be entitled to be present at the Governing Board when any matter is under consideration which specially concerns the State he represents, and to take part in the discussion.

(13) The Governing Board shall be entitled to reduce the quotas of members, all in the same specified proportion, if it seems necessary to correct in this manner an excess of world purchasing power. In that event, the provisions of 6 (8) shall be held to apply to the quotas as so reduced, provided that no member shall be required to reduce his actual overdraft at the date of the change, or be entitled by reason of this reduction to alter the value of his currency under 6 (8) (a), except after the expiry of two years. If the Governing Board subsequently desires to correct a potential deficiency of world purchasing power, it shall be entitled to restore the general level of quotas towards the original level.

(14) The Governing Board shall be entitled to ask and receive from each member State any relevant statistical or other information, including a full disclosure of gold, external credit and debit balances and other external assets and liabilities, both public and private. So far as circumstances permit, it will be desirable that the member States shall consult with the Governing Board on important matters of policy likely to affect substantially their bancor balances or their financial relations with other members.

(15) Executives offices of the Union shall be situated in London and New York, with the Governing Board meeting alternately in London and Washington.

(16) Members shall be entitled to withdraw from the Union on a year's notice, subject to their making satisfactory arrangements to discharge any debit balance. They would not, of course, be able to employ any credit balance except by making transfers from it, either before or after their withdrawal, to the Clearing Accounts of other Central Banks. Similarly, it should be within the power of the Governing Board to require the withdrawal of a member, subject to the same notice, if the latter is in breach of agreements relating to the Clearing Union.

(17) The Central Banks of non-member States would be allowed to keep credit clearing accounts with the Union; and, indeed, it would be advisable for them to do so for the conduct of their trade with member States. But they would have no right to overdrafts and no say in the management.

(18) The Governing Board shall make an annual Report and shall convene an annual Assembly at which every member State shall be entitled to be represented individually and to move proposals. The principles and governing rules of the Union shall be the subject of reconsideration after five years' experience, if a majority of the Assembly desire it.

III.—WHAT LIABILITIES OUGHT THE PLAN TO PLACE ON CREDITOR COUNTRIES?

7. It is not contemplated that either the debit or the credit balance of an individual country ought to exceed a certain maximum—let us say, its *quota*. In the case of debit balances this maximum has been made a rigid one, and, indeed, counter-measures are called for long before the maximum is reached. In the case of credit balances no rigid maximum has been proposed. For the appropriate provision might be to require the eventual cancellation or compulsory investment of persistent bancor credit balances accumulating in excess of a member's quota; and, however desirable this may be in principle, it might be felt to impose on creditor countries a heavier burden than they can be asked to accept before having had experience of the benefit to them of the working of the plan as a whole. If, on the other hand, the limitation were to take the form of the creditor country not being required to accept bancor in excess of a pre-

scribed figure, this might impair the general acceptability of bancor, whilst at the same time conferring no real benefit on the creditor country itself. For, if it chose to avail itself of the limitation, it must either restrict its exports or be driven back on some form of bilateral payments agreements outside the Clearing Union, thus substituting a less acceptable asset for bancor balances which are based on the collective credit of all the member States and are available for payments to any of them, or attempt the probably temporary expedient of refusing to trade except on a gold basis.

8. The absence of a rigid maximum to credit balances does not impose on any member State, as might be supposed at first sight, an unlimited liability outside its own control. The liability of an individual member is determined, not by the quotas of the other members, but by its own policy in controlling its favourable balance of payments. The existence of the Clearing Union does not deprive a member State of any of the facilities which it now possesses for receiving payment for its exports. In the absence of the Clearing Union a creditor country can employ the proceeds of its exports to buy goods or to buy investments, or to make temporary advances and to hold temporary overseas balances, or to buy gold in the market. All these facilities will remain at its disposal. The difference is that in the absence of the Clearing Union, more or less automatic factors come into play to restrict the volume of its exports after the above means of receiving payment for them have been exhausted. Certain countries become unable to buy and, in addition to this, there is an automatic tendency towards a general slump in international trade and, as a result, a reduction in the exports of the creditor country. Thus, the effect of the Clearing Union is to give the creditor country a choice between voluntarily curtailing its exports to the same extent that they would have been involuntarily curtailed in the absence of the Clearing Union, or, alternatively, of allowing its exports to continue and accumulating the excess receipts in the form of bancor balances for the time being. Unless the removal of a factor causing the involuntary reduction of exports is reckoned a disadvantage, a creditor country incurs no burden but is, on the contrary, relieved, by being offered the additional option of receiving payment for its exports through the accumulation of a bancor balance.

9. If, therefore, a member State asks what governs the maximum liability which it incurs by entering the system, the answer is that this lies entirely within its own control. No more is asked of it than that it should hold in bancor such surplus of its favourable balance of payments as it does not itself choose to employ in any other way, and only for so long as it does not so choose.

IV.—SOME ADVANTAGES OF THE PLAN

10. The plan aims at the substitution of an expansionist, in place of a contractionist, pressure on world trade.

11. It effects this by allowing to each member State overdraft facilities of a defined amount. Thus each country is allowed a certain margin of resources and a certain interval of time within which to effect a balance in its economic relations with the rest of the world. These facilities are made possible by the constitution of the system itself and do not involve particular indebtedness between one member State and another. A country is in credit or debit with the Clearing Union as a whole. This means that the overdraft facilities, whilst a relief to some, are not a real burden to others. For the accumulation of a credit balance with the Clearing Union would resemble the importation of gold in signifying that the country holding it is abstaining voluntarily from the

immediate use of purchasing power. But it would not involve, as would the importation of gold, the withdrawal of this purchasing power from circulation or the exercise of a deflationary and contractionist pressure on the whole world, including in the end the creditor country itself. Under the proposed plan, therefore, no country suffers injury (but on the contrary) by the fact that the command over resources, which it does not itself choose to employ for the time being, is not withdrawn from use. The accumulation of bancor credit does not curtail in the least its capacity or inducement either to produce or to consume.

12. In short, the analogy with a national banking system is complete. No depositor in a local bank suffers because the balances, which he leaves idle, are employed to finance the business of someone else. Just as the development of national banking systems served to offset a deflationary pressure which would have prevented otherwise the development of modern industry, so by extending the same principle into the international field we may hope to offset the contractionist pressure which might otherwise overwhelm in social disorder and disappointment the good hopes of our modern world. The substitution of a credit mechanism in place of hoarding would have repeated in the international field the same miracle, already performed in the domestic field, of turning a stone into bread.

13. There might be other ways of effecting the same objects temporarily or in part. For example, the United States might redistribute her gold. Or there might be a number of bilateral arrangements having the effect of providing international overdrafts, as, for example, an agreement by the Federal Reserve Board to accumulate, if necessary, a large sterling balance at the Bank of England, accompanied by a great number of similar bilateral arrangements, amounting to some hundreds altogether, between these and all the other banks in the world. The objection to particular arrangements of this kind, in addition to their greater complexity, is that they are likely to be influenced by extraneous, political reasons; that they put individual countries in a position of particular obligation towards others; and that the distribution of the assistance between different countries may not correspond to need and to the real requirements, which are extremely difficult to foresee.

14. It should be much easier, and surely more satisfactory for all of us, to enter into a general and collective responsibility, applying to all countries alike, that a country finding itself in a creditor position *against the rest of the world as a whole* should enter into an arrangement not to allow this credit balance to exercise a contractionist pressure against world economy and, by repercussion, against the economy of the creditor country itself. This would give everyone the great assistance of multilateral clearing, whereby (for example) Great Britain could offset favourable balances arising out of her exports to Europe against unfavourable balances due to the United States or South America or elsewhere. How, indeed, can any country hope to start up trade with Europe during the relief and reconstruction period on any other terms?

15. The facilities offered will be of particular importance in the transitional period after the war, as soon as the initial shortages of supply have been overcome. Many countries will find a difficulty in paying for their imports, and will need time and resources before they can establish a readjustment. The efforts of each of these debtor countries to preserve its own equilibrium, by forcing its exports and by cutting off all imports which are not strictly necessary, will aggravate the problems of all the others. On the other hand, if each feels free from undue pressure, the volume of international exchange will be increased and everyone will find it easier to re-establish equilibrium

without injury to the standard of life anywhere. The creditor countries will benefit, hardly less than the debtors, by being given an interval of *time* in which to adjust their economies, during which they can safely move at their own pace without the result of exercising deflationary pressure on the rest of the world, and, by repercussion, on themselves.

16. It must, however, be emphasised that the provision by which the members of the Clearing Union start with substantial overdraft facilities in hand will be mainly useful, just as the possession of any kind of reserve is useful, to allow time and method for necessary adjustments and a comfortable safeguard behind which the unforeseen and the unexpected can be faced with equanimity. Obviously, it does not by itself provide any long-term solution against a continuing disequilibrium, for in due course the more improvident and the more impecunious, left to themselves, would have run through their resources. But, if the purpose of the overdraft facilities is mainly to give time for adjustments, we have to make sure, so far as possible, that they *will* be made. We must have, therefore, some rules and some machinery to secure that equilibrium is restored. A tentative attempt to provide for this has been made above. Perhaps it might be strengthened and improved.

17. The provisions suggested differ in one important respect from the pre-war system because they aim at putting some part of the responsibility for adjustment on the creditor country as well as on the debtor. This is an attempt to recover one of the advantages which were enjoyed in the nineteenth century, when a flow of gold due to a favourable balance in favour of London and Paris, which were then the main creditor centres, immediately produced an expansionist pressure and increased foreign lending in those markets, but which has been lost since New York succeeded to the position of main creditor, as a result of gold movements failing in their effect, of the breakdown of international borrowing and of the frequent flight of loose funds from one depository to another. The object is that the creditor should not be allowed to remain entirely passive. For if he is, an intolerably heavy task may be laid on the debtor country, which is already for that very reason in the weaker position.

18. If, indeed, a country lacks the productive capacity to maintain its standard of life, then a reduction in this standard is not avoidable. If its wage and price levels in terms of money are out of line with those elsewhere, a change in the rate of its foreign exchange is inevitable. But if, possessing the productive capacity, it lacks markets because of restrictive policies throughout the world, then the remedy lies in expanding its opportunities for export by removal of the restrictive pressure. We are too ready to-day to assume the inevitability of unbalanced trade positions, thus making the opposite error to those who assumed the tendency of exports and imports to equality. It used to be supposed, without sufficient reason, that effective demand is always properly adjusted throughout the world; we now tend to assume, equally without sufficient reason, that it never can be. On the contrary, there is great force in the contention that, if active employment and ample purchasing power can be sustained in the main centres of the world trade, the problem of surpluses and unwanted exports will largely disappear, even though, under the most prosperous conditions, there may remain some disturbances of trade and unforeseen situations requiring special remedies.

V.—THE DAILY MANAGEMENT OF THE EXCHANGES UNDER THE PLAN

19. The Clearing Union restores unfettered multilateral clearing between its members. Compare this with the difficulties and complications of a large number of bilateral

agreements. Compare, above all, the provisions by which a country, taking improper advantage of a payments agreement (for the system is, in fact, a *generalised* payments agreement), as Germany did before the war, is dealt with not by a single country (which may not be strong enough to act effectively in isolation or cannot afford to incur the diplomatic odium of isolated action), but by the system as a whole. If the argument is used that the Clearing Union may have difficulty in disciplining a misbehaving country and in avoiding consequential loss, with what much greater force can we urge this objection against a multiplicity of separate bilateral payments agreements.

20. Thus we should not only obtain the advantages, without the disadvantages, of an international gold currency, but we might enjoy these advantages more widely than was ever possible in practice with the old system under which at any given time only a minority of countries were actually working with free exchanges. In conditions of multilateral clearing, exchange dealings would be carried on as freely as in the best days of the gold standard, without its being necessary to ask anyone to accept special or onerous conditions.

21. The principles governing transactions are: first, that the Clearing Union is set up, not for the transaction of daily business between individual traders or banks, but for the clearing and settlement of the ultimate outstanding balances between Central Banks (and certain other super-national Institutions), such as would have been settled under the old gold standard by the shipment or the earmarking of gold, and should not trespass unnecessarily beyond this field; and, second, that its purpose is to increase *freedom* in international commerce and not to multiply interferences or compulsions.

22. Many Central Banks have found great advantage in centralising with themselves or with an Exchange Control the supply and demand of all foreign exchange, thus dispensing with an outside exchange market, though continuing to accommodate individuals through the existing banks and not directly. The further extension of such arrangements would be consonant with the general purposes of the Clearing Union, inasmuch as they would promote order and discipline in international exchange transactions in detail as well as in general. The same is true of the control of Capital Movements, further described below, which many States are likely to wish to impose on their own nationals. But the structure of the proposed Clearing Union does not *require* such measures of centralisation or of control on the part of a member State. It is, for example, consistent alike with the type of Exchange Control now established in the United Kingdom or with the system now operating in the United States. The Union does not prevent private holdings of foreign currency or private dealings in exchange or international capital movements, if these have been approved or allowed by the member States concerned. Central Banks can deal direct with one another as heretofore. No transaction in bancor will take place except when a member State or its Central Bank is exercising the right to pay in it. In no case is there any direct control of capital movements by the Union, even in the case of 6 (8) (*b*) (ii) above, but only by the member States themselves through their own institutions. Thus the fabric of international banking organisation, built up by long experience to satisfy practical needs, would be left as undisturbed as possible.

23. It is not necessary to interfere with the discretion of countries which desire to maintain a special intimacy within a particular group of countries associated by geographical or political ties, such as the existing sterling area, or groups, like the Latin Union of former days, which may come into existence covering, for example, the countries of North America or those of South America, or the groups now under

active discussion, including Poland and Czechoslovakia or certain of the Balkan States. There is no reason why such countries should not be allowed a double position, both as members of the Clearing Union in their own right with their proper quota, and also as making use of another financial centre along traditional lines, as, for example, Australia and India with London, or certain American countries with New York. In this case, their accounts with the Clearing Union would be in exactly the same position as the independent gold reserves which they now maintain, and they would have no occasion to modify in any way their present practices in the conduct of daily business.

24. There might be other cases, however, in which a dependency or a member of a federal union would merge its currency identity in that of a mother country, with a quota appropriately adjusted to the merged currency area as a whole, and *not* enjoy a separate individual membership of the Clearing Union, as, for example, the States of a Federal Union, the French colonies or the British Crown Colonies.

25. At the same time countries, which do not belong to a special geographical or political group, would be expected to keep their reserve balances with the Clearing Union and not with one another. It has, therefore, been laid down that balances may not be held in another country except with the approval of the monetary authorities of that country; and, in order that sterling and dollars might not appear to compete with bancor for the purpose of reserve balances, the United Kingdom and the United States might agree together that they would not accept the reserve balances of other countries in excess of normal working balances except in the case of banks definitely belonging to a Sterling Area or Dollar Area group.

VI.—THE POSITION OF GOLD UNDER THE PLAN

26. Gold still possesses great psychological value which is not being diminished by current events; and the desire to possess a gold reserve against unforeseen contingencies is likely to remain. Gold also has the merit of providing in point of form (whatever the underlying realities may be) an uncontroversial standard of value for international purposes, for which it would not yet be easy to find a serviceable substitute. Moreover, by supplying an automatic means for settling some part of the favourable balances of the creditor countries, the current gold production of the world and the remnant of of gold reserves held outside the United States may still have a useful part to play. Nor is it reasonable to ask the United States to de-monetise the stock of gold which is the basis of its impregnable liquidity. What, in the long run, the world may decide to do with gold is another matter. The purpose of the Clearing Union is to supplant gold as a governing factor, but not to dispense with it.

27. The international bank-money which we have designated *bancor* is defined in terms of a weight of gold. Since the national currencies of the member States are given a defined exchange value in terms of bancor, it follows that they would each have a defined gold content which would be their official buying price for gold, above which they must not pay. The fact that a member State is entitled to obtain a credit in terms of bancor by paying actual gold to the credit of its clearing account, secures a steady and ascertained purchaser for the output of the gold-producing countries, and for countries holding a large reserve of gold. Thus the position of producers and holders of gold is not affected adversely, and is, indeed, improved.

28. Central Banks would be entitled to retain their separate gold reserves and

ship gold to one another, provided they did not pay a price above parity; they could coin gold and put it into circulation, and, generally speaking, do what they liked with it.

29. One limitation only would be, for obvious reasons, essential. No member State would be entitled to demand gold from the Clearing Union against its balance of bancor; for bancor is available only for transfer to another clearing account. Thus between gold and bancor itself there would be a one-way convertibility, such as ruled frequently before the war with national currencies which were on what was called a "gold exchange standard." This need not mean that the Clearing Union would only receive gold and never pay it out. It has been provided above that, if the Clearing Union finds itself in possession of a stock of gold, the Governing Board shall have discretion to distribute the surplus between those possessing credit balances in bancor, proportionately to such balances in reduction of their amount.

30. The question has been raised whether these arrangements are compatible with the retention by individual member States of a full gold standard with two-way convertibility, so that, for example, any foreign central bank acquiring dollars could use them to obtain gold for export. It is not evident that a good purpose would be served by this. But it need not be prohibited, and if any member State should prefer to maintain full convertibility for internal purposes it could protect itself from any abuse of the system or inconvenient consequences by providing that gold could only be exported under licence.

31. The value of bancor in terms of gold is fixed but not unalterably. The power to vary its value might have to be exercised if the stocks of gold tendered to the Union were to be excessive. No object would be served by attempting further to peer into the future or to prophesy the ultimate outcome.

VII.—THE CONTROL OF CAPITAL MOVEMENTS

32. There is no country which can, in future, safely allow the flight of funds for political reasons or to evade domestic taxation or in anticipation of the owner turning refugee. Equally, there is no country that can safely receive fugitive funds, which constitute an unwanted import of capital, yet cannot safely be used for fixed investment.

33. For these reasons it is widely held that control of capital movements, both inward and outward, should be a permanent feature of the post-war system. It is an objection to this that control, if it is to be effective, probably requires the machinery of exchange control for *all* transactions, even though a general permission is given to all remittances in respect of current trade. Thus those countries which have for the time being no reason to fear, and may indeed welcome, outward capital movements, may be reluctant to impose this machinery, even though a general permission for capital, as well as current, transactions reduces it to being no more than a machinery of record. On the other hand, such control will be more difficult to work by unilateral action on the part of those countries which cannot afford to dispense with it, especially in the absence of a postal censorship, if movements of capital cannot be controlled *at both ends*. It would, therefore, be of great advantage if the United States, as well as other members of the Clearing Union, would adopt machinery similar to that which the British Exchange Control has now gone a long way towards perfecting. Nevertheless, the universal establishment of a control of capital movements cannot be regarded as essential to the operation of the Clearing Union; and the method and degree of such control should therefore be left to the decision of each member State. Some less drastic way might be found by which countries, not themselves controlling outward capital

movements, can deter inward movements not approved by the countries from which they originate.

34. The position of abnormal balances in overseas ownership held in various countries at the end of the war presents a problem of considerable importance and special difficulty. A country in which a large volume of such balances is held could not, unless it is in a creditor position, afford the risk of having to redeem them in bancor on a substantial scale, if this would have the effect of depleting its bancor resources at the outset. At the same time, it is very desirable that the countries owning these balances should be able to regard them as liquid, at any rate over and above the amounts which they can afford to lock up under an agreed programme of funding or long-term expenditure. Perhaps there should be some special over-riding provision for dealing with the transitional period only by which, through the aid of the Clearing Union, such balances would remain liquid and convertible into bancor by the creditor country whilst there would be no corresponding strain on the bancor resources of the debtor country, or, at any rate, the resulting strain would be spread over a period.

35. The advocacy of a control of capital movements must not be taken to mean that the era of international investment should be brought to an end. On the contrary, the system contemplated should greatly facilitate the restoration of international loans and credits for legitimate purposes. The object, and it is a vital object, is to have a means—

(a) of distinguishing long-term loans by creditor countries, which help to maintain equilibrium and develop the world's resources, from movements of funds out of debtor countries which lack the means to finance them; and

(b) of controlling short-term speculative movements or flights of currency whether out of debtor countries or from one creditor country to another.

36. It should be emphasised that the purpose of the overdrafts of bancor permitted by the Clearing Union is, not to facilitate long-term, or even medium-term, credits to be made by debtor countries which cannot afford them, but to allow time and a breathing space for adjustments and for averaging one period with another to all member States alike, whether in the long run they are well-placed to develop a forward international loan policy or whether their prospects of profitable new development in excess of their own resources justifies them in long-term borrowing. The machinery and organisation of international medium-term and long-term lending is another aspect of post-war economic policy, not less important than the purposes which the Clearing Union seeks to serve, but requiring another, complementary institution.

VIII.—RELATION OF THE CLEARING UNION TO COMMERCIAL POLICY

37. The special protective expedients which were developed between the two wars were sometimes due to political, social or industrial reasons. But frequently they were nothing more than forced and undesired dodges to protect an unbalanced position of a country's overseas payments. The new system, by helping to provide a register of the size and whereabouts of the aggregate debtor and creditor positions respectively, and an indication whether it is reasonable for a particular country to adopt special expedients as a temporary measure to assist in regaining equilibrium in its balance of payments, would make it possible to establish a general rule *not* to adopt them, subject to the indicated exceptions.

38. The existence of the Clearing Union would make it possible for member States contracting commercial agreements to use their respective debit and credit positions

with the Clearing Union as a test, though this test by itself would not be complete. Thus, the contracting parties, whilst agreeing to clauses in a commercial agreement forbidding, in general, the use of certain measures or expedients in their mutual trade relations, might make this agreement subject to special relaxations if the state of their respective clearing accounts satisfied an agreed criterion. For example, an agreement might provide that, in the event of one of the contracting States having a debit balance with the Clearing Union exceeding a specified proportion of its quota on the average of a period it should be free to resort to import regulation or to barter trade agreements or to higher import duties of a type which was restricted under the agreement in normal circumstances. Protected by the possibility of such temporary indulgences, the members of the Clearing Union should feel much more confidence in moving towards the withdrawal of other and more dislocating forms of protection and discrimination and in accepting the prohibition of the worst of them from the outset. In any case, it should be laid down that members of the Union would not allow or suffer among themselves any restrictions on the disposal of receipts arising out of current trade or "invisible" income.

IX.—THE USE OF THE CLEARING UNION FOR OTHER INTERNATIONAL PURPOSES

39. The Clearing Union might become the instrument and the support of international policies in addition to those which it is its primary purpose to promote. This deserves the greatest possible emphasis. The Union might become the pivot of the future economic government of the world. Without it, other more desirable developments will find themselves impeded and unsupported. With it, they will fall into their place as parts of an ordered scheme. No one of the following suggestions is a necessary part of the plan. But they are illustrations of the additional purposes of high importance and value which the Union, once established, might be able to serve:—

(1) The Union might set up a clearing account in favour of international bodies charged with post-war relief, rehabilitation and reconstruction. But it could go much further than this. For it might supplement contributions received from other sources by granting preliminary overdraft facilities in favour of these bodies, the overdraft being discharged over a period of years out of the Reserve Fund of the Union, or, if necessary, out of a levy on surplus credit balances. So far as this method is adopted it would be possible to avoid asking any country to assume a burdensome commitment for relief and reconstruction, since the resources would be provided in the first instance by those countries having credit clearing accounts for which they have no immediate use and are voluntarily leaving idle, and in the long run by those countries which have a chronic international surplus for which they have no beneficial employment.

(2) The Union might set up an account in favour of any super-national policing body which may be charged with the duty of preserving the peace and maintaining international order. If any country were to infringe its properly authorised orders, the policing body might be entitled to request the Governors of the Clearing Union to hold the clearing account of the delinquent country to its order and permit no further transactions on the account except by its authority. This would provide an excellent machinery for enforcing a financial blockade.

(3) The Union might set up an account in favour of international bodies charged with the management of a Commodity Control, and might finance stocks of commodities held by such bodies, allowing them overdraft facilities on their accounts up to an

agreed maximum. By this means the financial problem of buffer stocks and "ever-normal granaries" could be effectively attacked.

(4) The Union might be linked up with a Board for International Investment. It might act on behalf of such a Board and collect for them the annual service of their loans by automatically debiting the clearing account of the country concerned. The statistics of the clearing accounts of the member-States would give a reliable indication as to which countries were in a position to finance the Investment Board, with the advantage of shifting the whole system of clearing credits and debits nearer to equilibrium.

(5) There are various methods by which the Clearing Union could use its influence and its powers to maintain stability of prices and to control the Trade Cycle. If an International Economic Board is established, this Board and the Clearing Union might be expected to work in close collaboration to their mutual advantage. If an International Investment or Development Corporation is also set up together with a scheme of Commodity Controls for the control of stocks of the staple primary products, we might come to possess in these three Institutions a powerful means of combating the evils of the Trade Cycle, by exercising contractionist or expansionist influence on the system as a whole or on particular sections. This is a large and important question which cannot be discussed adequately in this paper; and need not be examined at length in this place because it does not raise any important issues affecting the fundamental constitution of the proposed Union. It is mentioned here to complete the picture of the wider purposes which the foundation of the Clearing Union might be made to serve.

40. The facility of applying the Clearing Union plan to these several purposes arises out of a fundamental characteristic which is worth pointing out, since it distinguishes the plan from those proposals which try to develop the same basic principle along bilateral lines and is one of the grounds on which the Plan can claim superior merit. This might be described as its "anonymous" or "impersonal" quality. No particular member States have to engage their own resources as such to the support of other particular States or of any of the international projects or policies adopted. They have only to agree in general that, if they find themselves with surplus resources which for the time being they do not themselves wish to employ, these resources may go into the general pool and be put to work on approved purposes. This costs the surplus country nothing because it is not asked to part permanently, or even for any specified period, with such resources, which it remains free to expend and employ for its own purposes whenever it chooses; in which case the burden of finance is passed on to the next recipient, again for only so long as the recipient has no use for the money. As pointed out above, this merely amounts to extending to the international sphere the methods of any domestic banking system, which are in the same sense "impersonal" inasmuch as there is no call on the particular depositor either to support as such the purposes for which his banker makes advances or to forgo permanently the use of his deposit. There is no countervailing objection except that which applies equally to the technique of domestic banking, namely that it is capable of the abuse of creating excessive purchasing power and hence an inflation of prices. In our efforts to avoid the opposite evil, we must not lose sight of this risk, to which there is an allusion in 39 (5) above. But it is no more reason for refusing the advantages of international banking than the similar risk in the domestic field is a reason to return to the practices of the seventeenth century goldsmiths (which are what we are still following in

the international field) and to forgo the vast expansion of production which banking principles have made possible. Where financial contributions are required for some purpose of general advantage, it is a great facility not to have to ask for specific contributions from any named country, but to depend rather on the anonymous and impersonal aid of the system as a whole. We have here a genuine organ of truly international government.

X.—THE TRANSITIONAL ARRANGEMENTS

41. It would be of great advantage to agree the general principles of the Clearing Union before the end of the war, with a view to bringing it into operation at an early date after the termination of hostilities. Major plans will be more easily brought to birth in the first energy of victory and whilst the active spirit of united action still persists, than in the days of exhaustion and reaction from so much effort which may well follow a little later. Such a proposal presents, however, something of a dilemma. On the one hand, many countries will be in particular need of reserves of overseas resources in the period immediately after the war. On the other hand, goods will be in short supply and the prevention of inflationary international conditions of much more importance for the time being than the opposite. The expansionist tendency of the plan, which is a leading recommendation of it as soon as peace-time output is restored and the productive capacity of the world is in running order, might be a danger in the early days of a sellers' market and an excess of demand over supply.

42. A reconciliation of these divergent purposes is not easily found until we know more than is known at present about the means to be adopted to finance post-war relief and reconstruction. If the intention is to provide resources on liberal and comprehensive lines outside the resources made available by the Clearing Union and additional to them, it might be better for such specific aid to take the place of the proposed overdrafts during the "relief" period of (say) two years. In this case credit clearing balances would be limited to the amount of gold delivered to the Union, and the overdraft facilities created by the Union in favour of the Relief Council, the International Investment Board or the Commodity Controls. Nevertheless, the immediate establishment of the Clearing Union would not be incompatible with provisional arrangements, which could take alternative forms according to the character of the other "relief" arrangements, qualifying and limiting the overdraft quotas. Overdraft quotas might be allowed on a reduced scale during the transitional period. Or it might be proper to provide that countries in receipt of relief or Lend-Lease assistance should not have access at the same time to overdraft facilities, and that the latter should only become available when the former had come to an end. If, on the other hand, relief from outside sources looks like being inadequate from the outset, the overdraft quotas may be even more necessary at the outset than later on.

43. We must not be over-cautious. A rapid economic restoration may lighten the tasks of the diplomatists and the politicians in the resettlement of the world and the restoration of social order. For Great Britain and other countries outside the "relief" areas the possibility of exports sufficient to sustain their standard of life is bound up with good and expanding markets. We cannot afford to wait too long for this, and we must not allow excessive caution to condemn us to perdition. Unless the Union is a going concern, the problem of proper "timing" will be nearly insoluble. It is sufficient at this stage to point out that the problem of timing must not be overlooked, but that the Union is capable of being used so as to aid rather than impede its solution.

XI.—CONCLUSION

44. It has been suggested that so ambitious a proposal is open to criticism on the ground that it requires from the members of the Union a greater surrender of their sovereign rights than they will readily concede. But no greater surrender is required than in a commercial treaty. The obligations will be entered into voluntarily and can be terminated on certain conditions by giving notice.

45. A greater readiness to accept super-national arrangements must be required in the post-war world. If the arrangements proposed can be described as a measure of financial disarmament, there is nothing here which we need be reluctant to accept ourselves or to ask of others. It is an advantage, and not a disadvantage, of the scheme that it invites the member States to abandon that licence to promote indiscipline, disorder and bad-neighbourliness which, to the general disadvantage, they have been free to exercise hitherto.

46. The plan makes a beginning at the future economic ordering of the world between nations and "the winning of the peace." It might help to create the conditions and the atmosphere in which much else would be made easier.

The White Plan

The first definitive version of Mr. White's plan for a Stabilization Fund was a mimeographed draft dated April 1942. This covered both the Fund and the Bank. It comprised an Introduction, an Outline of the Articles proposed for the Fund and for the Bank, and extensive commentaries on these Articles. The extract (A) below omits the Articles for the Bank and also the commentary on them except for a section which dealt with "A new international currency."

The final version of Mr. White's plan was issued by the U.S. Treasury in printed form on July 10, 1943. This is reproduced in (B) below.

(A) Preliminary Draft Proposal for a United Nations Stabilization Fund and a Bank for Reconstruction and Development of the United and Associated Nations

(April 1942)

H. D. WHITE, Assistant to the Secretary, U.S. Treasury Department

This report has been prepared at the request of Secretary Morgenthau that I draft a plan for an International Stabilization Fund and an International Unit of Currency.

He felt that the requirements of furthering the war effort and preparing for the financial needs of the reconstruction period called for the immediate preparation and study of preliminary proposals.—H. D. WHITE

INTRODUCTION

Suggested Plan for a United and Associated Nations Stabilization Fund and a Bank for Reconstruction and Development of the United and Associated Nations

It is yet too soon to know the precise form or the approximate magnitude of post-war monetary problems. But one thing is certain. No matter how long the war lasts nor how it is won, we shall be faced with three inescapable problems: to prevent the disruption of foreign exchanges and the collapse of monetary and credit systems; to assure the restoration of foreign trade; and to supply the huge volume of capital that will be needed virtually throughout the world for reconstruction, for relief, and for economic recovery.

If we are to avoid drifting from the peace table into a period of chaotic competition, monetary disorders, depressions, political disruption, and finally into new wars within as well as among nations, we must be equipped to grapple with these three problems and to make substantial progress toward their solution.

Specific plans must be formulated now.

Clearly the task can be successfully handled only through international action. In most discussions of post-war problems this fact has been recognized, yet to date—though a number of persons have pointed to the solution in general terms—no detailed plans sufficiently realistic or practical to give promise of accomplishing the task have been formulated or discussed. It is high time that such plans were drafted. It is time that detailed and workable plans be prepared providing for the creation of agencies with resources, powers and structure adequate to meet the three major post-war needs.

Such agencies should, of course, be designed to deal chiefly with post-war problems. But their establishment must not be postponed until the end of hostilities. It takes many months to set up such agencies. First, a plan has to be perfected. Then it has to be carefully considered by a number of countries. In each country, again, acceptance can follow only upon legislation. That alone will consume many months and possibly longer. And even when the plan is finally accepted, much time will be further consumed in the collection of personnel, and the performance of the preliminary ground work which must be done before effective operations can begin. Altogether, a year may be required before a proposal can be transformed into an operating agency.

Obviously, therefore, even though no important immediate ends will be served by having such agencies functioning during war time, it will be an error to wait until the end of the war is in sight before beginning serious discussion of plans for establishing such agencies. No one knows how soon the war will end, and no one can know how long it will take to get plans approved and the agencies started. Yet, if we are to "win the peace," which will follow the war, we must have adequate economic instruments with which to carry on effective work as soon as the war is over. It would be ill-advised, if not positively dangerous, to leave ourselves at the end of the war unprepared for the stupendous task of world-wide economic reconstruction.

Specific proposals will help win the war.

But there is an additional important reason for initiating at once serious discussion of specific proposals. Such discussion will be a factor toward winning the war. It has been frequently suggested, and with much cogency, that the task of securing the defeat of the Axis powers would be made easier if the victims of aggression, actual and potential, could have more assurance that a victory by the United Nations will not mean in the economic sphere, a mere return to the pre-war pattern of every-country-for-itself, or inevitable depression, of possible widespread economic chaos with the weaker nations succumbing first under the law-of-the-jungle that characterized international economic practices of the pre-war decade. That assurance must be given now. The people of the anti-Axis powers must be encouraged to feel themselves on solid international ground, they must be given to understand that a United Nations victory will not usher in another two decades of economic uneasiness, bickering, ferment, and disruption. They must be assured that something will be done in the sphere of international economic relations that is new, that is powerful enough and comprehensive enough to give expectation of successfully filling a world need. They must have assurance that methods and resources are being prepared to provide them with capital to help them rebuild their devastated areas, reconstruct their war-distorted economies, and help free them from the strangulating grasp of lost markets and depleted reserves. Finally, they must have assurance that the United States does not intend to desert the war-worn and impoverished nations after the war is won, but proposes to help them in the long and difficult task of economic reconstruction. To help them, not primarily for altruistic motives, but from recognition of the truth that prosperity, like peace, is indivisible. To give that assurance now is to unify and encourage the anti-Axis forces, to greatly strengthen their will and effort to win.

Nor will the effect be on the anti-Axis powers alone. Whether within the Axis countries the will to fight would be weakened by such arrangements is not certain, but assuredly it would not be strengthened. And certainly the people in the invaded countries, and the wavering elements in the Axis dominated and Axis-influenced countries would be given additional cause to throw in their lot more definitely and openly with the anti-Axis forces if there is real promise that an orderly prosperous world will emerge from a United Nations victory.

Two International Government Agencies must be established—a Stabilization Fund and a Bank for Reconstruction.

A vital part of that promise rests on international monetary and banking collaboration. The United Nations and the Nations associated with them must undertake cooperatively two tasks as soon as possible: first, to provide an instrument with the means and the procedure to stabilize foreign exchange rates and strengthen the monetary systems of the United Nations; and second, to establish an agency with resources and powers adequate to provide capital for economic reconstruction, to facilitate rapid and smooth transition from war-time economies to peace-time economies, to provide relief for stricken people during the immediate post-war period, to increase foreign trade and permanently increase the productivity of the United Nations.

Those two tasks should be kept distinct. Though in some of their facets and in many of their consequences there is considerable interdependence and interaction, the two are different enough to call for separate instrumentalities. Each is sufficiently specialized to require different resources, different responsibilities, and different procedures and criteria for action. To supply the United Nations with necessary capital not otherwise available except possibly on too costly terms should be the function of a bank created for that specific purpose; whereas monetary stabilization—a highly specialized function calling for a special structure, special personnel, and special organization—would best be performed by a stabilization fund created to perform that special function.

It is therefore recommended that immediate consideration be given to formulating plans for the establishment of two separate institutions:

1. A United and Associated Nations Stabilization Fund, and
2. A Bank for Reconstruction and Development of the United and Associated Nations.

While either agency could function without the existence of the other, the creation of both would nevertheless aid greatly in the functioning of each. Doubtless one agency with the combined functions of both could be set up, but it could operate only with a loss of effectiveness, risk of over-centralization of power, and danger of making costly errors of judgment. The best promise of successful operation seems to lie in the creation of two separate institutions, linked together by one or two directors in common.

Proposals must be drafted by experts of many governments meeting for that purpose.

It is hoped that some time soon, representatives of various interested governments will meet in conference to explore the possibility of working out a plan for the establishment of an international stabilization fund and bank. To facilitate the preliminary work of such a committee, and to provide the officials of the interested governments with a proposal set in specific enough terms to encourage and justify fruitful discussion prior to a meeting, the following report has been prepared. It contains a suggested plan for a fund and for a bank, and also some discussion of the various points involved.

Anyone familiar with the task of setting up new and complex organizations such as the two envisaged will fully appreciate that no single person, no matter how well informed on the subject, can hope to draft a plan that would meet with general approval. This is especially true of a proposal calling for international collaboration and requiring acceptance by several governments. To draft a plan that is likely to meet with approval of various governments is a task beyond the competence even of a group of economists from any single country. The details of any plan submitted for consideration would have to be subjected to careful evaluation and examination by a number of men, some of whom should be expert in the handling of international economic problems and monetary theory, and others at home in related fields. In addition to monetary problems, questions of sovereignty, of national interest, and of broad economic policy are involved in some of the more important provisions, and these inevitably must be the subject of controversy and compromise. They are also matters that must be discussed in detail and at length by high officials whose responsibilities include the shaping and administration of monetary and financial policy.

The proposals and comments that follow are submitted with the intent of providing a starting point for intelligent discussion and of calling attention to some of the difficulties which would have to be satisfactorily met before a workable and acceptable plan may emerge. The proposals have been set forth only in outline and for the most part only those points are included which are essential to an understanding of the plan.

It is certain that some of the powers and requirements included in the outline of the Fund and the Bank will not survive discussion, prejudice and fear of departure from the usual. Some may not stand the test of political reality, and some may be unacceptable on technical grounds, while others may be generally regarded as going too far toward "internationalism." Yet most of them appear as desirable objectives in most writings or conferences on post-war economies and are worth considering.

Willingness to depart from tradition and break new ground is essential if meaningful results are to be obtained.

It will perhaps help toward understanding and induce a more sympathetic approach to the proposals which follow to state at the outset that something much more than the usual banking and stabilization functions are envisaged in the plan. There is urgent need for instruments which will pave the way and make easy a high degree of cooperation and collaboration among the United Nations in economic fields hitherto held too sacrosanct for international action or multilateral sovereignty. A breach must be made and widened in the outmoded and disastrous economic policy of each-country-for-itself-and-the-devil-take-the-weakest. Just as the failure to develop an effective League of Nations has made possible two devastating wars within one generation, so the absence of a high degree of economic collaboration among the leading nations will, during the coming decade, inevitably result in economic warfare that will be but the prelude and instigator of military warfare on an even vaster scale.

The Fund and the Bank described in the following pages are envisaged as economic instruments that most easily and effectively can facilitate that high degree of economic collaboration. It will be at once apparent that the resources, powers and requirements for membership, accorded both agencies go far beyond the usual attributes of monetary stabilization and of banking. They must if they are to be the stepping stone from shortsighted disastrous economic nationalism to intelligent international collaboration. Timidity will not serve. It is my conviction that the long-time effectiveness of both agencies will be measured by the degree to which boldness and vision are displayed in their organization and objectives.

Part I, which follows, consists of an outline of (1) a United and Associated Nations Stabilization Fund, and (2) of a Bank for Reconstruction of the United and Associated Nations.

Part II consists of a brief explanation and discussion of the proposed Fund, and Part III of the proposed Bank.

PART I
A. SUGGESTED OUTLINE OF A UNITED AND ASSOCIATED NATIONS STABILIZATION FUND.

I. The Purposes of the Fund are:
   1. To stabilize foreign exchange rates of the United Nations.
   2. To encourage the flow of productive capital among the United Nations.
   3. To liberate blocked balances.
   4. To help correct the maldistribution of gold among the United Nations.
   5. To facilitate the settlement and servicing of international debts—both public and private.
   6. To shorten the periods of disturbing disequilibrium in the international accounts of member countries and help stabilize price levels.
   7. To reduce the necessity and use of foreign exchange controls.
   8. To eliminate multiple currency practices and bilateral clearing arrangements.
   9. To promote sound note issuing and credit policies and practices among the United Nations.
   10. To reduce barriers to foreign trade.
   11. To promote more efficient and less expensive clearings of international exchange transactions.

II. Powers.

   To help attain the objectives listed above, the Fund shall have the following powers:
   1. Buy, sell and hold gold, currencies, foreign exchange, bills of exchange, and government bonds of the "member" countries, and act as a clearing house for international movement of funds, balances, checks, drafts, acceptances, gold.
   2. The Treasury of each member country (or its agent, a stabilization fund or central bank) shall have the privilege of purchasing from the Fund the currency of any member country which the Fund holds, provided:
      a. The currency demanded from the Fund is required to meet adverse balance of payments to the country whose currency is being demanded.
      b. The sum in the Fund of the currency of the country making the purchase shall be, after adding the sum proposed to be purchased, not more than

100 percent of the total sum—gold, currency, and notes—originally contributed to the Fund.

    c. The rate of exchange shall be the one determined by the Fund.

3. Should a country wish to sell its currency to the Fund in an amount in excess of the above quota, approval by four-fifths of the member votes would be required. The Fund could decide to purchase the excess of the currency in question if:

    a. It is believed the anticipated balance of payments of the country in question was such as to warrant the expectation that the "excess" could be disposed of within a reasonable time, or

    b. The country in question had gold holdings which, together with gold it expected to accumulate within a reasonable time, were adequate to replace the excess, and

    c. The country in question agreed to adopt and carry out measures designed to correct the disequilibrium in the country's balance of payments, which the Fund recommended—after careful examination of the situation.

4. The governments of member countries may sell to the Fund, blocked foreign balances acquired from their nationals, provided all the following conditions are met:

    a. The foreign balances were in member countries and were either partly or wholly blocked.

    b. The foreign balances were included in the sum reported (for the purpose of this provision) by the member government as blocked on date of its becoming a member.

    c. The country selling the blocked balances to the Fund agreed to begin repurchasing 40 percent of the amount sold to the Fund, at the price received, and at a rate not to be less than 2 percent a year. The repurchases to begin not later than three years after date of sale, and the currency to be used in repayment to be either the currency received or the local currency, as desired by the Fund.

    d. The country in which the blocked balances are held agrees to transfer those balances to the Fund, and purchase back 40 percent of them from the Fund, at the rate of 2 percent a year, beginning not later than three years after the date of transfer. The Fund may accept government bonds payable in gold in lieu of part of the blocked balances, and shall be free to sell such bonds under certain conditions.

    e. If the country selling the blocked foreign balances to the Fund asks for foreign exchange rather than local currency, it must need the foreign exchange for the purpose of meeting adverse balance of payments arising from any cause except acquisitions of gold, or accumulation of foreign balances.

    f. The country in which the blocked funds are kept agrees not to impose any restrictions on the installments of the 40 percent portion gradually to be repurchased by country owning the blocked balances.

    g. A charge of 1 percent, payable in the currency of the country paying shall be levied against the country selling its blocked funds, and a charge of 1 percent payable by country in which blocked account exists.

- h. The Fund shall determine from time to time what shall be the maximum proportion of the blocked balances it can afford to take over under this provision.
- i. The Fund on its part agrees not to sell the blocked balances acquired under the above authority, except with the permission, or at the request of the country in which the blocked balances are being held but can invest those balances in regular or special government securities of that country.

5. The Fund would fix the rates at which it will exchange one member's currency for another, and the rates at which it will buy and sell gold with local currencies. The guiding principle in the fixing of such rates shall be stability in exchange relationships. Changes in the rates shall be made only when essential to correction of a fundamental disequilibrium, and only with the consent of four-fifths of member votes.

6. The Fund shall have authority to deal only with the Treasuries of the participating countries, or with official stabilization funds of those countries, and with the bank designated by participating government as its fiscal agent, and with international banks owned by governments.

7. The Fund shall not have the authority to engage in any transactions within a member country, or with any corporation or part of the government of that country without the consent of the Board representative of that country.

8. The Fund shall have the authority to buy and sell currencies of non-member countries, but shall not be authorized to hold such currencies beyond sixty days after date of purchase, except with the approval of four-fifths of the member votes.

9. The Fund shall have the authority to borrow, at such rates as the Fund may recommend, the currency of any country, provided four-fifths of the member votes approve the terms, amount and condition of such borrowing.

10. The Fund shall have the authority to invest any currency it holds in "short-term" securities—commercial or government—of the country of that currency provided a four-fifths vote of the member votes shall approve, and provided further that the approving votes shall include that of the Board representative of the country in which the investment is to be made.

11. The Fund shall have authority to sell the obligation it holds of the member countries provided four-fifths of the member votes approve, and provided the representative of the country in which the securities are to be sold approves.

12. No sale of any currency from the Fund shall be made to a member without approval of four-fifths of member votes when the currency so sold is to be used or is to make possible adjustment of a foreign debt, including, of course, debts already in default.

13. Any member country can borrow local currency from the Fund for one year or less up to 75 percent of the currency of that country held by the Fund, provided such loan is approved by three-fourths of the member votes. A country borrowing such funds shall pay to the Fund an interest rate of 1 percent a year.

14. A very moderate service charge shall be made by the Fund on all exchange and gold transactions.

III. Eligibility for membership.

Any member of the United or Associated Nations is eligible for membership in the Fund provided it agrees:

1. To abandon, not later than one year after joining the Fund, or after the cessation of hostilities, whichever is later, all restrictions and controls over foreign exchange transactions with member countries, except with the approval of the Fund.
2. To alter exchange rates on the currencies of other countries only with the consent of the Fund and only to the extent and in the direction approved by the Fund, with the exception of a narrow range fixed by the Fund and permitted to all member currencies.
3. (a) Not to accept or permit deposits or investments from any member country except with the permission of the government of that country, and
   (b) To make available to the government of any member country at its request all property in form of deposits, investments, securities of the nationals of that member country.
4. Not to enter upon any bilateral clearing arrangements.
5. Not to adopt any monetary or general price measure or policy, the effect of which, in the opinion of a majority of the member votes, would be to bring about sooner or later a serious disequilibrium in the balance of payments, if four-fifths of the member votes of the Fund submitted to the country in question their disapproval of the adoption of the measure.
6. To embark upon a program of gradual reduction of existing trade barriers— import duties, import quotas, administrative devices—and further agree not to adopt any increase in tariff schedules, or other devices having as their purpose higher trade obstacles, without giving reasonable opportunity for the Fund to study the effect of the contemplated change on exchange rates and register its opinion. In rendering its opinion, the Fund will make recommendation to which the member governments agree to give serious consideration.
7. Not to permit any defaults on foreign obligations of the government, Central Bank or government agency without approval of the Fund.
8. Not to subsidize—directly or indirectly—the exportation of any commodity or services to member countries without consent of the Fund.

IV. Composition of the Fund.
1. The Fund shall consist of gold, currencies of member countries, and member government securities in such amounts as shall be indicated by a formula set forth in the agreement.

    The total subscription to the Fund shall be the equivalent of at least $5 billion. The Bank of the United Nations should subscribe $100 million to the Fund.

2. The contribution of each country shall consist of 25 percent cash and 25 percent in interest-bearing government securities (interest and principal payable in gold or its equivalent). The remaining 50 percent to be paid in such installments and in such form as shall be determined from time to time by the Fund.

    The initial payment of 25 percent cash shall consist of at least one-half in gold, the remainder in local currency.

V. Management.
1. The management of the Fund shall be vested in a Board of Directors consisting

of the representatives appointed by the member governments. Each government shall appoint one representative.

2. The Board shall elect a chairman and a small operating committee. The Chairman shall be chief of the operating committee. The members of the operating committee should devote full time to the management of the Fund, should be assisted by an appropriate technical staff, and should receive an adequate salary. The Chief of the operating committee with the approval of the Board shall appoint the heads of the departments.

3. In all voting by the Board each representative shall have one hundred votes, plus one vote for the equivalent of every million dollars subscribed to the Fund by his government.

4. A country can replace, wholly or in part, its bonds with currency or gold. The number of votes its representatives can cast will alter accordingly.

5. All decisions, except where specifically provided otherwise, shall be decided by the majority of the votes cast.

6. The President of the Bank for the United Nations shall be a member of the Board and shall have 100 votes. He shall have no additional votes notwithstanding the Bank's participation in the Fund.

VI. The rules and regulations regarding the type, amount and conditions of day-to-day transactions to be handled by the operating committee, shall be promulgated by four-fifths of the member votes.

VII. No change in the gold value of any currency of the participating countries shall be permitted to alter the gold value of the total currency holdings in the Fund. Thus, if the currency of any of the participating countries should depreciate, that country must deliver to the Fund an amount of its local currency equal to the decreased value of that currency held by the Fund. Likewise, if the currency of a particular country should increase, the Fund must deliver to that country an amount (in the currency of that country) equal to the resultant increase in the gold value of the Fund's holdings. This provision does not apply to currencies acquired under paragraph 4 under section on "Powers."

VIII. A country failing to contribute to the Fund sums due the Fund shall be dropped as a member, provided a majority of the member votes so decide. Any member dropped shall have returned to it an amount (in its own currency) equal to its contribution minus any sum due by that country to the Fund.

IX. Net profits earned by the Fund shall be distributed in the following manner:

1. 50 percent to reserves until the reserves are equal to 10 percent of the assets of the Fund.

2. 50 percent to be divided each year among the members in form of the local currency. That is, each country shall distribute its dividends in its own currency.

X. The member governments agree to furnish the Fund with all information it needs for its operations, and to furnish such reports as it may require, in the form and at the times requested by the Fund.

[Part I.B, outlining proposals for an International Bank, has been omitted here.]

PART II
A UNITED NATIONS STABILIZATION FUND

The outline of the purposes, powers and structure of a stabilization fund presented in the previous pages is hardly enough to supply the interested reader with more than very general idea of how the proposed institution would function and what they would be expected to accomplish. A brief discussion of some of the points outlined should serve to give a clearer idea of what is proposed, and also suggest some of the difficulties involved in the proposal.

In the following pages the outline presented in Part I is somewhat elaborated and some brief discussion is ventured of the more troublesome or important points. This section is devoted to discussion of the Fund and Part III to discussion of the Bank.

I. Purposes of the Fund

The various purposes enumerated in the outline are to a considerable extent interdependent and overlapping and in some instances may even represent apparently conflicting tendencies. Yet, progress in the attainment of almost any one of them facilitates progress toward the attainment of many of the others. Each of them represents a different phase of international monetary arrangements and calls in the main for different procedure, different powers, and in some cases, different kinds of resources.

The fact that some of the objectives may be at times harmonious and at other times conflicting, indicates that the management of an international stabilization fund cannot be reduced to a matter of simple rules. The successful operation of the Fund calls for constant examination of a large variety of pertinent factors and the continual evaluation of various effects which might be expected to follow any particular action or failure to act.

There follows a brief amplification and justification of each of the objectives.

Stabilization of foreign exchange rates.

The advantages of obtaining stable exchange rates are patent. The maintenance of stable exchange rates means the elimination of exchange risk in international economic and financial transactions. The cost of conducting foreign trade is thereby reduced, and capital flows much more easily to the country where it yields the greatest return because both short-term and long-term investments are greatly hampered by the possibility of loss from exchange depreciation. As the expectation of continued stability in foreign exchange rates is strengthened there is also more chance of avoiding the disrupting effects of flights of capital and of inflation.

Altogether, if the Fund were successful in bringing about a much greater degree of stability in foreign exchange relationships than existed during the 'twenties and 'thirties, it will have justified its existence on that score alone.

Flow of productive capital, blocked balances, and redistribution of gold.

The desirability of encouraging the flow of productive capital to areas where it can be most profitably employed needs no emphasis. The Fund can help encourage that flow by reducing exchange risks, and also by making the imposition of restrictions on exchange transactions less likely to happen. Also, insofar as the Fund can help strengthen the monetary and banking system of the country, it increases that country's attraction to funds of private foreign investors.

Balances owned by residents of another country which have been blocked because holdings of gold and other liquid foreign exchange assets are inadequate (this does not apply to the United States where restrictions have been imposed for reasons other than because of any scarcity of gold reserves) will constitute after the war one of the danger spots to monetary stability, and to resumption of liberal trade policies. If the Fund can eliminate that danger spot it will have justified its existence—even were it to accomplish little else.

The Fund has the possibility of utilizing more effectively the gold resources of any given country, and thereby encourage countries to hold larger gold reserves. By facilitating an easier adjustment of the international balance of payments, it reduces the volume of hectic gold movements. Machinery can be developed under the aegis of the Bank, with which countries can more easily develop a favorable balance of payments vis-à-vis the gold-holding and producing countries. By providing strength to countries with weakened economic and credit systems, the Fund can also encourage the return flow of gold from the United States.

Servicing of international debts.

The reduction in risk of exchange loss and progress toward elimination of restrictions on foreign exchange transactions should make easier debt adjustments of foreign debts now in default—both public and private—and continued servicing of debts not in default.

To help stabilize price levels.

Any development which would contribute toward stability of price levels is greatly to be welcomed. Wide swings in price levels are one of the destructive elements in domestic as well as international trade. An intelligent use of an international stabilization fund could contribute something toward reducing the fluctuations, and even the cyclical movements of prices within a country and in the relationship of price levels between countries.

To reduce the necessity and use of foreign exchange controls.

Foreign exchange controls usually constitute an interference with trade and capital flows. Unfortunately, such controls are too often preferable to the alternatives facing a particular country. Insofar as an international stabilization fund can reduce the necessity for such controls and can prevent the use of such controls where they are not necessary, it will serve to substantially increase foreign trade of nations and encourage the flow of production capital.

To eliminate multiple currency practices and bilateral clearing arrangements.

The developments during the last twenty years of multiple currency devices and bilateral clearing arrangements served to disrupt trade, increase economic difficulties in some countries, and stimulate the worst kind of competitive practices among countries seeking to increase their foreign markets or protect the foreign markets they already have. These practices frequently arise from difficulties which are subject to mitigation by an appropriately handled stabilization fund. An international stabilization fund with ample resources and broad powers could do much to eliminate the justification for resorting to trade practices that are an obstacle to a high level of foreign trade for all countries.

Promotion of sound note issuing and credit policies and practices.

The sounder the monetary and banking policies of governments, the less sensitive are they to economic disturbances, and the quicker will be the recovery from any depression. There are numerous ways in which an international stabilization fund could add to the strength of monetary systems of member governments.

Reduction of trade barriers.

The existence of high tariff policies and other obstacles to trade and the tendency during the post-war period to heighten those barriers, are serious barriers to recovery and maintenance of a high level of economic activity among countries. It will be readily admitted that if an international stabilization fund can assist in bringing about a reduction in the unnecessary barriers to international trade, it will have performed a valuable service toward maintaining business recovery after the war.

The establishment of an efficient clearing house for international monetary transactions.

The advantage of providing such a clearing house would not be negligible, particularly among countries who transact a small volume of business with each other. The spread between the buying and selling rates of some foreign currencies is much larger in some countries than it should be. Thus transactions between those countries are subject to handicaps that are unnecessary. To the extent that exchange rate spreads are adjuncts to fiscal or commercial policy, the Fund will deal with the problem in other ways. It is impossible to measure the gains that accrue from more efficient handling of clearances, but they could be substantial.

Can these objectives be reached?

Each of the objectives listed, if achieved, would help in some degree to restore and maintain world prosperity. If the Fund is to make much progress toward achieving the objectives enumerated in the previous pages, it must have broad powers and courageous and intelligent direction. It is a task that is surely within the competence of the present generation.

II. Powers of the Fund

The Fund should have the power to buy, sell and hold gold, currencies, foreign exchange, bills of exchange, and government securities of the "member" countries and act as a clearing house for international movements of gold and balances.

The purchase and sale of gold would be an essential part of the operations of the Fund. The Fund might well become the most attractive depository for earmarked gold, and be the means of greatly reducing the need for physical transfers of gold among members.

To promote the practice of "earmarking" gold its storing and transfer could be made without charge to members, and agreement between countries could accord a maximum of legal security to such holdings. It should even be possible to secure written assurance by the government of the country where the gold was to be held that such gold would not be subject to any controls. Earmarked gold could be given a special status so that countries could unhesitatingly earmark large amounts with the Fund and still record such gold as part of their own reserve. The Fund might find it convenient to have a branch office on each continent. This would still further cut down gold shipments. It would also speed up other kinds of transactions.

Dealings in foreign exchange would constitute, of course, the chief business of the Fund. It is through such transactions that the Fund would be expected to carry out many of its objectives. It might therefore be helpful if this part of the Fund's operations were described with little more detail. Tedious though it may be, this part of the Fund's activities must be elaborated to permit a proper evaluation of the role an international stabilization fund can play. In the several pages which follow the exchange operations with which the Fund would be chiefly occupied are briefly described.

The Treasury, or its fiscal agent, of each member country shall have the privilege of purchasing from the Fund the currency of any member country which the Fund holds.

Since the Fund would deal only with and for Treasuries (or their fiscal agents and the Bank) the regular private channels through which foreign exchange transactions are now consummated by commercial banks, and other dealers and brokers, would continue to serve. It is presumed that the Treasuries would deal in foreign exchange only when exchange situation warranted government operation. They might also employ the Fund to transact foreign exchange business between governments.

Certain restrictions on operations are necessitated by the wide differences in the strength of the various currencies. If any country could purchase from the Fund as much of any currency as it pleased at a fixed rate without reducing the supply of the strong currency available in the open market, countries with weak currencies would be tempted to accumulate stocks of strong currencies. The Fund's supply of gold and strong currencies would soon be depleted and in their place would be weak currencies, i.e. currencies of countries which prefer other currencies to their own. Some restrictions are therefore necessary.

The first condition of purchase from the Fund might be that the currency purchased must be needed to meet an adverse balance of payments to the country whose currency is being demanded. Thus, a country could not obtain gold or other currency from the Fund if the direct result were to increase the gold or foreign exchange holdings of the Government, its Stabilization Fund, or fiscal agent, except, of course, possibly for short periods.

There would be no justification for a member government to use the Fund's assets as a means of converting its currency into gold or foreign exchange, unless it needed that gold or foreign exchange to meet claims or liabilities due or soon to be due. It is quite true that one of the possible reasons why a government would need more foreign exchange might be that its nationals were building up their foreign balances, or increasing their foreign investments. That, however, is a quite different matter than the government or Central Bank building up its foreign balances. The Fund might wish to supply the foreign exchange when the demand arises from an outflow of private funds. Whether or not it would wish to do so depends on a number of factors, including the cause of the outflow, the rate of outflow, the countries involved, the reserve position of the capital losing country, and the rapidity with which the mechanism of adjustment in the balance of payments is operating. Each episode would have to be considered on its own merits. It is, therefore, important that when there is present in the balance of payments of the country in question substantial outflow of capital which may be contributing to the disequilibrium the Fund have the authority to provide the exchange or not, as it sees fit. It would have this authority in any case, as indicated below, if the country in question had already obtained its maximum quota of foreign exchange from the Fund but the Fund should also have the privilege of not responding to demand for exchange, even before the quota was reached, where capital movements are involved.

What this matter boils down to is that the Fund should have the authority to determine whether the transactions causing a balance to turn unfavorable include transactions which the Fund would judge "illegitimate" under the circumstances. There are times when some types of capital outflow for some countries would be considered "legitimate," whereas the same type for other countries or even for the same country under different circumstances would be regarded as "illegitimate." There might also be instances in which all types of capital outflows for a given country might be considered "illegitimate," whereas for another country, all types might be considered "legitimate." No generalization can be made without all the circumstances being given. It is necessary only that the Fund have authority to make the decision on this matter and, as explained later, that the Fund have the authority to obtain the kind of information that would enable it to make an intelligent decision.

To aid in the settlement of international balance is the legitimate use of the Fund and this use is in no way interfered with by the above restriction. Better information on foreign balances and volume of exchange transactions than is now available in most countries will be necessary before it will be possible for the Fund to operate wisely under this restriction, but the development of such statistical data should not be difficult, especially since exchange controls in most countries are prevalent.

The restriction that the foreign exchange should be needed to meet adverse balances is not enough, however, to protect the strong assets of the Fund. If that were the only restriction imposed, a country could continue for a long time to permit an unfavorable balance of payments without calling forth the usual restraints. Without additional restrictions the Fund would in effect be placing the entire gold and foreign exchange assets at the disposal of any member country. The purpose of the Fund could not be to supply an unlimited amount of foreign exchange to any country which might not wish to adopt the proper measures to correct a prolonged disequilibrium in its transactions with foreign countries.

The sum in the Fund of the currency of the country making the purchase shall be, after adding the sum proposed to be sold to the Fund, not more than 100 percent of the total sum (currency, gold and notes) originally contributed to the Fund.

A quantitative limit is therefore also necessary on the amount of foreign exchange a country could purchase from the Fund, without special action.

What limit it were best to set is difficult to decide. It should be large enough to take care of fluctuations in the country's balance of payments that occur within a year or two, but should not be so large as to make it unlikely that the currency sold to the Fund would be repurchased by the country in question within a reasonable time. It is suggested that a country should be able to purchase with its currency any other country's currency so long as the Fund's holdings of the purchasing country is not more than 100 percent of that country's original total contribution to the Fund. Since one-fourth of the original contribution was in form of gold (plus $1/4$ in local currency and $1/2$ in notes or bonds) the 100 percent increase in the holdings of the Fund actually represents an increase of 300 percent of the local currency subscribed. In other words, a country subscribing $100 million, consisting of $25 million gold, $25 million local currency, and $50 million obligations would be able to buy with local currency as much as $75 million of any currency needed. Since $25 million of gold had been subscribed, the net immediate possible gain to the country needing foreign exchange would be $50 million of foreign exchange. That may seem a small sum and doubtless is for some countries. However, it should be noted the limit is not a rigid nor final one. It is supplemented by an important qualification, to be described in a moment.

How the assistance by the Fund would operate may be more easily understood by following through the steps of a transaction using a simplified illustration:

The Government (or fiscal agent) of Country A finds that the demand by its nationals for foreign exchange, arising out of trade and service transactions, is increasing relative to the supply, to the point where it must (a) give up more gold than it feels desirable, or (b) impose restrictions on imports—either through exchange controls or import controls, or (c) permit its currency to depreciate. In that situation, being a member of the Fund, it turns to the Fund for the assistance it is entitled to receive.

It purchases from the Fund as much of the types of currencies it needs, paying for it with its own currency. This it can do as its right so long as the sum of its currency which the Fund possesses is not in excess of 100 percent of Country A's original total contribution.

Sooner or later other countries will turn to the Fund to buy currency of Country A, and Country A will then again be able to buy other currencies from the Fund if necessary. It might happen that a long time would elapse before Country A's balance of payments would turn favorable (i.e. before Country A's inpayments exceeded her outpayments so that some stabilization fund or central bank would be confronted with the same choice vis-à-vis Country A that Country A had been earlier). So long as Country A had not used up its maximum allowance permitted without special decision by the Fund, the duration of the period during which Country A would not be decreasing the Fund's holdings of her currency would not matter very much.

If the balance of payments position among all the member countries did not stray from equilibrium by large amounts (relative to their foreign exchange assets) or for long periods, then the Fund would serve as a sort of reserve pillow absorbing the shock of pressures on exchange rates, thus safeguarding trade from unnecessary restrictions and exchange from unnecessary fluctuations. But it would be unwarranted to expect all the balance of payments situations to return quickly to equilibrium. For some countries it would frequently happen, and for almost all countries it would sometimes happen that an adverse balance of payment situation would persist. There are a number of reasons for this, but it would take more space to explain them than is justified in this report. Suffice to say that it would be wholly to be expected that some member countries would frequently find they have sold so much of their currency to the Fund that the Fund held the maximum permitted by usual majority procedures. When that point will have been reached by any country it will have already obtained substantial assistance.

Let it be assumed, for example, that Country A had originally contributed $100 million to the Fund, and due to the development of an adverse balance it has sold to the Fund $75 million in addition to the $25 million originally subscribed. When that point is reached Country A will have received what is virtually a costless "loan" of $50 million of other countries' currencies. It really is not a loan since Country A has given its own currency in exchange, yet Country A has been able to buy $75 million of foreign exchange with its own currency, whereas without access to the Fund it would have had to use gold or other foreign exchange resources. Since Country A has subscribed $25 million in gold to the Fund which it otherwise could have used to purchase foreign exchange the gain it is able to make through its membership in the Fund is the use of an additional $50 million. That, however, need be only the beginning.

There is a provision which permits the Fund to increase its purchase of Country A's currency after the above-described maximum is reached, as follows:

A country can exceed the limit imposed by the regulation provided it can obtain approval of four-fifths of the member votes.

This approval should be given only if four-fifths of the member votes were of the opinion that (a) the anticipated balance of payments prospects of the country in question were such as to warrant the expectation that the "excess" could be disposed of within a "reasonable" time, or (b) if the country in question had gold holdings which together with the gold it expected to accumulate within a reasonable time was adequate to replace the excess, and (c) if the country in question agreed to adopt and carry out measures designed to correct the disequilibrium measures which the Fund either approved or suggested, and (d) some time limit be imposed on the country during which the excess shall be repurchased—a time limit that shall be long enough to permit the country to adjust its international accounts without too great a strain.

This provision gives the desired flexibility. No country need suffer from lack of foreign exchange necessary to meet temporary drains. It need not even suffer from shortage of foreign exchange during a prolonged period of disequilibrium provided the Fund was satisfied proper steps were being taken to restore equilibrium.

Admittedly the operation of that flexible provision would call for technical knowledge, careful examination and good judgment by the Fund's staff. It is hoped that the technical staff which the Fund would gradually develop would be the most competent available in that special field. It would need to be because the problems it will have to deal with are difficult and because the success of the Fund in reducing fluctuations in foreign trade and in preventing monetary disturbances will depend largely upon the wisdom of the technical staff's advice. The Fund would doubtless be free from political pressure from any one country in its decisions, and should be able to make recommendations more apt to be in the long-run interest of the country concerned, than would likely be the case where decisions are dominated by short-run considerations or by domestic political considerations.

To what extent the Fund will be called upon to purchase and accumulate local currencies cannot be forecast. It depends on a number of changing factors, such as: how many countries will participate in the Fund, and how much each will invest; how rapidly foreign exchange controls will be eliminated; how much capital will be available for foreign investment, and finally, the pattern of world trade which will emerge shortly after peace is resumed.

Much also will depend on the extent to which some of the countries have foreign balances to which they will prefer to resort when experiencing adverse balances. That will mean that the Fund will not be able to convert some of the currencies which it had acquired as rapidly as would seem to be called for by the then-prevailing pattern of trade. Thus, for example, the Fund may accept sterling from England because England has turned to the Fund to meet an adverse balance of payments. Other countries, however, later developing adverse balances with England might not turn to the Fund for sterling. They might utilize sterling balances which they already have, or dip into ample gold holdings. The Fund would in that case be unable to diminish its holdings of sterling and therefore England would not be able to sell the Fund more sterling later if necessary except by action under the flexible provision.

The fact that the countries which will participate to the largest extent in the Fund are likely to be those least in need of resorting to the Fund for assistance of the character indicated above, would make it possible for the Fund to help most where it would be most needed. Only experience can show how far the Fund could go in eliminating fluctuations in exchange rates and in making the imposition of exchange and trade controls unnecessary. It is certain that the Fund cannot perform miracles, nor solve all problems involved in the maintenance of equilibrium in international accounts. The Fund cannot and should not make it possible for countries to ignore the cardinal principle of international economic relations, namely, that a country must in the long run buy only as much goods and services as it sells. An important exception, of course, is a country which has a balance due it on current borrowing, but sooner or later even that country will have to sell more than it buys in order to pay interest and principal on its borrowings. To be sure, the country which has foreign exchange resources, in the form of gold or income from foreign investments, can continue to buy more than it sells so long as those resources last, but for most countries these resources are not present in abundance, and hence for most countries the Fund can operate to make their path much smoother provided the countries themselves approach their own balance of payments problem intelligently.

Gold producing countries would not be immune from needing help from the Fund. It is true that such countries usually have an "unfavorable" balance of payments in the sense that they need constant exports of gold to help pay for the exchange they need. But such countries may and frequently do need more foreign exchange than they can buy with current gold production. At such times they can be helped by the Fund just as can countries which do not produce gold.

Even if countries ignore the basic limitations set upon any country's ability to buy more than it sells, the Fund can exercise considerable influence in helping them to correct this situation in time, and in ways which will create the smallest amount of destruction to world trade and least disturbance to their own economy.

It may be that experience will demonstrate that the limitations set upon the Fund's authority to agree to purchase currencies offered it are too strict. It may be that the commercial policies pursued by numerous countries, including more liberal tariff policies, will reduce the length of time in which countries are apt to experience adverse balance of payments and also the magnitudes of the disequilibrium. If so, the Fund can undertake much greater obligations. In any case the Fund is well protected against loss.

It should be remembered that the Fund in its operations is not undertaking the same risk of loss that would be involved in a usual extension of credit. The Fund gets foreign exchange in return for the currency it gives up, and each member government is required to make good any exchange loss suffered by the Fund through depreciation of its currency. Thus, the Fund not only has the foreign exchange which is always worth something, but it also has the obligation of the government to make good any exchange loss that might result. More than that, each government has invested with the Fund gold, currency, and its obligations, which the Fund would, in effect, have as collateral against potential exchange losses.

The Fund would receive additional protection against loss from the fact that a member government not meeting its obligations to the Fund could be dropped. Without knowing how many members will participate or how influential the Fund will become, we cannot say how serious a punishment being dropped from the Fund would be, but it is not unlikely that it would be serious enough to induce any country to make good its obligations to the Fund, difficult though that might prove to be.

Because the Fund will be undertaking so little risk, it can go further in the assistance it gives to foreign countries than would be the case were the risk of loss great. Should the Fund find itself pressed for certain kinds of currencies, it has of course both assets and borrowing power which can, if necessary, be used to purchase the desired currencies.

The power of the Fund to deal in the bonds of participating governments is an important one. It would, for example, make it possible for the Fund to come to the aid of any country which is being subjected to pressure on its exchange arising out of some types of capital flights. The Fund could, of course, buy the currency of the country, but the circumstances might, under certain conditions, be better handled by buying bonds and it might even help countries which for one reason or another do not have or cannot exercise adequate open-market powers and whose money market has become unduly tight because of a capital flight.

Unfreezing of blocked funds.

Special powers are called for to deal with the problem created by the growing magnitude of blocked balances. The countries in which large totals of balances are blocked are the United States and England (Germany is, of course, excluded) whereas the countries to whom those balances belong include almost the rest of the world.

The balances blocked in the United States present no monetary problem. They were not blocked because of any scarcity of gold or foreign exchange assets and their unblocking will not leave the United States short of gold or foreign exchange poor. There will doubtless be many cases in which for political or legal reasons, unfreezing will be delayed, but the cause of the delay will not be any scarcity of gold which may safely leave the country. There are more than two billion of earmarked gold, three billion of deposits, and possibly several hundred million of short-term investments, the withdrawal of which has been placed under some restrictions. A rapid withdrawal of any part of it, or all of it, can be handled with the utmost ease by the United States because of its large gold reserves. At most, it may prove necessary to lower reserve requirements to prevent a tightening of the credit situation here—should the outflow be great enough. With the cessation of war the release of dollar funds (equivalent to gold) capable of purchasing goods anywhere will prove a very important factor in stimulating trade and aiding reconstructions. The trouble, if any, is apt to be that nationals and governments of foreign countries will not elect to withdraw their funds from the United States rapidly enough.

The situation with respect to blocked balances in England is quite different. The gold and foreign exchange reserves which England will have at the close of the war are certain to be far too small relative to the sterling balances blocked there to permit England to remove restrictions on the withdrawal of funds by foreign owners. England may end the war with more than 5 billion dollars of deposits belonging to residents of other countries, while her liquid foreign exchange resources are likely to be much less than that. Moreover, England will need whatever gold she will be able to accumulate, and indeed should have more foreign exchange available than she is likely to have, in order to operate properly even were the total of foreign balances in England much smaller. Most of these balances belong to the Dominions who would wish to keep substantial sums in England in any case—unless there was imminent danger of sterling depreciation. Against some of the remainder there are offsetting blocked currencies. Nonetheless, the drain on British foreign liquid exchange reserves could easily be greater than England could safely permit.

The unblocking of these sterling funds is highly to be desired. Probably, no single action would do more to stimulate world trade, prevent pressure on numerous exchanges, and reduce the probability of widespread depreciation of currencies. The restoration of confidence in the soundness of British currency, the assurance that international monetary problems are to be intelligently handled, and renewed hope that currency stability will be achieved after the war that would follow a successful unfreezing of sterling, would alone justify every effort to solve through international action the problem of blocked balances in Britain.

The Fund would seem to be the appropriate agency to use for the solution of that problem. The method that could be employed to accomplish this is a bit complicated to describe and may seem at first reading difficult to follow but the importance of the subject warrants the attempt.

To accomplish a maximum of results with a minimum of risks the Fund should be given the power to purchase sterling, or any other currency offered to it, from any country other than the country whose currency is being purchased, provided:

a. The government selling its foreign balances (blocked in another country) to the Fund under this provision guarantees to repurchase 40 percent of the currency from the Fund at the price paid. The repurchase to begin after 3 years and to be made at the rate of not less than 2 percent a year of the amount acquired by the Fund under this authority.

b. The country whose local currency belonging to residents of another country is being offered for sale to the Fund agrees first to transfer title to the balances from the foreign nationals to the Fund, and to begin 3 years after sale to repurchase from the Fund 40 percent of the sterling acquired under this provision at a rate of not less than 2 percent a year, at the purchase price.

c. Not more than 20 percent of the currency offered should be paid for by the Fund with gold, half of which should be exempt from the condition imposed in paragraph (d) below.

d. The particular currency paid over by the Fund in exchange for the currency offered should be either local currency or currency needed by the country to meet an adverse balance of payments, with the exception of the 10 percent of gold. Thus, for example, if Canada wishes to sell to the Fund some of its blocked sterling balances in exchange for United States dollars, Canada would either have to accept Canadian dollars or the Fund would have to be assured that Canada needs the United States dollars to make payments to the United States (for trade, services, interest payments, or even investments) and not to make possible an increase in Canada's gold holdings or an increase in her United States dollar exchange. In other words, if Canada wished to use the sterling accumulated by herself, or her nationals, to convert into funds to be spent in United States, or in Mexico or in Netherlands, the Fund could make that possible without, on the one hand, putting any strain on England and, on the other hand, without denuding the Fund of its gold assets. Canada would be able, according to the above provision, to add to her gold holdings by 10 percent of the blocked balances she sold to the Fund.

e. If the Fund's stocks of sterling or other currencies should decline the Fund can offer to reduce the rate of repurchase required of both governments as specified above, but should it do so, the countries involved must be relieved by the same percentage, and shall be deemed to have repurchased the amount by which they are so released.

A service charge of possibly 1 percent would be imposed by the Fund on countries involved.

Perhaps the operation would be more easily understood if the specific steps were outlined which a country would have to go through under the plan suggested to realize on its blocked funds.

For convenience of illustration, let us take a specific case. Let us assume that the Chinese Government has £50 million blocked in England and wishes to utilize £10 million of it in the ensuing quarter. The steps would be as follows:

1. China makes application to the Fund. The Fund after investigation is satisfied that the use of at least 90 percent of the £10 million is not to accumulate gold or foreign exchange. (China can if it wishes add 10 percent of the £10 million of gold to her holdings.)
2. The £10 million is transferred by the British banks from the Chinese Government to the Fund. The Chinese Government pays 1 percent (in yuan) to the Fund and the British pay 1 percent (in sterling) as a "service" charge.
3. The Fund gives to China
   a. the equivalent of £1 million in gold (if China wishes it), and
   b. the equivalent of £9 million in one or more currencies needed and requested by China—say, $12 million in United States dollars and 120 million Mexican pesos. If the Fund doesn't have enough Mexican pesos, it purchases what it needs.
4. After three years from the date of the transaction:
   a. China begins to repurchase from the Fund each year £200,000 (2 percent of 40 percent of £10 million) of British sterling, at the same rates of exchange she received, paying for the sterling either in yuan or other currencies she received, depending upon the wishes of the Fund.
   b. England begins to repurchase the same amount of sterling each year, paying for the sterling either gold or "New International Units".
   c. China is free to do what she likes with her repurchased sterling, England having agreed in the first place that there would be no restrictions on its withdrawal.
5. Not later than 23 years after the transaction the situation would be as follows:
   a. China would have utilized the £10 million, while her balance of payments would be burdened not at all for 3 years and by not more than 1.2 percent of the £10 million a year after three years.
   b. England would have been able to unfreeze China's balances, while imposing no burden on her (England's) foreign exchange resources for the first three years, and from then on 1.6 percent to 3.2 percent a year (2 percent of from 40 to 80 percent), depending upon what China elects to do with her repurchased 2 percent.
   c. The Fund will have first exchanged some of her gold assets for £1 million, or possibly more if she had to purchase currencies with gold to satisfy China's demands, and will have exchanged the remainder of the £10 million of various currencies for sterling.

      Then the Fund would get back each year gold from England to a sum not less than 2 percent of £4 million until the Fund will have received £4 million in gold. The Fund would also get £4 million of certain currencies from China, leaving the Fund with 2 million pounds sterling.

      The Fund will also have earned 2 percent (1 percent in yuan and 1 percent

in sterling) in the transactions, and some interest on her investment of sterling balances in British Government securities.

At the end of 23 years—or sooner if England permits—the Fund could sell the remaining £2 million of sterling and the transaction would be complete.

The above is the transaction under most unfavorable conditions. A more likely outcome is that either or both China and England could purchase back the sterling from the Fund a great deal sooner than 23 years. Nonetheless, a long period is permitted to assure an easy adjustment for both England and China in the event the situation would not be favorable to a rapid adjustment.

The illustration has been that of Government-owned funds. If, as is equally likely, the British sterling balances were owned by nationals of China instead of the Government of China, the general process would be the same but some details would differ.

First, the Chinese nationals would have to indicate to their Government that they wished their blocked balances released. It might be found desirable to give private persons only local currencies in exchange for blocked foreign balances. How important this restriction would be is uncertain since they could later buy any currency desired. The Chinese Government would then make the arrangements with the Fund, after which the Chinese Government would transfer to its nationals the money which the Fund puts at China's disposal in exchange for their sterling balances. Title to the sterling balances would be transferred to the Fund.

So long as China is willing to take yuan for the blocked sterling, the Fund would supply it, if necessary buying or borrowing yuan for the purpose. If, however, China's Treasury asks for United States dollars or Brazilian milreis, the Fund might wish to satisfy itself first that China needed those currencies for "legitimate" purposes.

The Treasury of China would be permitting its nationals to avoid the risk of exchange that holders of blocked sterling would otherwise have to bear. Forty percent of that risk would be borne by the Treasury of China since it would be committed to repurchase 40 percent of the sterling unblocked to it; forty percent would be borne by the British Treasury for a similar reason. The Fund would accept the other 20 percent of the exchange risk.

The Treasury of China might impose a two or three percent charge on its nationals for the transaction. That would help cover the service charge imposed by the Fund, and leave a small profit after expense of administration.

Consideration might be given to the possibility that a small annual charge could be imposed by the Fund on the blocked balances it held. In the above illustration, for example, a charge of 1 percent a year could be placed on both China and England on the blocked sterling not yet repurchased.

Arrangements for the transaction might take some time, but for the individual holder of the blocked balance the transaction would be simple. After the initial arrangements had been completed, the transactions between the Fund and the two Governments involved would assume an almost routine character. Careful watching of the balance of payments of the various countries concerned in the transactions would be necessary continuously. That task, however, would be one of the important current responsibilities of the Fund's technical staff at all times and with all countries. The condition and movements of the international accounts of the member countries would be to the Fund's research staff, what the thermometer, stethoscope, x-ray, and microscope, etc., are to the diagnostician. Without a carefully drawn up and compiled quarterly balance of payments account of member countries the technical staff of the Fund would be greatly handicapped in their recommendation of decisions and policies. With adequate data in their hands they would be in a position to know and understand what was going on in matters pertinent to the work of the Fund.

How much could the Fund be expected to do with blocked balances? The sum of blocked balances which the Fund would be called upon to purchase might be greater than the Fund felt it could afford to take. If, for example, it were asked to absorb two billion dollars of blocked balances it might well hesitate if such assets were not to be liquid. It might be three years before they could sell any of it, and even then they might not be able to sell it at a rate faster than 4 percent a year. The Fund could, it is true, invest the assets in interest-bearing Government obligations (of the country in which the currency is blocked), but they could not convert those into gold or other currencies without either risking a loss on the transaction or adding to the possible drain of gold from the country whose obligations they were selling.

If the Fund attempted to sell a substantial amount of (say) British Government obligations payable in sterling to residents of United States, the price the Fund would get might be substantially less than what the Fund paid for the bonds.

Moreover, if the Fund invested the blocked sterling in British Government bonds, and then sold them in New York, and later the Americans sold the bonds in London getting sterling which would not be blocked, the end result would be that England would be subjected to the drain on her foreign exchange resources which she wished in the first place to avoid. It seems, therefore, that if the Fund is to be permitted to invest its sterling in British Government obligations, it should not be permitted to sell them except as England repurchased them according to the schedule, or unless the British Government approved the sale.

Yet the Fund would like to take over as much of the blocked balances as possible, but, on the other hand, could not tie up too much of her liquid resources in frozen currencies. A way out of the dilemma might be to permit the Fund to borrow in New York (or anywhere else except England) using as collateral the British Government bonds. With that possibility for converting a frozen asset into a liquid resource the Fund could afford to take more blocked balances. It might even be feasible to arrange that the bonds be special ones payable in either gold or sterling (at the holder's will), in order to increase their collateral value. Since 40 percent of the blocked sterling the Fund acquires would have to be repurchased with gold anyway, this latter possibility might be acceptable to the Government concerned.

The end result of the exercise of this authority should be:

1. Private holders of blocked sterling balances should be able to convert them at once into their local currencies by selling them to their Government. With that currency nationals, as distinct from the Government, could purchase any currency they wished.

2. Their Government would be in possession of sterling which at small risk of exchange on 40 percent of its purchases it could sell to the Fund for any currency it wished.

3. England could at once remove restrictions on the withdrawal of foreign-owned sterling balances without fearing any serious drain on her gold or other foreign exchange assets. She would have to purchase back only 40 percent of the funds withdrawn under this authority at the rate of 2 percent a year, beginning after three years.

Two gains would quickly emerge: one, the demand for withdrawal would be greatly lessened by the fact that foreign holders would have no reason to hurry their withdrawal, and two, the post-war pressure against sterling would be dissipated and hence the sterling rate could be more easily maintained.

If adjustment of the price of sterling in terms of other currencies were later justified by a basic unbalance, then only 40 percent of the resultant exchange loss would be borne by England, and not more than 40 percent by the country having blocked balances, and 20 percent by the Fund.

4. Finally, foreign purchasing power would be released to be spent wherever desired, and one of the potent obstacles to a return to fair trade practices removed.

This provision on blocked balances is not proposed as a method of freeing balances which might accumulate after the war. Unless the funds to which this particular power are to apply is clearly delimited, the provision would overlap and largely nullify other provisions contained in the proposal specifically designed to meet current and developing situations in a country's balance of payments. The provision described in the previous several pages is not intended to make it possible for owners of foreign balances—whatever the source of these balances may be—to withdraw those balances at will at the expense of the Fund's assets. It is hoped that the Fund will make it possible for all countries to remove restrictions on exchange transactions, but this particular provision should be used as the vehicle to free only the blocked balances in existence at the date the country joins the Fund. It is for the purpose of clearing up the present bad situation with respect to blocked currencies that this provision is included.

In the event a similar situation develops in the future, authority is granted to the Fund provided four-fifths of the member votes approve to initiate a similar program which would apply to the then-existing balances.

To provide the data necessary for the operation of this provision each member country should be required to file with the Fund a record of the balances in its country owned by residents of foreign countries, and also a record of the balances of its nationals held abroad. These balances should be broken down in the significant categories as required by the Fund A quarterly report should be filed keeping the information up to date.

The fact that each of the parties concerned, i.e. the country in which the balances are blocked, the country whose nationals own the balances, and the Fund—will be undertaking an exchange risk should help prevent undesirable practices or misapplication of this provision.

In evaluating the effectiveness of this provision to liberate blocked balances, it must be borne in mind that the mere existence of this power will remove much of the eagerness to withdraw funds in the near future. That reaction would in turn make it easier for England (and other countries) to remove exchange restrictions. Even though the blocked balances in various countries outside of the United States were as high as the equivalent of 6 billion dollars, only a portion of this amount would be involved unless there were strong fears of depreciation of sterling—a development the Fund could do much to prevent. The greater the assurance that foreign exchange rates will be stable, and the knowledge that large portions of the funds will be unblocked periodically would encourage holders of these balances to diminish their withdrawal requests.

However, since the amount that the Fund might be called upon to absorb might be larger than it wished to handle at the beginning, the Fund is given the authority to set a maximum percentage of blocked balances that could be handled through this provision in any given period. It would be easy enough to adjust that percentage upward if circumstances indicated it could be safely done.

The fixing of rates.

The Fund would fix the rates at which it would exchange a member's currency for another, and the rates at which it would buy and sell gold in exchange for local currency.

The guiding principle in the fixing of such rates should be stability in exchange relationships. To assure the maximum stability in rates, it is suggested that alterations in rates set by the Fund beyond the range of narrow fluctuations applying to all rates be permitted only with the consent of four-fifths of the member votes. If a country does not wish to accept or pay the rate fixed by the Fund, it can, of course, attempt to complete its transactions through other channels. Nonetheless the authority to set the rates of exchange at which the Fund is willing to operate can be an important and in some cases a decisive influence on the rate at which transactions are made outside of the Fund.

The service charge for exchange transactions should be no larger than necessary to cover the direct costs of the operations.

Borrowing from the Fund.

Any member country can borrow its local currency from the Fund for one year or less up to 75 percent of the currency of that country held by the Fund, provided such loan is approved by three-fourths of the member votes.

A country borrowing such funds shall pay to the Fund an interest rate of 1 percent a year. Revenue from such loans shall constitute a reserve for the Fund which can be drawn upon to meet expenses or losses of the Fund.

The object of the provision permitting any member country to borrow local currency from the Fund for one year or less up to 75 percent of the currency of that country held by the Fund, provided such loan is approved by three-fourths of the member votes, is to make it possible for a member country to reduce the burden of participation on its budget. Some of the countries may at times be confronted with deficits, and the investment that they would have in the Fund should be a source to which they could turn in time of need to borrow at very low rates of interest. It may well prove to be the case that every country operating at a deficit would prefer to borrow up to the maximum of its local currency, at 1 percent, rather than go into the market and possibly pay 2 or more percent. Inasmuch as a fund could, if necessary, always obtain such local currency by rediscounting the paper in that market, there would seem to be no reason why the Fund should object to such practice on the part of those countries wishing to avail themselves of the low rate of interest. Also, from the Fund's point of view, it would be desirable to permit such loans since it would prove a source of revenue with which to meet expenses or losses of the Fund.

Borrowing by the Fund.

It is suggested that the Fund should have authority to borrow at such rates as the Fund may recommend, the currency of any country, provided four-fifths of the member votes approve the terms, amount and conditions of such borrowing.

This provision gives the Fund power to obtain any currency it may feel it will need only for a short time. It also makes it possible for the Fund to expand its resources to meet short-term special demands.

Currency sold to a government in default.

No sale of any currency from the Fund should be made to a member without approval of four-fifths of the member votes when the sale of such currency so sold is to make possible adjustment of a government foreign debt which had been defaulted. This provision is probably necessary in order to prevent utilizing the Fund for the purpose of servicing a foreign debt. The resources of the Fund should be used for such purpose only when most of the Board feels that the borrowing for debt adjustment is temporary, or when they are satisfied that basic adjustments are being undertaken.

Accept deposits, act as clearing house for international movements of funds, balances, checks, etc.

The power to accept deposits and perform clearing functions would enable the Fund to operate more efficiently in its foreign exchange operations. It is not intended that the Fund shall perform banking functions other than those supplementary to the task of foreign exchange stabilization.

Deal only with (a) the Treasuries of the participating countries, or with the official stabilization funds of those countries, and (b) with the bank designated by the participating government as its fiscal agent, and (c) with international banks and international corporations owned by at least five governments.

The Fund is envisaged as an intergovernmental agency which should interfere as little as possible with the operations of private banks, brokers and dealers. It is only when the supply-demand relationship of exchange arising out of usual transactions through the customary channels are causing pressure in an undesired direction, that the Fund begins to operate.

The Fund will also wish to deal with any intergovernmental financial institutions such as the proposed Inter-American Bank. The Fund shall have the authority to invest any currency it holds in "short-term" securities—commercial or government— of the country of that currency provided a four-fifths vote of the member votes shall approve and provided further that the approving votes shall include those of the country in which the investment is to be made.

The Fund shall also have authority to sell the obligation it holds of the member countries provided four-fifths of the member votes approve, and provided the representative of the country in which the securities are to be sold approves.

Value of total holdings should remain unchanged.

No change in the gold value of any currency of the participating countries shall be permitted to alter the gold value of the total currency holdings of the Fund. Through the day-to-day operations of the Fund, the proportion of various local currencies held by the Fund will constantly change, but the book value of the total assets would remain the same in terms of the unit of account (presuming the small service charges and interest revenue would cover operating expenses). The unit of account used should either be gold or a new international unit defined in terms of gold. If the currency of any of the participating countries should depreciate, that country must deliver to the Fund an amount of its local currency equal to the decrease in the value of that currency held by the Fund. Likewise, if the currency of a particular country should increase, the Fund must deliver to that country an amount (in the currency of that country) equal to the resultant increase in the gold value of the Fund's holdings.

An exception to the above would be the blocked balances purchased by the Fund under provision described earlier. Those currencies could be kept in a separate account until repurchased or sold. The only portion upon which there might be a loss is in the 20 percent portion, the exchange risk on which is borne by the Fund. The sole justification for placing that exchange risk on the Fund is the desire to spread some of the risk of sterling accumulations resulting from the war on all nations benefiting by the successful outcome. If that is not considered adequate justification, the Fund can be relieved of any risk.

The only serious bookkeeping loss that could be experienced would be in the event the unit of account—either a new international unit fixed in terms of gold or the dollar having a fixed gold content—were to appreciate in terms of all or most of the currencies. That is equivalent to saying that all other currencies depreciated in terms of the unit of account. There is no way to avoid that possibility unless the unit of account were defined in terms of an index of other currencies—a complicated device and of doubtful utility.

A country failing to contribute to the Fund sums due the Fund shall be dropped as a member, provided a majority of the member votes so decide. Any member dropped shall have returned to it an amount (in its own currency) equal to its contribution minus any sum due by that country to the Fund.

III. Eligibility for Membership

The conditions selected to be fulfilled before any country can be eligible for membership in the Fund constitute an important part of the plan. It will also prove to be one of the most disputed parts. Serious differences of opinion as to the wisdom of including many of the conditions listed are certain to exist. It will be said of some of them that they embrace far too wide an area of economic policy. Others on the list will be opposed on the grounds that they involve policy decisions which cannot be shared by or delegated to any combination of nations. And against some of the conditions listed opposition will arise because there will be differing views as to the economic soundness of some of the requirements, and of the political feasibility of others. Finally, some of the requirements for eligibility listed may be very difficult for many countries to accept because acceptance would involve abandonment, or rather suspension, during period of membership, of certain legislative powers. Nonetheless, the list is submitted because the chief purpose of this memorandum is to suggest possibilities and stimulate discussion.

It is vital to the success of any international stabilization fund designed to play a really useful role that there be a suspension of certain economic elements of national sovereignty in favor of international collaboration. It is well to recognize at the outset that unless there is willingness to keep dormant, for a trial period at least, certain rights to unilateral economic action which directly affect other countries, there is no hope that any international instrument can be devised to help bring about the kind of collaboration among nations essential to a prosperous and peaceful world. If no government is prepared to sacrifice for the sake of a larger though possibly a less obvious good what it regards as an advantage when that advantage is obtained at the expense of some friendly power, then the world will revert to the barbaric international economic relationships of the 'twenties and 'thirties.

The strength of the position of those who call for the temporary transfer to an international body of certain sovereign economic powers rests in the conviction that the long-run interests of most countries are best served when no country seeks to gain at the expense of another. It is true that rich and powerful countries can for long periods safely and easily ignore the interests of poorer or weaker neighbors or competitors, but by doing so they will imperil the future and reduce the potentiality of their own level of prosperity. The lesson that must be learned is that prosperous neighbors are the best neighbors; that a higher standard of living in one country begets higher standards in others, and that a high level of trade and business is most easily attained when generously and widely shared.

It is with these thoughts in mind that the following list of conditions for eligibility should be examined.

Any member of the United or Associated Nations is eligible for membership in the Fund provided it agrees:

To abandon, not later than one year after joining the Fund, all restrictions and controls over foreign exchange transactions with member countries, except with the approval of the Fund.

It is important that participating countries be motivated by common objectives in conceiving their foreign exchange policies and desirous of adopting basically harmonious procedures in implementing such policies. Some allowance will, of course, have to be made for reasonable differences because of dissimilarities in the economies of various countries, and early in the Fund's existence there would need to be toleration of lack of uniformity in policy. In general, however, and as basic and long-run prerequisites to participation, it would seem necessary for each member country to subscribe to the general policies of permitting foreign exchange trading in an open, free and legal market, and to abandon, as rapidly as conditions permit, all restrictions or controls by which various classes of foreign exchange transactions have been prohibited or interfered with, other than from consummation in such a free market.

This requirement calls for careful examination. There has been too easy an acceptance of the view that an enlightened trade and monetary policy requires complete abandonment of controls over international economic transactions. There is a tendency to regard foreign exchange controls, or any interference with the free movement of funds and of goods as, ipso facto, bad. This view is both unrealistic and unsound. It ignores the fact that there are situations in which many countries frequently find themselves, and which all countries occasionally meet, that make inevitable the adoption of controls of one character or another. There are times when it is in the best economic interests of a country to impose restrictions on movements of capital, and on movements of goods. There are periods in a country's history when failure to impose exchange controls, or import or export controls, have led to serious economic and political disruption.

It probably would be fatal to the Fund if the conditions of participation in it were based upon the assumption that no restrictions upon exchange or upon trade were permissible.

It would be equally unfortunate, however, if it were to be assumed that restrictions on foreign exchange transactions, on the international movement of goods, and the use of multiple currency devices were desirable instruments to employ under all circumstances for safeguarding or controlling international economic relationships. It is as easy to exaggerate the need for such instruments and the benefits derived from the use thereof, as it is to exaggerate their adverse effects.

The theoretical bases for the belief still so widely held, that interference with trade and with capital and gold movements, etc., are harmful, are hangovers from a Nineteenth Century economic creed, which held that international economic adjustments, if left alone, would work themselves out toward an "equilibrium" with a minimum of harm to world trade and prosperity.

It is doubtful whether that belief was ever sound. Certainly few competent students of international economic affairs would hold that it applied to present conditions or to conditions likely to prevail during the post-war period. The forces of adjustment set into motion by changing trade balances, flows of gold or of purchasing power, changes in price levels and all the phenomena that the expert in the subject recognizes as instrumentalities in the so-called mechanism of adjustment of international balances of payment, rarely, if ever, work out quickly enough or effectively enough to be depended upon to achieve good results. In fact, it is doubtful if they ever were depended upon, unaided, to bring about the desired "equilibrium". In modern times, particularly, there has always been somewhere in the picture some measure of control over, some measure of interference with the movement of funds and goods in order to bring about certain desired ends.

The task before us is not to prohibit instruments of control but to develop those measures of control, those policies of administering such control, as will be the most effective in obtaining the objectives of world-wide sustained prosperity. To cast aside certain effective instrumentalities of control because they may be and have been abused, is just as foolish as it would be to rely solely on the self-interest motive of individuals as a means of solving our economic problems.

The requirement suggested above that there be accepted the general policy of foreign exchange trading in open, free and legal markets, and the abandonment as rapidly as conditions permit of restrictions on exchange controls, should be taken to mean that there shall be acceptance of the principle that controls and restrictions will be employed only when they are clearly justified by the economic circumstances, and only to the extent necessary to carry out a purpose contributing to general prosperity. The chief difficulty in the application of the principle will be agreement as to what is in the interests of general prosperity. The danger of conflicting policies lies not only in the difficulty of distinguishing between real and specious advantage, i.e. between the advantages of a special group as against the advantages of the whole—but much more in the difficulty of reconciling short-run interests with long-run interests. One of the purposes of this Fund is to provide for a more reasonable basis for such distinction, and to supply the means through which it should be possible to pursue long-run and broader interests, without too great a sacrifice of the narrower and short-run interests.

The second requirement or condition for participation should be the acceptance of the principle that no participating country will alter its exchange rate on currencies of other countries without the consent of the Fund.

This condition is very important. Its obvious purpose is to eliminate the possibility of competitive depreciation of currencies. It recognizes that there are occasions when it may be economically wise for a country to increase or decrease the value of its currency in terms of other currencies. When a country's balance of payments is in disequilibrium for causes that do not appear to be temporary, and if that disequilibrium uncorrected will deplete a country's foreign exchange reserve, then altering the value of that currency in terms of other currencies is one of the ways in which the disequilibrium could be corrected. Other ways of correcting disequilibrium in the balance of payments are the imposition of restrictions on imports and subsidy of exports, either directly through import and export controls, or through use of exchange controls or multiple currencies. Which method or methods are best suited to accomplish the objective depends on the cause of the disequilibrium, the circumstances, the country, and the time.

The circumstances under which it may be wise to alter an exchange rate in order to correct maladjustments of the balance of payments have long been a matter of controversy among monetary theorists. But there is general agreement that an alteration in the value of a currency in terms of gold (or in terms of important currencies) is a very serious business and one not to be undertaken lightly. The change in the value of a currency in terms of gold or other currencies means that a change has by that act been imposed on the other currencies. When, for example, the dollar changes in terms of sterling, obviously sterling changes in terms of the dollar. Because all countries are to a lesser or greater degree affected by the action of any one country with respect to the value of its currency, it is only reasonable to demand that such action should not be undertaken without careful—and, if possible, impartial—weighing of the consequences of the action on other countries.

The purpose of requiring approval by the Fund as a condition of alteration of currency is to assure joint consideration of the merits of the proposed action and thereby avoid unilateral action taken to obtain presumed competitive short-run advantages irrespective of the consequences of the impact of the step on other countries or even on the same country. The mere fact that membership would be forfeited if a country acted in so important a matter contrary to the wishes of the majority would make countries hesitate to undertake lightly a change in their currency. The very discussion of the problem by competent representatives of various countries should in itself be a potent influence to avoid unnecessary changes. It would, moreover, be an assurance that when a change is made it would not be a signal for numerous other countries to follow in their own real or presumed interest.

There will be difficulties surrounding the operation of this condition, the most important of which would be the necessity for secrecy when a country is contemplating a step such as altering the value of its currency in terms of other currencies. If a country believes that it should depreciate its currency relative to others, it could hardly throw that matter open for public discussion. By so doing it would stimulate speculative activities in the exchange market which might have the effect of precipitating the very action being considered. Some procedure would have to be devised to make possible deliberations without publicity. It might be that an Executive Committee could undertake to pass on such cases, or it might be possible to arrange that during such discussions no country will accept or permit movements of capital to and from a country considering the step.

Some objection to this requirement will doubtless be raised on the ground that such a provision means that other countries pass judgment on what is a domestic monetary matter. The necessity for obtaining approval of other countries on such a matter will be regarded in some quarters as a serious infringement of sovereignty. There is some measure of truth in this but hardly enough to constitute a decisive reason for not participating in the Fund. Alteration of a currency affects other countries as well as the country making the change. It is, therefore, only reasonable to demand that the other countries have some say in the decision. Furthermore, all members would be surrendering their "rights" to an equal extent. Unless nations are willing to sacrifice some of their power to take unilateral action in matters of international economic relations, there is very little hope of any significant international cooperation—let alone collaboration.

To avoid giving richer nations greater authority on such matters, by virtue of their larger number of votes, it may be desirable to give each participant only one vote when questions of altering currency rates are being voted upon. As a last resort, a country always has the choice of withdrawing from the Fund so that it can always preserve its sovereignty in monetary matters if it feels it is being prevented by the Fund from taking action deemed important to its own interest.

The principle worked only tolerably well in the Tripartite Accord during 1935, 1936 and 1937, and better machinery for more adequate discussion and greater willingness to recognize the legitimate interests of other countries, needs to be developed to achieve best results. In evaluating the need for collaboration on questions of foreign exchange rates, it is well to remember that unilateral action can easily be neutralized by similar action on the part of other countries. When a competitive advantage is sought it is essential if it is to be successful that other countries do not take similar action. Otherwise the advantage hoped for is lost. Where the chief objective sought is not a competitive trade advantage in the international market but modification of the domestic price structure or money market, the favorable effects cannot be wholly negated by action of other countries. Since, however, the chief reason for establishing the requirement is to avoid competitive depreciation of currencies, the fact that unilateral action can be easily neutralized constitutes an important argument for securing approval of the Fund before taking such action.

Each country agrees (a) not to accept or permit deposits or investments from any member country except with the permission of that country, and (b) to make available to the government of any member country at its request all property in form of deposits, investments, securities, of the nationals of member countries, under such terms and conditions as will not impose an unreasonable burden on the country of whom the request is made.

This is a far-reaching and important requirement. Its acceptance would go a long way toward solving one of the very troublesome problems in international economic relations, and would remove one of the most potent disturbing factors of monetary stability. Flights of capital, motivated either by prospect of speculative exchange gain, or desire to avoid inflation, or evade taxes or influence legislation, frequently take place especially during disturbed periods. Almost every country, at one time or another, exercises control over the inflow and outflow of investments, but without the cooperation of other countries such control is difficult, expensive, and subject to considerable evasion.

It would seem to be an important step in the direction of world stability if a member government could obtain the full cooperation of other member governments in the control of capital flows. For example, after the war a number of countries could request the United States not to permit increases in the deposits or holdings of their nationals, or to do so only with a license granted by the government making the request. Or, some countries greatly in need of capital might request the United States to supplement their efforts to attract capital back to the native country by providing information, or imposing special regulations or even special taxes, on certain types of holdings of the nationals of the foreign countries.

The search for speculative exchange gains or desire to evade the impact of new taxes or burdens of social legislation have been one of the chief causes of foreign exchange disturbances. Less hectic and less dramatic yet in the case of some countries during some stages of their development capable in the long run of even greater harm, is the steady drain of capital from a country that needs the capital but is unable for one reason or another to offer sufficient monetary return to keep its capital at home. The assumption that capital serves a country best by flowing to countries which offer most attractive terms is valid only under circumstances that are not always present.

A good case could be made for the thesis that a government should have the power to control the influx and efflux of capital, just as it has the authority to control the inflow and outflow of goods and of gold. In fact, virtually every participating government has already practiced these controls to some extent during this war. The consequence of cooperation in this matter among the member governments would give each government much greater measure of control in carrying out its monetary and tax policies. Such an increase in the effectiveness of control means, however, less freedom for owners of liquid capital. It would constitute another restriction on the property rights of the 5 or 10 percent of persons in foreign countries who have enough wealth or income to keep or invest some of it abroad, but a restriction that presumably would be exercised in the interests of the people—at least so far as the government is competent to judge that interest.

The inclusion of this provision does not mean that capital flows between foreign countries would disappear or even greatly subside; it means only that they would not be permitted to operate against what the government deemed to be the interests of any country.

A fourth condition might be that each country agrees not to enter upon any bilateral clearing arrangements except with non-member countries, and then only with the consent of the Fund, and to establish no geographically preferential exchange rates.

The justification for setting up this requirement for participation is to eliminate discriminatory practices in foreign trade which result in friction, unfair competition, retaliation, and sharp trade policies which serve to disrupt good economic and political relations. It means that for the sake of the larger good to be obtained countries agree to give up opportunities for making certain advantageous arrangements. If each country is to operate in accordance with its own immediate interest, irrespective of long-run effects and irrespective of the impact of its actions on other countries, a repetition of the pre-war chaotic conditions in trade will result and again threaten political and economic stability of other nations. The task which confronts the high officials of all nations is to make possible a high level of business activity and of foreign trade within the framework of reasonable and fair foreign trade practices. Just as individuals subscribe to a government of law to obtain maximum prosperity and effectiveness for the whole group, even though adherence to that law involves restrictions on individual behavior at numerous points, so must nations give up lesser advantages for greater good. The concept of sacrificing some immediate benefits for the sake of larger good is the foundation stone of peace and economic collaboration among nations, just as it is the keystone of peace and prosperity within a nation.

The operations of the two agencies discussed in this report should help considerably to remove the justification for trade practices adopted to protect or strengthen an exchange position.

There are times when gains could accrue from bilateral clearing arrangements without significant adverse effects on other countries, but in general the operation of the Fund should have the effect of making such clearing arrangements much less profitable as among members of the Fund. One of the specific objectives of the Fund is to make available for each member a supply of foreign exchange adequate to enable it to operate more freely and with a higher level of trade than would otherwise be the case. Nevertheless, in the interest of flexibility, and to take care of those situations in which circumstances may warrant a bilateral clearing arrangement, it should be possible for a country to enter upon such an arrangement provided it can obtain the Fund's approval. Discussions by the Fund of such proposals do not require the secrecy or the speed involved in consideration of alterations of exchange rate, and discussions of the advantages and disadvantages of the particular proposal should prove beneficial. An objective decision on the economic wisdom of such proposal is more likely to emerge from the discussion by the appropriate committee of the Fund than from the consideration by one or two countries alone where vested or political interests are likely to dominate the decision.

A fifth requisite for membership might be subscription to the principle that no monetary or banking or price measure or policy would be adopted, the effect of which, in the opinion of a majority of the member votes, would be to bring about sooner or later a serious disequilibrium in the balance of payments, if four-fifths of the member votes of the Fund submitted to the country in question their disapproval of the adoption of the measure.

This provision would prove to be more troublesome than any of the others and yet it would seem to be important to the successful functioning of the Stabilization Fund. Serious inflation or deflation in any one country would affect not only exchange rates and trade, but price levels in other countries as well. It is impossible for any country to take action of that character which does not have important effects on other countries with whom it competes or with whom it carries on trade. The decision as to whether a particular measure or policy contemplated would bring about a serious disequilibrium in the balance of payments would be a difficult one on which to get agreement. To estimate even very roughly the quantitative effects of any given measure on a country's balance of payments is a very difficult task at best. After sufficient agreement was reached on that point it would be even more difficult in many cases to get any measure of agreement as to whether the adoption of the measure in question was economically wise or not.

There are times when domestic consequences are sought which are more important to a country than the adverse effects that might follow in some directions from the accompanying disequilibrium in the balance of payments. There are other instances in which disequilibrium provides a necessary corrective, and frequently a country is confronted with only poor choices and disequilibrium is the least undesirable of them.

To assume that it would ever prove easy to get four-fifths of the member votes to take so drastic a step as to disapprove a measure proposed by a sovereign government deemed by it to be in its own interest, is to ignore the known complexities of the monetary problems, and the political realities of international relationships.

Notwithstanding the difficulties involved in exercise of a veto power by the Fund over monetary measures, there will be instances in which the case is clear enough and the consequences important enough to justify the exercise of that power. It is assumed that the Fund would not concern itself with minor measures. To help avoid the error of attempting to evaluate measures which are not important, the requirement provides that a majority of the members would have to be of the opinion that the results of any given measure are likely to be serious. It then requires four-fifths of the member votes to authorize official disapproval. It may well be that despite this degree of protection against arbitrary action or needless interference most countries would object to subjecting what they believe to be purely domestic affairs to international supervision. If compromise with this view is found feasible, it is hoped that it takes the form of requiring a larger majority—say 90 percent instead of 80 percent of the member votes, or, as a last resort, requiring that the disapproval of the Fund call forth the promise of the offending country to reexamine her position in the light of the Fund's report.

In any case, the discussion which would take place by an international committee of the character envisaged—men expert in their fields, international in their outlook, and scientific in their approach—could not help but prove very salutary. The educational process to which officials, administrative and legislative, in each country would be subjected in defending specific policies or measures before such a committee would in itself go a long way toward improving the quality of monetary, credit and banking policy. It probably would be necessary for the committee, certainly during the early years, to be very tolerant of policies pursued by participating countries. Gradually, however, there should develop a greater reluctance on the part of member countries to take measures which do not meet the approval of the majority of the members of the Fund. The success of the Fund in this field would depend in large measure upon the wisdom with which matters of this kind are examined and the degree of sympathetic understanding the Fund was capable of displaying.

The member countries agree (a) to embark within a year after joining upon a program of gradual reduction of existing trade barriers—import duties, import quotas, administrative devices—and further agree (b) not to adopt any increase in tariff schedules, or other devices having as their purposes higher obstacles to imports, without giving reasonable opportunity for the Fund to study the effects of the contemplated change on exchange rates and to register its opinion. In rendering an opinion the Fund will make recommendations to which member governments agree to give serious consideration.

It might contribute notably to conditions tending to promote exchange stability if participating countries, particularly those with large reserve of foreign exchange, were to agree to a gradual reduction of duties on imports. It might be possible to devise an acceptable formula for general and gradual tariff reduction to a level more in harmony than were tariff policies of the twentieth century with the objectives of reducing the causes for international friction and increasing the standard of living the world over. Those high tariff policies in the main reflect adherence to the traditional, crude, mercantilist fallacies. So widely held are those fallacies, so persistently clung to by persons who should know better, so potent are they in shaping many aspects of domestic and foreign policy, and so unfortunate in their effects on world peace and prosperity, that one is tempted to list "mercantilism" or its more expressive heir "protectionism" as "World Enemy No. 1," in the economic sphere.

Yet, though there is no doubt as to the evils of crude protectionist policies, caution must be exercised in attempting to translate a policy of lower tariff schedules into an actual program. There is danger of retarding progress by advocating a trade policy which ignores the sound basis for the existence of some import duties. There is too easy an assumption that as much reduction as possible in all duties is desirable; that any movement toward free trade is, ipso facto, a good thing for the world.

In the reaction against the crude protectionist fallacies that a country with high standards of living must adhere to a policy of high tariff schedules if it is to prevent widespread unemployment or deterioration of its high standard of living, there is an inclination to throw the baby out with the bath and assume that all duties are bad; that free trade, or rather tariff for revenue only, is the ideal toward which all enlightened nations should move as rapidly as possible.

The belief that reduction in all import duties increases trade and yields a higher standard of living for all countries under all circumstances and in all stages of their economic evolution assumes that countries are usually utilizing virtually all their capital and labor; that a country chiefly agricultural in its economy has as many economic, political and social advantages as a country whose economy is chiefly industrial, or as a country which has a balanced economy; that there are no gains to be achieved by great diversification of output. These assumptions, essential to the belief that "Free Trade" policy is ideal, are not valid. They are unreal and unsound. "Free Trade" policy grossly underestimates the extent to which a country can virtually lift itself by its bootstraps in one generation from a lower to a higher standard of living, from a backward agricultural to an advanced industrialized country, provided always it is willing to pay the price. The view further overlooks the very important fact that political relationships among countries being what they are, vital considerations exist in the shaping of the economic structure of a country other than that of producing goods with the least labor.

The subject of the best tariff policy for a given country at a given period in its history is a most interesting one, but justice could not be done to it in the space that could reasonably be allocated to it here. A great deal has been written on the subject and the interested reader in his search for sound policy will find that the complexity of the problem is apt to increase with the profundity of his reading. Yet one conclusion is certain to emerge from his study of the subject, namely, that most import duties are too high, that many duties remain too long, that few are imposed for sound reasons, and almost none of them are reevaluated often enough by the law-making bodies in the light of changing needs and conditions.

The value of requiring participating governments to agree to a general policy of lower tariffs lies solely in the recognition that most duties in the tariff schedules of every country, at their present level, are inexcusable on any economic, political or social grounds. Their existence merely reflects uncritical adhesion to protectionist policies or the successful pressure of some powerful vested interest, or both. It is to place on the defensive obstructions to trade, whether in the form of unreasonably high duties or in any other form, that commitment to lower tariff policies might be justified.

Yet, it cannot be overlooked that the shaping of tariff policy has been for too long the prerogative of lawmaking bodies and the battleground of legislative maneuvering to expect the Congresses and Parliaments to subordinate to an international body their authority on such matters. If the sugar, wool, wheat growers of the United States, and the shoe and textile, pottery, and steel manufacturers—to name only a few of the industries insisting on high protective duties—were to see in any suggested agency a definite threat to what they regard as necessary protection to their industry, they would combine and probably rally enough support to their crusade to ruin the prospects of acceptance by Congress of any proposal no matter how attractive the scheme might be to economists, statesmen, foreign trade associations, college professors and bankers.

It would seem to be a far wiser policy not to attempt too much and thereby jeopardize any but an innocuous program. On this issue, as on no other, prudence dictates compromise. The most one can hope to get is adherence to a principle without surrender of any authority. Hence the requirement calls only for public adherence to the stated principle, and permission to the Fund to submit a report giving reasons for its disapproval of an added barrier to trade if the Fund deems it harmful. If any international agency or organization wrings more than that out of the American and other publics, a miracle in economic morality will have been wrought by this war.

Another possible condition of participation that merits attention is the agreement that no Government or Central Bank shall default on its external obligations, or any part thereof, without consent of the Fund.

This requirement has considerable possibilities for good. If the flow of private capital from capital-rich to capital-poor countries is to be stimulated and the flow of specialized capital among countries is to be fostered, something drastic must be done to reestablish confidence of private investors in the integrity of foreign borrowers. Defaults by governments and states have been in the past too easy a way out of foreign exchange and budgetary difficulties. The defaulting country frequently experiences an immediate gain but unfortunately the long-run losses have far more than outweighed the gains. If the Fund and the Bank could be a potent force for preventing defaults (as well as keeping interest rates reasonably low), a long step forward will have been made toward the increased productiveness of all countries.

It can hardly be expected that objective decisions on defaults can be made by the defaulting country or by the country gaining most by continued servicing of a debt. To make what takes on the character of compulsory arbitration in debt adjustment an acceptable and workable instrument, the proposed judgment must be that of a large group of nations, the majority of whom are not directly and immediately affected by the decision. Consideration of the pros and cons of a contemplated default by the Fund would seem to promise that kind of objectivity, and therefore not be a requirement that would stand in the way of acceptance by any government.

Not to subsidize—directly or indirectly—the exportation of any commodity or service to member countries without consent of the Fund.

One of the unfair trade practices frequently resorted to in the past has been export subsidies. Most countries have been guilty of subsidizing some exports either by direct or indirect methods. It is easy for the practice to grow as there are in every country powerful interests who because of a monopoly position or political influence, at the expense of the public, are able to keep up the price of a product at home by practicing subsidized dumping on foreign markets. This device in essence is no different from the use of multiple currencies or special clearing arrangements except that the gain in the latter case is shared by more persons. They all aim to undersell a foreign competitor not by offering the same goods at a lower price, or better goods at the same price, but by undercutting a foreign competitor at the expense of the taxpayer of the exporting country.

It is just such practices that give rise to rivalries which constitute fertile soil for international friction. If subsidies to exports are condoned there is no logical justification for objecting to any kind of trade device designed to increase exports or decrease imports. The result would be a repetition of the ruthless fight for foreign markets that characterized international trade in the pre-war decade.

It might be possible to obtain acquiescence among the member countries not to resort to the more obvious forms of subsidies without consent of the Fund. Since the Fund would be a sort of court of appeal, the possibility of subsidizing the export of a commodity or service exists. Yet presumably it would be invoked only under special circumstances. The fact that approval of the Fund were necessary would be helpful to governments in their struggle against vested groups seeking special advantages. Though it will be found very difficult to get a satisfactory working definition of an indirect subsidy, it should be at least possible to define the term so as to apply to the more obvious devices.

The Fund would probably have to permit subsidies to shipping and air travel. Almost every country subsidizes these two for military reasons, for economic reasons, and reasons of national prestige. It is irrelevant that much of the defense for ship-building and shipping based on economic and patriotic grounds is specious. These subsidies are so deeply imbedded in custom and policy that it is useless to attempt to modify them through an agency such as we are discussing.

Subsidies to tourists, to student voyages, etc., are of a different character. It may well be in the interests of all countries, and certainly is in the interests of some countries, to attract tourists by subsidies of one form or another. This subsidizing of exports of services seems to arouse little objection in the importing country (i.e. in the countries whose nationals do the touring) and can at least be defended on social and cultural grounds. Since United States is probably the most generous producer of profitable tourists, there is an added justification for attracting Americans abroad by subsidies if necessary, namely it will help the United States to develop a much desired "unfavorable" balance of payments through the most desirable available channels.

All considered it were probably better to exclude "services" altogether from the prohibition of subsidies, and save the Fund much trouble. It would, moreover, make it less unlikely that the requirement would find acceptance by enough nations.

It may be properly questioned whether an agency of this character is the appropriate instrument for obtaining fair trade practices in foreign trade. It might be that some other agency like a league of nations should be the vehicle, or possibly dependence should be on a program of multilateral treaties. However, it does seem that it should be less difficult to obtain agreement on such matters when the vehicle is an agency, membership in which has obvious economic advantages. Moreover, a country could feel it could always withdraw from the Fund if it deems its interests significantly harmed by failure to obtain approval of the Fund for a contemplated action, and hence would be less reluctant to try giving up the privilege.

Restrictions on membership.

No restrictions as to membership should be imposed on grounds of the particular economic structure adopted by any country.

There are certain to be some persons or governments, who either out of fear, or prejudice, or dislike would wish to exclude countries with socialist economies from participation in an international undertaking of the character described in the previous pages. Yet to exclude a country such as Russia would be an egregious error. Russia, despite her socialist economy could both contribute and profit by participation. To deny her the privileges of joining in this cooperative effort to improve world economic relations would be to repeat the tragic errors of the last generation, and introduce a very discordant note in the new era millions everywhere are hoping for. If the Russian Government is willing to participate, her counsel in the preliminary negotiations should be as eagerly sought as that of any other country, and her membership in both Fund and Bank equally as welcome.

A socialist economy like a capitalistic economy engages in international trade and financial transactions which can be either beneficial or harmful to other countries. In fact, because the conduct of foreign trade and international financial transactions is so completely under the control of the government in a socialist economy, there is all the more reason to attempt to get them to join in a cooperative attempt to introduce stability in international economic relationships and a higher level of trade.

Furthermore, no one can know what direction some of the smaller liberated states will take in the shaping of their economic structures. There is likely to be, during the next decade or two, a variety of economic systems and it would seem desirable that these should not be discouraged from cooperating with the others so long as they are willing to agree to conduct their international economic affairs in accordance with principles acceptable to the United Nations.

IV. Composition of the Fund

The Fund shall consist of gold, member country currencies, and member government securities, in such amounts as shall be indicated by a formula set forth in the Agreements. The total subscription to the Fund shall be the equivalent of at least $5 billion.

The task which the Fund would be expected to perform would involve transactions of large magnitude; it therefore should have large resources available. Moreover, the greater its resources the more potent could the Fund be in preventing monetary disruption and in reducing the frequency and duration of periods of disequilibrium. Considering the likelihood that the number of participating governments might be at least a score, a total subscription of the equivalent of two to five billion dollars would seem to be both possible and desirable.

To avoid tying up funds that would not be needed for some time, if ever, the participants could be required to subscribe only 25 percent of their participation in cash. An additional 25 percent could be subscribed in obligations of the participating government. These obligations would yield revenue to the Fund, and would also supply a source of additional funds to be tapped if and when needed. They would also provide the Fund with the means of conducting open-market operations in any given country when desired. To reduce the cost to participating countries, it might be found preferable to make the securities a renewable three to five-year note, rather than a long-term bond, thus reducing the interest rate and increasing their marketability.

The remaining 50 percent of the subscription should be paid in such installments and in such form as shall be determined from time to time by the Fund.

The Fund would need local currencies and gold to carry on its operations. The provision that half the initial payment of 25 percent be in gold and half in local currencies takes care of that, and also makes participation easier for those countries having little gold. For a few of the countries—e.g. the United States—gold and local currencies are synonymous for purposes of international transactions. One of the objectives of the Fund is to increase the number of countries about which that could be said.

In view of the fact that the gains from participation in the Fund would not take the form of a distribution of substantial profits, the sum each member country should subscribe can hardly be left to the decision of each country. It is hoped that the Fund would show an annual profit but the purpose of the Fund is not to make profits but to help achieve much more important objectives that are not susceptible of measurement in terms of money profits. The Fund would be a cooperative enterprise operated for the benefit of all the participating nations, and each participant should subscribe at least its reasonable share of the total capital necessary, though it could subscribe more if it wished to do so. The share of the total each country subscribes should be determined by some agreed upon formula which would give due weight to various pertinent considerations.

There follows an illustrative formula that attempts to measure the minimum amount of funds each participant should be required to subscribe. The items listed are those which seem most pertinent, and the weights ascribed to each attempt roughly to reflect the importance of that item to the benefits that might be expected to result from participation and the ability to contribute to the Fund's capital.

1. Gold holdings — 100 points for every billion dollars
2. Gold production — 50 " " " " "
3. National income — 2 " " " " "
4. Foreign trade — 25 " " " " "
5. Population — 1 " " " ten million
6. Foreign investments — 25 " " " billion dollars
7. Foreign debts — 10 " " " $50 million of annual interest payments on external public debt

Applying the above weights to the situation in some selected countries, the following approximate scores would result:

United States	2,905	U.S.S.R.	149
United Kingdom	577	China	78
Canada	125	Mexico	24
Netherlands and Colonies	143	Brazil	45
Norway	15	Colombia	12

Converted into dollars, the contributions would be something like the following:

TABLE
(In millions of U.S. dollars)

(Though the contributions or investments would be in the form of gold or local currency, they are converted, for convenience, into U.S. dollar units in the table below.)

United States	3,196	Argentina	72
England	635	Mexico	26
U.S.S.R.	164	Brazil	50
Canada	138	Colombia	13
Netherlands and Colonies	157	Cuba	9

The purpose of the table is merely to suggest a pattern of quotas for discussion, and not to lay down any precise pattern or formula. An attempt was made to present a pattern of quotas, the general character of which probably could be defended on logical grounds, but it is certain that a more appropriate formula could be worked out if several minds focused on the problem.

If only 50 percent of the participation were called for, and only half of that in cash, the amounts indicated in the above table would not be erroneous. The United States would be called upon to subscribe $500 million in cash and Cuba only $12½ million.

That would be the minimum. They could, of course, subscribe more if they wished. Experience would show whether the total was much more than was needed, or much less. If more were needed the securities could be converted into cash and the remaining half called in. On the other hand, if after long experience it is found that even the initial payments were greatly in excess of needs, it would be an easy matter to return the excess. Since the Fund should be ample to take care of periods of special stress, many years would have to pass, however, before enough experience is acquired to determine the most appropriate size of the Fund. It would certainly be better in the beginning to err on the side of having too much rather than not enough. The effective strength of the Fund and its ability to instill confidence in the currency stability of its participants will be enhanced with the ease with which the Fund can be expected to meet all legitimate claims on its resources. A sum of several billions of dollars does not, therefore, seem inappropriate to the task.

Inasmuch as some of the assistance the Fund can give to member countries is directly proportional to the sum of participation of that country, there will be a strong incentive for some countries to make their participation larger than the scheduled amount.

The Bank for Reconstruction and Development of the United and Associated Nations could be called upon to participate to the extent of possibly $100 million.

Contributions made according to the scale at the bottom of page 74 would result in total assets of $5,225,000,000. The following table summarizes the proportionate share which would be contributed by significant groups of countries. The second column of the table indicates the percentage of the total votes which would be allotted to each area, on the basis of these minimum contributions.

	Participation	Number of Votes on Board
	(In percent of total)	
United States	61.03	25.32
Argentina and Chile	1.68	3.93
Other Latin America	2.93	30.54
British Empire	20.20	17.56
U.S.S.R.	3.13	2.85
Netherlands and Colonies	3.01	2.81
Other European Countries	4.24	13.10
China	1.64	2.26
Bank for Reconstruction	2.14	1.63
	100.00	100.00

V. Management

Where control of the Fund shall be vested is a matter of paramount importance in the formulation of a workable plan. The magnitude of the Fund, the broad scope of its likely powers, the requirements for continued eligibility of participants, together make the question of situs of control important.

The management of the Fund should be vested in a Board of Directors consisting of the representatives appointed by the member governments, each government to appoint one representative.

It would be easy to reach agreement that the most convenient and simplest device would be to vest control of the Fund in a board of directors, to consist of representatives appointed by member governments, each government appointing one representative. It probably would be desirable to have each government appoint an alternate as well. In view of the technical nature of many of the problems, the governments might wish to select as alternates men who would be more qualified than are likely to be the representatives to take up the kind of problems that would most frequently come before the Fund. The representatives would probably be selected from more responsible posts than the alternates, and would likely be concerned with the larger and less technical issues involved in decisions.

The Board shall elect a chairman and a small operating committee.

With a body so unwieldy as it would likely be with representatives from each government, added to the fact that many of such representatives could devote only brief periods away from their home governments, it is virtually essential that the day-to-day operations of the Fund be handled by a small operating committee of representatives. Such a committee would be able to devote full time to the task of managing the Fund, and would, of course, have to be adequately compensated. The election of this operating committee by the member participants would insure the selection of a competent group and the brief period of their tenure of office before reelection would assure also a responsiveness to the wishes of the board. Delegation of authority by the whole board to the committee on many matters could be safely made, leaving larger policy decisions to be referred to the entire board. It is to be expected that the operating committee would have the assistance of a competent technical staff.

If a Fund were to be established with anything like the powers and resources outlined in this report, it would need the services of a large staff of the best experts available. Nothing would injure the chances of effective and successful operation and of making a major contribution to the solution of some of our most troublesome international economic problems than mediocrity in directors and technical staff. A board the size of the one recommended here can, of course, assimilate without serious damage some stuffed shirts, some narrow-minded nationalists, and a few bankers with counting house ideals. But the board will have to include more than a sprinkling of economic statesmen, forward looking and of broad vision, comprehensive experienced world outlook and tenacity of social purpose. The technical staff will have to be headed up by experienced analysts with a thorough knowledge of monetary theory and international economics, with intellectual integrity and aggressiveness, and also include a generous quota of eager, able, young men who have been at or near the top in their scholastic achievements and technical writings. The United and Associated Nations can produce plenty of such men.

In all voting by the Board, each representative should have one hundred votes, plus one vote for the equivalent of every million dollars turned over to the Fund.

There would be little difficulty in reaching agreement that some such set-up as the board working through a committee as outlined above would provide a satisfactory working arrangement, but the real problem is how to distribute the voting power. If each member of the board were to be given an equal vote, then a small country that invested one million dollars would have as much power in making decisions as a country that has subscribed a hundred or a thousand times that amount. With the possibility that the number of small countries participating will be much greater than the large countries, a one-vote-one-member arrangement is palpably unwise. On the other hand, to accord voting power strictly proportionate to the value of the subscription would give the one or two powers control over the Fund. To do that would destroy the truly international character of the Fund, and seriously jeopardize its success. Indeed, it is very doubtful if many countries would be willing to participate in an international organization with wide powers if one or two countries were to be able to control its policies.

It is clear that the voting power must be so arranged as to steer between these two evils. This might be accomplished by working out some compromise between the two bases of voting power referred to above. By giving each member 100 votes plus one vote for every million dollars invested in the Fund, a satisfactory distribution of control might be approximated. Thus, if the United States subscribes $1 billion it would have 100 plus 1,000 votes, or a total of 1,100 votes, whereas a country contributing $10 million would have 100 plus 10 votes, or a total of 110. With such an arrangement ten small countries could outvote the United States. If any country felt the arrangement agreed upon did not give it an adequate share of control, it could increase its contribution.

A country should have the privilege of replacing, wholly or in part, its securities, with currency or gold. The number of votes its representatives can cast would alter accordingly.

This provision would supply some flexibility in the assets a country turns over to the Fund, and also provides a means whereby a country could increase its voting power. How important the provision might prove to be is uncertain, but in the beginning at least it would appear desirable to introduce flexibility wherever possible.

All decisions, except where specifically provided otherwise, should be decided by a simple majority of the votes cast.

To give adequate protection to each country, most of the important decisions could be made to require more than a simple majority of the votes.

The President of the Bank should be a member of the Board, and would have 100 votes.

Because of the interdependence of the two institutions—the Fund and the Bank—close liaison and opportunities to harmonize policies would be helpful. Both agencies would have broad objectives, both would be international in their outlook, and both would be motivated by the desire to promote worldwide peace, prosperity, and stability. Each would be undertaking responsibilities that call for analyses and judgments of economic situations and trends. The operations of each would affect the other, and the decisions of each should be partly based on the knowledge, plan and judgment of the other. There, therefore, is much to be gained by close liaison between them. That is why the head of each should be a director of the other.

To avoid cumulating voting power, however, the Bank should not be able to cast votes in excess of the minimum, irrespective of the extent of its monetary participation.

Reports and information

The possession by the Fund of adequate, timely and appropriate information is a vital necessity to its proper functioning. The Fund should have the authority to require that all members file with it a quarterly itemized balance of payments. This balance of payments record—which is of particular importance in the operation of this Fund—should be standardized in form, and carefully designed by the technical staff of the Fund. The Fund would also need special reports from members from time to time, and should have the authority to obtain them.

[The following paragraphs are from Part III, commenting on the plans for an International Bank.]

A new international currency

We frequently hear expressed a desire or hope for a new international currency, but the specific nature of the new currency is never described, nor are the gains that are presumed to result from such a currency ever stated in meaningful language. They are either taken for granted or referred to only in the vaguest of generalities. So much misunderstanding of the nature and utility of a new international currency seems to prevail that it is probably worth attempting to indicate the limits of usefulness possessed by such a currency. The reader not interested in the confusions surrounding the demand for an international currency can omit the next few pages.

There are some persons who seem to think that all foreign exchange problems would be solved if only all countries adopted the same international unit for use in international transactions. A little thought will demonstrate how absurd that belief is. The fact that Canada adopted a "dollar" unit containing 100 cents and having the same *de jure* gold content as the United States dollar, did not prevent the adoption of foreign exchange controls in Canada nor did it keep the United States dollar-Canadian dollar exchange rate from moving, any more than did Australia, South Africa and New Zealand, by adopting the same unit as England, prevent the value of the currencies of those countries from changing in relation to the British £ sterling. There are innumerable instances of different currency units keeping the same value, in terms of each other, for many years; and other instances of similar currency units beginning with identical values and only to have those values change greatly. Thus, the pound sterling hovered around $4.86 for thirty-five years (1878–1914), and the Swiss franc was about 20 cents for fifty years; whereas, the exchange rates between the British £ and Australian £ and New Zealand £ and the Egyptian £ have moved greatly notwithstanding the fact that to begin with they all were the same unit, not only in designation—pound—but in the sense that their value was 1 to 1.

The value of any currency in terms of any other currency is a consequence of a complex of monetary and economic forces, changes in these forces influence the value of one currency in terms of others. The adoption of a new international currency would not modify those forces one whit. If all of the Western Hemisphere were to adopt the "dollar" as their own unit of currency, it would not be long before it would be necessary to distinguish between the "U. S. dollar," the "Mexican dollar," the "Colombian dollar," etc., because the exchange rates between those currencies had moved away from the 1 to 1 ratio. In fact, even now there are a number of "dollars" in use in the foreign exchange systems of the American Republics. The adoption of the same unit of currency no more eliminates foreign exchange problems than would the general adoption of Esperanto solve international political problems or no more than does the use of a common language, e.g. Spanish, eliminate international political problems between all Spanish-speaking nations.

Occasionally, one hears expressed the view that if only there could be created some unit of currency that could be universally used in trade—"a trade dollar" or "export dollar" (Presumably no reference is intended to a special kind of dollar which costs less to the foreigner than a regular dollar, yet which buys as much in the U. S. as a regular dollar. That would be a clear example of multiple currencies which involve government subsidies, and which constitutes one of the devices the U. S. is opposed to on principle), or any unit with a new name—considerable advantages in trade and other international transactions would result. Unfortunately, this view is fallacious. The obstacles to trade do not lie in the fact that different countries use different units of currency. Insofar as currency has anything to do with obstructing trade, it is the scarcity of foreign exchange and the variations in exchange rates which are responsible. Neither of these two obstacles to trade will be dissipated by the adoption of a new international unit of currency. There are, it is true, possibilities of developing machinery which will make foreign exchange more plentiful to countries that lack adequate foreign exchange, and there is also machinery which may be developed to reduce the fluctuation in exchange rates. The proposal here made for the Fund and the Bank is designed to help achieve those very objectives among others. Neither proposal involves, or needs, or is dependent upon the adoption of an international unit of currency.

We already have an international medium of exchange, namely, gold. An ounce of gold .999 fine is the same in United States as it is in China or South Africa or Iceland. Any exporter or importer or banker or investor can liquidate a monetary debt with gold just as easily as would be possible with a new international unit. Such difficulties as exist in the use of gold as a medium of international exchange lie in difficulties imposed by war conditions. In peace time nothing could be simpler than to send or receive gold, or send or receive dollar or other exchange convertible into gold.

Some who clamor for a new international currency to replace gold would concede this, but claim gold is too expensive to be used. This is quite another matter. It may be possible to develop a satisfactory international medium of exchange that costs less to produce than more gold, but certainly not significantly less than gold already in monetary stock. It is important to remember in thinking about this subject that the monetary gold stock of the country *has already been paid for. It is very inexpensive to use the gold already in world monetary stocks.* Even the cost of shipping from one country to another can be avoided through development of earmarking. The only expense of using gold already mined is the small value that gold would have for industrial uses if it had no monetary value.

The situation is quite different with respect to further additions to the gold stock—and more complex. Obviously there is a real cost as well as a monetary cost involved in mining and refining gold. Insofar as the gold would not be produced had it only commodity value, and insofar as the labor and material used in gold mining would be used for some other purpose, it is true that additions to our monetary gold stock are expensive. The solution to that, however, is simple—namely, just limit or control the additions of newly-mined gold to the world's monetary stock. This is not the place to discuss the method; suffice to say it is entirely feasible should it ever be deemed desirable. There are some advantages and disadvantages to the proposal, but it is possible that the time may come when the advantages may outweigh the disadvantages. In any case, the utility of *additions* to the world's monetary stock is a separate question from that of use of *existing* stocks. There is no advantage in substituting a new medium of international exchange for existing gold—even if it could be done—and I am confident it could not be done. But it may be worthwhile giving the Bank note-issuing powers—based on some gold reserve—solely in order to make the world's monetary gold stock do more work, and at the same time help correct the maldistribution of gold.

To be sure, the United States already does just that when for one reason or another, by one method or another, it increases its supply of currency and demand deposits.

The only difference between what the United States (and virtually every other country) already does, and what it is proposed the Bank shall do is that in the United States note issues are regulated by the law of the country, whereas the proposed note issues of the Bank will be regulated by the by-laws of the Bank as drawn up by the member Governments.

The belief previously referred to as being held in some quarters that a common unit of currency will solve the world's foreign exchange problems, and help promote foreign trade in goods and services, and the international flow of capital does not concern itself with either the scarcity of gold, or its maldistribution. It seems to take the form of something much less intelligible. It seems to assume that these benefits are to be attained by a new international unit which is to be adopted by many countries as a *substitute* for their own currency.

The belief that countries will find it helpful to replace their own currency in favor of a currency to be used by all, or by a group of nations, is based on a fundamental misunderstanding of the factors which determine the value of any currency. So long as most countries insist on shaping their own monetary policies so long will it be impossible to replace local currencies with a new international currency. The adoption of a common currency by several countries is possible only if they each surrender separate sovereignty in monetary and credit policies in favor of sovereignty exercised by one over all of them, or by an international organization. For example, it was impossible for the states in the American colonies to have a common currency with a common value until the United States was formed and the Federal Government given sole authority over currency. Even then scores of different bank notes existed, many of them with changing values, because the State rather than the Federal Government exercised sovereignty in matters of bank note issue. It was only until the Federal Government became supreme in the matter of all note issues that the United States was able to keep all bank notes at par.

It is possible for a group of countries to agree to adopt a common currency, but such adoption is of little use unless they also agree not to exercise separate sovereign powers with respect to note issues, exchange rates, rediscount rates and privileges and other aspects of monetary policy. If country A is going to agree to adopt the same currency as country B, country A will want assurance that country B cannot do whatever it pleases with its monetary policy.

But, it may be asked, would not the use of a new international unit as a *supplement* to local currency facilitate international trade and finance? The answer is an unqualified "No."

A "trade dollar" or "Demos" or "Victor" or "what-have-you" unit of currency supplementing the United States dollar, whether of the same or different value, would no more help foreign trade than would the adoption of a new flag. The only difference in trade between Massachusetts and Texas and trade between Massachusetts and Mexico—aside from tariffs—is that in the first case both buyer and seller deal in dollars only, whereas in trade between Mexico and United States two currencies are involved— the Mexican peso and United States dollar. (The supply of either currency to either country would be no different with a supplementary currency than without it; therefore, the matter of supply and demand for currency can be ignored in this discussion.) An importer, exporter, bank, or a tourist has simply to make conversions from one currency into another in his transactions. Were it possible to eliminate by use of an international currency unit the arithmetical labors involved in the conversions, it would indeed be a convenient device, though by no means a very important one. Unfortunately, however, the use of a new international currency unit does not obviate the necessity of calculating conversion values any more than does the use of gold in settling international transactions.

Let us, for example, consider the case of a tourist. As it is now, when an American travels to Mexico he converts his dollars into Mexican pesos, when he enters Colombia he converts his dollars into Colombian pesos, and when he goes to Brazil he converts his dollars into milreis, etc. Yet, if there existed a new international unit of currency he would be no better off; his purchases and sales would be consummated with no less inconvenience. On the contrary, he would have to make more calculations and more monetary adjustments in his price judgments. Upon leaving the United States he would have to convert his dollars into the new international unit and then when he came to Mexico he'd have to convert the international unit into pesos since most prices in any country are expressed in terms of the local currency unit. He would have had to do just that had he carried with him dollars instead of an international currency. Only this time, if he wanted to judge the value of an article tagged, say 50 pesos, he would have to make two mental conversions instead of one, because most of his life he has been dealing in dollars and cents, not in a new international currency. Then, when he enters Colombia he would have to again calculate conversions and again make the necessary mental adjustments in evaluating his purchases. It would be possible, of course, to have price tags or price schedules in shops and hotels frequented by tourists expressed in the international unit, but such a practice would be a nuisance to the seller and would be only a slight convenience to the buyer.

Nor does a buyer of imported goods purchase those goods in one country rather than in another because of ease of an arithmetical calculation. Where there is any difficulty and the seller meets with any sales resistance on this score, he can easily overcome it by quoting his price in the buyer's currency even if a bill is to be paid in the seller's currency.

Is there then no advantage to be obtained from the adoption of a new international unit of currency aside from the advantage of increasing the Bank's lending resources described earlier?

Yes, there is one advantage, though of minor importance. It is in the realm of economic research. A universally recognized international monetary unit of account would be helpful in the presentation of those statistical series which are pertinent to international comparisons and of use in discussions involving international comparisons of quantitative data measured in money terms. For many purposes it would be convenient to set up tables that involved summation of money values in more than one currency. It would also prove useful in statistical data involving comparisons of various money values over long periods of time.

Were values set in terms of a local currency which had undergone substantial changes in purchasing power relative to other countries, certain significant comparisons would be easier to make.

Altogether, the introduction of a new currency unit would not be of sufficient importance to warrant its introduction at this time, were the Bank not to be established with note issuing power. But if the Bank were to be established and given the authority to issue notes, what unit should it be?

It would probably be preferable to adopt a new unit. The adoption of a new international unit of currency of account would probably meet with little opposition, whereas an attempt to use any one of the existing currencies, such as dollars, sterling, or francs for that purpose would be opposed on the grounds that it would seem to give the country possessing that currency some slight advantage in publicity or trade. There are deemed to be some national prestige values and possibly slight economic gains in trade and financial transactions that adhere to a country having a currency that is widely used as an international unit of account. For that reason a new unit belonging to no country would be more welcome to most countries than the unit of any selected country.

A new unit of currency would have to be defined. It would have to be fixed in terms of something, whether by international agreement or by general acquiescence, or unilateral action. To set the value of the new currency unit in terms of some existing currency has the disadvantage of subjecting the new unit to the variations of the currency to which it is tied and also raises the question of "favoritism." The simplest course is to fix the value of the new unit in terms of gold. A unit of account does not have to be set in terms of gold, it could be set in terms of some commodity other than gold—tin, platinum, or any material. It could even be set in terms of an average basket of goods, or an aggregate of goods. But examination of the various possibilities will show that the only practical solution is to set the new currency unit in terms of a given physical volume of gold.

For convenience of arithmetical calculation it would probably be well to define the new unit as being equivalent to 14.62 grains nine-tenths fine. This would make the new unit worth 50 U.S. [cents] or 10 yuan or 2 s. at current rates of exchange and at present price for gold in the United States.

(B) Preliminary Draft Outline of a Proposal for an International Stabilization Fund of the United and Associated Nations
(Revised July 10, 1943)

The plan for post-war international currency stability set forth in this pamphlet is a revision of the preliminary draft outline of a proposal for an International Stabilization Fund of the United and Associated Nations made public by the Secretary of the Treasury on April 7, 1943.

The preliminary draft was sent by the Secretary of the Treasury to the finance ministers of the United Nations and the countries associated with them with a request that it be studied by their technical experts. The finance ministers were also invited to send representatives to Washington for informal discussions with the experts of this Government.

Such informal discussions have been held with nearly 30 countries. On the basis of these discussions, the experts of the Treasury with the cooperation of experts of other Departments of this Government have revised the preliminary draft proposal for an international stabilization fund. While suggestions of the representatives of other countries have been included in the revised draft, it does not necessarily reflect the views of the experts of any other country.

This revised draft is in every sense still a preliminary document representing the views of the technical experts of the Treasury and of other Departments of this Government. It has not received the official approval either of the Treasury or this Government.

FOREWORD

By HENRY MORGENTHAU, Jr., *Secretary of the Treasury*

When the United Nations have brought this war to a successful conclusion, they will be faced with many urgent international economic and financial problems. Some of these are new problems arising directly from this war; others are continuing consequences of failure to solve the problems that have been with us since the last war. The solution of these problems is essential to the development of a sound economic foundation for world peace and prosperity.

All of the important international economic and financial problems are closely interrelated. Monetary stabilization, commercial policy, the provision of long-term international credit, promotion of stability in the prices of primary products, and arrangements for relief and rehabilitation are problems that join at innumerable points. Nevertheless, because of their complexity, they must be taken up separately, although each in turn must be integrated with the rest.

It is generally recognized that monetary stability and protection against discriminatory currency practices are essential bases for the revival of international commerce and finance. For this reason, an appropriate starting point might well be the consideration of post-war international monetary problems. Success in dealing with international monetary problems in the post-war period will contribute toward final solution of the other international financial and economic problems. Despite the technical difficulties involved, the common interest which all countries have in the solution of post-war monetary problems provides a basis for agreement.

It is still too soon to know the precise form and magnitude of post-war monetary problems. But it is certain that we shall be confronted with three inseparable monetary tasks: to prevent the disruption of foreign exchanges, to avoid the collapse of monetary systems, and to facilitate the restoration and balanced growth of international trade. Clearly, such formidable problems can be successfully handled only through international action.

The creation of instrumentalities adequate to deal with the inevitable post-war monetary problems should not be postponed until the end of hostilities. It would be ill-advised, if not dangerous, to leave ourselves unprepared at the end of the war for the difficult taks of international monetary cooperation. Specific and practical proposals must be formulated by the experts and must be carefully considered by the policy-shaping officials of the various countries. In each country acceptance of a definitive plan can follow only upon legislative or executive action. And even when a plan is finally adopted, much time will be consumed in preparation before an international institution for monetary cooperation can begin effective work.

There is another important reason for initiating now concrete discussions of specific proposals. A plan for international monetary cooperation can be a factor in winning the war. It has been suggested, and with much cogency, that the task of assuring the defeat of the Axis powers would be made easier if the victims of aggression could have greater assurance that a victory of the United Nations will not mean in the economic sphere a repetition of the exchange instability and monetary collapse that followed the last war. The people in all of the United Nations must be given some assurance that there will not again be two decades of post-war economic disruption. The people must know that we at last recognize the fundamental truth that the prosperity of each country is closely linked to the prosperity of other countries.

One of the appropriate agencies to deal with international economic and monetary problems would be an international stabilization fund with resources and powers adequate to the task of helping to achieve monetary stability and of facilitating the restoration and balanced growth of international trade. A proposal along these lines was drafted by American technical experts and made public on April 7, 1943. There have been informal discussions on this draft in which nearly thirty countries have participated. These discussions have shown that all countries think joint action in this field is necessary for the reconstruction of the world economy.

It is recognized that an international stabilization fund is only one of the instrumentalities which may be needed in the field of international economic cooperation. Other agencies may be needed to provide long-term international credit for post-war reconstruction and development, to provide funds for rehabilitation and relief, and to promote stability in the prices of primary international commodities. There is a strong inclination on the part of some to entrust to a single agency the responsibility for dealing with these and other international economic problems. We believe, however, that an international economic institution can operate most effectively if it is not burdened with diverse duties of a specialized character.

Although an international stabilization fund can provide the facilities for cooperation on monetary questions, the establishment of such an institution would not of itself assure the solution of these difficult problems. The operations of such a fund can be successful only if the powers and resources of the fund are used wisely, and if member countries cooperate with the fund's endeavors to maintain international equilibrium at a high level of international trade. Such cooperation must include commercial policies designed to reduce trade barriers and to terminate discriminatory practices that have in the past hampered the balanced growth of international trade. The nations of this world can be prosperous only if they are good neighbors in their economic as well as their political relations.

The draft proposals that have been put forward on a tentative basis have received wide publicity in the United States, the United Kingdom, Canada, and in other countries. It is in the best democratic tradition that the people should have the fullest opportunity to express their views and to shape the policies of their Governments on the important problems affecting national well-being. And it is an extension of this tradition that all the United Nations should have an opportunity to participate in the formulation of a program for international monetary cooperation.

This revised draft is published with the hope that it will call forth further comments and constructive suggestions. It aims to present only the essential elements of a workable international stabilization fund, and its provisions are in every sense tentative. Obviously, there are many details that have been omitted and that can be better formulated after there is agreement on the more important points. We believe that a workable and acceptable plan can emerge only from the joint efforts of the United Nations support by enlightened public opinion.

PRELIMINARY DRAFT OUTLINE OF A PROPOSAL FOR AN INTERNATIONAL STABILIZATION FUND OF THE UNITED AND ASSOCIATED NATIONS

Preamble

1. There is a growing recognition that progress toward establishment of a functioning democratic world in the post-war period will depend on the ability of free peoples to work together in solving their economic problems. Not the least of these is the problem of how to prevent a widespread breakdown of currencies with resultant international economic disorder. We must assure a troubled world that the free countries will solve these perplexing problems, and that they will not resort to competitive exchange depreciation, multiple currency practices, discriminatory bilateral clearing, or other destructive foreign exchange devices.

2. These are not transitory problems of the immediate postwar period affecting only a few countries. The history of the past two decades shows that they are continuing problems of vital interest to all countries. There must be a general realization that world prosperity, like world peace, is indivisible. Nations must act together to restore multilateral international trade, and to provide orderly procedure for the maintenance of balanced economic growth. Only through international cooperation will it be possible for countries successfully to apply measures directed toward attaining and maintaining a high level of employment and income which must be the primary objective of economic policy.

3. The International Stabilization Fund of the United and Associated Nations is proposed as a permanent institution for international monetary cooperation. The

resources of this Fund would be available under adequate safeguards to maintain currency stability, while giving member countries time to correct maladjustments in their balance of payments without resorting to extreme measures destructive of international prosperity. The resources of the Fund would not be used to prolong a basically unbalanced international position. On the contrary, the Fund would be influential in inducing countries to pursue policies making for an orderly return to equilibrium.

4. The Fund would deal only with member governments and their fiscal agents, and would not intrude in the customary channels for conducting international commerce and finance. The Fund is intended to provide supplemental facilities for the successful functioning of the established foreign exchange institutions and to free international commerce from harmful restrictions.

5. The success of the Fund must ultimately depend upon the willingness of nations to act together on their common problems. International monetary cooperation should not be regarded as a matter of generosity. All countries have a vital interest in the maintenance of international monetary stability, and in the balanced growth of multilateral international trade.

I. Purposes of the Fund

The United Nations and the countries associated with them recognize, as declared in the Atlantic Charter, the need for the fullest cooperation among nations with the object of securing economic advancement and rising standards of living for all. They believe that attainment of these objectives will be facilitated by international monetary cooperation. Therefore, it is proposed that there be established an International Stabilization Fund with the following purposes:

1. To help stabilize the foreign exchange rates of the currencies of the United Nations and the countries associated with them.

2. To shorten the periods and lessen the degree of disequilibrium in the international balance of payments of member countries.

3. To help create conditions under which the smooth flow of foreign trade and of productive capital among the member countries will be fostered.

4. To facilitate the effective utilization of the blocked foreign balances accumulating in some countries as a consequence of the war situation.

5. To reduce the use of such foreign exchange restrictions, bilateral clearing arrangements, multiple currency devices, and discriminatory foreign exchange practices as hamper world trade and the international flow of productive capital.

II. Composition of the Fund

1. The Fund shall consist of gold and the currencies and securities of member governments.

2. Each of the member countries shall subscribe a specified amount, to be called its *quota*. The aggregate of quotas of the member countries shall be the equivalent of at least $5 billion.

3. Each member country shall meet its quota contribution in full on or before the date set by the Board of Directors for the Fund's operations to begin.

(a) A country shall pay in gold not less than an amount determined as follows. If its gold and free foreign exchange holdings are:

(i) In excess of three times its quota, it shall pay in gold 50 percent of its quota.

(ii) More than two but less than three times its quota, it shall pay in gold 40 percent of its quota plus 10 percent of its holdings in excess of twice its quota.

(iii) More than its quota but less than twice its quota, it shall pay in gold 30 percent of its quota plus 10 percent of its holdings in excess of its quota.

(iv) Less than its quota, it shall pay in gold 30 percent of its holdings.

The gold payment required of a member country substantial parts of whose home areas have been wholly or partly occupied by the enemy, shall be only three-fourths of the above. (For other gold provisions, Cf. V–2–a and V–6, 7.)

A member country may include in the legal reserve account and in the published statement of the reserves of gold and foreign exchange in its Treasury or Central Bank, an amount not to exceed its gold contribution to the Fund, minus its net purchases of foreign exchange from the Fund paid for with local currency.

(b) It shall pay the remainder of its quota in local currency, except that a member country may substitute government securities (redeemable at par) for local currency up to 50 percent of its quota.

4. A quota for each member country shall be computed by an agreed upon formula which gives due weight to the important relevant factors, *e. g.*, a country's holdings of gold and free foreign exchange, the magnitude and the fluctuations of its balance of international payments, its national income, *etc.*

Before computing individual quotas on the basis of the agreed upon formula, there shall be reserved an amount equal to 10 percent of aggregate quotas to be used as a special allotment for the equitable adjustment of quotas. Where the initial quota of a member country as computed by the formula is clearly inequitable, the quota may be increased from this special allotment.

5. Quotas shall be adjusted on the basis of the most recent data 3 years after the establishment of the Fund, and at intervals of 5 years thereafter, in accordance with the agreed upon formula. In the period between adjustment of quotas, the Fund may increase the quota of a country, where it is clearly inequitable, out of the special allotment reserved for the equitable adjustment of quotas.

6. Any changes in the formula by which the quotas of member countries are determined shall be made only with the approval of a four-fifths vote of the Board.

7. No increase shall be made in the quota of a member country under II–4, 5 or 6 without the consent of the representative of the country concerned.

8. The resources of the Fund shall be used exclusively for the benefit of the member countries.

III. Monetary Unit of the Fund

1. The monetary unit of the Fund shall be the *unitas* (UN) equal in value to $137\frac{1}{2}$ grains of fine gold (equivalent to $10). No change in the gold value of the unitas shall be made except with the approval of 85 percent of the member votes. When such change is made, the gain or loss sustained by the Fund on its holdings of gold shall be distributed equitably among the members of the Fund.

The accounts of the Fund shall be kept and published in terms of unitas.

2. The value of the currency of each member country shall be established in terms of unitas and may not be altered except as provided in IV–5, below. (Cf. IV–1, 2, below.)

No member country shall purchase or acquire gold, directly or indirectly, at a price in terms of its national currency in excess of the parity which corresponds to the value of its currency in terms of unitas and to the value of unitas in terms of gold; nor shall any member country sell or dispose of gold, directly or indirectly, at a price in terms of its national currency below the parity which corresponds to the value of its currency in terms of unitas and to the value of unitas in terms of gold. (Cf. VII–1.)

3. No change in the value of the currencies of member countries shall be permitted to alter the value in unitas of the assets of the Fund. Whenever the currency of a member country has depreciated to a significant extent, that country must deliver to the Fund when requested an amount of its local currency or securities equal to the decrease in the unitas value of the Fund's holdings of the local currency and securities of the country. Likewise, if the currency of a member country should appreciate to a significant extent, the Fund must return to that country an amount (in the currency or securities of that country) equal to the resulting increase in the unitas value of the Fund's holdings.

IV. Exchange Rates

1. The rates at which the Fund will buy and sell one member currency for another and at which the Fund will buy and sell gold for local currency shall be established in accordance with the provisions below. (Cf. also III–2 and V–2.)

2. The initial rates of exchange for member countries' currencies shall be determined as follows:

(a) For any country which becomes a member prior to the date on which the Fund's operations begin, the rates initially used by the Fund shall be based upon the value of the currency in terms of United States dollars which prevailed on July 1, 1943.

If, in the judgment of either the member country or the Fund, the above rate is clearly inappropriate, the initial rate shall be determined by consultation between the member country and the Fund. No operations in such currency shall be undertaken by the Fund until a rate has been established which has the approval of the Fund and of the member country in question.

(b) For any member country which has been occupied by the enemy, the Fund shall use the exchange rate fixed by the government of the liberated country in consultation with the Fund and acceptable to the Fund. Prior to the fixing of a definitive rate, operations in such currency may be undertaken by the Fund with the approval of the Board at a tentative rate of exchange fixed by the member country in consultation with the Board. No operations shall be continued under this provision for more than 3 months after the liberation of the country or when the local currency holdings of the Fund exceed the quota of the country, except that under special circumstances the period and the amount of such operations may be extended by the Fund.

3. The Fund shall not come into operation until agreement has been reached on the exchange rates for currencies of countries representing a majority of the aggregate quotas.

4. The Fund shall determine the range within which the rates of exchange of member currencies shall be permitted to fluctuate. (Cf. VII–1.)

5. Changes in the exchange value of the currency of a member country shall be considered only when essential to the correction of fundamental disequilibrium in its balance of payments, and shall be made only with the approval of three-fourths of the member votes including the representative of the country concerned.

Because of the extreme uncertainties of the immediate post-war period, the following exceptional provisions may be used during the first 3 years of the Fund's operations:

(a) When the existing rate of exchange of a member country is clearly inconsistent with the maintenance of a balanced international payments position for that country, changes from the established rate may be made at the special request of that country and with the approval of a majority of the member votes.

(b) A member country may change the established rate for its currency by not more than 10 percent provided that the member country shall notify the Fund of its intention and shall consult with the Fund on the advisability of its action.

V. Powers and Operations

The Fund shall have the following powers:

1. To buy, sell and hold gold, currencies, and government securities of member countries; to earmark and transfer gold; to issue its own obligations, and to offer them for discount or sale in member countries.

The Fund shall purchase for local currency or needed foreign exchange any member currency in good standing acquired by another member country in settlement of a balance of payments on current account, where such currency cannot be disposed of in the foreign exchange markets within the range established by the Fund.

2. To sell to the Treasury of any member country (or Stabilization Fund or Central Bank acting as its agent) at the accepted rate of exchange, currency of any member country which the Fund holds, provided that:

(a) The foreign exchange demanded from the Fund is required to meet an adverse balance of payments predominantly on current account with any member country. (Cf. V–3, for capital transfers.)

When the gold and free foreign exchange holdings of a member country exceed 50 percent of its quota, the Fund in selling foreign exchange to such member country shall require that one-half of such exchange shall be paid for with gold or foreign exchange acceptable to the Fund. (Cf. V–6, 7; on gold collateral, see V–2–c.)

(b) The Fund's total holdings of the currency and securities of any member country shall not exceed the quota of such country by more than 50 percent during the first year of operation of the Fund, and thereafter shall not exceed such quota by more than 100 percent (except as otherwise provided below). The total holdings thus permitted are termed the *permissible quota* of a country. When the Fund's holdings of local currency and securities are equal to the permissible quota of a country, the Fund may sell foreign exchange for such additional local currency only with the specific approval of the Board of Directors (cf. VI–3–a, below), and provided that at least one of the following two conditions is met:

(i) In the judgment of the Fund satisfactory measures are being or will be taken by the country whose currency is acquired by the Fund, to correct the disequilibrium in the country's balance of payments; or

(ii) It is believed that the balance of payments of the country whose currency is acquired by the Fund will be such as to warrant the expectation that the excess currency holdings of the Fund can be disposed of within a reasonable time;

Provided further, that when the Fund's holdings of the currency of any member country or countries fall below 20 percent of their respective quotas, the sale shall also require the approval of the representatives of these countries.

(c) When the Fund's holdings of local currency and securities exceed the permissible quota of a country, the Board may require the member country to deposit collateral in accordance with regulations prescribed by the Board. Such collateral shall take the form of gold, foreign or domestic currency or Government bonds, or other suitable collateral within the capacity of the member country.

(d) When, in the judgment of the Fund, a member country, whose currency and securities held by the Fund exceed its quota, is exhausting its permissible quota more rapidly than is warranted, or is using its permissible quota in a manner that clearly has the effect of preventing or unduly delaying the establishment of a sound balance in its international accounts, the Fund may place such conditions upon additional sales of foreign exchange to that country as it deems to be in the general interest of the Fund.

3. The Fund may sell foreign exchange to a member country, under conditions prescribed by the Fund, to facilitate a transfer of capital, or repayment or adjustment of foreign debts, when in the judgment of the Board such a transfer is desirable from the point of view of the general international economic situation, provided the Fund's holdings of the currency and securities of the member country do not exceed 150 percent of the quota of that country. When the Fund's holdings of the local currency and securities of a member country exceed 150 percent of the quota of that country, the Fund may, in exceptional circumstances, sell foreign exchange to the member country for the above purposes with the approval of three-fourths of the member votes. (Cf. V–2–a, above; on voting, VI–3–a, below.)

4. When the Fund's holdings of the currency and securities of a member country become excessively small in relation to prospective acquisitions and needs for that currency, the Fund shall render a report to that country. The report shall embody an analysis of the causes of the depletion of the Fund's holdings of that currency, a forecast of the prospective balance of payments in the absence of special measures, and finally, recommendations designed to increase the Fund's holdings of that currency. The representative of the country in question shall be a member of the Fund committee appointed to draft the report. This report shall be sent to all member countries and, if deemed desirable, be made public. Member countries agree that they will give immediate and careful attention to recommendations made by the Fund.

5. Whenever it becomes evident to the Board of Directors that the anticipated demand for any particular currency may soon exhaust the Fund's holdings of that currency, the Fund shall inform the member countries of the probable supply of the currency and of a proposed method for its equitable distribution, together with suggestions for helping to equate the anticipated demand for and supply of that currency.

The Fund shall make every effort to increase the supply of the scarce currency by acquiring that currency from the foreign balances of member countries. The Fund may make special arrangements with any member country for the purpose of providing an emergency supply under appropriate conditions which are acceptable to both the Fund and the member country.

To facilitate appropriate adjustment in the balance of payments position of member countries, and to help correct the distortions in the pattern of trade balances, the Fund shall apportion its sales of such scarce currency. In such apportionment, it shall be guided by the principle of satisfying the most urgent needs from the point of view of the general international economic situation. It shall also consider the special needs and resources of the particular countries making the request for the scarce currency.

The right of any member country to acquire an amount of other currencies equal to its permissible quota shall be limited by the necessity of assuring an appropriate distribution among the various members of any currency the supply of which is scarce.

6. In order to promote the most effective use of the available and accumulating supply of foreign exchange resources of member countries, each member country agrees that it will offer to sell to the Fund, for its local currency or for foreign currencies which the member country needs, one-half of the foreign exchange resources and gold it acquires in excess of its official holdings at the time it became a member of the Fund, but no country need sell gold or foreign exchange under this provision unless its official holdings (*i. e.*, Treasury, Central Bank, Stabilization Fund, *etc.*) are in excess of 25 percent of its quota. For the purpose of this provision, only free and liquid foreign exchange resources and gold shall be considered. The Fund may accept or reject the offer. (Cf. II–3–a, V–2–a, and V–7.)

To help achieve this objective each member country agrees to discourage the excessive accumulation of foreign exchange resources and gold by its nationals. The Fund shall inform any member country when, in its opinion, any further growth of privately held foreign exchange resources and gold appears unwarranted.

7. When the Fund's holdings of the local currency and securities of a member country exceed the quota of that country, the Fund shall, upon request of the member country, resell to the member country the Fund's excess holdings of the currency of that country for gold or acceptable foreign exchange. (Cf. V–14, for charges on holdings in excess of quota.)

8. To buy from the governments of member countries, blocked foreign balances held in other member countries, provided all the following conditions are met:

(a) The blocked balances are held in member countries and are reported as such (for the purpose of this provision) by the member governments and are verified by the Fund.

(b) The member country selling the blocked balances to the Fund agrees to transfer these balances to the Fund and to repurchase from the Fund 40 percent of them (at the same price) with gold or such free currencies as the Fund may wish to accept, at the rate of 2 percent of the transferred balances each year for 20 years beginning not later than 3 years after the date of transfer.

(c) The country in which the blocked balances are held agrees to transfer to the Fund the balances described in (b) above, and to repurchase from the Fund 40 percent of them (at the same price) with gold or such free currencies as the Fund may wish to accept, at the rate of 2 percent of the transferred balances each year for 20 years beginning not later than 3 years after the date of transfer.

(d) A charge of 1 percent on the amount of blocked balances sold to the Fund, payable in gold, shall be levied against the country selling its blocked balances and against the country in which the balances are held. In addition a charge of not less than one percent, payable in gold, shall be levied annually against each country on the amount of such balances remaining to be purchased by it.

(e) If the country selling blocked balances to the Fund asks for foreign exchange rather than local currency, the request will not be granted unless the country needs the foreign exchange for the purpose of meeting an adverse balance of payments not arising from the acquisition of gold, the accumulation of foreign balances, or other capital transactions.

(f) Either country may, at its option, increase the amount it repurchases annually. But, in the case of the country selling blocked balances to the Fund, not more than 2 percent per annum of the original sum taken over by the Fund shall become free, and only after 3 years shall have elapsed since the sale of the balances to the Fund.

(g) The Fund has the privilege of disposing of any of its holdings of blocked balances as free funds after the 23-year period is passed, or sooner under the following conditions:

   (i) Its holdings of the free funds of the country in which the balances are held fall below 20 percent of its quota; or

   (ii) The approval is obtained of the country in which the balances are held.

(h) The country in which the blocked balances are held agrees not to impose any restrictions on the use of the installments of the 40 percent portion gradually repurchased by the country which sold the balances to the Fund.

(i) The Fund agrees not to sell the blocked balances acquired under the above authority, except with the permission or at the request of the country in which the balances are being held. The Fund may invest these balances in the ordinary or special government securities of that country. The Fund shall be free to sell such securities in any country under the provisions of V–11, below.

(j) The Fund shall determine from time to time the maximum proportion of the blocked balances it will purchase under this provision.

Provided, however, that during the first 2 years of its operation, blocked balances purchased by the Fund shall not exceed in the aggregate 10 percent of the quotas of all member ccountries. At the end of 2 years of operation, the Fund shall propose a plan for the gradual further liquidation of blocked balances still outstanding indicating the proportion of the blocked balances which the Board considers the Fund can appropriately purchase.

Blocked balances acquired under this provision shall not be included either in computing the amount of foreign exchange available to member countries under their quotas (cf. V–2, 3), or in computing charges on balances of local currency in excess of the quotas (cf. V–14).

9. To buy and sell currencies of non-member countries but shall not acquire more than $10 million of the currency of any one non-member country nor hold such currencies beyond 60 days after date of purchase except with the approval of the Board.

10. To borrow the currency of any member country provided the additional amount is needed by the Fund and provided the representative of that country approves.

11. To sell member-country obligations owned by the Fund provided that the representatives of the country issuing the securities and of the country in which the securities are to be sold approve, except that the approval of the representative of the issuing country shall not be necessary if the obligations are to be sold in its own market.

To use its holdings to obtain rediscounts or advances from the Central Bank of any country whose currency the Fund needs.

12. To invest any of its currency holdings in government securities of the country of that currency provided that the representative of the country approves.

13. To lend to any member country its local currency from the Fund for 1 year or less up to 75 percent of the currency of that country held by the Fund, provided the local currency holdings of the Fund are not reduced below 20 percent of the quota.

14. To make a service charge on all gold and exchange transactions.

To levy a charge uniform to all countries, at a rate not less than 1 percent per annum, payable in gold, against any country on the amount of its currency held by the Fund in excess of the quota of that country. An additional charge, payable in gold, shall be levied by the Fund against any member country on the Fund's holdings of its currency in excess of the permissible quota of that country.

In case the Fund finds it necessary to borrow currency to meet the demands of its members, an additional charge, payable in gold, shall be made by the Fund sufficient to cover the cost of the borrowing.

15. To levy upon member countries a *pro rata* share of the expenses of operating the Fund, payable in local currency, not to exceed one-tenth percent per annum of the quota of each country. The levy may be made only to the extent that the earnings of the Fund are inadequate to meet its current expenses.

16. The Fund shall deal only with or through:

(a) The Treasuries, Stabilization Funds, or Central Banks acting as fiscal agents of member governments.

(b) Any international banks owned predominantly by member governments.

The Fund may, nevertheless, with the approval of the representatives of the governments of the countries concerned, sell its own securities, or securities it holds, directly to the public or to institutions of member countries.

VI. Management

1. The administration of the Fund shall be vested in a Board of Directors. Each government shall appoint a director and an alternate, in a manner determined by it, who shall serve for a period of 5 years, subject to the pleasure of their government. Directors and alternates may be reappointed.

2. In all voting by the Board, the director or alternate of each member country shall be entitled to cast an agreed upon number of votes.

The distribution of *basic votes* shall be closely related to the quotas of member countries, although not in precise proportion to the quotas. An appropriate distribution of basic voting power would seem to be the following: Each country shall have 100 votes, plus 1 vote for the equivalent of each 100,000 unitas ($1 million) of its quota.

No country shall be entitled to cast more than one-fifth of the aggregate basic votes, regardless of its quota.

3. All voting shall be according to basic votes except as follows:

(a) In voting on proposals to authorize the sale of foreign exchange, each country shall cast a number of votes modified from its basic vote:

   (i) By the addition of one vote for each $2 million of net sales of its currency by the Fund (adjusted for its net transactions in gold), and

   (ii) By the subtraction of one vote for each $2 million of its net purchases of foreign exchange from the Fund (adjusted for its net transactions in gold).

(b) In voting on proposals to suspend or restore membership, each member country shall cast one vote, as provided in VI–11, below.

4. All decisions, except where specifically provided otherwise, shall be made by a majority of the member votes.

5. The Board of Directors shall select a Managing Director of the Fund and one or more assistants. The Managing Director shall become an *ex officio* member of the Board and shall be chief of the operating staff of the Fund. The operating staff shall be selected in accordance with regulations established by the Board of Directors.

6. The Board of Directors shall appoint from among its members an Executive Committee of not less than 11 members. The Chairman of the Board shall be Chairman of the Executive Committee, and the Managing Director of the Fund shall be an *ex officio* member of the Executive Committee.

The Executive Committee shall be continuously available at the head office of the Fund and shall exercise the authority delegated to it by the Board. In the absence of any member of the Executive Committee, his alternate shall act in his place. Members of the Executive Committee shall receive appropriate remuneration.

7. The Board of Directors may appoint such other committees as it finds necessary for the work of the Fund. It may also appoint advisory committees chosen wholly or partially from persons not employed by the Fund.

8. The Board of Directors may at any meeting authorize any officers or committees of the Fund to exercise any specified powers of the Board not requiring more than a majority vote.

The Board may delegate any authority to the Executive Committee, provided that the delegation of powers requiring more than a majority of the member votes can be authorized only by a majority (of the Board) of the same size as specified, and can be exercised by the Executive Committee only by like majority.

Delegated powers shall be exercised only until the next meeting of the Board, and in a manner consistent with the general policies and practices of the Board.

9. The Board of Directors may establish procedural regulations governing the operations of the Fund. The officers and committees of the Fund shall be bound by such regulations.

10. The Board of Directors shall hold an annual meeting and such other meetings as it may be desirable to convene. The annual meeting shall be held in places designated by the Executive Committee, but not more than one annual meeting in any 5-year period shall be held within the same member country.

On request of member countries casting one-fourth of the votes, the Chairman shall call a meeting of the Board for the purpose of considering any matters placed before it.

11. A country failing to meet its obligations to the Fund may be suspended provided a majority of the member countries so decides. While under suspension, the country shall be denied the privileges of membership but shall be subject to the same obligations as any other member of the Fund. At the end of 1 year the country shall be automatically dropped from membership unless it has been restored to good standing by a majority of the member countries.

Any country may withdraw from the Fund by giving notice, and its withdrawal will take effect 1 year from the date of such notice. During the interval between notice of withdrawal and the taking effect of the notice, such country shall be subject to the same obligations as any other member of the Fund.

A country which is dropped or which withdraws from the Fund shall have returned to it an amount in its own currency equal to its contributed quota, plus other obligations of the Fund to the country, and minus any sum owed by that country to the Fund. Any losses of the Fund may be deducted *pro rata* from the contributed quota to be returned to the country that has been dropped or has withdrawn from membership. Local currency holdings of the Fund in excess of the above shall be repurchased by that country with gold or foreign exchange acceptable to the Fund.

When any country is dropped or withdraws from membership, the rights of the Fund shall be fully safeguarded. The obligations of a country to the Fund shall become due at the time it is dropped or withdraws from membership; but the Fund shall have 5 years within which to liquidate its obligations to such country.

12. Net profits earned by the Fund shall be distributed in the following manner:

(a) Fifty percent to reserves until the reserves are equal to 10 percent of the aggregate quotas of the Fund.

(b) Fifty percent to be divided each year among the members in proportion to their quotas. Dividends distributed to each country shall be paid in its own currency or in gold at the discretion of the Fund.

VII. Policies of Member Countries

Each member country of the Fund undertakes the following:

1. To maintain by appropriate action exchange rates established by the Fund on the currencies of other countries, and not to alter exchange rates except as provided in IV–5, above.

Exchange rates of member countries may be permitted to fluctuate within the specified range fixed by the Fund.

2. Not to engage in exchange dealings with member or non-member countries that will undermine stability of exchange rates established by the Fund.

3. To abandon, as soon as the member country decides that conditions permit, all restrictions (other than those involving capital transfers) over foreign exchange transactions with other member countries, and not to impose any additional restrictions (except upon capital transfers) without the approval of the Fund.

The Fund may make representations to member countries that conditions are favorable for the abandonment of restrictions over foreign exchange transactions, and each member country shall give consideration to such representations.

All member countries agree that all of the local currency holdings of the Fund shall be free from any restrictions as to their use. This provision does not apply to blocked foreign balances acquired by the Fund in accordance with the provisions of V-8, above.

4. To cooperate effectively with other member countries when such countries, with the approval of the Fund, adopt or continue controls for the purpose of regulating international movements of capital. Cooperation shall include, upon recommendation by the Fund, measures that can appropriately be taken, such as:

(a) Not to accept or permit acquisition of deposits, securities, or investments by nationals of any member country imposing restrictions on the export of capital except with the permission of the government of that country and the Fund;

(b) To make available to the Fund or to the government of any member country such information as the Fund considers necessary on property in the form of deposits, securities and investments of the nationals of the member country imposing the restrictions.

5. Not to enter upon any new bilateral clearing arrangements, nor engage in multiple currency practices, which in the judgment of the Fund would retard the growth of world trade or the international flow of productive capital.

6. To give consideration to the views of the Fund on any existing or proposed monetary or economic policy, the effect of which would be to bring about sooner or later a serious disequilibrium in the balance of payments of other countries.

7. To furnish the Fund with all information it needs for its operations and to furnish such reports as the Fund may require in the form and at the times requested by the Fund.

8. To adopt appropriate legislation or decrees to carry out its undertakings to the Fund.

The French Plan

In May 1943 Messrs. Hervé Alphand and André Istel, with the help of certain studies made by one of the high officials of the French Treasury, put forward the plan reproduced below. The greater part of it was reproduced in The New York Times *on May 9, 1943. A French version was published by the Bank for International Settlements as HS.99.*

In the summary in The New York Times *the proposed permanent institution was called an "International Clearing Office," instead of a "Monetary Stabilization Office" as in the French version and in the English text reproduced below.*

Suggestions Regarding International Monetary Relations
(May 1943)

1. *Preliminary remarks.*

There is little doubt that a return to a generalized system of multilateral international trade, excluding foreign-trade control and foreign-exchange control, cannot be expected for some time after the end of hostilities. For numerous countries, a premature suppression of these controls would have ominous effects.

The states of Continental Europe, in particular, devastated by war and by the consequences of German occupation, will have first to feed their population, to import essential supplies, and then to reconstruct their capacity of production for national consumption and for foreign export. It is out of the question to let private importers, each acting independently, import foreign products without restrictions. By reason of the huge size of the requirements and the extreme urgency of some of them, the Government will have to control for a while both the volume and the nature of imports.

Foreign-exchange control will also probably have to be maintained for a while, not so much because of the considerable amount of internal capital requirements, but because it is difficult to visualize how rigid foreign-trade control can be enforced without exchange control.

Anyhow Russia will maintain, for an unpredictable period of time, both foreign-trade and foreign-exchange control.

Also ex-enemy countries will have, for a period of time, to be subjected, under United Nations supervision, to strict foreign-trade and foreign-exchange control.

It is thus necessary to conceive and achieve a practical system of exchange stability and of trade financing with the following characteristics:

a) It must be applicable as soon as hostilities are over and even earlier wherever possible.

b) It must be applicable simultaneously to those countries which will practice foreign-trade control and foreign-exchange control, and to others which will enjoy freedom of foreign trade and foreign exchange.

c) It must be adaptable to the evolution of internal systems of exchange control and of foreign-trade control.

d) Far from paralyzing evolution toward a better system of international economic relations, it should constitute in itself a step toward such a system.

2. *Fundamental conditions of satisfactory monetary relations.*

No international monetary system can work satisfactorily unless certain fundamental political and economic conditions are fulfilled. Military security and social order are of course paramount. But among the general conditions, it appears useful to lay particular stress on the following:

a) Commercial treaties should be concluded permitting a rational distribution of productive activities among nations. Such a distribution ought to take into account the natural resources, the geographic and demographic conditions, the level of education as well as various other elements of the cost of production; it ought furthermore, to take into account the creditor or debtor situation of the balance of payments.

b) Certain regulatory measures of an international character should be adopted, designed to stabilize business conditions and to reduce as far as possible the swing of economic cycles.

These measures ought to have a double character: they should operate on the one hand, on the volume of instruments of payment or of credit, in order to adapt them to needs; they ought to operate, on the other hand, directly on the volume of goods in order to adapt them to outlets.

This latter action should, itself, be of a double character: on raw materials, by some kind of regulatory action on stocks and output; on finished goods, by methods devised to accelerate or slow down the rhythm of production.

c) International long term credits should be favored, and might consist, not only in traditional loans, but in direct participation of industry, agriculture, real estate, etc. . . . . through the establishment of national or international public or private Investment Trusts, or other forms of financing.

d) Methods should be devised to remedy persistent disequilibria of balances of payments, through fundamental economic adjustments.

During the period immediately after the war it will be necessary to take care of permanent deficits in the balance of payments arising from reconstruction of devastated countries and development of backward countries. This is a problem of long term financing outside of the scope of the present memorandum.

3. *Analysis of precedents supplied by previous monetary agreements.*

Various monetary agreements entered in recent years supply interesting precedents and give useful indications concerning the requisites for satisfactory international monetary relations.

Among the most useful precedents, it appears worthwhile to mention the Franco-British agreement of December 1939 which was designed to stabilize the two currencies and to finance trade between the two countries during the war. Its distinctive feature was that the two governments agreed to acquire and keep, through their exchange equalization funds, at the official rates, the other country's exchange offered through authorized channels. Thus was initiated, instead of the traditional method of financial assistance based on credits opened in terms of the money of the creditor country, a new method based on the acquisition by the creditor country of bank balances expressed in terms of the money of the debtor country.

The advantage of this new method arises in part from its flexibility; it arises also from the additional guarantee which it provides to the creditor country. Indeed, when a country opens to another a credit expressed in the currency of the creditor country, the creditor country holds exclusively a promissory note expressed in a currency which the debtor country might be unable to obtain for redeeming its debt. If, however, the creditor country holds the currency of the debtor country, it holds an internal purchasing power inside the country. True, it is conceivable that the debtor country might "freeze" its own currency owned by another country; but between friendly countries, violation of a promise not to "freeze" its own currency is a much more serious offense than failure to refund a foreign currency which the debtor country might be unable to obtain.

Several features of monetary agreements entered during the war were well suited to the special situation involved, but are not satisfactory for purposes of international financial collaboration in the future. Thus, the Franco-British agreement specified an unlimited mutual assistance, which implies risks unsuitable to a peace-time system; it specified also a prohibition of utilizing in third markets the other partner's exchange, which constitutes a bilateral regulation incompatible with the multilateral character of international trade and credit.

4. *Explanation of the proposed monetary system.*

Let us assume that the principal nations, as in the case of the tripartite agreement of 1936, might conclude a monetary accord among themselves, to which the other United Nations might be invited to adhere, under certain conditions.

a) This agreement would, in the first place, fix the official parities of the currencies of the participating countries; these official rates would not be changed without preliminary consultation (or preferably agreement) of the interested countries. A suitable mechanism of consultation (or preferably agreement) should be set up.

b) The stability of exchange rates thus determined would be assured by the undertaking, on the part of the monetary authorities (either Exchange Equalization Fund or Central Bank) to acquire at the specified rate and to conserve, at their own risks, but with the limitations and guarantees hereafter specified, the exchange of other participating countries offered through *authorized* channels. (The word "authorized" applies to countries with foreign-exchange control.)

In order to facilitate to participating countries the relaxation of foreign exchange control, treatment, both as regards limitations and guarantees, should be made more favorable as control is relaxed.

c) The foreign exchange thus acquired by the monetary authorities of the participating countries could be utilized for payments to be made in such currencies (purchase of goods, payments for services, payments of interests or dividends, purchase of securities, of real estate, etc.); it might also, under certain conditions, be sold to the monetary authorities of other participating countries.

d) A limit would be fixed, for each participating country, of the amount of exchange of each participating country which its monetary authorities would agree to acquire, if offered, at the specified rate, and conserve if required.

While the limits should correspond to a reasonable amount of international trade, the authors of this memorandum have not attempted, at the present stage, to establish the basis of the determination of these limits.

e) As a guarantee against loss arising from depreciation of its own exchange, each participating country would not only undertake to protect each other participating country against such loss, but would also agree to deposit, on demand, collateral (gold, foreign bills, raw materials, approved securities, etc.) up to a specified percentage (10 to 30% for instance) of the amount of its own currency held by the monetary authorities of another participating country. This collateral should be deposited with the monetary authorities (or warehouses, in the case of raw materials) of the country holding the currency, or a third approved country. Should the currency of the debtor country depreciate, additional collateral might be demanded, like in the case of commercial loans.

f) The proposed monetary system, which amounts to the opening of mutual credits, undoubtedly entails inflationary risks. A method must therefore be devised to counteract, whenever considered advisable, the inflationary effects of the mutual purchases of exchange. The method suggested is a method of sterilization, which would work as follows:

In a normal period, the monetary authorities of a country holding the currency of another country would use this currency so as to favor flow of credit; for instance in the form of current accounts in commercial banks, of Treasury obligations, of discounted bills, etc. In periods of inflation, this currency would be kept in the form of an account with the Central Bank of the debtor country which would refrain from basing credits on them. Thus the debtor country would be enabled to maintain the foreign exchange value of its currency without losing the control of its internal circulation.

5. *Optional constitution of a Monetary Stabilization Office.*

To assure the smooth working of the system, it would be necessary that the monetary authorities of the participating countries should be constantly in close contact, either by means of periodical meetings or by setting up a permanent committee. It would probably be still preferable to establish a central board which might be called the Monetary Stabilization Office.

This Stabilization Office would keep account of all exchange transactions effected by the monetary authorities of the participating countries. It would not only facilitate clearings, but could also receive and scrutinize collateral. Furthermore, it would be in a position to know the balance of payments of each of the participating countries and thus to furnish valuable information concerning disequilibria of an accidental or permanent character, which should be corrected by financial or economic measures. Thus the Monetary Stabilization Office could serve both as a barometer of economic conditions and as a counsellor on economic affairs.

It should be noted, nevertheless, that the establishment of a Monetary Stabilization Office is not an essential condition for the operation of the proposed system.

6. *The place of gold in the future monetary system.*

Under the proposed system, monetary parities are fixed by mutual reference, and mutual credits are opened without movements of gold (except when used as collateral). However, the suggested system may be considered as a first step toward a general return to an international gold standard. Indeed, the establishment of fixed monetary parities,—even if tentative and even if affected by exchange control is tantamount to the adoption of a common monetary unit. Thus the link to gold of the U.S. dollar becomes a link for all other currencies also.

The role of gold could be enhanced by stipulating that any nation which so desired would be authorized to redeem in gold the credits received. Gradually, the various monetary units, as experience would show that parities are well established, could be defined anew in gold ounces.

Nevertheless, the place of gold has undergone deep modifications since 1914 and will remain considerably altered. Gold has ceased, for three decades, to be an instrument of internal circulation. Unlike platinum and silver, which have found new outlets in the chemical industry, gold has found none. So that its industrial use has been greatly reduced and has now become an infinitesimal proportion of an annual production which, in 1940, was three times as high, in dollars, as in 1920. The conception of gold as a "pledge" of internal monetary circulation has been pointedly criticized. Gold, however, has not ceased to be of valuable service for settlement of balances of payment between countries. It has also remained in use for the purpose of hoarding, notwithstanding administrative restrictions in most countries; such restrictions increase the risk of gold hoarding, but increase also its psychological attraction.

To sum up, use of gold is considerably restricted, while its world stock is now, in dollars, about four times as high as in 1914.

The facts themselves, in their evolution, seem to designate the new place of gold. Inasmuch as its stock, considerably increased, is in the hands of the monetary authorities of certain countries, predominantly in the United States, and inasmuch as its other uses have become insignificant, *therefore its value depends mainly on the action of monetary authorities, particularly in the United States.* The value of gold has thus become similar to the value of a fiduciary currency. Considering the difficulties which nations would encounter if they attempted to agree upon the adoption of a new international currency, is it not providential that they have at hand such a currency, consecrated by a mystic thousands of years old, in the form of yellow metal? Gold is the international currency of the future.

While gold should thus resume its role as an instrument of settlement of international balances and as a common monetary unit, its function as chief economic regulator should not be revived. The latter function should be exercised mainly through the concerted action of the competent authorities on the volume of credits and of goods. (It should be pointed out that the action of competent authorities on credits was already an inherent part of the traditional gold standard which, widely held opinion to the contrary, did not work automatically, but was managed through discount rates.)

7. *Conclusion.*

It may be pointed out that the proposed system is intermediate between two systems which were widely in use in the period 1920–1940. Before Great Britain devalued in 1931, central banks customarily held currencies of certain other countries, without limit nor protection. Under this system, usually designated as the "gold exchange standard," the Bank of France and the Netherlands Central Bank had accumulated large sterling balances. After the heavy losses thus incurred, monetary authorities adhered to the practice of requesting conversion into gold of the foreign exchange balances which they acquired. This system, usually called the "gold bullion standard," was utilized in the tripartite monetary agreement, where each adhering country promised to redeem in gold, within 24 hours the amounts of its own currency acquired by the exchange equalization fund of another adhering country.

Both these systems are unsatisfactory. It is unreasonable, under the "gold exchange standard," to expect one country to hold, without some limit and guarantee, another country's currency. It is also unreasonable, under the "gold bullion standard," to consider the currency of a friendly country as worthless. The proposed system does not, like the gold exchange standard, imply one hundred percent confidence in another country's currency, nor, like the gold bullion standard, imply one hundred percent lack of confidence.

There seems to be no reason why the proposed system, or a similar one, could not be started immediately between the United Nations without waiting for the end of hostilities. The only real problem is to find a proper basis for fixing the limits of the amounts of exchange to be purchased. But should important difficulties arise in this connection, the system could be started nevertheless in an experimental way by fixing at the outset very low limits which could be gradually increased later.

The Canadian Plan

Following discussions between U.S. and Canadian officials in May 1943, the Canadian Government decided to put forward its own plan as an alternative to the White and Keynes Plans. A first draft was sent to Lord Keynes on June 3, 1943 and a slightly revised version was tabled in the Canadian House of Commons by the Minister of Finance on July 12, 1943. It is the latter version which is reproduced below.

Tentative Draft Proposals of Canadian Experts for an International Exchange Union

(July 12, 1943)

CONTENTS

	PAGE
General Observations of Canadian Experts on Plans for Post-War Monetary Organization	103
Tentative Draft Proposals of Canadian Experts for an International Exchange Union*	108

OTTAWA: *June 9, 1943*

GENERAL OBSERVATIONS OF CANADIAN EXPERTS ON PLANS FOR POST-WAR MONETARY ORGANIZATION

1. Officials of the Canadian Government have had an opportunity of examining the United States Treasury Department Preliminary Draft Outline of a Proposal for a United and Associated Nations Stabilization Fund, and have received explanations of this proposal from American officials. A similar procedure was followed in connection with the paper containing proposals by British experts for an International Clearing Union. The discussions with both British and American officials have been entirely exploratory and the Canadian Government has not been committed to any course of action as a result of these conversations. The American and British experts, for their part, have laid stress on the fact that their proposals are tentative in character, and have made it clear to representatives of the Canadian Government (as well as to those of other governments) that they would welcome critical comment and constructive

---

* It might be preferable to refer to the proposed organization as the International Exchange Fund. However, to avoid any possible misunderstanding which might arise through the use of the term Fund to describe both the association of members and the resources of the institution, the term Union has been used throughout this document to describe the organization itself.

suggestions. Canadian experts who have been studying the British and the American proposals are, therefore, led to make certain observations of a general character and to submit an alternative plan. Like the British and the American plans, the proposals of the Canadian experts are provisional and tentative in character; they incorporate important features of both the American and the British plans and add to them certain new elements.

2. The main objectives of the American and the British proposals appear to be identical, namely, the establishment of an international monetary mechanism which will aid in the restoration and development of healthy international trade after the war, which will achieve a high degree of exchange stability, and which will not conflict with the desire of countries to carry out such policies as they may think appropriate to achieve, so far as possible, economic stability at a high level of employment and incomes. To aid in the achievement of these objectives, the British and American experts have proposed the establishment of a new international monetary institution. Their proposals are large in conception, but no larger than the problem itself. There is every reason to improve the structure and operation of the monetary mechanism on the basis of experience. But there is no reason why proposals should be based exclusively on the limited, and on the whole, bad experience of the past two decades. Unless dependable exchange and credit relations between countries can be achieved before the stresses and strains of the post-war period begin, there is little likelihood that irreparable damage can be avoided.

3. If plans for international monetary organization are to be successful, other problems—by no means less difficult or less important—will also have to be faced and solved by joint international action. It would, indeed, be dangerous to attach too much importance to monetary organization of and by itself, if this resulted in neglect of other problems which may be even more important and difficult, or in a misguided faith that with a new form of monetary organization the other problems would solve themselves. In the international field alone (to say nothing of the innumerable domestic problems involved in the profound changes in the structure of production and employment which have taken place in all belligerent and many non-belligerent countries due to the exigencies of the war) it will be necessary to attack frontally such problems as commercial policy, international investment, the instability of primary product prices—to name but a few. No international monetary organization, however perfect in form, could long survive economic distortions resulting from bilateralist trade practices, continued refusal of creditor countries to accept imports in payment of the service on their foreign investment or to invest their current account surplus abroad, or enormous fluctuations in food and raw material prices such as characterized the years between the two wars. But the fact that there are many problems to be faced cannot be used as an excuse for facing none. A start must be made somewhere, and for the reasons given in paragraph 5, the problem of international monetary organization is a logical and fruitful starting-place.

4. The establishment of an international monetary organization is no substitute for the measures of international relief and rehabilitation which will be required as the war draws to its conclusion and afterwards; and in the view of the Canadian experts any monetary organization which is set up should not be called upon to finance transactions of this nature. Some continuing and stable arrangements regarding international long-term investment are also clearly essential if equilibrium is to be achieved and maintained. Nor should it be thought that the proposed international monetary institu-

tion is merely an instrument of the transition period from war to peace. True, it has special importance in this period, but it should be designed as a permanent institution and not as a stop-gap to function during a relatively short period of time.

5. An important, perhaps the most important, feature of the British and the American proposals is the provision in both plans for the extension of credit between countries. The two plans differ as regards the precise techniques to be used in extending credit and as regards the amounts which may be involved; but both plans provide that foreign credits are to be available under certain conditions to countries having need of them, and that they shall be made available through an international monetary organization rather than through bilateral arrangements between pairs of countries. The provision for credit extension is nothing more nor less than a straightforward and realistic recognition of the fact that at the end of the war a large number of countries, whose import requirements will be considerable, will not have immediately available a sufficient reserve of foreign assets to enable them to expose themselves to the risk of participation in a world economic system. An interval will be needed to give time for adjustment and re-organization. If the penury in foreign means of payment of certain important countries is to be allowed to fix the pattern of post-war trading and domestic policies, then all can look forward to penury—no country, rich or poor, will escape the impoverishment resulting from the throttling of international trade which will result.

6. It is useful to consider what would happen if no action were taken to set up international machinery of the general character suggested by the experts of the United States and the United Kingdom. Theoretically, one alternative would be immediate cash settlement for all international transactions. But how can cash be produced for purchases abroad? Only by selling goods or services abroad, or by disposing of acceptable foreign assets such as securities and gold. The facts regarding the distribution of the world's monetary gold reserves and the changes which have taken place in the course of the war in various countries' holdings of foreign securities are too well known to require elaboration. Broadly speaking, and allowing for certain exceptions and time-lags, a cash basis for the settlement of international transactions would mean that any country's capacity to export would be limited to the amount of its own currency it made available to foreign countries through its imports and other current payments abroad—in other words, trade would in effect be reduced to barter. In point of fact, however, there is no possibility that countries would for long allow themselves to be confined in such a strait-jacket. Faced with the problem of an unsalable surplus of export goods and with consequent domestic unemployment, they would refuse to accept the penalty of disorganization of export trade if that penalty could be avoided, even temporarily, by the extension of credit. Countries would embark on bilateral credit arrangements, no doubt linked with deals relating to the purchase and sale of goods; and as soon as certain countries began to adopt this course others would find that they had to follow suit to protect their trade interests. It is difficult to imagine a more fruitful source of international dissension than a competitive trade and credit extension program of this character.

The Canadian experts believe it to be true, therefore, that the Stabilization Fund or Clearing Union plans do not involve a decision as to whether foreign credits shall be extended or withheld. In some form or other, credit will in fact be extended; and the decision which has to be taken relates primarily to the method employed. For the reasons given above, international arrangements are greatly to be preferred to bilateral deals.

7. This leads to the question, how much credit should be made available through the international monetary mechanism? A vital feature of any plan of this sort is the provision it makes for the borrowing power of each participant and for the contribution to the resources of the organization by the participating countries through the provision of capital, the accumulation of balances or through loans. Some concern has been expressed in regard to the size of the commitment which may be assumed by prospective creditors. It is probable that Canada will be a creditor country on current account, and the Canadian experts have therefore given careful thought to this aspect of the arrangements.

8. There is one preliminary observation which should be made in this connection. It would be a distortion of the realities of the situation for any country, or its citizens, to regard the willingness to provide resources to an international organization of the general character proposed by the British and American experts as an act of generosity which is performed for the sake of foreign countries. Resources are provided to the organization first, because all have a stake in re-creating a functioning international economic system and secondly, because for each individual country the realistic alternatives in the form of trade disorganization are costlier than the provision of resources. Moreover, and most important of all, the resources provided are not given away; they are fully secured by the organization's holdings of gold and national currencies. It can only lead to confusion of thought to regard participation in such plans as these as in any way similar in character to participation in international relief schemes, important and necessary though the latter may be.

9. It seems apparent that, in one way or another, substantial unregulated movements of capital between countries will be prevented. In these circumstances, countries will, by and large, lose or gain foreign exchange to the extent, but only to the extent, of the unbalance in their current account transactions with the rest of the world. If a country is building up a substantial credit position, it will know that this situation is produced because it is selling more goods and services abroad than it is buying abroad. If it is dissatisfied with this position, if it wishes to reduce its credit balance, it has through participation in the proposed organization lost no single one of the courses of action ever open to it. True, it is by no means easy for a country, acting alone, to solve problems of unbalance. But as a last resort a country *can* find a solution by unilateral action. It can do the only things it ever could do in these circumstances; it can buy more abroad—goods, services or investments; or it can sell less abroad. It is therefore quite wrong to assume that countries participating in the proposed institution would, because of this participation, be left without control over their international commitments. It may be, and no doubt is, useful to erect danger signals at various stations along the road followed by both debtors and creditors. Such signals are useful reminders. But there is nothing to prevent either creditor or debtor from taking remedial action at any time.

10. If the foregoing is a correct analysis of the situation—and it would appear to be a simple statement of fact—creditors need not be unduly concerned about the possible size of their investment in the Fund, knowing that the ultimate actual size of their stake can be determined by their own course of action from day to day and from year to year. Nevertheless, even the appearance of an unlimited commitment is probably undesirable and in the tentative proposals of Canadian experts, a limit is placed on the obligation of each participant to provide resources to the institution. But there is less real danger to the interests of creditor countries in the establishment of a Fund

or a Union whose potential resources are unnecessarily large (and may in consequence never be entirely used) than there is in the establishment of an institution whose resources are obviously too small. The interests of all will best be served by providing a fair degree of latitude, a satisfactory breathing-space—to debtors and creditors alike. If its objectives are to be achieved, the resources must be large enough to permit time for basic re-adjustments to be accomplished; they must be such that the organization will command general confidence in its own stability. For if this is not the case, what will happen? It will be believed that certain currencies are likely to become "scarce" currencies—a belief which will be reinforced by the reduction in the institution's holdings of that particular currency. Countries which are likely to require a "scarce" currency will hasten to make their purchases which are payable in that currency. As the holdings of the "scarce" currency are used up, as discussions and arguments commence regarding an enlargement of the quota or some other form of extension of credit, grave misgivings in regard to the international situation will arise. The position will be very much akin to that of a bank whose cash reserves are feared to be insufficient. There will be a run on that currency in the institution; and if the currency concerned is an important one, the international effects will be very serious indeed. No form of international monetary organization can continuously compensate for chronic maladjustments in the current account balance of payments of the countries which may be concerned, but it would be most unwise to set up machinery which stood a fair chance of facing a crisis at a comparatively early date.

11. To avoid misunderstanding it should be emphasized that it would be extremely dangerous to use short-term credits as a device to cover up basically unsound positions. This would be no less disastrous in the international than in the domestic field, and any monetary system which made such an attempt on a large scale would inevitably break down. A chronic unbalance in current account balances of international payments which is not matched by voluntary long-term capital movements—lending abroad by creditor countries, and borrowing abroad by debtor countries—is symptomatic of a deep-seated maladjustment which has to be dealt with if equilibrium is to be restored. No debtor country can live beyond its resources indefinitely; and no creditor country can persistently refuse to lend its surplus abroad or make other adjustments to its creditor position without ripping the international fabric. But time is required for adjustments to be made and for remedial measures to have their effects, and the contention of this paper is that the time allowed must be adequate. More time may be purchased at a smaller real cost than less time.

12. There is one final observation of a general character which should be made. The new international monetary institution which it is proposed to establish will be neither omniscient nor omnipotent. Its aim will be to promote conditions in which member countries are free to carry out sound economic policies for the welfare of their own people and in which they will not be induced or forced, for lack of organized co-operation, to pursue policies which impoverish themselves and contribute to the impoverishment of the world. The organization should be international and not supernational. Nations should enter into the proposed agreement for common purposes and advantages, realizing that without such agreement the common purposes cannot be achieved. In their national policies, countries should be limited only by their own will in entering and remaining in the organization. If the proposed institution functions well, it will have at its disposal more information regarding the currents of international financial transactions and the causes of disequilibrium than has ever been available before. It will be in a position to offer informed and disinterested advice

to its members. It may be hoped that the quality of the advice offered will be such that it will carry great weight. But no member state should be asked to bind itself in all circumstances to follow the advice given by the organization. Moreover, if a country feels at any time that its national interests are being jeopardized by the actions of the organization, and is willing to sacrifice the advantages of continued membership, it should be free to withdraw, after making provision to liquidate its obligations to the organization or, if the country is a creditor, it should have returned to it its original contribution to the resources of the organization. The proposals here advanced are put forward in the belief that a soundly conceived international agreement can give greater scope for national policies than can exist outside it.

13. To sum up these general observations, it is suggested that:

(a) An international agreement for the establishment of an international monetary organization which involves the extension of credit is essential if international co-operation in the post-war world is to be achieved.

(b) Such machinery will deal with only one of the numerous problems which must be faced, but it is a logical and convenient starting place for joint international action.

(c) The credit made available through the international monetary organization should be adequate to deal with that portion of current account surpluses and deficits which is not met by relief and other concerted international action in the years immediately after the war; it should be sufficient to provide a firm basis on which multilateral world trade can be re-established after the war; and it should provide time to countries which find their international accounts unbalanced to take the necessary corrective measures to adjust their position.

(d) The extension of credit is not a cure-all; it merely provides time for adjustments; and unless unbalanced positions (except those accompanying long-term capital movements) are brought into equilibrium, any arrangements made will break down.

(e) No country participating in the arrangements loses control over the size of its international commitments, since it can determine their size by its own action, if it wishes to do so.

(f) No country participating in the arrangements loses control over its domestic economic policies.

TENTATIVE DRAFT PROPOSALS OF CANADIAN EXPERTS FOR AN INTERNATIONAL EXCHANGE UNION

I. PURPOSES OF THE UNION

1. To provide for stability of exchange rates and to provide an orderly method for their determination.

2. To provide a convenient clearing mechanism to settle balances in international payments.

3. To provide to all countries access to foreign exchange resources in order to reduce the danger that economic and commercial policies in the period immediately after the war will be largely determined by a shortage of foreign exchange and to enable

countries thereafter to be guided in their economic and commercial policies by long-run considerations when faced with a temporary reduction of foreign markets.

4. To aid in the achievement of international equilibrium by measures designed to prevent excessive short-term borrowing through the Union or the excessive accumulation of uninvested foreign surpluses.

5. To contribute to the re-establishment and development of a multilateral trading system and to the elimination of discriminatory trading and currency practices.

II. Resources of the Union

Member countries shall agree to make the following resources available to the Union:

1. A capital subscription to the amount of the quota assigned to each member country, the aggregate of such quotas to be $8,000 million.

DETAILED PROVISIONS
REGARDING 1—QUOTAS AND CAPITAL SUBSCRIPTION

(a) *Determination of Quotas*

The quota for each member country shall be determined by a formula which will give due regard to factors such as international trade, national income, and holdings of gold and foreign exchange convertible into gold. A special assessment may be levied in any case where this formula would be inappropriate.

(b) *Payment of Capital Subscriptions*

The capital subscription of each member country shall be paid up in full on or before the date set by the Governing Board of the Union on which the Union's operations are to begin. Each member country shall pay in at least 15 per cent. of its quota in gold and the balance in national currency; a country may substitute gold for national currency in meeting its quota requirements. The Union may make such arrangements as it deems appropriate to provide a period of time within which countries having less than $300 million in gold or foreign exchange convertible into gold in official exchange reserves may pay up their gold contribution in full, the equivalent in national currency to be paid in the interval. Notwithstanding the provisions of subsequent paragraphs, the Union shall sell foreign exchange to such member countries for the purpose of acquiring gold to pay their capital subscriptions.

(c) *Change in Quotas*

The Board may from time to time change the quotas of particular member countries, provided, however, that in voting on proposals to increase quotas the voting strength of each member shall be increased or decreased to take account of the Union's net sales or purchases of the currency of each member country in accordance with the weighted voting formula set out in paragraph IX 3 below. No increase shall, however, be made in the quota of any country without the consent of the representative of the country concerned.

2. Loans to the Union, as required, in amounts not exceeding 50 per cent. of the quota of each member country.

DETAILED PROVISIONS
REGARDING 2—LOANS TO THE UNION

(a) *Conditions of Borrowing*

The terms and conditions of loans made by member countries to the Union under the provisions of paragraph II.2 shall be set out in the rules and regulations of the Union. The Union's authority to borrow domestic currency from member countries in amounts up to 50 per cent. of their quotas shall be a revolving authority. The Union shall not exercise its right to borrow until it has used its available gold resources to acquire additional supplies of the currency in question. Subject to the provisions of the preceding sentence, the Union must exercise its right to borrow when its holdings of the currency of any member country have been reduced to 10 per cent. of the quota of that member country. When the Union exercises its right under the provisions of paragraph II.2 to borrow additional supplies of the currency of any member country it shall have the duty to attempt to improve its position in the currency concerned by acquiring the currency or gold from the holdings of other member countries for payment in their national currencies or in other foreign exchange they need.

(b) *Conditions of Repayment*

The Union shall have the right to repay loans contracted under the provisions of paragraph II.2 at any time. The member country making the loan shall have the right to demand repayment in gold to the extent of the Union's gold holdings at any time and shall also have the right to demand repayment in its national currency provided that such repayment does not reduce the Union's holdings of that currency below 50 per cent. of the quota of the member country. Member countries shall agree to give 30 days' notice of demand for repayment of loans made to the Union under the provisions of the present article.

III. MONETARY UNIT OF THE UNION

1. The monetary unit of the Union shall be an international unit of such name as may be agreed (hereafter referred to as the Unit) and it shall consist of 137 1/7 grains of fine gold. The accounts of the Union shall be kept and published in terms of the Unit.

2. The value of the Unit in terms of gold shall not be changed without the approval of four-fifths of member votes.

3. Member countries shall agree with the Union the initial values of their currencies in terms of gold or the Unit and, except as provided in paragraph IV.2 below, shall undertake not to alter these values without the approval of the Union.

4. Deposits in terms of the Unit may be accepted by the Union from member countries upon the delivery of gold to the Union. Such Unit deposits shall be transferable to other member countries. They shall be redeemable in gold and the Union shall maintain at all times a 100 per cent. reserve in gold against all Unit deposits.

IV. EXCHANGE RATES

1. The Union shall fix, on the basis of exchange rates initially agreed between it and each member country, the rates at which it will buy and sell one member's currency for another's and the rates in local currencies at which it will buy and sell gold. The spread between the Union's buying and selling rates for member currencies and for gold shall not exceed 1 per cent. Except as provided in paragraph IV.2 below, member countries shall agree not to change the initially agreed exchange rates without the approval of the Union and any country which alters the value of its currency without the consent of the Union shall be declared in default of its obligations and become subject to the penalties provided in paragraph XI.1 below.

2. Notwithstanding the provisions of paragraph IV.1 above, any member country which is a net purchaser of foreign exchange from the Union (arising from other than capital account transactions) to the extent of at least 50 per cent. of its quota and has so been on the average of the preceding 12 months shall be entitled to depreciate its exchange to the maximum extent of 5 per cent.; provided, however, that the provisions of this paragraph shall not apply to any country which holds independent official reserves of gold and foreign currencies freely convertible into gold in amounts exceeding 50 per cent. of its quota. No country shall be entitled to repeat the exchange depreciation provided for in this paragraph without the specific approval of the Union.*

3. No change in the value of the currencies of member countries shall be permitted to alter the value of the assets of the Union in terms of gold or the Unit. Thus, if the Union approves a reduction in the value of the currency of a member country, or if a country depreciates its exchange under the provisions of the preceding paragraph, or if a significant depreciation in the value of the currency of a member, as determined by quotations on the exchange markets of other member countries, has in fact occurred, that country must on request deliver to the Union an amount of its local currency equal to the decrease in the value of that currency held by the Union. Likewise, if the currency of a particular country should appreciate, the Union must return to that country an amount in the currency of that country or in gold equal to the resulting increase in the value of the Union's holdings.

V. OPERATIONS OF THE UNION—PROVISIONS OF SPECIAL APPLICABILITY TO DEFICIT COUNTRIES

1. The Union shall have the power to sell to the Treasury of any member country (or exchange fund or central bank acting as its agent for the purpose) at the rate of exchange established by the Union, currency of any country which the Union holds, subject to the following provisions:

(a) Without special permission, no country shall be a net purchaser of foreign exchange from the Union except for the purpose of meeting an adverse balance of payments on current account and the Union may at any time limit the amounts of foreign exchange to be sold to any member country which is permitting significant exports of capital while having an adverse balance of payments on current account.

---

* In the course of conversations in Washington the Canadian experts expressed the view that it might be desirable to provide for a somewhat greater permissive range of depreciation in exchange rates with somewhat different safeguards than those incorporated in paragraph IV.2. The following is a draft of a paragraph which might be substituted for paragraph IV.2 of the text:

"Notwithstanding the provisions of paragraph IV.1 above, any member country which has had an adverse balance of payments on current account during a two year period of such magnitude that it has utilized, to cover this deficit, 50 per cent. of its independent gold and foreign exchange reserves and is, in addition, a net purchaser of foreign exchange from the Union to the extent of 50 per cent. of its quota shall be entitled to depreciate its exchange rate to the maximum extent of 10 per cent. The provisions of this paragraph shall only be applicable once in respect of each member country unless the specific approval of the Union has been obtained. Any member country intending to depreciate its exchange rate under the provisions of this paragraph shall inform the management of the Union in advance and shall afford it an opportunity to make such observations as it deems appropriate before taking such action."

DETAILED PROVISIONS

REGARDING (a)—RESTRICTION OF RIGHT OF DEFICIT COUNTRIES TO PURCHASE FOREIGN EXCHANGE TO AMOUNTS REQUIRED TO MEET AN ADVERSE BALANCE OF PAYMENTS ON CURRENT ACCOUNT.

(i) A country shall be regarded as a net purchaser of foreign exchange if as a result of the Union's purchases and sales of currencies the Union's holdings of its currency rise above the amount originally provided to the Union by way of capital subscription.

(ii) The Union may require any member country to furnish at periodic intervals statistics of its balance of international payments on current account and on capital account and statistics of gold and foreign exchange holdings, public and private. Each such member country shall agree to furnish officers of the Union with detailed explanations of the basis on which such statistics are computed. If at any time the Governing Board has reason to believe that an overflow of capital from any member country is resulting directly or indirectly in net purchases of foreign exchange by that country from the Union, it shall have the right to request a control of outward capital movements as a condition of making additional sales of foreign exchange to such country. Without limiting the generality of the foregoing, the Union shall normally require any member country which has been a net purchaser of foreign exchange to the extent of 25 per cent. of its quota to impose restrictions on outward capital movements if none exist.

(iii) In considering applications from countries which have been net purchasers of foreign exchange from the Union for the special permission referred to in paragraph V.1 (a) to purchase foreign exchange for purposes other than the meeting of an adverse balance of payments on current account, the Governing Board shall give careful attention to applications for foreign exchange to facilitate the adjustment of foreign debts where this is deemed to be desirable from the point of view of the general economic situation and shall also give special attention to applications for foreign exchange by member countries not in default on their foreign obligations for the purpose of maintaining contractual principal payments on foreign debt.

(b) In order to promote the most effective utilization of existing stocks of gold and foreign exchange, no member country shall have the right to be a net purchaser of foreign exchange from the Union so long as that country's holdings of gold and foreign currencies freely convertible into gold (including private as well as official holdings) exceed its quota.

DETAILED PROVISION

REGARDING (b)—RESTRICTION OF RIGHT OF COUNTRIES HOLDING LARGE INDEPENDENT GOLD AND FOREIGN EXCHANGE RESERVES TO PURCHASE FOREIGN EXCHANGE FROM THE UNION

In interpreting this provision the Governing Board shall give special consideration to the position of certain Asiatic countries where gold has long been used as private treasure.

(c) In general, the Union shall have the power to sell foreign exchange for domestic currency to member countries up to 200 per cent. of the quota of each such member country. Net sales of foreign exchange shall not exceed 50 per cent.

of the quota of each member country during the first year and the cumulative net sales shall not exceed 100 per cent., 150 per cent. or 200 per cent. during the first two, three and four years of the operation of the union.

> DETAILED PROVISION
> REGARDING (c)—RESTRICTION OF SALES OF FOREIGN EXCHANGE TO SPECIFIED LIMITS
>
> On special vote of the Governing Board, in which voting strength shall be weighted to allow for the Union's net purchases and sales of each member country's currency in accordance with the provisions described in paragraph IX.3 below, the Union may purchase any currency in excess of these limits provided that (a) the country whose currency is being acquired by the Union agrees to adopt and carry out measures recommended by the Union to correct the disequilibrium in its balance of payments, or (b) it is the view of the Governing Board that the country's prospective balance of payments is such as to warrant the expectation that the excess currency holdings of the Union can be disposed of in a reasonable time.

(d) In order to promote the most effective utilization of existing stocks of gold and foreign exchange, the Union may, as a condition of making further sales of foreign exchange to any member country which would bring its net purchases to an amount in excess of 50 per cent. of its quota, require such country to sell the Union, for domestic currency, appropriate amounts of any reserves it (or its residents) may hold of gold or foreign exchange acceptable to the Union.

(e) Notwithstanding the provisions of paragraph (c) above, whenever a member country is exhausting its quota more rapidly than is warranted in the judgment of the Governing Board, the Board may make such recommendations to that country as it thinks appropriate with a view to correcting the disequilibrium, and may place such conditions upon additional sales of foreign exchange to that country as it deems to be in the general interest of the Union.

2. A charge of 1 per cent. per annum payable in gold shall be levied against member countries on the amount of their currency held by the Union in excess of the quotas of such countries.

VI. OPERATIONS OF THE UNION—PROVISIONS OF SPECIAL APPLICABILITY TO SURPLUS COUNTRIES

1. In order to promote the most effective utilization of the available and accumulating supply of gold and foreign exchange resources of member countries, each member country shall, on request of the Union, sell to the Union, for its local currency or for foreign currencies which it needs, all gold and foreign exchange it acquires in excess of the amounts held immediately after joining the Union.

> DETAILED PROVISION
> REGARDING 1—ACCUMULATING SUPPLIES OF GOLD AND FOREIGN EXCHANGE
>
> For the purpose of this provision, only free foreign exchange and gold are considered. Each member country shall agree to furnish the Union with periodic reports of gold and foreign exchange holdings, public and private.

2. When the Union's operations have resulted in net sales of the currency of any member country to the extent of 75 per cent. of the quota of that country the Union may, in order to increase its resources of the currency in question, attempt to arrange, in co-operation with such agencies as may be established to promote international

investment, with the member country a program of foreign capital investment (or repatriation) and may sell foreign exchange to facilitate such capital movements.

3. When the Union's holdings of the currency of a member country are being exhausted more rapidly than is warranted in the judgment of the Governing Board, the Board may make a report on the situation. Without restricting the generality of the foregoing, whenever the Union's operations have resulted in net sales of the currency of any member country to the extent of 85 per cent. of the quota of that country, the Union has the authority and the duty to render to the country a report embodying an analysis of the causes of the depletion of its holdings of the currency and recommendations appropriate to restore the equilibrium of the international balances of the country concerned. Such recommendations may relate to monetary and fiscal policies, exchange rate, commercial policy and international investment.

>DETAILED PROVISION
>REGARDING 3—REPORT ON COUNTRIES WHOSE CURRENCY IS BECOMING SCARCE
>
>The Board member of the country in question shall be a member of the Union Committee appointed to draft the report. The report shall be sent to all member countries and, if deemed desirable, made public.

4. The Union shall have the right at any time to enter into arrangements with any member country to borrow additional supplies of its currency on such terms and conditions as may be mutually satisfactory.

5. The Union shall have the right at any time to enter into special arrangements with any member country for the purpose of providing an emergency supply of the currency of any other member country on such terms and conditions as may be mutually satisfactory.

6. Whenever it becomes apparent to the Governing Board that the anticipated demand for any currency may soon exhaust the Union's holdings, the Governing Board shall inform the member countries of the probable supply of this currency and of a proposed method for its equitable distribution together with suggestions for helping to equate the anticipated demand and supply.

>DETAILED PROVISIONS
>REGARDING 6—RATIONING OF SCARCE CURRENCIES

(a) The provisions of paragraph VI.6 shall come into force only after the Union has exercised in full its right under paragraph II.2 to borrow additional supplies of the currency of the member country and after the Union has taken such further steps to increase its supply of this currency as it has deemed appropriate and found possible.

(b) The provisions of paragraph V.1 (c) shall, if necessary, be restricted by the duty of the Union to assure an appropriate distribution among various members of any currency the Union's supply of which is being exhausted.

(c) In rationing its sales of any scarce currency the Union shall be guided by the principle of satisfying the most urgent needs from the point of view of the general international economic situation. It shall also consider the special needs and resources of the various countries making the request for the scarce currency.

(d) Member countries shall agree that restrictions imposed by other member countries on the importation of goods from a country whose currency is being rationed by the Union shall, for the duration of such rationing, not be regarded as constituting an infraction of the most-favoured nation obligations of commercial treaties except in the case of countries holding official reserves of gold and the currencies of member countries in amounts exceeding 50 per cent. of their quotas.*

7. Whenever the Governing Board has, under the provisions of the preceding paragraph, taken steps to ration the Union's supply of the currency of any member country, it may require the remaining member countries to prevent the sale by their residents of each other's currencies, including bills of exchange, in the country whose currency is being rationed and to prevent the purchase by their residents of the rationed currency through the exchange markets of non-member countries. In addition, whenever the Board has taken steps to ration the Union's supply of the currency of any member country, it shall have the duty to re-examine the prevailing exchange rates and to recommend such changes as it may regard as appropriate to the changed circumstances.

VII. POWERS OF THE UNION—GENERAL

1. The Union shall have the powers to take such actions as are required to carry out the operations enumerated in the preceding paragraphs. For greater clarity, the Union shall have the power to buy, sell and hold gold, currencies and government securities of member countries; to accept deposits and to earmark gold; to issue its own obligations and to discount or offer them for sale in member countries; and to act as a clearing house for the settling of international movements of funds and gold.

> DETAILED PROVISION
> REGARDING 1—GENERAL POWERS OF THE UNION
>
> Member countries agree that all of the Union's local currency holdings shall be free from any restrictions as to their use for payments within the country concerned.

2. When the Union's holdings of the local currency of a member country exceed the quota of that country the Union shall have the power to resell to the member country, upon its request, the Union's excess holdings of its currency for gold or acceptable foreign exchange.

3. The Union shall have the power to invest any of its currency holdings in government securities of the country of that currency, provided that the Board representative of the country concerned approves.

4. The Union shall have the power to buy and sell currencies of non-member countries, but shall not normally hold the currencies of non-member countries beyond 60 days after the date of purchase.

5. The Union shall have the power to levy upon member countries a pro rata share of the expenses of operating the Union, such levy to be made, however, only to the extent that the earnings of the Union are inadequate to meet its current expenses.

6. The Union shall make a service charge of one-quarter per cent. on all gold transactions.

7. In conducting its own operations, the Union shall have the power to deal only with or through (a) the Treasuries, exchange funds or fiscal agents of governments,

---

* This proposal will clearly have to be reviewed in the light of such general arrangements as may be made regarding international commercial policy and co-ordinated with those arrangements.

(b) central banks, with the consent of the member of the Board representing the country in question, and (c) any international banks owned predominantly by member countries. The Union may, nevertheless, with the approval of the member of the Board representing the country concerned, sell its own securities directly to the public or to institutions of member countries.

8. The Union shall have the power and the duty to co-operate with such other institutions of an international character as may exist or be established to deal with matters of international concern, including but not restricted to international investment and commercial policy.

VIII. ABNORMAL WAR-TIME BALANCES

During the first two years of operation the Union shall have the right to purchase abnormal war time balances held by member countries in other member countries for the national currency of the country selling such balances or for foreign exchange needed to meet current account deficits in such country's balance of international payments; in amounts not exceeding in the aggregate 5 per cent. of the quotas of all member countries. At the end of two years of operation the Governing Board shall propose a plan for the gradual further liquidation, in whole or in part, through the Union, of abnormal war time balances lying to the credit of member countries in other member countries and other financial indebtedness of a similar character. If the Governing Board feels unable to recommend that the Union's resources be used for this purpose it shall have the duty to propose some other method by which the problem can be considered.

IX. VOTING POWER

1. Each member country shall have 100 votes, plus one vote for the equivalent of each 100,000 Units of its quota.

2. All decisions, except where specifically provided otherwise, shall be made by majority of the member votes.

3. Notwithstanding the provisions of paragraph I above, in any vote on a proposal to increase the quota of any member country, member countries shall acquire one additional vote for each 100,000 Units of its contribution to the resources of the Fund (by way of original capital subscription or by way of loans made under the provisions of paragraph II.2) which has been utilized, net, on the average of the preceding year by the Union for sale to other member countries; and member countries shall lose one vote for each 100,000 Units of their net utilization of the resources of the Union on the average of the preceding year.

X. MANAGEMENT

1. The administration of the Union shall be vested in a Governing Board. Each government shall appoint a representative and an alternate who shall serve on the Board for a period of three years subject to the pleasure of their government. Representatives and alternates may be re-appointed.

2. The Governing Board shall select a Governor of the Union and one or more assistants. The Governor shall become an *ex officio* member of the Board and shall be chief of the operating staff of the Board. The Governor and his assistants shall hold office for five years and shall be eligible for re-election and may be removed for cause at any time by the Board.

3. The Governor of the Union shall select the operating staff in accordance with regulations established by the Governing Board. Members of the staff may be made available upon request of member countries or of other institutions of an international character for consultation in connection with economic problems and policies.

4. The Governing Board shall appoint from among its members an Executive Committee to consist of not fewer than eleven members. The Chairman of the Board shall be the Chairman of the Executive Committee and the Governor of the Union shall be *ex officio* a member of the Executive Committee. Meetings of the Executive Committee shall be held at least once every two months and more frequently if the Executive Committee shall so decide.

5. The Governing Board shall hold an annual meeting and such other meetings as it may be desirable to convene. On request of member countries casting one-fourth of the votes the Chairman shall call a meeting of the Board for the purpose of considering any matters placed before it.

6. Net profits earned by the Union shall be distributed in the following manner:

(a) 50 per cent. to reserves until the reserves are equal to 10 per cent. of the aggregate quotas of the Union;

(b) 50 per cent. to be divided each year among the members in proportion to their quotas.

XI. WITHDRAWAL AND EXPULSION FROM THE UNION

1. A country failing to meet its obligations to the Union may be suspended provided a majority of the member votes so decides. While under suspension the country shall be denied the privileges of membership but shall be subject to the same obligations as any other member of the Union. At the end of one year the country shall be automatically dropped from membership unless it has been restored to good standing by a majority of the member votes.

2. Any country which has been a net purchaser of foreign exchange from the Union may withdraw from the Union by giving notice and its withdrawal shall take effect one year from the date of such notice. During the interval between notice of withdrawal and the taking effect of the notice such country shall be subject to the same obligations as any other member of the Union.

3. Any country which has not been a net purchaser of foreign exchange from the Union may withdraw from the Union by giving notice and its withdrawal shall take effect 30 days from the date of such notice. During the interval between notice of withdrawal and the taking effect of notice such country shall be subject to the same obligations as any other member of the Union; except, however, that no country which has given notice of withdrawal shall be required to make loans to the Union under the provisions of paragraph II.2 above.

4. A country which is dropped or which withdraws from membership shall have returned to it an amount in its own currency equal to its contributed quota plus other obligations of the Union to the country and minus any sums owed by that country to the Union. The Union shall have 5 years in which to liquidate its obligation to such country.

XII. POLICIES OF MEMBER COUNTRIES

In addition to the obligations assumed under the preceding paragraphs, each member country shall undertake the following:

1. To maintain by appropriate action the exchange rates initially agreed with the Union on the currencies of other countries and not to alter exchange rates except under the provisions of paragraph IV.2 above, or with the consent of the Union and only to the extent and in the direction approved by the Union. Exchange rates of member countries may be permitted to fluctuate within a range not exceeding the spread fixed by the Union itself for its own purchases and sales of foreign exchange.

2. To abandon, as soon as the member country decides that conditions permit, all restrictions on foreign exchange transactions, other than those required effectively to control capital movements, with other member countries; and not to impose any additional restrictions, except for the purpose of controlling capital movements, without the approval of the Union.

DETAILED PROVISION

REGARDING 2—ABANDONMENT OF EXCHANGE CONTROL OTHER THAN ON CAPITAL MOVEMENTS

The Union may make representations to member countries that conditions are favourable for the abandonment or relaxation of foreign exchange restrictions other than those required effectively to control capital movements and each member country shall agree to give consideration to such representations.

3. To co-operate effectively with other member countries when such countries, with the approval of the Union, adopt or continue controls for the purpose of regulating international movements of capital.

DETAILED PROVISIONS

REGARDING 3—CO-OPERATION IN ENFORCING APPROVED EXCHANGE CONTROLS ON CAPITAL MOVEMENTS

Co-operation shall include, upon recommendation by the Union, measures that can appropriately be taken

(a) not to accept or permit acquisitions of deposits, securities or investments by residents of any member country imposing restrictions on the export of capital except with the permission of the government of that country and the Union;

(b) to make available to the Union or to the government of any member country full information on all property in the form of deposits, securities and investments of the residents of that country; and

(c) such other measures as the Union may recommend.

4. Not to enter into any new bilateral foreign exchange clearing arrangements nor engage in multiple currency practices except with the approval of the Union.

5. To give careful consideration to the views of the Union on existing or proposed monetary or economic policy the effect of which would be to cause a serious disequilibrium in the balance of payments of the country adopting such policy or of other countries.

6. To furnish the Union with all information it needs for its operations and to furnish such reports as it may require in the forms and at the times requested by the Union.

7. To adopt appropriate legislation or decrees to carry out its undertakings to the Union and to facilitate the activities of the Union.

Professor Williams' Key-Currency Plan

Professor John H. Williams expounded his proposals for a "key-currency" approach to the problems of international monetary organization in two places. The first was at the end of a paper delivered at a joint meeting of the American Statistical Association and the American Economic Association on December 28, 1936; this was reproduced in The American Economic Review, Vol. XXVII, No. 1, Supplement *(March 1937), pages 151–68. The extract (A) below consists of the final section of this paper. His second reference to the plan was at the end of his article entitled "Currency Stabilization: The Keynes and White Plans" in* Foreign Affairs, Vol. 21, No. 4 *(July 1943), pp. 645–58. Extract (B) below contains the final section of this article.*

Both the paper and the article were reprinted in Professor Williams' Postwar Monetary Plans and Other Essays, *3rd edition (New York, 1947), on pages 199–227 and pages 3–21, respectively.*

(A) Extract from a Paper on "The Adequacy of Existing Currency Mechanisms Under Varying Circumstances" *

(December 28, 1936)

I have presented the view, first, that there must be some form of compromise system, second, that this compromise should be one which will give the largest measure of internal monetary protection and control which is consistent with exchange stability, and third, that exchange variation, while not excluded, should be resorted to only when other means of control have been exhausted.

I want to conclude with three points which, I believe, have a special bearing upon the present trends and developments with respect to international monetary organization and policy:

1. The views expressed are not inconsistent with a keen and sympathetic interest in the new developments which have been growing out of the recent "gentlemen's agreement."

2. There are grounds for thinking that we do not need or want any single pattern of compromise in all countries, such as the gold standard pattern was before the War. Different kinds of countries require different kinds of monetary systems.

3. The best prospect for stability in individual countries and in the world as a whole, so far as it can be achieved by monetary means, lies in more efficient

---

* Reproduced by permission of Professor Williams and *The American Economic Review.*

monetary control within the major countries, especially the United States and England, coupled with co-operation between them; and on this basis, there is no such dilemma between internal and external monetary stability as has been frequently emphasized in abstract analysis.

1. *The "Gentlemen's Agreement."* The gentlemen's agreement is a form of de facto stabilization, less definite and binding than any which had been previously proposed and for that reason more acceptable and feasible. Whatever kind of system is ultimately to emerge, it has been commonly recognized that a trial period would be necessary before any more permanent and formal kind of stabilization could be ventured upon.

Moreover, the device—as set up under this agreement—for converting stabilization fund holdings of foreign currency into gold at a price that is based from day to day on the exchange rate may provide a new and better kind of exchange stability. Pressure on a currency will lead to its support through purchase by stabilization funds (or through sales of the other currencies) and to conversion of these balances into gold at a known price. If the pressure continues unabated it can be relieved by varying the exchange rate through varying the price of gold. With this instrument of flexibility at the disposal of the respective stabilization fund authorities, the result may be a greater assurance of exchange rates which are both more stable and more under control than has previously been the case. It will certainly make possible a more orderly change to new levels, if that is required; and it provides, moreover, a better possibility than we have previously had of effecting alterations in the exchange rate structure, of varying a currency with relation to some other without that change being communicated to all the others.[10]

It should be noted that, as it has thus far operated, this mechanism includes a fixed buying and selling price of gold in terms of dollars. Prior to the devaluation of the franc, the British Equalization Account operated against a fixed buying and selling price for gold in terms of francs. There is no evidence thus far that this kind of exchange stabilization can operate without being anchored to a fixed price of gold in one or more markets. In some respects, it would seem to be more feasible with only one, or a few countries, having a variable price of gold and operating against the fixed gold price maintained by the others. There is also the question whether operations cannot be conducted more effectively by one, or a few, stabilization funds rather than by a larger number. The objection to having one country on a variable basis, in this sense, and the others on a fixed basis is, of course, that it implies a large measure of trust in the integrity and the freedom from nationalistic motives of the variable exchange country which would act as the stabilizing agency. But perhaps the knowledge that other countries could retaliate by devaluation, either by new legislation or under an authority previously granted and held in readiness, might be a sufficient deterrent. The possible difficulty in having more than one stabilizing agency is, of course, that they might not be able to agree when any major change in exchange rates is desirable. England might think it desirable to put the pound down, but other countries might not think it desirable to have their currencies go up in consequence. Again it seems clear that nations could co-operate better on some plan of monetary control which leaves exchanges stable than they could upon a plan involving variable exchange rates.

2. *Different Currency Mechanisms for Different Countries.* The discussion of the gentlemen's agreement indicates that it may be both desirable and feasible to have

---

[10] It may, for example, be desired to lower currency A relative to B but to raise it relative to C.

different currency mechanisms for different countries. Already there are included in (or attached to) the agreement countries with stabilization funds and a variable price of gold, countries with stabilization funds and a fixed price of gold and countries with a fixed price of gold and without stabilization funds. It may be an open question whether France, which now has the first type (but whose variable price of gold is limited by law within a range) may not, as Belgium did, return eventually to a fixed price of gold with no stabilization fund. And it may be a question whether the American fund will prove eventually to be primarily a gold sterilization fund or equally an exchange stabilization fund.

Some light can be thrown on the question whether the world needs a single, uniform system or a combination of different systems by consideration of the diversity of countries, and in particular the differences in their proportions of home and foreign trade. It would seem that the relatively self-contained countries should, in most circumstances, be less concerned about exchange variation as a means of correction of their business cycle maladjustments, and must rely mainly upon their powers of internal control. On the other hand, countries chiefly dependent upon foreign trade and foreign capital have most both to gain and to lose by exchange variation; they most need exchange stability when foreign trade is prosperous, and they most need a currency adjustment when capital inflow is threatening to produce a boom, or when depression in the outside world is threatening their foreign markets. From this point of view, countries like the United States, and probably France, could best afford to have an unchanging currency, once a generally sustainable structure of exchange rates had been attained. Countries like Australia or Argentina would probably want fixed exchanges the larger part of the time, but with some provision for both depreciation and appreciation. Currency appreciation would be indeed a new phenomenon in the history of young countries, which like most others have been less concerned to stop booms than to stop depressions; but currency depreciation in depression would be only repeating what they have always done. The only new suggestion is that it might be worked out in some more orderly and deliberate fashion, as a conscious instrument of policy. For such countries, internal money management must be at best the minor part of policy. Since these countries are a minor part of the world economy, currency variations by them would probably not hurt others so much as it might help them. In these countries, as in all, there would be some conflict of interests. Currency depreciation, which might help export trade, would impair ability to pay interest charges, but this sacrifice is at the expense of the foreign creditor, who may be more able to bear it and should have been better able to calculate the risk in the first place.

Consideration of countries largely dependent on foreign trade suggests consideration of the sterling area. The development of the sterling area when England went off gold represents the emergence, in a more limited sphere, of the same type of international trade organization and hence of the same type of monetary system that existed before the War, when in a very real sense it could be said that England was on gold and much of the rest of the world on sterling. Within such an area, among nations closely tied by trade and financial relations, the need for stability of exchange is so compelling that when the center country varies its currency it is apt to carry all the other members of the group with it. In such an area, also, as was largely true before the War, the monetary control exerted at the center is likely to have a powerful influence throughout the area, which suggests that through stable exchanges forces of expansion or contraction can be initiated at the center and be transmitted throughout the area.

To hold such a unit together and to maintain exchange stability within it, it is probably unnecessary that all the countries, or indeed any of them, should be on the gold standard. What the constituents of this area need chiefly are foreign exchange balances in London; and as the exchange stabilizing agency, what it needs is a sterling balance which the foreign country's central bank holds and which this bank can control by decreasing or increasing its purchases and sales of sterling at a price that is stable but which it reserves the right to vary. If there is need of gold, it is as an internal reserve for notes or deposits, as a protection against an unrestricted credit expansion; but this function could be performed, also, as it can in other countries, by a central bank control of member bank reserves, without gold.

There is left for consideration those countries whose position is intermediate, whose foreign trade, though less in quantity or value than home trade, is nevertheless essential, in the long run, to a high level of productivity and real income. In this group are such countries as England, pre-eminently, and also Germany. In so far as such countries have trade areas, their concern for stability of exchange in support of their foreign trade has been already dealt with. Exchange stability within the trade area appears to be the less troubling aspect of their problem; and in a sense is self-insured by the closeness of trade ties. But there trade with the rest of the world is on a different footing. It is here that the conflict of objectives as between internal and external monetary stability chiefly arises. In depression, such countries are likely to strike out for freedom of internal policy, even though the protective devices which are set up, including currency depreciation, work out their effects at the expense of others. How their freedom of action is limited in other phases of the cycle, particularly by rising costs of imports, has already been discussed. Whether England would appreciate its currency substantially to help ward off an internal boom, we have yet to see. We must remember that she is occupied and perhaps somewhat complacent with her internal recovery, for which the ground was laid not only by cheap imports, but in addition by an easy money policy which is supporting both an extensive housing program (England having had no such construction activity as we had in the twenties) and now also a feverish armament program. The fundamental question at the moment, then, is whether England, in the light of her present situation, may not be less concerned about her foreign trade, which has been noticeably backward in the recovery, than in the longer run she will need to be. In considerable measure, the problem of monetary policy, in so far as there is conflict of internal and external considerations, is a problem of business cycle versus the longer run forces which govern national productivity and income. The question, as stated earlier, is how to control short-time change without doing damage to the basic trade relationships.

3. *The Solution Mainly Turns on Internal Stability in the Major Countries, Coupled with Co-operation.* The discussion of the sterling area suggests that for such a group monetary stability mainly depends upon the behavior of the center country. This suggestion has a larger application. The economic activities of the United States and England combined represent more than half of total world activity; and these countries are, in normal times, the main sources of capital. World booms and depressions are more likely to spring from changes originating in them and carried outward than by the reverse process. As has been indicated repeatedly by the course of events, international capital movements are likely to be mainly a phase of expansion or contraction in the major countries. We are likely to export capital at the same time that we expand investment at home. If we also attract capital, as in a major rise of the stock market, it is most apt to come from England or some other major country.

From this point of view, the problem of monetary stability appears to be one which calls in large measure for an over-all control, rather than for a compensatory mechanism operating as between countries, and to require as its main foundation effective internal monetary control in the leading countries. It ought not to be impossible in a matter of such mutual interest and serious importance to achieve, after the experiences which the nations have gone through in pursuing their own narrower ends, some community of action in monetary and general economic policy; but I must add that I am not altogether sanguine. Even without such formal co-operation, I believe that the best prospect for general stability is to be found in internal stability in the leading countries if it is intelligently, which means not too narrowly, conceived.

But it is not to be expected that economic change would or should exactly keep pace in all countries; that is far from true even in the different parts of our own country. There will always be diversity of change and of pace and character of development. There will be business cycle lags and leads as between countries. There will be crises here and there, registering their effects not only in the countries of origin but in others, and perhaps especially in the center countries. What an effective system of compromise must do is to provide slacks and elements of variability which will lessen shocks, permit monetary change to be slowed down to the pace which the economic structure can tolerate, and leave freedom of action in directing the impact and extent of change. For this purpose, it seems preferable to have some compromise, or combination of compromise systems, which, while excluding no form of variation which might be serviceable in a constantly changing world, would resort to currency variation only sparingly and when other means had failed.

(B) Extract from "Currency Stabilization: The Keynes and White Plans" *

(July 1943)

The most important question, however, is whether in the longer run, when the transition to peace has been achieved, the general type of monetary organization outlined in the Keynes and White plans promises to give the best assurance of achieving and maintaining international currency stability, with all that implies for a stable and orderly economic world. This, too, I do not find an easy question, and my present attitude is one of wanting to hear more and think more about it as the debate develops. One of the dangers involved in the present technique of concentrating upon the comparison of the two plans, and taking the visiting experts of the allied and associated governments through them point by point, is that no other plan is likely to get an adequate hearing—unless it be later on, at the legislative stage, which may not be the best method of arriving at well and calmly reasoned conclusions.

The difficulty for me is that I have long believed that there is another kind of approach to the problem, and one that deserves equally well the name of international collaboration even though it is constructed on less elaborate lines. This is what might be called the key countries, or central countries, approach to the problem.[8] It is closer in conception than either the Keynes or White plan to the way the gold standard actually worked, around England as the central country, in the nineteenth century; whereas I have the feeling that those plans have a closer family relationship with what might be called the textbook type of gold standard, which implied that monetary stability was maintained by the compensatory action of a large number of countries of equal economic weight. What I call the key countries approach to monetary stabilization could be tried with or without an international governing board, though I think this is not the main point of difference between the two ways of going at the problem.

The main difference is in the conception of how trade and finance are organized in the world, and of the importance of stabilizing the truly international currencies whose behavior dominates and determines what happens to all the others. Though the organization of trade and finance has undergone much change since the nineteenth century, it still seems true that stabilization of the leading currencies with reference to each other, combined with coöperation among the countries concerned for the promotion of their own internal stability, would be the best foundation for monetary and economic stability throughout the world.

The importance of coöperation upon internal as well as external monetary and economic policies in the leading countries is in line with the current of thought among economists in recent years. One of the most interesting points in Keynes' White Paper is the lightness of touch with which he deals with internal policies. "There should be the least possible interference with internal national policies, and the plan should not wander from the international terrain. Since such policies may have important repercussions on international relations they cannot be left out of account. Nevertheless,

---

* Reproduced by permission of Professor Williams and *Foreign Affairs*.

[8] See again my paper, "The Adequacy of Existing Currency Mechanisms under Varying Circumstances," *American Economic Review*, March 1937, Supl., p. 151–168.

in the realm of internal policy, the authority of the governing board of the proposed institution should be limited to recommendations, or, at most, to imposing conditions for more extended enjoyment of the facilities which the institution offers." As I read over his provisions as to what debtor countries may be required to do to adjust their position as their net debit balances mount from a quarter to a half to three-fourths of their quotas, I am not overly convinced that the board's powers of control have very strong or sharp teeth. On exceeding a quarter of its quota on the average for two years, the debtor country may depreciate its currency up to 5 percent. On reaching a half of its quota, it may be required to deposit collateral. As a condition of exceeding a half of its quota, it may be required to do all or any of the following at the governing board's discretion: reduce the value of its currency; control outward capital movements; and/or surrender a suitable proportion of any separate gold or other liquid reserve in reduction of its debit balance. It is at this point that the governing board may "recommend . . . any internal measures . . . which may appear to be appropriate." On exceeding three-fourths of its quota, the debtor country "may, in addition, be asked by the governing board to take measures to improve its position, and, in the event of its failing to reduce its debit balance accordingly within two years" may be declared in default and no longer entitled to draw against its account.

All of these measures seem desirable. In particular, I have long believed that the younger countries, whose economic conditions primarily reflect the conditions existing in the great world markets, for which they are only secondarily responsible, should be permitted to vary their currencies. It might help them somewhat, without too seriously affecting the larger countries. Such countries do not often have major difficulties arising out of the outward movement of capital; for them the exchange problem is usually presented by the stoppage of the inward movement. When this happens, they are not unacquainted with being declared in default. The same circumstances which stop capital inflow restrict the markets for their products and produce a severe shrinkage in the value of their merchandise exports, so that these countries are frequently unable to maintain interest payments or even to pay for their current imports. The classical economists would have insisted upon internal reduction of their costs; and some countries, like Australia in the great depression, have proved that internal cost reductions can be a feasible and a potent method of adjustment of the international position.[9] But, broadly speaking, the whole experience of the inter-war period proved nothing more clearly than the fact that the economic condition and the balance of payments position of these countries are primarily a reflection of the conditions in the larger countries, and that if those conditions are bad enough, there can be no real escape, even though the countries are driven—as most of them were—to exchange control as a desperate last resort.

From this experience of the inter-war period, I come back always to the conclusion that the problem of international monetary stability is primarily that of maintaining a state of proper economic health in the leading countries; and that this is the only workable answer to the whole conflict between internal and external monetary stability, about which discussions of the gold standard for years revolved.[10] This means collaboration to maintain both a high level of real income within the leading countries and

---

[9] Australia also depreciated her currency and adopted expansive monetary and fiscal policies.

[10] See my paper, "The World's Monetary Dilemma—Internal Versus External Monetary Stability," *Proceedings of the Academy of Political Science*, April 1934, p. 62–68.

a high degree of exchange stability between them. If this could be done, the problem of maintaining exchange stability for the other countries, and a reasonable state of economic well-being within them, would probably not present major difficulties.

But such a program implies a degree of coöperation among the leading countries which goes far beyond what is outlined for the governing bodies in either the Keynes or the White plan. I doubt whether the requirements could be spelled out at present, or even whether it would be wise to try to do so. But I heartily agree with Herbert Feis when he says in his article in the April number of FOREIGN AFFAIRS that the best augury for success lies in the intimate collaboration upon numerous problems which has already been developed between this country and the British Empire in our conduct of the war.

Between the two approaches to the problem of monetary stabilization which I have discussed, the Keynes or the White proposal on the one hand and the closer collaboration among leading countries on the other, there may be no inherent or fundamental disagreement. A French plan of the kind I have suggested was prepared prior to the release of the British and American plans and has since been published in the *New York Times*.[11] One of the reasons advanced in favor of it by the authors was that it could be put into effect promptly, whereas in their judgment "If the international monetary system is so ambitious that it cannot become of general use until political and economic conditions are peacefully settled in the whole world, it may have to wait a long while." It might be more feasible to start with a scheme embracing fewer countries, which is less ambitious only in the sense that it is less extensive and more ambitious in the degree of coöperation contemplated, and tie in other countries as conditions warrant. This was the method followed in the Tripartite Agreement of 1936. I am not suggesting that agreement as the model, however, unless it can be greatly strengthened in its provisions for external collaboration and supplemented by provisions for coöperation on internal policies, to which it made no reference. There might be many advantages in such a piecemeal procedure. We could start, for example, with plans for stabilizing the dollar-sterling rate and for measures of coöperation on internal policy, while postponing until later the many difficult questions about the relation of sterling and the dollar to the European currencies which cannot conceivably be settled, I think, except after a period of European reconstruction.

Since I have dealt here exclusively with the proposals for currency stabilization, I should say in conclusion that monetary mechanics is only the lesser part of the problem, as the authors of the plans discussed fully recognize. Keynes begins his White Paper by suggesting four main lines of approach to the problem of how to achieve a stable and prosperous world, of which the mechanism of currency and exchange is only one. The others are international commercial policy; orderly conduct of production, distribution and price of primary products; and investment aid, both medium and long-term, for countries whose economic development needs assistance from the outside. Work is going forward on these other lines of approach, and upon the success of this work will depend fundamentally the success of our efforts, by whatever plan, to achieve inter-

---

[11] The *New York Times*, May 9, 1943, p. 5. The plan was prepared by André Istel, former financial adviser to the Reynaud Ministry and one of the negotiators of the Franco-British Financial Agreement of 1939, and Hervé Alphand, former financial attaché in Washington, former head of Trade Agreements in the French Ministry of Commerce, and French representative at the International Food Conference at Hot Springs.

national monetary stability. In all phases of it the United States has a vital interest and carries a unique responsibility. This will be the leading and probably the only important creditor country after the war. If we are to have an orderly and stable world, our responsibilities must not be shirked. But our rôle being what it is, and must be, we owe it to ourselves and to the rest of the world to think through the problems with all the intelligence and care and breadth of outlook of which we are capable.

The Joint Statement

The Joint Statement by Experts on the Establishment of an International Monetary Fund *was the outcome of discussions between Lord Keynes and Mr. White in Washington in September–October 1943. After extensive redrafting a final version was agreed upon in April 1944 and was then published. The text reproduced below is taken from the British White Paper, Cmd. 6519, and includes the British Government's foreword and Explanatory Notes indicating the British attitude to the Statement.*

Joint Statement by Experts on the Establishment of an International Monetary Fund [1]
(April 1944)

His Majesty's Government have authorised the publication of this Statement of Principles for an International Monetary Fund, which is the result of close study over many months at the expert level. It in no way commits the Governments concerned. It is conceived as part of a general plan for international co-operation, the objectives of which, as a whole, would be the progressive development of international trade, active employment, reasonable stability of prices and the machinery for the orderly adjustment of exchanges.

The purpose of publication in this way and at this stage is to promote informed discussion in all quarters from which valuable guidance can be obtained by the Governments in preparation for the formulation in due course of policies by the States concerned.

I. EXPLANATORY NOTES BY UNITED KINGDOM EXPERTS ON THE PROPOSAL FOR AN INTERNATIONAL MONETARY FUND.

Some of the more important respects in which the *Joint Statement by Experts on the Establishment of an International Monetary Fund*, set forth below as agreed between the British and American technical experts, differs from, or resembles, the *Proposals for an International Clearing Union* published as Cmd. 6437 are briefly explained below:—

(1) Under the *Clearing Union* the member countries might have been said to bank with the Union with which they were to keep balances or run overdrafts. Under the *International Monetary Fund*, on the other hand, the Fund may be said to bank with the member countries, which undertake to grant to the *Fund* facilities to hold and to draw on their local funds. Thus if under the *Clearing Union* a member country drew resources from the *Union* this meant that its own balance with the *Union* would be diminished and the balance of some other member would be increased; whereas, if a member country draws resources from the *Fund*, this means that the *Fund's* balances with that member are increased and its balances with some other member are decreased.

---

[1] Reproduced by permission of the Controller, Her Britannic Majesty's Stationery Office.

These two arrangements represent alternative technical setups, capable of performing precisely the same functions. The same purposes and provisions in all other respects can be carried into effect under the one as under the other. It has, however, proved easier to obtain agreement on the mechanism of the proposed *Fund*, which has the appearance of being closer to what is already familiar.

(2) As a consequence of this, it is no longer necessary to introduce a new international unit, whether bancor or unitas, since it is only if the member countries bank with the Fund that the use of a new common unit becomes unavoidable.

(3) The provisions of the *Clearing Union*, by which only the Central Banks of member countries were in a position to engage in transactions with the *Union*, are replaced by the analogous provisions of III (1) (2) and (3) under which the *Fund* can only engage in transactions with the Monetary Authority of member countries and is not free to enter the market or deal with other banks or persons.

(4) The aggregate facilities, guaranteed by the initial subscriptions of the members under II (1), are smaller than were proposed for the *Clearing Union*. But they are substantial and, if necessary, can be increased later on by general agreement. It has been argued that the present proposals involve as large a commitment as it is prudent to ask in favour of an, as yet, untried institution. Moreover, in estimating the sufficiency of the facilities proposed, it is necessary to bear in mind X (1), where it is made clear that the facilities of the *Fund* are not intended to provide facilities for relief or reconstruction or to deal with international indebtedness arising out of the war.

(5) The *Clearing Union* proposals were criticised on the ground that they made insufficient provision for elasticity of exchange rates and for subsequent modification in the rates initially established. The new proposal explicitly provides for alteration of exchange rates, whilst maintaining the general principle that, exchange rates being two-ended so that a change in the parity of any currency affects the currencies of all countries, not only that of the country making the change, a proposed change is a proper subject for international consultation. The *Fund*, acting in a judicial capacity, is required under IV (3) to approve any change which is essential to the correction of a fundamental disequilibrium, and shall, in determining the matter, accept the domestic, social or political policies of the country applying for a change as facts of the situation to be accepted and not criticised. Moreover, during the transitional period immediately after the war it shall under X (4) give the member country presenting a proposal the benefit of any reasonable doubt, and shall under IV (3) at all times take into consideration the extreme uncertainties prevailing at the time the parities of exchange were initially agreed upon. In addition member countries are allowed under IV (4) a certain margin for making unilateral changes. Finally, if a member feels unable to accept a decision of the Fund on this or on any other matter, it is entitled under VIII (1) to withdraw from membership without notice and without penalty, apart from an undertaking under VIII (2) to liquidate any outstanding obligations to the Fund within a reasonable time. Thus no member is under any obligation to continue its adherence to the conditions of membership if it comes to the conclusion that, taken as a whole, they are no longer to its advantage.

(6) The provisions for securing, apart from certain temporary relaxations, an eventual free inter-convertibility of all national currencies, on the basis of the parities of the exchange rates established for the time being, are the same in effect as those under the *Clearing Union*.

(7) Clauses III (5) and IX (3) provide that a member's obligation to maintain free convertibility of its currency applies only to transactions of a current account nature. It does not apply to capital transfers or to the removal of balances accumulated prior to the acceptance of the obligation of convertibility. Clause V (1) contemplates the control of the outflow of capital by members using the resources of the *Fund*, so as to ensure that the *Fund* shall not be drawn upon to finance a large or sustained outflow of a capital nature. Thus the proposal allows the maintenance of exchange control in so far as it is required to carry out the above defined purposes, and may even require a member to exercise control of some kind.

(8) The proposals of the *Clearing Union*, to prevent a country from using up its quota too rapidly and from drawing on the *Fund* too freely in conditions in which its own resources are adequate without drawing on the *Fund*, are worked out more fully in clauses III (2) and (7) but without difference of intention. The provisions of II (3) and III (6) and (7) are new, under which the *Fund* has some gold resources which may be gradually increased with the intention that such gold in the hands of the *Fund* will be freely available in the interests of equilibrium.

(9) It was a feature of the *Clearing Union* proposals that they introduced certain provisions for placing on creditor countries, as well as on debtor countries, some pressure to share the responsibility in appropriate circumstances for maintaining a reasonable stability in the balances of international payments. These have been replaced in the new proposal by a different, but perhaps more far-reaching, provision with the same object in view. This is under VI, which provides that, if the requirements of the *Fund* for the currency of a country, in an unbalanced creditor position with the rest of the world, seem likely to exceed the supply of that currency which the *Fund* is in a position to acquire to meet the applications of the other members, the *Fund* shall issue a report covering the causes of the unbalanced position and containing recommendations designed to bring it to an end. Meanwhile the available supplies of the scarce currency will be apportioned, and the other members become entitled to resume complete freedom of action in relation to the affected currency. They are allowed to take any steps at their discretion to curtail imports from the country in question and to restrict and regulate exchange transactions, so as to keep their purchases in terms of the affected currency within the limits of their ability to pay. Rather than allow such a situation to develop, it would be open to a creditor country to use any of various means to prevent the development of an unmanageable unbalanced situation with the rest of the world as a whole.

(10) The provisions for the management of the new Institution have not been worked out in detail in this Statement of Principles. This is an important matter left over for further discussion and development at a later date.

(11) The *Clearing Union* proposals, which were put forward at a relatively early stage of the war, did not attempt to deal adequately with the transitional arrangements in the period following the conclusion of hostilities. Whilst there are still too many uncertainties in other directions to allow of clear-cut conclusions, Clause X of the Joint Statement carries matters somewhat further. It is there provided that a member need not assume the full obligations of membership until satisfactory arrangements are at its disposal to facilitate the settlement of its balance of payments difficulties arising out of the war. Furthermore X (2) contemplates a gradual evolution towards the attainment of the objects of the *Fund* by progressive stages and no country is committed to an immediate removal of war-time restrictions and regulations. Whilst the *Fund*

may, within three years of the *Fund's* coming into force, make representations that the time has come for a further withdrawal of restrictions, no member is committed as to any fixed date for this final removal and is entitled to use its own judgment as to when it is strong enough to undertake the free convertibility of its currency which it has accepted as the desirable aim. The drafting of this Clause, as the experts on both sides understand it, allows, during the transition period, the maintenance and adaptation by the members of the sterling area of the arrangements now in force between them. Nor is the scheme intended, when the obligation of free convertibility has been accepted, to interfere with the traditional ties and other arrangements between the members of the sterling area and London.

(12) In most other respects the general aims and purposes of the new scheme are the same as those set forth in Cmd. 6437 in presenting the *Clearing Union Proposals*.

II. JOINT STATEMENT BY EXPERTS ON THE ESTABLISHMENT OF AN INTERNATIONAL MONETARY FUND.

Sufficient discussion of the problems of international monetary co-operation has taken place at the technical level to justify a statement of principles. It is the consensus of opinion of the experts of the United and Associated Nations who have participated in these discussions that the most practical method of assuring international monetary co-operation is through the establishment of an International Monetary Fund. The principles set forth below are designed to constitute the basis of this Fund. Governments are not asked to give final approval to these principles until they have been embodied in the form of definite proposals by the delegates of the United and Associated Nations meeting in a formal conference.

I. *Purposes and Policies of the International Monetary Fund.*

The Fund will be guided in all its decisions by the purposes and policies set forth below:

1. To promote international monetary co-operation through a permanent institution which provides the machinery for consultation on international monetary problems.

2. To facilitate the expansion and balanced growth of international trade and to contribute in this way to the maintenance of a high level of employment and real income, which must be a primary objective of economic policy.

3. To give confidence to member countries by making the Fund's resources available to them under adequate safeguards, thus giving members time to correct maladjustments in their balance of payments without resorting to measures destructive of national or international prosperity.

4. To promote exchange stability, to maintain orderly exchange arrangements among member countries, and to avoid competitive exchange depreciation.

5. To assist the establishment of multilateral payments facilities on current transactions among member countries and the elimination of foreign exchange restrictions which hamper the growth of world trade.

6. To shorten the periods and lessen the degree of disequilibrium in the international balance of payments of member countries.

II. *Subscription to the Fund.*

1. Member countries shall subscribe in gold and in their local funds amounts (quotas) to be agreed, which will amount altogether to about $8 billion if all the

United and Associated Nations subscribe to the Fund (corresponding to about $10 billion for the world as a whole).

2. The quotas may be revised from time to time, but changes shall require a four-fifths vote, and no member's quota shall be changed without its assent.

3. The obligatory gold subscription of a member country shall be fixed at 25 per cent. of its subscription (quota) or 10 per cent. of its holdings of gold and gold-convertible exchange, whichever is smaller.

III. *Transactions with the Fund.*

1. Member countries shall deal with the Fund only through their Treasury, Central Bank, Stabilization Fund or other fiscal agencies. The Fund's account in a member's currency shall be kept at the Central Bank of the member country.

2. A member shall be entitled to buy another member's currency from the Fund in exchange for its own currency on the following conditions:

(a) The member represents that the currency demanded is presently needed for making payments in that currency which are consistent with the purposes of the Fund.

(b) The Fund has not given notice that its holdings of the currency demanded have become scarce in which case the provisions of VI, below, come into force.

(c) The Fund's total holdings of the currency offered (after having been restored, if below that figure, to 75 per cent. of the member's quota) have not increased by more than 25 per cent. of the member's quota during the previous twelve months, and do not exceed 200 percent of the quota.

(d) The Fund has not previously given appropriate notice that the member is suspended from making further use of the Fund's resources on the ground that it is using them in a manner contrary to the purposes and policies of the Fund; but the Fund shall not give such notice until it has presented to the member concerned a report setting forth its views and has allowed a suitable time for reply.

The Fund may in its discretion and on terms which safeguard its interests, waive any of the conditions above.

3. The operations on the Fund's account will be limited to transactions for the purpose of supplying a member country on the member's initiative with another member's currency in exchange for its own currency or for gold. Transactions provided for under 4 and 7, below, are not subject to this limitation.

4. The Fund will be entitled at its option with a view to preventing a particular member's currency from becoming scarce:

(a) To borrow its currency from a member country;

(b) To offer gold to a member country in exchange for its currency.

5. So long as a member country is entitled to buy another member's currency from the Fund in exchange for its own currency, it shall be prepared to buy its own currency from that member with that member's currency or with gold. This requirement does not apply to currency subject to restrictions in conformity with IX (3) below or to holdings of currency which have accumulated as a result of transactions of a current account nature effected before the removal by the member country of restrictions on multilateral clearing maintained or imposed under X (2) below.

6. A member country desiring to obtain directly or indirectly the currency of another member country for gold is expected, provided that it can do so with equal advantage,

to acquire the currency by the sale of gold to the Fund. This shall not preclude the sale of newly-mined gold by a gold-producing country on any market.

7. The Fund may also acquire gold from member countries in accordance with the following provisions:

(a) A member country may repurchase from the Fund for gold any part of the latter's holdings of its currency.

(b) So long as a member's holdings of gold and gold-convertible exchange exceed its quota, the Fund in selling foreign exchange to that country shall require that one-half of the net sales of such exchange during the Fund's financial year be paid for with gold.

(c) If at the end of the Fund's financial year a member's holdings of gold and gold-convertible exchange have increased, the Fund may require up to one-half of the increase to be used to repurchase part of the Fund's holdings of its currency so long as this does not reduce the Fund's holdings of a country's currency below 75 per cent. of its quota or the member's holdings of gold and gold-convertible exchange below its quota.

IV. *Par Values of Member Currencies.*

1. The par value of a member's currency shall be agreed with the Fund when it is admitted to membership and shall be expressed in terms of gold. All transactions between the Fund and members shall be at par subject to a fixed charge payable by the member making application to the Fund; and all transactions in member currencies shall be at rates within an agreed percentage of parity.

2. Subject to 5, below, no change in the par value of a member's currency shall be made by the Fund without the country's approval. Member countries agree not to propose a change of parity of their currency unless they consider it appropriate to correct a fundamental disequilibrium. Changes shall be made only with the approval of the Fund subject to the provisions below.

3. The Fund shall approve a requested change in the par value of a member's currency if it is essential to correct a fundamental disequilibrium. In particular, the Fund shall not reject a requested change necessary to restore equilibrium because of domestic social or political policies of the country applying for a change. In considering a requested change, the Fund shall take into consideration the extreme uncertainties prevailing at the time the parities of currencies of member countries were initially agreed upon.

4. After consulting the Fund a member country may change the established parity of its currency provided the proposed change inclusive of any previous change since the establishment of the Fund does not exceed 10 per cent. In the case of application for a further change not covered by the above and not exceeding 10 per cent., the Fund shall give its decision within two days of receiving the application if the applicant so requests.

5. An agreed uniform change may be made in the gold value of member currencies, provided every member country having 10 per cent. or more of the aggregate quotas approves.

V. *Capital Transactions.*

1. A member country may not use the Fund's resources to meet a large or sustained outflow of capital and the Fund may require a member country to exercise control to

prevent such use of the resources of the Fund. This provision is not intended to prevent the use of the Fund's resources for capital transactions of reasonable amount required for the expansion of exports or in the ordinary course of trade, banking and other business. Nor is it intended to prevent capital movements which are met out of a member country's own resources of gold and foreign exchange, provided such capital movements are in accordance with the purposes of the Fund.

2. Subject to VI, below, a member country may not use its control of capital movements to restrict payments for current transactions or to delay unduly the transfer of funds in settlement of commitments.

VI. *Apportionment of Scarce Currencies.*

1. When it becomes evident to the Fund that the demand for a member country's currency may soon exhaust the Fund's holdings of that currency, the Fund shall so inform member countries and propose an equitable method of apportioning the scarce currency. When a currency is thus declared scarce, the Fund shall issue a report embodying the causes of the scarcity and containing recommendations designed to bring it to an end.

2. A decision by the Fund to apportion a scarce currency shall operate as an authorization to a member country, after consultation with the Fund, temporarily to restrict the freedom of exchange operations in the affected currency and, in determining the manner of restricting the demand and rationing the limited supply amongst its nationals, the member country shall have complete jurisdiction.

VII. *Management.*

1. The Fund shall be governed by a board on which each member will be represented, and by an executive committee. The executive committee shall consist of at least nine members including representatives of the five countries with the largest quotas.

2. The distribution of voting power on the board of directors and the executive committee shall be closely related to the quotas.

3. Subject to II (2) and IV (5), all matters shall be settled by a majority of votes.

4. The Fund shall publish at short intervals a statement of its position showing the extent of its holdings of member currencies and of gold and its transactions in gold.

VIII. *Withdrawal.*

1. A member country may withdraw from the Fund by giving notice in writing.

2. The reciprocal obligations of the Fund and the country are to be liquidated within a reasonable time.

3. After a member country has given notice in writing of its withdrawal from the Fund, the Fund may not dispose of its holdings of the country's currency except in accordance with arrangements made under 2, above. After a country has given notice of withdrawal its use of the resources of the Fund is subject to the approval of the Fund.

IX. *The Obligations of Member Countries.*

1. Not to buy gold at a price which exceeds the agreed parity of its currency by more than a prescribed margin and not to sell gold at a price which falls below the agreed parity by more than a prescribed margin.

2. Not to allow exchange transactions in its market in currencies of other members at rates outside a prescribed range based on the agreed parities.

3. Not to impose restrictions on payments for current international transactions with other member countries (other than those involving capital transfers or in accordance with VI, above) or to engage in any discriminatory currency arrangements or multiple currency practices without the approval of the Fund.

X. *Transitional Arrangements.*

1. Since the Fund is not intended to provide facilities for relief or reconstruction or to deal with international indebtedness arising out of the war, the agreement of a member country to III (5) and IX (3), above, shall not become operative until it is satisfied as to the arrangements at its disposal to facilitate the settlement of the balance of payments differences during the early post-war transition period by means which will not unduly encumber its facilities with the Fund.

2. During this transition period member countries may maintain and adapt to changing circumstances exchange regulations of the character which have been in operation during the war, but they shall undertake to withdraw as soon as possible by progressive stages any restrictions which impede multilateral clearing on current account. In their exchange policy they shall pay continuous regard to the principles and objectives of the Fund; and they shall take all possible measures to develop commercial and financial relations with other member countries which will facilitate international payments and the maintenance of exchange stability.

3. The Fund may make representations to any member that conditions are favourable to the withdrawal of particular restrictions or for the general abandonment of restrictions inconsistent with IX (3), above. Not later than three years from the coming into force of the Fund any member still retaining any restrictions inconsistent with IX (3) shall consult the Fund as to their further retention.

4. In its relations with member countries the Fund shall recognize that the transition period is one of change and adjustment and in deciding on its attitude to proposals presented by members it shall give the member country the benefit of any reasonable doubt.

U.S. Commentary

In preparation for the discussions at Atlantic City in June 1944 and at Bretton Woods in the following month, the U.S. Treasury issued Questions and Answers on the International Monetary Fund *(June 10, 1944). While this was not an internationally agreed document, it usefully elaborates the U.S. view on many of the subjects which were being publicly discussed at the time.*

Questions and Answers on the International Monetary Fund
(June 10, 1944)

CONTENTS

	PAGE
Part One: The Fund and International Economic Cooperation	136
Part Two: Quotas and Composition of the Fund	140
Part Three: Gold and the Operations of the Fund	150
Part Four: Exchange Rates	154
Part Four [bis]: Operations of the Fund	163
Part Five: Policies of the Fund	171

PART ONE: THE FUND AND INTERNATIONAL ECONOMIC COOPERATION

QUESTION 1

Will the operations of the International Monetary Fund be limited to the immediate post-war period?

REPLY

In the Foreword to the Joint Statement by the experts on the establishment of an International Monetary Fund, Secretary Morgenthau said:

"The tentative proposals that have been under discussion by the experts are part of a broad program for cooperation on international economic problems among the United Nations. The objectives of this program are the expansion and development of international trade, the revival of international investment for productive purposes, the establishment of orderly and stable exchange rates, and the elimination of discriminatory exchange practices that hamper world trade. The attainment of these objectives will go far toward preventing serious economic disruption in many countries during the critical decade after the war."

It is still too soon to know the precise form and magnitude of post-war monetary problems. But it is certain that we shall be confronted with three inseparable monetary tasks: to prevent the disruption of foreign exchanges, to avoid the collapse of monetary systems, and to facilitate the restoration and balanced growth of international trade. Clearly, such formidable problems can be successfully handled only through international action.

While the Fund can be of enormous help in the solution of the monetary problems growing out of the war, it would be a serious mistake to regard the Fund as an agency designed exclusively or even largely for the immediate post-war period. To think of international monetary problems as simply an aftermath of the war is to overlook the fundamental realities. For two decades before the war the world suffered from serious monetary disorders without having any means to act together to prevent or to remedy the ills out of which they grew and the evils which were their fruit.

Long before the war, the necessary monetary and financial basis for international prosperity had been weakened by competitive currency depreciation, by exchange restrictions, by multiple currency devices, and by other discriminatory foreign exchange practices that hampered and even throttled world trade and the international flow of productive capital. Unless the United Nations cooperate to provide a sound foundation for the balanced growth of international trade, we must expect a recurrence of the same monetary disorders.

These are not transitory problems of the immediate post-war period affecting only a few countries. They are continuing problems of vital interest to all countries. There must be a general realization that world prosperity, like world peace, is indivisible. Nations must act together to restore multilateral international trade, and to provide orderly procedure for the maintenance of balanced economic growth. Only through international cooperation will it be possible for countries successfully to apply measures directed toward attaining and maintaining a high level of employment and real income which must be the primary objective of economic policy.

International monetary problems cannot be solved by occasional cooperation improvised among a few great countries to meet a threatened disaster. Such monetary difficulties can be met only by continuous cooperation, to prevent them if possible, to remedy them when necessary. It is for this reason that the International Monetary Fund of the United and Associated Nations is proposed as a permanent institution for international monetary cooperation.

QUESTION 2
Will the Fund provide resources for relief and reconstruction?

REPLY

It is recognized that an International Monetary Fund is only one of the instrumentalities which may be needed in the field of international economic cooperation. Other agencies may be needed to provide long-term international credit for post-war reconstruction and development and to provide funds for rehabilitation and relief. Within the scope of its functions the Fund can and should collaborate with other international agencies. It is our view that the operations of the Fund can contribute to the solution of other economic problems and the operations of other international agencies can facilitate the work of the Fund. Because international economic problems touch each other at innumerable points, it is essential that there be some degree of collaboration of the Fund with other international agencies.

The question, therefore, is as to the form and degree of collaboration. The Fund is designed to help maintain stability of exchange rates by providing resources for meeting temporary adverse balances on current account, while giving a member country time to take appropriate measures to adjust its balance of payments. If in the judgment of the member country and the Fund such an adjustment can best be made through the alteration of the exchange rate, provision is made for the necessary adjustment through cooperative action. In this connection, it should not be overlooked that the primary objective of the Fund is to assure a pattern of stable and orderly exchange rates that will make possible the expansion of international trade and the maintenance of a high level of business activity.

The Fund is not designed to provide resources for relief, nor is it designed to provide capital for reconstruction. Such specialized types of economic aid can be best given by agencies designed for these purposes, and it is expected that provision will be made for such agencies. There is no advantage in burdening the Fund with duties it is not suited to perform and which might impair its usefulness for maintaining exchange stability and bringing about the restoration and balanced growth of international trade.

While the Fund cannot place any part of its resources at the disposal of the other international agencies, it can and presumably would cooperate with other agencies. Because of the close interrelationship of all important international economic and financial problems, it will undoubtedly be necessary to have consultation between the Fund and other international agencies. For example, it is quite clear that in dealing with the problem of persistent favorable or unfavorable balances on current international account, the Fund and a Bank for Reconstruction and Development would have to pursue related policies.

The mere establishment of international agencies will not solve the international economic and financial problems. While such agencies are necessary, their successful operation requires policies that will encourage the growth of international trade and the maintenance of a high level of business activity.

QUESTION 3

Is the Fund intended to provide for international expansion of production and exchange which is one of the objectives stated in Article VII of the Mutual Aid Agreement? Is it intended to introduce measures for controlling the trade cycle?

REPLY

As is stated in the Joint Statement on the International Monetary Fund, the primary objective of economic policy must be the maintenance of a high level of employment and real income. It is recognized that only through international cooperation will it be possible for nations successfully to apply measures for achieving this end. It is a fundamental purpose of the Fund proposal to provide an agency for monetary cooperation among nations to aid in the securing of economic advancement and rising standards of living for all.

The operations of the International Monetary Fund are designed in the first instance to prevent discriminatory and restrictive exchange devices and to promote exchange stability through the cooperation of member countries. Obviously, a greater degree of stability of exchange rates is not an end in itself. It would be a complete inversion of objectives if a high level of business activity were to be sacrificed in order to maintain any given structure of exchange rates. Nor can we expect that a high level of production and employment will be automatically brought about through international monetary cooperation. But the Fund can contribute to the success of national policies intended to facilitate the attainment of a high level of production and employment by providing an international economic environment favorable to the development of such policies.

By helping to keep exchange rates relatively stable and removing the fear of large and sudden changes in exchange rates, the Fund will contribute to the revival of international trade and the resumption of international investment. With international cooperation on exchange policy, it will be possible to avoid the "beggar my neighbor" tactics of the 1930's which contributed to the spread of depression from country to country.

By discouraging bilateral clearing arrangements and putting an end to the use of multiple currencies and other restrictive exchange devices, the Fund will make it possible for member countries to enjoy the advantages of multilateral international trade without which the possibilities for the balanced growth of international commerce can never be fully realized.

Finally, by providing member countries with exchange resources when they are needed to meet an adverse balance of payments on current account, the Fund will free member countries from the necessity of taking extreme measures that have the effect of contracting income and employment in order to restrict imports and adjust an adverse balance of payments.

Under the Fund, corrective measures can be taken to adjust an adverse balance of payments which need not involve domestic contraction and a drastic reduction of imports. Under adequate safeguards, the Fund will provide the necessary exchange to maintain imports while more fundamental adjustments are being made. Likewise, in the case of member countries with a favorable balance on current account, the operations of the Fund will enable them to maintain their exports while adjustments are made, instead of being forced to undertake a sharp reduction in exports with the resulting adverse effects on domestic employment.

The Fund is not designed directly to control business fluctuations. In our opinion no international agency could assume the responsibility for the control of the trade cycle. To a considerable degree the volume of international trade is a reflection of the internal economic health of the trading nations. The work of the Fund is confined to the provision of some of the conditions necessary for international prosperity.

The maintenance of a high level of employment and the expansion of production can be achieved ultimately only through the development of its productive capacity by each member country. We may reasonably assume that while national policy in each country should and would be concerned with such development, the principal purpose of the Fund is the creation of a healthy international monetary environment in which the economies of member countries can enjoy a high level of employment and production.

We believe that to the extent the Fund is successful in realizing its objectives, fluctuations in the trade cycle will be mitigated. The Fund can minimize the deflationary monetary pressure that adverse balances of payments have had in the past. It can eliminate competitive currency depreciation and a variety of discriminatory trade practices. In this way it will help prevent a recurrence of the unfortunate policies that have had the effect of intensifying international depression and spreading it from country to country through nationalistic policies designed to secure recovery of one country at the cost of depression in other countries. Because the Fund holds resources to which all member countries have access, member countries may more freely undertake policies designed to stimulate investment and employment during periods of recession, without fear that such policies will lead to a serious depletion of their exchange resources and imperil the stability of exchange rates.

PART TWO: QUOTAS AND COMPOSITION OF THE FUND

QUESTION 4

What are the aggregate quotas of all member countries of the International Monetary Fund expected to be?

REPLY

The Joint Statement on the International Monetary Fund states that the aggregate quotas of the member countries shall be about $8 billion if all the United and Associated Nations subscribe to the Fund. This corresponds to about $10 billion for the world as a whole. The precise amount of the aggregate quotas cannot of course be determined until it is known how many countries will become members of the Fund.

The aggregate quotas represent the subscribed resources of the Fund. The primary consideration in deciding on this range of aggregate quotas is that resources of this magnitude will probably be sufficient for the purpose of the Fund. It should be borne in mind that the resources of the Fund are not intended to be used to finance flights of capital. Nor is the Fund expected to provide the resources for relief and rehabilitation, or for reconstruction and development. The needs for these purposes can more appropriately be met by international agencies designed to meet these specific problems.

In considering the adequacy of aggregate quotas of $8 billion for all of the United and Associated Nations it is necessary to bear in mind the prescribed purposes for which the resources of the International Monetary Fund may be used. The Fund is intended to provide exchange resources which may be purchased by member countries to meet their adverse balances on current account. But it is not proposed that the resources of the Fund be used to maintain indefinitely an unbalanced position in the economy of a country that has suffered a structural change in its relative international economic situation, though such resources may be used to facilitate the transition to a new position of internation equilibrium. There are adequate safeguards against the use of the Fund's resources to prevent or unduly delay the establishment of a sound pattern in international balances of payments. When a member country persistently shows a considerable favorable or unfavorable balance of payments that affects adversely the distribution of the resources of the Fund, a committee of the Fund will study the problem and report upon possible corrective measures.

While the resources of the Fund are intended primarily for use by member countries in meeting adverse balances on current account, they may be used to a limited extent to facilitate a transfer of capital or repayment of a foreign debt. In some instances such transfers will reduce the need of member countries to purchase foreign exchange from the Fund with which to meet their adverse balances on current account. This point is further elaborated in the reply to Question 26.

The resources of the International Monetary Fund will be used to finance adverse balances on current transactions. The question to be considered is whether resources of approximately $8 billion for all of the United and Associated Nations will be enough for this purpose in the years after the war. A preliminary test of the adequacy of the aggregate quotas may be made on the basis of the prewar situation. Specifically, would the Fund have had resources sufficient to meet all of the calls on the Fund for foreign exchange?

An examination was made of the balance of payments on current account of all countries for which such data were available in the years 1936 to 1938. For other countries, trade data were adjusted to give an approximation of their balance of payments on current account. In the case of countries that are large producers of gold, their exports of gold were regarded as part of their current trade. For other countries, neither gold movements nor capital movements were included in their balance of payments on current account.

In 1936, the total of all debit balances on current account was approximately $1 billion. In 1936 and 1937, the total of all debit balances for the two-year period was approximately $1.8 billion, and for the three-year period 1936 to 1938, the total of all debit balances was approximately $2.5 billion. Allowance should be made for the fact that even with a Fund many countries with debit balances would have preferred to meet their adverse balances by drawing on their holdings of gold and foreign exchange, or by importing capital from abroad. On the other hand the magnitude of the volume of trade and fluctuations in the balances of payments would undoubtedly have been larger during the period if nations had not resorted to restrictive exchange practices and bilateralism during this period. The purpose of the Fund is to remove such restrictive and discriminatory practices and to obviate the need for them.

It would appear from the above analysis that an International Monetary Fund with resources of $8 billion for all the United and Associated Nations could have met without difficulty the calls that would have been made upon it by member countries for the sale of foreign exchange to meet their adverse balances on current account in the period 1936 to 1938. It should be added that shortages of specific currencies would not be likely to present a serious problem so long as the aggregate resources of the Fund are ample since a considerable portion of the Fund's resources would be in the form of gold. This is particularly true if credit balances are widely distributed among a number of countries. If a serious one-sidedness in the balance of payments should develop in the post-war period, the Fund might be faced with the scarcity of an important currency. This problem is further discussed in the answers to questions 22 and 30. It is doubtful, however, whether the solution can be found in a general expansion of quotas.

The fact that a Fund with the amount and character of resources called for in the tentative proposal would have been in a position before the war to meet all calls to sell foreign exchange needed for adverse balances on current account does not prove that a Fund with the same resources would necessarily be in a position to meet all calls for this purpose after the war. Unquestionably, the distortion in the normal pattern of international trade will result in relatively large unbalanced positions during the early post-war period. Even so, a Fund with about forty-five member countries holding resources of approximately $8 billion, of which a considerable part is in gold, should be in a position to meet all legitimate calls for the sale of foreign exchange to meet adverse balances on current account. This is particularly so because it is not intended that the Fund continue to sell foreign exchange to any member country that uses the resources of the Fund to prevent or unduly delay the establishment of equilibrium in its international accounts.

In considering the adequacy of aggregate quotas of members of the Fund, it should not be overlooked that some countries already have relatively large reserves of gold and foreign exchange. Such reserves will be used along with resources of the Fund in meeting adverse balances of payments. The Fund will not have to provide resources for relief, a function it is not suited to perform. Furthermore, with the establishment of orderly and stable exchange rates, there will probably be a revival of international investment, particularly if encouragement is given to private investors through a Bank for Reconstruction and Development. Finally, no Fund can function successfully unless some measure of balance is attained in international trade. The maintenance of a high level of business activity, particularly in the United States, will contribute to the attainment of the necessary balance in international trade.

While it is expected that the Fund will hold adequate resources, provision is made for increasing the resources of the Fund if this should become necessary and desirable. The Fund may borrow the currency of any member country provided the country approves. It would appear, therefore, that the aggregate quotas will probably provide the Fund with adequate resources, and additional resources may be borrowed if and when they are needed under conditions that safeguard the member country and the Fund. Aggregate quotas may also be increased periodically in the future although no increase can be made in the quota of a member country without its consent.

QUESTION 5

How much foreign exchange can member countries purchase from the International Monetary Fund?

REPLY

The amount of foreign exchange which a member country can generally purchase from the Fund is related to the total amount of its currency which the Fund is permitted to hold. According to the provisions of the Joint Statement, the Fund's holdings of the currency of a member country may not exceed the quota of that country by more than 100 percent, unless additional local currency is acquired with the approval of the Board and on conditions that safeguard the interests of the Fund. In addition it is provided that the Fund's total holdings of the currency offered, after having been restored, if below that figure, to 75 percent of the member's quota, may not increase by more than 25 percent of that member's quota over a period of 12 months.

The significance of these provisions and their relations to the facilities that may be put at the disposal of a member country can be brought out more clearly by a concrete illustration. Assume that a member country has a quota of $100 million and that it meets its quota by paying $20 million in gold and $80 million in local currency. The total amount of that member's currency which the Fund can hold is $200 million. As the Fund will already hold $80 million in local currency it could acquire an additional $120 million in local currency before the country will have used up its maximum privilege to purchase foreign exchange from the Fund for local currency. Allowing for the gold contribution, $20 million, which could have been used to acquire foreign exchange without the Fund, the country can purchase $100 million in foreign exchange from the Fund for its local currency in excess of what it could get exclusively through use of its own resources.

A member country cannot, however, use up its total rights to acquire foreign exchange from the Fund over a short period of time. In the case of the example given above the member country could not acquire a net amount of foreign exchange from the Fund for local currency in excess of $25 million in any one year. The purpose of this provision is two-fold: It protects the member country from using up its privilege to acquire foreign exchange from the Fund before taking appropriate steps to adjust its balance of payments position; and it protects the Fund from a too rapid use of its resources. This provision is designed to prevent a member country from using the resources of the Fund to prolong an unbalanced international position.

While the normal amount of local currency of a member country which the Fund is permitted to hold is 200 percent of the quota of that member country the Fund is not rigidly limited to this amount and a member country is not assured that the Fund will necessarily be willing to hold this amount. The Fund may sell foreign exchange for additional local currency, even when its holdings exceed the prescribed limits, if the Board of Directors approves the sale and the member country is taking satisfactory measures to correct the disequilibrium or to reduce the excess local currency holdings of the Fund. In this connection, the Fund will prescribe the terms and conditions under which it will permit this, and it may require the deposit of collateral as one of the conditions. On the other hand, if a member country is using its quota in a manner contrary to the purposes and policies of the Fund, the Fund may give appropriate notice that the member is suspended from further use of the resources of the Fund.

By its very nature, the Fund cannot be called upon to provide all countries simultaneously with foreign exchange with which to meet their adverse balances on current account with other member countries. An adverse balance for some member countries must mean a favorable balance for other countries. If there were a fairly even distribution of favorable and adverse balances, there could be no question whatever of the Fund's capacity to provide member countries with the maximum facilities each could call for under its permissible quota. The Fund would not only have available for such use its holdings of the currencies of member countries with favorable balances, but it could draw upon its gold holdings to acquire additional amounts of whatever member currencies it might need.

There is, of course, a possibility that only a few member countries will have favorable balances for some years, the great bulk of the member countries having adverse balances on current account during this period. Let us assume that the Fund would be willing to provide the countries having unfavorable balances with the maximum facilities they could request within their permissible quotas. Could the Fund provide such facilities?

To put the case more concretely, let us assume that with 45 member countries having aggregate quotas of $8 billion, only 4 countries—the United States, Canada, Mexico and Brazil—have favorable balances, the remaining 41 countries having unfavorable balances on current account. Let us assume further these four countries have aggregate quotas of $3.5 billion, and that the gold contribution to the Fund of all other member countries is $700 million. Then, the 41 countries with unfavorable balances could purchase from the Fund $5.2 billion before every one of the countries would have exhausted its normal rights to purchase exchange from the Fund. To meet these demands the Fund would have $4.2 billion in the currencies of the four countries and in gold. Under the assumption the Fund would either have to restrict by $1 billion the total demand of the 41 countries with unfavorable balances, or borrow an additional $1 billion in the four countries with favorable balances.

The assumed case is clearly an extreme one. Unfavorable balances are not likely to be so general and widespread, or so concentrated in time, without the Fund's having previously taken steps to restore a greater degree of equilibrium. It is unreal to assume that the Fund must hold immediately available resources equal to the gross amount of foreign exchange all member countries could purchase from the Fund within their normal rights. The resources of the Fund may be considered as a revolving fund from which countries temporarily in need of foreign exchange resources can purchase what they require. There is no need, therefore, for the Fund to hold assets of a particular type equal to the aggregate of all individual demands which may be made upon it.

As a revolving fund, there is no definitive limit to the ability of the Fund to furnish foreign exchange to member countries. In the first place, the Fund does not lend foreign exchange but sells foreign exchange to member countries in return for their own local currencies. As it depletes its holdings of some currencies, it builds up correspondingly its holdings of other currencies. If, therefore, the member countries of the Fund, in cooperation with the Fund, succeed in preventing large and persistent favorable and unfavorable balances of payments, the Fund will always be in a position to provide member countries with the facilities they require. Under such conditions, the resources of the Fund would be adequate to meet the needs of member countries for foreign exchange to help maintain the stability of their exchanges while they put into effect measures that will restore balance in their international accounts.

In order to place the Fund in as strong a position as possible, there are several provisions which make it possible for the Fund to mobilize as much gold as the members can reasonably be expected to take out of their independent reserves. Original subscriptions in gold are scaled to the capacity of each member country as determined by its gold and gold-convertible exchange holdings and its quota. A member country purchasing exchange from the Fund must pay for one-half of such exchange in gold so long as its holdings of gold and gold-convertible exchange exceed its quota. It is expected that a member country desiring to obtain another member currency with gold will do so, if it is equally advantageous, by the sale of gold to the Fund. Half of the increase in a member country's official gold and gold-convertible exchange holdings in excess of its quota is to be used to repurchase its currency from the Fund. While exerting a minimum of pressure on the reserves of member countries, these provisions will serve to strengthen the Fund and will enable it to use all of its resources in meeting the needs of member countries for foreign exchange.

The Fund's resources will probably be adequate for all ordinary needs of member countries. When the Fund has been strengthened and a larger proportion of its assets are in the form of gold it will undoubtedly be able to meet even extraordinary needs for any particular currency or currencies. In the meantime, if the Fund should find its holdings of any member currency inadequate, it may borrow the needed amounts of that currency with the approval of the member country concerned and on terms and conditions agreed between them.

QUESTION 6

In what form will the Fund hold the quota subscriptions of the member countries?

REPLY

The subscriptions of the member countries to the Fund will be in the form of local currencies and gold. The Fund will keep a portion of its holdings of the currency of each member as a deposit in the Central Bank of that country, such portion being in accordance with the needs of the Fund for its current operations. It is the view of the technical experts of the United States that the balance of the Fund's holdings of the member countries' currencies should be in the form of bills, notes, or other forms of indebtedness, issued by the governments of the member countries. These securities would be non-negotiable, non-interest bearing and payable at their par value on demand by a credit to the deposit account of the Fund at the Central Bank of the member country.

Why is it desirable for the Fund to keep its surplus currency holdings in the form of securities of the member countries?

There are some countries for whom the required subscription of currency to the Fund can be made only with great difficulty. For such countries the problem is created by the existence of a monetary system under which the issue of currency (or the creation of central bank deposits) requires a high marginal reserve of gold.

For example, some countries can issue local currency only when secured in whole or in large part by gold or foreign exchange. It is not possible for such countries to issue local currency as a means of meeting the required subscription to an International Monetary Fund. Nor can such countries borrow at once the needed resources from the banks or the public except at rates of interest that would be burdensome. Such countries could, however, meet the subscription requirement if the Fund were to hold their subscriptions in the form of their own obligations.

There is another reason why some countries would find it desirable if a part of their subscription were held in the form of their own obligations. Clearly, the Fund is not going to use the entire local currency subscription of a country at the time operations of the Fund begin. For the Fund's purposes it would be satisfactory to have an adequate working balance at the Central Bank of the member country, holding the remainder of the local currency subscription in the form of government obligations. This would avoid the appearance of inflation or illiquidity of the Central Bank, which might be mistakenly inferred from the sudden increase of its deposit liabilities.

To meet the needs of countries that would find it more convenient not to pay all of the local currency subscription at once, it is proposed that part of the quota subscription be held in the form of government obligations, redeemable at par on demand. Whenever the working balance of the Fund in local currency is depleted by its sales of such currency, the Fund can replenish the balance by presenting for redemption the securities it holds.

There is no reason for believing that the Fund takes any more risk in holding Government obligations than in holding local currency. When the Fund requires local currency for its operations, the national monetary authorities will presumably wish, as a matter of monetary policy, to redeem the securities held by the Fund and to borrow from the market.

QUESTION 7

In determining the Fund's holdings of a country's currency at a given date does "currency" include or exclude securities expressed in that currency?

REPLY

The Fund's holdings of a currency for purposes of determining the maximum amount of this currency which the Fund is normally permitted to hold are regarded as the net position of the Fund with respect to that currency. The Fund's holdings of the currency may be defined, therefore, as all of the assets of the Fund in a given currency minus all of the liabilities of the Fund in that currency. Quite definitely, in calculations on the amount of foreign exchange which a country may normally purchase from the Fund, the security holdings of the Fund in any local currency should be included as part of the local currency

It should be understood, of course, that the Fund is not authorized to deal in securities. The Fund is permitted to acquire securities redeemable on demand at par in part payment of the initial subscription. The Fund might require the deposit of securities as collateral when selling foreign exchange for local currency. The Fund cannot otherwise acquire securities.

The way in which the Fund acquires assets in terms of a given local currency does not affect the inclusion of the assets in the Fund's holdings so far as determining the maximum permissible holdings of that currency by the Fund is concerned. Therefore, the Fund's holdings of local currency include initial subscriptions in these forms, and currency acquired by the purchase of foreign exchange from the Fund. The Fund's position in a local currency may be modified whenever the local currency is sold to the Fund or bought from the Fund by a member country. Devaluation does not affect the calculated holdings of the currency and securities of a member country as the gold value of such holdings are not affected by devaluation.

QUESTION 8

What is the formula for determining the quotas of member countries?

REPLY

A formulation of a method to be used in measuring the participation of the various member countries was not included in the Joint Statement by the experts on the establishment of an International Monetary Fund. This was considered to be a matter on which a decision should be reached only after there has been ample opportunity for consultation with all of the prospective participants. Considerable attention has been given this matter in discussions among the technical experts of the United and Associated Nations.

After examining a great number of suggested bases for quotas, it is the view of the technical experts of the United States that no single factor can allocate participation among the various nations in a satisfactory manner. Several methods for combining a number of factors were tested. The method which is discussed below seems to combine the important relevant factors in a reasonable way and to give relative quotas that seem fair when applied to the approximate data available for a number of countries.

A satisfactory quota formula must give consideration to the multiple functions of the quota. The size of a member country's quota determines the amount of the subscription which that country makes to the resources of the Fund and is the basis for determining the normal rights of that country to purchase foreign exchange from the Fund. The size of the quota is also one of the factors which determines the relative voice of that country in the management of the Fund. The aggregate size of the quotas will determine the total subscribed resources of the Fund.

In view of the functions of the quotas, it would seem that the formula for the determination of relative quotas for member countries should take into account the ability of a country to subscribe resources to the Fund, the need of a country for use of the resources of the Fund, and the economic significance of a country.

The ability of a country to subscribe resources to the Fund is best indicated by its national income. In a sense, participation in the Fund is an investment. The extent to which a country can devote resources to this or other purposes depends very largely on its national income. However, because the Fund is an international institution that can function more effectively if some of its resources are in the form of gold, it has been thought desirable to require payment of part of the quota subscription in this form. Under the circumstances, the ability of a country to subscribe resources to the Fund in the form of gold is also indicated by its holdings of gold and gold-convertible exchange.

The probable need of a country for use of the resources of the Fund is best indicated by the magnitude of the fluctuations in its balance of payments. There is a good deal of difficulty in dealing directly with fluctuations in the balance of payments. For this reason it was found preferable to utilize import and export data. A country's need for foreign exchange generally arises from the fact that its imports may be maintained when its exports fall off. We have, therefore, made use of average annual imports and maximum fluctuations in exports as indications of a country's need for use of the resources of the Fund.

The economic significance of a country in the world's economy is an intangible factor impossible to measure even approximately. It depends on its national output, its foreign trade, its foreign investment, its economic and political strength. In the final determination of quotas allowance is made for this factor through use of a special allotment for the equitable adjustment of quotas, which is further discussed below.

In order to take account of the above factors it is suggested that the quota of a country be determined by the following formula:

(a) 2 percent of the national income of 1940;
(b) 5 percent of the holdings of gold and gold-convertible exchange as of January 1, 1944;
(c) 10 percent of average annual imports, 1934–1938, inclusive;
(d) 10 percent of maximum variation in annual exports 1934–1938, inclusive.

It is further proposed that the total so determined be increased for each country by the percentage ratio of its average annual exports (1934–1938) to its national income. In this way, special consideration is given to those countries whose national income is particularly affected by international trade.

After testing this formula for a number of countries, we have come to the conclusion that on the whole the results are as satisfactory as can be obtained through the use of any formula. We recognize that under this formula some countries may, for various reasons, be given entirely inadequate quotas. With any formula, provision must be made for adjustment of inequitable quotas. We have proposed that before determining individual quotas 10 percent of aggregate quotas be reserved as a special allotment for the equitable adjustment of quotas. For example, if the aggregate quotas for all member countries should be equivalent to $8 billion, the formula would be used to apportion 90 per cent ($7.2 billion) of the authorized aggregate quotas among the member countries. The remaining 10 percent ($800 million) could be used to increase the quotas of any countries whose quotas, as determined by application of the formula, seem inadequate. The adjustment of the quota need not always be based upon a country's need for access to the Fund. Since no formula can take account of the intangible factors, the special allotment will also be needed to assure to each country a share in the responsibility for management of the Fund commensurate with its potential position in international economic affairs.

It is provided in the Joint Statement that quotas may be revised from time to time by changes which require a four-fifths vote and no member's quota may be changed without its consent. It is the view of the technical experts of the United States that provision should be made for the adjustment of quotas on the basis of the most recent data three years after the establishment of the Fund and at intervals of five years thereafter, in accordance with an agreed upon formula. At the time of revision of quotas, the special allotment mentioned above may be used to increase the quota of a country if the quota as determined by the formula is still termed inequitable. This special allotment may also be used in the periods between recurrent adjustments, if developments indicate that a country is entitled to a larger quota.

QUESTION 9

If quotas are to be based in part on holdings of gold and gold-convertible exchange would not this give most facilities to those members needing them least and vice versa?

REPLY

As indicated in the answer to the previous question gold and gold-convertible exchange holdings would be only one of several factors in the determination of the quotas of member countries.

The quotas assigned to member countries in the International Monetary Fund proposal have a three-fold purpose: to provide a measure of the appropriate subscription to the Fund by member countries; to provide a measure of the appropriate utilization of resources of the Fund by member countries; and to provide a basis for responsibility in the management of the Fund. It is not regarded as feasible to set up one formula for subscription to the Fund, a separate formula for the utilization of resources of the Fund, and still another formula for voting power in the Fund. For each country the use of the resources of the Fund must be related to its subscription although in practice countries will necessarily use varying proportions of their quotas. Finally, the voting power in the Fund must be related to each country's subscription to the Fund, although it need not be in precise proportion to subscriptions.

Holdings of gold and gold-convertible exchange are regarded as one of the appropriate factors in the determination of quotas because they indicate the capacity of a country to provide an important type of asset that will be required in the operations of the Fund. It has not been given preponderant importance in the formula for quotas that has been suggested for consideration. The proportion of aggregate quotas arising from the use of this factor is something over 16 percent of the whole. All of the other elements used—national income, variability of exports, average imports, and relation of exports to national income—measure characteristics of the national economy which reflect past or potential need for the use of foreign exchange resources to meet adverse balances on current account and to maintain stability of the exchanges. Finally, when the formula does not give a country a quota properly reflecting its prospective need for use of the resources of the Fund, the quota can be adjusted from the special allotment.

It should be added that a number of provisions are included in the draft proposal intended to give consideration to the position of countries with relatively small holdings of gold and gold-convertible exchange. The subscription in the form of gold is smaller in proportion to the quota for such countries than for countries with relatively large holdings. Countries with gold and gold-convertible exchange holdings which are less than their quotas need not use any part of their gold holdings in purchasing foreign exchange from the Fund. And countries with official holdings which are less than their quotas need not offer to sell to the Fund any part of the increment of gold they acquire so long as their official holdings are below this level.

QUESTION 10

Does the Fund proposal provide for a quasi-automatic increase in quotas to facilitate the financing of an increasing volume of international trade?

REPLY

The characteristic feature of the Fund proposal as outlined in the Joint Statement on the Fund is its flexibility. In general, the Fund proposal does not depend on quasi-automatic provisions for its effectiveness. Instead, the Board of Directors is commonly given authority to adjust the policies of the Fund to the conditions prevailing in particular cases, acting within broad provisions intended to safeguard the resources of the Fund and the interests of member countries.

As was stated in the reply to Question 8, it is the recommendation of the technical experts of the United States that the quotas of member countries should be adjusted on the basis of the most recent data three years after the establishment of the Fund and at intervals of five years thereafter, in accordance with an agreed formula. The quota formula itself could only be changed with the approval of a four-fifths vote of the Board of Directors. However, it would not be necessary to wait for the termination of the initial three-year period, or subsequent five-year periods, to adjust quotas. It would be within the power of the Board to increase the quota of a member country at any time out of a special allotment reserved for the equitable adjustment of quotas. To safeguard any country from being compelled to subscribe additional resources to the Fund, it is provided that an increase in the quota of a country can be made only with its consent.

Under the provisions outlined above there will be an expansion of quotas periodically as national incomes rise, as the stock of monetary gold increases, and as the volume of international trade grows. With the expansion of quotas the resources of the Fund and the ability of member countries to purchase foreign exchange will be increased correspondingly. More important, however, is the fact that neither the resources of the Fund nor the ability of member countries to purchase foreign exchange from the Fund are rigidly determined by the quotas. There are flexible provisions for increasing the resources of the Fund as needed. No limitations are placed on the Fund's ability to obtain resources through borrowing scarce currencies from member countries on terms agreed between the countries and the Fund. Likewise member countries may secure foreign exchange for their needs when they have exceeded the ordinary limits provided under the quota limitations under provisions that safeguard the interests of the Fund.

It would be a mistake to put too much stress on quasi-automatic changes in quotas. For example, if quotas were adjusted automatically to short-run changes in the volume of trade there would be an expansion of quotas in boom years and a contraction in years of slump. While the expansion of quotas in boom periods may not be disturbing of itself because the excessive use of quotas can be controlled, there can be no doubt that a contraction of quotas in depression periods would tend to have a depressing influence.

The fact is that the need for use of the resources of the Fund is not a simple function of the volume of trade. When international trade expands gradually, the growth may well be balanced, and there may be little need for help from the Fund. The need is likely to be greatest at the very time when the total volume of trade has fallen, for it is at such times that the greatest distortion in the normal balance of payments takes place. It is for this reason that the Fund proposal places great stress on fluctuations in the balance of payments on current account as a factor in the determination of quotas.

Automatic devices are unreliable guides to policy in troubled times. What is needed is not a new series of automatic signals to replace the discarded ones of the past. On monetary problems, there can be no automatic substitute for a rational policy implemented with flexible powers. While the American technical experts favor a provision for periodic adjustment of quotas, this feature is regarded as less significant than the provisions that give the Fund flexibility in acquiring resources and in permitting member countries to use resources.

QUESTION 11

In what form will member countries meet supplementary subscriptions if their quotas are increased?

REPLY

No specific provision is made for the form in which member countries may meet supplementary subscriptions if their quotas are increased. Unless specific provision is regarded as necessary by some member countries, it would be desirable to give the Board of Directors complete authority to require member countries to meet supplementary subscriptions in the form which seems most appropriate to the Board at the time the supplementary subscriptions are made.

It would not be possible to specify in advance in what form it would be most desirable to have supplementary subscriptions to the resources of the Fund. If the Fund has experienced a period of successful operation, with its resources appropriately distributed among different member currencies and with adequate holdings of gold, there could be no objection to having supplementary subscriptions paid largely in member currencies. On the other hand, if the Fund has experienced some difficulty in meeting the demands for some currencies, it would be preferable to strengthen the Fund by having some part of the supplementary subscriptions paid in gold.

There may be some member countries that would wish to assure themselves against a requirement that they meet supplementary subscriptions with an excessive payment in gold. While a country could withhold its consent to an increase in its quota if too large a part of the supplementary subscription is called for in gold, this may not be regarded as an adequate safeguard. Such countries might prefer a provision that supplementary subscriptions should be made in the same proportions as the original subscriptions and on the basis of the relation of gold and gold-convertible exchange holdings to the revised quota at the time supplementary subscriptions would be made.

An alternative provision could provide the necessary safeguard to member countries while retaining for the Fund considerable flexibility in determining the form in which supplementary subscriptions should be made. The Fund could be given authority to call for subscriptions in whatever form it deems in the general interest, but limiting the subscription to be paid in gold to not more than the proportion specified for the original subscriptions. Of course, any schedule for payments in gold in connection with supplementary subscriptions should be applied uniformly to all member countries.

PART THREE: GOLD AND THE OPERATIONS OF THE FUND

QUESTION 12

What is the purpose of requiring that a portion of the subscribed quota be paid in gold?

REPLY

Because of the unquestioned acceptability of gold as an international exchange medium the power of the Fund to serve its members will depend in part upon the size of its gold holdings. With gold the Fund can buy the currency of any member country. If the assets of the Fund consisted solely of currencies of member countries, there would be a danger that relatively small disturbances in the balance of payments positions of member countries would leave the Fund short of certain currencies.

So long as the Fund holds gold it can acquire additional amounts of any member currency. The lack of such generally acceptable resources as gold could in time compel the Fund to take measures to restrict its sales of foreign exchange to the currencies that are available. It is of utmost importance, therefore, that the Fund hold resources that can be used, as needed, to acquire any currency that becomes temporarily scarce.

In many respects, an ideal Fund would be one consisting predominately of gold. It is recognized that such an ideal Fund cannot be immediately established. There is every reason, however, to provide the Fund with as much of such general exchange resources as is within the power of member countries to furnish through their quota subscriptions. For this reason, part of the quota subscription is to be made in gold, graduated for each member country according to its capacity to meet part of its quota in this form. While large gold holdings would strengthen the Fund, such holdings will have to be accumulated gradually in order to avoid pressure on the reserves now held by member countries. Gold subscriptions of 25 percent of the quota or 10 percent of the official gold and gold-convertible exchange holdings of a member country, whichever is the smaller, would appear to meet the immediate needs of the Fund and to be within the present capacity of member countries.

Apart from the original contributions in gold, there are provisions for strengthening the Fund by gradually increasing its holdings of gold. Provision is made for sale of gold to the Fund by member countries desiring to obtain other member currencies. Part of the payment for foreign exchange purchased from the Fund must be made in gold if the member country's official gold and gold-convertible exchange holdings exceed its quota. And member countries are required to use part of the increase in their official gold and gold-convertible exchange holdings, if they exceed their quotas, to repurchase their local currencies from the Fund. These provisions will in time add to the gold holdings of the Fund without putting pressure on the gold reserves of member countries.

It should be noted that a member country will not necessarily in fact find its foreign exchange position impaired by making part of its quota subscription in the form of gold, or by substituting gold for its local currency in the Fund, since the right of a member country to purchase foreign exchange from the Fund is directly related to the Fund's holdings of its local currency. The greater the original subscription in gold and the later replacement of local currency holdings with gold, the more foreign exchange a member country has the right to purchase from the Fund. The net foreign exchange position of a member country (its own holdings of gold and foreign exchange, plus its unused right to purchase foreign exchange from the Fund) is unaffected by its use of gold in payment of part of its subscription and by its sale of gold to the Fund. On the other hand, the liquidity of the Fund's assets, and hence its usefulness to member countries, is increased when local currency is in part replaced with gold.

There is, of course, the possibility that a member country will find that although the unused portion of its right to purchase foreign exchange from the Fund is large, the one currency it requires is scarce and can be acquired from the Fund only in limited amounts. It is true for such a country that its gold subscription to the Fund is not fully equivalent to holding gold for itself. Such a difficulty can be overcome only by strengthening the Fund and by avoiding in this and in other ways the development of a situation in which a currency must be declared scarce.

QUESTION 13

Would the Fund contribute in any way to the maintenance of a market for gold?

REPLY

Because gold has a world-wide market, it is superfluous to speak of the Fund as contributing to the maintenance of a market for gold. With or without the Fund, gold will continue to be held as monetary reserves and to be used throughout the world in the settlement of international balances. The provisions of the Fund in no way change the established position of gold. They are designed to utilize the recognized status of gold as the accepted medium of international payments in order to facilitate the settlement of international balances and the maintenance of stable exchanges.

The Fund utilizes the accepted position of gold in a number of ways. In the first place, the Fund itself is expected to hold gold, entirely for the purpose of assuring to member countries an adequate supply of any member currency that may be demanded. As has been indicated in the reply to Question 5, the Fund must hold an adequate amount of general resources such as gold.

The Fund is authorized to buy and sell gold and provision is made for strengthening the Fund by adding to its holdings of gold to enable it to more effectively meet the needs of member countries. Part of the quota subscription is required in gold and member countries are required to pay for part of their foreign exchange purchases from the Fund in gold unless their own gold and exchange holdings are inadequate. Member countries holding a stated minimum of gold must repurchase the Fund's holdings of their local currencies with part of the gold they acquire in excess of their holdings at the time of becoming members of the Fund. Member countries that wish to sell gold for member currencies are expected to offer the gold for sale to the Fund if this is equally advantageous to them.

The Fund also utilizes the accepted position of gold to facilitate the maintenance of exchange stability. It is generally recognized that when a currency is defined in terms of gold and the monetary authorities are prepared to buy and sell gold (or currencies equivalent to gold) at approximately fixed prices in terms of local currency, the exchange rates can be maintained stable within an appropriate range. Various provisions of the Fund proposal make use of these customary devices.

The assets of the Fund are guaranteed against depreciation with respect to gold. Member countries may not induce a *de facto* depreciation of their currencies by purchasing gold, directly or indirectly, at a price in local currency in excess of a stated maximum above the gold parity; nor may member countries induce a *de facto* appreciation of their currencies by selling gold, directly or indirectly, at a price in local currency below a stated minimum under this parity.

The Fund itself is expected to buy and sell local currencies for gold when this becomes necessary for avoiding a fluctuation in exchange rates beyond the range established by the Fund. Member countries, in turn, are expected to take appropriate action to maintain exchange rates within the prescribed range. By established custom, such appropriate action includes the use of gold and foreign exchange resources to prevent depreciation and the acquisition of gold to prevent appreciation of the exchanges.

While the Fund utilizes the recognized status of gold to facilitate its operations, the Fund does not impose any specific obligations on member countries to hold or use gold for any purposes other than to help maintain stability of the exchanges. While member countries must buy back their own currencies acquired by other member countries from current transactions either with the currency of the other member country or with gold, there is no general obligation on the part of any member country to redeem its local currency in gold. Nor is it expected that the Fund will regard appropriate action to maintain exchange rates as requiring a member country to exhaust all of its reserves of gold and foreign exchange.

QUESTION 14

Are all countries that are members of the International Monetary Fund under obligation to buy all gold offered to them at a fixed price?

REPLY

The Fund proposal provides no explicit obligation on the part of member countries to buy all gold offered to them at a fixed price. Provision IX-1 of the Joint Statement on the Fund Proposal is intended to prevent member countries from depreciating or appreciating their currencies through an increase in the price at which gold is bought or a decrease in the price at which gold is sold. While this provision does place limitations on the prices at which gold transactions may be undertaken, it does not itself require a member country either to buy or sell gold at all.

Despite the fact that there is no explicit provision requiring member countries to buy all gold offered to them, it is our view that provision IX-2 implicitly requires member countries to buy gold offered to them by member countries when this becomes necessary to prevent an appreciation of the exchange beyond the range established by the Fund. Appropriate action to prevent exchange transactions in its market in currencies of other members at rates outside the prescribed range involves the acquisition of gold offered by other member countries or by the Fund.

Obviously, a member country can take steps to limit the demand for its currency by the nationals of other countries and in this way it can minimize the import of gold. It may, with the approval of the Fund, restrict capital movements when the influx of foreign funds is regarded as undesirable. It may even adopt measures that will reduce the demand for its exports in other countries, although certain forms of such measures can be adopted only with the approval of the Fund. But in any case, so long as there is a demand for its currency to settle international transactions on current account, a member country is implicitly obligated to provide its currency for gold.

Also, it is clearly expected that the Fund can replenish its supply of the currency of any member country through the sale of gold when this is necessary to provide exchange for the purposes for which the Fund is authorized to sell exchange. Because the Fund's gold holdings are regarded as a liquid asset equivalent to any member currency, provision is made for the gradual replacement of local currency by gold. It would be contrary to the purposes of these provisions if gold were not purchased freely by member countries when this becomes necessary to prevent an appreciation of the exchanges.

QUESTION 15

Would the Fund be able to create credit in the course of its operations?

REPLY

The Fund proposal as outlined by the Joint Statement makes no provision for transferable currency or deposits in terms of a new or special monetary unit. The operations of the Fund are exclusively in currencies of member countries and in gold.

The Fund does not have any means of creating, holding or transferring currencies or deposits which do not originate with the member countries themselves.

In fact, the Fund proposal does not anywhere provide for the creation by the Fund of transferable credits whether denominated in gold or in the currencies of the member countries or in some special unit. The resources of the Fund in currencies and gold plus what resources the Fund can borrow, represent the facilities the Fund can put at the disposal of member countries. The resources of the Fund are not indefinitely expandable in the sense that international credits are created by the process of a country's getting into debt to the Fund. The creation of credit remains exclusively a function of the monetary authorities of member countries.

We believe that this arrangement is more desirable for the following reasons:

First, with this restriction the management of the Fund is likely to be more vigilant in taking steps which will correct a persistent disequilibrium in the balance of payments position of member countries than if there were no definite limit to the total volume of credit balances which could be created by means of loans or overdrafts.

Second, a system under which a member country assumes a known and limited obligation to subscribe resources for the Fund gives needed protection to all countries, and Governments will be more willing to enter into such an arrangement with a definite and specified limit to their obligations.

Third, the financial strength and stability will be greater in the case of a Fund which possesses a substantial amount of tangible resources for carrying on its operations than in the case of an international institution which has no resources other than an agreement on the part of member countries to accept the credits created by that institution in exchange for real goods and services.

Fourth, if the operations of the Fund reveal a need for additional resources for its successful functioning, such resources can be secured through the borrowing power of the Fund, without the indirect compulsion inherent in the creation of credit.

PART FOUR: EXCHANGE RATES

QUESTION 16

What will be the procedure for establishing initial rates of exchange?

REPLY

Initial rates of exchange are to be established for the currencies of all member countries by defining the parity of each currency in terms of gold. Once established, the initial parity of a member country's currency can be changed only after consultation with or approval by the Fund. All transactions between the Fund and member countries, and all transactions in member currencies, will be at rates of exchange within an agreed percentage of parity.

The Joint Statement on the Fund proposal provides that initial par values of the currencies of the member countries shall be fixed by agreement between the member countries and the Fund. Before the Fund can be established it will be necessary for the member countries to agree with the Fund as to the exchange rates which these countries will fix upon entering the Fund. At the initial meeting of the members of the Fund, the Fund will accept or reject the initial rates proposed by each of the member countries. An agreement must be reached with the Fund on the par values of their currencies by the members at the initial meeting of the Fund before the Fund can begin operations.

The task of considering and determining the initial rates of exchange for all countries that will become members of the Fund would seem at first glance to be overwhelming. If the process of determining initial exchange rates by extended negotiation can be avoided it would simplify the problem of the organization of the Fund. What is wanted is a criterion for the initial fixing of rates of exchange which can be applied generally without prolonged and difficult negotiations with each member country.

It is believed that for most countries that will be invited to become members of the Fund the prevailing rates of exchange will prove entirely satisfactory. In the case of such countries there is clearly no need for the negotiation of a new rate of exchange. For this reason it is the recommendation of the technical experts of the United States that for any country which becomes a member prior to the date on which the Fund's operation began, the rates initially used by the Fund shall be based on the value of the currency in terms of U.S. dollars which prevailed on July 1, 1943. In the event that either the member country or the Fund regards the rate prevailing on July 1, 1943 as clearly inappropriate, it will be necessary for the initial rate to be determined by consultation between the member country and the Fund.

In countries occupied by the enemy there were no dollar rates on July 1, 1943. Moreover, because of the drastic economic changes that have taken place in occupied countries it would not be feasible to apply a general rule, such as a pre-war rate, as a guide for determining the initial rates of exchange for these currencies. In such cases the Fund will use the exchange rate fixed by the government of the liberated country in consultation with the Fund, provided this rate is not considered by the Fund to be inappropriate. No operations in the currency of the member country may be undertaken by the Fund until an acceptable rate has been determined.

Because of the great uncertainty of their postwar situation, some occupied countries may be justly reluctant to fix a definitive rate of exchange immediately after their liberation. Adequate provision has been made in the Joint Statement for changing rates of exchange which prove to be unsatisfactory to the member country. These provisions will be discussed in the reply to Question 17. It would naturally be in the interest of the Fund to correct any maladjustment which was the outgrowth of the fixing of an improper rate at the time a country joined the Fund.

Although under the present provisions of the Joint Statement member countries must establish definitive par values for their currencies before they can purchase foreign exchange from the Fund, it may be desirable to provide that countries which have been occupied in whole or in part during the present war may with the approval of the Fund establish provisional rates. The Fund might be permitted to undertake limited operations in such currencies under adequate safeguards for the resources of the Fund.

Question 17

What facilities are provided by the Fund for correcting an initial rate of exchange that proves unsatisfactory?

Reply

The provisions of the Joint Statement on the Fund proposal recognize certain fundamental concepts with respect to exchange rates. First, it is not desirable to alter exchange rates unnecessarily or when there are other satisfactory means of restoring equilibrium in a country's international balance of payments. Second, it is not possible to support indefinitely an exchange rate that does not reflect a country's international economic position. Third, an alteration of the exchange rate affects the economic life of other countries and should, therefore, be undertaken only after consultation with other countries. Fourth, the interest of a country in its own exchange is paramount, and no change in the exchange rate for a currency should be made except with the consent of that country.

In order to avoid the unnecessary changing of exchange rates, it is provided in the Joint Statement that the par value of each member's currency shall be fixed by agreement between the Fund and the member country. Normally this will be the rate which prevails at the time the member country joins the Fund; but where the prevailing rate is deemed to be inappropriate by either the Fund or the member country, the initial rate must be determined by consultation between the member country and the Fund.

It is recognized in the Fund proposal that alteration in exchange rates may be necessary to correct fundamental disequilibrium. Neither a member country nor the Fund can succeed in supporting indefinitely an exchange rate which does not reflect a country's international economic position. Where other satisfactory measures cannot be taken to restore equilibrium in a country's balance of payments position, it is necessary to adjust the rate of exchange. There is general agreement that because of the extreme uncertainties prevailing at the time, some exchange rates that are fixed during and immediately after the war may have to be altered. For this reason, it is believed that some changes in such exchange rates should be permitted with more freedom than would be justified after international economic relationships have attained a greater degree of stability. The Fund should not, of course, reject a requested change in an exchange rate that is necessary to restore equilibrium because of the domestic social or political policies of the country applying for the change.

An alteration in an established rate of exchange is a matter of interest not only to the country whose currency is changed but to other countries whose economies may be affected by the alteration of the rate of exchange. A change in exchange rates should not be made, therefore, unless it is essential to the correction of fundamental disequilibrium, and except in cooperation with other countries. The Fund proposal provides that no change in exchange rates can be made without prior consultation with the Fund, and that changes that alter the established rate by more than 10 percent can be made only with the approval of the Fund.

It is provided in the Joint Statement that a member country may, after first consulting the Fund, change the established parity of its currency provided the proposed change, inclusive of any changes made since the establishment of the Fund, does not exceed 10 percent. If a member country believes that a change in its exchange rate, not covered by the above, is necessary for the correction of a fundamental disequilibrium, it may make application to the Fund for such change. If the requested change does not exceed 10 percent the Fund is required to give its decision on such application within two days of receiving the application, if the applicant so requests. In the case of requests for changes beyond those covered by the above provisions the Fund will allow sufficient time for a thorough investigation of the need for the change in the exchange rate requested by the member country before giving its decision. It should be noted that in all cases of requests for changes in exchange rates member countries agree not to propose a change in the parity of their currency unless they consider it appropriate to the correction of a fundamental disequilibrium.

Although there are times when an alteration of exchange rates is in the general interest, the significance of the rate of exchange is of such paramount importance in the economic life of a country, that a change in the exchange rate for a currency should not be imposed on a country. The Fund proposal recognizes the special interest of a country in its own exchange rate and provides that a change in the exchange rate for a currency can be made only at the request of the country concerned.

Where the Fund's approval for a change in the par value of a member currency is required, the decision is by majority of the votes of the member countries.

While the Fund cannot compel a country to accept an exchange rate it does not regard as desirable or to change an exchange rate it wishes to keep, the Fund need not make its resources available to support an exchange rate it regards as inappropriate. The Fund cannot undertake operations in a currency until an initial rate is fixed which has its approval. Further, the Fund may give appropriate notice that it will not continue to sell foreign exchange to a country that is using the resources of the Fund in a manner contrary to the purposes and policies of the Fund. Obviously, under this provision the Fund would not provide an exchange rate which prevents the restoration of equilibrium.

QUESTION 18

What will be the position of countries, members of the International Monetary Fund, whose currencies are customarily tied to the dollar or sterling?

REPLY

The practice followed by many countries of maintaining close relationships between their currencies and either the dollar or sterling has undoubtedly been very useful to them. To a considerable extent, such relationships have been helpful in maintaining a greater degree of exchange stability than would otherwise be possible. There is nothing in this practice that is necessarily contrary to the purposes of the Fund, and there is much in this practice that can facilitate the operations of the Fund.

Countries whose currencies have been tied to the dollar or to sterling can continue their customary relationship. They may by law define their currencies in terms of the dollar or sterling; they may hold their monetary reserves in the form of dollar or sterling balances; they may make their currencies redeemable in dollars or sterling. In general, there will be for such countries no need to terminate or to alter the prevailing relationship between their currencies and the dollar or sterling.

Such countries will be particularly interested in the stability of the exchange rates for their currencies in terms of dollars or sterling. When the initial gold parities of their currencies are determined, it is expected that in most instances the Fund will use parities based on the exchange rates prevailing at the time the Fund is established. Unless such rates are clearly inappropriate, and they do not appear to be for most currencies which were tied to the dollar or to sterling, there will be no reason to disturb the existing rates between such currencies and the dollar or sterling.

Once established, the gold parity for a currency continues in effect so long as a member country is satisfied, for the Fund cannot on its own initiative compel a country to alter the parity of its currency. There is no reason for assuming, therefore, that the Fund would in the future require a country to discontinue the special relationship of its currency to the dollar or sterling.

The only occasion when a country could experience any difficulty, as a member of the Fund, in retaining the customary relationship of its currency to the dollar or to sterling would be if the parity for either the dollar or sterling were altered. Even so, there is reason for believing that the difficulty is more apparent than real. A change in the gold parity of a currency can be made only after consultation with the Fund and, with one exception, only with the approval of the Fund. Assuming that the gold parity for either the dollar or sterling were changed, would countries whose currencies are linked to the dollar or sterling be able to alter the parities for their currencies correspondingly?

Aside from the exception previously referred to, a country desiring to alter the parity for its currency in order to maintain its previous relationship to the dollar or sterling would have to secure the prior approval of the Fund. Such approval would be granted if it were shown that a change in the parity is necessary to correct a fundamental disequilibrium. In most instances in which a currency is tied to the dollar or sterling, the special relationship has been established because of the close ties of the two countries in international commerce or finance. If this is so, a change in the dollar or sterling parity is likely to lead to a change for such a country in the demand for exports to or imports from the United States or England. Obviously if such a change in the dollar or sterling parity would have the effect of bringing about a disequilibrium in a country's international payments position, the Fund would undoubtedly permit a country to make the corresponding change for its own currency.

It should be noted that there is no provision in the Fund proposal for pooling or transferring the permissible quotas of member countries. Undoubtedly, to some small extent it is possible for member countries to use their quotas to support the currencies of other countries. The Fund, however, could prevent any considerable use of its resources for this purpose.

QUESTION 19

How will the range of permissible fluctuation in exchange rates, as fixed by the Fund, compare with the old spread between gold points?

REPLY

There would appear to be three sets of limits on exchange rates to be considered in connection with this question: (1) the gold import and gold export points; (2) the highest and lowest points within which exchange rates established by the Fund may be permitted to fluctuate; and (3) the Fund's buying and selling rates for foreign exchange in terms of local currency.

In the opinion of the technical experts of the United States it is on the whole desirable to have the range established by the Fund somewhat broader than the range of the gold points. It is a moot question whether the Fund's buying and selling rates should be the same as the lower and upper limits of the range established by the Fund. There are, however, some disadvantages in having the Fund's buying and selling rates lie within the range of fluctuations permitted by the Fund, and some advantages in having the Fund's buying and selling rates lie outside this range.

In general, it is our view that the range that the Fund would establish would be somewhat greater than the traditional gold points that prevailed in the 1920's. A broader range within which exchange rates could fluctuate might have some effect in inducing member countries to use their independent resources of gold and foreign exchange before resorting to the Fund. It would be in the general interest if member countries would undertake to meet normal and moderate needs for additional exchange by their nationals out of their holdings of gold and foreign exchange, while the resources of the Fund would be reserved for occasions when member countries experience a real need for supplementary resources to be used while working out the basic adjustments in their international position. The inducement to a country to use its resources of gold and foreign exchange is further increased if the Fund's buying and selling rates for exchange lie outside the range of permitted fluctuations, as this would directly penalize the monetary authorities of a member country for using the resources of the Fund.

It is too much to hope that even a relatively broad range, say 2 percent, within which member currencies might be permitted to fluctuate would provide sufficient flexibility for adjusting a country's international balance of payments through a movement in exchange rates. There will, nevertheless, be seasonal or even small cyclical pressures that can be considerably offset by a movement of exchange rates within such a broad range prescribed by the Fund.

There is to this extent something to be said even on the economic side for broadening the range of exchange rates prescribed by the Fund as compared with the old spread between gold points. On the other hand, the permissible variations must not introduce a risk of exchange fluctuations so considerable as to deter short-term financing of international trade or long-term lending for investment. Neither should the permissible fluctuation encourage speculation of a character that would tend to weaken the established structure of exchange rates, or too easily introduce a disrupting influence in the money and exchange markets.

The range prescribed by the Fund should for administrative reasons be greater than the spread between the gold points. In the post-war period, it is almost certain that under any circumstances the spread between the gold points will be considerably greater than it was in the 1920's. While lower interest rates, the higher monetary value of gold, and perhaps improved transport facilities will tend to narrow the gold points, other factors, particularly the difference between the buying and selling prices for gold in various countries, will tend to broaden the gold points.

In the 1920's there was in fact no difference between the buying and selling prices for gold in the United States and a difference of less than 1/6 of 1 percent in the United Kingdom. Differences between the buying and selling prices of gold were an insignificant factor in determining the dollar-sterling gold points in the 1920's. Now, under the Gold Reserve Act of 1934 there is a charge of 1/4 percent for buying or selling gold. If this difference of 1/2 percent were to be adopted by the United Kingdom, there would be a spread of approximately 1 percent between the exchange rate equivalents for gold in New York and London. Probably another 3/5 of 1 percent should be allowed for actual costs of moving gold in both directions. Under these conditions, the spread between the gold points would be 1.6 percent.

It would seem, therefore, that if the range of fluctuations in exchange rates permitted by the Fund is to be somewhat greater than the spread between the gold points, the Fund's range will have to be very close to 2 percent. This would seem to be sufficient inducement to a country to utilize its own gold and exchange resources rather than to draw upon the resources of the Fund to meet normal and moderate needs for foreign exchange. As already stated, a further penalty would be placed upon a country using the Fund's resources if the Fund's buying and selling rates for exchange were outside the range of permitted fluctuations.

In this connection, it should be noted that the range of exchange rates permitted by the Fund has been compared with the normal gold points that might be expected in the post-war period. Some countries may have so large a difference between the official buying and selling prices for gold that their gold points might in fact lie outside any broad but reasonable range the Fund might be expected to establish. In such cases the Fund might recommend that the member country narrow the spread between its buying and selling prices for gold.

There is another point of some interest that may be mentioned. In general, the spread between the gold points is a function of the distance between the two exchange markets under consideration. In the 1920's, the spread between the gold points was much narrower between New York and Montreal than between New York and Bombay. It may be desirable to standardize the range established by the Fund in order to give all member countries whatever advantage there may be in a broad range within which exchange rates may be permitted to fluctuate.

Because of the importance of these unsettled questions and the difference of opinion on the technical merits of alternative policies, it was considered best not to include in our tentative proposal any specific provisions on such technical matters until agreement has been reached on these questions. There is no doubt that decisions on such technical questions can be worked out to the satisfaction of member countries.

QUESTION 20

Would differential rates of exchange for different classes of imports and exports (visible and invisible) be permitted by the Fund?

REPLY

Differential rates of exchange would come under the provision of the Joint Statement which deals with multiple currency practices. This provision, IX-3, is based on a view that the use of such methods should not be encouraged because they may so easily become the means for discrimination in trade relationships and because they usually involve control of the exchanges so complete as to offer a strong temptation to restrict transactions on current account.

According to provision IX-3 member countries agree not to engage in multiple currency practices without the approval of the Fund. Undoubtedly such approval would not be given in the case of multiple currency practices which in the judgment of the Fund do retard international trade and the flow of productive capital.

Where a country has centralized the exchange dealings of its nationals for purposes of supervision, differential rates on imports may provide a convenient substitute for customs duties. At the time the exchange authorities make foreign exchange available to importers it is very simple for them to collect what are in effect import duties. Insofar as various classes of imports are distinguished and different exchange rates are assigned to them, the same result is produced as by an ad valorem tariff with different rates of duty on the various classes of merchandise. Differential rates that are not the same for all currencies are obviously discriminatory. Of course, if the exchange rates for some classes of imports are extremely low (say, lower than the exchange rates for some classes of exports) there may in fact be a subsidy for some imports. Obviously, differential exchange rates for imports may easily lead to restriction of international trade.

Differential rates of exchange for exports act as a subsidy for some exports and an export duty on others. This may create important although disguised discrimination among the importing countries, especially where the differentials are not the same for all currencies. On the whole, the case for differential rates of exchange for exports is even weaker than for differential rates for imports.

While differential rates have some administrative advantages in a country which has centralized its foreign exchange dealings and which secures substantial revenues from them, there are serious disadvantages and dangers inherent in their use. Comparability of international values becomes much more tenuous where there are multiple exchange rates. Also, differential rates can hardly be prevented from channelizing trade in a fashion that results in intentional or unintentional discrimination among countries. Differential exchange rates can become an instrument for the worst form of unfair competition in international trade. There is also the risk that multiple currencies may again be used, as Germany used them, to produce division and domination of weaker countries for political purposes. On the whole, differential exchange rates open the way to dangerous abuses, while offering few offsetting advantages that cannot be equally well achieved in other ways.

For these reasons, it is provided that member countries may not engage in multiple currency practices which in the judgment of the Fund restrict international transactions. In countries where differential rates of exchange for different classes of imports and exports are used, their continuances would require the approval of the Fund. It is conceivable that the Fund would in some instances decide that multiple currencies are being used by a member country in such a way that they do not conflict with the purposes of the Fund. In other cases the Fund may permit adequate time for the abandonment of the practice, in order to give member countries ample opportunity to arrange for collection of revenue by other methods based on the foreign transactions of their nationals.

There is, nevertheless, one category of invisible exports where a differential exchange rate would seem to be within the purposes of the Fund. For social and political reasons it may be desirable to attract tourists and students from other countries. A differential rate of exchange for these purposes could very well be regarded by the Fund as an appropriate means of encouraging friendly relations between countries, and in some instances may be found to be an effective device for helping to correct disequilibrium in a country's balance of payments. It would seem undesirable, therefore, not to allow some flexibility in this matter. The Fund, of course, would have to give its approval before such differential exchange rates were established.

QUESTION 21

If a country has exhausted its rights of recourse to the Fund, does its undertaking to maintain a stable rate of exchange lapse?

REPLY

The obligations of a country to other member countries and to the Fund are not terminated when it has exhausted its permissible quota or for any other reason has no further access to the resources of the Fund.

Specifically, a member country is obligated to prevent exchange transactions in its market in currencies of other members at rates outside the range prescribed by the Fund by taking whatever appropriate measures are necessary for this purpose. Such measures cannot, of course, include the practices opposed to the purposes of the Fund and prescribed in Section IX of the Joint Statement. Obviously, one appropriate measure is the use of the gold and foreign exchange resources of a country to support its currency.

A country cannot succeed indefinitely in maintaining a stable exchange rate by the use of its own resources of gold and foreign exchange if the established rate does not reflect approximately its international economic position. Where the disequilibrium in a country's balance of payments is of a fundamental character, measures will ultimately have to be taken to restore equilibrium either through an approved change in the exchange rate or through other appropriate means.

When a country has reached the stage where its rights of recourse to the resources of the Fund are exhausted the Fund may at its discretion waive the limitation on the Fund's holdings of that currency provided in III-2(c) under conditions which safeguard the interest of the Fund. The conditions which the Fund will normally impose on a country which has exhausted its normal rights of recourse to the Fund will be the adoption of measures by the member country which in the view of the Fund will restore the necessary balance in the country's position. Such measures might include alteration of the exchange rate, control of capital movements, or in extreme cases direct measures to limit the volume of imports.

It would be unfortunate if any member country should adopt the attitude that its obligations to the Fund could be disregarded when it has exhausted its right to further use of the Fund. The provision of resources to facilitate the maintenance of exchange stability is only one aspect of the Fund's functions. The Fund must be regarded as an agency with general responsibilities for international monetary cooperation. The duty to take all possible measures to avoid unilateral exchange depreciation is not a qualified duty.

Alteration of exchange rates can only be undertaken with the approval of the Fund, except that a member country may change the established rate for its currency by not more than 10 percent, provided the Fund is notified and consulted on the advisability of the action. Both a member country and the Fund have a duty to cooperate in taking measures to prevent an authorized depreciation in exchange rates.

QUESTION 22

When a country's currency becomes scarce, does that country's obligation to keep constant by "appropriate action" its rate of exchange on the currencies of all other countries remain unaffected?

REPLY

As indicated in the answer to the previous question, it is the view of the technical experts of the United States that the obligation of a member country to prevent its exchange rate from fluctuating beyond the range specified by the Fund cannot be terminated without the consent of the Fund. The fact that a currency has become scarce within the meaning of provision VI-1 is indicative of a demand for the currency which, if not met or restricted, will tend to appreciate that currency. It is clearly the intention of provision VI-1, if no additional supply is forthcoming, to restrict the demand for the currency in some equitable manner, in order to prevent an appreciation of the exchange rate.

As one of its obligations as a member of the Fund, each member country agrees not to allow exchange rates in its market to fluctuate outside a prescribed range based on the agreed parities of the currencies. This implies that a member country must undertake by appropriate action to maintain exchange rates within the range established by the Fund. For a country with a favorable balance of payments, the obligation to maintain exchange rates by appropriate action includes the acquisition of gold that is offered for its currency to support the exchanges of the gold selling countries and to prevent the appreciation of the currency of the country with a favorable balance of payments.

The acquisition of unlimited amounts of the currencies of any other countries cannot reasonably be regarded as appropriate action within the meaning of the Fund proposal. It is not intended that any provision of the Fund proposal shall make it mandatory for any member country to acquire and to hold the currency of another member country. Instead, it is the Fund as a cooperative enterprise which undertakes to acquire the currencies of member countries in accordance with the provisions of the proposal.

When a country's currency becomes scarce, the Fund itself takes steps either to increase the supply or to restrict the demand. By apportioning the available supply, the demand is directly restricted. In general, such action by the Fund would prevent an appreciation of a scarce currency. Member countries are, after consultation with the Fund, authorized to restrict freedom of exchange operations in currencies which have been declared by the Fund to be scarce. In the countries where a scarce currency must be rationed, the controls should be effective in restricting imports. It follows that the exporters of the country whose currency is scarce will not, in fact, have foreign exchange to offer for sale, and there will be no need for placing limitations on the sale of foreign currencies by exporters. However, a member country could apply such direct limitations with the approval of the Fund and in cooperation with other member countries.

For further discussion of the problem related to a scarce currency, see the answers to questions 30 and 31.

PART FOUR [BIS]: OPERATIONS OF THE FUND

QUESTION 23

Will the International Monetary Fund sell foreign exchange to a member country to support its rate of exchange if that rate is not in accord with the country's international economic position?

REPLY

While it is a major purpose of the Fund to help stabilize exchange rates, the Fund cannot and should not undertake to provide foreign exchange to prolong a basically unbalanced position. Numerous provisions of the Fund proposal are intended to provide safeguards against the use of the Fund's resources to support an exchange rate not in accord with a member country's international economic position.

When initial rates of exchange are determined, the rate established for a currency must, in the judgment of the Fund, be appropriate. Until the Fund has given its approval to an initial rate of exchange, no operations may be undertaken by the Fund in such a currency. Even after the initial rate of exchange has been fixed with its approval, the Fund is not required to sell exchange to a member country if that country is using the resources of the Fund in a manner contrary to the purposes and policies of the Fund. One of the fundamental purposes of the Fund as stated in provision I-3 is to enable members to correct maladjustments in their balances of payments by making the Fund's resources available to them with adequate safeguards. The Fund is not required therefore to sell exchange to a member country to support an unbalanced position.

When a member country is using the resources of the Fund in a manner that clearly has the effect of preventing or unduly delaying the establishment of a sound balance in its international accounts, the Fund, after notice, may suspend the member country from making further use of the Fund's resources on the grounds that it is using them in a manner contrary to the purposes and policies of the Fund. The Fund is, however, required to present to such country a report setting forth the reasons for that country's being suspended from the privilege of purchasing foreign exchange from the Fund and the Fund must allow a suitable time for reply before notice of actual suspension is given. The Fund in its report to the member country will undoubtedly stipulate certain conditions whereby the member country can avoid suspension of the right to draw on the resources of the Fund. If in its reply to the Fund, the member country agrees to the conditions stipulated by the Fund, notice of suspension of the privilege of purchasing foreign exchange from the Fund would not be given.

The Fund is also expected to limit its sales of foreign exchange to member countries that use the resources of the Fund at an unwarranted rate. In general, the presumption is that a country that purchases foreign exchange for local currency at an annual rate in excess of 25 percent of its quota is making unwarranted use of the Fund and except under special circumstances members will not be permitted to purchase foreign exchange from the Fund at an annual rate in excess of 25 percent of their quotas provided the Fund's total holdings of their currency are not below 75 percent of their quota. Such use of the Fund is an indication of an unbalanced position that should be corrected.

A limitation on the Fund's holdings of the local currency of a member country is established for each country because it is regarded as desirable to have an objective indication of a limit to the Fund's acquisition of local currency to help a country to support its exchange rate. There is implicit in this provision the view that when the Fund's holdings have reached 200 percent of the quota, it is generally an indication that there is a fundamental disequilibrium in a country's international position that calls for remedial action. While the Fund may sell additional foreign exchange to such a country, the sale requires specific approval and can be made only if satisfactory measures are being or will be taken to correct the disequilibrium, or if it is believed that the disequilibrium is temporary and the excess holdings of the Fund can be disposed of within a reasonable time.

It cannot be emphasized too frequently that the Fund is not designed simply to sell foreign exchange needed by member countries to meet their adverse balances on international account. The resources of the Fund may properly be used to help a country through a period of temporary disequilibrium. The resources of the Fund are available to member countries under adequate safeguards to help them maintain stability of their currencies, while giving them time to correct maladjustments in their balance of payments without resorting to extreme measures destructive of international prosperity. A Fund operating successfully should be influential in inducing member countries to adopt policies making for an orderly return to equilibrium.

QUESTION 24

Does the Fund provide facilities for multilateral clearing to a country which has its overall international payments on current account in balance but has an adverse balance of payments on current account with some countries?

REPLY

According to the present provisions of the Joint Statement on the Fund proposal there can be no doubt that in almost all circumstances a member country will be able to use freely the proceeds of its transactions in one country for the settlement of balances due on current account in another country.

Let us suppose that England has a favorable balance with France and an adverse balance of equal amount with the Netherlands. France and the Netherlands are in equilibrium with each other, and so is each of the three countries with all countries other than the three. This situation may manifest itself in an accumulation of francs by England and a need by England for guilders. It might be possible for England to offer all or part of its accumulated holdings of francs for sale in the exchange market and secure payments in guilders.

Assuming, however, that there is no franc-guilder market, it would then be necessary for England to offer the francs for sale to France. Under provision III-5, France is obligated to buy francs from England with sterling or with gold, if such francs were acquired by England from current transactions with France, and if France has access to sterling in the Fund. France might have to apply to the Fund for sterling for the purpose. If the Fund supplied sterling, the Fund's holdings of sterling would be reduced by the amount made available for the purpose.

If the Fund's holdings of sterling are not outside the limits specified in the proposal (which is unlikely in view of the fact that the Fund's holdings of sterling would have been reduced by support of the franc), and if England is not making unwarranted use of the Fund's resources (which is unlikely in view of the fact that there is no net change in the Fund's holdings of sterling), the Fund could under the provisions of the proposal make available the necessary guilders.

Under provision III-2 of the Joint Statement on the Fund proposal the Fund is permitted to sell foreign exchange to a member country so long as the currency demanded is presently needed for making payments in that currency which are consistent with the purposes and policies of the Fund and so long as the member country is not making unwarranted use of the Fund's resources. It is not necessary for a member country to have an over-all adverse balance of payments to obtain a particular member's currency which that country needs to correct a temporary maladjustment in her balance of payments with another member.

Question 25

Would it be possible for the Fund to provide the foreign exchange needed to maintain stability of the currency of a member country if the deficit giving rise to this need for foreign exchange is in the balance of payments with a third country?

Reply

The resources of the Fund are intended to be used to aid member countries in meeting adverse balances of payments predominantly on current account. The Fund is not intended to enter the exchange markets or to provide the means for carrying out arbitrage transactions.

Under the provisions of the Joint Statement the Fund cannot use the currency of one country to help maintain stability of the exchange of another country if the deficit giving rise to the pressure on the exchange is with a third country. Concretely, if Canada has a favorable balance of payments on current account with England, the Fund cannot use U.S. dollars for the purpose of enabling England to meet payments in Canada.

If England has an adverse balance on current account with Canada, the Fund can sell Canadian dollars to England for sterling in order to enable England to settle this balance. If the Fund's holdings of Canadian dollars are inadequate, it may use gold to purchase Canadian dollars. The Fund is not authorized to use any member currency for the purpose of acquiring another.

No hardship is inflicted on Canada because of this regulation. Under provision III-5 of the Joint Statement, Canada can require England to purchase the sterling acquired from current transactions, payment to be made either in Canadian dollars or in gold. If England may acquire Canadian dollars from the Fund (Canadian dollars not being a scarce currency and England not being suspended from making use of the Fund's resources), England is obligated to purchase such sterling from Canada. The reduction in the Fund's holdings of Canadian dollars would increase correspondingly Canada's ability to purchase foreign exchange from the Fund within the terms of the Joint Statement.

No doubt, there would be some advantages if the Fund could use any of its resources to aid any member country in meeting adverse balances on current account. If all member currencies were freely convertible into gold, such restrictions might be safely dropped. It is not feasible, however, to permit the free use of some currencies (say, U.S. dollars) for meeting an adverse balance of payments with any country, while restricting the use of another currency exclusively for meeting adverse balances with that country.

QUESTION 26

Would member countries exporting capital be permitted to purchase foreign exchange from the Fund?

REPLY

If a member country is in present need of the currency of another member country for making payments in that currency in order to correct a maladjustment in its balance of payments toward which capital exports are contributing only in small part, the Fund would undoubtedly permit its resources to be utilized by the member. Provision V-1 prevents a member country from using the resources of the Fund to meet a large or sustained outflow of capital, and gives the Fund power to require a member to exercise controls to prevent such use of the resources of the Fund. This provision is not intended however to prevent the use of the Fund's resources for capital transactions of a reasonable amount required in the ordinary course of trade, banking, or other business. Nor is it intended to prevent capital movements which are met out of a member country's own resources of gold and foreign exchange, provided such capital movements are in accordance with the purposes of the Fund. A capital export for the purpose of expanding exports does not in fact represent a net loss of exchange resources of the amount involved, since the expansion of exports tends to provide a favorable current balance of approximately the same amount. Capital exports for this purpose are therefore permitted, even when a country is making some use of the Fund.

In general it would appear to be more desirable for the Fund to provide a member country with some resources to help maintain exchange stability than to require the imposition of a system of exchange control merely to prevent the export of a moderate amount of capital. The Fund can safely take this position so long as its holdings of the local currency in question are not excessive. But the Fund cannot allow its resources of other currencies to be seriously depleted to facilitate the speculative movement of funds; nor can it sanction the dissipation in this way of resources of the Fund which should be reserved for the maintenance of international interchange of goods and services. It is expected that as the Fund's holdings of a member currency increase, the Fund will be less lenient with respect to the volume of capital exports which that country will be permitted to have without being deprived of the use of the resources of the Fund.

It is clear from the above provisions that it is not intended that the Fund should ever rigidly exclude the utilization of its resources when a country has an export of capital. It is recognized that there will be instances when permitting an export of capital will not involve a net drain on the resources of the Fund and will be beneficial from the point of view of the general international economic situation. Under such circumstances, the Fund will want to allow its resources to be used in moderation by a country exporting capital.

It may be of interest to consider the conditions under which the Fund might regard the export of capital as in the general interest and as not in conflict with the primary objectives of the Fund. In fact, an export of capital, even when some of the foreign exchange is provided by the Fund, may reduce the net call on the Fund's resources and may give the Fund a more balanced distribution of its assets. For example, one member country may export capital to another member country which has an adverse balance on current account and may wish to purchase from the Fund part of the exchange needed for this purpose. Such a capital export may reduce correspondingly the need of the second country to call upon the Fund for exchange with which to meet its adverse balance on current account. The net amount of exchange sold by the Fund under such conditions would be less because it facilitated the capital export. Further, if this capital export is from a country whose currency the Fund holds in a moderate amount to a country whose currency the Fund holds in an excessive amount, the distribution of the Fund's assets would become more balanced, and as a result of the transaction the Fund would be in a better position to serve all member countries.

Apart from such general conditions, the Fund might be more favorably disposed toward permitting certain types of capital transfer than toward permitting others. The repayment of a short-term credit is, in a sense, a capital movement. However, if the credit was acquired to finance trade, it may have served when made to obviate a corresponding use of the Fund, and the Fund would ordinarily provide exchange for the repayment of such a credit. The meeting of normal sinking fund installments on a debt is usually regarded as a capital movement. Nevertheless, if such sinking fund payments are not large relative to the Fund's holdings of the currency of a member country, the Fund would ordinarily provide foreign exchange to facilitate a capital export by a country with a maturing obligation which cannot be fully met at once but which its balance of payments could absorb within two or three years.

In considering the probable attitude of the Fund toward the sale of foreign exchange to facilitate a transfer of capital, it should be borne in mind that the provisions of the Fund proposal are designed to give effect to the general principle that the Fund's resources should be used primarily for settling international balances on current account. However, sufficient flexibility is provided so that the resources of the Fund can be used for meeting a capital export where it is deemed to be generally desirable. There is no reason to believe that a country making payments of a capital nature will be debarred entirely from recourse to the Fund unless and until the Fund has given sufficient notice to the member country that such payments are not in the general interest.

It is important for the Fund to build up in the course of its operations accurate statistics on international payments of all types, as it easily can do under its authority to require full reports from member countries. In the period before these records are available, however, completely accurate records of a country's capital inflow or outflow are not essential to the proper execution of the policy outlined above. The Fund will be concerned only with large movements, not with flows that are small relative to a country's volume of international transactions. Large non-recurring capital flows—like a large redemption operation, or defaulted loan settlement—would be known to the Fund, while recurring net outflows of significant size would be difficult to obscure. It is not necessary to know precisely the amount of net outflow; it is enough to be able to ascertain whether the net outflow is significantly large or not. It would be desirable, of course, for member countries to arrange to receive regular reports on capital movements into and out of their countries, and to make such data available to the Fund.

An extended discussion of the control of capital movements will be found in the answers to questions 33 and 34.

QUESTION 27

What provision is made to permit a country with abnormally low holdings of foreign currencies and gold to accumulate such resources while a member of the Fund?

REPLY

Provision III-7-c requires each member country to offer to sell to the Fund one-half of the gold and gold-convertible exchange it acquires in excess of its official holdings at the time it became a member of the Fund so long as this does not reduce the Fund's holdings of the member's currency below 75 percent of its quota. However, no country need sell gold or gold-convertible exchange under this provision unless its official holdings are in excess of its quota.

The significance of this provision can best be brought out by an explanation of its purpose.

1. Some member countries may be tempted to use the resources of the Fund to build up independent holdings of gold and foreign exchange. The Fund is not devised to facilitate the accomplishment of such a purpose. On the contrary, the Fund's resources are intended only for needs arising from an adverse balance of payments predominantly on current account.

Although the Fund would not sell foreign exchange for local currency to permit a member country to acquire additional balances of gold or foreign exchange, some provision is necessary to prevent the Fund from being used indirectly for such a purpose. Without such provision, a member country could resort to the Fund when it has a temporary adverse balance of payments, and keep any increment of gold or foreign exchange which it may acquire when it has a favorable balance of payments.

With provisions III-7-b and III-7-c, a member country cannot build up excessive gold and foreign exchange balances while at the same time drawing upon the resources of the Fund. A member country must pay with gold for one-half its net purchases of foreign exchange from the Fund, provided its gold and gold-convertible exchange holdings exceed its quota; and it must offer to sell to the Fund for its local currency one-half of the gold and gold-convertible exchange it may acquire in excess of its official holdings at the time it became a member of the Fund (provided its official holdings exceed its quota).

2. The Fund proposal does not generally specify a definite time compelling the repurchase of local currency which has been acquired by the Fund from the sale of

foreign exchange to a member country. Presumably when the Fund sells foreign exchange in excess of the amounts normally permitted under provision III-2-c, there would be an understanding that the Fund's holdings of local currency would be brought within appropriate limits in some specified period. Similarly, when the Fund sets conditions upon additional sales of foreign exchange to a country in accordance with provision III-2-d one condition could be that a reduction in the Fund's holdings of local currency be effected in some specified period.

The great bulk of the exchange transactions of the Fund with member countries will not require specific approval, as the Fund's holdings of the currencies of member countries will in general not exceed the prescribed limits. The Fund would not in such instances prescribe conditions for the repurchase of local currencies, although the penalty provisions will be a strong inducement to repurchase local currencies from the Fund. It is necessary, however, that some obligation should rest on member countries utilizing the resources of the Fund to repurchase their own currencies. Otherwise, the Fund's resources would tend to become unbalanced in the form of unnecessarily large holdings of some local currencies. Provision III-7-c is in fact a method of requiring the repurchase of local currency by member countries as their balances of payments become favorable and as they acquire additional gold and gold-convertible exchange.

3. The Fund starts with resources of local currencies and gold. In general, resources of this character should be adequate for the operations of the Fund. With its local currency resources the Fund may meet any moderate calls for any currency; and with its gold holdings the Fund can supplement its local currencies and meet very large calls for any new currencies. Nevertheless, it would be desirable to strengthen the Fund by gradually converting its local currency holdings into gold. Provision III-7 makes this possible.

For the world as a whole, the balance of payments, as ordinarily defined, is always active to the extent of the annual increment in gold reserves resulting from the production and distribution of newly-mined gold (perhaps modified for changes in private hoards of gold). The normal balance of payments for a country should tend to provide for an expansion in its holdings of gold and gold-convertible exchange. There is no good reason why part of the increment in gold and gold-convertible exchange should not be used by member countries to repurchase from the Fund its holdings of their local currencies. It is in the interest of all member countries that the strength and liquidity of the Fund be increased by the gradual replacement of local currencies with gold, particularly as such replacement would not involve any reduction in the reserves of member countries.

It should be emphasized that no hardship is incurred by a member country in offering to sell to the Fund part of its increment of gold and gold-convertible exchange. The member country offering the resources for sale is under no obligation to accept any currency other than its own. To the extent that a member country reduces the Fund's holdings of its local currency, it increases its right to acquire foreign exchange from the Fund with its local currency. In view of the general advantages that would be conferred by a strong and liquid Fund, the right to acquire foreign exchange from a Fund adequately supplied with gold is not inferior to the actual holding of gold and foreign exchange (except, of course, in the acquisition of scarce currencies).

These provisions by no means indicate a policy of discouraging the maintenance of independent monetary reserves. It is, on the contrary, the view of the technical experts of the United States that it is desirable for member countries to build up adequate holdings of gold and foreign exchange. For this reason a reduced subscription in the form of gold may be made by countries with small or moderate holdings, since the obligatory gold subscription of a member country is 25 percent of its quota or 10 percent of its holdings of gold and gold-convertible exchange whichever is smaller. To take account of the greater need of countries which have been occupied by the enemy, a further reduction in the subscription of gold might be permitted for such countries. It is the recommendation of the U.S. technical experts that the countries whose home areas have suffered substantial damage from enemy action or occupation during the present war, should be permitted to reduce their obligatory gold subscriptions to 75 percent of the amount they would otherwise pay.

In addition, a country with gold and gold-convertible exchange holdings less than its quota need not use gold in paying for exchange purchased from the Fund. In countries in which working balances, other than official balances, are at a very low level at the time of adherence to the Fund, these private working balances may be built up (but not excessively) without any obligation to offer to sell such increments of gold and gold-convertible exchange to the Fund.

The requirement to offer to sell to the Fund gold and gold-convertible exchange acquired by a member country is also subject to qualifications designed to permit a country to accumulate some holdings of gold and gold-convertible exchange. The provision applies only to gold and gold-convertible exchange acquired by a member country in excess of its *official* holdings at the time it became a member of the Fund, and no country need offer to sell gold or gold-convertible exchange under this provision unless its official holdings are in excess of its quota. Furthermore, only one-half of the increase in gold and gold-convertible exchange holdings must be offered to the Fund. Finally, a member country is not required to sell additional gold to the Fund after the Fund's holdings of its local currency are below 75 percent of its quota.

QUESTION 28

When does newly-mined gold become subject to the provision that member countries must under certain conditions offer for sale to the Fund half of the increase in their official holdings of gold?

REPLY

The provision that the Fund may require up to half of the increase in a member's holdings of gold and gold-convertible exchange to be used to repurchase part of the Fund's holdings of its currency applies only to the increase in official holdings of gold or gold-convertible exchange. Newly-mined gold held by the producers or by bullion dealers awaiting sale is not to be regarded as part of the official holdings of a country.

It is conceivable that newly-mined gold will regularly be offered for sale to the monetary authorities of a country soon after its production. It then becomes subject to the obligations of III-7-c. It should be noted that the Fund may require a member country to sell half of its increase in gold and gold-convertible exchange only at the end of the Fund's financial year, so that a gold producing country in which newly-mined gold is sold to the monetary authorities will only need to offer for sale to the Fund one-half of the net increment in its gold holdings as represented by its holdings at the end of the Fund's financial year.

As a matter of administrative convenience the Fund would probably provide some period during which newly-mined gold would be deemed not to have entered into the official holdings. This might be necessary in order to avoid innumerable minor adjustments. In some countries, Treasury or Mint agencies temporarily include in their holdings newly-mined gold delivered to them for assaying and refining or for safekeeping. To avoid hardship, holdings of such a character should be excluded by establishing a period during which such holdings are deemed not to have entered into the official holdings.

It may be pointed out again that a country holding newly-mined gold awaiting distribution does not suffer any hardship (the scarce currency problem aside) if half of the increment of such gold is offered to the Fund for its local currency. To the extent that the gold was held to acquire foreign exchange, the capacity of the country to acquire such exchange is not impaired by sale of half of the increment of gold to the Fund for local currency. The member country can acquire foreign exchange to the full value of the gold held for the purpose by purchasing needed foreign exchange from the Fund, payment to be made half in gold and half in local currency.

QUESTION 29

In computing the increment of gold and gold-convertible exchange that member countries must offer for sale to the Fund is any allowance made for increased foreign liabilities?

REPLY

In computing the amount of gold and gold convertible exchange that must be offered for sale to the Fund under this provision, no explicit allowance is made for increased liabilities to foreigners. It should be noted, however, that it is only half the increase in official holdings that must be offered for sale to the Fund. The intention is not to restrict the acquisition of such resources when they are needed by commercial banks and other nationals as working balances for international transactions. It is desirable, however, to avoid the accumulation of excessive holdings in this form by countries utilizing the resources of the Fund. In the event that the commercial banks and nationals of a member country using the resources of the Fund are accumulating gold or gold-convertible exchange in excessive amounts the Fund might consider bringing to the attention of the monetary authorities of the country concerned, the undesirability of utilizing the resources of the Fund while excessive balances of foreign exchange are held by its nationals. Undoubtedly, in determining whether such holdings are excessive, consideration would be given to the foreign liabilities of commercial banks and other nationals.

No explicit allowance is made for offsetting the official holdings of Treasuries and central banks with their foreign liabilities. If it is regarded as desirable to make some allowance for such liabilities against official holdings of gold and foreign exchange, consideration can be given to the manner in which this may be most appropriately done. Provision for such offsets, if regarded as desirable, could be made in the operating regulations that are adopted to implement III-7.

PART FIVE: POLICIES OF THE FUND

QUESTION 30

What kind of action is it contemplated that the International Monetary Fund would recommend to a country whose currency is in scarce supply?

REPLY

The Joint Statement provides that when the Fund's holdings of the currency of a member country become excessively small in relation to prospective acquisitions and needs for that currency, the Fund is required to render a report embodying an analysis of the causes of the depletion of the Fund's holdings and recommending measures designed to increase the Fund's holdings of that currency (VI-1).

The specific recommendations which the Fund might make to a member country whose currency is in scarce supply would be formulated in accordance with the nature of the existing disequilibrium in the balance of payments position of that country and the forces responsible for its development. It would be desirable to have a special committee appointed to study the problem and to draft a report on the recommendations to be made. It would also be desirable for the Board member of the country whose currency is declared scarce to be a member of the Fund committee appointed to draft the report.

No limitation on the scope of such recommendations is provided in the Fund proposal. It would, however, be necessary for the Fund to give full consideration to the effects of its recommendation on the internal economy of the member country to whom the recommendations are made as well as to any constitutional or other legal limitations which might make difficult or impossible positive action on some of the recommendations under consideration.

It may be assumed that such obvious measures as the control of capital movements have already been taken to ease the strain on the exchange position of member countries and the Fund with relation to the scarce currency. In the event that the disequilibrium in the balance of the payments position of a member country was the result of an inflow of capital and not the result of persistent forces operating on current account items, the Fund would undoubtedly make recommendations which look toward a reversal of this flow. The control of capital inflow is not, however, the primary responsibility of the member country experiencing such inflows. If capital movements are responsible for a serious drain on the Fund's supply of that currency, the member countries exporting capital to the country whose currency is in short supply could be required by the Fund to take the initiative in restricting such exports.

The Fund may propose to a member country whose currency is in scarce supply that it lend currency to the Fund. Such an additional supply would provide the member countries with the additional time needed to work out a more satisfactory balance in international payments with the country whose currency is scarce. No member country is under any obligation to make any loan to the Fund. If a loan is made, the terms and conditions of the loan would be agreed between the member country and the Fund.

This question regarding the Fund's recommendations is not primarily concerned with these intermediate measures but with corrective measures. It is impossible at this point to state specifically what the Fund would recommend in any given situation, since each case would be a problem of its own, involving a large number of variables, and concerning which intensive study would be necessary. If, for example, the disequilibrium stems from an excess of exports over imports which is not likely to correct itself in a reasonable period of time, the Fund might recommend measures for an expansion of imports and a reduction of artificial stimulants to exports if any are operating. Specifically, appropriate recommendations for increasing imports might include a reduction of tariff rates and the encouragement of tourist travel abroad. We believe it would be contrary to the best interests of the members of the Fund to recommend a reduction of exports; but it might be quite proper to recommend that nations eliminate subsidies on exports provided such elimination would make a significant contribution to the adjustment.

When a country shows a persistently favorable balance of payments on current account, it may be that the most appropriate and the most effective means of restoring a balance in its international accounts would be an expansion in its foreign investments. If there are factors prevalent in the country discouraging the flow of private investment to foreign countries, the report might well recommend their correction. The Fund might even recommend measures designed to promote repatriation of foreign funds.

In general, there is little reason to expect that it will be necessary to recommend measures designed to encourage domestic expansion in the country whose currency is scarce. Nevertheless, if such recommendations are needed, they should be made, including recommendations on credit policy, investment policy, and other measures which have a bearing on the level of economic activity and employment within a member country. It is quite possible that the rise in production has been greater than the rise in wage rates, efficiency rates of remuneration have fallen, and that an upward adjustment should be encouraged.

In extreme cases it may also be desirable to recommend a change in exchange rates for the country whose currency is scarce. An upward change in the foreign exchange value of a currency, however, should be considered only if other measures appear to be inadequate, and only if such a step does not contribute to further deterioration in the general international economic situation. It should be emphasized that what is desired is not merely a reduction in a country's exports, but, remedial action that will correct its balance of payments without generating deflationary forces at home and abroad.

The recommendations of the Fund will unquestionably be given careful consideration. It is in the interests of a country whose currency is scarce to avoid the need by the Fund to allot its holdings of such a currency, and to take measures to obviate the need for such action by the Fund. While the Fund itself cannot correct the situation, it provides a means for facilitating the adoption of appropriate measures by the cooperating member countries.

It should not be overlooked that a disequilibrium in the balance of payments cannot be manifested as a problem peculiar to one country. Whenever the supply of a member country's currency is scarce, this scarcity is likely to be accompanied by excessive supplies of the currencies of other countries. In such cases the responsibility for the correction of the maladjustment is not a unilateral one. It will be the duty of the Fund to make a report not only to the country whose currency is scarce but also to the member countries who are exhausting or are using the resources of the Fund in a manner which is not consistent with the purposes of the Fund. The report should provide a comprehensive analysis of the causes of the scarcity and practical recommendations for remedying the situation.

QUESTION 31

What is the purpose of requiring the Fund to apportion a scarce currency?

REPLY

As was pointed out in the answer to the previous question, the Fund will make recommendations to a member country whose currency is in scarce supply, with a view to correcting the conditions in its balance of payments relations giving rise to the scarcity of its currency. It is in the interest of such a member country to carry out the Fund's recommendations since otherwise it will be faced with the alternative of reducing its exports and making other undesirable adjustments.

It should be noted that the scarcity of an important currency is likely to be accompanied by an excess in the Fund's holdings of the currencies of other member countries. A disequilibrium in the balance of payments is of necessity not confined to one country; and it is well to recognize that the responsibility for the scarcity of a currency in the Fund need not be primarily that of the country whose currency becomes scarce. We may presume the Fund will study the problem in all its aspects and will make appropriate recommendations to all interested countries.

There can be no assurance that the action of the Fund under VI-1 will always be adequate to remedy the situation. The recommendations of the Fund should be given the utmost consideration in the formulation of the monetary, economic, and commercial policies of member countries. The Fund's recommendations will have behind them the enormous force of the world's opinion. Within each country there is certain to be developed a growing recognition of the importance of effective cooperation with other countries through the Fund and in other ways. Even though the Fund's recommendations carry with them no element of compulsion, it will be difficult for any country cognizant of its responsibility to disregard them.

It is to be hoped that the Fund will not find it necessary to utilize provision VI-2 on the apportionment of scarce currencies. Ordinarily, the Fund will be able to borrow enough of a scarce currency to meet the needs of member countries during the period in which the recommendations made by the Fund take effect. Nevertheless, it is necessary to establish the basis for the apportionment of a scarce currency if such action should become essential for a limited time.

The fact that a currency has become scarce is evidence of a distortion in the pattern of trade balances that must be corrected through fundamental adjustments. In the meantime action may have to be taken to limit the demand for a scarce currency. The apportionment of a scarce currency by the Fund and its rationing by the monetary authorities of member countries are one means of promptly limiting the demand and even of helping to correct the disturbances in the pattern of trade balances. In time, the measures recommended by the Fund, if adopted by member countries, would probably have the effect of establishing a more balanced international payments position. Until these measures can be made effective, some direct control is necessary in extreme cases.

The apportionment of scarce currencies by the Fund is probably the most certain means of promptly directing excessive demand away from a member country with a large and persistently favorable balance of payments to other member countries with an unfavorable balance of payments. In a sense such action involves a type of direct control and of bilateralism that should be avoided. It is important, therefore, to bear in mind that apportionment of a scarce currency is regarded as a temporary measure of an emergency character. Under the direction of the Fund, this method of adjusting the demand for a scarce currency to the available supply would be free from dangers of discrimination. Ultimately, of course, it is expected that fundamental adjustments will remove the need for apportioning a currency.

QUESTION 32

May a country to whom the Fund has granted an allocation of a scarce currency restrict imports from the country whose currency has become scarce?

Reply

It is intended that when the Fund's holdings of a currency become scarce steps will first be taken to increase the supply of the scarce currency. Under provision VI-1, the Fund is authorized to render a report to the member country embodying an analysis of the causes of the depletion of the Fund's holdings of that currency and making recommendations designed to increase the Fund's holdings of that currency.

The recommendations are likely to be of two types. Some of the recommendations will probably be designed to provide member countries and the Fund with additional amounts of the scarce currency, through encouragement of foreign investment in member countries and through loans or advances to the Fund. Other recommendations will probably be designed to correct the fundamental maladjustment in the balance of payments position of the member countries. It is hoped, of course, that the recommended measures will be effective.

Nevertheless, the Fund must take account of the possibility that whatever measures are taken will not immediately alleviate the scarcity of a currency. Under such circumstances, with a continuing scarcity for a currency, the Fund must adopt measures on its own account to assure the proper use of its limited holdings. Provision VI-2 provides for the apportionment of a scarce currency.

The technical experts of the United States interpret this provision as applying only to the Fund's holdings of a scarce currency. Member countries would be free to use the scarce currency accruing to them directly to meet their own needs, with the qualification, of course, that half of the increases in their accumulated holdings of gold and gold-convertible exchange must be offered for sale to the Fund in accordance with provision III-7. Similarly, member countries could utilize their holdings of gold and foreign exchange to supplement the allocation of a scarce currency made to them by the Fund.

The apportionment of a scarce currency by the Fund would take the form of allotting to member countries an amount of scarce currency (to be paid for with local currency and gold, as provided in III-7), the Fund taking into consideration the special needs and resources of member countries requesting an allotment. The actual distribution of its allotment by any member country among its importers and other users of a scarce currency would be a matter for the member country to decide.

Obviously, with a limited allotment of a scarce currency, some member countries will find it necessary to restrict the demand of their nationals for such a currency. The decision by the Fund to apportion a scarce currency is in effect an authorization to member countries temporarily to restrict the freedom of exchange transactions in the affected currency. Thus, their action would not be inconsistent with provision IX-3 in which they undertake not to impose restrictions on current transactions except with the Fund's consent. In determining the manner of restricting the demand, and in rationing the limited supply among its nationals, it is provided that the member country shall have complete jurisdiction.

Question 33

Will the Fund require all member countries to prohibit or restrict the outflow of capital?

Reply

The purpose of the Fund is to provide, through stability of exchanges and through cooperation in the maintenance of exchanges, the conditions necessary for the restoration and balanced growth of international trade. In accordance with this purpose, it is not intended as a general policy to have the resources of the Fund used to finance substantial outflows of capital from member countries.

The decades of the 20's and the 30's showed that many countries could not withstand the drains on their gold resources resulting from widespread conversion of local currency and flights of capital. Out of this experience has come general recognition that the gold and foreign exchange resources of a country should be reserved primarily for the settlement of international balances on current account. In line with this view, the general policy of the Fund should be to give countries access to the resources of the Fund only when such resources are needed to meet an adverse balance of payments predominantly on current account.

It would be incorrect to assume that most capital exports are prohibited under the Fund's provisions or that the policy of the Fund with respect to capital exports requires the maintenance of exchange controls or exchange restrictions in all or even the majority of cases. A careful examination of the Fund proposal will reveal that most capital exports can probably take place freely, and only in a minority of cases will exchange restrictions have to be imposed. The conditions under which capital exports may take place freely are described in the following paragraph:

1. Capital exports of any type can take place freely from countries with a favorable balance on current account.

It is recognized that there will be many countries in need of foreign capital for reconstruction and development after the war, and that there will be some countries whose international economic position will permit them to export capital. The provision of capital under these conditions can contribute to the balanced growth of international trade. Most of the capital exports of this type are likely to be from countries with a credit balance of payments on current account, and serve to help maintain monetary stability. It is one of the purposes of the Fund to facilitate the resumption of such international lending by restoring confidence in the greater stability of exchange rates, and in the greater freedom from injurious restrictive exchange practices.

The only limit on the free outflow of capital from a country experiencing a favorable balance on current account might be the case where a country has been previously experiencing an unfavorable balance and had sold the Fund more of its currency than the Fund found it desirable to keep. In that event, the Fund might prefer to have the country employ part of its favorable balance of payments to repurchase some of the Fund's holdings for its currency before or *pari passu* with the country's undertaking significant amounts of capital exports. In fact, provision III-7 is intended to do this.

2. Some countries experiencing an *unfavorable* balance of payments on current account could regard with complete equanimity an efflux of capital of any character, because their holdings of gold and foreign exchange are entirely adequate to meet all likely drains. Provision V specifically states that the limitation on capital exports is not intended to prevent capital movements which are made out of a member country's own gold and foreign exchange resources, provided such capital movements are in accordance with the purposes of the Fund. For example, the United States could permit very substantial and continued capital exports for a long time even if its balance of payments turned unfavorable on current account. There are doubtless a number of other countries which could permit capital exports under these circumstances, either because the unfavorable balance of payments on current account is small relative to

their foreign exchange resources, or the volume of capital outflow is small compared to the unfavorable balance or current account.

3. Also, a country having an unfavorable balance of payments on current account could freely permit foreign investments, or capital exports if at the same time it was itself a recipient of capital inflow. It usually happens that a country is at the same time both an importer of capital and an exporter of capital. Sometimes both inflow and outflow of capital may be long-term in character. For example, British firms may be building branch plants in South America or Africa, at the same time that Americans are investing in British securities, newly issued or held by residents of the United Kingdom. In some instances, the capital may be predominantly of short term character and the outflow predominantly long-term in character.

The significant drain of foreign exchange resources on capital account is the drain on *net* capital account, though it is also true that attention must be paid to the predominant character of the inflow or outflow. The movement of what may be classified as short term capital has different significance in different countries and at different periods. Nevertheless, it is not to be assumed that a country with an unfavorable balance of payments on current account could not continue to purchase foreign exchange from the Fund unless it curtailed its capital exports. A country could continue indefinitely having large gross capital flows and small net flows.

4. All countries could permit capital exports such as are reflected, even with a moderate lag, wholly or chiefly in exports of goods or services. It has been a common practice in the past, and there is no reason to expect that it will cease in the future, for some foreign loans to be tied to exports in such a way that the granting of the loan is accompanied sooner or later by a net export of goods and services almost of the same magnitude as the loan. The Joint Statement specifically provides that the Fund's resources may be used for capital transactions of reasonable amount required for expansion of exports or in the ordinary course of trade, banking or other business (V-1).

The mechanism of adjustment of international accounts does not always, or even usually, operate smoothly or rapidly enough to translate a net export of capital to a net flow of goods and services (unless the foreign investment is "tied" to the export of goods). But it would be an error to overlook the fact that the mechanism of adjustment does operate to some extent. The rapidity of operation differs greatly with the countries affected, the period, the magnitudes involved, the make-up of the international accounts, the phase of the business cycle, and other factors.

Countries with limited foreign exchange resources making loans to other countries should be very reluctant to make loans in excess of the amount absolutely needed to finance the additional exports effectuated directly or indirectly through the loan. The borrowing countries should be equally reluctant to burden their balance of payments unnecessarily by borrowing more for a particular project than is required to pay for the imports necessary for that project, making due allowance for secondary effects of the borrowing. Countries with inadequate foreign exchange resources should rarely borrow abroad merely for the purpose of domestic financing.

5. Finally, even where a country has an unfavorable balance of payments and inadequate foreign exchange resources, the Fund would not be disturbed by capital exports from that country if the amount were small or if the Fund did not have large holdings of that country's currency, or if the capital exports were sporadic or of brief duration. Provision V-1 prohibits a member country from using the Fund's resources to meet a large or sustained outflow of capital. It is only when the capital exports are (a) net,

(b) large, (c) sustained, and (d) are motivated chiefly by the desire for speculative profit that the Fund is likely to require a restriction of capital exports as a condition for continued use of the Fund's resources.

The flow of capital from one country to another seeking political and economic security, or speculative profit is frequently undesirable. Such flows are particularly disturbing when they take place from countries with a debit balance of payments to countries with a credit balance of payments on current account. Such flows serve to disturb monetary stability, and it is not the purpose of the Fund to facilitate such capital movements.

Until, however, the Fund considers a continuation of capital exports of that character and under these conditions to be injurious, no restrictive action over capital exports need be taken by the country exporting capital. It is only when the Fund deems it undesirable to continue to sell foreign exchange to the country in question, unless its capital exports are curtailed, that the latter must seek ways of curtailing undesirable forms of capital exports. In some cases, the country may be able to do without the necessity of imposing exchange controls and restrictions. When it cannot do so, then the country will have to restrict the flow of capital through the exercise of carefully imposed exchange controls. The existence of the Fund should make resort to such restrictions less urgent and less frequent.

A proper evaluation of this aspect of the Fund's powers can be made only against alternative courses. It would be quite erroneous to assume that in the absence of the Fund, countries could permit uncontrolled capital outflow of any character at all times. Restriction of capital movements is, of course, not a novel practice. One needs only to recall the history of the last 20 years to make clear that controls over capital movements were adopted in a large number of countries even though no such institution as a Fund existed.

It should be clear that under any circumstances the Fund does not of itself require that any country impose control over capital exports unless and until the member country wishes to purchase excessive amounts of foreign exchange from the Fund and then only if they are regarded as in the general interest of the Fund and its members.

In summary, it is clear that the Fund does not expect a member country to use exchange provided by the Fund exclusively for current account purposes. So long as the exchange purchased from the Fund is used to meet an adverse balance of payments predominantly on current account, the Fund would regard a member country as fulfilling its obligations. No definite proof would be required that the resources of the Fund are being used predominantly for current account. The Fund would expect to utilize reports on the balance of payments and on capital movements. Although such reports would not always be complete and accurate, they should be sufficient to reveal a substantial and continued outflow of capital. Only when the resources of the Fund are used to finance capital movements of this character would the Fund require a member country, as a condition for the sale of additional exchange, to restrict the outflow of capital.

The regulatory devices a member country might use are discussed more fully in the reply to the next question.

QUESTION 34

What provision must be made by countries that are members of the Fund to control capital movements if this should become necessary?

Reply

The Fund proposal provides for the control of capital movements by member countries in two ways.

First, member countries have the right to control capital exports when such control is regarded by them as desirable. This right is subject to the limitation that a member country may not use its control of capital movements to restrict payments for current transactions or to delay the transfer of funds in settlement of commitments (V-2).

Second, under certain conditions, discussed in the reply to the previous question, the Fund itself may require that member countries control capital exports as a condition for further use of the Fund's resources (V-1). It may be presumed that member countries will take the necessary steps, including in some instances supervision of the exchange market, to assure their capacity to fulfill the above obligations. The manner in which member countries organize and control their exchange markets is not prescribed by the Fund. It is a matter for each country to decide. Presumably, organization and control would differ from country to country depending upon the nature of a country's exchange market, the state of its monetary reserves, its balance of payments position, and the position of its currency in the Fund.

In some countries, particularly those not purchasing exchange from the Fund, no elaborate system of government organization and control of the exchange market will be necessary in order to assure fulfillment of their cooperative obligation to members of the Fund.

As a minimum, each country would certainly set up a system for collecting information on its balance of payments position and on capital movements. The receipt of such information would be helpful to the proper functioning of the Fund. Even though it never becomes necessary for a country to prevent a flight of capital, a country may find it helpful to cooperate with other member countries in controlling capital movements. Such cooperative measures might appropriately include a refusal to accept or permit acquisition of deposits, securities, or investments by nationals of any member country imposing restrictions on the export of capital except with the permission of the government of that country and the Fund. Member countries might also undertake to make available to the Fund or to the government of any member country information on property, deposits, securities, and investments of the nationals of that member country.

To supply this current information, most countries will have to have at all times an adequate system of reporting capital movements. This is not to be confused with exchange controls. They are quite different. The United States for many years has had a reporting system for capital movements, but not until the outbreak of the war were any restrictions imposed on the transfer of funds. The only countries that might find it necessary to adopt exchange controls are those whose foreign exchange resources do not permit a free and continued export of capital.

Apart from the arrangements for providing the Fund with data on capital movements, there are no measures that must be taken by member countries in anticipation of a possible need for controlling capital movements. It is a matter for each country to decide whether, while imposing no restrictions on current transactions, it wishes to establish or retain any administrative supervision over foreign exchange transactions. The Fund does not require member countries either to control capital movements or to supervise them, unless and until such member countries make considerable use of the resources of the Fund.

Some countries, foreseeing the need for control of capital movements, might require prior notification on international transactions in order to keep close control of their exchange position by scrutiny of international transactions. Such scrutiny of exchange transactions would not be in conflict with the obligations of the member country under provision IX-3 unless it were used in fact as a device to impose exchange restrictions on current international transactions in the guise of a control of the export of capital. Since the imposition of restrictions on current international transactions would be contrary to the obligations of a member country, it may be presumed that the Fund would make representations to member countries if such scrutiny of exchange transactions were used contrary to the purposes of the Fund (V-2).

Still other countries may find it desirable to set up a licensing system to assure an effective control over capital movements. Thus a country might require that all foreign exchange must be bought and sold through licensed dealers. No exchange need then be sold unless the purchaser showed proof that the foreign exchange was needed for the purchase of goods and services or the payment of interest and dividends or other payments of a non-capital nature; and the delivery of foreign exchange receipts would be required of exporters and other recipients of funds from abroad. Banks and other institutions licensed to engage in foreign exchange operations might not be permitted to increase their foreign exchange holdings or holdings of other foreign assets beyond an amount necessary to carry on their normal business operations. The government might require that any additional amounts of foreign exchange acquired by banks and by other licensed dealers be sold to the central bank or the exchange authority.

Presumably in some countries effective control could be assured only through an official monopoly of exchange transactions. There is no provision in the Fund proposal that would bar a country from instituting a monopoly of exchange transactions, provided that such techniques are not administered to restrict current international transactions without the consent of the Fund. It is not with administrative techniques but with policies that the Fund is primarily concerned.

It is not contemplated that control of international capital transactions or of exchange transactions generally will be exercised directly by the Fund. On the contrary, it is expected that in many countries the usual channels for buying and selling exchange will continue to be utilized. Within the provisions set forth in the proposal, the Fund will sell to member governments such foreign exchange as they may require to meet an adverse balance of payments predominantly on current account. The manner of channeling into the exchange market the foreign exchange sold by the Fund is a matter for each member country to decide. While in the ordinary course of events the Fund would not scrutinize exchange transactions, it may be expected that the Fund may require assurances in some instances that the exchange sold by the Fund is in fact intended to meet an adverse balance of payments predominantly on current account and not to meet a large or sustained outflow of capital. In the main, however, the Fund's decision would be based on information revealed by the balance of payments of the country in question rather than by supervision over its foreign exchange transactions.

Our conclusions with respect to the control of capital movements may be summarized as follows:

1. All countries should have machinery for adequate reporting of capital movements by type and totals with geographical breakdowns.

2. A number of countries will find it necessary from time to time to maintain some form of supervision over foreign exchange transactions.

3. Some of these countries will have to impose restrictions at one time or another on the outward movement of certain types of capital.

4. The Fund itself will never exercise authority as an agency controlling exchange transactions in any member country.

QUESTION 35

What are the purposes of the provisions requiring more than a majority vote to authorize action by the Fund?

REPLY

There are only two provisions in the Joint Statement requiring more than a majority to authorize action by the Fund. In these cases, the requirement is for the purpose of safeguarding the resources of the Fund or safeguarding the interests of member countries on matters affecting their national policies.

The ordinary business of the Fund would be undertaken by the management in accordance with the provisions of the Fund and the regulations prescribed by the Board of Directors. For the most important operations of the Fund, no positive action by the Board is needed at all.

In those instances where approval of the Board is needed all ordinary operations of the Fund require only a simple majority vote. The following important operations are included in this category:

1. To permit the sale of exchange to a member country in excess of the limitations prescribed in III-2-c and determine the conditions for such sale.
2. To permit and determine the conditions for the sale of additional exchange where a country is purchasing exchange at an annual rate in excess of 25 percent of its quota (III-2).
3. To report to a member country whose currency in the Fund is becoming scarce (VI-1).
4. To allocate among member countries available amounts of a scarce currency (VI-2).
5. To propose to a member country that it lend its currency to the Fund (III-4).
6. To approve of any multiple currency arrangements and similar practices engaged in by a member country (IX-3).
7. To suspend a country from making further use of the Fund's resources on the ground that it is using them in a manner contrary to the purposes and policies of the Fund (III-2-d).
8. To approve the initial par value of a member's currency fixed by that member (IV-1).
9. To grant a request by a member country for a change in the par value of its currency in accordance with provisions IV-3 and IV-4.

It would appear from the above that the Fund can unquestionably engage in all transactions necessary for the ordinary conduct of its business without prior approval or with the approval of only a majority of the member votes.

There are two matters of an extraordinary character involving the safeguarding of the resources of the Fund and of member countries and matters of the highest policy which are reserved for decision by a larger than majority vote of the Board:

1. According to the present provisions of the Joint Statement changes in the quotas require a four-fifths vote. It is the recommendation of the United States technical experts that this provision be changed to read that changes in the quota formula require a four-fifths vote (see question 8). The purpose of this requirement is to assure member countries that having joined the Fund with assurance of their relative position within the Fund, they will not be confronted with a change in the quota formula which will seriously affect their status. This is the more important because many countries will subscribe large resources to the Fund the use of which will depend in part upon the relative position of countries within the Fund.

2. A uniform change in the gold value of the member currencies can be made only by a majority including the approval of every member country having 10 percent or more of the votes. Because a uniform change in the price of gold can have far-reaching effects, it is thought essential to require the unanimous approval of the countries with the largest gold holdings and the greatest production of gold for such action.

It will be observed that the two actions of the Fund requiring more than a majority vote would only be necessary as a result of special circumstances and can in no way be considered as a part of the ordinary operations of the Fund. It is felt that on policy questions of such far-reaching importance, a safeguard against hasty and unwarranted action is needed in the form of a favorable vote larger than a majority.

PART II

Basic Documents

Articles of Agreement

The Final Act of the United Nations Monetary and Financial Conference held at Bretton Woods from July 1 to July 22, 1944 included, inter alia, the Articles of Agreement of the International Monetary Fund. These are reproduced below. For convenience, the list of Articles and Sections printed at the end of the Articles in the Final Act has here been transferred to the beginning as a Table of Contents.

Articles of Agreement of the International Monetary Fund
(July 22, 1944)

TABLE OF CONTENTS

	PAGE
Introductory Article	187
I. Purposes	187
II. Membership	188
1. Original members	188
2. Other members	188
III. Quotas and Subscriptions	188
1. Quotas	188
2. Adjustment of quotas	188
3. Subscriptions: time, place, and form of payment	188
4. Payments when quotas are changed	189
5. Substitution of securities for currency	189
IV. Par Values of Currencies	189
1. Expression of par values	189
2. Gold purchases based on par values	189
3. Foreign exchange dealings based on parity	189
4. Obligations regarding exchange stability	190
5. Changes in par values	190
6. Effect of unauthorized changes	190
7. Uniform changes in par values	190
8. Maintenance of gold value of the Fund's assets	191
9. Separate currencies within a member's territories	191
V. Transactions with the Fund	191
1. Agencies dealing with the Fund	191
2. Limitation on the Fund's operations	191
3. Conditions governing use of the Fund's resources	191
4. Waiver of conditions	192
5. Ineligibility to use the Fund's resources	192

	PAGE
6. Purchases of currencies from the Fund for gold	192
7. Repurchase by a member of its currency held by the Fund	192
8. Charges	193

VI. Capital Transfers 193
    1. Use of the Fund's resources for capital transfers 193
    2. Special provisions for capital transfers 194
    3. Controls of capital transfers 194

VII. Scarce Currencies 194
    1. General scarcity of currency 194
    2. Measures to replenish the Fund's holdings of scarce currencies 194
    3. Scarcity of the Fund's holdings 195
    4. Administration of restrictions 195
    5. Effect of other international agreements on restrictions 195

VIII. General Obligations of Members 195
    1. Introduction 195
    2. Avoidance of restrictions on current payments 195
    3. Avoidance of discriminatory currency practices 195
    4. Convertibility of foreign-held balances 196
    5. Furnishing of information 196
    6. Consultation between members regarding existing international agreements 197

IX. Status, Immunities, and Privileges 197
    1. Purposes of Article 197
    2. Status of the Fund 197
    3. Immunity from judicial process 197
    4. Immunity from other action 197
    5. Immunity of archives 197
    6. Freedom of assets from restrictions 197
    7. Privilege for communications 197
    8. Immunities and privileges of officers and employees 197
    9. Immunities from taxation 198
   10. Application of Article 198

X. Relations with Other International Organizations 198

XI. Relations with Non-member Countries 198
    1. Undertakings regarding relations with non-member countries 198
    2. Restrictions on transactions with non-member countries 199

XII. Organization and Management 199
    1. Structure of the Fund 199
    2. Board of Governors 199
    3. Executive Directors 200
    4. Managing Director and staff 201
    5. Voting 201
    6. Distribution of net income 202
    7. Publication of reports 202
    8. Communication of views to members 202

XIII. Offices and Depositories 202
    1. Location of offices 202
    2. Depositories 202
    3. Guarantee of the Fund's assets 202

		PAGE
XIV.	Transitional Period	203
	1. Introduction	203
	2. Exchange restrictions	203
	3. Notification to the Fund	203
	4. Action of the Fund relating to restrictions	203
	5. Nature of transitional period	203
XV.	Withdrawal from Membership	203
	1. Right of members to withdraw	203
	2. Compulsory withdrawal	203
	3. Settlement of accounts with members withdrawing	204
XVI.	Emergency Provisions	204
	1. Temporary suspension	204
	2. Liquidation of the Fund	204
XVII.	Amendments	205
XVIII.	Interpretation	205
XIX.	Explanation of Terms	205
XX.	Final Provisions	207
	1. Entry into force	207
	2. Signature	207
	3. Inauguration of the Fund	208
	4. Initial determination of par values	208

SCHEDULES

A.	Quotas	210
B.	Provisions with Respect to Repurchase by a Member of its Currency Held by the Fund	210
C.	Election of Executive Directors	211
D.	Settlement of Accounts with Members Withdrawing	212
E.	Administration of Liquidation	213

The Governments on whose behalf the present Agreement is signed agree as follows:

INTRODUCTORY ARTICLE

The International Monetary Fund is established and shall operate in accordance with the following provisions:

ARTICLE I. PURPOSES

The purposes of the International Monetary Fund are:

(i) To promote international monetary cooperation through a permanent institution which provides the machinery for consultation and collaboration on international monetary problems.

(ii) To facilitate the expansion and balanced growth of international trade, and to contribute thereby to the promotion and maintenance of high levels of employment and real income and to the development of the productive resources of all members as primary objectives of economic policy.

(iii) To promote exchange stability, to maintain orderly exchange arrangements among members, and to avoid competitive exchange depreciation.

(iv) To assist in the establishment of a multilateral system of payments in respect of current transactions between members and in the elimination of foreign exchange restrictions which hamper the growth of world trade.

(v) To give confidence to members by making the Fund's resources available to them under adequate safeguards, thus providing them with opportunity to correct maladjustments in their balance of payments without resorting to measures destructive of national or international prosperity.

(vi) In accordance with the above, to shorten the duration and lessen the degree of disequilibrium in the international balances of payments of members.

The Fund shall be guided in all its decisions by the purposes set forth in this Article.

ARTICLE II. MEMBERSHIP

SECTION 1. *Original members.*—The original members of the Fund shall be those of the countries represented at the United Nations Monetary and Financial Conference whose governments accept membership before the date specified in Article XX, Section 2 (*e*).

SEC. 2. *Other members.*—Membership shall be open to the governments of other countries at such times and in accordance with such terms as may be prescribed by the Fund.

ARTICLE III. QUOTAS AND SUBSCRIPTIONS

SECTION 1. *Quotas.*—Each member shall be assigned a quota. The quotas of the members represented at the United Nations Monetary and Financial Conference which accept membership before the date specified in Article XX, Section 2 (*e*), shall be those set forth in Schedule A. The quotas of other members shall be determined by the Fund.

SEC. 2. *Adjustment of quotas.*—The Fund shall at intervals of five years review, and if it deems it appropriate propose an adjustment of, the quotas of the members. It may also, if it thinks fit, consider at any other time the adjustment of any particular quota at the request of the member concerned. A four-fifths majority of the total voting power shall be required for any change in quotas and no quota shall be changed without the consent of the member concerned.

SEC. 3. *Subscriptions: time, place, and form of payment.*—(*a*) The subscription of each member shall be equal to its quota and shall be paid in full to the Fund at the appropriate depository on or before the date when the member becomes eligible under Article XX, Section 4 (*c*) or (*d*), to buy currencies from the Fund.

(*b*) Each member shall pay in gold, as a minimum, the smaller of

(i) twenty-five percent of its quota; or

(ii) ten percent of its net official holdings of gold and United States dollars as at the date when the Fund notifies members under Article XX, Section 4 (*a*) that it will shortly be in a position to begin exchange transactions.

Each member shall furnish to the Fund the data necessary to determine its net official holdings of gold and United States dollars.

(c) Each member shall pay the balance of its quota in its own currency.

(d) If the net official holdings of gold and United States dollars of any member as at the date referred to in (b) (ii) above are not ascertainable because its territories have been occupied by the enemy, the Fund shall fix an appropriate alternative date for determining such holdings. If such date is later than that on which the country becomes eligible under Article XX, Section 4 (c) or (d), to buy currencies from the Fund, the Fund and the member shall agree on a provisional gold payment to be made under (b) above, and the balance of the member's subscription shall be paid in the member's currency, subject to appropriate adjustment between the member and the Fund when the net official holdings have been ascertained.

SEC. 4. *Payments when quotas are changed.*—(a) Each member which consents to an increase in its quota shall, within thirty days after the date of its consent, pay to the Fund twenty-five percent of the increase in gold and the balance in its own currency. If, however, on the date when the member consents to an increase, its monetary reserves are less than its new quota, the Fund may reduce the proportion of the increase to be paid in gold.

(b) If a member consents to a reduction in its quota, the Fund shall, within thirty days after the date of the consent, pay to the member an amount equal to the reduction. The payment shall be made in the member's currency and in such amount of gold as may be necessary to prevent reducing the Fund's holdings of the currency below seventy-five percent of the new quota.

SEC. 5. *Substitution of securities for currency.*—The Fund shall accept from any member in place of any part of the member's currency which in the judgment of the Fund is not needed for its operations, notes or similar obligations issued by the member or the depository designated by the member under Article XIII, Section 2, which shall be non-negotiable, non-interest bearing and payable at their par value on demand by crediting the account of the Fund in the designated depository. This Section shall apply not only to currency subscribed by members but also to any currency otherwise due to, or acquired by, the Fund.

ARTICLE IV. PAR VALUES OF CURRENCIES

SECTION 1. *Expression of par values.*—(a) The par value of the currency of each member shall be expressed in terms of gold as a common denominator or in terms of the United States dollar of the weight and fineness in effect on July 1, 1944.

(b) All computations relating to currencies of members for the purpose of applying the provisions of this Agreement shall be on the basis of their par values.

SEC. 2. *Gold purchases based on par values.*—The Fund shall prescribe a margin above and below par value for transactions in gold by members, and no member shall buy gold at a price above par value plus the prescribed margin, or sell gold at a price below par value minus the prescribed margin.

SEC. 3. *Foreign exchange dealings based on parity.*—The maximum and the minimum rates for exchange transactions between the currencies of members taking place within their territories shall not differ from parity

(i) in the case of spot exchange transactions, by more than one percent; and

(ii) in the case of other exchange transactions, by a margin which exceeds the margin for spot exchange transactions by more than the Fund considers reasonable.

SEC. 4. *Obligations regarding exchange stability.*—(a) Each member undertakes to collaborate with the Fund to promote exchange stability, to maintain orderly exchange arrangements with other members, and to avoid competitive exchange alterations.

(b) Each member undertakes, through appropriate measures consistent with this Agreement, to permit within its territories exchange transactions between its currency and the currencies of other members only within the limits prescribed under Section 3 of this Article. A member whose monetary authorities, for the settlement of international transactions, in fact freely buy and sell gold within the limits prescribed by the Fund under Section 2 of this Article shall be deemed to be fulfilling this undertaking.

SEC. 5. *Changes in par values.*—(a) A member shall not propose a change in the par value of its currency except to correct a fundamental disequilibrium.

(b) A change in the par value of a member's currency may be made only on the proposal of the member and only after consultation with the Fund.

(c) When a change is proposed, the Fund shall first take into account the changes, if any, which have already taken place in the initial par value of the member's currency as determined under Article XX, Section 4. If the proposed change, together with all previous changes, whether increases or decreases,

(i) does not exceed ten percent of the initial par value, the Fund shall raise no objection;

(ii) does not exceed a further ten percent of the initial par value, the Fund may either concur or object, but shall declare its attitude within seventy-two hours if the member so requests;

(iii) is not within (i) or (ii) above, the Fund may either concur or object, but shall be entitled to a longer period in which to declare its attitude.

(d) Uniform changes in par values made under Section 7 of this Article shall not be taken into account in determining whether a proposed change falls within (i), (ii), or (iii) of (c) above.

(e) A member may change the par value of its currency without the concurrence of the Fund if the change does not affect the international transactions of members of the Fund.

(f) The Fund shall concur in a proposed change which is within the terms of (c) (ii) or (c) (iii) above if it is satisfied that the change is necessary to correct a fundamental disequilibrium. In particular, provided it is so satisfied, it shall not object to a proposed change because of the domestic social or political policies of the member proposing the change.

SEC. 6. *Effect of unauthorized changes.*—If a member changes the par value of its currency despite the objection of the Fund, in cases where the Fund is entitled to object, the member shall be ineligible to use the resources of the Fund unless the Fund otherwise determines; and if, after the expiration of a reasonable period, the difference between the member and the Fund continues, the matter shall be subject to the provisions of Article XV, Section 2 (b).

SEC. 7. *Uniform changes in par values.*—Notwithstanding the provisions of Section 5 (b) of this Article, the Fund by a majority of the total voting power may make uniform proportionate changes in the par values of the currencies of all members, provided each such change is approved by every member which has ten percent or more of the total of the quotas. The par value of a member's currency shall, however, not be changed under this provision if, within seventy-two hours of the Fund's action, the member informs the Fund that it does not wish the par value of its currency to be changed by such action.

Sec. 8. *Maintenance of gold value of the Fund's assets.*

(a) The gold value of the Fund's assets shall be maintained notwithstanding changes in the par or foreign exchange value of the currency of any member.

(b) Whenever (i) the par value of a member's currency is reduced, or (ii) the foreign exchange value of a member's currency has, in the opinion of the Fund, depreciated to a significant extent within that member's territories, the member shall pay to the Fund within a reasonable time an amount of its own currency equal to the reduction in the gold value of its currency held by the Fund.

(c) Whenever the par value of a member's currency is increased, the Fund shall return to such member within a reasonable time an amount in its currency equal to the increase in the gold value of its currency held by the Fund.

(d) The provisions of this Section shall apply to a uniform proportionate change in the par values of the currencies of all members, unless at the time when such a change is proposed the Fund decides otherwise.

Sec. 9. *Separate currencies within a member's territories.*—A member proposing a change in the par value of its currency shall be deemed, unless it declares otherwise, to be proposing a corresponding change in the par value of the separate currencies of all territories in respect of which it has accepted this Agreement under Article XX, Section 2 (g). It shall, however, be open to a member to declare that its proposal relates either to the metropolitan currency alone, or only to one or more specified separate currencies, or to the metropolitan currency and one or more specified separate currencies.

ARTICLE V. TRANSACTIONS WITH THE FUND

Section 1. *Agencies dealing with the Fund.*—Each member shall deal with the Fund only through its Treasury, central bank, stabilization fund, or other similar fiscal agency and the Fund shall deal only with or through the same agencies.

Sec. 2. *Limitation on the Fund's operations.*—Except as otherwise provided in this Agreement, operations on the account of the Fund shall be limited to transactions for the purpose of supplying a member, on the initiative of such member, with the currency of another member in exchange for gold or for the currency of the member desiring to make the purchase.

Sec. 3. *Conditions governing use of the Fund's resources.*—(a) A member shall be entitled to buy the currency of another member from the Fund in exchange for its own currency subject to the following conditions:

(i) The member desiring to purchase the currency represents that it is presently needed for making in that currency payments which are consistent with the provisions of this Agreement;

(ii) The Fund has not given notice under Article VII, Section 3, that its holdings of the currency desired have become scarce;

(iii) The proposed purchase would not cause the Fund's holdings of the purchasing member's currency to increase by more than twenty-five percent of its quota during the period of twelve months ending on the date of the purchase nor to exceed two hundred percent of its quota, but the twenty-five percent limitation shall apply only to the extent that the Fund's holdings of the member's currency have been brought above seventy-five percent of its quota if they had been below that amount;

(iv) The Fund has not previously declared under Section 5 of this Article, Article IV, Section 6, Article VI, Section 1, or Article XV, Section 2 (a), that the member desiring to purchase is ineligible to use the resources of the Fund.

(b) A member shall not be entitled without the permission of the Fund to use the Fund's resources to acquire currency to hold against forward exchange transactions.

SEC. 4. *Waiver of conditions.*—The Fund may in its discretion, and on terms which safeguard its interests, waive any of the conditions prescribed in Section 3 (a) of this Article, especially in the case of members with a record of avoiding large or continuous use of the Fund's resources. In making a waiver it shall take into consideration periodic or exceptional requirements of the member requesting the waiver. The Fund shall also take into consideration a member's willingness to pledge as collateral security gold, silver, securities, or other acceptable assets having a value sufficient in the opinion of the Fund to protect its interests and may require as a condition of waiver the pledge of such collateral security.

SEC. 5. *Ineligibility to use the Fund's resources.*—Whenever the Fund is of the opinion that any member is using the resources of the Fund in a manner contrary to the purposes of the Fund, it shall present to the member a report setting forth the views of the Fund and prescribing a suitable time for reply. After presenting such a report to a member, the Fund may limit the use of its resources by the member. If no reply to the report is received from the member within the prescribed time, or if the reply received is unsatisfactory, the Fund may continue to limit the member's use of the Fund's resources or may, after giving reasonable notice to the member, declare it ineligible to use the resources of the Fund.

SEC. 6. *Purchases of currencies from the Fund for gold.*—(a) Any member desiring to obtain, directly or indirectly, the currency of another member for gold shall, provided that it can do so with equal advantage, acquire it by the sale of gold to the Fund.

(b) Nothing in this Section shall be deemed to preclude any member from selling in any market gold newly produced from mines located within its territories.

SEC. 7. *Repurchase by a member of its currency held by the Fund.*—(a) A member may repurchase from the Fund and the Fund shall sell for gold any part of the Fund's holdings of its currency in excess of its quota.

(b) At the end of each financial year of the Fund, a member shall repurchase from the Fund with gold or convertible currencies, as determined in accordance with Schedule B, part of the Fund's holdings of its currency under the following conditions:

(i) Each member shall use in repurchases of its own currency from the Fund an amount of its monetary reserves equal in value to one-half of any increase that has occurred during the year in the Fund's holdings of its currency plus one-half of any increase, or minus one-half of any decrease, that has occurred during the year in the member's monetary reserves. This rule shall not apply when a member's monetary reserves have decreased during the year by more than the Fund's holdings of its currency have increased.

(ii) If after the repurchase described in (i) above (if required) has been made, a member's holdings of another member's currency (or of gold acquired from that member) are found to have increased by reason of transactions in terms of that currency with other members or persons in their territories, the member whose holdings of such currency (or gold) have thus increased shall use the increase to repurchase its own currency from the Fund.

(c) None of the adjustments described in (b) above shall be carried to a point at which

(i) the member's monetary reserves are below its quota, or
(ii) the Fund's holdings of its currency are below seventy-five percent of its quota, or
(iii) the Fund's holdings of any currency required to be used are above seventy-five percent of the quota of the member concerned.

SEC. 8. *Charges.*—(a) Any member buying the currency of another member from the Fund in exchange for its own currency shall pay a service charge uniform for all members of three-fourths percent in addition to the parity price. The Fund in its discretion may increase this service charge to not more than one percent or reduce it to not less than one-half percent.

(b) The Fund may levy a reasonable handling charge on any member buying gold from the Fund or selling gold to the Fund.

(c) The Fund shall levy charges uniform for all members which shall be payable by any member on the average daily balances of its currency held by the Fund in excess of its quota. These charges shall be at the following rates:

(i) *On amounts not more than twenty-five percent in excess of the quota:* no charge for the first three months; one-half percent per annum for the next nine months; and thereafter an increase in the charge of one-half percent for each subsequent year.
(ii) *On amounts more than twenty-five percent and not more than fifty percent in excess of the quota:* an additional one-half percent for the first year; and an additional one-half percent for each subsequent year.
(iii) *On each additional bracket of twenty-five percent in excess of the quota:* an additional one-half percent for the first year; and an additional one-half percent for each subsequent year.

(d) Whenever the Fund's holdings of a member's currency are such that the charge applicable to any bracket for any period has reached the rate of four percent per annum, the Fund and the member shall consider means by which the Fund's holdings of the currency can be reduced. Thereafter, the charges shall rise in accordance with the provisions of (c) above until they reach five percent and failing agreement, the Fund may then impose such charges as it deems appropriate.

(e) The rates referred to in (c) and (d) above may be changed by a three-fourths majority of the total voting power.

(f) All charges shall be paid in gold. If, however, the member's monetary reserves are less than one-half of its quota, it shall pay in gold only that proportion of the charges due which such reserves bear to one-half of its quota, and shall pay the balance in its own currency.

ARTICLE VI. CAPITAL TRANSFERS

SECTION 1. *Use of the Fund's resources for capital transfers.*—(a) A member may not make net use of the Fund's resources to meet a large or sustained outflow of capital, and the Fund may request a member to exercise controls to prevent such use of the resources of the Fund. If, after receiving such a request, a member fails to exercise appropriate controls, the Fund may declare the member ineligible to use the resources of the Fund.

(b) Nothing in this Section shall be deemed

(i) to prevent the use of the resources of the Fund for capital transactions of reasonable amount required for the expansion of exports or in the ordinary course of trade, banking or other business, or

(ii) to affect capital movements which are met out of a member's own resources of gold and foreign exchange, but members undertake that such capital movements will be in accordance with the purposes of the Fund.

SEC. 2. *Special provisions for capital transfers.*—If the Fund's holdings of the currency of a member have remained below seventy-five percent of its quota for an immediately preceding period of not less than six months, such member, if it has not been declared ineligible to use the resources of the Fund under Section 1 of this Article, Article IV, Section 6, Article V, Section 5, or Article XV, Section 2 (a), shall be entitled, notwithstanding the provisions of Section 1 (a) of this Article, to buy the currency of another member from the Fund with its own currency for any purpose, including capital transfers. Purchases for capital transfers under this Section shall not, however, be permitted if they have the effect of raising the Fund's holdings of the currency of the member desiring to purchase above seventy-five percent of its quota, or of reducing the Fund's holdings of the currency desired below seventy-five percent of the quota of the member whose currency is desired.

SEC. 3. *Controls of capital transfers.*—Members may exercise such controls as are necessary to regulate international capital movements, but no member may exercise these controls in a manner which will restrict payments for current transactions or which will unduly delay transfers of funds in settlement of commitments, except as provided in Article VII, Section 3 (b), and in Article XIV, Section 2.

ARTICLE VII. SCARCE CURRENCIES

SECTION 1. *General scarcity of currency.*—If the Fund finds that a general scarcity of a particular currency is developing, the Fund may so inform members and may issue a report setting forth the causes of the scarcity and containing recommendations designed to bring it to an end. A representative of the member whose currency is involved shall participate in the preparation of the report.

SEC. 2. *Measures to replenish the Fund's holdings of scarce currencies.*—The Fund may, if it deems such action appropriate to replenish its holdings of any member's currency, take either or both of the following steps:

(i) Propose to the member that, on terms and conditions agreed between the Fund and the member, the latter lend its currency to the Fund or that, with the approval of the member, the Fund borrow such currency from some other source either within or outside the territories of the member, but no member shall be under any obligation to make such loans to the Fund or to approve the borrowing of its currency by the Fund from any other source.

(ii) Require the member to sell its currency to the Fund for gold.

Sec. 3. *Scarcity of the Fund's holdings.*—(*a*) If it becomes evident to the Fund that the demand for a member's currency seriously threatens the Fund's ability to supply that currency, the Fund, whether or not it has issued a report under Section 1 of this Article, shall formally declare such currency scarce and shall thenceforth apportion its existing and accruing supply of the scarce currency with due regard to the relative needs of members, the general international economic situation, and any other pertinent considerations. The Fund shall also issue a report concerning its action.

(*b*) A formal declaration under (*a*) above shall operate as an authorization to any member, after consultation with the Fund, temporarily to impose limitations on the freedom of exchange operations in the scarce currency. Subject to the provisions of Article IV, Sections 3 and 4, the member shall have complete jurisdiction in determining the nature of such limitations, but they shall be no more restrictive than is necessary to limit the demand for the scarce currency to the supply held by, or accruing to, the member in question; and they shall be relaxed and removed as rapidly as conditions permit.

(*c*) The authorization under (*b*) above shall expire whenever the Fund formally declares the currency in question to be no longer scarce.

Sec. 4. *Administration of restrictions.*—Any member imposing restrictions in respect of the currency of any other member pursuant to the provisions of Section 3 (*b*) of this Article shall give sympathetic consideration to any representations by the other member regarding the administration of such restrictions.

Sec. 5. *Effect of other international agreements on restrictions.*—Members agree not to invoke the obligations of any engagements entered into with other members prior to this Agreement in such a manner as will prevent the operation of the provisions of this Article.

ARTICLE VIII. GENERAL OBLIGATIONS OF MEMBERS

Section 1. *Introduction.*—In addition to the obligations assumed under other articles of this Agreement, each member undertakes the obligations set out in this Article.

Sec. 2. *Avoidance of restrictions on current payments.*—(*a*) Subject to the provisions of Article VII, Section 3 (*b*), and Article XIV, Section 2, no member shall, without the approval of the Fund, impose restrictions on the making of payments and transfers for current international transactions.

(*b*) Exchange contracts which involve the currency of any member and which are contrary to the exchange control regulations of that member maintained or imposed consistently with this Agreement shall be unenforceable in the territories of any member. In addition, members may, by mutual accord, co-operate in measures for the purpose of making the exchange control regulations of either member more effective, provided that such measures and regulations are consistent with this Agreement.

Sec. 3. *Avoidance of discriminatory currency practices.*—No member shall engage in, or permit any of its fiscal agencies referred to in Article V, Section 1, to engage in, any discriminatory currency arrangements or multiple currency practices except as authorized under this Agreement or approved by the Fund. If such arrangements and practices are enagaged in at the date when this Agreement enters into force the member concerned shall consult with the Fund as to their progressive removal unless they are maintained or imposed under Article XIV, Section 2, in which case the provisions of Section 4 of that Article shall apply

SEC. 4. *Convertibility of foreign held balances.*—(a) Each member shall buy balances of its currency held by another member if the latter, in requesting the purchase, represents

(i) that the balances to be bought have been recently acquired as a result of current transactions; or

(ii) that their conversion is needed for making payments for current transactions.

The buying member shall have the option to pay either in the currency of the member making the request or in gold.

(b) The obligation in (a) above shall not apply

(i) when the convertibility of the balances has been restricted consistently with Section 2 of this Article, or Article VI, Section 3; or

(ii) when the balances have accumulated as a result of transactions effected before the removal by a member of restrictions maintained or imposed under Article XIV, Section 2; or

(iii) when the balances have been acquired contrary to the exchange regulations of the member which is asked to buy them; or

(iv) when the currency of the member requesting the purchase has been declared scarce under Article VII, Section 3 (a); or

(v) when the member requested to make the purchase is for any reason not entitled to buy currencies of other members from the Fund for its own currency.

SEC. 5. *Furnishing of information.*—(a) The Fund may require members to furnish it with such information as it deems necessary for its operations, including, as the minimum necessary for the effective discharge of the Fund's duties, national data on the following matters:

(i) Official holdings at home and abroad, of (1) gold, (2) foreign exchange.

(ii) Holdings at home and abroad by banking and financial agencies, other than official agencies, of (1) gold, (2) foreign exchange.

(iii) Production of gold.

(iv) Gold exports and imports according to countries of destination and origin.

(v) Total exports and imports of merchandise, in terms of local currency values, according to countries of destination and origin.

(vi) International balance of payments, including (1) trade in goods and services, (2) gold transactions, (3) known capital transactions, and (4) other items.

(vii) International investment position, *i. e.*, investments within the territories of the member owned abroad and investments abroad owned by persons in its territories so far as it is possible to furnish this information.

(viii) National income.

(ix) Price indices, *i. e.*, indices of commodity prices in wholesale and retail markets and of export and import prices.

(x) Buying and selling rates for foreign currencies.

(xi) Exchange controls, *i. e.*, a comprehensive statement of exchange controls in effect at the time of assuming membership in the Fund and details of subsequent changes as they occur.

(xii) Where official clearing arrangements exist, details of amounts awaiting clearance in respect of commercial and financial transactions, and of the length of time during which such arrears have been outstanding.

(b) In requesting information the Fund shall take into consideration the varying ability of members to furnish the data requested. Members shall be under no obligation to furnish information in such detail that the affairs of individuals or corporations are disclosed. Members undertake, however, to furnish the desired information in as detailed and accurate a manner as is practicable, and, so far as possible, to avoid mere estimates.

(c) The Fund may arrange to obtain further information by agreement with members. It shall act as a centre for the collection and exchange of information on monetary and financial problems, thus facilitating the preparation of studies designed to assist members in developing policies which further the purposes of the Fund.

Sec. 6. *Consultation between members regarding existing international agreements.*— Where under this Agreement a member is authorized in the special or temporary circumstances specified in the Agreement to maintain or establish restrictions on exchange transactions, and there are other engagements between members entered into prior to this Agreement which conflict with the application of such restrictions, the parties to such engagements will consult with one another with a view to making such mutually acceptable adjustments as may be necessary. The provisions of this Article shall be without prejudice to the operation of Article VII, Section 5.

ARTICLE IX. STATUS, IMMUNITIES AND PRIVILEGES

Section 1. *Purposes of Article.*—To enable the Fund to fulfill the functions with which it is entrusted, the status, immunities and privileges set forth in this Article shall be accorded to the Fund in the territories of each member.

Sec. 2. *Status of the Fund.*—The Fund shall possess full juridical personality, and in particular, the capacity

(i) to contract;

(ii) to acquire and dispose of immovable and movable property;

(iii) to institute legal proceedings.

Sec. 3. *Immunity from judicial process.*—The Fund, its property and its assets, wherever located and by whomsoever held, shall enjoy immunity from every form of judicial process except to the extent that it expressly waives its immunity for the purpose of any proceedings or by the terms of any contract.

Sec. 4. *Immunity from other action.*—Property and assets of the Fund, wherever located and by whomsoever held, shall be immune from search, requisition, confiscation, expropriation or any other form of seizure by executive or legislative action.

Sec. 5. *Immunity of archives.*—The archives of the Fund shall be inviolable.

Sec. 6. *Freedom of assets from restrictions.*—To the extent necessary to carry out the operations provided for in this Agreement, all property and assets of the Fund shall be free from restrictions, regulations, controls and moratoria of any nature.

Sec. 7. *Privilege for communications.*—The official communications of the Fund shall be accorded by members the same treatment as the official communications of other members.

Sec. 8. *Immunities and privileges of officers and employees.*—All governors, executive directors, alternates, officers and employees of the Fund

(i) shall be immune from legal process with respect to acts performed by them in their official capacity except when the Fund waives this immunity;

(ii) not being local nationals, shall be granted the same immunities from immigration restrictions, alien registration requirements and national service obligations and the same facilities as regards exchange restrictions as are accorded by members to the representatives, officials, and employees of comparable rank of other members;

(iii) shall be granted the same treatment in respect of traveling facilities as is accorded by members to representatives, officials and employees of comparable rank of other members.

Sec. 9. *Immunities from taxation.*—(a) The Fund, its assets, property, income and its operations and transactions authorized by this Agreement, shall be immune from all taxation and from all customs duties. The Fund shall also be immune from liability for the collection or payment of any tax or duty.

(b) No tax shall be levied on or in respect of salaries and emoluments paid by the Fund to executive directors, alternates, officers or employees of the Fund who are not local citizens, local subjects, or other local nationals.

(c) No taxation of any kind shall be levied on any obligation or security issued by the Fund, including any dividend or interest thereon, by whomsoever held

(i) which discriminates against such obligation or security solely because of its origin; or

(ii) if the sole jurisdictional basis for such taxation is the place or currency in which it is issued, made payable or paid, or the location of any office or place of business maintained by the Fund.

Sec. 10. *Application of Article.*—Each member shall take such action as is necessary in its own territories for the purpose of making effective in terms of its own law the principles set forth in this Article and shall inform the Fund of the detailed action which it has taken.

ARTICLE X. RELATIONS WITH OTHER INTERNATIONAL ORGANIZATIONS

The Fund shall cooperate within the terms of this Agreement with any general international organization and with public international organizations having specialized responsibilities in related fields. Any arrangements for such cooperation which would involve a modification of any provision of this Agreement may be effected only after amendment to this Agreement under Article XVII.

ARTICLE XI. RELATIONS WITH NON-MEMBER COUNTRIES

Section 1. *Undertakings regarding relations with non-member countries.*—Each member undertakes:

(i) Not to engage in, nor to permit any of its fiscal agencies referred to in Article V, Section 1, to engage in, any transactions with a non-member or with persons in a non-member's territories which would be contrary to the provisions of this Agreement or the purposes of the Fund;

(ii) Not to cooperate with a non-member or with persons in a non-member's territories in practices which would be contrary to the provisions of this Agreement or the purposes of the Fund; and

(iii) To cooperate with the Fund with a view to the application in its territories of appropriate measures to prevent transactions with non-members or with persons in their territories which would be contrary to the provisions of this Agreement or the purposes of the Fund.

SEC. 2. *Restrictions on transactions with non-member countries.*—Nothing in this Agreement shall affect the right of any member to impose restrictions on exchange transactions with non-members or with persons in their territories unless the Fund finds that such restrictions prejudice the interests of members and are contrary to the purposes of the Fund.

ARTICLE XII. ORGANIZATION AND MANAGEMENT

SECTION 1. *Structure of the Fund.*—The Fund shall have a Board of Governors, Executive Directors, a Managing Director, and a staff.

SEC. 2. *Board of Governors.*—(a) All powers of the Fund shall be vested in the Board of Governors, consisting of one governor and one alternate appointed by each member in such manner as it may determine. Each governor and each alternate shall serve for five years, subject to the pleasure of the member appointing him, and may be reappointed. No alternate may vote except in the absence of his principal. The Board shall select one of the governors as chairman.

(b) The Board of Governors may delegate to the Executive Directors authority to exercise any powers of the Board, except the power to:

(i) Admit new members and determine the conditions of their admission.

(ii) Approve a revision of quotas.

(iii) Approve a uniform change in the par value of the currencies of all members.

(iv) Make arrangements to cooperate with other international organizations (other than informal arrangements of a temporary or administrative character).

(v) Determine the distribution of the net income of the Fund.

(vi) Require a member to withdraw.

(vii) Decide to liquidate the Fund.

(viii) Decide appeals from interpretations of this agreement given by the Executive Directors.

(c) The Board of Governors shall hold an annual meeting and such other meetings as may be provided for by the Board or called by the Executive Directors. Meetings of the Board shall be called by the Directors whenever requested by five members or by members having one-quarter of the total voting power.

(d) A quorum for any meeting of the Board of Governors shall be a majority of the governors exercising not less than two-thirds of the total voting power.

(e) Each governor shall be entitled to cast the number of votes alloted under Section 5 of this Article to the member appointing him.

(f) The Board of Governors may by regulation establish a procedure whereby the Executive Directors, when they deem such action to be in the best interests of the Fund, may obtain a vote of the governors on a specific question without calling a meeting of the Board.

(g) The Board of Governors, and the Executive Directors to the extent authorized, may adopt such rules and regulations as may be necessary or appropriate to conduct the business of the Fund.

(h) Governors and alternates shall serve as such without compensation from the Fund, but the Fund shall pay them reasonable expenses incurred in attending meetings.

(i) The Board of Governors shall determine the remuneration to be paid to the Executive Directors and the salary and terms of the contract of service of the Managing Director.

SEC. 3. *Executive Directors.*—*(a)* The Executive Directors shall be responsible for the conduct of the general operations of the Fund, and for this purpose shall exercise all the powers delegated to them by the Board of Governors.

(b) There shall be not less than twelve directors who need not be governors, and of whom

(i) five shall be appointed by the five members having the largest quotas;

(ii) not more than two shall be appointed when the provisions of *(c)* below apply;

(iii) five shall be elected by the members not entitled to appoint directors, other than the American Republics; and

(iv) two shall be elected by the American Republics not entitled to appoint directors.

For the purposes of this paragraph, members means governments of countries whose names are set forth in Schedule A, whether they become members in accordance with Article XX or in accordance with Article II, Section 2. When governments of other countries become members, the Board of Governors may, by a four-fifths majority of the total voting power, increase the number of directors to be elected.

(c) If, at the second regular election of directors and thereafter, the members entitled to appoint directors under *(b)* (i) above do not include the two members, the holdings of whose currencies by the Fund have been, on the average over the preceding two years, reduced below their quotas by the largest absolute amounts in terms of gold as a common denominator, either one or both of such members, as the case may be, shall be entitled to appoint a director.

(d) Subject to Article XX, Section 3 *(b)* elections of elective directors shall be conducted at intervals of two years in accordance with the provisions of Schedule C, supplemented by such regulations as the Fund deems appropriate. Whenever the Board of Governors increases the number of directors to be elected under *(b)* above, it shall issue regulations making appropriate changes in the proportion of votes required to elect directors under the provisions of Schedule C.

(e) Each director shall appoint an alternate with full power to act for him when he is not present. When the directors appointing them are present, alternates may participate in meetings but may not vote.

(f) Directors shall continue in office until their successors are appointed or elected. If the office of an elected director becomes vacant more than ninety days before the end of his term, another director shall be elected for the remainder of the term by the members who elected the former director. A majority of the votes cast shall be required for election. While the office remains vacant, the alternate of the former director shall exercise his powers, except that of appointing an alternate.

(g) The Executive Directors shall function in continuous session at the principal office of the Fund and shall meet as often as the business of the Fund may require.

(h) A quorum for any meeting of the Executive Directors shall be a majority of the directors representing not less than one-half of the voting power.

(i) Each appointed director shall be entitled to cast the number of votes allotted under

Section 5 of this Article to the member appointing him. Each elected director shall be entitled to cast the number of votes which counted towards his election. When the provisions of Section 5 (b) of this Article are applicable, the votes which a director would otherwise be entitled to cast shall be increased or decreased correspondingly. All the votes which a director is entitled to cast shall be cast as a unit.

(j) The Board of Governors shall adopt regulations under which a member not entitled to appoint a director under (b) above may send a representative to attend any meeting of the Executive Directors when a request made by, or a matter particularly affecting, that member is under consideration.

(k) The Executive Directors may appoint such committees as they deem advisable. Membership of committees need not be limited to governors or directors or their alternates.

SEC. 4. *Managing Director and staff.*—(a) The Executive Directors shall select a Managing Director who shall not be a governor or an executive director. The Managing Director shall be chairman of the Executive Directors, but shall have no vote except a deciding vote in case of an equal division. He may participate in meetings of the Board of Governors, but shall not vote at such meetings. The Managing Director shall cease to hold office when the Executive Directors so decide.

(b) The Managing Director shall be chief of the operating staff of the Fund and shall conduct, under the direction of the Executive Directors, the ordinary business of the Fund. Subject to the general control of the Executive Directors, he shall be responsible for the organization, appointment and dismissal of the staff of the Fund.

(c) The Managing Director and the staff of the Fund, in the discharge of their functions, shall owe their duty entirely to the Fund and to no other authority. Each member of the Fund shall respect the international character of this duty and shall refrain from all attempts to influence any of the staff in the discharge of his functions.

(d) In appointing the staff the Managing Director shall, subject to the paramount importance of securing the highest standards of efficiency and of technical competence, pay due regard to the importance of recruiting personnel on as wide a geographical basis as possible.

SEC. 5. *Voting.*—(a) Each member shall have two hundred fifty votes plus one additional vote for each part of its quota equivalent to one hundred thousand United States dollars.

(b) Whenever voting is required under Article V, Section 4 or 5, each member shall have the number of votes to which it is entitled under (a) above, adjusted

(i) by the addition of one vote for the equivalent of each four hundred thousand United States dollars of net sales of its currency up to the date when the vote is taken, or

(ii) by the subtraction of one vote for the equivalent of each four hundred thousand United States dollars of its net purchases of the currencies of other members up to the date when the vote is taken;

provided, that neither net purchases nor net sales shall be deemed at any time to exceed an amount equal to the quota of the member involved.

(c) For the purpose of all computations under this Section, United States dollars shall be deemed to be of the weight and fineness in effect on July 1, 1944, adjusted for any uniform change under Article IV, Section 7, if a waiver is made under Section 8 (d) of that Article.

(*d*) Except as otherwise specifically provided, all decisions of the Fund shall be made by a majority of the votes cast.

SEC. 6. *Distribution of net income.*—(*a*) The Board of Governors shall determine annually what part of the Fund's net income shall be placed to reserve and what part, if any, shall be distributed.

(*b*) If any distribution is made, there shall first be distributed a two percent noncumulative payment to each member on the amount by which seventy-five percent of its quota exceeded the Fund's average holdings of its currency during that year. The balance shall be paid to all members in proportion to their quotas. Payments to each member shall be made in its own currency.

SEC. 7. *Publication of reports.*—(*a*) The Fund shall publish an annual report containing an audited statement of its accounts, and shall issue, at intervals of three months or less, a summary statement of its transactions and its holdings of gold and currencies of members.

(*b*) The Fund may publish such other reports as it deems desirable for carrying out its purposes.

SEC. 8. *Communication of views to members.*—The Fund shall at all times have the right to communicate its views informally to any member on any matter arising under this Agreement. The Fund may, by a two-thirds majority of the total voting power, decide to publish a report made to a member regarding its monetary or economic conditions and developments which directly tend to produce a serious disequilibrium in the international balance of payments of members. If the member is not entitled to appoint an executive director, it shall be entitled to representation in accordance with Section 3 (*j*) of this Article. The Fund shall not publish a report involving changes in the fundamental structure of the economic organization of members.

ARTICLE XIII. OFFICES AND DEPOSITORIES

SECTION 1. *Location of offices.*—The principal office of the Fund shall be located in the territory of the member having the largest quota, and agencies or branch offices may be established in the territories of other members.

SEC. 2. *Depositories.*—(*a*) Each member country shall designate its central bank as a depository for all the Fund's holdings of its currency, or if it has no central bank it shall designate such other institution as may be acceptable to the Fund.

(*b*) The Fund may hold other assets, including gold, in the depositories designated by the five members having the largest quotas and in such other designated depositories as the Fund may select. Initially, at least one-half of the holdings of the Fund shall be held in the depository designated by the member in whose territories the Fund has its principal office and at least forty percent shall be held in the depositories designated by the remaining four members referred to above. However, all transfers of gold by the Fund shall be made with due regard to the costs of transport and anticipated requirements of the Fund. In an emergency the Executive Directors may transfer all or any part of the Fund's gold holdings to any place where they can be adequately protected.

SEC. 3. *Guarantee of the Fund's assets.*—Each member guarantees all assets of the Fund against loss resulting from failure or default on the part of the depository designated by it.

ARTICLE XIV. TRANSITIONAL PERIOD

Section 1. *Introduction.*—The Fund is not intended to provide facilities for relief or reconstruction or to deal with international indebtedness arising out of the war.

Sec. 2. *Exchange restrictions.*—In the post-war transitional period members may, notwithstanding the provisions of any other articles of this Agreement, maintain and adapt to changing circumstances (and, in the case of members whose territories have been occupied by the enemy, introduce where necessary) restrictions on payments and transfers for current international transactions. Members shall, however, have continuous regard in their foreign exchange policies to the purposes of the Fund; and, as soon as conditions permit, they shall take all possible measures to develop such commercial and financial arrangements with other members as will facilitate international payments and the maintenance of exchange stability. In particular, members shall withdraw restrictions maintained or imposed under this Section as soon as they are satisfied that they will be able, in the absence of such restrictions, to settle their balance of payments in a manner which will not unduly encumber their access to the resources of the Fund.

Sec. 3. *Notification to the Fund.*—Each member shall notify the Fund before it becomes eligible under Article XX, Section 4 (c) or (d), to buy currency from the Fund, whether it intends to avail itself of the transitional arrangements in Section 2 of this Article, or whether it is prepared to accept the obligations of Article VIII, Sections 2, 3, and 4. A member availing itself of the transitional arrangements shall notify the Fund as soon thereafter as it is prepared to accept the above-mentioned obligations.

Sec. 4. *Action of the Fund relating to restrictions.*—Not later than three years after the date on which the Fund begins operations and in each year thereafter, the Fund shall report on the restrictions still in force under Section 2 of this Article. Five years after the date on which the Fund begins operations, and in each year thereafter, any member still retaining any restrictions inconsistent with Article VIII, Sections 2, 3, or 4, shall consult the Fund as to their further retention. The Fund may, if it deems such action necessary in exceptional circumstances, make representations to any member that conditions are favorable for the withdrawal of any particular restriction, or for the general abandonment of restrictions, inconsistent with the provisions of any other article of this Agreement. The member shall be given a suitable time to reply to such representations. If the Fund finds that the member persists in maintaining restrictions which are inconsistent with the purposes of the Fund, the member shall be subject to Article XV, Section 2 (a).

Sec. 5. *Nature of transitional period.*—In its relations with members, the Fund shall recognize that the post-war transitional period will be one of change and adjustment and in making decisions on requests occasioned thereby which are presented by any member it shall give the member the benefit of any reasonable doubt.

ARTICLE XV. WITHDRAWAL FROM MEMBERSHIP

Section 1. *Right of members to withdraw.*—Any member may withdraw from the Fund at any time by transmitting a notice in writing to the Fund at its principal office. Withdrawal shall become effective on the date such notice is received.

Sec. 2. *Compulsory withdrawal.*—(a) If a member fails to fulfill any of its obligations under this Agreement, the Fund may declare the member ineligible to use the resources of the Fund. Nothing in this Section shall be deemed to limit the provisions of Article IV, Section 6, Article V, Section 5, or Article VI, Section 1.

(b) If, after the expiration of a reasonable period the member persists in its failure to fulfill any of its obligations under this Agreement, or a difference between a member and the Fund under Article IV, Section 6, continues, that member may be required to withdraw from membership in the Fund by a decision of the Board of Governors carried by a majority of the governors representing a majority of the total voting power.

(c) Regulations shall be adopted to ensure that before action is taken against any member under (a) or (b) above, the member shall be informed in reasonable time of the complaint against it and given an adequate opportunity for stating its case, both orally and in writing.

SEC. 3. *Settlement of accounts with members withdrawing.*—When a member withdraws from the Fund, normal transactions of the Fund in its currency shall cease and settlement of all accounts between it and the Fund shall be made with reasonable despatch by agreement between it and the Fund. If agreement is not reached promptly, the provisions of Schedule D shall apply to the settlement of accounts.

ARTICLE XVI. EMERGENCY PROVISIONS

SECTION 1. *Temporary suspension.*—(a) In the event of an emergency or the development of unforeseen circumstances threatening the operations of the Fund, the Executive Directors by unanimous vote may suspend for a period of not more than one hundred twenty days the operation of any of the following provisions:

(i) Article IV, Sections 3 and 4 (b).

(ii) Article V, Sections 2, 3, 7, 8 (a) and (f).

(iii) Article VI, Section 2.

(iv) Article XI, Section 1.

(b) Simultaneously with any decision to suspend the operation of any of the foregoing provisions, the Executive Directors shall call a meeting of the Board of Governors for the earliest practicable date.

(c) The Executive Directors may not extend any suspension beyond one hundred twenty days. Such suspension may be extended, however, for an additional period of not more than two hundred forty days, if the Board of Governors by a four-fifths majority of the total voting power so decides, but it may not be further extended except by amendment of this Agreement pursuant to Article XVII.

(d) The Executive Directors may, by a majority of the total voting power, terminate such suspension at any time.

SEC. 2. *Liquidation of the Fund.*—(a) The Fund may not be liquidated except by decision of the Board of Governors. In an emergency, if the Executive Directors decide that liquidation of the Fund may be necessary, they may temporarily suspend all transactions, pending decision by the Board.

(b) If the Board of Governors decides to liquidate the Fund, the Fund shall forthwith cease to engage in any activities except those incidental to the orderly collection and liquidation of its assets and the settlement of its liabilities, and all obligations of members under this Agreement shall cease except those set out in this Article, in Article XVIII, paragraph (c), in Schedule D, paragraph 7, and in Schedule E.

(c) Liquidation shall be administered in accordance with the provisions of Schedule E.

ARTICLE XVII. AMENDMENTS

(a) Any proposal to introduce modifications in this Agreement, whether emanating from a member, a governor or the Executive Directors, shall be communicated to the chairman of the Board of Governors who shall bring the proposal before the Board. If the proposed amendment is approved by the Board the Fund shall, by circular letter or telegram, ask all members whether they accept the proposed amendment. When three-fifths of the members, having four-fifths of the total voting power, have accepted the proposed amendment, the Fund shall certify the fact by a formal communication addressed to all members.

(b) Notwithstanding (a) above, acceptance by all members is required in the case of any amendment modifying

(i) the right to withdraw from the Fund (Article XV, Section 1);
(ii) the provision that no change in a member's quota shall be made without its consent (Article III, Section 2);
(iii) the provision that no change may be made in the par value of a member's currency except on the proposal of that member (Article IV, Section 5 (b)).

(c) Amendments shall enter into force for all members three months after the date of the formal communication unless a shorter period is specified in the circular or letter or telegram.

ARTICLE XVIII. INTERPRETATION

(a) Any question of interpretation of the provisions of this Agreement arising between any member and the Fund or between any members of the Fund shall be submitted to the Executive Directors for their decision. If the question particularly affects any member not entitled to appoint an executive director it shall be entitled to representation in accordance with Article XII, Section 3 (j).

(b) In any case where the Executive Directors have given a decision under (a) above, any member may require that the question be referred to the Board of Governors, whose decision shall be final. Pending the result of the reference to the Board the Fund may, so far as it deems necessary, act on the basis of the decision of the Executive Directors.

(c) Whenever a disagreement arises between the Fund and a member which has withdrawn, or between the Fund and any member during liquidation of the Fund, such disagreement shall be submitted to arbitration by a tribunal of three arbitrators, one appointed by the Fund, another by the member or withdrawing member and an umpire who, unless the parties otherwise agree, shall be appointed by the President of the Permanent Court of International Justice or such other authority as may have been prescribed by regulation adopted by the Fund. The umpire shall have full power to settle all questions of procedure in any case where the parties are in disagreement with respect thereto.

ARTICLE XIX. EXPLANATION OF TERMS

In interpreting the provisions of this Agreement the Fund and its members shall be guided by the following:

(a) A member's monetary reserves means its net official holdings of gold, of convertible currencies of other members, and of the currencies of such non-members as the Fund may specify.

(b) The official holdings of a member means central holdings (that is, the holdings of its Treasury, central bank, stabilization fund, or similar fiscal agency).

(c) The holdings of other official institutions or other banks within its territories may, in any particular case, be deemed by the Fund, after consultation with the member, to be official holdings to the extent that they are substantially in excess of working balances; provided that for the purpose of determining whether, in a particular case, holdings are in excess of working balances, there shall be deducted from such holdings amounts of currency due to official institutions and banks in the territories of members or non-members specified under (d) below.

(d) A member's holdings of convertible currencies means its holdings of the currencies of other members which are not availing themselves of the transitional arrangements under Article XIV, Section 2, together with its holdings of the currencies of such non-members as the Fund may from time to time specify. The term currency for this purpose includes without limitation coins, paper money, bank balances, bank acceptances, and government obligations issued with a maturity not exceeding twelve months.

(e) A member's monetary reserves shall be calculated by deducting from its central holdings the currency liabilities to the Treasuries, central banks, stabilization funds, or similar fiscal agencies of other members or non-members specified under (d) above, together with similiar liabilities to other official institutions and other banks in the territories of members, or non-members specified under (d) above. To these net holdings shall be added the sums deemed to be official holdings of other official institutions and other banks under (c) above.

(f) The Fund's holdings of the currency of a member shall include any securities accepted by the Fund under Article III, Section 5.

(g) The Fund, after consultation with a member which is availing itself of the transitional arrangements under Article XIV, Section 2, may deem holdings of the currency of that member which carry specified rights of conversion into another currency or into gold to be holdings of convertible currency for the purpose of the calculation of monetary reserves.

(h) For the purpose of calculating gold subscriptions under Article III, Section 3, a member's net official holdings of gold and United States dollars shall consist of its official holdings of gold and United States currency after deducting central holdings of its currency by other countries and holdings of its currency by other official institutions and other banks if these holdings carry specified rights of conversion into gold or United States currency.

(i) Payments for current transactions means payments which are not for the purpose of transferring capital, and includes, without limitation:
   (1) All payments due in connection with foreign trade, other current business, including services, and normal short-term banking and credit facilities;
   (2) Payments due as interest on loans and as net income from other investments;
   (3) Payments of moderate amount for amortization of loans or for depreciation of direct investments;
   (4) Moderate remittances for family living expenses.

The Fund may, after consultation with the members concerned, determine whether certain specific transactions are to be considered current transactions or capital transactions.

ARTICLE XX. FINAL PROVISIONS

SECTION 1. *Entry into force.*—This Agreement shall enter into force when it has been signed on behalf of governments having sixty-five percent of the total of the quotas set forth in Schedule A and when the instruments referred to in Section 2 (*a*) of this Article have been deposited on their behalf, but in no event shall this Agreement enter into force before May 1, 1945.

SEC. 2. *Signature.*—(*a*) Each government on whose behalf this Agreement is signed shall deposit with the Government of the United States of America an instrument setting forth that it has accepted this Agreement in accordance with its law and has taken all steps necessary to enable it to carry out all of its obligations under this Agreement.

(*b*) Each government shall become a member of the Fund as from the date of the deposit on its behalf of the instrument referred to in (*a*) above, except that no government shall become a member before this Agreement enters into force under Section 1 of this Article.

(*c*) The Government of the United States of America shall inform the governments of all countries whose names are set forth in Schedule A, and all governments whose membership is approved in accordance with Article II, Section 2, of all signatures of this Agreement and of the deposit of all instruments referred to in (*a*) above.

(*d*) At the time this Agreement is signed on its behalf, each government shall transmit to the Government of the United States of America one one-hundredth of one percent of its total subscription in gold or United States dollars for the purpose of meeting administrative expenses of the Fund. The Government of the United States of America shall hold such funds in a special deposit account and shall transmit them to the Board of Governors of the Fund when the initial meeting has been called under Section 3 of this Article. If this Agreement has not come into force by December 31, 1945, the Government of the United States of America shall return such funds to the governments that transmitted them.

(*e*) This Agreement shall remain open for signature at Washington on behalf of the governments of the countries whose names are set forth in Schedule A until December 31, 1945.

(*f*) After December 31, 1945, this Agreement shall be open for signature on behalf of the government of any country whose membership has been approved in accordance with Article II, Section 2.

(*g*) By their signature of this Agreement, all governments accept it both on their own behalf and in respect of all their colonies, overseas territories, all territories under their protection, suzerainty, or authority and all territories in respect of which they exercise a mandate.

(*h*) In the case of governments whose metropolitan territories have been under enemy occupation, the deposit of the instrument referred to in (*a*) above may be delayed until one hundred eighty days after the date on which these territories have been liberated. If, however, it is not deposited by any such government before the expiration of this period the signature affixed on behalf of that government shall become void and the portion of its subscription paid under (*d*) above shall be returned to it.

(*i*) Paragraphs (*d*) and (*h*) shall come into force with regard to each signatory government as from the date of its signature.

Sec. 3. *Inauguration of the Fund.*—(a) As soon as this Agreement enters into force under Section 1 of this Article, each member shall appoint a governor and the member having the largest quota shall call the first meeting of the Board of Governors.

(b) At the first meeting of the Board of Governors, arrangements shall be made for the selection of provisional executive directors. The governments of the five countries for which the largest quotas are set forth in Schedule A shall appoint provisional executive directors. If one or more of such governments have not become members, the executive directorships they would be entitled to fill shall remain vacant until they become members, or until January 1, 1946, whichever is the earlier. Seven provisional executive directors shall be elected in accordance with the provisions of Schedule C and shall remain in office until the date of the first regular election of executive directors which shall be held as soon as practicable after January 1, 1946.

(c) The Board of Governors may delegate to the provisional executive directors any powers except those which may not be delegated to the Executive Directors.

Sec. 4. *Initial determination of par values.*—(a) When the Fund is of the opinion that it will shortly be in a position to begin exchange transactions, it shall so notify the members and shall request each member to communicate within thirty days the par value of its currency based on the rates of exchange prevailing on the sixtieth day before the entry into force of this Agreement. No member whose metropolitan territory has been occupied by the enemy shall be required to make such a communication while that territory is a theater of major hostilities or for such period thereafter as the Fund may determine. When such a member communicates the par value of its currency the provisions of (d) below shall apply.

(b) The par value communicated by a member whose metropolitan territory has not been occupied by the enemy shall be the par value of that member's currency for the purposes of this Agreement unless, within ninety days after the request referred to in (a) above has been received, (i) the member notifies the Fund that it regards the par value as unsatisfactory, or (ii) the Fund notifies the member that in its opinion the par value cannot be maintained without causing recourse to the Fund on the part of that member or others on a scale prejudicial to the Fund and to members. When notification is given under (i) or (ii) above, the Fund and the member shall, within a period determined by the Fund in the light of all relevant circumstances, agree upon a suitable par value for that currency. If the Fund and the member do not agree within the period so determined, the member shall be deemed to have withdrawn from the Fund on the date when the period expires.

(c) When the par value of a member's currency has been established under (b) above, either by the expiration of ninety days without notification, or by agreement after notification, the member shall be eligible to buy from the Fund the currencies of other members to the full extent permitted in this Agreement, provided that the Fund has begun exchange transactions.

(d) In the case of a member whose metropolitan territory has been occupied by the enemy, the provisions of (b) above shall apply, subject to the following modifications:

(i) The period of ninety days shall be extended so as to end on a date to be fixed by agreement between the Fund and the member.

(ii) Within the extended period the member may, if the Fund has begun exchange transactions, buy from the Fund with its currency the currencies of other members, but only under such conditions and in such amounts as may be prescribed by the Fund.

(iii) At any time before the date fixed under (i) above, changes may be made by agreement with the Fund in the par value communicated under (a) above.

(e) If a member whose metropolitan territory has been occupied by the enemy adopts a new monetary unit before the date to be fixed under (d) (i) above, the par value fixed by that member for the new unit shall be communicated to the Fund and the provisions of (d) above shall apply.

(f) Changes in par values agreed with the Fund under this Section shall not be taken into account in determining whether a proposed change falls within (i), (ii), or (iii) of Article IV, Section 5 (c).

(g) A member communicating to the Fund a par value for the currency of its metropolitan territory shall simultaneously communicate a value, in terms of that currency, for each separate currency, where such exists, in the territories in respect of which it has accepted this Agreement under Section 2 (g) of this Article, but no member shall be required to make a communication for the separate currency of a territory which has been occupied by the enemy while that territory is a theater of major hostilities or for such period thereafter as the Fund may determine. On the basis of the par value so communicated, the Fund shall compute the par value of each separate currency. A communication or notification to the Fund under (a), (b) or (d) above regarding the par value of a currency, shall also be deemed, unless the contrary is stated, to be a communication or notification regarding the par value of all the separate currencies referred to above. Any member may, however, make a communication or notification relating to the metropolitan or any of the separate currencies alone. If the member does so, the provisions of the preceding paragraphs (including (d) above, if a territory where a separate currency exists has been occupied by the enemy) shall apply to each of these currencies separately.

(h) The Fund shall begin exchange transactions at such date as it may determine after members having sixty-five percent of the total of the quotas set forth in Schedule A have become eligible, in accordance with the preceding paragraphs of this Section, to purchase the currencies of other members, but in no event until after major hostilities in Europe have ceased.

(i) The Fund may postpone exchange transactions with any member if its circumstances are such that, in the opinion of the Fund, they would lead to use of the resources of the Fund in a manner contrary to the purposes of this Agreement or prejudicial to the Fund or the members.

(j) The par values of the currencies of governments which indicate their desire to become members after December 31, 1945, shall be determined in accordance with the provisions of Article II, Section 2.

Done at Washington, in a single copy which shall remain deposited in the archives of the Government of the United States of America, which shall transmit certified copies to all governments whose names are set forth in Schedule A and to all governments whose membership is approved in accordance with Article II, Section 2.

SCHEDULE A. QUOTAS

[In millions of United States dollars]

Country	Quota	Country	Quota
Australia	200	India	400
Belgium	225	Iran	25
Bolivia	10	Iraq	8
Brazil	150	Liberia	.5
Canada	300	Luxembourg	10
Chile	50	Mexico	90
China	550	Netherlands	275
Colombia	50	New Zealand	50
Costa Rica	5	Nicaragua	2
Cuba	50	Norway	50
Czechoslovakia	125	Panama	.5
Denmark	([1])	Paraguay	2
Dominican Republic	5	Peru	25
Ecuador	5	Philippine Commonwealth	15
Egypt	45	Poland	125
El Salvador	2.5	Union of South Africa	100
Ethiopia	6	Union of Soviet Socialist Republics	1,200
France	450	United Kingdom	1,300
Greece	40	United States	2,750
Guatemala	5	Uruguay	15
Haiti	5	Venezuela	15
Honduras	2.5	Yugoslavia	60
Iceland	1	**Total**	**8,800**

[1] The quota of Denmark shall be determined by the Fund after the Danish Government has declared its readiness to sign this Agreement but before signature takes place.

SCHEDULE B. PROVISIONS WITH RESPECT TO REPURCHASE BY A MEMBER OF ITS CURRENCY HELD BY THE FUND

1. In determining the extent to which repurchase of a member's currency from the Fund under Article V, Section 7 (b), shall be made with each type of monetary reserve, that is, with gold and with each convertible currency, the following rule, subject to 2 below, shall apply:

(a) If the member's monetary reserves have not increased during the year, the amount payable to the Fund shall be distributed among all types of reserves in proportion to the member's holdings thereof at the end of the year.

(b) If the member's monetary reserves have increased during the year, a part of the amount payable to the Fund equal to one-half of the increase shall be distributed among those types of reserves which have increased in proportion to the amount by which each of them has increased. The remainder of the sum payable to the Fund shall be distributed among all types of reserves in proportion to the member's remaining holdings thereof.

(c) If after all the repurchases required under Article V, Section 7 (b), had been made, the result would exceed any of the limits specified in Article V, Section 7 (c), the Fund shall require such repurchases to be made by the members proportionately in such manner that the limits will not be exceeded.

2. The Fund shall not acquire the currency of any non-member under Article V, Section 7 *(b)* and *(c)*.

3. In calculating monetary reserves and the increase in monetary reserves during any year for the purpose of Article V, Section 7 *(b)* and *(c)*, no account shall be taken, unless deductions have otherwise been made by the member for such holdings, of any increase in those monetary reserves which is due to currency previously inconvertible having become convertible during the year; or to holdings which are the proceeds of a long-term or medium-term loan contracted during the year; or to holdings which have been transferred or set aside for repayment of a loan during the subsequent year.

4. In the case of members whose metropolitan territories have been occupied by the enemy, gold newly produced during the five years after the entry into force of this Agreement from mines located within their metropolitan territories shall not be included in computations of their monetary reserves or of increases in their monetary reserves.

SCHEDULE C. ELECTION OF EXECUTIVE DIRECTORS

1. The election of the elective executive directors shall be by ballot of the governors eligible to vote under Article XII, Section 3 *(b)* (iii) and (iv).

2. In balloting for the five directors to be elected under Article XII, Section 3 *(b)* (iii), each of the governors eligible to vote shall cast for one person all of the votes to which he is entitled under Article XII, Section 5 *(a)*. The five persons receiving the greatest number of votes shall be directors, provided that no person who received less than nineteen percent of the total number of votes that can be cast (eligible votes) shall be considered elected.

3. When five persons are not elected on the first ballot, a second ballot shall be held in which the person who received the lowest number of votes shall be ineligible for election and in which there shall vote only *(a)* those governors who voted in the first ballot for a person not elected, and *(b)* those governors whose votes for a person elected are deemed under 4 below to have raised the votes cast for that person above twenty percent of the eligible votes.

4. In determining whether the votes cast by a governor are to be deemed to have raised the total of any person above twenty percent of the eligible votes the twenty percent shall be deemed to include, first, the votes of the governor casting the largest number of votes for such person, then the votes of the governor casting the next largest number, and so on until twenty percent is reached.

5. Any governor part of whose votes must be counted in order to raise the total of any person above nineteen percent shall be considered as casting all of his votes for such person even if the total votes for such person thereby exceed twenty percent.

6. If, after the second ballot, five persons have not been elected, further ballots shall be held on the same principles until five persons have been elected, provided that after four persons are elected, the fifth may be elected by a simple majority of the remaining votes and shall be deemed to have been elected by all such votes.

7. The directors to be elected by the American Republics under Article XII, Section 3 *(b)* (iv) shall be elected as follows:

(a) Each of the directors shall be elected separately.

(b) In the election of the first director, each governor representing an American Republic eligible to participate in the election shall cast for one person all the votes

to which he is entitled. The person receiving the largest number of votes shall be elected provided that he has received not less than forty-five percent of the total votes.

(c) If no person is elected on the first ballot, further ballots shall be held, in each of which the person receiving the lowest number of votes shall be eliminated, until one person receives a number of votes sufficient for election under (b) above.

(d) Governors whose votes contributed to the election of the first director shall take no part in the election of the second director.

(e) Persons who did not succeed in the first election shall not be ineligible for election as the second director.

(f) A majority of the votes which can be cast shall be required for election of the second director. If at the first ballot no person receives a majority, further ballots shall be held in each of which the person receiving the lowest number of votes shall be eliminated, until some person obtains a majority.

(g) The second director shall be deemed to have been elected by all the votes which could have been cast in the ballot securing his election.

SCHEDULE D. SETTLEMENT OF ACCOUNTS WITH MEMBERS WITHDRAWING

1. The Fund shall be obligated to pay to a member withdrawing an amount equal to its quota, plus any other amounts due to it from the Fund, less any amounts due to the Fund, including charges accruing after the date of its withdrawal; but no payment shall be made until six months after the date of withdrawal. Payments shall be made in the currency of the withdrawing member.

2. If the Fund's holdings of the currency of the withdrawing member are not sufficient to pay the net amount due from the Fund, the balance shall be paid in gold, or in such other manner as may be agreed. If the Fund and the withdrawing member do not reach agreement within six months of the date of withdrawal, the currency in question held by the Fund shall be paid forthwith to the withdrawing member. Any balance due shall be paid in ten half-yearly installments during the ensuing five years. Each such installment shall be paid, at the option of the Fund, either in the currency of the withdrawing member acquired after its withdrawal or by the delivery of gold.

3. If the Fund fails to meet any installment which is due in accordance with the preceding paragraphs, the withdrawing member shall be entitled to require the Fund to pay the installment in any currency held by the Fund with the exception of any currency which has been declared scarce under Article VII, Section 3.

4. If the Fund's holdings of the currency of a withdrawing member exceed the amount due to it, and if agreement on the method of settling accounts is not reached within six months of the date of withdrawal, the former member shall be obligated to redeem such excess currency in gold or, at its option, in the currencies of members which at the time of redemption are convertible. Redemption shall be made at the parity existing at the time of withdrawal from the Fund. The withdrawing member shall complete redemption within five years of the date of withdrawal, or within such longer period as may be fixed by the Fund, but shall not be required to redeem in any half-yearly period more than one-tenth of the Fund's excess holdings of its currency at the date of withdrawal plus further acquisitions of the currency during such half-

yearly period. If the withdrawing member does not fulfill this obligation, the Fund may in an orderly manner liquidate in any market the amount of currency which should have been redeemed.

5. Any member desiring to obtain the currency of a member which has withdrawn shall acquire it by purchase from the Fund, to the extent that such member has access to the resources of the Fund and that such currency is available under 4 above.

6. The withdrawing member guarantees the unrestricted use at all times of the currency disposed of under 4 and 5 above for the purchase of goods or for payment of sums due to it or to persons within its territories. It shall compensate the Fund for any loss resulting from the difference between the par value of its currency on the date of withdrawal and the value realized by the Fund on disposal under 4 and 5 above.

7. In the event of the Fund going into liquidation under Article XVI, Section 2, within six months of the date on which the member withdraws, the account between the Fund and that government shall be settled in accordance with Article XVI, Section 2, and Schedule E.

SCHEDULE E. ADMINISTRATION OF LIQUIDATION

1. In the event of liquidation the liabilities of the Fund other than the repayment of subscriptions shall have priority in the distribution of the assets of the Fund. In meeting each such liability the Fund shall use its assets in the following order:

(a) the currency in which the liability is payable;

(b) gold;

(c) all other currencies in proportion, so far as may be practicable, to the quotas of the members.

2. After the discharge of the Fund's liabilities in accordance with 1 above, the balance of the Fund's assets shall be distributed and apportioned as follows

(a) The Fund shall distribute its holdings of gold among the members whose currencies are held by the Fund in amounts less than their quotas. These members shall share the gold so distributed in the proportions of the amounts by which their quotas exceed the Fund's holdings of their currencies.

(b) The Fund shall distribute to each member one-half the Fund's holdings of its currency but such distribution shall not exceed fifty percent of its quota.

(c) The Fund shall apportion the remainder of its holdings of each currency among all the members in proportion to the amounts due to each member after the distributions under (a) and (b) above.

3. Each member shall redeem the holdings of its currency apportioned to other members under 2 (c) above, and shall agree with the Fund within three months after a decision to liquidate upon an orderly procedure for such redemption.

4. If a member has not reached agreement with the Fund within the three-month period referred to in 3 above, the Fund shall use the currencies of other members apportioned to that member under 2 (c) above to redeem the currency of that member apportioned to other members. Each currency apportioned to a member which has not reached agreement shall be used, so far as possible, to redeem its currency apportioned to the members which have made agreements with the Fund under 3 above.

5. If a member has reached agreement with the Fund in accordance with 3 above, the Fund shall use the currencies of other members apportioned to that member under

2 (*c*) above to redeem the currency of that member apportioned to other members which have made agreements with the Fund under 3 above. Each amount so redeemed shall be redeemed in the currency of the member to which it was apportioned.

6. After carrying out the preceding paragraphs, the Fund shall pay to each member the remaining currencies held for its account.

7. Each member whose currency has been distributed to other members under 6 above shall redeem such currency in gold or, at its option, in the currency of the member requesting redemption, or in such other manner as may be agreed between them. If the members involved do not otherwise agree, the member obligated to redeem shall complete redemption within five years of the date of distribution, but shall not be required to redeem in any half-yearly period more than one-tenth of the amount distributed to each other member. If the member does not fulfill this obligation, the amount of currency which should have been redeemed may be liquidated in an orderly manner in any market.

8. Each member whose currency has been distributed to other members under 6 above guarantees the unrestricted use of such currency at all times for the purchase of goods or for payment of sums due to it or to persons in its territories. Each member so obligated agrees to compensate other members for any loss resulting from the difference between the par value of its currency on the date of the decision to liquidate the Fund and the value realized by such members on disposal of its currency.

Agreement with the United Nations

The Agreement reproduced below was approved by the Board of Governors of the Fund on September 17, 1947 and by the General Assembly of the United Nations on November 15, 1947. Accordingly, the Agreement came into force on November 15, 1947.

Agreement Between the United Nations and the International Monetary Fund

(November 15, 1947)

ARTICLE I

General

1. This agreement, which is entered into by the United Nations pursuant to the provisions of Article 63 of its Charter, and by the International Monetary Fund (hereinafter called the Fund), pursuant to the provisions of article X of its Articles of Agreement, is intended to define the terms on which the United Nations and the Fund shall be brought into relationship.

2. The Fund is a specialized agency established by agreement among its member governments and having wide international responsibilities, as defined in its Articles of Agreement, in economic and related fields within the meaning of Article 57 of the Charter of the United Nations. By reason of the nature of its international responsibilities and the terms of its Articles of Agreement, the Fund is, and is required to function as, an independent international organization.

3. The United Nations and the Fund are subject to certain necessary limitations for the safeguarding of confidential material furnished to them by their members or others, and nothing in this agreement shall be construed to require either of them to furnish any information the furnishing of which would, in its judgment, constitute a violation of the confidence of any of its members or anyone from whom it shall have received such information, or which would otherwise interfere with the orderly conduct of its operations.

ARTICLE II

Reciprocal representation

1. Representatives of the United Nations shall be entitled to attend, and to participate without vote in, meetings of the Board of Governors of the Fund. Representatives of the United Nations shall be invited to participate without vote in meetings especially called by the Fund for the particular purpose of considering the United Nations point of view in matters of concern to the United Nations.

2. Representatives of the Fund shall be entitled to attend meetings of the General Assembly of the United Nations for purposes of consultation.

3. Representatives of the Fund shall be entitled to attend, and to participate without vote in, meetings of the committees of the General Assembly, meetings of the Economic and Social Council, of the Trusteeship Council and of their respective subsidiary bodies, dealing with matters in which the Fund has an interest.

4. Sufficient advance notice of these meetings and their agenda shall be given so that, in consultation, arrangements can be made for adequate representation.

Article III
Proposal of agenda items

In preparing the agenda for meetings of the Board of Governors, the Fund will give due consideration to the inclusion in the agenda of items proposed by the United Nations. Similarly, the Council and its commissions and the Trusteeship Council will give due consideration to the inclusion in their agenda of items proposed by the Fund.

Article IV
Consultation and recommendations

1. The United Nations and the Fund shall consult together and exchange views on matters of mutual interest.

2. Neither organization, nor any of their subsidiary bodies, will present any formal recommendations to the other without reasonable prior consultation with regard thereto. Any formal recommendations made by either organization after such consultation will be considered as soon as possible by the appropriate organ of the other.

Article V
Exchange of information

The United Nations and the Fund will, to the fullest extent practicable and subject to paragraph 3 of article I, arrange for the current exchange of information and publications of mutual interest, and the furnishing of special reports and studies upon request.

Article VI
Security Council

1. The Fund takes note of the obligation assumed, under paragraph 2 of Article 48 of the United Nations Charter, by such of its members as are also Members of the United Nations, to carry out the decisions of the Security Council through their action in the appropriate specialized agencies of which they are members, and will, in the conduct of its activities, have due regard for decisions of the Security Council under Articles 41 and 42 of the United Nations Charter.

2. The Fund agrees to assist the Security Council by furnishing to it information in accordance with the provisions of article V of this agreement.

Article VII

Assistance to the Trusteeship Council

The Fund agrees to co-operate with the Trusteeship Council in the carrying out of its functions by furnishing information and technical assistance upon request, and in such other similar ways as may be consistent with the Articles of Agreement of the Fund.

Article VIII

International Court of Justice

The General Assembly of the United Nations hereby authorizes the Fund to request advisory opinions of the International Court of Justice on any legal questions arising within the scope of the Fund's activities other than questions relating to the relationship between the Fund and the United Nations or any specialized agency. Whenever the Fund shall request the Court for an advisory opinion, the Fund will inform the Economic and Social Council of the request.

Article IX

Statistical services

1. In the interests of efficiency and for the purpose of reducing the burden on national Governments and other organizations, the United Nations and the Fund agree to co-operate in eliminating unnecessary duplication in the collection, analysis, publication and dissemination of statistical information.

2. The Fund recognizes the United Nations as the central agency for the collection, analysis, publication, standardization and improvement of statistics serving the general purposes of international organizations, without prejudice to the right of the Fund to concern itself with any statistics so far as they may be essential for its own purposes.

3. The United Nations recognizes the Fund as the appropriate agency for the collection, analysis, publication, standardization and improvement of statistics within its special sphere, without prejudice to the right of the United Nations to concern itself with any statistics so far as they may be essential for its own purposes.

4. (*a*) In its statistical activities the Fund agrees to give full consideration to the requirements of the United Nations and of the specialized agencies.

(*b*) In its statistical activities the United Nations agrees to give full consideration to the requirements of the Fund.

5. The United Nations and the Fund agree to furnish each other promptly with all their non-confidential statistical information.

Article X

Administrative relationships

1. The United Nations and the Fund will consult from time to time concerning personnel and other administrative matters of mutual interest, with a view to securing as much uniformity in these matters as they shall find practicable and to assuring the most efficient use of the services and facilities of the two organizations. These consultations shall include determination of the most equitable manner in which special services furnished by one organization to the other should be financed.

2. To the extent consistent with the provisions of this agreement, the Fund will participate in the work of the Co-ordination Committee and its subsidiary bodies.

3. The Fund will furnish to the United Nations copies of the annual report and the quarterly financial statements prepared by the Fund pursuant to section 7 (a) of article V of its Articles of Agreement. The United Nations agrees that, in the interpretation of paragraph 3 of Article 17 of the United Nations Charter it will take into consideration that the Fund does not rely for its annual budget upon contributions from its members, and that the appropriate authorities of the Fund enjoy full autonomy in deciding the form and content of such budget.

4. The officials of the Fund shall have the right to use the *laissez-passer* of the United Nations in accordance with special arrangements to be negotiated between the Secretary-General of the United Nations and the competent authorities of the Fund.

Article XI

Agreements with other Organizations

The Fund will inform the Economic and Social Council of any formal agreement which the Fund shall enter into with any specialized agency, and in particular agrees to inform the Council of the nature and scope of any such agreement before it is concluded.

Article XII

Liaison

1. The United Nations and the Fund agree to the foregoing provisions in the belief that they will contribute to the maintenance of effective co-operation between the two organizations. Each agrees that it will establish within its own organization such administrative machinery as may be necessary to make the liaison, as provided for in this agreement, fully effective.

2. The arrangements provided for in the foregoing articles of this agreement shall apply, as far as is appropriate, to relations between such branch or regional offices as may be established by the two organizations, as well as between their central machinery.

Article XIII

Miscellaneous

1. The Secretary-General of the United Nations and the Managing Director of the Fund are authorized to make such supplementary arrangements as they shall deem necessary or proper to carry fully into effect the purposes of this agreement.

2. This agreement shall be subject to revision by agreement between the United Nations and the Fund from the date of its entry into force.

3. This agreement may be terminated by either party thereto on six months' written notice to the other party, and thereupon all rights and obligations of both parties hereunder shall cease.

4. This agreement shall come into force when it shall have been approved by the General Assembly of the United Nations and the Board of Governors of the Fund.

Selected Decisions

The decisions reproduced below are those contained in Selected Decisions of the Executive Directors and Selected Documents, Third Issue, January 1965. They comprise the decisions of a general nature which have been cited in Volumes I and II above. They are arranged in the order of the Articles of Agreement to which they refer, and not chronologically.

Decisions embodied in Rules and Regulations are not included here; they will be found in the document following this one (beginning on p. 287).

Selected Decisions of the Executive Directors
(As at December 31, 1965)

CONTENTS

DECISION NO.	PAGE	DECISION NO.	PAGE	DECISION NO.	PAGE
2-1	267	521-3	273	708-(57/57)	276
71-2	227, 245	534-3	266	876-(59/15)	232
117-1	269	574-2	268	904-(59/32)	226
124-2	244	595-3	222	905-(59/32)	277
180-5	268	597-4	268	955-(59/45)	260
196-2	268	7-(648)	244	1033-(60/26)	275
233-2	225	75-(705)	225	1034-(60/27)	260
237-2	261	102-(52/11)	228	1107-(60/50)	277
269-2	226	103-(52/12)	274	1116-(60/51)	275
278-3	227	119-(52/30)	243	1151-(61/6)	234
284-2	272	144-(52/51)	257	1238-(61/43)	245
284-3	234	155-(52/57)	230	1245-(61/45)	224
284-4	227	201-(53/29)	258	1272-(61/53)	277
286-1	234	270-(53/95)	231	1283-(61/56)	224
287-3	228	316-(54/27)	274	1289-(62/1)	246
292-3	235	321-(54/32)	222	1345-(62/23)	233
298-3	220, 269	343-(54/47)	269	1371-(62/36)	235
408-2	220	433-(55/42)	258	1477-(63/8)	238
419-1	244	451-(55/52)	228	1529-(63/33)	222
446-4	256	488-(56/5)	275	1543-(63/39)	240
447-5	244	541-(56/39)	246	1687-(64/22)	243
486-2	271, 272	572-(56/55)	274	1712-(64/29)	254
493-3	272	649-(57/33)	265	1745-(64/46)	243
510-2	273	705-(57/55)	245	1813-(65/4)	245

Article III, Section 2

ADJUSTMENT OF QUOTAS

The first interval of five years, at the end of which the Fund shall review the quotas of the members in accordance with Article III, Section 2, began on the date when the Fund Agreement, in accordance with Article XX, Section 1, entered into force: i.e. on December 27, 1945.

Decision No. 408-2
March 11, 1949

Article III, Section 3

SUBSCRIPTIONS

Net Official Holdings: Principles of Interpretation

In order to ensure the uniform application of the relevant Articles of Agreement as they apply to determinations of members' net official holdings of gold and U.S. dollars for the purposes of Article III, Section 3 (b) (ii), the Fund adopts or reaffirms the following principles of interpretation for the indicated provisions of the Fund Agreement:

(a) *Article III, Section 3 (b)* : "Each member shall pay in gold, as a minimum, the smaller of

  (i) twenty-five per cent of its quota; or

  (ii) ten per cent of its net official holdings of gold and United States dollars as at the date when the Fund notifies members under Article XX, Section 4 (a), that it will shortly be in a position to begin exchange transactions.

Each member shall furnish to the Fund the data necessary to determine its net official holdings of gold and United States dollars."

  (1) The concept of "holdings" of gold or United States dollars involves the ownership of gold or United States dollars.

  (2) A claim to gold or dollars, unsupported by title to them, is not a "holdings."

  (3) "United States dollars" means "without limitation coins, paper money, bank balances, bank acceptances, and government obligations issued with a maturity not exceeding twelve months." This definition appears in Article XIX (d) and has been adopted by analogy in the calculation of net official holdings. The government obligations referred to must have been issued with an original maturity not exceeding twelve months, and it does not suffice that a government obligation will simply mature within twelve months from September 12, 1946.

  (4) Dollars drawn by a member under a loan and in its ownership, for example, because deposited in a bank account which it owns, are part of its "holdings." Dollars which a member has not drawn under a loan agreement or commitment and which it does not yet own, although it may later get ownership of them, are not a "holding."

(5) The usability of gold or dollars for the payment of the gold subscription is not necessary in order to constitute "holdings." A member does not pay 10 per cent of each item of gold or dollars, but the equivalent of 10 per cent of its total "holdings" of gold and dollars. Thus, segregated dollar balances are "holdings." So, too, are gold or dollars blocked under wartime freezing arrangements, if a member has title to them. This means, in the case of gold, that the member has title to specific gold (e.g., earmarked gold) or to a fixed share of specific gold (e.g., one-quarter of earmarked gold). There is no "holding" if a member has merely a claim to unidentified gold (e.g., such looted gold as may be discovered and restored to it) or to an uncertain share of specific or unidentified gold (e.g., a share of such looted gold as may be or has been recovered, to be determined in proportion to all claims).

(6) Under a pledge of gold or dollars, title remains in the pledgor, for which reason pledged gold or dollars are the "holdings" of the pledgor.

(7) Since local law cannot override international obligations, gold or dollars are "holdings" even though inalienable under local law or allocated to some special purpose.

(8) Gold must be valued in accordance with Article IV, Section 1.

(9) If a member had no "holdings" of gold or dollars on September 12, 1946, its total subscription will be payable in its own currency.

(b) *Article III, Section 3 (d)*: "If the net official holdings of gold and United States dollars of any member as at the date referred to in (b) (ii) above are not ascertainable because its territories have been occupied by the enemy, the Fund shall fix an appropriate alternative date for determining such holdings. If such date is later than that on which the country becomes eligible under Article XX, Section 4 (c) or (d), to buy currencies from the Fund, the Fund and the member shall agree on a provisional gold payment to be made under (b) above, and the balance of the member's subscription shall be paid in the member's currency, subject to appropriate adjustment between the member and the Fund when the net official holdings have been ascertained."

(1) Where a member was occupied by the enemy and its net official holdings of gold and United States dollars as of September 12, 1946, are not ascertainable, the Fund may postpone the date as of which the calculation shall be made. This means that some later date may be substituted for September 12, 1946, as the effective date for the purposes of Article III, Section 3 (b) (ii).

(2) The postponement must relate to the determination of the whole of a member's net official holdings of gold and U.S. dollars. That is to say, there cannot be a postponement of only those items whose status on September 12, 1946, cannot be ascertained.

(c) Pertains to Article XIX (b); see p. 270.

(d) Pertains to Article XIX (c); see p. 270.

(e) Pertains to Article XIX (h); see p. 270.

Decision No. 298-3
April 14, 1948

Article III, Section 4

PAYMENTS WHEN QUOTAS ARE CHANGED

Interpretation

It is determined as a matter of interpretation that Art. III, Sec. 4, and not Art. III, Sec. 3, applies to all changes in quotas.

Decision No. 595-3
July 20, 1950

Quota Increases: Gold Subscriptions

In connection with any quota increases granted in accordance with the Fund's decision on "Compensatory Financing of Export Fluctuations" and any quota increases granted as the result of requests received before the decision referred to, it is decided:

(a) to recommend to the Board of Governors, where a member represents, for reasons which it shall submit to the Fund, that its reserves should not be reduced by an immediate 25 per cent gold payment, that such member shall be permitted in accordance with an appropriate resolution to have its quota increased in five annual installments, with the right to accelerate the payment of such installments;

(b) to give sympathetic consideration to a request for an exchange transaction up to 25 per cent of the increase by any member which wishes to have the full increase in its quota take effect immediately or to expedite the full increase in its quota if it is paying under the installment schedule. This facility will be available where: (i) the member would encounter undue payments difficulties through the reduction in its reserves by the payment of the 25 per cent gold subscription or of the outstanding balance; and (ii) the request is made within two years after the date of the consent to the increase or, in the case of an increase in installments, within two years after the payment of the first installment; and (iii) the member requesting such an exchange transaction beyond the gold tranche represents that it will make a repurchase corresponding to any drawing in equal annual installments, to commence one year after the drawing and to be completed not later than three years after the drawing.

Decision No. 1529-(63/33)
June 14, 1963

Article IV, Section 1

TRANSACTIONS AND COMPUTATIONS INVOLVING FLUCTUATING CURRENCIES

Transactions and Computations Involving Fluctuating Currencies

The Fund has examined certain problems relating to the adjustment of its holdings of fluctuating currencies and to transactions and computations involving such currencies and has come to the following conclusions:

I. The Fund does not intend to apply the rules set forth in II below to its holdings of members' currencies having fluctuating rates when there is no practical interest for the Fund or members to do so. To avoid misunderstanding, it may be useful to point out that these rules do not constitute a formula for dealing with the currencies of countries in which current transactions are conducted at multiple rates.

II. Subject to I above, the following rules are adopted:

Where the foreign exchange value of a currency fluctuates so that exchange transactions in that currency are not based on parity in accordance with Article IV, Section 3, and the Fund decides to apply Article IV, Section 8, computations by the Fund relating to that currency (hereinafter referred to as "fluctuating currency") for the purpose of applying the provisions of the Articles of Agreement of the Fund will be made as follows:

1. (i) Computations will be based on the mid-point between the highest rate and the lowest rate for the United States dollar quoted, for cable transfers for spot delivery, in the main financial center of the country of the fluctuating currency on the day specified in sub-paragraph (ii) below; provided, however, that when prescribed by sub-paragraph (iii) below computations will be based on the mid-point between the highest rate and the lowest rate for the fluctuating currency quoted in New York for cable transfers for spot delivery. Arrangements will be made with the Fund's depository in the country of the appropriate exchange market as determined hereunder to communicate to the Fund the rates referred to in this sub-paragraph (i).

(ii) For the purpose of sub-paragraph (i) the specified day will be:

(a) For the sale or purchase by the Fund of a fluctuating currency in exchange for another currency, or the purchase of gold by the Fund under Article V, Section 6 (a), or voluntary repurchase, the last business day, in the main financial center of the country of the fluctuating currency, before the Fund instructs its depository to transfer or receive the fluctuating currency.

(b) For computations for the purpose of Article V, Section 7 (b) or Article V, Section 8 (f), the day as of which the computation is made.

(iii) If a mid-point cannot be determined in the main financial center of the country of the fluctuating currency in accordance with sub-paragraph (i) for the day specified in sub-paragraph (ii), there will be substituted therefor the mid-point for the fluctuating currency in New York determined in accordance with sub-paragraph (i) for the same calendar day. If no such mid-point can be determined for that day, there will then be substituted, to the extent necessary, first the previous business day in the main financial center of the country of the fluctuating currency, and secondly the same calendar day in New York. This procedure will be followed to the extent necessary, until a mid-point is determined in accordance with sub-paragraph (i), except where the Fund decides to make a special determination under paragraph 6 below.

2. Where as the result of the application of paragraph 1 the amount of currency which the Fund has agreed to sell would exceed the amount that the purchasing member is entitled to purchase under Article V, Section 3 (a) (iii), the amount of currency to be sold will be reduced to the amount the purchasing member is entitled to purchase under that provision unless the Fund makes a waiver under Article V, Section 4.

3. The Fund will revalue all of its holdings of a fluctuating currency on the basis of the mid-point employed for a computation under paragraph 1, and such revaluation will take effect as of the day specified for the computation in sub-

paragraph (ii) of paragraph 1. As a minimum, revaluation will be made as of each July 31, October 31, January 31, and April 30.

4. Whenever the Fund revalues its holdings of a fluctuating currency under paragraph 3, it will establish an account receivable or an account payable, as the case may be, in respect of the amount of the currency payable by or to the member under Article IV, Section 8. For the purpose of applying the provisions of the Articles as of any date, the Fund's holdings of the fluctuating currency will be deemed to be its actual holdings plus the balance in any such account receivable or minus the balance in any such account payable as of that date.

5. Any account receivable or payable established under paragraph 4 above will be settled promptly after each July 31, October 31, January 31, and April 30, provided, however, that settlement will not be necessary for any July 31, October 31, or January 31 on which the mid-point as determined under paragraph 1 above does not differ by more than five per cent from the rate for the last settlement. Settlement of any account receivable or payable established under paragraph 4 above will always be made when requested by either the Fund or the member.

6. In any case in which it appears to the Fund that any of the provisions of paragraphs 1 to 5 above are not adequate or satisfactory, the Fund will make a special determination for the treatment of such case.

III. Sections I and II above of this decision shall be communicated to members together with SM/54/25 as amended by SM/54/25, Supplement 1 as an explanatory memorandum.

Decision No. 321-(54/32)
June 15, 1954

TRANSACTIONS AND COMPUTATIONS INVOLVING FLUCTUATING CURRENCIES

The foregoing Decision No. 321-(54/32) was amended as follows:—

1. [Expired.]

2. There shall be added after "Article V, Section 6 (a)," in paragraph II.1 (ii) (a) of Executive Board Decision No. 321-(54/32) the words "or the sale of gold by the Fund under Article VII, Section 2,".

3. [Expired.]

Decision No. 1245-(61/45)
August 4, 1961

TRANSACTIONS AND COMPUTATIONS INVOLVING FLUCTUATING CURRENCIES

Paragraph II.1 (ii) (a) of Executive Board Decision No. 321-(54/32) is amended to read as follows:

For the sale or purchase by the Fund of a fluctuating currency in exchange for another currency, or the purchase of gold by the Fund under Article V, Section 6 (a), or the sale of gold by the Fund under Article VII, Section 2, or voluntary repurchase, or borrowing or the repayment of borrowing under Article VII, Section 2, the last business day in the main financial center of the country of the fluctuating currency, before the Fund instructs its depository to transfer or receive the fluctuating currency.

Decision No. 1283-(61/56)
December 20, 1961

Article IV, Section 2

GOLD

Premium Gold Transactions: Statement to Members

The following statement should be communicated to members and made public without delay:

In June 1947, the Fund issued a statement recommending to its members that they take effective action to prevent external transactions in gold at premium prices, because such transactions tend to undermine exchange stability and to impair monetary reserves. From time to time the Fund has reviewed its recommendations and the effectiveness of the action taken by its members.

Despite the improvement in the payments position of many members, sound gold and exchange policy of members continues to require that to the maximum extent practicable, gold should be held in official reserves rather than go into private hoards. It is only as gold is held in official reserves that it can be used by the monetary authorities to maintain exchange rates and meet balance of payments needs.

However, the Fund's continuous study of the situation in gold-producing and -consuming countries shows that their positions vary so widely as to make it impracticable to expect all members to take uniform measures in order to achieve the objectives of the premium gold statement. Accordingly, while the Fund reaffirms its belief in the economic principles involved and urges the members to support them, the Fund leaves to its members the practical operating decisions involved in their implementation, subject to the provisions of Art. IV, Sec. 2 and other relevant articles of the Articles of Agreement of the I.M.F.

The Fund will continue to collect full information about gold transactions, will watch carefully developments in this field and will be prepared in consultation with members to consider problems relating to exchange stability and any other problems which may arise.

Decision No. 75-(705)
September 28, 1951

For the statement of June 1947, see below, p. 310.

Statement of Policy Concerning Subsidies for Gold Production

The following statement of policy concerning subsidies for the production of gold is adopted, and the Managing Director is asked to send copies to members and release the statement for publication on December 12.

The International Monetary Fund has a responsibility to see that the gold policies of its members do not undermine or threaten to undermine exchange stability. Consequently every member which proposes to introduce new measures to subsidize the production of gold is under obligation to consult with the Fund on the specific measures to be introduced.

Under Article IV, Section 2, of the Articles of Agreement of the Fund members are prohibited from buying gold at a price above parity plus the prescribed margin. In the view of the Fund, a subsidy in the form of a uniform payment per ounce for all or part of the gold produced would constitute an increase in price which would not be permissible if the total price paid by the member for gold were thereby to become in excess of parity plus the prescribed margin. Subsidies involving payments in another form may also, depending upon their nature, constitute an increase in price.

Under Article IV, Section 4 (a), each member of the Fund "undertakes to collaborate with the Fund to promote exchange stability, to maintain orderly exchange arrangements with other members, and to avoid competitive exchange alterations." Subsidies on gold production regardless of their form are inconsistent with Article IV, Section 4 (a) if they undermine or threaten to undermine exchange stability. This would be the case, for example, if subsidies were to cast widespread doubt on the uniformity of the monetary value of gold in all member countries.

Subsidies which do not directly affect exchange stability may, nevertheless, contribute directly or indirectly to monetary instability in other countries and hence be of concern to the Fund.

A determination by the Fund that a proposed subsidy is not inconsistent with the foregoing principles will depend upon the circumstances in each case. Moreover, the Fund may find that subsidies which are justified at any one time may, because of changing conditions and changing effects, later prove to be inconsistent with the foregoing principles. In order to carry out its objectives, the Fund will continue to study, and to review with its members, their gold policies and any proposed changes, to determine if they are consonant with the provisions of the Fund Agreement and conducive to a sound international policy regarding gold.

Decision No. 233-2
December 11, 1947

ARTICLE IV, SECTIONS 3 AND 5

PAR VALUES AND MARGINS

FOREIGN EXCHANGE DEALINGS BASED ON PARITY: ARTICLE IV, SECTION 3

Dealings in paper money and coins are deemed to be "other exchange transactions" within the meaning of Article IV, Section 3, whether or not the importation and exportation of such money and coins to and from the country of origin are subject to restrictions. The dealings are in consequence subject to the provisions of that Section. Members shall not permit transactions in such paper money and coins within their territories in a manner or to an extent which will negate the par values agreed with the Fund. Where transactions in fact have such an effect the Fund will be obliged to intervene.

Decision No. 269-2
February 11, 1948

EXCHANGE DEALINGS AND MARGINS UNDER CONDITIONS OF INCREASING CONVERTIBILITY

The Fund does not object to exchange rates which are within 2 per cent of parity for spot exchange transactions between a member's currency and the currencies of other members taking place within the member's territories, whenever such rates result from the maintenance of margins of no more than 1 per cent from parity for a convertible, including externally convertible, currency.

Decision No. 904-(59/32)
July 24, 1959

Interpretation of Articles of Agreement

[A member] has stated its intention to maintain full employment and has requested an interpretation of the Articles of Agreement as to whether steps necessary to protect a member from unemployment of a chronic or persistent character, arising from pressure on its balance of payments, shall be measures necessary to correct a fundamental disequilibrium.

The Executive Directors interpret the Articles of Agreement to mean that steps which are necessary to protect a member from unemployment of a chronic or persistent character, arising from pressure on its balance of payments, are among the measures necessary to correct a fundamental disequilibrium; and that in each instance in which a member proposes a change in the par value of its currency to correct a fundamental disequilibrium the Fund will be required to determine, in the light of all relevant circumstances, whether in its opinion the proposed change is necessary to correct the fundamental disequilibrium.

Pursuant to Decision No. 71-2
September 26, 1946

Changes in Par Values: Fundamental Disequilibrium

The Fund has authority under Article IV, Section 5 (c) (ii) or (iii), to object to a change in par value proposed by a member when the extent of the proposed change, in the judgment of the Fund, is insufficient to correct a fundamental disequilibrium. The Executive Board recognizes, however, that the extent of the change in par value, necessary to correct a fundamental disequilibrium, cannot be determined with precision and that in reaching a decision on a member's proposal to change its par value, whether during the transitional period or thereafter, the member should be given the benefit of any reasonable doubt. In addition, due consideration should be given the views of the member regarding the political and social consequences of a change in par value greater than the one proposed.

Decision No. 278-3
March 1, 1948

Article V, Sections 3, 4, and 5

USE OF FUND'S RESOURCES AND STAND-BY ARRANGEMENTS

Use of Fund's Resources: Meaning of Article V, Section 3 (a) (i)

The word "represents" in Article V, Section 3 (a) (i), means "declares." The member is presumed to have fulfilled the condition mentioned in Article V, Section 3 (a) (i), if it declares that the currency is presently needed for making payments in that currency which are consistent with the provisions of the Agreement. But the Fund may, for good reasons, challenge the correctness of this declaration, on the grounds that the currency is not "presently needed" or because the currency is not needed for payment "in that currency," or because the payments will not be "consistent with the provisions of this Agreement." If the Fund concludes that a particular declaration is not correct, the Fund may postpone or reject the request, or accept it subject to conditions. The phrase "presently needed" cannot be defined in terms of a formula uniformly applicable to all cases, but where there is good reason to doubt that the currency is "presently needed," the Fund will have to apply the phrase in each case in the light of all the circumstances.

Decision No. 284-4
March 10, 1948

Use of Fund's Resources: Meaning of "Consistent with the Provisions of This Agreement" in Article V, Section 3

The phrase "consistent with the provisions of this Agreement" in Article V, Section 3, mean consistent both with the provisions of the Fund Agreement other than Article I and with the purposes of the Fund contained in Article I.

Decision No. 287-3
March 17, 1948

Extent of Drawing Rights: Meaning of Article V, Section 3 (a) (iii)

The Executive Board, acting pursuant to Article XVIII (a) of the Fund Agreement, interprets the quantitative limit of twenty-five per cent of quota in relation to drawing rights under Article V, Section 3 (a) (iii) as follows:

Where the Fund's holdings of a member's currency are not less than seventy-five per cent of its quota, and to the extent that such holdings would not be increased above two hundred per cent of its quota, the purchases which the member may make during a period of twelve months ending on the date of a proposed purchase shall be determined as follows:

(a) The total purchases shall not exceed twenty-five per cent of its quota;

(b) Provided that, if the member has made purchases during the period, it may then purchase an amount equal to the difference between twenty-five per cent of its quota and the total of such purchases adjusted on the basis that a repurchase by the member or sale of its currency during the period is deducted from a previous, but not subsequent, purchase or purchases during the period.

Decision No. 451-(55/52)
August 24, 1955

Use of Fund's Resources and Repurchases

1. The Managing Director has made the following statement which should be the framework for his discussions with members on use of the Fund's resources:

"The present proposals are designed to provide a practical basis for use of the Fund's resources in accordance with the purposes of the Fund. When the proposals are agreed they will, of course, have to be carried into effect through actual cases. Decisions will have to be made in accordance with the particular circumstances, and in this manner a body of practical criteria will gradually be built up. However, even at the outset I think it must be clear that access to the Fund should not be denied because a member is in difficulty. On the contrary, the task of the Fund is to help members that need temporary help, and requests should be expected from members that are in trouble in greater or lesser degree. The Fund's attitude toward the position of each member should turn on whether the problem to be met is of a temporary nature and whether the policies the member will pursue will be adequate to overcome the problem within such a period. The policies, above all, should determine the Fund's attitude.

"In addition, the Fund should pay attention to a member's general credit-worthiness, particularly its record with the Fund. In this respect, the member's record of prudence in drawing, its willingness to offer voluntary repayment when its situation permitted, and its promptness in fulfilling the obligation to transmit monetary reserves data and in discharging repurchase obligations would be important.

I would expect that in the years to come, with extended activities of the Fund, we shall be able more and more to rely on the Fund's own experience, thus providing a further and most useful link between Fund drawings and repurchases.

"After a period of relative inactivity of the Fund, it would be too much to expect that we should be able to solve with one stroke the entire problem of access to the Fund's resources so that each member would always know how any request would be received by the Fund. We shall have to feel our way. Sometimes a member may want to submit to the Fund a specific request for drawings, with adequate information as to the particular situation which prompts the request. At other times discussions between the member and the Fund may cover its general position, not with a view to any immediate drawing, but in order to ensure that it would be able to draw if, within a period of say 6 or 12 months, the need presented itself. The Fund itself might take the initiative in discussing with one or more members transactions which it believes suitable for the Fund and helpful to the members concerned. In cases where it would appear appropriate and useful, the Fund might arrange drawings to deal with special short-run situations accompanied by arrangements for repurchase in a period not exceeding 18 months."

2. a. In view of the Executive Board's interpretation of September 26, 1946, concerning the use of the Fund's resources, and considering especially the necessity for ensuring the revolving character of the Fund's resources, exchange purchased from the Fund should not remain outstanding beyond the period reasonably related to the payments problem for which it was purchased from the Fund. The period should fall within an outside range of three to five years. Members will be expected not to request the purchase of exchange from the Fund in circumstances where the reduction of the Fund's holdings of their currencies by an equivalent amount within that time cannot reasonably be envisaged.

b. The Fund has recently determined that when the charges on the Fund's holdings of a member's currency in any bracket have reached a rate of 3½ per cent per annum, the Fund and the member, in accordance with Article V, Section 8 (d) "shall consider means by which the Fund's holdings of the currency can be reduced" (EB Meeting 717, 11/19/51). In the course of consultations arising from purchases of exchange taking place after December 1, 1951, the Fund and the member will agree upon appropriate arrangements to ensure the reduction of the Fund's holdings of the member's currency as soon as possible, with the maximum period to be permitted in any such agreed arrangement requiring that within five years of each purchase made by the member there will be an equivalent repurchase of the Fund's holdings unless they have otherwise been reduced.

c. With respect to each future purchase which raises the Fund's holdings of the member's currency from not less than 75 per cent to not more than 100 per cent of its quota, a member whose currency held by the Fund has not been otherwise reduced within three years will be requested by the Fund to agree upon an arrangement providing that within five years of each purchase made by the member there will be an equivalent repurchase of the Fund's holdings unless they have otherwise been reduced.

d. When unforeseen circumstances beyond the member's control would make unreasonable the application of the principles set forth in paragraph 2 above, the Fund will consider extensions of time.

e. When requesting use of the resources of the Fund in accordance with the arrangements described above, a member will be expected to include in its authenticated request a statement that it will comply with the above principles.

f. These principles will be an essential element in any determination by the Fund as to whether a member is using the resources of the Fund in accordance with the purposes of the Fund.

3. Each member can count on receiving the overwhelming benefit of any doubt respecting drawings which would raise the Fund's holdings of its currency to not more than its quota.

4. The Managing Director should communicate with members concerning means to speed the collection and reporting of monetary reserves data and means to reduce the delays in reaching agreement under Rule I-6 in cases where a repurchase obligation has been computed. The Fund should also make it clear that an important element in its judgment respecting the use of its resources will be the co-operation of the member in helping to make Article V, Section 7 effective, including the timely provision of information and the facilitating of settlement.

5. This decision will be effective until December 31, 1953, and will be reviewed by the Executive Board before that date.

Decision No. 102-(52/11)
February 13, 1952

STAND-BY CREDIT ARRANGEMENTS

The Fund is prepared to consider requests by members for stand-by arrangements designed to give assurance that, during a fixed period of time, transactions up to a specified amount will be made whenever a member requests and without further consideration of its position, unless the ineligibility provisions of the Fund Agreement have been invoked. The following paragraphs set forth the general framework for stand-by arrangements:

1. Stand-by arrangements would be limited to periods of not more than six months. They could be renewed by a new decision of the Executive Board.

2. In considering the request for a stand-by arrangement or a renewal of a stand-by arrangement, the Fund would apply the same policies that are applied to requests for immediate drawings, including a review of the member's position, policies and prospects in the context of the Fund's objectives and purposes. The Fund would agree to a stand-by arrangement only for a member that would be in a position to make purchases of the same amount of exchange from the Fund.

3. Such arrangements would cover the portion of the quota which a member would be allowed, under Article V, Section 3, to draw within the period provided in the arrangement. However, this does not preclude the Fund from making stand-by arrangements for larger amounts on terms in accordance with Article V, Section 4.

4. A charge of $\frac{1}{4}$ of 1 per cent per annum would be payable to the Fund at the time a stand-by arrangement is agreed. This charge would be payable in gold (or United States dollars in lieu of gold) or the member's currency as specified for other charges by Article V, Section 8 (f). In the event that a stand-by arrangement is renewed, a new charge at the rate of $\frac{1}{4}$ of 1 per cent per annum would be payable to the Fund.

5. A member having a stand-by arrangement would have the right to engage in the transactions covered by the stand-by arrangement without further review by the

Fund. This right of the member could be suspended only with respect to requests received by the Fund after: (a) a formal ineligibility, or (b) a decision of the Executive Board to suspend transactions either generally (under Article XVI, Section 1 (a) (ii)) or in order to consider a proposal, made by an Executive Director or the Managing Director, formally to suppress or to limit the eligibility of the member.

6. In view of the policy of the Fund with respect to drawings within the so-called "gold tranche," it is not considered likely that members will request stand-by arrangements confined to transactions within the "gold tranche." Accordingly, the policy set forth in this decision is designed primarily to deal with stand-by arrangements for drawings beyond the "gold tranche." If at any time a member proposes a stand-by arrangement which would, in part or entirely, involve drawings within the "gold tranche," the Fund will reconsider the charge set forth in paragraph 4 above as applied to "gold tranche" transactions.

7. This decision will be effective until December 31, 1953, and will be reviewed by the Executive Board before that date.

Decision No. 155-(52/57)
October 1, 1952

I. Use of Fund's Resources and Repurchases
II. Stand-By Credit Arrangements

I. *Use of Fund Resources and Repurchases*

The decision taken at Meeting 52/11 on February 13, 1952, relating to use of the Fund's resources and repurchases, shall continue in effect subject to review by the Executive Board from time to time as circumstances warrant.

II. *Stand-by Arrangements*

The Fund is prepared to consider requests by members for stand-by arrangements designed to give assurance that, during a fixed period of time, transactions up to a specified amount will be made whenever a member requests and without further consideration of its position, unless the ineligibility provisions of the Fund Agreement have been invoked. The following paragraphs set forth the general framework for stand-by arrangements:

1. Stand-by arrangements will be limited to periods of not more than six months. They can be renewed by a new decision of the Executive Board. If a member believes that the payments problems it anticipates (for example, in connection with positive problems for maintaining or achieving convertibility) can be adequately provided for only by a stand-by arrangement of more than six months, the Fund will give sympathetic consideration to a request for a longer stand-by arrangement in the light of the problems facing the member and the measures being taken to deal with them. With respect to stand-by arrangements for periods of more than six months, the Fund and the member might find it appropriate to reach understandings additional to those set forth in this decision.

2. In considering the request for a stand-by arrangement or renewal of a stand-by arrangement, the Fund will apply the same policies that are applied to requests for immediate drawings, including a review of the member's position, policies and prospects in the context of the Fund's objectives and purposes. The Fund will agree to a stand-by arrangement only for a member that is in a position to make purchases of the same amount of exchange from the Fund.

3. There will be specified in each stand-by arrangement the transactions which may be made under that arrangement.

4. A member having a stand-by arrangement will have the right to engage in the transactions covered by the stand-by arrangement without further review by the Fund. This right of the member can be suspended only with respect to requests received by the Fund after: (a) a formal ineligibility, or (b) a decision of the Executive Board to suspend transactions either generally (under Article XVI, Section 1 (a) (ii)) or in order to consider a proposal, made by an Executive Director or the Managing Director, formally to suppress or to limit the eligibility of the member.

5. (a) A charge of ¼ of 1 per cent per annum will be payable to the Fund for stand-by arrangements. The charge will be payable in advance for each six months' period that the arrangement or any renewal is in effect.

(b) Charges for stand-by arrangements will be payable in gold, or U.S. dollars in lieu of gold, or in the member's currency as specified for other charges by Article V, Section 8 (f).

(c) There will be credited against the service charge payable for a transaction under a stand-by arrangement the charges paid for that part of the stand-by arrangement (or renewal of it) for the six months' period in which the transaction takes place and for the preceding six months' period; provided that the amount of charge paid for a stand-by arrangement (or renewal of it) for any six months' period will not be credited more than once in that period and the succeeding six months' period.

(d) In order to effect a credit against a service charge, the Fund will repay the portion of the charge paid for a stand-by arrangement that is to be credited under (c) above and collect the service charge in full.

(e) If a member notifies the Fund that it wishes to cancel a stand-by arrangement, the Fund will repay to the member a portion of the charge. The portion repaid will represent the charge paid for the period remaining unexpired at the time of cancellation with respect to the maximum amount of the stand-by arrangement that has never been drawn.

(f) Repayment under (d) or (e) above of a charge paid for a stand-by arrangement will be made in gold, U.S. dollars, and the member's currency in the same proportions as the charge was paid.

6. The Fund will not levy the charge set forth in paragraph 5 above with respect to that part of the stand-by arrangement covering "gold tranche" transactions.

7. This decision shall continue in effect subject to review by the Executive Board from time to time as circumstances warrant.

Decision No. 270-(53/95)
December 23, 1953

CHARGES FOR TRANSACTIONS AND STAND-BY ARRANGEMENTS

I. [Amendment to a Rule]

II. A stand-by arrangement shall provide for a fixed amount that can be purchased under it augmented by amounts equivalent to repurchases in respect of drawings made under the stand-by arrangement or made at the time when the stand-by arrangement is entered into, unless when any such repurchase is made the member informs the Fund that it does not wish the stand-by arrangement to be augmented by the amount of that repurchase. In exceptional circumstances, however, a stand-by arrangement may provide for purchases that increase the Fund's holdings of the currency of the member having the stand-by arrangement up to a specified level, provided that the amounts the member may purchase shall in no case be increased by other members' purchases of its currency.

III. 1. Paragraph II.5 (a) and (c) of Decision No. 270-(53/95) shall be amended to read as follows:

(a) When a stand-by arrangement is entered into or renewed, a charge of ¼ of 1 per cent per annum will be payable to the Fund in advance for the period of the stand-by arrangement or renewal. For any additional drawing rights that arise in the course of a stand-by arrangement, a further charge will be payable to the Fund in advance at the rate of ¼ of 1 per cent per annum calculated on the basis of the amount of the additional drawing rights and the unexpired period of the stand-by arrangement.

(c) There will be credited against the service charge for a transaction under a stand-by arrangement the charges actually paid in respect of that amount under the stand-by arrangement and any stand-by arrangement which preceded it without interval at the rate of ¼ of 1 per cent per annum and up to a maximum of ¼ of 1 per cent on that amount, due allowance being made for any refunds under paragraph II.6 of this decision. For the purpose of calculating such credits and for the purpose of calculating refunds under (e) below, it shall be assumed that drawings are made in respect of drawing rights in the order in which such drawing rights arose.

2. [Applies to individual countries.]

IV. Paragraph II.5 (e) of Decision No. 270-(53/95) is amended to read:

If a member notifies the Fund that it wishes to cancel a stand-by arrangement, the Fund will repay to the member a portion of the charge. The portion repaid will represent the charge for the period remaining unexpired at the date of cancellation for the amount that could still be drawn under the stand-by arrangement at the date of cancellation for which the member has paid a charge.

V. The following shall be added to Paragraph II.6 of Decision No. 270-(53/95):

To the extent that a charge has been levied on a part of the stand-by arrangement which falls into the gold tranche in the course of the stand-by arrangement, the Fund will refund the charge on that part for the unexpired period of the stand-by arrangement.

VI. Sections II, III.1, IV, and V above shall apply to stand-by arrangements entered into or renewed after the date of the adoption of this decision.

Decision No. 876-(59/15)
April 27, 1959

STAND-BY ARRANGEMENTS: REFUND OF CHARGES

(a) Refunds pursuant to Paragraph II.6 of Executive Board Decision No. 270-(53/95), as amended, of charges paid for stand-by arrangements entered into before the date of this decision will be calculated as of the date of each repurchase, drawing of the member's currency by other members, or increase of the member's quota, and will be based on the Fund's total holdings of the member's currency as of the date of each such calculation. If no such repurchase, drawing or increase of quota has taken place before the expiration of the stand-by arrangement the calculation will be based on the Fund's holdings at the end of the quarters of the Fund's financial year and at the date of expiration.

(b) In determining the Fund's holdings of a member's currency for the purposes of all calculations involving charges payable for stand-by arrangements entered into after the date of this decision, no account will be taken of amounts, not in excess of $\frac{1}{100}$ of 1% of the member's quota, in a special account to meet administrative expenses.

Decision No. 1345-(62/23)
May 23, 1962

STAND-BY ARRANGEMENTS

1. There shall be added to the end of paragraph II.4 of Executive Board Decision No. 270-(53/95) the following sentence for use in all future stand-by arrangements:

When notice of a decision for formal ineligibility or of a decision to consider a proposal is given pursuant to this paragraph, purchases under this stand-by arrangement will be resumed only after consultation has taken place between the Fund and the member and agreement has been reached on the terms for the resumption of such purchases.

2. "Prior notice" provisions appearing in existing stand-by arrangements, except for the one approved at EBM/60/53, shall be understood as if the sentence set forth in paragraph 1 above were substituted for such provisions.

Decision No. 1151-(61/6)
February 20, 1961

USE OF FUND'S RESOURCES: LIMITATION AND INELIGIBILITY UNDER ARTICLE V, SECTION 5

The Fund has, in the case of a member which has had a previous exchange transaction with the Fund, power to declare the member ineligible or limit its use of the resources of the Fund if the member is, in the opinion of the Fund, using the resources of the Fund in a manner contrary to the purposes of the Fund.

Decision No. 284-3
March 10, 1948

USE OF FUND'S RESOURCES: POSTPONEMENT AND LIMITATION UNDER ARTICLE V, SECTION 5

If the Fund receives a request from a member to purchase exchange and either, (1) the Fund is considering sending the member a report pursuant to Article V, Section 5, or (2) the Fund finds when the request is before it that action pursuant to that Section should be considered; then the Fund has the authority, pursuant to Article V, Section 5, of the Fund Agreement, to postpone the transfer as permitted under the provisions of Rules and Regulations G-3 for such time as may reasonably be necessary to decide the question of applying Article V, Section 5, and, if it decides to apply it, to prepare and send to the member a report and subject its use of the Fund's resources to limitations. Under such circumstances the limitations imposed will apply to the pending request for the purchase of exchange as well as to future requests.

Decision No. 286-1
March 15, 1948

USE OF FUND'S RESOURCES: MEANING OF "IS USING" IN ARTICLE V, SECTION 5

A member "is using" the resources of the Fund within the meaning of Article V, Section 5, where it is either actually disposing of the exchange purchased from the Fund, or, having purchased exchange from the Fund, the Fund's holdings of its currency are in excess of 75 per cent of its quota.

Decision No. 292-3
March 30, 1948

CURRENCIES TO BE DRAWN AND TO BE USED IN REPURCHASES

The Board approves the statement entitled "Currencies to be Drawn and to be Used in Repurchases" (SM/62/62, Revision 2), and this statement shall be incorporated in the Annual Report for 1962.

Decision No. 1371-(62/36)
July 20, 1962

Currencies to be Drawn and to be Used in Repurchases

From the beginning of the Fund's operations through 1957, drawings were overwhelmingly made in U.S. dollars. Starting in 1958, however, the Fund has increasingly encouraged drawings in other currencies, and this has been facilitated by the introduction of *de facto* convertibility for the currencies of the main industrial countries. Since the same currencies have become formally convertible under Article VIII in February 1961, repurchases have also begun to be made in these currencies.

Certain practices have been developed which take into account the new situation of the increasing number of currencies usable for the transactions of the Fund. These practices are still in a state of evolution as increased experience is being gained. The following paragraphs set out what may be regarded as appropriate practices to be followed for the time being.

I. *Procedure*

When a substantial number of currencies other than the U.S. dollar became usable for drawings, the drawing countries began to discuss with the Managing Director what currencies might be drawn. It gradually became the practice that consultation should take place between the drawing country and the Managing Director about the currencies to be drawn, and this practice has now become established in connection with all stand-by arrangements and drawings. Before giving advice to the drawing country, the Managing Director has got into contact with countries whose currencies might be drawn, even in circumstances where speed in arranging the drawing was essential. These consultations and the contacts with the countries concerned have thus become an integral part of the procedure which has been evolved.

In addition, an attempt is being made to indicate from time to time the amounts likely to be drawn and what might be a proper distribution of drawings among different currencies. Since under stand-by arrangements even fairly large drawings may be made suddenly, such indications as will be given can only be tentative and informal but they can, even so, serve a useful purpose in contributing to the maintenance of close contact between the Managing Director and the countries whose currencies may be drawn.

It has been concluded that the Fund has the legal authority to specify the convertible currencies to be used in making repurchases in discharge of obligations to repurchase that do not arise under Article V, Section 7 (b), and that, accordingly members are required to obtain the prior agreement of the Fund on the convertible currencies to be used in making such repurchases. Such repurchases must not increase the Fund's holdings of a member's currency beyond 75 per cent of that member's quota or decrease the Fund's holdings of the repurchasing member's currency below 75 per cent of that member's quota.

Until further notice, and in order to maintain conditions which foster repurchases and the revolving character of the Fund's resources, the Fund will accept any convertible currency fulfilling the conditions set forth in the last sentence above, provided that the repurchasing member has consulted the Managing Director on the currencies, and the amounts of each, to be used by the member in making its repurchase. Before giving his advice, the Managing Director will consult with countries whose currencies could be used in repurchase, and he will also attempt to give advance indications comparable to those relating to the currencies to be drawn. In all of these consultations, the Managing Director's recommendations will be guided by the principles regarding the currency composition of repurchases set out in Section II below.

The preceding paragraph shall apply to those repurchase obligations outside Article V, Section 7 (b) that are entered into after July 20, 1962. Members that entered into such obligations before that date shall be invited to consult the Managing Director on the currencies to be used in discharging these obligations, and the Managing Director will follow the procedure and be guided by the considerations referred to in the preceding paragraph.

The Managing Director will notify the Executive Directors at least two business days before any repurchase under the preceding paragraphs is carried out.

Where consultations with a country are referred to in this document they will normally be conducted with the Executive Director appointed or elected by such country.

II. *Criteria for the Selection of Currencies for Drawings and Repurchases*

The experience of the Fund in recent years has made it possible to indicate the main considerations which govern the selection of currencies for drawings and repurchases.

Drawings

With regard to the question of the selection of currencies for a particular drawing or for drawings in general, account has been taken of the balance of payments and reserve positions of the countries whose currencies are considered for drawing, as well as of the Fund's holdings of these currencies.

It has been found in practice that weight has to be given to all these three considerations, with some differentiation according to specific circumstances, and perhaps most particularly according to the size of the transaction or transactions involved.

During periods when aggregate drawings were moderate in amount, little difficulty was experienced in distributing these drawings among countries with reasonably satisfactory balance of payments positions on the basis of the level of these countries' reserves. When the volume of drawings has been large, it has been necessary to give more importance to the relative balance of payments positions of the countries to be drawn upon, so as to prevent excessive declines in their primary reserves as a result of Fund sales of their currencies. In connection with large drawings, in particular when they are associated with short-term capital movements, it is usually fairly easy to single out the countries whose reserves have benefited from an inflow of capital and to direct drawings more particularly towards the currencies of these countries.

By the attention thus given to the balance of payments position, the Fund has been able to arrange drawings in large measure to offset movements of funds in the exchange markets, and thus contribute to the strengthening of the international payments position. In considering a country's balance of payments position, seasonal fluctuations have not been allowed great weight, and the Fund has avoided drawing prematurely the currency of a country which is in the process of building up reserves from a relatively low position.

In applying the third consideration, account has to be taken of prevailing circumstances. For example, when the Fund's holdings of a particular currency have become very low, this has precluded substantial sales of that currency irrespective of the balance of payments and reserve position of the country concerned. In practice, the Fund has taken account of the level of its holdings of any currency well before the point of actual exhaustion, by gradually—rather than abruptly—reducing its sales of that currency on account of this factor.

Small drawings have normally been executed in one currency only, preferably the currency in which the drawing country holds the bulk of its reserves, even in circumstances where the payments position of the reserve center drawn upon has not been strong. Somewhat larger drawings have usually been distributed over more than one currency, but only exceptionally more than three to five currencies have been involved in a single drawing unless it has been a very large one. As far as possible, factors relevant to the particular drawing country, such as closeness of trade and payments relations, have been taken into account in the selection of the currencies to be drawn.

Repurchases

With regard to repurchases, the range of currencies is, as mentioned in Section I above, limited to currencies that are formally convertible and of which the Fund's holdings are below 75 per cent of the quota. As a result, repurchases in currencies have, until early 1961, been made almost exclusively in U.S. dollars. The U.S. dollar was also, in recent years, a currency that was available in the exchange market at favorable rates which reflected the prevailing balance of payments position.

Increasingly, however, weight has been given, in suggesting the allocation of repurchases among the countries whose currencies can be received in repurchase, to the Fund's holdings of these currencies compared to quotas. It would seem from the point of view of equity, and also with due regard to the liquidity position of the Fund, that great weight should be given to this criterion. But consideration should also be given, when appropriate, to the prevailing balance of payments position. In the case of relatively small repurchases it has been found practical that they be made in the currency in which a country holds its reserves, provided of course that such currency can be received by the Fund.

III. *Conversion*

It has been the experience in the Fund that a country drawing one or more currencies, after consultation with the Managing Director, has often wanted to convert either the whole or part of the amount drawn in a particular currency into one or more other currencies depending upon the payments that country has to meet or the currencies it normally holds in its reserves. The conversions thus effected have made it possible for the drawing country to meet its payments obligations and to strengthen its reserves in the most effective manner.

In the case of drawings in dollars, sterling and moderate amounts of certain other currencies, there has been no difficulty in effecting conversion at the going rate by transactions in the exchange market. Since the currencies drawn have generally been strong currencies for which there is a demand in the market, such conversion has generally been carried out without any disturbance to the market. For several currencies, arrangements have often been made between central banks, i.e., between the central banks in the drawing country and in the country whose currency is drawn, which provide for direct conversion into the latter's main reserve currency at the prevailing market rate without any commission being charged. In certain cases, however, especially when the amounts involved have been large, consideration has been given to the fact that conversion on the market would have affected exchange rates, and in some cases an allowance for this has been made. A preference has been indicated by two central banks for conversion at par, especially for large drawings.

In accordance with normal central banking procedure, whenever a country desires conversion of a currency it is drawing, it would get in touch with the central bank of the country drawn upon in order to reach an understanding on the most convenient way to arrange such conversion. When conversion has presented a country with difficulties, the assistance of the Managing Director has been sought in order to arrive at an appropriate solution.

The practices outlined above for drawings can, *mutatis mutandis*, be applied when a country needs to obtain a currency in order to make a repurchase from the Fund with that currency.

The Fund will keep the practices with respect to conversion as described above under study, and will re-examine them in the light of further experience.

COMPENSATORY FINANCING OF EXPORT FLUCTUATIONS

I. The report entitled "Compensatory Financing of Export Fluctuations" is approved for transmittal to the United Nations.

II. The following shall be recorded as the decision of the Executive Board on the compensatory financing of fluctuations in exports of primary exporting countries:

(1) The financing of deficits arising out of export shortfalls, notably those of primary exporting member countries, has always been regarded as a legitimate reason for the use of Fund resources, which have been drawn on frequently for this purpose. The Fund believes that such financing helps these members to continue their efforts to adopt adequate measures toward the solution of their financial problems and to avoid the use of trade and exchange restrictions to deal with balance of payments problems, and that this enables these members to pursue their programs of economic development with greater effectiveness.

(2) The Fund noted in its 1962 Annual Report that trends in prices of basic commodities in the past few years have adversely affected the export earnings of many Fund members, which has increased the strain on their reserves. In view of this and in order to ensure the maximum effectiveness for its support to members—in particular, primary exporting members—that are faced with fluctuations in export proceeds, the Fund is taking the action set forth below.

A. *Quotas*

(3) The quotas of many primary exporting countries, taken in conjunction with a reasonable use of their own reserves, are at present adequate for dealing with export fluctuations such as have occurred during the past decade. In those instances, however, where adjustment of the quotas of certain primary exporting countries, and in particular of countries with relatively small quotas, would be appropriate to make them more adequate in the light of fluctuations in export proceeds and other relevant criteria, the Fund is willing to give sympathetic consideration to requests for such adjustment.

B. *Drawing policies*

(4) Under the present policies and practices on the use of Fund resources, any member is given the overwhelming benefit of the doubt in relation to requests for transactions within the gold tranche, and the Fund's attitude to requests for transactions within the first credit tranche is a liberal one provided the member itself is making reasonable efforts to solve its problems. In the higher credit tranches too, where a member's policies are consistent with Fund policies and practices on the use of Fund resources in these tranches, the Fund gives assistance, on a substantial scale, toward meeting temporary payments deficits, including deficits arising out of export shortfalls. The policies and practices of the Fund on drawings and stand-by arrangements have been developed in order to help members to meet more effectively their temporary balance of payments difficulties and to enable them, where necessary, to pursue policies aimed at restoring external and internal equilibrium. Fund assistance in accordance with these policies and practices has made an effective contribution to the solution of the difficulties of these members and the achievement of equilibrium. It has often led, moreover, to the provision of further resources from public and private resources for meeting immediate and longer-term needs. In the application of its policies and practices governing the use of its resources, the Fund's attitude has been a flexible one, and account has been taken of special difficulties facing members.

(5) The Fund has reviewed its policies to determine how it could more readily assist members, particularly primary exporters, encountering payments difficulties produced by temporary export shortfalls, and has decided that such members can expect that their requests for drawings will be met where the Fund is satisfied that

   (a) the shortfall is of a short-term character and is largely attributable to circumstances beyond the control of the member; and
   (b) the member will cooperate with the Fund in an effort to find, where required, appropriate solutions for its balance of payments difficulties.

The amount of drawings outstanding under this decision will not normally exceed 25 per cent of the member's quota, and the drawings will be subject to the Fund's established policies and practices on repurchase. When drawings are made under this decision, the Fund will so indicate in an appropriate manner.

(6) In order to implement the Fund's policies in connection with compensatory financing of export shortfalls, the Fund will be prepared to waive the limit on Fund holdings of 200 per cent of quota, where appropriate. In particular, the Fund will be prepared to waive this limit (i) where a waiver is necessary to permit compensatory drawings to be made under paragraphs (4) and (5) above, or (ii) to the extent that drawings in accordance with paragraph (5) are still outstanding.

Whenever the Fund's holdings of a member's currency resulting from an outstanding compensatory drawing under paragraph (5) are reduced, by the member's repurchase or otherwise, this will restore *pro tanto* the member's facility to make a further compensatory drawing under that paragraph, should the need arise.

(7) In order to identify more clearly what are to be regarded as export shortfalls of a short-term character, the Fund, in conjunction with the member concerned, will seek to establish reasonable estimates regarding the medium-term trend of the member's exports on the basis of appropriate statistical data in conjunction with qualitative information about its export prospects.

(8) The provision of credit to deal with the balance of payments effects of export fluctuations provides immediate relief for a country's short-term difficulties. In many cases, however, it will also be necessary to introduce measures of a policy character in order to attain a satisfactory and lasting solution to a country's balance of payments problems. Members generally have actively cooperated with the Fund to find and adopt the measures necessary to this end. Beyond immediate balance of payments difficulties, the primary exporting countries are, in many instances, facing unfavorable long-term export trends, and all are trying to meet the challenge of achieving more rapid and sustained development through a strengthening and broadening of their economies. The last mentioned problem will require action in many fields and over many years by both the primary exporting countries and the industrial countries, separately and in concert, including readier access to the markets of the developed countries for the products of the developing countries and an appropriate and sustained flow of technical and financial assistance to the developing countries. The Fund considers that its activities can provide valuable assistance in helping to establish a climate within which longer-term measures can be more effectively pursued.

Decision No. 1477-(63/8)*
February 27, 1963

GOLD COLLATERAL TRANSACTIONS

Where the Fund decides in exceptional circumstances to enter into a gold collateral transaction with a member because this would promote the purposes of the Fund and give the member the opportunity, in consultation with the Fund, to adopt policies, during the period referred to in (a) below, that would be consistent with the policies and practices of the Fund on the use of its resources:

(a) the period for repurchase of the Fund's holdings of the member's currency resulting from the transaction, to the extent that they are not otherwise reduced, shall normally not exceed six months after the transfer of exchange by the Fund;

(b) the repurchase shall be made with gold or convertible currencies acceptable to the Fund in accordance with its Decision of July 20, 1962;

(c) the provisions of the pledge agreement shall be on the lines of those set forth in the draft letter annexed to SM/63/30.

Decision No. 1543-(63/39)
July 1, 1963

---

* Regarding gold subscriptions in connection with quota increases granted in accordance with this decision, see Decision No. 1529-(63/33), p. 222.

Draft Letter to Member Entering into a Gold Collateral Transaction

Dear Sir:

On_____, the Fund decided to enter into an exchange transaction with_____in an amount equivalent to US$_____ secured by the pledge of gold as collateral, [and granted the necessary waiver under Article V, Section 4,] subject to the conditions set forth in this letter. The amount of_____, equivalent to US$_____ and_____, equivalent to US$_____, will be transferred to your account(s) after the steps set forth in Section B below have been taken.

Section A

1. The collateral for the transaction shall consist of gold bars containing fine gold having a value not less than $_____ calculated on the basis of US$35 per troy ounce of fine gold. The fine gold content will be determined to the satisfaction of the Fund and at your expense.

2. The gold bars will be transferred by you by way of pledge at a gold depository selected by you from among the Fund's gold depositories (Federal Reserve Bank of New York, New York; the Bank of England, London; Banque de France, Paris; the Reserve Bank of India, Nagpur, India). You will irrevocably instruct the depository in accordance with the attached exhibit that the gold is to be transferred to, earmarked, and held in a special account in the name of and for the sole account of the International Monetary Fund, that the special account shall be at the sole order of the Fund, and that the depository shall accept and act upon any and all instructions of the Fund with respect to part or all of the gold in the special account. The Fund will arrange with the depository for the establishment of the special account. The depository will not be informed that the gold is held under pledge to the Fund.

3. You will represent to the Fund that the gold is free from any claims, liens or encumbrances in favor of any other party and subject to paragraph 9 below will remain free therefrom during the pledge. You will further represent to the Fund that under your law the gold may be freely pledged and disposed of as provided in this letter.

4. The gold will continue to be owned by you. Accordingly, the Fund will enter the gold in its books in your name, and will not show the gold in its books or accounts as owned by the Fund.

5. Not later than the repurchase date, namely the close of business six months after the value date for transfer of the exchange by the Fund to your account(s), you will repurchase the Fund's holdings of your currency resulting from the transaction, to the extent that such holdings are not otherwise reduced, with gold in the special account if you so request or with other gold or convertible currencies acceptable to the Fund in accordance with the Fund's Decision of July 20, 1962.

6. On any reduction at any time of the Fund's holdings of your currency resulting from the transaction otherwise than by repurchase with gold in the special account, the Fund will, on your request, release to you or to your order at the depository gold from the special account in an amount not exceeding the equivalent of the reduction, provided that the amount of gold remaining in the special account shall not be less than the equivalent of the outstanding balance of the transaction.

7. To the extent that the Fund's holdings of your currency resulting from the transaction have not been reduced by the close of business on the repurchase date, the Fund will give you notice of the balance due and payable by way of repurchase in respect of the transaction, and you will complete such repurchase with gold in the special account if you so request or other gold or convertible currencies acceptable to the Fund in accordance with the Fund's Decision of July 20, 1962 not later than the close of business thirty days after the repurchase date. In the absence of such repurchase by the close of business thirty days after the repurchase date, repurchase will be effected with gold in the special account on the instructions of the Fund and without the need for further notice or request to you.

8. Where repurchase is effected with gold in the special account pursuant to paragraph 5 or 7, the gold in the special account will be transferred, on the instructions of the Fund, to the ordinary gold account of the Fund at the depository, which gold shall then be deemed to have been transferred by you to the Fund and shall thereupon be owned by the Fund free from any claim, including any right of redemption. Any surplus balance of gold beyond the full amount of the repurchase will be returned to you but any balance less than one bar will be held under earmark for you pursuant to Rule I-1 of the Fund's Rules and Regulations.

9. At any time before the repurchase date or the close of business thirty days after the repurchase date, you may, after consulting the Fund, arrange for the sale of the gold in the special account, and the Fund will be prepared to give appropriate instructions to facilitate the sale, provided that on or before the close of business thirty days after the repurchase date the Fund's holdings of your currency resulting from the transaction will be repurchased with gold or convertible currencies acceptable to the Fund in accordance with the Fund's Decision of July 20, 1962, and provided further that the gold will not be released from pledge before such repurchase is effected.

10. All charges and costs connected with or resulting from the transfer to the special account (including without limitation transportation, earmarking, and holding), release, and redelivery, as well as converting the gold into good delivery bars if deemed necessary by the Fund under paragraph 1 above or if the gold is transferred to the Fund's ordinary gold account by way of repurchase will be borne by you.

Section B

The transfer of currencies pursuant to the transaction agreed by the Fund will be made by the Fund after the Fund has received from you:

   (i) acceptance of all of the conditions of this letter; and

   (ii) a copy of the instructions referred to in Section A 2 above; and

   (iii) the representations referred to in Section A 3 above;

and, in addition, has received from the depository:

   (iv) confirmation that the depository has established the special account, earmarked the gold, and will act in accordance with Section A 2 above; and

   (v) information satisfactory to the Fund as to the fine gold content of the bars.

Very truly yours,
International Monetary Fund
By:

EXCHANGE TRANSACTIONS PRIOR TO THE ESTABLISHMENT OF INITIAL PAR VALUE

(a) Where the Fund prescribes the conditions and amount of an exchange transaction by a member before the establishment of an initial par value, the member will be required to complete the payment of its subscription on the basis of a provisional rate of exchange for its currency proposed by the member and agreed by the Fund.

(b) In deciding whether to permit exchange transactions before the establishment of an initial par value, the Fund, in accordance with the last sentence of Article I, will be guided by the purposes of the Articles; the Fund will encourage members to follow policies leading to the establishment of realistic exchange rates and to the adoption at the earliest feasible date of effective par values, and will take into account the efforts that are being made to achieve this objective. However, the Fund will give the overwhelming benefit of any doubt to requests for exchange transactions within the gold tranche and members can expect that requests for drawings will be met where they are made in accordance with paragraph 5 of E.B. Decision No. 1477-(63/8), adopted February 27, 1963.

Decision No. 1687-(64/22)
April 22, 1964

PROCEDURE FOR DRAWINGS IN THE GOLD TRANCHE

When a duly authenticated request to draw in the gold tranche is received from a member, the request shall be notified to the Executive Board on the day it is received, whenever possible, or on the next business day, and unless, by the close of that business day, the Managing Director decides or an Executive Director requests that the matter be placed on the Board's agenda for discussion, the Fund shall, at the close of the first business day following the date of the receipt of the request, instruct the appropriate depository to make the transfer on the next business day after the instruction or as soon as possible thereafter.

Decision No. 1745-(64/46)
August 3, 1964

ARTICLE V, SECTION 7

REPURCHASE OBLIGATIONS

REPURCHASE AND RULE G-7

Until further notice, where a member has an accrued repurchase obligation in currency under Art. V, Sec. 7 (b), and Schedule B and discharges part or all of that obligation by a sale of gold to the Fund for that currency under Art. V, Sec. 6 (a), as provided in paragraph 3 of the decision of the Executive Board at EBM 648 (3/8/51), such gold shall be purchased by the Fund without collecting the estimated costs of later possible conversion of the gold into that currency as permitted under Rule G-7 of the Rules and Regulations, it being understood that the existing requirements as to the form and delivery of such gold would remain in effect.

Decision No. 119-(52/30)
June 2, 1952

Effect of Payment of Gold Subscriptions on Repurchase Obligations

RESOLVED:

. . . that, for the purpose of the repurchase obligations prescribed by Article V, Section 7, increases and decreases in the monetary reserves of a member shall not be considered if they occur on or before the latest date on which the member's subscription must be paid in accordance with this Resolution; and the payment of subscriptions, whether actually made before or after such latest date for payment, shall not be regarded as resulting in a decrease in monetary reserves.

Decision No. 124-2
January 22, 1947

Repurchase Obligations: Article V, Section 7 (c)

In the application of the repurchase obligations of the Fund Agreement the limits specified in Article V, Section 7 (c), apply solely as of the end of the financial year for which the repurchase obligations are calculated.

Decision No. 419-1
April 11, 1949

Repurchase Obligations: Article V, Section 7 (b) (i) or (ii)

Whenever a member uses its monetary reserves to repurchase its currency from the Fund in accordance with the provisions of Article V, Section 7 (b) (i) or (ii), the resulting reduction in its monetary reserves and in the Fund's holdings of its currency must be regarded as having occurred, for the purpose of calculating subsequent repurchase obligations under the same provisions of the Fund Agreement, at the end of the financial year of the Fund in respect of which the obligation to make the repurchase arose. Members shall be informed of the foregoing.

Decision No. 447-5
June 17, 1949

Voluntary Repurchases

(1) Subject to paragraph 3 below, a member may offer in voluntary repurchase, and the Fund has the power to accept, if it so decides, gold or convertible currencies to the extent that (a) the Fund's holdings of the convertible currency of a member which is offered would not be increased above 75% of the quota of that member, and (b) the Fund's holdings of the repurchasing member's currency would not be decreased below 75% of its quota.

(2) As a matter of legal interpretation it is determined that the consent of the member whose currency is offered in voluntary repurchase is not necessary as a condition precedent to the acceptance by the Fund of such currency.

(3) Where a member has an accrued and undischarged repurchase obligation under Art. V, Sec. 7 (b), and Schedule B in respect of any financial year of the Fund, the member must discharge the obligation in accordance with those provisions; provided, however, that the payment of currency under those provisions may be combined with the sale of gold to the Fund for the currency under Art. V, Sec. 6 (a).

Decision No. 7-(648)
March 8, 1951

Minimal Repurchase Obligations Procedure

In cases where a repurchase obligation of less than the equivalent of $500 is calculated the member will be notified, and the obligation collected, on the next occasion thereafter that a repurchase obligation accrues which, together with the first one, will total the equivalent of $500 or more.

Decision No. 705-(57/55)
November 7, 1957

Calculation of Repurchase Obligations: Prompt Reporting of Monetary Reserves Data

1. Where on any April 30 the Fund holds a member's currency in an amount exceeding 75 per cent of the member's quota, the member shall make a provisional monetary reserves report to the Fund not later than May 31, preferably by cable.

2. The Fund will make a provisional calculation of the amount and distribution of the repurchase obligations of such members and will inform them of the results of the calculation not later than June 15. Members shall discharge within thirty days any repurchase obligations as thus provisionally calculated and agreed with the member.

3. All provisional repurchases shall be subject to adjustment by members and the Fund in accordance with Rule I-6 of the Fund's Rules and Regulations.

Decision No. 1813-(65/4)
January 18, 1965

Article VI, Section 1
USE OF FUND'S RESOURCES FOR CAPITAL TRANSFERS

Interpretation of Articles of Agreement

The Executive Directors of the International Monetary Fund interpret the Articles of Agreement to mean that authority to use the resources of the Fund is limited to use in accordance with its purposes to give temporary assistance in financing balance of payments deficits on current account for monetary stabilization operations.

Pursuant to Decision No. 71-2
September 26, 1946

Use of Fund's Resources for Capital Transfers

After full consideration of all relevant aspects concerning the use of the Fund's resources, the Executive Directors decide by way of clarification that Decision No. 71-2 does not preclude the use of the Fund's resources for capital transfers in accordance with the provisions of the Articles, including Article VI.

Decision No. 1238-(61/43)
July 28, 1961

Article VI, Section 3

CONTROLS ON CAPITAL TRANSFERS

The report of the Committee on Interpretation on controls on capital transfers (EBD/56/71, 7/11/56) is approved and the following conclusions are adopted:

Subject to the provisions of Article VI, Section 3 concerning payments for current transactions and undue delay in transfers of funds in settlement of commitments:

(a) Members are free to adopt a policy of regulating capital movements for any reason, due regard being paid to the general purposes of the Fund and without prejudice to the provisions of Article VI, Section 1.

(b) They may, for that purpose, exercise such controls as are necessary including making such arrangements as may be reasonably needed with other countries, without approval of the Fund.

Decision No. 541-(56/39)
July 25, 1956

Article VII, Section 2

GENERAL ARRANGEMENTS TO BORROW *

Preamble

In order to enable the International Monetary Fund to fulfill more effectively its role in the international monetary system in the new conditions of widespread convertibility, including greater freedom for short-term capital movements, the main industrial countries have agreed that they will, in a spirit of broad and willing cooperation, strengthen the Fund by general arrangements under which they will stand ready to lend their currencies to the Fund up to specified amounts under Article VII, Section 2 of the Articles of Agreement when supplementary resources are needed to forestall or cope with an impairment of the international monetary system in the aforesaid conditions. In order to give effect to these intentions, the following terms and conditions are adopted under Article VII, Section 2 of the Articles of Agreement.

Paragraph 1. *Definitions*

As used in this Decision the term:

(i) "Articles" means the Articles of Agreement of the International Monetary Fund;

(ii) "credit arrangement" means an undertaking to lend to the Fund on the terms and conditions of this Decision;

(iii) "participant" means a participating member or a participating institution;

(iv) "participating institution" means an official institution of a member that has entered into a credit arrangement with the Fund with the consent of the member;

(v) "participating member" means a member of the Fund that has entered into a credit arrangement with the Fund;

(vi) "amount of a credit arrangement" means the maximum amount expressed in units of its currency that a participant undertakes to lend to the Fund under a credit arrangement;

---

* See p. 252.

(vii) "call" means a notice by the Fund to a participant to make a transfer under its credit arrangement to the Fund's account;

(viii) "borrowed currency" means currency transferred to the Fund's account under a credit arrangement;

(ix) "drawer" means a member that purchases borrowed currency from the Fund in an exchange transaction or in an exchange transaction under a stand-by arrangement;

(x) "indebtedness" of the Fund means the amount it is committed to repay under a credit arrangement.

Paragraph 2. *Credit Arrangements*

A member or institution that adheres to this Decision undertakes to lend its currency to the Fund on the terms and conditions of this Decision up to the amount in units of its currency set forth in the Annex to this Decision or established in accordance with Paragraph 3 (b).

Paragraph 3. *Adherence*

(a) Any member or institution specified in the Annex may adhere to this Decision in accordance with Paragraph 3 (c).

(b) Any member or institution not specified in the Annex that wishes to become a participant may at any time, after consultation with the Fund, give notice of its willingness to adhere to this Decision, and, if the Fund shall so agree and no participant object, the member or institution may adhere in accordance with Paragraph 3 (c). When giving notice of its willingness to adhere under this Paragraph 3 (b) a member or institution shall specify the amount, expressed in terms of its currency, of the credit arrangement which it is willing to enter into, provided that the amount shall not be less than the equivalent at the date of adherence of one hundred million United States dollars of the weight and fineness in effect on July 1, 1944.

(c) A member or institution shall adhere to this Decision by depositing with the Fund an instrument setting forth that it has adhered in accordance with its law and has taken all steps necessary to enable it to carry out the terms and conditions of this Decision. On the deposit of the instrument the member or institution shall be a participant as of the date of the deposit or of the effective date of this Decision, whichever shall be later.

Paragraph 4. *Entry into Force*

This Decision shall become effective when it has been adhered to by at least seven of the members or institutions included in the Annex with credit arrangements amounting in all to not less than the equivalent of five and one-half billion United States dollars of the weight and fineness in effect on July 1, 1944.

Paragraph 5. *Changes in Amounts of Credit Arrangements*

The amounts of participants' credit arrangements may be reviewed from time to time in the light of developing circumstances and changed with the agreement of the Fund and all participants.

Paragraph 6. *Initial Procedure*

When a participating member or a member whose institution is a participant approaches the Fund on an exchange transaction or stand-by arrangement and the Managing Director, after consultation, considers that the exchange transaction or stand-by arrangement is necessary in order to forestall or cope with an impairment of the international monetary system, and that the Fund's resources need to be supplemented for this purpose, he shall initiate the procedure for making calls under Paragraph 7.

Paragraph 7. *Calls*

(a) The Managing Director shall make a proposal for calls for an exchange transaction or for future calls for exchange transactions under a stand-by arrangement only after consultation with Executive Directors and participants. A proposal shall become effective only if it is accepted by participants and the proposal is then approved by the Executive Directors. Each participant shall notify the Fund of the acceptance of a proposal involving a call under its credit arrangement.

(b) The currencies and amounts to be called under one or more of the credit arrangements shall be based on the present and prospective balance of payments and reserve positions of participating members or members whose institutions are participants and on the Fund's holdings of currencies.

(c) Unless otherwise provided in a proposal for future calls approved under Paragraph 7 (a), purchases of borrowed currency under a stand-by arrangement shall be made in the currencies of participants in proportion to the amounts in the proposal.

(d) If a participant on which calls may be made pursuant to Paragraph 7 (a) for a drawer's purchases under a stand-by arrangement gives notice to the Fund that in the participant's opinion, based on the present and prospective balance of payments and reserve position, calls should no longer be made on the participant or that calls should be for a smaller amount, the Managing Director may propose to other participants that substitute amounts be made available under their credit arrangements, and this proposal shall be subject to the procedure of Paragraph 7 (a). The proposal as originally approved under Paragraph 7 (a) shall remain effective unless and until a proposal for substitute amounts is approved in accordance with Paragraph 7 (a).

(e) When the Fund makes a call pursuant to this Paragraph 7, the participant shall promptly make the transfer in accordance with the call.

Paragraph 8. *Evidence of Indebtedness*

(a) The Fund shall issue to a participant, on its request, nonnegotiable instruments evidencing the Fund's indebtedness to the participant. The form of the instruments shall be agreed between the Fund and the participant.

(b) Upon repayment of the amount of any instrument issued under Paragraph 8 (a) and all accrued interest, the instrument shall be returned to the Fund for cancellation. If less than the amount of any such instrument is repaid, the instrument shall be returned to the Fund and a new instrument for the remainder of the amount shall be substituted with the same maturity date as in the old instrument.

Paragraph 9. *Interest and Charges*

(a) The Fund shall pay a charge of one-half of one per cent on transfers made in accordance with Paragraph 7 (e).

(b) The Fund shall pay interest on its indebtedness at the rate of one and one-half per cent per annum. In the event that this becomes different from a basic rate determined as follows:

the charge levied by the Fund pursuant to Article V, Section 8 (a) plus the charge levied by the Fund pursuant to Article V, Section 8 (c) (i), as changed from time to time under Article V, Section 8 (e), during the first year after a purchase of exchange from the Fund, minus one-half of one per cent,

the interest payable by the Fund shall be changed by the same amount as from the date when the difference in the basic rate takes effect. Interest shall be paid as soon as possible after July 31, October 31, January 31, and April 30.

(c) Interest and charges shall be paid in gold to the extent that this can be effected in bars. Any balance not so paid shall be paid in United States dollars.

(d) Gold payable to a participant in accordance with Paragraph 9 (b) or Paragraph 11 shall be delivered at any gold depository of the Fund chosen by the participant at which the Fund has sufficient gold for making the payment. Such delivery shall be free of any charges or costs for the participant.

Paragraph 10. *Use of Borrowed Currency*

The Fund's policies and practices on the use of its resources and stand-by arrangements, including those relating to the period of use, shall apply to purchases of currency borrowed by the Fund.

Paragraph 11. *Repayment by the Fund*

(a) Subject to the other provisions of this Paragraph 11, the Fund, five years after a transfer by a participant, shall repay the participant an amount equivalent to the transfer calculated in accordance with Paragraph 12. If the drawer for whose purchase participants make transfers is committed to repurchase at a fixed date earlier than five years after its purchase, the Fund shall repay the participants at that date. Repayment under this Paragraph 11 (a) or under Paragraph 11 (c) shall be, as determined by the Fund, in the participant's currency whenever feasible, or in gold, or, after consultation with the participant, in other currencies that are convertible in fact. Repayments to a participant under the subsequent provisions of this Paragraph 11 shall be credited against transfers by the participant for a drawer's purchases in the order in which repayment must be made under this Paragraph 11 (a).

(b) Before the date prescribed in Paragraph 11 (a), the Fund, after consultation with a participant, may make repayment to the participant, in part or in full, with any increases in the Fund's holdings of the participant's currency that exceed the Fund's working requirements, and participants shall accept such repayment.

(c) Whenever a drawer repurchases, the Fund shall promptly repay an equivalent amount, except in any of the following cases:

(i) The repurchase is under Article V, Section 7 (b) and can be identified as being in respect of a purchase of currency other than borrowed currency.

(ii) The repurchase is in discharge of a commitment entered into on a purchase of currency other than borrowed currency.

(iii) The repurchase entitles the drawer to augmented rights under a stand-by arrangement pursuant to Section II of Decision No. 876-(59/15) of the Executive Directors, provided that, to the extent that the drawer does not exercise such augmented rights, the Fund shall promptly repay an equivalent amount on the expiration of the stand-by arrangement.

(d) Whenever the Fund decides in agreement with a drawer that the problem for which the drawer made its purchases has been overcome, the drawer shall complete repurchase, and the Fund shall complete repayment and be entitled to use its holdings of the drawer's currency below 75 per cent of the drawer's quota in order to complete such repayment.

(e) Repayment under Paragraph 11 (c) and (d) shall be made in the order established under Paragraph 11 (a) and in proportion to the Fund's indebtedness to the participants that made transfers in respect of which repayment is being made.

(f) Before the date prescribed in Paragraph 11 (a) a participant may give notice representing that there is a balance of payments need for repayment of part or all of the Fund's indebtedness and requesting such repayment. The Fund shall give the overwhelming benefit of any doubt to the participant's representation. Repayment shall be made after consultation with the participant in the currencies of other members that are convertible in fact, or made in gold, as determined by the Fund. If the Fund's holdings of currencies in which repayment should be made are not wholly adequate, individual participants shall be requested, and will be expected, to provide the necessary balance under their credit arrangements. If notwithstanding the expectation that the participants will provide the necessary balance, they fail to do so, repayment shall be made to the extent necessary in the currency of the drawer for whose purchases the participant requesting repayment made transfers. For all of the purposes of this Paragraph 11, transfers under this Paragraph 11 (f) shall be deemed to have been made at the same time and for the same purchases as the transfers by the participant obtaining repayment under this Paragraph 11 (f).

(g) All repayments to a participant in a currency other than its own shall be guided, to the maximum extent practicable, by the present and prospective balance of payments and reserve positions of the members whose currencies are to be used in repayment.

(h) The Fund shall at no time reduce its holdings of a drawer's currency below an amount equal to the Fund's indebtedness to the participants resulting from transfers for the drawer's purchases.

(i) When any repayment is made to a participant, the amount that can be called for under its credit arrangement in accordance with this Decision shall be restored *pro tanto* but not beyond the amount of the credit arrangement.

Paragraph 12. *Rates of Exchange*

(a) The value of any transfer shall be calculated as of the date of the transfer in terms of a stated number of fine ounces of gold or of the United States dollar of the weight and fineness in effect on July 1, 1944, and the Fund shall be obliged to repay an equivalent value.

(b) For all of the purposes of this Decision, the equivalent in currency of any number of fine ounces of gold or of the United States dollar of the weight and fineness in effect on July 1, 1944, or *vice versa*, shall be calculated at the rate of exchange at which the Fund holds such currency at the date as of which the calculation is made; provided however that the provisions of Decision No. 321-(54/32) of the Executive Directors on Transactions and Computations Involving Fluctuating Currencies, as amended by Decision No. 1245-(61/45) and Decision No. 1283-(61/56), shall determine the rate of exchange for any currency to which that decision, as amended, has been applied.

Paragraph 13. *Transferability*

A participant may not transfer all or part of its claim to repayment under a credit arrangement except with the prior consent of the Fund and on such terms and conditions as the Fund may approve.

Paragraph 14. *Notices*

Notice to or by a participating member under this Decision shall be in writing or by cable and shall be given to or by the fiscal agency of the participating member designated in accordance with Article V, Section 1 of the Articles and Rule G-1 of the Rules and Regulations of the Fund. Notice to or by a participating institution shall be in writing or by cable and shall be given to or by the participating institution.

Paragraph 15. *Amendment*

This Decision may be amended during the period prescribed in Paragraph 19 (a) only by a decision of the Fund and with the concurrence of all participants. Such concurrence shall not be necessary for the modification of the Decision on its renewal pursuant to Paragraph 19 (b).

Paragraph 16. *Withdrawal of Adherence*

A participant may withdraw its adherence to this Decision in accordance with Paragraph 19 (b) but may not withdraw within the period prescribed in Paragraph 19 (a) except with the agreement of the Fund and all participants.

Paragraph 17. *Withdrawal from Membership*

If a participating member or a member whose institution is a participant withdraws from membership in the Fund, the participant's credit arrangement shall cease at the same time as the withdrawal takes effect. The Fund's indebtedness under the credit arrangement shall be treated as an amount due from the Fund for the purpose of Article XV, Section 3, and Schedule D of the Articles.

Paragraph 18. *Suspension of Exchange Transactions and Liquidation*

(a) The right of the Fund to make calls under Paragraph 7 and the obligation to make repayments under Paragraph 11 shall be suspended during any suspension of exchange transactions under Article XVI of the Articles.

(b) In the event of liquidation of the Fund, credit arrangements shall cease and the Fund's indebtedness shall constitute liabilities under Schedule E of the Articles. For the purpose of Paragraph 1 (a) of Schedule E, the currency in which the liability of the Fund shall be payable shall be first the participant's currency and then the currency of the drawer for whose purchases transfers were made by the participant.

Paragraph 19. *Period and Renewal*

(a) This Decision shall continue in existence for four years from its effective date.

(b) This Decision may be renewed for such period or periods and with such modifications, subject to Paragraph 5, as the Fund may decide. The Fund shall adopt a decision on renewal and modification, if any, not later than twelve months before the end of the period prescribed in Paragraph 19 (a). Any participant may advise the Fund not less than six months before the end of the period prescribed in Paragraph 19 (a) that it will withdraw its adherence to the Decision as renewed. In the absence of such notice, a participant shall be deemed to continue to adhere to the Decision as renewed. Withdrawal of adherence in accordance with this Paragraph 19 (b) by a participant, whether or not included in the Annex, shall not preclude its subsequent adherence in accordance with Paragraph 3 (b).

(c) If this Decision is terminated or not renewed, Paragraphs 8 through 14, 17 and 18 (b) shall nevertheless continue to apply in connection with any indebtedness of the Fund under credit arrangements in existence at the date of the termination or expiration of the Decision until repayment is completed. If a participant withdraws its adherence to this Decision in accordance with Paragraph 16 or Paragraph 19 (b), it shall cease to be a participant under the Decision, but Paragraphs 8 through 14, 17 and 18 (b) of the Decision as of the date of the withdrawal shall nevertheless continue to apply to any indebtedness of the Fund under the former credit arrangement until repayment has been completed.

Paragraph 20. *Interpretation*

Any question of interpretation raised in connection with this Decision which does not fall within the purview of Article XVIII of the Articles shall be settled to the mutual satisfaction of the Fund, the participant raising the question, and all other participants. For the purpose of this Paragraph 20 participants shall be deemed to include those former participants to which Paragraphs 8 through 14, 17 and 18 (b) continue to apply pursuant to Paragraph 19 (c) to the extent that any such former participant is affected by a question of interpretation that is raised.

ANNEX
Participants and Amounts of Credit Arrangements

			Units of Participant's Currency
1.	United States of America	US$	2,000,000,000
2.	Deutsche Bundesbank	DM	4,000,000,000
3.	United Kingdom	£	357,142,857
4.	France	NF	2,715,381,428
5.	Italy	Lit	343,750,000,000
6.	Japan	Yen	90,000,000,000
7.	Canada	Can$	216,216,000
8.	Netherlands	f.	724,000,000
9.	Belgium	BF	7,500,000,000
10.	Sveriges Riksbank	SKr	517,320,000

Decision No. 1289-(62/1)*
January 5, 1962

Letter from Mr. Baumgartner, Minister of Finance, France, to Mr. Dillon, Secretary of the Treasury, United States

December 15, 1961

Dear Mr. Secretary:

The purpose of this letter is to set forth the understandings reached during the recent discussions in Paris with respect to the procedure to be followed by the Participating Countries and Institutions (hereinafter referred to as "the participants") in connection with borrowings by the International Monetary Fund of Supplementary Resources under credit arrangements which we expect will be established pursuant to a decision of the Executive Directors of the Fund.

This procedure, which would apply after the entry into force of that decision with respect to the participants which adhere to it in accordance with their laws, and which would remain in effect during the period of the decision, is as follows:

---

* As amended: with effect from August 1, 1962 (Decision No. 1362-(62/32) dated July 9, 1962) and with effect from October 12, 1962 (Decision No. 1415-(62/47) dated September 19, 1962).

The General Arrangements to Borrow entered into force on October 24, 1962.

A. A participating country which has need to draw currencies from the International Monetary Fund or to seek a stand-by agreement with the Fund in circumstances indicating that the Supplementary Resources might be used, shall consult with the Managing Director of the Fund first and then with the other participants.

B. If the Managing Director makes a proposal for Supplementary Resources to be lent to the Fund, the participants shall consult on this proposal and inform the Managing Director of the amounts of their currencies which they consider appropriate to lend to the Fund, taking into account the recommendations of the Managing Director and their present and prospective balance of payments and reserve positions. The participants shall aim at reaching unanimous agreement.

C. If it is not possible to reach unanimous agreement, the question whether the participants are prepared to facilitate, by lending their currencies, an exchange transaction or stand-by arrangement of the kind covered by the special borrowing arrangements and requiring the Fund's resources to be supplemented in the general order of magnitude proposed by the Managing Director, will be decided by a poll of the participants.

The prospective drawer will not be entitled to vote. A favorable decision shall require the following majorities of the participants which take part in the vote, it being understood that abstentions may be justified only for balance of payments reasons as stated in paragraph D:

(1) a two-thirds majority of the number of participants voting; and

(2) a three-fifths majority of the weighted votes of the participants voting, weighted on the basis of the commitments to the Supplementary Resources.

D. If the decision in paragraph C is favorable, there shall be further consultations among the participants, and with the Managing Director, concerning the amounts of the currencies of the respective participants which will be loaned to the Fund in order to attain a total in the general order of magnitude agreed under paragraph C. If during the consultations a participant gives notice that in its opinion, based on its present and prospective balance of payments and reserve position, calls should not be made on it, or that calls should be for a smaller amount that that proposed, the participants shall consult among themselves and with the Managing Director as to the additional amounts of their currencies which they could provide so as to reach the general order of magnitude agreed under paragraph C.

E. When agreement is reached under paragraph D, each participant shall inform the Managing Director of the calls which it is prepared to meet under its credit arrangement with the Fund.

F. If a participant which has loaned its currency to the Fund under its credit arrangement with the Fund subsequently requests a reversal of its loan which leads to further loans to the Fund by other participants, the participant seeking such reversal shall consult with the Managing Director and with the other participants.

For the purpose of the consultative procedures described above, participants will designate representatives who shall be empowered to act with respect to proposals for use of the Supplementary Resources.

It is understood that in the event of any proposals for calls under the credit arrangements or if other matters should arise under the Fund decision requiring consultations among the participants, a consultative meeting will be held among all the participants. The representative of France shall be responsible for calling the first meeting, and at that time the participants will determine who shall be the Chairman. The Managing Director of the Fund or his representative shall be invited to participate in these consultative meetings.

It is understood that in order to further the consultations envisaged, participants should, to the fullest extent practicable, use the facilities of the international organizations to which they belong in keeping each other informed of the developments in their balances of payments that could give rise to the use of the Supplementary Resources.

These consultative arrangements, undertaken in a spirit of international cooperation, are designed to insure the stability of the international payments system.

I shall appreciate a reply confirming that the foregoing represents the understandings which have been reached with respect to the procedure to be followed in connection with borrowings by the International Monetary Fund under the credit arrangements to which I have referred.

I am sending identical letters to the other participants—that is, Belgium, Canada, Germany, Italy, Japan, the Netherlands, Sweden, the United Kingdom. Attached is a verbatim text of this letter in English. The French and English texts and the replies of the participants in both languages shall be equally authentic. I shall notify all of the participants of the confirmations received in response to this letter.

GENERAL ARRANGEMENTS TO BORROW: ASSOCIATION OF SWITZERLAND *

The understandings set forth in the letter which the Swiss Ambassador to the United States proposes to send to the Managing Director (EBD/64/73, Attachment I) are acceptable to the Fund and the Managing Director is authorized to send the letter attached to EBD/64/73 (Attachment II).

Decision No. 1712-(64/29)
June 8, 1964

* *Exchange of letters between the Ambassador of Switzerland to the United States and the Managing Director of the Fund*

June 11, 1964

The Managing Director
International Monetary Fund
19th and H Streets, N.W.
Washington, D.C. 20431

Sir:

I have the honor to refer to Mr. Jacobsson's letter of December 14, 1961 to the President of the Swiss Confederation and to conversations between representatives of the Swiss Confederation and the International Monetary Fund (hereinafter referred to as "the Fund") concerning the way in which the Swiss Confederation could be associated with the Fund's General Arrangements to Borrow, and thus contribute to the objectives of those Arrangements. The General Arrangements to Borrow (hereinafter referred to as "the General Arrangements") are those set forth in Decision No. 1289-(62/1) of January 5, 1962, of the Fund's Executive Directors, as amended by Decision No. 1362-(62/32) of July 9, 1962 and Decision No. 1415-(62/47) adopted on September 19, 1962.

In the light of the views that have been exchanged, the Swiss Federal Council, on behalf of the Swiss Confederation, is prepared to be associated with the General Arrangements as follows:

(1) The Swiss Confederation is prepared to make resources available to participants in the General Arrangements in accordance with this letter and in amounts not exceeding an outstanding total equivalent to 865,000,000 Swiss francs.

(2) The Swiss Confederation will be prepared to consider the conclusion of agreements (hereinafter referred to as "implementing agreements") with any of the participants in the General Arrangements if requested by such participants. The implementing agreements will prescribe the terms and conditions in accordance with which the Swiss Confederation will make resources available to the participant or the Swiss Confederation and the participant will make resources available to each other, which shall be on the basis of reciprocal terms if required. Immediately on the conclusion of an implementing agreement, or of any amendment of an implementing agreement, the Swiss Confederation will provide the Managing Director with a copy thereof.

(3) Whenever the Managing Director of the Fund initiates the procedure and makes a proposal for calls pursuant to Paragraphs 6 and 7 of the General Arrangements for the benefit of a participant that has entered into or enters into an implementing agreement, he may propose to the Swiss Confederation, after consultation with the Swiss Confederation, that it shall make a specified amount of resources available to the participant, which amount shall be in accordance with the implementing agreement with that participant. If the proposal for calls becomes effective under Paragraph 7 of the General Arrangements, the Swiss Confederation

will make the specified amount of resources available to the said participant in accordance with this letter and with the terms and conditions of the implementing agreement. If, however, the Swiss Confederation gives notice to the Managing Director that in its opinion, based on its present and prospective balance of payments and reserve position, it should not make resources available in accordance with this proposal, or should make available a smaller amount than that proposed, the Swiss Confederation will not be obliged to make any such resources available or more resources than it represents to the Managing Director that it should make available.

(4) If the Swiss Confederation makes resources available to a participant otherwise than in accordance with the procedure of paragraph (3), the Swiss Confederation, after consultation with the Managing Director, may deem such resources to be or to have been made available pursuant to this letter, provided that at the date of such deeming Switzerland has entered into an implementing agreement with that participant, that at the date of such deeming a proposal for calls for the benefit of that participant is in effect under Paragraph 7 of the General Arrangements and provided that the terms and conditions for repayment to Switzerland accord or are made to accord with paragraph (5).

(5) The effect of the terms and conditions for the timing of repayment of resources made available by Switzerland pursuant to this letter will correspond, to the maximum extent practicable, with the repayment provisions of Paragraph 11 of the General Arrangements.

(6) The Fund may, at the request of a party to an implementing agreement, make any determination, or use its good offices, to facilitate the operation of an implementing agreement, subject, however, to paragraph (9).

(7) Whenever the Swiss Confederation makes resources available pursuant to paragraph (3) or deems resources to be or to have been made available pursuant to paragraph (4), the Swiss Confederation will inform the Managing Director of the amount in terms of Swiss francs thus made available. The Swiss Confederation will inform the Managing Director of the amount in terms of Swiss francs of the repayment of any resources made available pursuant to paragraph (3) or (4).

(8) The Swiss Confederation and the Fund will provide each other with the general information necessary to facilitate the operation of this letter and implementing agreements.

(9) The Fund does not accept any responsibility or liability, whether as guarantor or otherwise, in connection with this letter or with respect to the performance of the terms and conditions of an implementing agreement.

(10) This letter will remain effective for four years from October 24, 1962, provided that the Swiss Confederation may rescind this letter, with immediate effect, within one month after an amendment of the General Arrangements becomes effective pursuant to Paragraph 15 of the General Arrangements. This letter may be amended or rescinded at any time if the Swiss Confederation and the Fund shall so agree.

(11) Any question of interpretation or application of these understandings will be settled to the mutual satisfaction of the Swiss Confederation and the Fund.

(12) For the purposes of this letter, references to participants shall be deemed to include the official institution of a participant with which an implementing agreement is made, even though such institution is not a "participating institution" under the General Arrangements.

(13) All communications by or to the Swiss Confederation pursuant to this letter shall be made by or to the Swiss National Bank.

I propose that, if this letter is approved by the International Monetary Fund, this letter and your reply constitute an agreement between the Swiss Federal Council and the International Monetary Fund, which shall enter into force on the date of your reply. I hereby declare that the Swiss Confederation has taken all steps necessary to implement the exchange of letters.

Accept, Sir, the assurances of my highest consideration.

/s/
A. ZEHNDER
Ambassador of Switzerland

June 11, 1964

Sir:

I am pleased to acknowledge receipt of your letter of June 11, 1964.

I have been authorized to inform you that the understandings set forth in your letter are accepted by the International Monetary Fund. Accordingly, your letter and this reply constitute an agreement between the International Monetary Fund and the Swiss Federal Council, which will enter into force on the date of this reply.

Accept, Sir, the assurances of my highest consideration.

Very truly yours,
/s/
PIERRE-PAUL SCHWEITZER
Managing Director

His Excellency
Alfred Zehnder
Ambassador of Switzerland
2900 Cathedral Avenue, N.W.
Washington, D.C. 20008

ARTICLE VIII, SECTION 2 (b)

UNENFORCEABILITY OF EXCHANGE CONTRACTS

UNENFORCEABILITY OF EXCHANGE CONTRACTS: FUND'S INTERPRETATION OF ARTICLE VIII, SECTION 2 (b)

The following letter shall be sent to all members:

The Board of Executive Directors of the International Monetary Fund has interpreted, under Article XVIII of the Articles of Agreement, the first sentence of Article VIII, Section 2 (b), which provision reads as follows:

Exchange contracts which involve the currency of any member and which are contrary to the exchange control regulations of that member maintained or imposed consistently with this Agreement shall be unenforceable in the territories of any member.

The meaning and effect of this provision are as follows:

1. Parties entering into exchange contracts involving the currency of any member of the Fund and contrary to exchange control regulations of that member which are maintained or imposed consistently with the Fund Agreement will not receive the assistance of the judicial or administrative authorities of other members in obtaining the performance of such contracts. That is to say, the obligations of such contracts will not be implemented by the judicial or administrative authorities of member countries, for example by decreeing performance of the contracts or by awarding damages for their non-performance.

2. By accepting the Fund Agreement members have undertaken to make the principle mentioned above effectively part of their national law. This applied to all members, whether or not they have availed themselves of the transitional arrangements of Article XIV, Section 2.

An obvious result of the foregoing undertaking is that if a party to an exchange contract of the kind referred to in Article VIII, Section 2 (b) seeks to enforce such a contract, the tribunal of the member country before which the proceedings are brought will not, on the ground that they are contrary to the public policy (*ordre public*) of the forum, refuse recognition of the exchange control regulations of the other member which are maintained or imposed consistently with the Fund Agreement. It also follows that such contracts will be treated as unenforceable notwithstanding that under the private international law of the forum, the law under which the foreign exchange control regulations are maintained or imposed is not the law which governs the exchange contract or its performance.

The Fund will be pleased to lend its assistance in connection with any problem which may arise in relation to the foregoing interpretation or any other aspect of Article VIII, Section 2 (b). In addition, the Fund is prepared to advise whether particular exchange control regulations are maintained or imposed consistently with the Fund Agreement.

Decision No. 446-4
June 10, 1949

Article VIII and Article XIV
PAYMENTS RESTRICTIONS

Payments Restrictions for Security Reasons: Fund Jurisdiction

Art. VIII, Sec. 2 (a), in conformity with its language, applies to all restrictions on current payments and transfers, irrespective of their motivation and the circumstances in which they are imposed. Sometimes members impose such restrictions solely for the preservation of national or international security. The Fund does not, however, provide a suitable forum for discussion of the political and military considerations leading to actions of this kind. In view of the fact that it is not possible to draw a precise line between cases involving only considerations of this nature and cases involving, in whole or in part, economic motivations and effects for which the Fund does provide the appropriate forum for discussion, and the further fact that the Fund must exercise the jurisdiction conferred by the Fund Agreement in order to perform its duties and protect the legitimate interests of its members, the following policy decision is taken:

1. A member intending to impose restrictions on payments and transfers for current international transactions that are not authorized by Art. VII, Sec. 3 (b) or Art. XIV, Sec. 2 of the Fund Agreement and that, in the judgment of the member, are solely related to the preservation of national or international security, should, whenever possible, notify the Fund before imposing such restrictions. Any member may obtain a decision of the Fund prior to the imposition of such restrictions by so indicating in its notice, and the Fund will act promptly on its request. If any member intending to impose such restrictions finds that circumstances preclude advance notice to the Fund, it should notify the Fund as promptly as circumstances permit, but ordinarily not later than 30 days after imposing such restrictions. Each notice received in accordance with this decision will be circulated immediately to the Executive Directors. Unless the Fund informs the member within 30 days after receiving notice from the member that it is not satisfied that such restrictions are proposed solely to preserve such security, the member may assume that the Fund has no objection to the imposition of the restrictions.

2. The Fund will review the operation of this decision periodically and reserves the right to modify or revoke, at any time, the decision or the effect of the decision on any restrictions that may have been imposed pursuant to it.

Decision No. 144-(52/51)
August 14, 1952

BILATERALISM AND CONVERTIBILITY

1. This decision records the Fund's views on the use of bilateral arrangements.

2. Fund policies and attitude on bilateral arrangements which involve the use of exchange restrictions and represent limitations on a multilateral system of payments are an integral part of its policy on restrictions. This policy aims at the elimination of foreign exchange restrictions and the earliest possible establishment of a multilateral system of payments in respect of current transactions between members. The Fund's policies and procedures on such restrictions rest on Articles I, VIII and XIV of the Fund Agreement.

3. Certain members have already taken steps to reduce their dependence on bilateral arrangements, but many members still use them. The Fund welcomes the reduced reliance on these arrangements and believes that the improvement in the international payments situation makes it less necessary for members to rely on such arrangements. The Fund urges the full collaboration of all its members to reduce and to eliminate as rapidly as practicable reliance on bilateralism. In this respect the Fund recommends close cooperation of those who plan to make their currencies convertible in the near future. Unless this policy is energetically pursued by all countries, both convertible and inconvertible, there is serious risk that widespread restrictions, particularly of a discriminatory character, will persist. Moreover, the persistence of bilateralism may impede the attainment and maintenance of convertibility. This whole problem is one not only for countries which maintain bilateral arrangements but also for other countries whose domestic and foreign economic policies may adversely affect the balance of payments of other members.

4. The Fund will have discussions with its members on their need to retain existing bilateral arrangements or their ability to facilitate the reduction of bilateral arrangements by other countries. During the coming year, the Fund will explore with all countries which are parties to bilateral arrangements which involve the use of exchange restrictions the need for the continuation of these arrangements, the possibilities of their early removal, and ways and means, including the use of the Fund's resources, by which the Fund can assist in this process. In its examination of the justification for reliance on such bilateral arrangements the Fund will, without excluding other considerations, have particular regard to the payments position and prospects of the members concerned.

Decision No. 433-(55/42)
June 22, 1955

RETENTION QUOTAS: DECISION AND LETTER OF TRANSMITTAL

In concluding consultations on restrictions on current payments and transfers as required under Article XIV of the Fund Agreement, the Fund postponed consideration of retention quotas and similar practices through which some members have sought to improve their earnings of specific currencies. The Fund has now examined these practices more fully than was possible at the consultations referred to above. The Fund has extended this examination to cover the terms of reference of the resolution adopted on September 9, 1952, by the Board of Governors and has come to the following conclusions:

1. Members should work toward and achieve as soon as feasible the removal of

these retention quotas and similar practices, particularly where they lead to abnormal shifts in trade which cause unnecessary damage to other countries. Members should endeavor to replace these practices by more appropriate measures leading to currency convertibility.

2. The Fund will enter into consultation with each of the members concerned with a view to agreeing on a program for the implementation of 1 above, including appropriate attention to timing of any action which may be decided upon.

3. The Fund does not object to those practices which, by their nature, can be regarded as devices designed solely to simplify the administration of official exchange allocations.

The Managing Director is asked to send the following letter to all members in transmitting the foregoing decision on retention quotas and similar practices:

The Fund has made a detailed study concerning retention quotas and other similar practices pursuant to the resolution passed at the Seventh Session of the Board of Governors in Mexico in September 1952. I am pleased to transmit herewith a decision of the Executive Board of the Fund based on this study.

The Fund has concluded that these practices stem from widespread difficulties presently existing in the international payments position of many countries. The Fund's consideration of this subject has shown that what is referred to as "retention quotas and similar practices" covers a wide range of exchange measures. Certain practices under this heading may be unobjectionable from the point of view of Fund policies. Other practices in this category, however, appear to result in adverse effects on exchange stability and to cause unnecessary damage to member countries. They also may lead to the adoption of retaliatory measures. The interest of the Fund in these matters clearly follows from the terms of Article VIII containing the general obligations of members with respect to the avoidance of exchange restrictions, discriminatory currency arrangements and multiple currency practices, and Article XIV dealing with these exchange measures during the transitional period.

In dealing with retention quotas and similar practices, the Board has not intended to change existing Fund standards and procedures with respect to exchange restrictions, discriminatory currency arrangements and multiple currency practices. Specifically, there was no intention to affect the existing requirements of prior consultation and approval with respect to measures of this character. Those requirements, so far as they concern multiple currency practices, were communicated to members in the Fund's letter of December 19, 1947 (Appendix II of the Fund's Annual Report of 1948). Accordingly, it is expected that members intending to maintain, introduce or enlarge those retention quotas and similar practices which constitute exchange restrictions, multiple currency practices or discriminatory currency arrangements will act in accordance with existing Fund requirements.

The decision recognizes that it is not practicable to deal with all of these practices on a general basis. The Fund, therefore, wishes to deal with these arrangements on a case-to-case basis. We shall communicate as quickly as practicable with members using these practices. We are confident that members will cooperate in these individual discussions in order to enable the Fund to reach appropriate conclusions.

Decision No. 201-(53/29)
May 4, 1953

DISCRIMINATION FOR BALANCE OF PAYMENTS REASONS

The following decision deals exclusively with discriminatory restrictions imposed for balance of payments reasons.

In some countries, considerable progress has already been made towards the elimination of discriminatory restrictions; in others, much remains to be done. Recent international financial developments have established an environment favorable to the elimination of discrimination for balance of payments reasons. There has been a substantial improvement in the reserve positions of the industrial countries in particular and widespread moves to external convertibility have taken place.

Under these circumstances, the Fund considers that there is no longer any balance of payments justification for discrimination by members whose current receipts are largely in externally convertible currencies. However, the Fund recognizes that where such discriminatory restrictions have been long maintained, a reasonable amount of time may be needed fully to eliminate them. But this time should be short and members will be expected to proceed with all feasible speed in eliminating discrimination against member countries, including that arising from bilateralism.

Notwithstanding the extensive moves toward convertibility, a substantial portion of the current receipts of some countries is still subject to limitations on convertibility, particularly in payments relations with state-trading countries. In the case of these countries the Fund will be prepared to consider whether balance of payments considerations would justify the maintenance of some degree of discrimination, although not as between countries having externally convertible currencies. In this connection the Fund wishes to reaffirm its basic policy on bilateralism as stated in its decision of June 22, 1955.

Decision No. 955-(59/45)
October 23, 1959

ARTICLE VIII AND ARTICLE XIV

There has been in recent years a substantial improvement in the balance of payments and the reserve positions of a number of Fund members which has led to important and widespread moves to the external convertibility of many currencies. Most international transactions are now carried on with convertible currencies, and many countries have progressed far with the removal of restrictions on payments. In consequence of these developments, it seems likely that a number of members of the Fund either have reached or are nearing a position in which they can consider the feasibility of formally accepting the obligations of Article VIII, Sections 2, 3, and 4. Previous decisions taken by the Fund, such as those on multiple currency practices, bilateral arrangements, discriminatory restrictions maintained for balance of payments purposes, and payments restrictions for security reasons, indicate the Fund's attitude on these matters. The present decision has been adopted as an additional guide to members in pursuance of the purposes of the Fund as set forth in Article I of the Articles of Agreement.

1. Article VIII provides in Sections 2 and 3 that members shall not impose or engage in certain measures, namely restrictions on the making of payments and transfers for current international transactions, discriminatory currency arrangements, or multiple currency practices, without the approval of the Fund. The guiding principle in ascertaining whether a measure is a restriction on payments and transfers for current transactions under Article VIII, Section 2, is whether it involves a direct governmental

limitation on the availability or use of exchange as such. Members in doubt as to whether any of their measures do or do not fall under Article VIII may wish to consult the Fund thereon.

2. In accordance with Article XIV, Section 3, members may at any time notify the Fund that they accept the obligations of Article VIII, Sections 2, 3, and 4, and no longer avail themselves of the transitional provisions of Article XIV. Before members give notice that they are accepting the obligations of Article VIII, Sections 2, 3, and 4, it would be desirable that, as far as possible, they eliminate measures which would require the approval of the Fund, and that they satisfy themselves that they are not likely to need recourse to such measures in the foreseeable future. If members, for balance of payments reasons, propose to maintain or introduce measures which require approval under Article VIII, the Fund will grant approval only where it is satisfied that the measures are necessary and that their use will be temporary while the member is seeking to eliminate the need for them. As regards measures requiring approval under Article VIII and maintained or introduced for nonbalance of payments reasons, the Fund believes that the use of exchange systems for nonbalance of payments reasons should be avoided to the greatest possible extent, and is prepared to consider with members the ways and means of achieving the elimination of such measures as soon as possible. Members having measures needing approval under Article VIII should find it useful to consult with the Fund before accepting the obligations of Article VIII, Sections 2, 3, and 4.

3. If members at any time maintain measures which are subject to Sections 2 and 3 of Article VIII, they shall consult with the Fund with respect to the further maintenance of such measures. Consultations with the Fund under Article VIII are not otherwise required or mandatory. However, the Fund is able to provide technical facilities and advice, and to this end, or as a means of exchanging views on monetary and financial developments, there is great merit in periodic discussions between the Fund and its members even though no questions arise involving action under Article VIII. Such discussions would be planned between the Fund and the member, including agreement on place and timing, and would ordinarily take place at intervals of about one year.

4. Fund members which are contracting parties to the GATT and which impose import restrictions for balance of payments reasons will facilitate the work of the Fund by continuing to send information concerning such restrictions to the Fund. This will enable the Fund and the member to join in an examination of the balance of payments situation in order to assist the Fund in its collaboration with the GATT. The Fund, by agreement with members which are not contracting parties to the GATT and which impose import restrictions for balance of payments reasons, will seek to obtain information relating to such restrictions.

Decision No. 1034-(60/27)
June 1, 1960

MULTIPLE CURRENCY PRACTICES

Statement to Members Transmitting Fund's Decisions on Multiple Currency Practices

The letter to members concerning multiple currency practices and the accompanying statement of the Fund's decisions with respect to such practices are agreed as revised (Executive Board Document No. 235, Revision 2) and shall be sent without delay to all members. The texts of earlier decisions on the same subject are modified as necessary to correspond with the agreed statement.

Decision No. 237-2
December 18, 1947

Letter to Members

December 19, 1947

To All Members:

During the past several months the Fund has been giving special consideration to multiple currency practices. I am writing to all of the members today in order to acquaint them with the results of our considerations. Enclosed is a memorandum containing the pertinent decisions taken by the Executive Board. These set forth the general lines of the Fund's policies toward multiple currency practices which the Fund has adopted to date, together with the obligations of the members and the jurisdiction of the Fund upon which the development of Fund policy will necessarily be based.

We intend, as rapidly as may be possible under the circumstances, to discuss with each member now engaging in a multiple currency practice how this general policy will be applied to its individual problems. In the meantime, all of the members are requested to be guided by the enclosed memorandum and to initiate with the Fund discussions of any pressing problems which may arise.

Sincerely yours,
/s/
Gutt
Managing Director

Multiple Currency Practices

This memorandum contains the decisions the Fund has so far taken concerning its policies toward multiple currency practices, and clarification of its jurisdiction with respect to such practices.

The exchange systems of the members who engage in multiple currency practices are frequently complex. For this reason various difficulties will be involved in the modification and removal of the practices, and the policy of the Fund in this regard must develop progressively as its consultations with the members concerned reveal problems which might otherwise be overlooked. The policies set forth below have been agreed as a basis for the initiation of discussions with the members affected:

I. *Policies*

 A. *General*

  1. *Consultation.* There should be continuing consultation on multiple currency practices between the Fund and the members concerned. Members should, as a minimum, consult the Fund before introducing a multiple currency practice, before making a change in any of the multiple rates of exchange, before reclassifying transactions subject to different rates, and before making any other type of significant change in their exchange systems.

  2. *Stability and Restrictions.* In most cases multiple currency practices are both systems of exchange rates and restrictions on payments and transfers for current international transactions. Whenever it is inconvenient to deal with both aspects of such multiple currency practice simultaneously, priority should be given to those

features which affect exchange stability and orderly exchange arrangements among members.

3. *Removal.* Early steps should be taken toward the removal of multiple currency practices which are clearly not necessary for balance of payments reasons. In such cases, ample time should be provided for members to take the necessary steps and to install appropriate substitutes where necessary.

The Fund will encourage members engaging in multiple currency practices for balance of payments reasons to establish as soon as possible conditions which would permit their removal, with the general objective of seeking removal not later than the end of the transitional period.

Where complete removal by the end of the transitional period proves impossible, the Fund will assist the members concerned to eliminate the most dangerous aspects of their multiple currency practices and to exercise reasonable control over those retained.

B. *Specific Practices*

1. *Fixed Exchange Rates.* When a multiple currency system includes fixed exchange rates, members should consult with the Fund on any changes in their practices, whether such changes concern the rates of exchange or the classification of transactions subject to particular practices. Should the step contemplated by a member be a part of a program made in agreement with the Fund, the member could, of course, act without prior consultation.

When a multiple rate system is used for restrictions on current and capital transactions, the elimination of the restriction on current transactions would be highly commendable even though restrictions on capital transactions might have to be retained.

2. *Taxes on Exchange Drafts.* The use by members of taxes on exchange drafts resulting in an unusually large difference between buying and selling rates for a currency is not in accord with the objectives of the Fund Agreement and the Fund shall, in consultation with members concerned, seek the elimination of such practices as rapidly as practicable.

3. *Fluctuating Rates of Exchange.*

(a) *Free Markets.* When a multiple currency practice includes a free market with a fluctuating rate, the member should agree with the Fund on the scope of the transactions permitted to take place in that market. Any changes in the scope of these transactions should, of course, be subject to agreement with the Fund. The objective should be to eliminate the fluctuations in the free market as soon as such action is reasonably practicable. When it is not reasonably practicable to eliminate such fluctuations, the Fund will encourage members to exclude current transactions from the free market to the extent that this would be reasonable in the circumstances of each case.

(b) *The Auction System*

(i) The purpose for which an auction system is to be used should be agreed with the Fund and any change in its scope should be agreed with the Fund. The fewer the transactions subject to the auction rate, and the less essential the goods involved, the better.

(ii) Depending upon the circumstances, the monetary authorities should undertake to keep the auction rate stable, or to maintain it within certain limits, or to make every effort to prevent brisk fluctuations.

(iii) Wherever auction rates exist or are proposed, the circumstances should be examined in order to determine whether a fixed rate should be substituted for the auction rate.

(iv) If, as is usually the case where an auction system exists, a reduction of the money supply is desirable, the proceeds of the auction market should be directed toward this end.

II. *Jurisdiction of the Fund*

Multiple currency practices, besides being in most cases restrictive practices, also constitute systems of exchange rates. Since exchange stability depends on effective rates, the general purposes of the Fund and the members' undertakings of Article IV, Section 4 (a) "to collaborate with the Fund to promote exchange stability, to maintain orderly exchange arrangements with other members, and to avoid competitive exchange alterations" are fundamental considerations in an interpretation of the rights and obligations of members under Article XIV, Section 2 or Article VIII, Section 3, to maintain, introduce, or adapt multiple currency practices. Subject to these general principles, the following conclusions are agreed with respect to the Fund's jurisdiction and the obligations of members.*

A. *Practices Subject to Article VIII, Section 3.*

1. *Maintenance.* A member maintaining multiple currency practices at the time the Agreement entered into force, if it does not take advantage of Article XIV, is required by Article VIII, Section 3, to consult with the Fund for their progressive removal or obtain the Fund's approval for their maintenance.

2. *Introduction.* Members that have not been occupied by the enemy, and former enemy-occupied members which have not taken advantage of the transitional arrangements, whether or not they have existing multiple rate practices, may introduce a new practice only under Article VIII, Section 3, which provides expressly for the necessity of approval by the Fund.

3. *Adaptation.* If a multiple currency practice is in force by virtue of Article VIII, Section 3, the member may change or adapt such practice only after consulting with the Fund and obtaining its approval.

4. *Reclassification.* Members maintaining multiple currency practices under Article VIII, Section 3, may reclassify commodities subject to the practices only after consultation with the Fund and Fund approval.

B. *Practices Subject to Article XIV, Section 2.*

1. *Restrictive Nature.* Multiple currency practices, when applied to current international transactions, constitute a type of restriction on payments and transfers for current international transactions for the purposes of Article XIV, Section 2.

2. *Representations by the Fund.* The following language in Article XIV, Section 4 of the Fund Agreement:

"The Fund may, if it deems such action necessary in exceptional circumstances, make representations to any member that conditions are favorable for the withdrawal of any particular restriction, or for the general abandonment of restrictions, inconsistent with the provisions of any other article of this Agreement."

---

* These conclusions concerning the Fund's jurisdiction and the obligation of members apply to all members including those for whose currencies par values have not been established.

(a) applies at any time after the entry into force of the Fund Agreement and

(b) gives to the Fund the power to determine what is meant by "in exceptional circumstances."

3. *Maintenance.* Members may maintain multiple currency practices during the transitional period under the provisions of Article XIV, Section 2, but only if the maintenance of such practices is necessary for settling members' balances of payments in a manner which does not unduly encumber their access to the resources of the Fund. Members are under a duty to withdraw such practices as soon as they are able without them to settle their balance of payments in a manner which will not unduly encumber their access to the resources of the Fund. Moreover, under Section 4 of Article XIV, the Fund has certain powers to make representations in exceptional circumstances, of which it is the judge, that conditions are favorable for the withdrawal of any particular restriction. The Fund may exercise this power even if a particular restriction is justified for balance of payments reasons, if the conditions are favorable for the substitution of some practice which is not inconsistent with the purposes of the Agreement.

4. *Introduction.* Only former enemy-occupied members, which are availing themselves of the transitional provisions, and then whether or not they have existing multiple currency practices, may introduce a new multiple currency practice under Article XIV, Section 2, provided the Fund agrees with the member that the practice is necessary and does not find that it is inconsistent with the purposes of the Fund Agreement or with Article IV, Section 4 (a).

5. *Adaptation.* A member maintaining multiple currency practices under Article XIV may adapt the existing restrictions, provided such action is consistent with the obligations of Article IV, Section 4 (a) and the Fund is satisfied that the adaptation is dictated by "changing circumstances." A duty to consult with and obtain the approval of the Fund before changing the practice is implicit in both Article IV, Section 4 (a) and in Article XIV, Section 2. The Fund has the power under Article XIV, Section 4, to represent in exceptional circumstances that circumstances are favorable to withdrawal of a proposal to change an existing multiple currency practice.

6. *Reclassification.* A member maintaining multiple currency practices under Article XIV may reclassify commodities subject to such practices, under the power to adapt restrictions in Section 2 of Article XIV, and under the same conditions, provided, however, that under the existing restrictions the effective rates are other than parity.

C. *Exchange Taxes.* When a tax affects an obligation undertaken by the members of the Fund, the relationship between the tax and the obligation is of direct concern to the Fund and subject to its jurisdiction. Whenever exchange taxes are used to modify par values, create multiple currency practices, or introduce restrictive exchange controls, they are subject to the Fund's jurisdiction. The Fund has authority to deal with these exchange matters irrespective of the official device or procedure involved.

D. *Rates Differing from Parity by More than One Per Cent.* An effective buying or selling rate which, as the result of official action, e.g. the imposition of an exchange tax, differs from parity by more than one per cent, constitutes a multiple currency practice.

MULTIPLE CURRENCY PRACTICES

1. The Executive Board has considered the staff paper on the "Review of Fund

Policies on Multiple Currency Practices" (SM/57/2, Rev. 1, 5/3/57) and is in agreement with the general approach of the paper.

II. Unification of the exchange rates in multiple rate systems is a basic objective of the Fund, and it is satisfying to record that several of the members which had followed such practices have been successful in achieving this objective, and that others have made considerable progress in this direction.

III. In reviewing the experience of the past ten years as summarized in the staff report, the Fund draws special attention to the fact that complex multiple rate systems damage the economies of countries maintaining them and harm other countries. These complex systems are difficult to administer, and involve frequent changes, discrimination, export subsidization, a considerable spread between rates, and undue differentiation between classes of imports.

IV. The Executive Board concludes that it is necessary and feasible to make more rapid progress in simplifying complex multiple rate systems, to remove those aspects of existing systems which adversely affect the interests of other members, and to avoid existing systems becoming more complex. Accordingly the following decision is taken:

1. Early and substantial steps should be taken to simplify complex multiple rate systems. The Fund will not approve such systems unless the countries maintaining them are making reasonable progress toward simplification and ultimate elimination of such systems, or are taking measures or adopting programs which seem likely to result in such progress.

2. As opportunity arises the Fund will continue to press for simplification in all cases where there is clear evidence that the multiple currency system in question is damaging to other members. It will in addition be reluctant to approve changes in multiple rate systems which make them more complex.

3. To assist members to simplify and eliminate complex rate systems the Fund wishes to intensify its collaboration with them. The Fund stands ready to meet members' requests for technical assistance in the preparation of economic programs and measures directed toward exchange simplification. These may in some cases include arrangements in other directions, especially in the fiscal and trade fields. If the Fund considers the proposed exchange simplification and related economic programs or measures to be adequate and appropriate, it will give sympathetic consideration, if requested, to the use of its resources.

Decision No. 649-(57/33)
June 26, 1957

ARTICLE IX, SECTION 7

PRIVILEGE FOR COMMUNICATIONS

INTERPRETATION OF ARTICLE IX, SECTION 7

WHEREAS the Executive Director for the [member concerned] has raised certain questions of interpretation of the provisions of Section 7 of Article IX of the Articles of Agreement of the Fund as to the treatment to be accorded by a member of the International Monetary Fund to official communications of the Fund, which questions of interpretation are set forth below;

WHEREAS the said Executive Director has requested that the Executive Directors, in accordance with Article XVIII of said Articles, decide such questions of interpretation;

NOW THEREFORE, the Executive Directors hereby decide such questions of interpretation as follows:

Question No. 1:

Does Section 7 of Article IX of the Articles of Agreement of the Fund apply to rates charged for official communications of the Fund?

Decision on Question No. 1:

Yes. Section 7 of Article IX applies to rates charged for official communications of the Fund.

Question No. 2:

If a member exercises regulatory powers over the rates charged for communications, is it relieved of the obligation of Section 7, Article IX, by reason of the fact that the facilities for transmitting communications are privately owned or operated or both?

Decision on Question No. 2:

No. A member which exercises regulatory powers over the rates charged for communications is not relieved of its obligation under Section 7 of Article IX by reason of the fact that the facilities for transmitting such communications are privately owned or operated or both.

Question No. 3:

Is the member's obligation under Section 7 of Article IX satisfied if official communications of the Fund may be sent only at rates which exceed the rates accorded the official communications of other members in comparable situations? For example, would the obligation of member "a", under Section 7 of Article IX, be satisfied if the rate charged the Fund for its official communications from the territory of member "a" to the territory of member "b" exceeds the rate charged member "b" for its official communications from the territory of "a" to that of "b"?

Decision on Question No. 3:

No. The obligation of a member under Section 7 of Article IX is not satisfied if official communications of the Fund may be sent only at rates which exceed the rates accorded the official communications of other members in comparable situations. For example, the obligation of member "a", under Section 7 of Article IX, would not be satisfied if the rate charged the Fund for its official communications from the territory of member "a" to the territory of member "b" exceeds the rate charged member "b" for its official communications from the territory of "a" to that of "b".

Decision No. 534-3
February 20, 1950

Article XII, Section 3

EXECUTIVE DIRECTORS

Interpretation of Article XII, Sections 3 (b) (i) and 3 (f)

The request for interpretation of the Articles of Agreement referred to the Executive Directors by Resolution No. 7 of the Board of Governors was considered [reference to document deleted]. It was unanimously agreed that Sections 3 (b) (i) and 3 (f) of

Article XII should be interpreted to mean that any member having one of the five largest quotas at the date of the regular election or at any date between regular elections shall be entitled to appoint an Executive Director who will hold office until the next regular election without prejudice to the right of a subsequently admitted member to appoint a Director if it has one of the five largest quotas.

Decision No. 2-1
May 8, 1946

EXECUTIVE DIRECTORS: ARTICLE XII, SECTION 3 (c)

Art. XII, Sec. 3 (c), should be understood as providing that the two members entitled to appoint additional directors are determined by the largest absolute amounts by which 75% of members' quotas exceed the average holdings by the Fund of their currencies during the two years preceding an election of directors, provided, of course, that they are not already entitled to appoint directors under Art. XII, Sec. 3 (b) (i).

In the calculation of average holdings under the provision, the Fund's special accounts for administrative purposes should not be included unless they exceed $\frac{1}{100}$ of one per cent of the member's quota. A member should not be entitled to the benefit of Art. XII, Sec. 3 (c) where the average holdings of its currency by the Fund have been reduced below 75% of its quota solely because of expenditures by the Fund for administrative purposes or because of the exclusion of the special accounts for administrative purposes from the calculation of average holdings.

Decision No. 574-2
May 18, 1950

ADDITIONAL APPOINTED DIRECTORS

The phrase "the preceding two years" as used in Art. XII, Sec. 3 (c), shall be deemed to be the two-year period ending on the July 31 preceding the dates of regular biennial elections of Executive Directors. However, this decision shall be reconsidered if such regular elections are held in other months than September.

Decision No. 597-4
July 28, 1950

ADJUSTMENT OF QUOTA AND VOTING POWER

A change in the quota of a member between regular biennial elections will change by the same amount the voting power of the elected Executive Director who casts the votes of the member.

Decision No. 180-5
June 25, 1947

ARTICLE XIV, SECTION 1

USE OF FUND'S RESOURCES: PURPOSE

USE OF FUND'S RESOURCES BY COUNTRIES UNDERGOING RECONSTRUCTION

The prohibition in the Fund Agreement, Article XIV, Section 1, was not meant to prevent countries which were undergoing reconstruction from using the Fund's resources.

Decision No. 196-2
July 31, 1947

ARTICLE XIV, SECTION 4

RESTRICTIONS ON PAYMENTS AND TRANSFERS: WITHDRAWAL

MEANING OF "EXCEPTIONAL CIRCUMSTANCES" IN ARTICLE XIV, SECTION 4

The following language in Article XIV, Section 4 of the Fund Agreement:

"The Fund may, if it deems such action necessary in exceptional circumstances, make representations to any member that conditions are favorable for the withdrawal of any particular restriction, or for the general abandonment of restrictions, inconsistent with the provisions of any other article of this Agreement."

(a) applies at any time after the entry into force of the Fund Agreement and

(b) gives to the Fund the power to determine what is meant by "in exceptional circumstances."

Decision No. 117-1
January 6, 1947

ARTICLE XV, SECTION 2

INTERPRETATION

In response to the request of the Government of [a member], and after having considered the arguments put forward by that Government, the Executive Directors, acting pursuant to Article XVIII (a) of the Fund Agreement, interpret Article XV, Section 2 as follows:

Action may be taken by the Fund to require a member to withdraw when the following conditions have been met:

1. The member has been declared ineligible to use the resources of the Fund pursuant to Article XV, Section 2 (a);

2. A reasonable time has passed since the member was declared ineligible to use the resources of the Fund pursuant to Article XV, Section 2 (a), whether or not a fixed period of time had been prescribed in connection with such action, and the member persists in failing to fulfill its obligations;

3. The member has been informed in reasonable time of the complaint against it and given adequate opportunity to state, both orally and in writing, any fact or legal argument relevant to the issue before the Fund.

Decision No. 343-(54/47)
August 11, 1954

The Board of Governors confirmed the foregoing decision on September 28, 1954.

ARTICLE XIX

MONETARY RESERVES AND OFFICIAL HOLDINGS

NET OFFICIAL HOLDINGS: PRINCIPLES OF INTERPRETATION

In order to ensure the uniform application of the relevant Articles of Agreement as they apply to determinations of members' net official holdings of gold and U.S. dollars for the purposes of Article III, Section 3 (b) (ii), the Fund adopts or reaffirms the following principles of interpretation for the indicated provisions of the Fund Agreement:

(a) [Pertains to Article III, Section 3 (b); see p. 220.]

(b) [Pertains to Article III, Section 3 (d); see p. 221.]

(c) *Article XIX (b)*: "The official holdings of a member means central holdings (that is, the holdings of its Treasury, central bank, stabilization fund, or similar fiscal agency)."

  (1) "Central holdings" are confined to holdings owned by the institutions set forth in Article XIX (b).

  (2) The term "similar fiscal agency" means an institution which performs an important function or functions similar to those normally performed by a Treasury, or central bank, or stabilization fund.

  (3) No distinction is made among the departments of a central bank or other central institution as specified in Article XIX (b). No distinction is made on the basis of the use to which gold or dollars may be put by any of the institutions covered by Article XIX (b). That is to say, all gold or dollars owned by such institutions are central holdings.

(d) *Article XIX (c)*: "The holdings of other official institutions or other banks within its territories may, in any particular case, be deemed by the Fund, after consultation with the member, to be official holdings to the extent that they are substantially in excess of working balances; provided that for the purpose of determining whether, in a particular case, holdings are in excess of working balances, there shall be deducted from such holdings amounts of currency due to official institutions and banks in the territories of members or nonmembers specified under (d) below."

  (1) "Other official institutions" and "other banks" are official institutions and banks not embraced by Article XIX (b). "Other official institutions" are those representing a member anywhere. "Other banks" are banks within its territories.

  (2) "Working balances" must be determined in the light of all the facts of the individual case, and no rigid rule can be formulated for their measurement. The general idea is that a working balance is one which is necessary to meet the requirements of its owner, taking into account normal receipts and payments, for a period not unreasonably protracted.

  (3) No deduction may be made from central holdings on the ground that they are said to represent, in whole or in part, "working balances," for example, because there are no commercial banks or because the holdings of commercial banks are alleged by the member to be inadequate for working purposes.

  (4) Gold or dollars owned by "other official institutions" and "other banks" may be included in a member's official holdings, after consultation with the member, to the extent that they are substantially in excess of "working balances."

  (5) The proviso in Article XIX (c) declares that in determining whether the holdings of other official institutions and other banks are substantially in excess of working balances, certain deductions shall be made. These deductions are in respect of liabilities arising from the holdings of the currency of the member whose official holdings are being calculated. Such liabilities must be owed by that member's official institutions and banks to the official institutions of and banks in the territories of countries which were members of the Fund on September 12, 1946.

(e) *Article XIX (h)*: "For the purpose of calculating gold subscriptions under Article III, Section 3, a member's net official holdings of gold and United States dollars shall consist of its official holdings of gold and United States currency after deducting central holdings of its currency by other official institutions and other banks if these holdings carry specified rights of conversion into gold or United States currency."

(1) Article XIX (h) establishes the only deduction from gross official holdings. That is to say, *gross* official holdings are the total of gold and dollars which a member owns; *net* official holdings are those holdings minus the one deduction which Article XIX (h) establishes.

(2) A deduction cannot be made under Article XIX (h) in the calculation of a member's net official holdings unless the following conditions are satisfied:

(a) There is a holding of the member's currency.

(b) There is a right of conversion of the currency into gold or U.S. dollars exercisable by virtue only of the holdings of the currency and not, for example, by reason of forward exchange contracts.

(c) The right of conversion is exercisable at the option of the holder of the currency and not at the option of the member whose currency is held.

(d) The option is exercisable by the central or other official institutions or other banks in the territories of other countries, and not by the member's own official institutions or by banks in the territories in respect of which it has accepted the Agreement in accordance with Article XX, Section 2 (g). "Other countries" embraces all countries, and not simply member countries or nonmember countries which have been specified under Article XIX (d).

(e) The right of conversion was in existence on September 12, 1946 (or any later date substituted under Article III, Section 3 (d)). However, the right of conversion need not have been exercisable on that date, but may be exercisable at any time thereafter.

(3) Liabilities payable in gold or dollars were the conditions of Article XIX (h) as set forth in 2 above are not otherwise met, e.g., where the creditor's right to gold or dollars is not attached to a holding of the currency of the member whose net official holdings are being calculated, are not deductible under Article XIX (h).

Decision No. 298-3
April 14, 1948

CURRENCY LIABILITIES: ARTICLE XIX (e)

1. [Expired.]

2. [Pertains to Schedule B; see p. 272.]

3. [A member has contended] that where, under a payment agreement, the other contracting party held [its currency and the member] held the currency of the other party, the full amount of the holdings of [the member's currency] should not be deducted but the two amounts should be offset for the purposes of calculating deductible currency liabilities under Article XIX (e) [*ibid.*]. It is determined that the meaning of the term "currency liabilities" under Article XIX (e) cannot be restricted in this way. It must be applied in the gross sense to include all of the holdings of a member's currency by another party under a payment agreement.

Decision No. 486-2
October 7, 1949

CURRENCY LIABILITIES: ARTICLE XIX (e)

The Executive Board has considered questions relating to the concept of currency liabilities in Article XIX (e), as set forth in Executive Board Special No. 107 (10/18/49), and agrees that the following principles apply:

1. The currency liabilities of a member are the liabilities represented by the holdings of its currency by the Treasuries, central banks, stabilization funds, similar fiscal agencies, other official institutions or other banks of other members, or of such nonmembers as have been specified by the Fund.

2. Currency liabilities are not confined to convertible currencies.

3. The deductibility of currency liabilities does not depend on whether the holder's currency is convertible.

4. "Currency" in the concept "currency liabilities" means "without limitation coins, paper money, bank balances, bank acceptances, and government obligations issued with a maturity not exceeding twelve months."

5. A blocked balance is not a currency liability.

Decision No. 493-3
November 4, 1949

ARTICLE XX, SECTION 4 (i)

USE OF FUND'S RESOURCES: POSTPONEMENT UNDER ARTICLE XX, SECTION 4 (i)

The Fund has, in the case of a member which has had no previous exchange transaction with the Fund, the power to postpone exchange transactions with it if its circumstances are such that, in the opinion of the Fund, they would lead to the use of the resources of the Fund in a manner contrary to the purposes of the Agreement or prejudicial to the Fund or its members. This power did not lapse as of the date the Fund began exchange transactions.

Decision No. 284-2
March 10, 1948

SCHEDULE B

CALCULATION OF REPURCHASE OBLIGATIONS

CALCULATION OF MONETARY RESERVES

1. [Expired.]

2. [A member has contended] that, in calculating its monetary reserves as of April 30, 1948, a sum greater than [the amount calculated by the staff] should have been deducted as the proceeds of a long-term or medium-term loan contracted during the financial year ending on that date . . . . It is determined that the deduction . . . calculated by the staff was correctly made, based on the following principles which are adopted:

(a) Before any exclusion of the proceeds of long-term or medium-term loans can be made under Schedule B, paragraph 3, of the Fund Agreement, it is necessary to identify that part of a member's holdings which can be regarded as representing the proceeds of such loans.

(b) Where the loan can be spent only for a specific project or purpose, the proceeds can be regarded as unspent only to the extent that the special project or purpose has not been completed and paid for. The formality of payment of the proceeds into a special or general account would not as a rule be considered a significant factor.

(c) Where the loan is not contracted for a special project or purpose, the proceeds of that loan which may be deducted should, as a rule of thumb, and in the absence of other evidence of identification, be determined as follows: (1) the member's lowest holdings of the currency in question between the date of receipt of the proceeds of the loan and the end of the financial year shall be determined, (2) the part of such lowest holdings which shall be excluded will be the proportion which the proceeds of the loan bear to the sum of the member's holdings of the currency as of the date of receipt of the proceeds of the loan plus other receipts in the same currency between that date and the day of the lowest holdings.

3. [Pertains to Article XIX (e); see p. 271.]

4. [Expired.]

Decision No. 486-2
October 7, 1949

CALCULATION OF MEMBERS' REPURCHASE OBLIGATIONS: SCHEDULE B, PARAGRAPH 3

In applying the provisions of Schedule B, paragraph 3 to the calculation of members' repurchase obligations, the following principles shall govern (Staff Memorandum No. 413, 12/8/49 and Supplement 1, 12/13/49):

1. Where exclusions have been made at the end of one year for holdings which are the proceeds of long-term or medium-term loans contracted during the year or for holdings which have been transferred or set aside for the repayment of a loan during the subsequent year, the exclusion continues to be made in the monetary reserve figures for the beginning of the succeeding year.

2. Where an exclusion has been made in respect of currency which became convertible during the year, this currency is included in the monetary reserve figures for the beginning of the subsequent year.

3. If the member indicates that certain holdings are the proceeds of loans or currency set aside, the reasonable implication is that the member wishes paragraph 3 to apply to such holdings. If the member does not provide such data, the implication is that it is not taking advantage of the provision.

Decision No. 510-2
December 16, 1949

ALLOCATION OF OBLIGATIONS: SCHEDULE B, PARAGRAPH 1 (c)

If part of a member's gross repurchase obligation for any financial year is allocated to a currency which the Fund cannot accept because of Article V, Section 7 (c) (iii), that part of the gross obligation is abated for that year under Schedule B, Paragraph 1 (c), and is not required to be discharged in gold or some other currency.

Decision No. 521-3
January 16, 1950

General

FUND ASSISTANCE IN GOLD TRANSACTIONS

Members' Gold Transactions

The Executive Board approves the Managing Director's continuing to assist members by bringing governmental buyers and sellers of gold into contact. If there is a demand, the function may be performed as a regular service on the basis outlined in SM/52/6 (2/7/52). It is understood that initially the service charge will be $\frac{1}{32}$ per cent for each partner in a completed transaction, and that the charge will be reviewed later on the basis of experience.

Decision No. 103-(52/12)
February 21, 1952

Fund Assistance in Gold Transactions *

The Executive Board approves the extension of the Fund's service in bringing buyers and sellers of gold into contact on the basis outlined in SM/52/6(2/7/52), to cases in which one of the parties to the gold transaction is a member and the other is one of the following nonmembers or international organizations:

> . . .
> Switzerland
> Bank for International Settlements
> International Bank for Reconstruction
>   and Development

In accordance with the foregoing, therefore, gold transactions under the service would always involve a member as buyer or seller, and all parties would be either governmental or international organizations.

Decision No. 316-(54/27)
May 27, 1954

Fund Assistance in Gold Transactions

1. The Executive Board approves the following extensions of the Fund's service in bringing buyers and sellers of gold into contact, on the basis outlined in SM/52/6 (2/7/52):

(a) the International Finance Corporation is added to the list of parties in the decision adopted at EBM/54/27(5/27/54);

(b) the service shall apply to gold transactions between an international organization covered by the service and any other party covered by the service.

Decision No. 572-(56/55)
November 21, 1956

---

* The decision lists certain countries which formerly were not members but are presently members.

FUND ASSISTANCE IN GOLD TRANSACTIONS

The Inter-American Development Bank is added to the list of parties in the decisions adopted at Executive Board Meetings 54/27(5/27/54) and 56/55(11/21/56).

Decision No. 1033-(60/26)
May 20, 1960

FUND ASSISTANCE IN GOLD TRANSACTIONS

The International Development Association is added to the list of parties in the decisions adopted at Executive Board Meetings 54/27(5/27/54), 56/55(11/21/56), and 60/26(5/25/60).

Decision No. 1116-(60/51)
December 8, 1960

INVESTMENT OF FUND'S ASSETS

INVESTMENT OF FUND'S ASSETS

The Executive Board, observing that the Fund has had and may continue to have an excess of expenditure over income and that the greater part of the Fund's administrative expenditures has been and will continue to be in United States dollars, considers that in the interest of good administration and conservation of the Fund's resources it would be appropriate to raise income towards meeting the deficit by the investment of a portion of the Fund's gold in a manner which will enable the Fund to reacquire gold at any time and will maintain the gold value of the investment.

In view of the foregoing and noting the willingness of the United States to consent to investment by the Fund in United States Treasury bills, the Executive Board takes the following decisions:

I. The Executive Board, acting pursuant to Article XVIII (a) of the Articles of Agreement, interprets the Articles of Agreement to permit the investment described in the present decisions, namely, sale of a portion of the Fund's gold to the United States for the purpose of investment of the proceeds in United States Treasury bills having not more than ninety-three days to run, subject to the following conditions:

(1) The amount of gold to be sold for investment:

(a) will not be such as to limit the ability of the Fund to make its resources available to members in accordance with the Articles of Agreement; and

(b) will be such as to produce an amount of income reasonably related to the deficit of the Fund;

(2) Whenever the Fund decides to reacquire gold after the sale or maturity of any United States Treasury bills invested in, it will be able to reacquire the same amount of gold as was sold for investment in such bills; and the United States, at the request of the Fund, will sell the said amount of gold to the Fund for U.S. dollars at the United States selling price at the time of the sale to the Fund;

(3) In any computations for the purpose of applying the provisions of the Articles of Agreement the Fund will treat the following assets as representing gold and not as holdings of United States currency:

(a) the dollar proceeds of the sale of gold before investment in United States Treasury bills; and

(b) the United States Treasury bills invested in; and

(c) the dollar proceeds resulting from the sale or maturity of any such bills before the purchase of gold therewith.

II. (1) The Executive Board, acting pursuant to Article XVIII (a) of the Articles of Agreement, interprets Article IV, Section 8 (a) to require the United States to maintain the gold value of the assets set forth in paragraph I (3) (a), (b) and (c) above, notwithstanding changes in the par or foreign exchange value of the currency of the United States. This obligation of the United States shall be fully discharged by its maintaining the gold value of the dollar proceeds resulting from the sale of the gold or from the sale or maturity of the U.S. Treasury bills purchased therewith.

(2) For the purposes of paragraphs I and II of these decisions the dollar proceeds resulting from the sale or maturity of the U.S. Treasury bills invested in shall not include the income of the investment.

III. Subject to the receipt of an assurance from the United States in accordance with paragraph I (2) above satisfactory to the Fund, the Executive Board decides that an amount of the Fund's gold sufficient to realize approximately but not more than two hundred million United States dollars shall be sold to the United States and the proceeds invested and reinvested in United States Treasury bills having not more than ninety-three days to run. The Executive Board will review the amount and operation of the investment at quarterly intervals and at such other times as may be appropriate.

Decision No. 488-(56/5)
January 25, 1956

FUND'S INVESTMENT PROGRAM

The Executive Board, observing that the Fund has had and in the future may again have an excess of expenditure over income and that the greater part of the Fund's administrative expenditure has been and will continue to be in United States dollars, considers that in the interest of good administration and conservation of the Fund's resources it would be appropriate to raise income and provide a reserve towards meeting possible future deficits by continuing the investment of a portion of the Fund's gold in a manner which will enable the Fund to reacquire gold at any time and will maintain the gold value of the investment.

In view of the foregoing and noting the willingness of the United States to consent to continued investment by the Fund in United States Treasury bills, the Executive Board takes the following decisions:

A. Paragraphs I, II and III of Executive Board Decision No. 488-(56/5) shall remain in effect except that the following shall be substituted for paragraph I (1) (b): "will be such as to produce an amount of income reasonably related to the purpose of the investment."

B. The income of the investment earned after October 31, 1957 shall be placed to a Special Reserve, and any administrative deficit for any fiscal year of the Fund shall be written off first against this reserve.

Decision No. 708-(57/57)
November 27, 1957

Fund's Investment Program

The Executive Directors (1) decide that for the purposes of Executive Board Decisions No. 488-(56/5) and No. 708-(57/57) on the investment of the proceeds of the sale of gold, the amount of $500,000,000 shall be substituted for $200,000,000 in Paragraph III of Executive Board Decision No. 488-(56/5), and (2) pursuant to Article XVIII-(a), interpret the Articles of Agreement to permit such investment in U.S. securities having a term to maturity not exceeding twelve months.

Decision No. 905-(59/32)
July 24, 1959

Fund's Investment Program

The amount of $200 million in paragraph III of Executive Board Decision No. 488-(56/5), which was subsequently increased to $500 million by Executive Board Decision No. 905-(59/32), shall be increased to $800 million for all of the purposes of those decisions and Executive Board Decision No. 708-(57/57).

Decision No. 1107-(60/50)
November 30, 1960

Fund's Investment Program

The authorization under (2) of Executive Board Decision No. 905-(59/32) is extended to permit an investment of the amount of $61,900,000 in 15-month U.S. Treasury securities maturing February 15, 1963.

Decision No. 1272-(61/53)
November 3, 1961

By-Laws and Rules and Regulations

The By-Laws and the Rules and Regulations of the Fund are reproduced below as they stood at December 31, 1965.

By-Laws of the International Monetary Fund
(As at December 31, 1965)

TABLE OF CONTENTS

	PAGE
1. Places of Business	278
2. Bank Represented	279
3. Meetings of the Board of Governors	279
4. Notice of Meetings of the Board of Governors	279
5. Attendance of Executive Directors and Observers at Meetings of the Board of Governors	279
6. Agenda of Meetings of the Board of Governors	280
7. Election of Chairman and Vice-Chairmen	280
8. Secretary	280
9. Minutes	280
10. Report of Executive Directors	280
11. Voting	280
12. Proxies	281
13. Voting Without Meeting	281
14. Terms of Service	281
15. Delegation of Authority	283
16. Rules and Regulations	283
17. Vacant Directorships	283
18. Additional Directors	283
19. Representation of Members Not Entitled to Appoint a Director	284
20. Budget and Audits	284
21. Applications for Membership	286
22. Compulsory Withdrawal	286
23. Settlement of Disagreements	286
24. Amendment of By-Laws	286

These By-Laws are adopted under the authority of, and are intended to be complementary to, the Articles of Agreement of the International Monetary Fund; and they shall be construed accordingly. In the event of a conflict between anything in these By-Laws and any provision or requirement of the Articles of Agreement, the Articles of Agreement shall prevail.

SEC. 1. PLACES OF BUSINESS

The principal office of the Fund shall be located within the metropolitan area of Washington, D. C., United States of America.

The Executive Directors may establish and maintain agencies or branch offices at any place in the territories of other members, whenever it is necessary to do so in order to facilitate the efficient conduct of the business of the Fund.

Adopted March 16, 1946

Sec. 2. Bank Represented

The Executive Directors are authorized to invite the International Bank for Reconstruction and Development to send a representative of the Bank to meetings of the Board of Governors and Executive Directors who may participate in such meetings, but shall have no vote.

The Executive Directors are authorized to accept invitations from the Bank to send a representative of the Fund to participate in meetings of the Board of Governors or Executive Directors of the Bank.

Adopted March 16, 1946

Sec. 3. Meetings of the Board of Governors

(a) The annual meeting of the Board of Governors shall be held at such time and place as the Board of Governors shall determine; provided, however, that, if the Executive Directors shall, because of special circumstances, deem it necessary to do so, the Executive Directors may change the time and place of such annual meeting.

(b) Special meetings of the Board of Governors may be called at any time by the Board of Governors or the Executive Directors and shall be called upon the request of five members of the Fund or of members of the Fund having in the aggregate one-fourth of the total voting power. Whenever any member of the Fund shall request the Executive Directors to call a special meeting of the Board of Governors, the Managing Director shall notify all members of the Fund of such request and of the reasons which shall have been given therefor.

(c) A quorum for any meeting of the Board of Governors shall be a majority of the Governors, exercising not less than two-thirds of the total voting power.

Adopted March 16, 1946, amended October 2, 1946

Sec. 4. Notice of Meetings of the Board of Governors

The Managing Director shall cause notice of the time and place of each meeting of the Board of Governors to be given to each member of the Fund by telegram or cable which shall be dispatched not less than 42 days prior to the date set for such meeting, except that in urgent cases such notice shall be sufficient if dispatched by telegram or cable not less than ten days prior to the date set for such meeting.

Adopted March 16, 1946, amended October 2, 1946

Sec. 5. Attendance of Executive Directors and Observers at Meetings of the Board of Governors

(a) The Executive Directors and their Alternates may attend all meetings of the Board of Governors and may participate in such meetings, but an Executive Director or his Alternate shall not be entitled to vote at any such meeting unless he shall be entitled to vote as a Governor or an Alternate or temporary Alternate of a Governor.

(b) The Chairman of the Board of Governors in consultation with the Executive Directors, may invite observers to attend any meeting of the Board of Governors.

Adopted March 16, 1946, amended October 2, 1946

Sec. 6. Agenda of Meetings of the Board of Governors

(a) Under the direction of the Executive Directors, the Managing Director shall prepare a brief agenda for each meeting of the Board of Governors and shall cause such agenda to be transmitted to each member of the Fund with the notice of such meeting.

(b) Additional subjects may be placed on the agenda for any meeting of the Board of Governors by any Governor provided that he shall give notice thereof to the Managing Director not less than seven days prior to the date set for such meeting. In special circumstances the Managing Director, by direction of the Executive Directors, may at any time place additional subjects on the agenda for any meeting of the Board of Governors. The Managing Director shall cause notice of the addition of any subjects to the agenda for any meeting of the Board of Governors to be given as promptly as possible to each member of the Fund.

(c) The Board of Governors may at any time authorize any subject to be placed on the agenda for any meeting of such Board even though the notice required by this section shall not have been given.

(d) Except as otherwise specifically directed by the Board of Governors, the Chairman of the Board of Governors jointly with the Managing Director, shall have charge of all arrangements for the holding of meetings of the Board of Governors.

Adopted March 16, 1946, amended October 2, 1946

Sec. 7. Election of Chairman and Vice-Chairmen

At each annual meeting the Board of Governors shall select a Governor to act as Chairman and at least two other Governors to act as Vice-Chairmen until the next annual meeting.

In the absence of the Chairman, the Vice-Chairman designated by the Chairman shall act in his place.

Adopted March 16, 1946

Sec. 8. Secretary

The Secretary of the Fund shall serve as Secretary of the Board of Governors.

Adopted March 16, 1946

Sec. 9. Minutes

The Board shall keep a summary record of its proceedings which shall be available to all members and which shall be filed with the Executive Directors for their guidance.

Adopted March 16, 1946

Sec. 10. Report of Executive Directors

The Executive Directors shall have prepared for presentation at the annual meeting of the Board of Governors an annual report in which shall be discussed the operations and policies of the Fund and which shall make recommendations to the Board of Governors on the problems confronting the Fund.

Adopted March 16, 1946

Sec. 11. Voting

Except as otherwise specifically provided in the Articles of Agreement, all decisions of the Board shall be made by a majority of the votes cast. At any meeting the Chair-

man may ascertain the sense of the meeting in lieu of a formal vote but he shall require a formal vote upon the request of any Governor. Whenever a formal vote is required the written text of the motion shall be distributed to the voting members.
Adopted March 16, 1946

Sec. 12. Proxies

No Governor or Alternate may vote at any meeting by proxy or by any other method than in person, but a member may make provision for the designation of a temporary Alternate to vote for the Governor at any Board session at which the regularly designated Alternate is unable to be present.
Adopted March 16, 1946

Sec. 13. Voting Without Meeting

Whenever, in the judgment of the Executive Directors, any action by the Fund must be taken by the Board of Governors which should not be postponed until the next regular meeting of the Board and does not warrant the calling of a special meeting of the Board, the Executive Directors shall present to each member by any rapid means of communication a motion embodying the proposed action with a request for a vote by its Governor. Votes shall be cast during such period as the Executive Directors may prescribe, provided that no Governor shall vote on any such motion until 7 days after dispatch of the motion, unless he is notified that the Executive Directors have waived this requirement. At the expiration of the period prescribed for voting, the Executive Directors shall record the results and the Managing Director shall notify all members. If the replies received do not include a majority of the Governors exercising two-thirds of the total voting power, which is usually required for a quorum of the Board of Governors, the motion shall be considered lost.
Adopted March 16, 1946

Sec. 14. Terms of Service

(a) Governors and Alternates shall receive their actual transport expenses to and from the place of meeting in attending meetings, and $75 for each night which attendance at such meetings requires them to spend away from their normal place of residence, this amount being reduced to $15 for each night when accommodation is included in the price of transportation.

(b) Pending the necessary action being taken by members to exempt from national taxation salaries and allowances paid out of the budget of the Fund, the Governors and the Executive Directors, and their Alternates, the Managing Director and the staff members shall be reimbursed by the Fund for the taxes which they are required to pay on such salaries and allowances.

In computing the amount of tax adjustment to be made with respect to any individual, it shall be presumed for the purposes of the computation that the income received from the Fund is his total income. All salary scales and expense allowances prescribed by this section are stated as net on the above basis.

(c) The salary of the Managing Director shall be $40,000 per annum. The Fund shall also pay any reasonable expenses incurred by the Managing Director in the interest of the Fund (including travel and transportation expenses for himself, and expenses for his family, and his personal effects in moving once to the seat of the Fund during or immediately before his term of office and in moving once from the seat during or immediately after his term of office). The contract of the Managing Director shall be for a term of five years and may be renewed for the same term or for a shorter term at the discretion of the Executive Directors, provided that no person shall be initially appointed to the post of Managing Director after he had reached his sixty-fifth birthday and that no Managing Director shall hold such post beyond his seventieth birthday.

(d) It shall be the duty of an Executive Director and his Alternate to devote all the time and attention to the business of the Fund that its interests require, and, between them, to be continuously available at the principal office of the Fund; however, in the event that both an Executive Director and his Alternate are unable to be available at the principal office of the Fund for reasons of health, absence while on business of the Fund, or similar reasons, the Executive Director may designate a temporary Alternate to act for him for periods of time which shall not in the aggregate exceed fifteen business days in the course of any financial year. A temporary Alternate shall receive no salary or expense allowance.

(e) The maximum salary and expense allowance including housing, entertainment and all other expenses [except those specified in subsection (f)] shall be $28,000 per year for Executive Directors and $22,000 per year for Alternates. It will be the duty of each Executive Director and each Alternate to state how much of these amounts he intends to draw whether as salary or as expense allowance, except that no Executive Director shall draw more than $25,000 and no Alternate shall draw more than $20,000 as salary.

(f) The Executive Directors and their Alternates are to be reimbursed, in addition, for all reasonable expenses incurred during absence from the seat of the Fund while on the designated service of the Fund. Executive Directors and their Alternates shall be reimbursed for authorized representation expenses actually incurred while they are absent from the seat of the Fund on a special mission at the request of the Fund. They shall also be reimbursed for travel and transportation expenses for themselves, their families, and their personal effects in moving once to the seat of the Fund during or immediately before their periods of service and in moving once from the seat during or immediately after their periods of service.

In addition, any Executive Director or Alternate shall in the third year of continuous full-time service in either capacity and in every second year of such service thereafter be entitled to reimbursement for the cost of transportation expenses for his family in traveling once to and from the country of which he or his wife is a national, provided that in cases where the wife is a national of another country the reimbursement for transportation expenses to and from her country does not exceed that to and from the country of which he is a national. For home leave travel more frequent than every third year, reimbursement shall be made on the basis of cabin- or economy-class accommodations.

(g) Where not specified, it is assumed that the Director and Alternate will be a full-time Director and Alternate. Where it is intended that he shall not devote his full time, it shall be so indicated. Where an Executive Director or Alternate indicates that he intends to devote only part of his time to the Fund, his remuneration shall be pro-rated on the basis of a representation by him of the proportion of his time he has devoted to the interests of the Fund. He may make such representation each month.

(h) Where an individual is serving both Fund and Bank, the aggregate of salary received from both shall not exceed the full annual single salary indicated above.

In all cases of salaries or expenses involving dual offices in the Fund or Bank, or both, the individual affected is entitled to take his choice as to which salary or expense he elects, but he shall not be entitled to both.

(i) An individual putting forward a claim for reimbursement for any expenses incurred by him shall include therewith a representation that he has not received and will not claim reimbursement in respect to those expenses from any other source.

(j) Secretarial, staff services, office space, and other services incidental to the performance of the duties of the Executive Directors and Alternates shall be provided by the Fund.

Adopted March 16, 1946; paragraph (a) amended March 18, 1946 and June 6, 1966; paragraph (c) amended July 27, 1951 and December 14, 1960, effective December 1, 1960; paragraph (d) amended September 17, 1947; paragraph (e) amended January 5, 1951, effective January 1, 1951; December 2, 1957, effective November 1, 1957; December 28, 1959, effective November 1, 1959; November 7, 1962, effective September 1, 1962; and August 8, 1966, effective November 1, 1965; paragraph (f) amended September 17, 1947, September 30, 1948, August 18, 1961, and September 10, 1964.

Sec. 15. Delegation of Authority

The Executive Directors are authorized by the Board of Governors to exercise all the powers of the Fund except those reserved to the Board by Article XII, Section 2 (b) and other provisions of the Articles of Agreement. The Executive Directors shall not take any action pursuant to powers delegated by the Board of Governors which is inconsistent with any action taken by the Board.

Adopted March 16, 1946

Sec. 16. Rules and Regulations

The Executive Directors are authorized by the Board of Governors to adopt such Rules and Regulations, including financial regulations, as may be necessary or appropriate to conduct the business of the Fund. Any Rules and Regulations so adopted, and any amendments thereof, shall be subject to review by the Board of Governors at their next annual meeting.

Adopted March 16, 1946

Sec. 17. Vacant Directorships

Whenever a new Director must be elected because of a vacancy requiring an election, the Managing Director shall notify the members who elected the former Director of the existence of the vacancy. He may convene a meeting of the Governors of such countries exclusively for the purpose of electing a new Director; or he may request nominations by mail or telegraph and conduct ballots by mail or telegraph. Successive ballots shall be cast until one candidate has a majority; and after each ballot, the candidate with the smallest number of votes shall be dropped from the next ballot.

When a new elective Director is named, the office of Alternate shall be deemed to be vacant and an Alternate shall be named by the newly-elected Director.

Adopted March 16, 1946

Sec. 18 Additional Directors

At least one month before the second and subsequent regular elections of Directors, the Managing Director shall notify all members of the two members whose currencies held by the Fund have been, on the average over the preceding two years, reduced below their quotas by the largest absolute amounts. He shall state whether either or both are entitled to appoint a Director in accordance with Article XII, Section 3 (c) of the Articles of Agreement.

When a member becomes entitled to appoint a Director in accordance with Article XII, Section 3 (b) (i) and 3 (c) of the Articles of Agreement, it shall not participate in the election of any Director.

Adopted March 16, 1946

Sec. 19. Representation of Members Not Entitled to Appoint a Director

(a) Each member not entitled to appoint a Director may, in accordance with the regulations provided in this section, send a representative to attend any meeting of the Executive Directors when a request made by, or a matter particularly affecting, that member is under consideration. A member, so electing, may waive its rights under this provision. The Executive Directors shall determine whether a matter under consideration particularly affects a member not entitled to appoint a Director, which determination shall be final.

(b) Whenever a member not entitled to appoint a Director desires to present its views at the meeting of the Executive Directors at which a request the member has made is to be considered, it shall so notify the Fund when it makes the request and shall designate a representative for this purpose who shall be available at the seat of the Fund. Failure to give such notice or to designate an available representative shall constitute a waiver of the member's right to present its views at the meeting.

(c) Whenever the Executive Directors are to consider a matter which has been determined particularly to affect a member not entitled to appoint a Director, the member shall be promptly informed by rapid means of communication of the date set for its consideration. No final action shall be taken by the Executive Directors with respect to such matter, nor any question particularly affecting such member submitted to the Board of Governors, until the member has either waived its rights under paragraph (a) of this section or has been given an opportunity to present its views through an appropriately authorized representative at a meeting of the Executive Directors, of which the member has had reasonable notice.

Adopted March 16, 1946, amended September 17, 1947

Sec. 20. Budget and Audits

(a) The Executive Directors shall instruct the Managing Director to prepare an annual administrative budget to be presented to them for approval. The budget so approved shall be incorporated in the annual report to be presented to the Board of Governors at their annual meeting.

(b) An external audit of the financial records and transactions of the Fund shall be made annually and such audit shall relate to the period representing the fiscal year of the Fund. The Executive Directors shall submit the Fund's audited balance sheet and audited statement of income and expense to the Board of Governors to be considered by them at their annual meeting.

The annual audit shall be made by an audit committee consisting of either three or five persons each of whom shall be nominated by a different member of the Fund and confirmed by the Executive Directors. At least one person serving on each audit committee shall be nominated by one of the six members of the Fund having the largest quotas. The Executive Directors shall determine, in the case of each audit, whether the audit committee shall consist of three or five persons and which members of the Fund shall be requested to nominate persons to serve on the committee. The service of the members of each audit committee shall terminate upon completion of the annual audit and submission of the report on audit.

Each audit committee shall elect one of its members as chairman, shall determine its own procedure, and shall otherwise be independent of the Management of the Fund in conducting the annual audit according to generally accepted auditing standards.

The annual audit shall be comprehensive with respect to examination of the financial records of the Fund; shall extend, insofar as practicable, to the ascertainment that financial transactions consummated during the period under review are supported by the necessary authority; and shall determine that there is adequate and faithful accounting for the assets of the Fund. It shall thereby establish an appropriate basis for conclusion concerning the financial position of the Fund at the close of the fiscal year and the results of its financial operations during that year. For this purpose, the audit committee shall have access to the accounting records of the Fund and other supporting evidence of its financial transactions and shall be furnished by the Management of the Fund with such information and representations as may be required in connection with the audit. The members of the audit committee shall respect the confidential nature of their service and the information made available for purposes of the audit.

All accounts shall be summarized in United States dollars; and for this purpose gold shall be valued in terms of United States dollars at the par value of the United States dollar, and all members' currencies shall be converted at their par values or in accordance with a decision of the Fund pursuant to Article IV, Section 8 (b) (ii) of the Articles of Agreement.

The Executive Directors shall decide all questions of policy raised by requests of the audit committee for particular information or the inspection of particular records or documents. The refusal of any such requests for reasons of policy shall be explained in the comments of the Executive Directors forwarded to the Board of Governors with the report on audit.

Any question the audit committee may have concerning interpretation of the Articles of Agreement, the By-Laws, or the Rules and Regulations shall be discussed with the Managing Director, or officials designated by him, and if the reply is not completely satisfactory to the audit committee, shall be referred to the Executive Directors through the Managing Director.

The audit committee shall submit its report on audit to the Board of Governors for consideration by them at their annual meeting. Such submission shall be made through the Managing Director and the Executive Directors who shall forward with the report on audit their comments thereon. The audit committee shall afford the Managing Director an opportunity for explanation to them before deciding that any matter seems to require criticism in the report on audit.

The audit committee may formally furnish the Managing Director and Executive Directors their views and suggestions concerning the system of accounting, internal financial control, and documentary or other procedure which may technically strengthen or improve the administration of the Fund's financial affairs. Such matters need not be dealt with in the report on audit unless the audit committee believes they are of such moment as to warrant inclusion.

The Managing Director shall determine what expenses are necessary and reasonable in connection with each annual audit and the Fund shall bear such expenses.

Adopted March 16, 1946, amended September 17, 1947

Sec. 21. Applications for Membership

Subject to any special provisions that may be made for countries listed in Schedule A of the Articles of Agreement, any country may apply for membership in the Fund by filing with the Fund an application setting forth all relevant facts.

When submitting an application to the Board of Governors, the Executive Directors after consultation with the applicant country shall recommend to the Board the amount of the quota, the form of payment, the parity of the currency, conditions regarding exchange restrictions, and such other conditions as, in the opinion of the Executive Directors, the Board of Governors may wish to prescribe.

Adopted March 16, 1946

Sec. 22. Compulsory Withdrawal

Before any member is required to withdraw from membership in the Fund, the matter shall be considered by the Executive Directors who shall inform the member in reasonable time of the complaint against it and allow the member an adequate opportunity for stating its case both orally and in writing. The Executive Directors shall recommend to the Board of Governors the action they deem appropriate. The member shall be informed of the recommendation and the date on which its case will be considered by the Board and shall be given a reasonable time within which to present its case to the Board both orally and in writing. Any member so electing may waive this provision.

Adopted March 16, 1946

Sec. 23. Settlement of Disagreements

The President of the International Court of Justice is prescribed as the authority to appoint an umpire whenever there arises a disagreement of the type referred to in Article XVIII (c) of the Articles of Agreement.

Adopted March 16, 1946

Sec. 24. Amendment of By-Laws

These By-Laws may be amended by the Board of Governors at any meeting thereof or by vote without a meeting as provided in Section 13.

Adopted October 2, 1946

Rules and Regulations of the International Monetary Fund
(As at December 31, 1965)

TABLE OF CONTENTS

	PAGE
A. Scope of Rules and Regulations	287
B. Terms, Definitions, and Symbols Employed in this Document	288
C. Meetings of the Executive Board	289
Meetings	289
Agenda	289
Voting	290
Language	290
Minutes	290
D. Application for Membership and Quotas	290
E. Subscriptions	291
F. Par Values	291
G. Fund Transactions	292
General	292
Foreign Exchange	292
Gold	293
H. Exchange Controls, Currency Practices, and Agreements	293
I. Repurchases and Charges	294
J. Accounts and Reports	299
K. Limitation and Ineligibility	299
L. Capital Transfers	300
M. Relations with Non-Members	300
N. Staff Regulations	301
Personnel	301
Travel	303

A—SCOPE OF RULES AND REGULATIONS

A-1. These Rules and Regulations supplement the Fund Agreement and the By-Laws adopted by the Board of Governors. They are not intended to replace any provision of either the Agreement or the By-Laws. The Rules and Regulations attempt to provide such operating rules, procedures, regulations, and interpretation as are necessary and desirable to carry out the purposes and powers contained in the Agreement, as supplemented by the By-Laws. If any provision in the Rules and Regulations is found to be in conflict with any provision in the Agreement or in the By-Laws, the Agreement and By-Laws shall prevail and an appropriate amendment should be made to these Rules and Regulations.

Adopted September 25, 1946

A-2. Additions to, and changes of, the Rules and Regulations will be made as experience brings to light new problems or suggests modifications in procedures already adopted.

Adopted September 25, 1946

B—Terms, Definitions, and Symbols Employed in this Document

B-1. Executive Director, except where otherwise specified, shall include the Alternate or the temporary Alternate, as the case may be.
Adopted September 25, 1946, amended August 14, 1947, effective September 17, 1947

B-2. Executive Board refers to the Executive Directors presided over by the Chairman.
Adopted September 25, 1946

B-3. Chairman, except where otherwise specified, shall refer to the Chairman or Acting Chairman of the Executive Board.
Adopted September 25, 1946

B-4. Agenda ordinarily refers to both the list of items to be considered at a meeting and the supplementary documents pertinent thereto.
Adopted September 25, 1946

B-5. Fund Agreement refers to the Articles of Agreement of the International Monetary Fund and, where the context is clear, Agreement shall also refer to the Articles of Agreement.
Adopted September 25, 1946

B-6. FA refers to the Fund Agreement.

BL refers to the By-Laws of the International Monetary Fund as adopted by the Board of Governors.

RR refers to these Rules and Regulations.
Adopted September 25, 1946

B-7. Executive Session refers to a Meeting of the Executive Directors in which no person is present except the Executive Directors, Managing Director, and, with the approval of the Board granted separately for each Executive Session, the Secretary of the Board.
Adopted September 25, 1946

B-8. Business day [1] refers to the normal working hours of the Fund, 9:00 a.m. to 5:30 p.m. at the official time for the District of Columbia, on Monday through Friday of each week with the following exceptions (which will include the preceding Friday whenever one of the dates below falls on a Saturday and the following Monday whenever one falls on a Sunday):

January 1	First Monday in September
February 22	November 11
May 30	Fourth Thursday in November
July 4	December 25

Adopted May 28, 1947, amended March 8, 1948 and October 27, 1961

---

[1] The definition of "business day" does not affect in any way the arrangements which have been made for the receipt of messages at all times and for prompt action upon them as required by circumstances and the Fund Agreement, By-Laws and Rules and Regulations.

C—Meetings of the Executive Board

Meetings

C-1. Meetings of the Executive Directors shall be called by the Chairman as the business of the Fund may require. Except in special circumstances the Chairman shall notify all Executive Directors of meetings at least two business days in advance.
Adopted September 25, 1946, amended May 28, 1947

C-2. The Chairman shall call a meeting at the request of any Executive Director.
Adopted September 25, 1946

C-3. Meetings of the Executive Board shall be open to attendance by the Secretary and such members of the staff as the Chairman indicates. At the request of the Chairman or any Executive Director meetings may be held in Executive Session, or the Executive Board may determine which particular members of the staff may attend any session.
Adopted September 25, 1946, amended January 15, 1948

C-4. The Executive Directors shall meet at the principal office of the Fund unless it is decided that a particular meeting shall be held elsewhere.
Adopted September 25, 1946

C-5. In the absence of the Managing Director, the Deputy Managing Director shall act as Chairman and shall have a deciding vote in case of an equal division. In the absence of both the Managing Director and the Deputy Managing Director, the Executive Director selected by the Executive Board shall act as Chairman. An Executive Director shall retain his right to vote when serving as Acting Chairman.
Adopted September 25, 1946, amended November 12, 1948

Agenda

C-6. The agenda for each meeting shall be prepared by the Chairman. The agenda shall include any item requested by an Executive Director.
Adopted September 25, 1946

C-7. Except in special circumstances the Chairman shall notify Executive Directors of new items on the agenda at least two full business days before their consideration in meetings. Additional advance notice shall be given at the discretion of the Chairman before the consideration of new items of especial importance which may require consultation with members or the return to the seat of the Fund of Executive Directors who are absent.
Adopted September 25, 1946, amended May 28, 1947

C-8. Matters not on the agenda for a meeting may be considered at that meeting only by unanimous consent of the Executive Directors present.
Adopted September 25, 1946

C-9. Any item of the agenda for a meeting, consideration of which has not been completed at that meeting, shall, unless the Executive Directors decide otherwise, be automatically included in the agenda of the next meeting.
Adopted September 25, 1946

Voting

C-10. The Chairman will ordinarily ascertain the sense of the meeting in lieu of a formal vote. Any Executive Director may require a formal vote to be taken with votes cast as prescribed in Article XII, Section 3 (i).

Adopted September 25, 1946

C-11. There shall be no formal voting in committees and subcommittees. The Chairman of the committee or subcommittee shall determine the sense of the meeting (including alternative points of view) which shall be reported.

Adopted September 25, 1946

C-12. No Executive Director may vote at any meeting by proxy or by any other method than in person.

Adopted September 25, 1946

Language

C-13. The working language of the Fund will be English. The discussion, documents, and reports of meetings will ordinarily be in English. Speeches or papers presented in other languages shall be translated into English.

Adopted September 25, 1946

Minutes

C-14. Under the direction of the Managing Director, the Secretary shall be responsible for the preparation of a summary record of the proceedings of the Executive Board.

Adopted September 25, 1946

C-15. Verbatim records will be taken only if the Chairman, the Executive Board or an Executive Director so requests. In such case, the Secretariat shall be given advance notice of the desire for verbatim recording.

Adopted September 25, 1946

C-16. Draft minutes will be circulated to all Executive Directors as quickly as possible after meetings. They will normally be submitted for approval at the next meeting of the Executive Board following the day they are circulated, and in any case will be submitted for approval not later than the third succeeding meeting.

Adopted September 25, 1946, amended May 28, 1947 and August 14, 1947

D—Application for Membership and Quotas

D-1. When a country applies for membership in the Fund, and the application is placed before the Executive Board, the Chairman shall announce a reasonable time to be allowed for discussion and preliminary investigation by the Executive Board before a decision is reached to proceed with the formal investigation. If this decision is in the affirmative the Fund may proceed to obtain all relevant information and discuss with the applicant any matters relating to its application. Any Executive Director may request such information to be added to the list requested of the applicant as in his opinion is relevant to the decision to be made. The Executive Board shall then decide whether to submit an application for membership with its views to the Board of Governors for a telegraphic vote or hold the application until the next meeting of the Board of Governors.

FA II-2; BL-21. Adopted September 25, 1946

D-2. When a member requests an adjustment of its quota, the Executive Board, after consulting the member, shall submit a written report on the request to the Board of Governors at its next meeting. If the Board of Governors approves an increase in the quota of a member, and on the date the member consents to the increase its monetary reserves are less than its new quota, the Executive Board may reduce the proportion of the increase to be paid in gold. The member shall, if it desires such a reduction, transmit to the Fund by rapid means of communication within ten days after its consent, the data necessary to determine its monetary reserves as at the date of the consent. The decision of the Executive Board shall be made within ten days after receipt of such data.

FA III-2 and 4. Adopted September 25, 1946, amended May 28, 1947

D-3. At least one year prior to the time when a review of quotas must be undertaken by the Fund, the Executive Board shall appoint a committee to study the problem and to prepare a written report.

FA III-2. Adopted September 25, 1946

E—Subscriptions

E-1. Gold depositories of the Fund shall be established in the United States, United Kingdom, France, and India. The gold of the Fund shall be held with the depositories designated by the members in whose territories they are located at places agreed with the Fund. A member may pay its gold subscription to the Fund at one or more of the specified gold depositories within the terms of Article XIII, Section 2.

FA XIII-2. Adopted September 25, 1946, amended November 29, 1956

E-2. A member shall pay its currency subscription to the Fund at the designated depository. Each member is authorized to substitute in accordance with Article III, Section 5, non-negotiable, non-interest bearing notes payable to the Fund on demand for that part of the currency holdings of the Fund which exceed 1 per cent of the member's quota, and the depository shall hold such notes for the account of the Fund. Such notes shall not be accepted until the Fund is satisfied that they are in proper form and that their issue has been authorized. The balances held in the administrative accounts of the Fund shall not be considered as part of the currency holdings of the Fund for the application of this Rule.

FA III-5. Adopted September 25, 1946, amended February 20, 1950

E-3. The Executive Board may agree to alter the 1 per cent requirement in the case of any member should circumstances in the opinion of the Executive Board warrant a different percentage.

Adopted September 25, 1946, amended February 20, 1950

E-4. The member is allowed 24 hours in which to deposit the currency necessary to maintain the amount required under E-2 and E-3.

Adopted September 25, 1946

E-5. For purposes of Article III, Section 3, initial gold payments in excess of the minimum shall be accepted on the same basis as the minimum payment.

Adopted September 25, 1946

F—Par Values

F-1. The Fund shall arrange through the fiscal agencies of members that frequent

and regular information as to the market rates of members' currencies bought and sold in their territories is made available to the Fund.
Adopted September 25, 1946

F-2. Members shall notify the Fund whether for the settlement of international transactions they, in fact, freely buy and sell gold within the prescribed limits of price and shall notify the Fund of any changes in such policy.
FA IV-4 (b). Adopted September 25, 1946

F-3. A member desiring to change the par value of its currency shall give the Fund as much notice as the circumstances allow, and shall submit a full and reasoned statement why, in its opinion, such a change is necessary to correct a fundamental disequilibrium.
FA IV-5. Adopted September 25, 1946

F-4. For transactions in gold by a member the margin above and below par value shall be, at the option of the member, either:

1. One quarter of one per cent plus the following charges:
   (a) The actual or computed cost of converting the gold transferred into good delivery bars at the normal center for dealing in gold of either the buying member or the member whose currency is exchanged for the gold;
   (b) The actual or computed cost of transporting the gold transferred to the normal center for dealing in gold of either the buying member or the member whose currency is exchanged for the gold;
   (c) Any charges made by the custodian of the gold transferred for effecting the transfer; or
2. One per cent, which one per cent shall be taken to include all of the charges set forth in 1 above.

Adopted June 10, 1947, amended October 15, 1954 and extended November 5, 1954

G—Fund Transactions

General

G-1. Each member shall designate a fiscal agency for its transactions with the Fund, in accordance with Article V, Section 1, before its subscription becomes due, and may change the agency after notifying the Fund.
FA V-1. Adopted September 25, 1946

Foreign Exchange

G-2. Each request from a member to purchase currency from the Fund shall be made by the fiscal agency designated in accordance with Article V, Section 1, such request to be authenticated in the manner agreed upon by the Fund and the agency. In its operations on behalf of the Fund a depository will act only on instructions authenticated in such manner as may be agreed upon by the Fund and the depository.
Adopted September 25, 1946, amended February 20, 1947

G-3. When a duly authenticated request for the purchase of foreign exchange in accordance with Article V, Section 3, is received, the Fund shall, on the third business day following the day of receipt of the request, instruct the appropriate depository to

make the transfer, except in cases which the Executive Board may indicate. The first business day after receipt of the request shall be regarded as the first of the three days.
Adopted September 25, 1946, amended February 7, 1947

G-4. When a member expects to purchase from the Fund, in a single transaction or a series of transactions, an unusually large sum of any other member's currency (unusually large relative to the quota of that other member), the member shall give the Fund as much notice of the proposed transaction or transactions as can reasonably be effected.
Adopted September 25, 1946

G-5. When the request of a member, if consummated, would increase to more than 5 per cent of its quota the aggregate purchases by the member pursuant to Article V, Section 3, during the thirty-day period preceding the date of action specified in G-3, the Managing Director shall notify each Executive Director (or his Alternate if the Executive Director is not available) on the first business day after receipt of the request. If neither the Executive Director nor the Alternate is in Washington or its environs, the notification will be assumed to have been duly delivered if appropriate notice is delivered to his office.

At the request of any Executive Director or on the initiative of the Managing Director, a special meeting shall be called by the Managing Director to discuss the request as soon as feasible, but not later than the morning of the second business day.
Adopted February 7, 1947

Gold

G-6. Gold due to the Fund may be delivered at any gold depository of the Fund. Whenever the Fund accepts gold situated elsewhere than at a gold depository of the Fund, the member delivering such gold may be required to assume the actual or estimated costs, as the case may be, of moving the gold to the Fund's nearest gold depository. Where the member is required to reimburse the Fund for such actual or estimated costs, the Fund shall advise the member in what form reimbursement shall be made.
Adopted July 30, 1948

G-7. When any member sells gold to the Fund pursuant to Article V, Section 6 (a), the member may be required to assume the estimated costs that would be incurred by the Fund if it used the gold so acquired to purchase the currency it has sold. The Fund shall advise the member in what form such payment shall be made.
Adopted July 30, 1948

H—Exchange Controls, Currency Practices, and Agreements

H-1. The Fund shall keep all exchange controls under review and shall consult with members with a view to the progressive removal of exchange restrictions in accordance with the Fund Agreement.
FA XIV-2. Adopted September 25, 1946

H-2. If a member complains to the Executive Board that another member is not complying with its obligations concerning exchange controls, discriminatory currency arrangements, or multiple currency practices, the complaint shall give all facts pertinent to an examination.
FA VIII-2 and 3. Adopted September 25, 1946

H-3. Upon receipt of a complaint from a member, the Executive Board shall make arrangements promptly for consultation with the members directly involved.
Adopted September 25, 1946

H-4. All requests by a member under Article VIII, Sections 2 and 3, that the Fund approve the imposition of restrictions on the making of payments and transfers for current international transactions, or the use of discriminatory currency arrangements or multiple currency practices, shall be submitted to the Executive Board in writing, with a statement of the reasons for making the request.
FA VIII-2 and 3. Adopted September 25, 1946

H-5. The Executive Board shall decide each request for approval expeditiously.
Adopted September 25, 1946

I—REPURCHASES AND CHARGES

I-1. The first time that a member has to make a gold payment to the Fund it shall deliver gold of designated weight and fineness at least sufficient in value to meet the payment. Any surplus balance of gold shall be held by the Fund under earmark at the disposal of the member and may be used to meet other payments incurred in the future.
Adopted September 25, 1946

I-2. The service charge payable by a member buying the currency of another member in exchange for its own currency shall be paid at the time the transaction is consummated. The service charge payable for such transactions taking place from December 1, 1951 through April 30, 1966, shall be ½ of 1 per cent.
FA V-8 (a). Adopted September 25, 1946, amended November 19, 1951, November 14, 1952, June 26, 1953, October 14, 1953, December 23, 1953, December 15, 1954, December 27, 1955, May 23, 1956, December 21, 1956, December 9, 1957, December 12, 1958, March 20, 1959, April 20, 1959, April 19, 1960, April 17, 1961, April 25, 1962, April 24, 1963, April 13, 1964, and April 28, 1965

I-3. Rule I-3, adopted September 25, 1946, was eliminated on July 30, 1948, and the substance of the Rule was incorporated into Rule G-6 on that date.

I-4. (a) As soon as possible after July 31, October 31, January 31 and April 30, the Fund shall notify each member by cable of the charges it owes to the Fund pursuant to Article V, Section 8 (c) or (d), for the three calendar months ending on each such date. These charges shall be payable within thirty days after the sending of such notice.
Adopted September 25, 1946, amended July 30, 1948 and February 24, 1954

(b) Such charges payable by each member shall be computed on the basis of the "average of the holdings" which, as used in this section, means the average daily balances of its currency held by the Fund in excess of its quota calculated as follows:
(i) At the end of each calendar month there shall be averaged for each member the daily amounts by which the Fund's holdings of its currency on the Fund's books at the close of each day during that month have exceeded its quota on each such day;

(ii) The Fund's holdings of each member's currency shall consist of all of its currency except amounts, not in excess of 1/100 of 1% of the member's quota, in a special account to meet administrative expenses.

Adopted July 30, 1948

(c) The period of time during which the Fund's holdings of a member's currency have been at a particular level shall be the continuous period of time during which the average of the holdings has not fallen below that level, and, in determining periods of time for the application of the charges, changes in the average of the holdings shall affect the calculation of time periods in the following way:

  (i) Each increase in the average of the holdings shall create a new segment of the holdings which will be equal to the amount of the increase and the period of time during which each segment is held shall be measured from the beginning of the month in which the increase in the average of the holdings occurs.

  (ii) Each decrease in the average of the holdings shall terminate the period of time during which the holdings have been in excess of the new average and the period of time shall terminate at the end of the month preceding that in which the decrease in the average of the holdings occurs.

Adopted July 30, 1948

[Rule I-4 (d) and (e) have been omitted because the charges provided thereunder are no longer applicable to any segment of the Fund's holdings.]

(f) (1) With respect to each segment of the holdings of a member's currency to the extent that it represents the acquisition of that currency by the Fund from January 1, 1954 through April 30, 1963:

  (i) The charge to be levied on each segment to the extent that it is within the first bracket of 50 per cent in excess of the quota shall be nil for the first three months, 2 per cent per annum for the next fifteen months, and an additional $1/2$ per cent per annum for each subsequent six months.

  (ii) The charge to be levied on each segment to the extent that it is within the second bracket of more than 50 per cent and not more than 75 per cent in excess of the quota shall be nil for the first three months, 2 per cent per annum for the next nine months, and an additional $1/2$ per cent per annum for each subsequent six months.

  (iii) The charge to be levied on each segment to the extent that it is within the third bracket of more than 75 per cent and not more than 100 per cent in excess of the quota shall be nil for the first three months, 2 per cent per annum for the next three months, and an additional $1/2$ per cent per annum for each subsequent six months.

Adopted as I-4 (f) December 23, 1953, amended December 15, 1954, December 27, 1955, May 23, 1956, December 21, 1956, December 9, 1957, December 12, 1958, March 20, 1959, April 20, 1959, April 19, 1960, April 17, 1961, April 25, 1962, and April 24, 1963

(2) With respect to each segment of the holdings of a member's currency to the extent that it represents the acquisition of that currency by the Fund from May 1, 1963 through April 30, 1966:

(i) The charge to be levied on each segment to the extent that it is within the first bracket of 50 per cent in excess of the quota shall be nil for the first three months, 2 per cent per annum for the next fifteen months, and an additional $1/2$ per cent per annum for each subsequent six months.

(ii) The charge to be levied on each segment to the extent that it is within the second bracket of more than 50 per cent and not more than 100 per cent in excess of the quota shall be nil for the first three months, 2 per cent per annum for the next nine months, and an additional $1/2$ per cent per annum for each subsequent six months.

(iii) The charge to be levied on each segment to the extent that it is within the third bracket of more than 100 per cent in excess of the quota shall be nil for the first three months, 2 per cent per annum for the next three months, and an additional $1/2$ per cent per annum for each subsequent six months.

Adopted April 24, 1963, amended April 13, 1964 and April 28, 1965

(g) The Fund and the member shall consider means by which the Fund's holdings of the currency can be reduced whenever the Fund's holdings of a member's currency are such that the charge under (f) above applicable to any segment for any period has reached the rate of 4 per cent per annum. Thereafter, the charges shall rise in accordance with (f) above, provided that the rate shall not increase beyond 5 per cent per annum when agreement is reached under this Rule for repurchase within three to five years after a drawing in accordance with Executive Board Decision No. 102-(52/11). In the case of agreements on means to reduce the Fund's holdings beyond five years, the Fund may adopt higher maximum rates. In the absence of agreement on means to reduce the Fund's holdings, the Fund may impose such charges as it deems appropriate after the rate of 5 per cent is reached. When an agreement for repurchase within three to five years after a drawing is not reached or observed, the charges to be imposed shall rise in accordance with (f) above, provided that when the charges payable on any segment have reached 6 per cent the Fund will review the charges to be imposed thereafter. In the case of non-observance, if 5 per cent is payable on any segment at the date of non-observance, it shall continue to be payable only for that part of a period of six months for which it has not yet been payable; and when the repurchases to which the non-observance relates are made or a new agreement for repurchase not later than five years after the drawing is made all charges in excess of 5 per cent shall be reduced to 5 per cent.

Adopted as I-4 (f) November 19, 1951, amended December 23, 1953, April 27, 1959, February 25, 1963, and April 24, 1963

FA V-8 (c) and (d).

I-5. (a) If, in accordance with Article V, Section 8 (f), a member wishes to pay in its own currency part of any charge due to the Fund pursuant to I-4, the proportion to be paid in such currency shall be calculated on the basis of its monetary reserves at the end of the quarter of the financial year of the Fund to which such charges apply.

Adopted September 25, 1946, amended May 28, 1947 and July 30, 1948

(b) If, in accordance with Article V, Section 8 (f), a member wishes to pay in its own currency part of any charge due to the Fund pursuant to I-2 or I-8, the proportion to be paid in such currency shall be calculated on the basis of its monetary reserves on the day before the day on which the charge is due; provided, however, that if the member would encounter undue difficulties in providing for that day the data required by the Fund in the monetary reserve report forms sent to members, the proportion to be paid in the member's currency shall be calculated on the basis of its monetary reserves at the end of the quarter of the financial year of the Fund in which the charge becomes due. The member, when making a provisional payment in accordance with (c) below, shall advise the Fund whether the member will provide monetary reserve data for the day before the day on which the charge becomes due or for the end of the quarter in which the charge becomes due.

Adopted July 30, 1948, amended March 24, 1950

(c) Whenever a charge is due under I-2, I-4, or I-8, and the member wishes to pay part thereof in its own currency, the member shall make a provisional payment in gold and currency on the basis of its own estimate of its monetary reserves for the appropriate day or end of quarter of the financial year of the Fund as specified in (a) or (b) above. The member shall provide the Fund with the data, for such appropriate day or end of quarter, required by the Fund in the monetary reserve report forms sent to members, and such data shall be provided to the Fund not later than six months from the aforesaid appropriate day or end of quarter. On the basis of such data, the Fund shall make a final determination of the proportions of the charge to be paid in gold and in currency, and final adjustment of the provisional payment shall be made on the date specified by the Fund. If the member fails to provide its monetary reserve data within the period prescribed herein, the whole of the charge shall be finally payable in gold.

Adopted July 30, 1948

FA V-8 (f)

I-6. (a) Within six months after the end of each financial year of the Fund, each member shall furnish the data necessary for the calculation of its monetary reserves and its repurchase obligation, if any. Such data shall be supplied to the Fund in the monetary reserve report forms send to members by the Fund.

(b) Each member's monetary reserves and repurchase obligation, if any, shall be computed on the basis of the aforesaid data.

(c) When a repurchase obligation has thus been computed for a member, the Managing Director, after consultation with the Executive Director appointed or elected by the member, shall notify the member by letter containing all the necessary details of the computation, including the distribution of the amount payable among the types of reserves.

(d) If the member is in agreement with the aforesaid computation, the member shall so advise the Fund within thirty days from the day on which the member receives notice thereof. The Managing Director shall then send to the member a formal request for payment, and shall at the same time notify the Board of such request. The member shall discharge the repurchase obligation within thirty days from the day on which the member receives the formal request for payment.

(e) If the member disagrees with the computation notified to it under (c) above, it shall so advise the Fund within thirty days from the day on which the member receives notice thereof, and shall at the same time or within the said thirty days inform the Fund of its reasoned objections. If agreement with the member is not reached within a period regarded by the Managing Director as reasonable in the circumstances of the case, the Managing Director, after consultation with the Executive Director appointed or elected by the member, shall refer the matter to the Executive Board.

(f) After agreement with the member if reached under (e) above, or after a decision by the Executive Board determining the member's repurchase obligation, the Managing Director shall send to the member a formal request for payment, and shall at the same time notify the Board of such request. The member shall discharge the repurchase obligation within thirty days from the day on which the member receives the formal request for payment or within such other period as may be decided by the Executive Board.

(g) The Managing Director shall report to the Executive Board any case in which it appears the above procedure has not been followed.

FA V-7 and Schedule B. Adopted September 25, 1946, amended July 28, 1950

I-7. For the purposes of Article V, Section 7, the term "financial year" shall be defined as beginning on May 1 and ending on the succeeding April 30; provided, however, that the first financial year shall begin on March 1, 1947 and end on April 30, 1948.

For purposes of the Fund's accounts and reports, its fiscal year shall begin on May 1 and end on the succeeding April 30; provided, however, that the fiscal year 1946/47 shall begin on July 1, 1946 and end on June 30, 1947, and the fiscal year 1947/48 shall begin on July 1, 1947 and end on April 30, 1948.

Adopted February 7, 1947, amended May 28, 1947, effective September 17, 1947

I-8. When any member sells gold to the Fund pursuant to Article V, Section 6 (a), or buys gold from the Fund, the Fund may levy a handling charge which shall be paid in accordance with Article V, Section 8 (f).

Adopted February 7, 1947, amended July 30, 1948

J—Accounts and Reports

J-1. The accounts of the Fund shall be kept in terms of the currencies held by the Fund and United States dollars on the basis of the established parities.
FA IV-1; BL-20. Adopted September 25, 1946

J-2. The accounts of the Fund shall be kept in a manner that will show clearly the nature of each transaction, the position of the Fund, and results of its operations.
Adopted September 25, 1946

J-3. A summary statement of the Fund's transactions and its holdings of gold and currencies of members shall be issued at intervals of three months or less, and a monthly statement of balances shall be sent to all members.
FA XII-7. Adopted September 25, 1946

J-4. The Managing Director shall prepare an annual administrative budget for presentation to the Executive Board for approval not later than April 1 of each year.
BL-20. Adopted September 25, 1946, amended February 20, 1948

J-5. Not later than June 30 of each year, the Managing Director shall present to the Executive Board a summary of the matters which in his opinion should be included in the annual report to the Board of Governors. At least one month before the annual meeting of the Board of Governors, the Managing Director shall submit to the Executive Board for its consideration, a draft of the annual report.
BL-10. Adopted September 25, 1946

J-6. At least one month before the annual meeting of the Board of Governors, the audited accounts of the Fund shall be submitted to the Executive Board for its consideration.
BL-20. Adopted September 25, 1946

K—Limitation and Ineligibility

K-1. The Managing Director shall report to the Executive Board any case in which it appears to him that a member is not fulfilling its obligations under the Fund Agreement.
Adopted September 25, 1946

K-2. Whenever the Executive Board would be authorized to declare a member ineligible to use the resources of the Fund it may refrain from making the declaration and indicate the circumstances under which, and/or the extent to which, the member may make use of the resources.
FA V-5, VI-1, and XV-2 (a). Adopted September 25, 1946

K-3. When a member has changed the par value of its currency despite the objection of the Fund, in cases where the Fund is entitled to object, the Executive Board may determine the circumstances under which, and the extent to which, a member may use the resources of the Fund.
Adopted September 25, 1946

K-4. Before any member is declared, pursuant to Article XV, Section 2 (a), ineligible to use the resources of the Fund, the matter shall be considered by the Executive Board, who shall inform the member in reasonable time of the complaint against it and allow the member an adequate opportunity for stating its case both orally and in writing.
FA XV-2 (a); BL-22. Adopted September 25, 1946

K-5. When any member that is ineligible to use the resources of the Fund, or whose use of the resources has been limited, according to K-2 or K-3 above, requests the Executive Board to permit the resumption of exchange transactions with or without special limitations and the Executive Board decides not to permit such resumption, a written report shall be made to the member stating what further action is required before such resumption will be permitted.
Adopted September 25, 1946, corrected October 18, 1950

L—Capital Transfers

L-1. If there is taking place a large or sustained outflow of capital from a member country:
- (a) that member or any other member may notify the Fund, presenting such information as it deems necessary; and may request the Fund's views with respect to such capital movement; and
- (b) the Fund may present to the member or members concerned a report setting forth its views, and may request the member or members to report on the situation within a suitable time.

Adopted September 25, 1946

L-2. Whenever the Fund has requested a member to exercise controls to prevent use of the resources of the Fund to meet a large or sustained outflow of capital, the Fund shall request the member to notify it promptly and in detail of the measures taken.
FA VI-1 (a). Adopted September 25, 1946

L-3. Each member shall inform the Fund in detail of the measures it is taking to regulate international capital movements and of changes made in such measures.
Adopted September 25, 1946

L-4. If the Fund is of the opinion that the controls exercised by a member to regulate international capital movements are restrictive of payments for current transactions, or unduly delay transfers of funds in settlement of commitments, the Fund shall, subject to the provisions of Article VII, Section 3 (b) and Article XIV, Section 2, consult with the member on the manner in which the controls are exercised. If, after consultation, the Fund is not satisfied that the controls are exercised in a manner consistent with the Fund Agreement, it shall so inform the member in a written report and request it to modify the controls.
FA VI-3. Adopted September 25, 1946

M—Relations with Non-Members

M-1. The Fund may request the cooperation of any member with a view to the application of appropriate measures to prevent transactions with non-members or with persons in their territories, contrary to the provisions of the Agreement or the purposes of the Fund.
FA XI-1 (iii). Adopted September 25, 1946

M-2. When the Fund finds that a member or any of its fiscal agencies referred to in Article V, Section 1, engages in any transaction with or cooperates in practices with a non-member or with persons in a non-member's territory, contrary to the provisions of the Agreement or the purposes of the Fund, it shall present to the member a report setting forth its views and may request the cessation or modification of the transactions or practices.

FA XI-1 (i) and (ii). Adopted September 25, 1946

M-3. A member shall inform the Fund promptly and in detail of any restrictions which it imposes on exchange transactions with non-members or with persons in their territories.

FA VIII-5 (a) (xi). Adopted September 25, 1946

M-4. Any member may notify the Fund of restrictions imposed by a member on exchange transactions with non-members or with persons in their territories which are deemed to prejudice the interests of members and to be contrary to the purposes of the Fund.

FA XI-2. Adopted September 25, 1946

M-5. When the Fund finds that the restrictions imposed by a member on exchange transactions with non-members or with persons in their territories are prejudicial to the interests of members and contrary to the purposes of the Fund, it shall present to the member a report setting forth its views and may request the abolition or modification of the restrictions.

FA XI-2. Adopted September 25, 1946

M-6. The Fund deems that it would be prejudicial to the interests of members and contrary to the purposes of the Fund for a member to impose restrictions on exchange transactions with those non-members having entered into special exchange agreements under the General Agreement on Tariffs and Trade, or with persons in their territories, which the member would not in similar circumstances be authorized to impose on exchange transactions with other members or persons in their territories. Therefore, pursuant to Article XI, Section 2, members should not institute restrictions on exchange transactions with such non-members, or persons in their territories, unless the restrictions (a) if instituted on transactions with other members, or persons in their territories, would be authorized under the Fund Agreement, or (b) have been approved in advance by the Fund. Requests for prior approval shall be submitted in writing with a statement of reasons.

FA XI-2. Adopted June 7, 1950

N—Staff Regulations

Personnel

N-1. The employment, classification, promotion, and assignment of personnel in the Fund shall be made without discriminating against any person because of sex, race or creed.

Adopted September 25, 1946

N-2. Persons on the staff of the Fund shall be nationals of members of the Fund unless the Executive Board authorizes exceptions in particular cases.

Adopted September 25, 1946

N-3. In the discharge of their functions, the persons on the staff shall owe their duty entirely to the Fund and to no other authority.

Adopted September 25, 1946

N-4. All persons on the staff must avoid any action, and in particular any kind of pronouncement, which may reflect unfavorably upon their position as employees of an international organization, either in their own country or elsewhere. They should always bear in mind the reserve and tact incumbent upon them by reason of their international functions, and they are required to exercise the utmost discretion in regard to matters of official business. At no time should they in any way use to private advantage information known to them by reason of their official position.
Adopted September 25, 1946

N-5. Except in the course of his official duties or by express authorization of the Managing Director, no person on the staff may, during the term of his appointment of service, publish, cause to be published, or assist in the publication of any book, pamphlet, article, letter, or other document relative to the policies or activities of the Fund or to any national political questions; deliver any speech, lecture, or radio broadcast, or grant any press interview on such policies, activities, or questions; or communicate to any person any unpublished information known to him by reason of his official position. After termination of his period of service with the Fund, a person formerly on the staff may not, without the express authorization of the Managing Director, disclose any confidential information he has received during his service with the Fund by reason of his official position.
Adopted September 25, 1946

N-6. No person on the staff shall hold other public or private employment or engage in any occupation or profession which in the Fund's opinion is incompatible with the proper performance of his official duties.
Adopted September 25, 1946

N-7. A person on the staff may retain re-employment rights or pension rights acquired in the service of a public or private organization.
Adopted September 25, 1946

N-8. Any person on the staff who accepts a public office of a political character shall immediately resign from the Fund.
Adopted September 25, 1946

N-9. No person on the staff may accept any honor, decoration, favor, gift, or bonus from any government, or from any other authority or person external to the Fund, for services rendered during the period of his appointment or service with the Fund.
Adopted September 25, 1946

N-10. Upon appointment, each person on the staff will subscribe in writing to the following affirmation:

I solemnly affirm:

That, to the best of my ability, I will carry out my responsibilities in a manner that will further the purposes of the International Monetary Fund;

That I will refrain from communicating confidential information to persons outside the Fund;

That I will not use to private advantage information known to me by reason of my official position; and

That I will accept no instruction in regard to the performance of my duties from any government or authority external to the Fund.

Adopted September 25, 1946

N-11. All persons appointed to permanent positions on the staff shall be classified by grades or positions according to the nature of their duties and responsibilities. Salary increases within each grade will be progressively available upon the successful completion of successive periods of work or upon the recommendation of supervisors.

Adopted September 25, 1946

N-12. The salary scale for permanent employees of the Fund shall, so far as practicable, conform to the salary scale of the United Nations.

Adopted September 25, 1946

N-13. The Managing Director shall inform the Executive Board at least two weeks in advance of any action to appoint or initiate the dismissal of any person at or above the rank of division chief within a department or office or receiving a salary equal to or more than that of a division chief within a department. All other appointments to the staff shall be made by the Managing Director or his designated representative.

Adopted September 25, 1946, amended July 1, 1959

N-14. The Managing Director is authorized to issue General Orders, with the approval of the Executive Board, concerning the general personnel policies which shall apply to the operating staff of the Fund.

Adopted September 25, 1946

Travel

N-15. (a) Official travel will be undertaken by staff members only with the approval of the Managing Director or officials designated by him. In the case of travel outside the continental United States, however, the specific approval of the Managing Director is required.

Adopted September 25, 1946, amended February 11, 1948

(b) The Managing Director will inform the Executive Board of all such travel at least once a month.

Adopted February 11, 1948

(c) Staff participation in activities of national agencies and staff travel to a member's territory require consultation in advance with the Executive Director appointed or elected by the member.

Adopted February 11, 1948

(d) Staff participation in deliberations or activities of international agencies or conferences as well as staff travel to a member's territory, undertaken in response to a formal invitation, require the advance approval of the Executive Board.

Adopted February 11, 1948

PART III

Fund Pronouncements

Use of the Fund's Resources

The date set for the commencement of Fund operations was March 1, 1947. Discussion in the Board of a number of relevant questions led to the issue, on June 7, 1947, of the following circular letter from the Managing Director to all members, enclosing a memorandum, also reproduced below, explaining the Board's policy in connection with the use of the Fund's resources.

Circular Letter to All Members
(June 7, 1947)

Gentlemen:

For some time the Executive Board has been discussing the policies to be followed in transactions between the Fund and its members. It is the purpose of this letter and its enclosure to acquaint you with the results of these discussions.

The enclosed memorandum contains a statement of policy concerning use of the Fund's resources. It is, of course, a general statement and does not attempt to cover all of the problems which may confront the Fund and the members in connection with use of the Fund's resources. It should, however, make clear the responsibilities of the Fund and the manner in which the members can make possible the execution of this responsibility with a minimum of inconvenience to themselves and to the Fund.

In the course of the discussions which led to the preparation of the enclosed memorandum, particular attention was given to the meaning of Article V, Section 3 (a) (i), which reads as follows:

"The member desiring to purchase the currency represents that it is presently needed for making in that currency payments which are consistent with the provisions of this Agreement."

This section, you will recall, is one of the conditions which must be met in order that "a member shall be entitled to buy the currency of another member from the Fund in exchange for its own currency."

At a meeting of the Executive Board on May 6 and May 29, 1947, the decision was as follows:

"The word 'represents' in Article V, Section 3 (a) (i) means 'declares.' The member is presumed to have fulfilled the condition mentioned in Article V, Section 3 (a) (i) if it declares that the currency is presently needed for making payments in that currency which are consistent with the provisions of the Agreement. But the Fund may, for good reason, challenge the correctness of this declaration, on the grounds that the currency is not 'presently needed' or because the currency is not needed for payments 'in that currency', or because the payments will not be 'consistent with the provisions of this Agreement'. If the Fund concludes that a particular declaration is not correct, the Fund may postpone or reject the request, or accept it subject to conditions.

"The phrase 'presently needed' cannot be defined in terms of a formula uniformly applicable to all cases, but where there is good reason to doubt that the currency is 'presently needed', the Fund will have to apply the phrase in each case in the light of all the circumstances."

The circumstances would of course clearly have to be unusual before the Fund felt that any representation by members might be open to question; but you will appreciate that the Fund must consider carefully all requests for currency in the light of circumstances existing at the time. This policy will ensure the Fund's resources against misapplication, without interfering with the ability of members to use the resources promptly when they do so in accordance with the purposes of the Fund Agreement.

It is our hope that this letter and its enclosure will be of assistance to you by clarifying the manner in which the resources will be administered.

Yours sincerely,
/s/   GUTT
Managing Director

Memorandum
(June 7, 1947)

The Fund Agreement sets up certain limitations on the use of its resources. These include the quantitative limitations. Equally important are the limitations as to the purposes for which use of the resources may be made.

1. They must be presently needed for payments in the currency requested. In short, the Fund cannot be used to increase a member's reserves.

2. They must be used to meet temporary needs—they cannot, for example, be used for large and sustained capital movements, for relief, reconstruction, or to meet indebtedness arising out of the war, or to support overvalued currencies when adequate measures are not being taken to correct the disequilibrium.

These are the principal matters covered by the representation members are required to make when they wish to purchase currencies from the Fund. With its large resources, the Fund must be concerned to see that they are used in accordance with its purposes. It must be in a position to know that the representations made by members are entirely correct and reflect a proper understanding of the Fund Agreement. In effect, this can best be done by keeping the officials of the Fund fully informed at all times of developments in each member country. This is the only way the Fund can judge for itself that aid it extends is not being used for financing a capital flight, that it will be repaid (and is not relief), and that it will be for a limited period (and is not for reconstruction).

In order that members may have the greatest possible assurance of access to the Fund when needed, the Fund ought to know these matters *before* rather than *after* a member applies for the purchase of exchange. A member should know that until it has been informed to the contrary, moderate purchases of exchange will be carried through promptly by the Fund. In that way a member can get the benefit of access to the Fund's resources as a second line of reserves. It would be undesirable to require a member to submit an extensive application to be considered at length in connection with each purchase of exchange.

From time to time, there will be cases where use of the Fund's resources would not be in accordance with the purposes of the Fund. Where a member is clearly not going to be in a position to repay the Fund, the Fund is duty bound not to engage in transactions with that member. Similarly, where a member has a fundamental disequilibrium, repayment to the Fund would require a correction of that disequilibrium, either through an adjustment of the exchange rate or through other measures. Aid to meet continuing balance of payments deficits, without prospect of a return to equilibrium, would be contrary to the Fund's purposes.

In every possible case, the Fund should know, from the information it receives and from discussion with the country's officials, the present and prospective position of the member and the use the member may be expected to make of the Fund. The Fund should know in advance of a request what its attitude will be toward use of its resources by a member.

As a general principle, the Fund should give as early notice as possible to a member that, in the view of the Fund, it ought to have only limited access or no access to the Fund's resources. In every instance, this should be done on an informal basis. The sanction of declaring a member ineligible should be used only in extreme cases where no other means of securing cooperation is forthcoming. There is no reason to believe that prior discussion with a member, in such cases where a limitation on use of the Fund's resources seems necessary, would fail to bring about the desired result. Consultation between the Fund and members should be a continuous process. Liaison should in time be so close that the Fund's advice may result in never reaching a stage that would warrant a sanction.

It would appear, therefore, that if the Fund can be kept fully informed as to the position and prospects of each member, any necessary measure of limitation can be taken informally before an application is made to the Fund for the purchase of exchange. In all other cases, the Fund would meet promptly each request in proper form for the purchase of exchange in moderate amount with a minimum of delay. The member could count on such aid from the Fund. However, in the case of unusually large requests in relatively short periods the Fund may have to take special account of the position of the member and consider over a longer period than a few days an application for the purchase of exchange. Such procedure gives to a member the greatest assurance of knowing that it will have access to the Fund's resources while enabling the Fund to make sure that the resources of the Fund are used in accordance with its purposes.

[For the definitive statement of the Fund's policy on the use of its resources, as later reached, see Executive Board Decision No. 102-(52/11) on pages 228–30 above.]

Transactions in Gold at Premium Prices

In May 1947 the Board set up a Committee on External Sales of Gold, charged with examining the legal and economic questions raised by member countries seeking to sell gold abroad at prices above parity. Following the committee's report, the Board communicated the following statement to all members on June 18, 1947.

Statement Communicated to All Members
(June 18, 1947)

The International Monetary Fund has given consideration to the international gold transactions at prices substantially above monetary parity which have been taking place in various areas of the world. Because of the importance of this matter the Fund has prepared this statement of its views.

A primary purpose of the Fund is world exchange stability and it is the considered opinion of the Fund that exchange stability may be undermined by continued and increasing external purchases and sales of gold at prices which directly or indirectly produce exchange transactions at depreciated rates. From information at its disposal, the Fund believes that unless discouraged this practice is likely to become extensive, which would fundamentally disturb the exchange relationships among the members of the Fund. Moreover, these transactions involve a loss to monetary reserves, since much of the gold goes into private hoards rather than into central holdings. For these reasons, the Fund strongly deprecates international transactions in gold at premium prices and recommends that all of its members take effective action to prevent such transactions in gold with other countries or with the nationals of other countries.

It is realized that some of these transactions are being conducted by or through non-member countries or their nationals. The Fund recommends that members make any representations which, in their judgment, are warranted by the circumstances to the governments of non-member countries to join with them in eliminating this source of exchange instability.

The Fund has not overlooked the problems arising in connection with domestic transactions in gold at prices above parity. The conclusion was reached that the Fund would not object at this time to such transactions unless they have the effect of establishing new rates of exchange or undermining existing rates of other members, or unless they result in a significant weakening of the international financial position of a member which might affect its utilization of the Fund's resources.

The Fund has requested its members to take action as promptly as possible to put into effect the recommendations contained in this statement.

[For the final decision of the Executive Board on the subject of premium gold transactions, see Decision No. 75-(705) on page 225 above.]

Adequacy of Monetary Reserves

On July 10, 1952, ECOSOC passed a resolution following an examination of a report entitled Measures for International Economic Stability. *This resolution, inter alia, asked the Fund to keep under continuous review the adequacy of monetary reserves, and to furnish an analysis on the subject for the meeting of ECOSOC in 1953.*

As a result, the staff prepared, in April 1953, a draft report on "The Adequacy of Monetary Reserves." This was discussed in the Board in May and after revision was sent to ECOSOC in June 1953, being described as a technical analysis and not a statement of Fund policy. The report as further revised and published in Staff Papers, *October 1953, is reproduced below.*

The Adequacy of Monetary Reserves
(October 1953)

On June 30, 1952, the Economic and Social Council of the United Nations (hereinafter referred to as ECOSOC) began consideration of a report, *Measures for International Economic Stability*, prepared by a group of experts [1] appointed by the Secretary-General pursuant to a resolution adopted by ECOSOC on August 15, 1950. Chapter IV of the report, entitled "International Monetary Reserves", states "Our examination of existing reserves has convinced us that they are not in general adequate." The chapter gives reasons for this conclusion and discusses means of increasing reserve adequacy—including increasing the size of the resources of the International Monetary Fund and making its resources more readily available to members. While the chapter considers the adequacy of monetary reserves generally, its primary emphasis (in accordance with the experts' terms of reference) is on their adequacy to protect countries from deflationary shocks of external origin and to check the international spread of depression.

After consideration of the report, ECOSOC adopted a resolution on July 10, 1952, the operative paragraphs of which referring to the International Monetary Fund are as follows:

"5. *Urges* the International Monetary Fund, in supporting the efforts of its members to meet balance of payments difficulties arising from recession:

---

[1] The group included James W. Angell, Professor of Economics and Executive Officer, Department of Economics, Columbia University; G. D. A. MacDougall, Fellow of Nuffield College and Reader in International Economics, Oxford University; Javier Marquez, Alternate Executive Director, International Monetary Fund, formerly Professor of Economics, National School of Economics, Mexico; Hla Myint, Lecturer in Colonial Economics, Oxford University, formerly Professor of Economics, Rangoon University; and Trevor W. Swan, Professor of Economics, Australian National University.

(a) To apply its rules flexibly and, in this connexion, to give careful consideration to the suggestions contained in chapter IV of the report entitled *Measures for International Economic Stability;* and

(b) To be prepared to use its resources as promptly and as fully as is consistent with its Articles of Agreement;

6. *Requests* the International Monetary Fund:

(a) To keep under continuing review the adequacy of monetary reserves for the purpose of helping countries to meet temporary disequilibria in their balances of international payments, having in mind the desirability of:

(i) Avoiding, to the extent practicable, recourse to restrictions on trade and payments imposed for balance of payments reasons, and of promoting general convertibility of currencies and liberalization of trade;

(ii) Creating conditions favourable to a steady expansion of international trade, and to high levels of production and consumption, employment and real income; and

(b) To furnish an analysis of this question to the Council in 1953."

Two aspects of reserve adequacy are stressed in the resolution. Paragraph 6 (a) (i) stresses adequacy of reserves to permit removal of trade and exchange restrictions imposed for balance of payments purposes and the attainment of general convertibility of currencies. Paragraph 6 (a) (ii) stresses adequacy of reserves to expand world trade and to maintain high levels of employment and real income—and so, inferentially, to check the spread of depression. This paper will be concerned with both aspects, which may be characterized as the *multilateral trade* and *high level employment* aspects, respectively.

The paper as a whole has been prepared on a technical level.[2] It is an analysis of the factors affecting reserve adequacy. It is not to be construed as a statement of Fund policy, and its general conclusions are not to be taken as indicating Fund attitude on specific country situations or day-to-day operating problems.

NATURE OF MONETARY RESERVES AND THE CONCEPT OF ADEQUACY

The concept of "adequacy" is a difficult one, and any standard of adequacy must be based upon a consideration of the purposes which monetary reserves are meant to serve and the obstacles which are expected to be encountered in fulfilling these purposes. While the concept of adequacy presents the greatest complexity, the concept of "monetary reserves" itself bristles with difficulties. It may be helpful, therefore, to start by considering first the nature of monetary reserves and then the meaning of the term adequacy.

Nature of monetary reserves

Monetary reserves may be defined narrowly or broadly. The most useful type of definition depends upon the purpose intended to be served. If the purpose is statistical

---

[2] This paper has been prepared under the supervision of Mr. Henry Murphy, Chief of the Financial Problems and Policies Division, Research Department. It was discussed in July 1953 at the sixteenth session of ECOSOC, held in Geneva. In the paper submitted to ECOSOC, the tables recorded figures for 1928, 1938, and 1951. In the present paper, the 1938 and 1951 figures have been revised, figures for 1952 have been added, and a number of consequential amendments to the text have been made.

or legal, the definition must, before all else, be precise. When the broader implications of reserves are taken into account, however, a precise definition is not possible without a loss of realism.

Some items are included in the term "reserves" by universal agreement. Beyond these, potential items shade away imperceptibly from those whose reserve character is almost as clear as those conventionally included in reserves to those which are scarcely reserves at all. A similar hierarchy exists for items which might be considered as deductions from reserves. Because of the essentially arbitrary character of all cutoff points, narrow definitions of reserves fail to give a true picture of the relative international liquidity of different countries. Precise reserve computations are also subject to discontinuous changes in time, as portions of a country's assets move into or out of the categories formally characterized as "reserves", or as portions of a country's liabilities are formally allowed, or cease to be formally allowed, as deductions. Consequently, when the purpose is to consider the over-all "deficit-financing power" of different countries or regions, as is true for this paper, it is desirable, in principle, to treat the concept of reserves broadly, even though only narrow and particular concepts can be measured and compared.

Viewed in this manner, the monetary reserves of a country [3] may be defined as the assets which its authorities have available to meet payments to other countries. The nature and ownership of these funds may be quite varied. The two tests of the reserve, or near-reserve, character of any item which may be in doubt are, first, its availability to the monetary authorities of the country in case of need and, second, its acceptability by potential creditors.

Gold and currencies readily convertible into gold held by monetary authorities meet both of these tests perfectly and so form the core of the monetary reserves of most countries. Very short-term securities of countries with convertible currencies or private securities or bankers' acceptances of unquestioned credit and short maturity payable in such currencies and held by the monetary authorities of other countries meet both tests about equally well. The same is true of gold and convertible currencies or of any of the above-mentioned assets held by commercial banks or other financial institutions in countries where such institutions are considered to be part of the "official family" and are closely accountable to the monetary authorities.

Other items that meet only one of the two tests may, depending on the country and the time, be equivalent to reserves as defined above, and for some purposes could be included in reserves. In any event, their availability in financing a deficit is an important factor in any consideration of the adequacy of reserves. For example, gold and convertible currencies and short-term securities held by others than the monetary authorities and their "official families" may in some countries and at some times function in much the same way as reserves. The holders may themselves use such assets to meet payments abroad, or they may sell such assets to the monetary authorities when required to do so by law or when induced to do so by financial considerations.

Apart from such assets, whose reserve character is diminished only by the fact that they are not held by the monetary authorities and their "official families", there are assets held by the monetary authorities which can perform the deficit-financing function, although not so widely or so readily as gold and convertible currencies,

---

[3] The reserve problems of the nonmetropolitan territories of a Fund member have special features which are not expanded in this paper.

including short-term securities. These assets include inconvertible currencies, credit balances in bilateral or multilateral payments agreements (as EPU), and debt-type securities (other than those already mentioned) payable in foreign currencies, whether convertible or inconvertible, and having an international market.

While access to foreign exchange under predetermined conditions cannot be regarded as reserves, such rights do perform some of the functions of reserves and affect the standard of adequacy of reserves. Stand-by agreements and the provisions for drawing needed currencies from the International Monetary Fund, the right to incur debit balances with the EPU or under bilateral payments agreements, and established lines of credit against which a foreign currency may be drawn all provide means of meeting balance of payments deficits.

Some countries include stocks of silver and precious stones in their monetary reserves under the provisions of their national laws. These assets are not reserves in the meaning of the term used here, because they are not readily salable at an approximately predetermined price. They may, nevertheless, be salable abroad and could be used to secure additional foreign exchange when necessary. This may also be true of other commodities readily salable in international markets and of equity securities similarly salable. The possession of such assets by the monetary authorities or by others may affect the level of what may be regarded as adequate reserves, even if they are not included in a definition of reserves.

Monetary reserves, however they may be calculated, may be stated at their full gross amount or they may be stated "net" after subtraction of liabilities on account of which near-term payments may have to be made to foreigners—as, for example, short-term debts of the government, the monetary authorities, or the banking and business communities, debit balances in clearing accounts, or foreign holdings of national currency.

As already noted, when it is necessary to give precision to the concept of monetary reserves, particular items (positive and sometimes negative) must be selected from the broad variety of reserve and near-reserve items just enumerated. Thus, a calculation of a member's monetary reserves pursuant to specified standards is necessary to determine its obligation, if any, to repurchase its currency from the Fund. Such calculations are based on the definitions of terms in Article XIX of the Fund Agreement. Reserve comparisons in which the need for precision is primarily statistical, rather than legal, present similar problems. Thus, data on movements of monetary reserves are presented in the Fund's annual *Balance of Payments Yearbook*, and data on their amount in its monthly publication, *International Financial Statistics*. Similarly, statistical comparisons of monetary reserves on several alternative bases are presented later in this paper. Each presentation or comparison helps in the understanding of over-all reserve adequacy. But any single basis of comparison can, at best, give only an approximation of the "real" amounts of the reserves actually available to the monetary authorities of each country in case of need.

The concept of adequacy

Adequacy of reserves depends on the prospective problems that confront a country and, therefore, will differ from country to country and from problem to problem. No amount of reserves can be adequate to finance a chronic or continuing imbalance in a country's payments. Therefore, the problem of reserve adequacy can be discussed meaningfully only for those countries prepared to take appropriate measures to balance their external accounts over an entire cycle—but which may, nevertheless, encounter substantial payments deficits in some years, or even occasionally for several years together.

It is obvious that this fundamental assumption of a strong and balanced payments position over the course of a cycle, which is essential for determining the adequacy of reserves for the only purpose for which reserves can ever be adequate, that is, to meet temporary needs, is not generally or even widely met by the situation currently prevailing. Some countries have failed to establish their exchange rates at appropriate levels, and other countries have been so concerned over assuring full employment or rapid economic development that their monetary policies have been too expansionist to enable them to bring their international payments into balance without severe exchange and import restrictions. Unless such countries are prepared to moderate their monetary policies, and, if necessary, readjust their exchange rates, they will be under steady pressure in their international payments, and they will necessarily find that their reserves are inadequate to establish and maintain multilateral trade without widespread and continuing restrictions and discriminations.

While satisfactory fiscal and monetary policies are indispensable to establishing a strong payments position, it does not follow that a country with noninflationary fiscal and monetary policies and an appropriate exchange rate will inevitably have a strong payments position. The international payments position of a country is affected not only by its own policies, but also by those of the countries with which it trades. An inflationary fiscal or monetary policy or an unsatisfactory exchange rate in another country may cut off the flow of imports from customary sources and force the country to seek other sources of supply. And a restrictive import or exchange policy in another country with inflationary fiscal or monetary policies or an unsatisfactory exchange rate may make it difficult for a country with sound policies to maintain its exports and to earn the gold, dollars, or foreign exchange which it could secure under better conditions. No doubt, with severely rigorous policies and a far-reaching shift in the pattern of production, a country may offset the effects of bad policies of its trading partners. But that is a costly step which countries will seek to avoid as long as there is hope of securing better policies elsewhere.

It must be pointed out, furthermore, that the magnitude of the task of establishing a strong payments position which confronts countries with a tendency toward deficit in their international accounts will be importantly affected by the policies of countries with a tendency toward surplus. This applies most clearly to the commercial policies of the surplus countries. The deficit countries want to buy—and, in some cases, desperately need—the exports of the surplus countries; but, as the deficit countries have no monetary reserves to spare, they can pay for the exports of the surplus countries only with their own goods. If the surplus countries place or maintain onerous trade barriers on the receipt of these goods, the effect must be a general lowering of the level of world trade to the mutual impoverishment of both groups of countries.

Particular attention should be called to restrictions of the "escape clause" or "peril point" type—which, in effect, serve notice on countries endeavoring to increase their sales in the markets of the surplus countries using them, or endeavoring to break into such markets with new types of goods, that success in such efforts may result merely in an increase in trade barriers sufficient to restore the earlier (low) trade volume. Where such attempts involve substantial investment in specialized plant or equipment or specialized inventories or involve substantial advertising, the value of which would be lost if the attempts should fail, the existence of "escape clause" or "peril point" provisions may often be a sufficient obstacle to prevent serious attempts at materially increasing sales from being made at all.

In addition to policies with respect to trade barriers, the surplus countries' policies with respect to stockpiling may make an important difference in the situations of countries with serious balance of payments problems. Changes in stockpiling policies, which may mean relatively little to the surplus countries pursuing them, may make a vital difference in the economies, and even in the social and political orientation, of hard-pressed raw material producing countries.

The investment policies of the surplus countries can also do much to ease the payments problems of underdeveloped countries. A flow of capital on a commercial basis from regions where it is relatively abundant to those where it is relatively scarce—and, consequently, of high productivity—is justified by investment considerations alone and is in the mutual interest of both the lending and the borrowing countries.

But most important of all are the policies of the surplus countries with respect to their domestic levels of activity. Experience has shown that, in the United States in particular, the level of industrial activity is a far more important determinant of import volume than is commercial policy. Even a moderate slump in the United States would place a substantial strain on the economies and balance of payments positions of other countries, particularly producers of raw materials. Some fluctuation in U.S. business volume is inevitable, and countries exporting to the United States must allow for it in their calculations of what they can "afford" to import over a normal cycle. But they cannot and should not be expected to make similar provision for a period of severe depression and mass unemployment in the United States. Just as no amount of reserves can be adequate to sustain a chronic deficit due to their own inappropriate policies, so no practicable amount of reserves can be adequate to maintain convertibility without discriminatory exchange restrictions in the event of a major depression in the United States. Provision against this contingency can be made only by the United States itself through domestic and international policies aimed at preventing the occurrence or continuance of the depression.

Let us consider a country which has established a balanced payments position. That is, through a period covering prosperity and depression—but not a deep or prolonged depression—its receipts are adequate to meet its payments. The exchange rate is correct, the monetary policy is correct, and restrictions and discriminations continuing throughout the cycle are not needed to shore up the payments position. For such a country, what is an adequate level of reserves? Four standards, each more rigorous than the preceding, can be suggested:

1. Enough to enable a country in bad years, by resort to restrictions, to maintain its external debt payments and to purchase the goods and services necessary to avoid hardship to its population or dislocation to its economy and the possible emergence of an exchange crisis, i.e., to permit a reasonable distribution over *time* of the payments which it can afford to make over the entire cycle;

2. Enough to maintain currency convertibility, barring a severe depression, but with occasional necessity to resort to trade and exchange restrictions for balance of payments purposes;

3. Enough to maintain currency convertibility, barring a severe depression, but without the necessity for occasional resort to trade and exchange restrictions;

4. Enough to maintain currency convertibility, even through severe depressions (but not through prolonged periods of international deflation such as occurred in the thirties), without either the necessity for occasional resort to trade and exchange restrictions or the necessity for resorting to domestic deflationary policies for the purpose of restraining imports, even if this involves a substantial drain on reserves.

It may be helpful to list some of the principal factors which must be taken into account in determining the "adequacy" category in which a given amount of reserves (expressed as a proportion of its trade) may place a country pursuing appropriate exchange rate and domestic financial policies. Without attempting to arrange them in order of importance (which would, in any event, vary greatly from country to country and from time to time), these factors may be listed as follows:

1. The normal seasonal variation in the country's imports and exports and in the service items in its balance of payments;

2. The extent to which the volume of its imports and exports is subject to extraordinary variation because of natural or other factors, e.g., crop failures, political or economic changes elsewhere, etc.;

3. The variability in the prices of its imports and in the prices of and demand for its exports;

4. The extent to which the country is dependent on imported raw materials, equipment, and essential foodstuffs to avoid dislocation of its economy or undue hardships to its population;

5. The size of its inventories of export goods and their components, and of import goods and their products, and the extent to which these inventories could be compressed without hardship in the event of pressure on the country's reserve position;

6. The extent, if any, to which the country may expect adverse changes in its reserve position to be offset by "equilibrating" movements of short-term credit;

7. The prospect that the supply of reserves can be supplemented by grants-in-aid or long-term loans from other countries;

8. The extent to which the use, for international purposes, of actual holdings of reserve-type assets may be prevented by legal or other restrictions.

The first three factors (each dealing with variations in the amount and value of a country's imports and exports) and the fourth (dealing with its need for imports) are the most fundamental in the list, and can be altered by the country itself only by basic changes in the structure of its economy.

The fifth factor deals with inventories. It has already been suggested that stocks of goods readily salable on international markets might be considered to have an important bearing on the adequacy of a country's holdings of the more conventional type of reserves. When used in this sense, the concept of inventories may be enlarged to include both stocks of materials entering into the production of export goods and import goods and their derivative products. All such inventories permit either exports to be expanded for a while or imports to be contracted for a while, in case of necessity, thereby easing strains on reserves. The reciprocal relationship between inventories and reserves appears most clearly during periods when reserves are being run down to build up inventories or during periods when reserves are being increased or maintained only at the expense of inventory run-downs. In such cases the *combined* changes in holdings of reserves *plus* inventories may give a better clue to a country's real external position than either of these quantities taken separately.

The sixth factor enumerated above is short-term credit movements. At one time short-term credit movements were extremely important as means of supplementing the reserves of individual countries, and so as means for making smaller amounts of reserves go further. In the environment which has prevailed during most of the period since the beginning of the depression of the thirties, however, short-term credit movements have been, on the whole, of a disequilibrating rather than of an equilibrating character for most countries—although they still operate to the advantage of countries with substantial amounts of mobile capital, in the event of temporary stringencies in their payments positions. It should be noted in this connection that there has been a great shrinkage during the past generation in the amount of one of the most important types of short-term international credit; bankers' acceptances created for the purpose of financing international trade, the outstanding amount of which ranged between the equivalent of $2 billion and $3 billion in the late twenties, have now very largely disappeared.

The seventh of the enumerated factors is the prospect that the balance of payments receipts of a country from other sources will be supplemented by long-term loans or grants-in-aid from other countries. Long-term loans are an important factor affecting reserve positions. Throughout most of the nineteenth century and well into the twentieth century, the United Kingdom and some other European countries were fairly consistent exporters of capital. When these countries were confronted with reserve stringencies they could often adjust their positions merely by cutting down on the outflow of long-term capital or by ceasing to export capital altogether. The capital exported by Europe was an important factor in the economic development of the newer countries. Long-term capital flows were not necessarily happy as far as their effects on the year-to-year *reserve* positions of the newer countries were concerned, however, as these countries often adjusted their levels of imports, exports, and reserves to an expected inflow of long-term capital and then suffered reserve crises whenever such inflows were suspended. But those newer countries with strong credit positions were often able to replenish their reserves in time of need by floating long-term loans for that purpose. The long-term capital movements brought about by such loans were decidedly equilibrating in character for the newer countries. Unfortunately, the possibility of floating such loans is much less today than it was even a few years ago, and the necessity of maintaining reserves is correspondingly greater.

The possibility of a deficit country receiving a grant-in-aid is principally a post-World War II development. Most grants-in-aid during the postwar period have been for the purpose of meeting balance of payments deficits arising from the physical devastation and disruption of trade and financial relationships caused by the war. Countries still in need of such grants are clearly in too weak a payments position to fall within the orbit of any of the categories of reserve adequacy used in this paper. Their problems are payments problems, not reserve problems. More recently, however, most grants have been for defense purposes. Such grants may be considered as part of the mechanism for financing the cost of a mutual defense system in which each country contributes resources, human and material, in proportion to its ability and situation. It seems proper, therefore, that the prospect of receiving such grants should be taken into consideration, along with other types of prospective balance of payments receipts, in determining the adequacy of the reserves of the recipient countries.

The eighth, and last, factor enumerated above is the extent to which the use for international purposes of the reserve-type assets actually held by the monetary authorities is restricted by law or custom. The laws of many countries require that the authorities hold reserve-type assets equal to a stipulated proportion of the outstanding currency or some other objectively determined criterion. The effect of such laws is to reduce the adequacy for international purposes of any given amount of total holdings of reserve-type assets. The same effect may be produced in the absence of law if the climate of public opinion in a country is such that the holding of some minimum amount of gold or of other reserve-type assets is considered a practical necessity by the monetary authorities.

Reserves and confidence

The discussion thus far has proceeded on the implicit assumption that reserves are meant to be used and that, except as qualified in the immediately preceding paragraph, all reserves are, in fact, available for use. Neither of these assumptions is strictly true in a world in which uncertainty is, and will continue to be, a major factor in all economic calculations. In practice, if they are to fulfill their functions efficiently, reserves must be considerably larger than would be indicated by any reasonable evaluation of the probabilities of their actual use.

Assume, for example, that $500 million is the most pessimistic estimate of the amount of reserves which a country might reasonably need to meet an existing current account deficit before the deficit would either halt of its own accord or could be halted by the adoption of appropriate policies. (It is assumed, for convenience, that capital transfers are controlled and that this control is tolerably well enforced.) Assume, also, that the country's reserves are of just the amount necessary to meet the maximum expected deficit—namely, $500 million. This amount, despite its superficial appearance of adequacy, will prove inadequate if the pessimistic possibilities are actually realized. This follows from the fact that, in spite of prior estimates, no one will know how far the adverse balance of payments will actually run; consequently, if reserves run low, traders will lose confidence in their adequacy and will take steps to protect their positions. These steps—such as stockpiling beyond ordinary requirements, expediting payments for imports, and delaying the receipt of payments for exports—will involve additional reserve drains which would not have occurred at all if reserves had been truly adequate. As a consequence, a reserve run-down which would have amounted to only $500 million if reserves had been, say, $1 billion, may result in a serious exchange crisis if reserves are actually only $500 million.

It follows that, in order to avoid the intermittent imposition of trade and exchange restrictions, reserves must be larger than any allowable current account deficit in order to maintain confidence and so hold down outpayments to the actual amount of the deficit. To secure the required confidence, it is necessary that there always be available, even at the very bottom of the cycle, a substantial volume of additional reserves which are uncommitted and available for immediate use.

Confidence, however, is a two-way street. Just as larger reserves promote confidence in a country's situation and so may make their use unnecessary, so confidence in a country's situation—and in its willingness to pursue appropriate policies—reduces the amount of reserves necessary to sustain this confidence. In the long run, the effect of "underlying" confidence upon the amount of necessary reserves is probably more important than the effect of adequate reserves upon confidence. The classic example, of course, is the United Kingdom before World War I, when London was the undisputed financial center of the world and operated on a minimal reserve base. At that time, other countries were able to hold a large portion of their reserves in sterling with full confidence in the universal acceptability of sterling which made it the practical equivalent of gold.

Over-all evaluations of reserve adequacy

The factors that determine the adequacy of reserves are not, in practice, precisely measurable. Basically, therefore, the adequacy of reserves is a matter of judgment—depending on the country, on the time, and on the purpose for which the reserves are intended. Furthermore, the prevalent opinion of the international business community concerning the adequacy of each country's reserves is itself a factor in determining their "real" adequacy—so that, in one sense, the reserves of a country are not adequate until the public thinks that they are adequate. Such opinions, it should be noted, are likely to be based as much on the trend in a country's reserve position as on its absolute amount; a moderate reserve position, well maintained, is likely to give an impression of greater adequacy than a large reserve position which has been rapidly declining, with no end clearly in sight.

That the adequacy of reserves cannot be precisely measured gives rise to the corollary that significant decisions depending in part upon reserve adequacy—e.g., decisions to impose or to relax exchange restrictions, to tighten or to relax monetary and fiscal policies, or to alter exchange rates—are based on the *opinions* of the relevant authorities, national and international, concerning this adequacy. The opinions of these authorities are seen most clearly by their actions in the field of international financial policy. For example, the decision of the Canadian authorities in late 1951 to eliminate all exchange controls expressed more clearly than words their opinion that their payments position had become strong and could be maintained strong, with their level of reserves, by appropriate monetary policies and a fluctuating rate of exchange—an opinion amply justified by the developments of the succeeding period.

It is much more difficult to draw conclusions from the actions of the authorities in the fields of monetary and fiscal policy. This is because actions in these fields are often determined with greater reference to their domestic than to their international effects. For example, the restrictive actions of the U.S. monetary authorities in 1951 and 1952 (which commenced during a period of heavy gold outflow) were undertaken for purely domestic reasons and not because of anxiety concerning the adequacy of the international reserves of the United States. Such inferences may be drawn more reasonably, however, with respect to actions in countries where international trade comprises a larger proportion of total activity. For example, it is probably not inaccurate to say that the relaxation in the rigor of monetary policy in the Federal Republic of Germany, Belgium, and the Netherlands during 1952 reflected in large part a lower degree of concern by the authorities in these countries with respect to the adequacy of their monetary reserves.

Reserves and total resources

An adequate reserve position permits both the monetary authorities and the private traders of a country to look ahead and to plan their affairs with confidence. When reserves are inadequate, a country's foreign trade may be subject to sudden starts and stops, as restrictions are imposed or relaxed, or its exchange rate may fluctuate sharply. In whatever way imports are suddenly restricted below the level suited to the economy under a strong payments position, the result may be a serious dislocation of the economy.

It must not be overlooked that reserves are real resources from the point of view of the countries holding them, and the holding of reserves is only one of the possible uses competing for the limited amount of resources at the disposal of each country. In a rich country, or in a country in which there is little prospect of economic development, the maintenance of an adequate reserve position may necessitate no practical sacrifice. In a poor country, however, or in one in which the tempo of economic development is greater than can be accommodated by available resources, the maintenance of an adequate reserve position may be at the expense of urgently needed industrial or agricultural equipment, or may even entail some hardship due to shortages of food or of other consumers' goods which might have been imported by using a portion of its reserves. It is inevitable, therefore, that poor and dynamic countries are tempted to sacrifice their reserve positions in favor of other uses of their real resources which they consider more urgent. This may often be sound policy. Indeed, such a transfer of resources would occur as a result of the operation of natural economic forces in the absence of state intervention, as it is of the essence of economics so to economize on scarce resources that the last unit employed in each use has an equal utility. If a country can improve its over-all position by transferring a portion of even an inadequate supply of reserves to some yet more urgent use, it is fully justified in doing so. On the other hand, countries may underestimate the real losses incurred because of inadequate reserves and so may tend to hold less reserves than they should, in their own interest.

In this respect, the reserves of countries have been compared with those of individuals. The monetary reserves of individuals (principally cash balances) serve much the same purposes as those of countries. They protect the individual's consumption from fluctuations in the amount and timing of his income, permit him to minimize his total outpayments by taking advantage of cash discounts, and allow him to prevent unfavorable developments in his situation from being magnified in their consequences because of the lack of adequate finances for dealing with them promptly. But, for individuals as well as for nations, monetary reserves are only one of a number of possible uses of resources competing for priority. Consequently, wealthy persons or persons with relatively few undertakings (although their incomes may fluctuate but little) are more likely than poorer or more active persons (although their incomes may fluctuate widely) to provide fully for reserves.

Therefore, it is normal to find, both for wealthy or more settled persons and for wealthy or more settled nations, that reserves are much larger in proportion to the apparent need for them than are the reserves of poorer or more dynamic individuals or of poorer or more dynamic nations. This tendency, at least on the international level, is often described as a "maldistribution of reserves". However, a high degree of maldistribution is normal and would reassert itself even if the reserves were redistributed—for, the poorer or more dynamic countries would apply part of their newly acquired reserves to higher priority uses, and the reserves disposed of in this way would return to the more wealthy or more settled countries. Of course, it does not follow that any given degree of maldistribution of reserves is compatible with a stable structure of world payments. An extremely high degree of maldistribution can, however, be corrected by appropriate changes in monetary and fiscal policies in low-reserve countries. The adjustment can be made gradual, although protracted, if the newly mined gold is added to the reserves of the countries with the greatest reserve deficiency. But the period of adjustment can be shortened and its unavoidable cost in terms of deflationary pressure on the economy can be lightened by liberalization of commercial and external investment policies on the part of high-reserve countries.

Interaction of reserves and policy

As already noted, reserves and policy interact on one another, the strength of the interaction varying with the importance of foreign trade in a country's total economy. Restrictive policies result in the accumulation of reserves, while adequate reserves tend to modify and soften policies. When world-wide inflationary and deflationary pressures are in balance, this interaction between reserves and policy tends to work out well and promotes a well-balanced distribution of the available reserves among the trading countries of the world in the light of their preference for reserves and other types of investment.

If no fundamental change in the basis of monetary standards is assumed, the world supply of reserves may be increased (1) by additions to the volume or value of the world monetary gold stock, or (2) by the creation of new international assets and contra-liabilities of such a character that the creditors will consider their asset holdings as part of their reserves, but the debtors will make no corresponding deduction of their liabilities in the calculation of their own reserve positions. Aside from changes in the world supply of reserves, all reserves gained by one country must be at the expense of another. Some year-by-year increase in the total stock of reserves is necessary in order to maintain an expanding volume of world trade and stable prices. An expansion of this magnitude in the world stock of reserves tends to promote sound policies, and countries pursuing sound policies tend to secure an appropriate share of the total available reserves. Indeed, a country can be said to have a strong payments position only when it is acquiring such an appropriate share of newly created reserves. On the other hand, a too rapid increase in the world stock of monetary reserves tends to promote inflationary policies generally and in individual countries, while an increase of less than the optimum amount (or a decrease) tends to promote deflationary policies.

These observations are, of course, true only when a number of years are taken into consideration. In a single year, or even for several years, characterized by general expansionary psychology, a stationary stock of reserves (or even a declining one) may be compatible with expanding trade and price stability. On the other hand, in a year, or series of years, characterized by general deflationary psychology, an extraordinarily large expansion in reserves may be necessary to support price stability and a continuing expansion in world trade.

Finally, it should be noted that the response of a country to an increase in its reserves or to an improvement in its balance of payments position is not likely to consist wholly in a relaxation or elimination of trade and exchange restrictions. It may consist wholly—and will probably consist partially—in a relaxation of its domestic fiscal and monetary policies. A general improvement in reserve positions during a time of world-wide inflationary pressures is likely, therefore, to reinforce those pressures.

Reserves and the growth of world trade

The necessary increment to reserves, if inadequacy of reserves is not to hamper the growth of multilateral trade, will depend primarily on the rate at which trade can grow. This in turn depends in large part on the growth of production throughout the world. Support of an appropriate rate of growth in world trade depends on the annual increment to the world's monetary gold stock and on other types of reserve assets created by national monetary systems and through the instrumentality of international agencies.

Newly mined gold is the principal source from which increments to gold reserves must be made. Unless this gold is in large part accumulated by the monetary authorities, it will not be effective in enabling countries to meet their needs for reserves. The increment to monetary gold stocks has been low in most postwar years. Monetary and exchange policies that leave doubt as to the future value of national currencies tend to divert newly mined gold into private hoards rather than into central holdings. Furthermore, little will be accomplished in securing adequate reserves for most countries for the future if all newly mined gold is regarded as an easy means of meeting continuing balance of payments deficits. Under such conditions, the newly mined gold will simply be concentrated in the reserves of a very few creditor countries, while the reserves of the rest of the world will be inadequate. A basic condition for adequate reserves in the long run is the maintenance of monetary and exchange policies that will enable countries not only to balance their international payments, but also to add part of the newly mined gold to their monetary reserves.

Adequacy of particular types of reserves

As already noted, assets are useful for reserve purposes only to the extent that they are acceptable for the external payments which the reserve holding country must meet. Before the depression of the thirties—when most currencies were convertible either through the medium of buying and selling prices for gold or foreign exchange maintained by the monetary authorities of the issuing countries, or by the purchase and sale of exchange in the market place—most currencies could be held for reserve purposes, subject to the qualification that holdings of currencies with fluctuating exchange rates involved greater risk than holdings of currencies with fixed exchange rates. Since the onset of the depression, and particularly since the end of World War II, a large number of currencies have become inconvertible and can no longer be legally exchanged (either officially or through the market place) by the monetary authorities of the countries holding them for such other currencies as they may need to meet their external payments. As a consequence, the reserve problem—which once could be viewed as a whole—has tended to break into fragments, and a country may now be short of reserves in some currencies but have a surplus of them in others.

Reserves and the spread of depression

A function of reserves upon which considerable emphasis was placed in the planning for the postwar period is that of preventing the spread of depression from one country to another. A depression in any country will tend to reduce its imports, as these are related more or less closely to its national income. Hence, a depression in an important country will tend to reduce substantially the exports of other countries. If these countries maintain their imports, they will deplete their monetary reserves; if they do not, the exports of other countries will be reduced further and so the depression will tend to spread in an ever widening circle. One of the principal purposes of the International Monetary Fund is to combat this mechanism for the international spread of depressions.

The amount of reserves necessary to prevent the spread of a depression depends upon the duration and intensity of the depression in the country of primary origin and the importance of that country in world trade. Even a minor depression in an important trading country, such as the United States, may have serious consequences in some other countries. If the depression is deep and protracted at its point of origin, the amount of monetary reserves necessary to prevent its spread may become indefinitely large. If such reserves should be supplied entirely by the Fund and be subject to reasonably firm undertakings with respect to their repayment in the foreseeable future, they might not be able—however large the amount available—to check the spread of a severe depression, because many countries would probably contract their imports (and so other countries' exports) substantially, rather than pile up large debts which they saw no prospects of repaying. The problem presented by such conditions is referred to later in this paper (pp. 342–43).

STATISTICS OF MONETARY RESERVES

A summary of monetary reserve statistics and a discussion of the methodology of their preparation are included in the June 1953 issue of *International Financial Statistics*, the monthly statistical publication of the International Monetary Fund. A reprint of part of that article is attached as an Appendix to this paper.

Monetary reserves are classified in that article as "gold", "foreign exchange", and "total", i.e., gold plus foreign exchange. It would be desirable if the "foreign exchange" item could be further subdivided into convertible and inconvertible currencies. Unfortunately, no comprehensive statistics are available on this basis. As will be seen by reference to the Appendix, the bulk of the monetary reserves of the world consists of holdings of gold, dollars, and sterling.

The official gold reserves and the total official reserves of gold and foreign exchange combined for a large number of countries, for the principal international monetary agencies, and for the world as a whole for the years 1928, 1938, 1951, and 1952 are given in Table 1. This table does not include data on reserve holdings for countries which are members of the Soviet bloc or for the dependent territories of the United Kingdom and of the continental EPU countries. The countries in the Soviet bloc are omitted because of inadequate data; the dependent territories are treated, for the purposes of this paper, as parts of the economies of their respective metropolitan countries. The reserves listed in the table include those held by monetary authorities only. Therefore, special caution should be used in interpreting comparisons between the data for 1951 and 1952 and those for earlier years for countries in which central banks have been established since 1928 or in which monetary reserves have been concentrated in the hands of the monetary authorities since that time. In such countries—Canada and Australia are especially in point—official reserve holdings in earlier years were, of course, supplemented by additional holdings of reserve-type assets in the hands of commercial banks.

In one sense it may be said that gold holdings constitute a "core within a core" of monetary reserves, as there are no contra-liabilities against them and they alone are "incompressible" and so must continue to exist in the same *physical* amount irrespective of any changes in their ownership. But the proportion of the total physical stock of gold held by the monetary authorities, and so counted as reserves, may vary; and the *monetary* value of this stock may also vary as a result of changes in the official price of gold. By far the most important price of gold is that in U.S. dollars, and it is in this unit that the gold reserves of all countries are stated throughout this paper.

The principal reason for the dramatic rise in the value of official gold stocks between 1928 and 1938 is, of course, the increase in the price of gold in U.S. dollars. This rise in the value of gold stocks is a "real" one, however, as the purchasing power of each U.S. dollar (in which the gold is measured) rose between 1928 and 1938. Conversely,

Table 1. Official Gold and Foreign Exchange Reserves, by Countries [1]

(In millions of U.S. dollars)

	Gold [2]				Gold plus Foreign Exchange [2]			
	1928	1938	1951	1952	1928	1938	1951	1952
United States	3,746	14,592	22,873	23,252	3,746	14,592	22,873	23,252
Canada	93	186	842	885	93	220	1,795	1,862
Latin American Republics	985[3]	690[3]	1,954	1,810[3]	1,160[3]	790[3]	3,025[3]	3,025[3]
Dollar countries	70[3]	130[3]	1,057	930[3]	125[3]	165[3]	1,535[3]	1,620[3]
Bolivia	9	3	23	23	9	5	32	28
Colombia	24	24	48	n.a.	62	29	123	152
Cuba	n.a.	1	311	214	n.a.	2	495	460
Dominican Republic	n.a.	—	12	12	n.a.	n.a.	30	32
Ecuador	1	3	22	23	8	4	31	44
El Salvador	5	7	20	20	5	8	42	44
Guatemala	2	7	27	27	5	9	40	43
Mexico	6	28	207	144	10	42	269	273
Venezuela	21	n.a.	373	373	21	n.a.	373	434
Other [4]	n.a.	1[3]	8[3]	8[3]	n.a.	5[3]	100[3]	110[3]
Non-dollar countries	915[3]	560[3]	897	880[3]	1,035[3]	625[3]	1,490[3]	1,400[3]
Argentina	607	n.a.	268	n.a.	607	n.a.	n.a.	n.a.
Brazil	149	32	317	317	177	59	514	525
Chile	65	30	45	42	120	44	59	71
Paraguay	n.a.	n.a.	—	—	n.a.	21	19	18
Peru	22	20	46	46	47	21	60	56
Uruguay	72	72	221	207	83	n.a.	n.a.	216
United Kingdom	748	2,877	2,200[5]	1,500[5]	748	2,877[6]	2,374	1,958
Other Sterling Countries [7]	385	535	627	620	754[3]	1,170[3]	5,055	4,400[3]
Australia	109	6	112	113	200	251	1,219	979
Burma	...[8]	...[8]	—	—	...[8]	...[8]	159	n.a.
Ceylon	...[8]	...[8]	1	—	...[8]	...[8]	218	163
Iceland	1	1	1	1	n.a.	1	9	9
India	202[9]	274[9]	247	247	440[9]	485[9]	1,888	1,729
Iraq	n.a.	—	—	—	n.a.	22	114	129
Ireland	n.a.	10	18	18	n.a.	59	206	219
New Zealand	35	23	32	33	35	43	217	183
Pakistan	...[8]	...[8]	27	38	...[8]	...[8]	639	n.a.
Union of South Africa	39	220	190	170	78	259	306	382

Table 1—Continued

	Gold[2]				Gold plus Foreign Exchange[2]			
	1928	1938	1951	1952	1928	1938	1951	1952
Continental EPU Countries	2,785[3]	6,060[3]	4,010[3]	4,485[3]	5,140[3]	6,500[3]	7,045[3]	7,935[3]
Austria	24	...[10]	n.a.	n.a.	126	...[10]	n.a.	n.a.
Belgium-Luxembourg	128	780	635	704	345	780	1,054	1,077
Denmark	46	53	31	31	77	77	118	142
France	1,254	2,757	548[11]	573[11]	2,541	2,791	800	676
Germany[12]	650	n.a.	28	140	776	n.a.	503	1,165
Greece	7	27	4	10	55	n.a.	n.a.	n.a.
Italy	266	193	333	n.a.	583	201	1,045	913
Netherlands	175	998	316	544	263	1,037	552	936
Norway	39	84	50	50	50	134	151	151
Portugal	9	86	264	286	25	n.a.	n.a.	n.a.
Sweden	63	321	152	184	121	520	484	446
Switzerland	103	701	1,452	1,422	152	764	1,594	1,648
Turkey	21	29	151	143	21	34	217	191
Other	1,060[3]	945[3]	950[3]	920[3]	1,400[3]	1,395[3]	3,665[3]	3,350[3]
Egypt	18	55	174	174	178	175	957	753
Finland	8	26	26	26	27	75	216	163
Indonesia	n.a.	80	280	235	n.a.	n.a.	511	314
Iran	n.a.	26	138	138	n.a.	38	190	177
Israel[13]	n.a.	—	—	—	n.a.	32	19	n.a.
Japan	541	230	n.a.	n.a.	598	289	n.a.	n.a.
Lebanon[14]	...	...	26	31	...	...	40	42
Philippines	n.a.	n.a.	7	9	50	n.a.	246	227
Spain	494	525	51	51	512	n.a.	n.a.	n.a.
Syria	n.a.	n.a.	11	14	n.a.	n.a.	33	38
Thailand	n.a.	—	113	113	43	56	358	349

Table 1—Continued

	Gold[2]				Gold plus Foreign Exchange[2]			
	1928	1938	1951	1952	1928	1938	1951	1952
International Agencies								
IMF	...[15]	...[15]	1,530	1,692	...[15]	...[15]	7,261	7,374
EPU	...[15]	...[15]	65	159	...[15]	...[15]	68	225
BIS	...[15]	14	115	196	...[15]	14[6]	283	442
Total, including international agencies and United States	9,800[3]	25,900[3]	35,150[3]	35,500[3]	13,050[3]	27,600[3]	53,450[3]	53,800[3]
Total, excluding international agencies and United States	6,050[3]	11,300[3]	10,600[3]	10,200[3]	9,300[3]	13,000[3]	22,950[3]	22,500[3]

[1] Data are as of end of year. Countries of the Soviet bloc and dependent territories of the United Kingdom and of continental EPU countries are excluded; see text. Totals and subtotals include estimated data for those countries for which definite totals are not available (marked n.a. in table). Dashes indicate less than $500,000. [The figures for Belgium-Luxembourg in 1928 have been corrected from those originally published in Staff Papers, with consequential changes in some totals and in related ratios in Table 3.]

[2] Gold valued at $20.67 per ounce in 1928, and $35.00 per ounce in 1938, 1951, and 1952.

[3] Estimate (rounded).

[4] Covers Costa Rica, Haiti, Honduras, Nicaragua, and Panama.

[5] Estimates of the U.S. Treasury and Board of Governors of the Federal Reserve System.

[6] Gold only.

[7] The total reserves of "Other Sterling Countries" cannot be added to those of the United Kingdom in order to obtain a meaningful aggregate for the total sterling area, as the reserves of the "Other Sterling Countries" are comprised largely of items which are, in turn, liabilities of the United Kingdom.

[8] Included with India.

[9] Undivided India.

[10] Part of Germany.

[11] Central bank holdings only.

[12] Undivided Germany, 1928 and 1938; Federal Republic of Germany, 1951 and 1952.

[13] Data for 1928 and 1938 refer to Palestine.

[14] Included with Syria in 1928 and 1938.

[15] Agency not yet established.

Sources: For 1928, United Nations, *Statistical Yearbook, 1948*, and League of Nations, *International Currency Experience* (1944); for 1938, 1951, and 1952, International Monetary Fund, *International Financial Statistics*, July 1953, and data supplied by the Statistics Division, Research Department, International Monetary Fund.

although the price of gold in dollars remained unchanged between 1938 and 1952, the purchasing power of the dollar fell.

The years used for comparison in the table were selected primarily on the basis of statistical convenience. The year 1928 was a good year in the twenties; the year 1938 was a fairly representative year in the thirties. It is true that 1938 was a low year for imports into the United States; however, it was not a particularly low year for U.S. exports or for imports into most other countries. It is, consequently, a satisfactory year for considering the reserve adequacy of most countries—and the adequacy of the reserves of the United States is not in question. The years 1951 and 1952 are the most recent ones for which comprehensive data are available. Particular years, of course, may not be representative for individual countries. Apart from the broad economic, industrial, and agricultural forces always operating to cause year-to-year variations, it should be noted that import levels are substantially affected by the reserve positions, the trade and exchange restrictions, the monetary and fiscal policies, and the exchange rates of individual importing countries, and by the convertibility of their own and other currencies.

Substantial changes have, of course, occurred in the reserve positions of individual countries and areas since the end of 1952, but they do not significantly change the long-term perspective to which this paper is directed. Data for the early months of 1953, as far as they are available, have been published in *International Financial Statistics*.

The foreign exchange reserves included in the figures for gold plus foreign exchange shown in Table 1 include holdings of "blocked" currencies. Consequently, for some countries (e.g., India) these total figures overstate the amount of reserves immediately available for settling adverse payments balances. For obvious reasons, special caution should be used in interpreting the world and regional totals for gold and foreign exchange combined. While gold is an asset in itself, with no corresponding contra-liability, foreign exchange other than gold is, in the nature of the case, both an asset to the holder and a liability to the issuer. The totals used in this table are, in every case, on a *gross* basis, i.e., the asset items are included but the liability items are ignored. This is the customary method of stating reserve statistics, and is, on the whole, more meaningful than an attempt to state them on a "net" basis, in which case foreign exchange would disappear completely as a reserve item for the world as a whole. The "double counting" involved in this procedure presents certain difficulties, however.

This "double counting" is important only for the United States and the United Kingdom, as dollars and sterling are the only currencies that other countries hold in substantial amounts as monetary reserves. The double counting results in overstating the reserve position of the United States, as the $10.5 billion of short-term liabilities to foreigners (including international institutions) outstanding on December 31, 1952 constituted, in an important sense, a first claim on the U.S. gold reserve of $23.3 billion on that same date.[4] A good part of these foreign claims are required as working balances, however, and, in any event, the reserve and payments positions of the United States are so strong that there is no practical difficulty in treating its reserve position on a gross basis. The case of the United Kingdom is rather different. The external

---

[4] The corresponding figures for December 31, 1951 are $22.9 billion for the gold reserve and $9.3 billion for total short-term liabilities to foreigners including international institutions.

sterling liabilities of the United Kingdom, counted as reserves by others, substantially exceed its own reserves. Its real reserve position, therefore, is not nearly so strong as might be inferred from the gross figures given in this table. Furthermore, no meaningful figure can be obtained by adding the total reserves of the United Kingdom and those of other sterling countries to obtain a "sterling area total", since the major portion of the reserves of the other sterling countries are comprised of liabilities of the United Kingdom. The amount of double counting in the table as a whole is, of course, substantially reduced by the omission of reserve statistics for the dependent territories of the United Kingdom and of the continental EPU countries.

Table 2 shows total imports on a c.i.f. basis for the countries for which reserve data are shown in Table 1. As in Table 1, members of the Soviet bloc and dependent territories of the United Kingdom and of the continental EPU countries are omitted. Table 3 shows the relationship which the official gold reserves and the total official reserves, respectively, of each country bore to its total c.i.f. imports in each of the reference years.

The relationship of reserves to imports serves as a common denominator on the basis of which reserves can be compared. It is the most comprehensive basis found practical to use in the general statistical comparisons in this paper. Strictly speaking, the most general basis for such comparisons would be total current account expenditures, but data on such expenditures are not available for many of the countries for many of the years. The necessary omission of invisible items has been repaired in part, however, by placing imports on a c.i.f. basis. The imports of each country are those from all other countries, including those from the country's own overseas dependencies. It is true that imports into metropolitan countries from their own overseas dependencies may often be financed in ways that do not place a strain on metropolitan reserves. The metropolitan country usually has a corresponding obligation, however, to assist in financing imports into the dependent territories from the outside world. These imports (like all other imports of the dependent territories) are omitted from the statistics, and may be considered as at least a partial offset to the inclusion of imports into the metropolitan countries from their dependent territories.

In any event, it should be emphasized that, whatever might be the character of the denominators by which the reserves of different countries were divided to place them on a comparable basis, they would not provide ready-made comparisons of reserve adequacy. The reserve figures themselves make no allowance for penumbral reserve items; and, were such allowances made, they would merely provide the starting point for the application of the various criteria of adequacy discussed earlier in this paper. This is brought out dramatically by the incongruity between the import-reserve percentages for a number of the countries in the tables and the generally accepted evaluations of the over-all reserve positions of these countries based upon the size of their reserves and all of the factors affecting reserve adequacy.

Table 1 does not distinguish between the convertible and inconvertible currency holdings of the International Monetary Fund. It is helpful, therefore, to say that the Fund's total holdings of gold and U.S. and Canadian dollars amounted to $3.1 billion at the end of 1951 and were equal to about 5 per cent of 1951 c.i.f. imports of all the countries included in the table, exclusive of the United States. By the end of 1952, the Fund's holdings of gold and U.S. and Canadian dollars had risen to $3.2 billion (6 per cent of 1952 c.i.f. imports).

Table 2. Merchandise Imports, C.I.F., by Countries[1]
(In millions of U.S. dollars)

	1928	1938	1951	1952
United States	*4,427*	*2,465*	*11,946*	*11,633*
Canada	*1,364*	*763*	*4,195*	*4,458*
Latin American Republics	*2,453*	*1,535*	*7,619*	*7,074*
Dollar countries	862	568	3,272	3,280
Bolivia	23	25	91	74[2]
Colombia	161	89	416	402
Cuba	234	119	691	667
Dominican Republic	30	13	64	63
Ecuador	16	12	64	65
El Salvador	18	9	62	68
Guatemala	31	21	81	76
Mexico	185	114	823	739
Venezuela	81	107	719	809
Other[3]	83	59	261	317
Non-dollar countries	1,591	967	4,347	3,794
Argentina	807	440	1,400[2]	860[2]
Brazil	441	295	2,011	2,010
Chile	163	103	329	371
Paraguay	13	9	30[2]	...[4]
Peru	70	58	261	288
Uruguay	97	62	316	237
United Kingdom	*5,795*	*4,600*	*10,942*	*9,747*
Other Sterling Countries	*2,670*	*2,299*	*8,054*	*7,554*
Australia	669[5]	571[5]	2,423	1,979
Burma	76[6]	79[7]	137	192
Ceylon	139	86	327	358
Iceland	17	11	57	56
India	837[6,8]	575[6,8]	1,816	1,672
Iraq	34	46	143	173
Ireland	288	203	573	482
New Zealand	218	225	596	739
Pakistan	...[9]	...[9]	534	609
Union of South Africa	393	503	1,448	1,294
Continental EPU Countries	*11,103*	*7,804*	*22,168*	*21,910*
Austria	456	...[10]	657	654
Belgium-Luxembourg	889	765	2,535	2,424
Denmark	441	354	1,013	962
France	2,097	1,324	4,551	4,431
Germany[11]	3,335	2,430	3,494	3,818
Greece	161	131	435	346
Italy	1,173	593	2,167	2,313
Netherlands	1,078	803	2,567	2,251
Norway	269	292	877	873
Portugal	120	102	330	350
Sweden	458	520	1,776	1,730
Switzerland	512	366	1,364	1,202
Turkey	114	119	402	556

Table 2, cont. Merchandise Imports, C.I.F., by Countries[1]
(In millions of U.S. dollars)

	1928	1938	1951	1952
Other	2,813	1,935	6,204	6,550
Egypt	249	185	667	608
Finland	202	182	676	792
Indonesia	403	275	805	972
Iran	76[12]	79[12]	248	165
Israel[13]	33	56	343	...[4]
Japan	990	759	1,995	2,028
Lebanon[14]	...	...	136	141
Philippines	149	153	539	477
Spain	580	...[4]	384	518
Syria	51	37	139	143
Thailand	80	57	272[2]	301[2]
Total, including United States	30,625	21,401	71,128	68,926
Total, excluding United States	26,198	18,936	59,182	57,293

[1] Countries of the Soviet bloc and dependent territories of the United Kingdom and of continental EPU countries are excluded; see text.
[2] Partly estimated.
[3] Covers Costa Rica, Haiti, Honduras, Nicaragua, and Panama.
[4] Estimate included in totals and subtotals.
[5] Year ending June.
[6] Year beginning April.
[7] Year ending September.
[8] Undivided India.
[9] Included with India.
[10] Included with Germany.
[11] Undivided Germany, 1928 and 1938; Federal Republic of Germany, 1951 and 1952.
[12] Year beginning June 21.
[13] Data for 1928 and 1938 refer to Palestine.
[14] Included with Syria in 1928 and 1938.
Sources: For 1928, League of Nations, *Network of World Trade* (1942); for 1938, 1951, and 1952, International Monetary Fund, *International Financial Statistics*, July 1953.

As stated previously, no comprehensive data are available separating foreign exchange reserves into those held in convertible and in inconvertible currencies. It is of interest, however, to present such data as are available with respect to reserve holdings of the major convertible currency—the U.S. dollar. These data are available from reports made to the U.S. Treasury by U.S. banks. They show that, for the world as a whole, holdings of U.S. dollars by official monetary authorities (excluding international agencies) amounted to $4.1 billion at the end of 1951 and to $5.1 billion at the end of 1952.[5] Data for official holdings only are not available for individual countries. In order to preserve the confidential character of the balances of individual foreign institutions, these data are published by the U.S. Treasury on a country basis only as a total of official and bank holdings of dollars. The total amount of such holdings (excluding international agencies) amounted to $6.0 billion at the end of 1951

---

[5] In each case reported official holdings of U.S. dollars by Japan are added to the total reported by the U.S. Treasury. See Appendix, p. 346.

Table 3. Ratios of Official Reserves to Total Merchandise Imports,
C.I.F., by Countries[1]

(In per cent)

	Ratio of Gold Reserves to Imports				Ratio of Gold plus Foreign Exchange Reserves to Imports			
	1928	1938	1951	1952	1928	1938	1951	1952
United States	85	592	191	202	85	592	191	202
Canada	7	24	20	20	7	29	43	42
Latin American Republics	40	45	26	26	47	51	40	43
Dollar countries	8	23	32	28	15	29	47	49
Bolivia	39	12	25	31	39	20	35	38
Colombia	15	27	12	—	39	33	30	38
Cuba	—	1	45	32	—	2	72	69
Dominican Republic	—	—	19	19	—	31	47	51
Ecuador	6	25	34	35	50	33	48	68
El Salvador	28	78	42	43	28	89	68	65
Guatemala	6	33	33	36	16	43	49	57
Mexico	3	25	25	19	5	37	33	37
Venezuela	26	—	52	46	26	—	52	54
Other[2]	—	2	3	3	—	8	38	35
Non-dollar countries	58	58	21	23	65	65	34	37
Argentina	75	—	19	—	75	—	—	—
Brazil	34	11	16	16	40	20	26	26
Chile	40	29	14	11	74	43	18	19
Paraguay	—	—	—	—	—	—	63	—
Peru	31	34	18	16	67	36	23	19
Uruguay	74	116	70	87	86	—	—	91
United Kingdom	13	63	20	15	13	63	22	20
Other Sterling Countries	14	23	8	8	28	51	63	58
Australia	16	1	5	6	30	44	50	49
Burma	—	—	—	—	—	—	116	—
Ceylon	—	—	—	—	—	—	67	46
Iceland	6	9	2	2	—	9	16	16
India	24	48	14	15	53	84	104	103
Iraq	—	—	—	—	—	48	80	75
Ireland	—	5	3	4	—	29	36	45
New Zealand	16	10	5	4	16	19	36	25
Pakistan	—	—	5	6	—	—	120	—
Union of South Africa	10	44	13	13	20	51	27	30
Continental EPU Countries	25	78	18	20	46	83	32	36
Austria	5	—	—	—	28	—	—	—
Belgium-Luxembourg	14	102	25	29	39	102	42	44
Denmark	10	15	3	3	17	22	12	15
France	60	208	12	13	121	211	18	15
Germany	19	—	1	4	23	—	14	24
Greece	4	21	1	3	34	—	—	—
Italy	23	33	15	—	50	34	48	39
Netherlands	16	124	12	24	24	129	22	42

Table 3, *cont.* Ratios of Official Reserves to Total Merchandise Imports, C.I.F., by Countries[1]

(In per cent)

	Ratio of Gold Reserves to Imports				Ratio of Gold plus Foreign Exchange Reserves to Imports			
	1928	1938	1951	1952	1928	1938	1951	1952
Continental EPU Countries, *cont.*								
Norway	14	29	6	6	19	46	17	17
Portugal	3	84	80	82	21	—	—	—
Sweden	14	62	9	11	26	100	27	26
Switzerland	20	192	106	118	30	209	117	137
Turkey	13	24	38	26	18	29	54	34
Other	35	49	15	14	50	73	59	40
Egypt	7	30	26	29	71	95	143	124
Finland	4	14	4	3	13	41	32	21
Indonesia	—	29	35	24	—	—	63	32
Iran	—	33	56	84	—	48	77	107
Israel	—	—	—	—	—	57	6	—
Japan	55	30	—	—	60	38	—	—
Lebanon	—	—	19	22	—	—	29	30
Philippines	—	—	1	2	34	—	46	48
Spain	85	—	13	10	88	—	—	—
Syria	—	—	8	10	—	—	24	27
Thailand	—	—	42	38	54	98	132	116
Total, including gold and reserves of international agencies, and gold and reserves *and* imports of the United States	32	121	49	52	43	129	75	78
Total, excluding gold and reserves of international agencies, and gold and reserves *and* imports of the United States	23	60	18	17	35	69	39	40

[1] Based on data in Tables 1 and 2. Dashes indicate less than one half of 1 per cent or nonavailability of data.
[2] Covers Costa Rica, Haiti, Honduras, Nicaragua, and Panama.

and to $6.6 billion at the end of 1952, and so exceeded by a considerable margin holdings of monetary authorities only.

For the various countries, the available data for holdings of gold and U.S. dollars by foreign monetary authorities and banks in 1951 and 1952, and the ratios of these data to the figures shown in Table 2 for the c.i.f. imports of each country, are given in Table 4. The comparisons here differ, of course, from those made earlier in this chapter in that they exclude holdings of all types of reserves other than gold and U.S. dollars and include holdings by banks as well as by monetary authorities.

COMPARISONS OF RESERVE ADEQUACY

To the preceding discussion of the factors affecting the need for reserves at any time and the statistics of actual reserve holdings in 1928, 1938, 1951, and 1952, it may

Table 4. Official and Bank Holdings of Gold and U.S. Dollars and Their Ratio to Total Merchandise Imports, C.I.F., by Countries, Excluding the United States

	Official and Bank Holdings of Gold and U.S. Dollars[1] (million dollars)		Ratio to Imports (per cent)	
	1951	1952	1951	1952
Canada	*1,953*	*2,047*	*47*	*46*
Latin American Republics	*2,838*	*2,755*	*37*	*39*
Dollar countries	1,585	1,631	48	50
Bolivia	40	37	44	50
Colombia	132	160[2]	32	40
Cuba	518	455	75	68
Dominican Republic	42	42	66	67
Ecuador	33[3]	47[3]	52	72
El Salvador	44	44	71	65
Guatemala	40	43	49	57
Mexico	294	283	36	38
Venezuela	399	465	55	57
Other[4]	43[3]	55[3]	16	17
Non-dollar countries	1,253	1,124	29	30
Argentina	482	370[2]	34	43
Brazil	377	352	19	18
Chile	71	92	22	25
Paraguay	5[3]	5[3]	17	18
Peru	70	70	27	24
Uruguay	248	235	78	99
United Kingdom	*2,530*	*2,027*	*23*	*21*
Other Sterling Countries	*798*	*810*	*10*	*11*
Australia	151	157	6	8
Ceylon	19[3]	14[3]	6	4
Iceland	5[3]	5[3]	9	9
India	305	308	17	18
Iraq	13[3]	14[3]	9	8
Ireland	34[3]	34[2]	6	7
New Zealand	37[3]	36[3]	6	5
Pakistan	40[3]	52[3]	7	9
Union of South Africa	194	190	13	15
Continental EPU Countries	*5,817*	*6,753*	*26*	*31*
Austria	102[2]	142[2]	16	22
Belgium-Luxembourg	715[5]	771[5]	28	32
Denmark	69	92	7	10
France	765	855	17	19
Germany	431	688	12	18
Greece	43	48	10	14
Italy	599	620[2]	28	27
Netherlands	443	726	17	32
Norway	126	138	14	16
Portugal	295	329	89	94
Sweden	218	268	12	15
Switzerland	1,851	1,929	136	160
Turkey	160	147	40	26

Table 4, cont. Official and Bank Holdings of Gold and U.S. Dollars and Their Ratio to Total Merchandise Imports, C I.F., by Countries, Excluding the United States

	Official and Bank Holdings of Gold and U.S. Dollars[1] (million dollars)		Ratio to Imports (per cent)	
	1951	1952	1951	1952
Other	2,286	2,393	37	37
Egypt	281	230	42	38
Finland	52	52	8	7
Indonesia	420	295	52	30
Iran	157	150	63	91
Israel	24	16	7	4
Japan	710[2]	920[2]	36	45
Lebanon	41	50[3]	30	35
Philippines	318	304	59	64
Spain	60	61	16	12
Syria	16	25[3]	12	17
Thailand	207	290	76	96
International Agencies				
IMF	2,854	2,980	—	—
EPU	68	226	—	—
BIS	283[6]	442[6]	—	—
Total, incl. international agencies	19,427	20,433	33	36
Total, excl. international agencies	16,222	16,785	27	29

[1] Data as of end of year.
[2] Partly estimated.
[3] Includes other than official and bank holdings.
[4] Covers Costa Rica, Haiti, Honduras, Nicaragua, and Panama.
[5] Belgian official and bank holdings; Luxembourg includes other than official and bank holdings.
[6] Includes currencies other than dollars.

Sources: Holdings of U.S. dollars are from U.S. Treasury Department, *Treasury Bulletin*, April 1952, May 1952, April 1953, and May 1953. For other sources used, see Tables 1 and 2.

be helpful to add a brief consideration of some changes in the need for reserves during the past few decades.

Reserve adequacy in 1928

Reserves in 1928 were adequate to support multilateral trade in the prosperous conditions prevailing at the time. It is futile to consider whether they would have continued to be adequate to support the newly established gold standard indefinitely through mild ups and downs in business conditions in the absence of deep depression. The fact is that the depression of the early thirties, spreading chiefly from the United States, but also from other leading industrial countries, placed the reserves of many countries, especially raw material countries, under great strain. At the same time, the loss of confidence in the exchange rates of the currencies of the reserve holding countries, especially the United Kingdom (due in part to inadequacies in their reserves), caused runs on these countries which induced them to contract their own credits, and so reduced the total amount of reserves available to other countries. A shortage of reserves was certainly not the principal cause of the depression of the thirties, but it did contribute to the scope, intensity, and duration of the depression because of the severe restrictions on trade and even because of the general deflationary policies that were instituted to protect reserves.

Effect of the low level of world trade on reserve adequacy in 1938

The situation in 1938 was quite different. The amount of reserves then available was doubtless adequate in the sense that a shortage of reserves was not the bottleneck restraining an expansion of trade, and probably would not have become one even if trade had expanded considerably. (Many countries—e.g., Germany, Japan, and some countries in eastern Europe, as well as some raw material producing countries—doubtless had inadequate reserves, but these countries were pursuing policies with respect to the disposition of their real resources which would have quickly dissipated some of their reserves even if somehow they had been made adequate.) It is probable that reserves in 1938 would have been adequate even if the total amount of world trade at that time had been at a volume corresponding to high level employment in, and the pursuit of liberal trade policies by, all or most trading countries. The important point is that the adequacy of 1938 reserves should be judged, not relative to actual 1938 trade but relative to the total amount of trade which would have been carried on under liberal trade policies and at a high level of employment. It follows that the shrinkage in the apparent adequacy of reserves relative to trade between 1938 and 1951 is not nearly so great as appears from the foregoing tables. This is true because the basis of comparison in one case is a volume of trade greatly shrunken by depression, and in the other case it is a volume which, despite illiberal trade policies, was at a high level.

Changes in the volatility of world trade

As pointed out previously, one of the principal factors affecting the need for reserves is the prospect of swings in the volume and prices of a country's imports and exports. The possibility of a downward swing in the demand for a country's exports increases its need for reserves and makes any given reserve holding less adequate.

There is some reason to believe that world trade is more volatile and the exports of most countries more vulnerable to sharp downward swings now than was the case in 1938. Before the war, economic conditions in the United States were generally subject to greater variation than those in most industrial countries. If this tendency should reappear in the postwar period (it has not thus far), an increase in the U.S. share of world trade would increase its over-all volatility. The ratio of U.S. imports (c.i.f.) to world imports decreased from 13 per cent in 1928 to 10 per cent in 1938, but again increased to 15 per cent in 1951 and 1952. It is possible, therefore, that the exports of other countries are somewhat more subject to sharp declines now than they were in 1938. Moreover, a larger proportion of the imports of the United States now consists of raw materials which are also produced in large volume in the United States, either directly or in the form of acceptable synthetic substitutes. The imported portion of these materials—copper and natural rubber are cases in point—represents a marginal supply which would be subject to sharp curtailment in the event of a U.S. recession. It appears, therefore, that, as far as trade factors are concerned, a larger amount of reserves relative to trade may be necessary now than would have been the case in 1938, in order to provide the same degree of relative adequacy.

RELATIONSHIP OF THE PAYMENTS AND RESERVES PROBLEMS IN THE POSTWAR PERIOD

The problem of assisting deficit countries to finance long-continuing, and possibly fundamental, disequilibria in their balances of payments is conceptually separate from the problem of building up their monetary reserves. The reserves problem of any country cannot be approached until its payments problem has been brought under control. But, in the last analysis, the funds obtained by each country are directly or indirectly transferable between the two uses, and the real character of any operation can be determined only *ex post*, after a study of the recipient countries' reserve and payments positions.

Viewed in this light, it is seen that the funds obtained by each country since the war (or during any other period) may be considered as interim installments toward its combined payments-reserves problem, with the final apportionment depending upon the policies of the country and the forces with which it has to contend.

As shown in Table 5, during the period 1946 to 1952, inclusive, the United States supplied the "rest of the world" with $125.9 billion, of which $89.9 billion was either earned or obtained through private donations or private capital movements, and $36 billion was obtained through official grants and loans from the U.S. Government and international agencies. Uses of dollars during this period totaled $129.2 billion, leaving a deficiency of $3.3 billion which was made up by a net transfer of reserves to the United States.[6] Gold production outside the United States during the same period totaled a little over $5 billion, which would have more than restored the reserves of the "rest of the world" to their original amount if it had all been added to monetary stocks—which, of course, was not the case.

During each of the past three years, the "rest of the world" has gained reserves from the United States, the amount being substantial in 1950. The proportion of the total dollar supply coming from official grants and loans (including military aid) has varied between 21 per cent and 24 per cent in the three-year period. During 1952, the total dollar supply exceeded the use of dollars by $0.8 billion (the net outflow of reserves from the United States). Official grants and loans (including military aid) totaled $5.2 billion and accounted for about 24 per cent of the total dollar supply of $21.7 billion in that year.

Military aid, which comprised a very small proportion of total official grants and loans prior to 1950, has increased rapidly since then, as shown in Table 6. In 1952, military aid comprised half of all official grants and loans of U.S. dollars. As suggested earlier in this paper, military aid, when considered as a means of financing the costs of a mutually shared defense system, may be viewed by the recipient countries in the same category as other current balance of payments receipts, rather than as a means of financing a deficit.

The significance of any given supply of dollars must, of course, be judged relative to the total needs which must be met and the purchasing power of each dollar. The dollar supply in 1952, exclusive of movements in reserves and of official grants and loans, and after subtracting an amount equal to the net investment income of the

---

[6] The figures in Table 5 are obtained by reversing the signs on the data for the balance of payments of the United States, published in International Monetary Fund, *Balance of Payments Yearbook*. The item "net errors and omissions" has been classified for this purpose as a "use" of funds by the "rest of the world" on the ground that such errors and omissions probably represent, for the most part, unrecorded private capital movements to the United States.

Table 5. Sources and Uses of U.S. Dollars by the Rest of the World, 1946-52[1]
(In billions of U.S. dollars, except for Col. 5)

	Sources						Uses				Net Movements in Reserves (Col. 6 minus Col. 10)
	Exports to U.S.	Services	Private donations and capital movements	Official grants and loans		Total sources	Imports from U.S.	Services	Net errors and omissions	Total uses	
				Amount	Per cent of total sources						
	(1)	(2)	(3)	(4)	(5)	(6)	(7)	(8)	(9)	(10)	(11)
1946	5.1	2.2	1.2	5.2	38	13.7	10.2	5.0	0.2	15.4	−1.6
1947	6.1	2.4	1.9	6.0	37	16.4	15.1	5.0	1.0	21.2	−4.8
1948	7.8	2.8	2.1	5.2	29	17.8	13.1	4.6	1.0	18.7	−0.9
1949	7.0	2.8	1.5	5.8	34	17.2	12.3	4.2	0.8	17.2	−[2]
1950	9.3	3.1	1.6	4.2	23	18.2	10.6	4.2	0.2	15.0	+3.2
1951	11.7	3.6	1.2	4.4	21	20.9	15.5	4.7	0.6	20.8	−[2]
1952	11.5	4.2	0.8	5.2	24	21.7	15.9	4.8	0.2	20.9	+0.8
Total	58.5	21.1	10.3	36.0	29	125.9	92.7	32.5	4.0	129.2	−3.3

[1] Totals and computations are based on unrounded figures.
[2] Less than $50 million.

Sources: 1946-51 data based on International Monetary Fund, *Balance of Payments Yearbook, 1948, 1949-50,* and *1950-51;* 1952 data are estimated.

United States,[7] was higher—both in real and in monetary terms—than it had been in any previous year. In real terms it was slightly greater than in 1950 and 1951,

Table 6. Official Grants and Loans by the United States to the Rest of the World, 1946-52[1]

	Military Aid	Other	Total	Military Aid	Other	Total
	←———(billion dollars)———→			(per cent of total dollar supply)		
1946	—	5.2	5.2	—	38	38
1947	0.1	5.9	6.0	1	36	37
1948	0.4	4.8	5.2	2	27	29
1949	0.2	5.6	5.8	1	33	34
1950	0.6	3.6	4.2	3	20	23
1951	1.5	2.9	4.4	7	14	21
1952	2.6	2.6	5.2	12	12	24

[1] For sources, see Table 5.

more than twice the amount in the thirties, and 60 per cent higher than in the twenties (see Chart 1 and Table 7). The dollars furnished by official grants and loans (including military aid) are in addition to this large supply from traditional sources. While the need for dollars has also increased since the twenties and the thirties, these figures make the dollar shortage seem much less hopeless than is sometimes assumed.

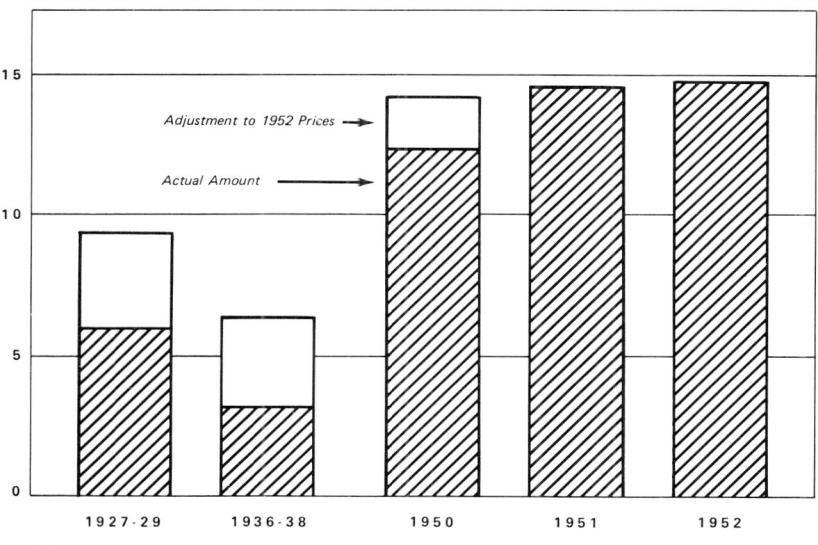

Chart 1. Annual Dollar Supply [1]
(In billions of U.S. dollars)

[1] See Table 7 and text.

The additional supply of dollars which has been furnished by official grants and loans has been an active factor in increasing the demand for dollars during the postwar period. This was, in part, inevitable, as an increase in the flow of dollars naturally relaxed the policies of the recipient countries and so caused them to make expenditures which they would otherwise have averted, although only at the cost of much hardship

[7] This subtraction is made in order to show the amount of dollars at the "free" disposal of the recipient countries after paying interest, dividends, etc., to the United States.

and political instability. It is also unlikely that so many dollars would have been furnished by the United States had a large portion of them been added to reserves. Indeed, most of the additional dollar expenditure was *planned* at the direct request of the United States, since one of the avowed purposes of the Marshall Plan was to stimulate investment in the recipient countries and thus strengthen their balance of payments positions in the long run. It would not be true, therefore, to say that the funds received from the United States in the form of official grants and loans could

Table 7. Annual Dollar Supply in Current and 1952 Dollars[1]
(In billions of U.S. dollars)

	1927-29 Average	1936-38 Average	1950	1951	1952
Actual amount	5.9	3.1	12.4	14.7	14.8
Amount adjusted to 1952 prices	9.3	6.3	14.2	14.7	14.8

[1] Excludes all dollars supplied by official financing and by movements of reserves; also excludes an amount of dollars supplied by other sources equal to the net investment income of the United States in each year. The adjustment to 1952 prices is made on the basis of the U.S. export price index. The data have been compiled by the International Monetary Fund.

have been added to reserves, even in large part, had the recipient countries adopted more rigorous policies. But the grants and loans did avert what might otherwise have been a disastrous run on reserves and contributed in some degree to an actual increase.

CONCLUSION

The preceding discussion has stressed three points which must be taken into account in any discussion of the adequacy of monetary reserves:

(1) Monetary reserves are meant to take care of swings between favorable and unfavorable payments positions. They are meant to cover recurrent balance of payments deficits that are temporary in character. No amount of monetary reserves is sufficient to finance a permanent disequilibrium in a country's balance of payments.

(2) The magnitude of the monetary reserves of a given country tends both to affect and to be affected by that country's domestic fiscal and monetary policies. The interaction between reserves and policies is stronger, the more important the role played by external trade in the economy of the country concerned. Rigorous fiscal and monetary policies tend to increase monetary reserves; strong reserve positions make the relaxation of fiscal and monetary policies possible. When world inflationary and world deflationary forces are in balance, this interaction is beneficial and helps both to promote sound policies and to achieve and maintain a viable distribution of monetary reserves throughout the trading world. When world inflationary forces are in the ascendancy, substantial accretions to world monetary reserves tend, through their interactions with policy, to increase these forces yet further; when world deflationary forces are in the ascendancy, substantial accretions to world monetary reserves tend to offset these forces. The foregoing should not be taken to imply that increases in reserves are *per se* undesirable even during periods of world inflation. Countries should be on guard in such situations, however, against relaxing their fiscal and monetary policies so far as to intensify domestic inflationary pressures.

(3) A world-wide distribution of monetary reserves in accordance with the apparent need for them is incompatible with the yet more fundamental consideration of the

distribution of the real resources of each country in accordance with the highest priority for their use. If the monetary reserves of the world were completely redistributed in accordance with apparent need, they would soon be re-redistributed, as each country would soon (quite properly) rearrange the changed amount of real resources at its disposal in accordance with its scale of preferences. In such a re-redistribution, wealthy or less dynamic countries would soon reacquire reserves which they either desired or merely accepted passively, but which, in any event, they could hold without sacrificing other deeply felt needs, while poorer or more dynamic countries would soon dispose of part of their newly acquired reserves in exchange for other types of real resources which they needed more urgently.

It is a corollary of the first of these points that the subject of reserve adequacy can be discussed meaningfully only on the assumption that countries which have not already done so adopt policies adequate to balance their accounts over a normal economic cycle. Upon the assumption that countries adopt such policies, the following four categories or standards of reserve adequacy were distinguished earlier in this paper:

1. Enough to enable a country in bad years, by resort to restrictions, to maintain its external debt payments and to purchase the goods and services necessary to avoid hardship to its population or dislocation to its economy and the possible emergence of an exchange crisis, i.e., to permit a reasonable distribution over *time* of the payments which it can afford to make over the entire cycle;

2. Enough to maintain currency convertibility, barring a severe depression, but with occasional necessity to resort to trade and exchange restrictions for balance of payments purposes;

3. Enough to maintain currency convertibility, barring a severe depression, but without the necessity for occasional resort to trade and exchange restrictions;

4. Enough to maintain currency convertibility, even through severe depressions (but not through prolonged periods of international deflation such as occurred in the thirties), without either the necessity for occasional resort to trade and exchange restrictions or the necessity for resorting to domestic deflationary policies for the purpose of restraining imports, even if this involves a substantial drain on reserves.

The determination of the "adequacy" category into which any country falls, assuming that it meets the fundamental condition of payments balance over a normal cycle, is a matter of judgment. It is probable, however, that almost all countries, assuming the adoption of appropriate policies, would qualify for category 1, many would qualify for category 2, some would qualify for category 3, and a few would qualify for category 4.[8]

---

[8] International Monetary Fund, *Annual Report, 1952*, p. 6, states: "An aggravating factor in the recurrent balance of payments crises of the postwar years is the inadequacy of international reserves available to monetary authorities outside the United States. Although the gold and dollar holdings of countries other than the United States have risen to some extent since 1938, the increase has not been in proportion to the expansion of world trade, and their value in real terms has been actually reduced by inflation. These trends, combined with the abnormally wide swings in balances of payments, have often produced situations in which reserves have appeared to be dangerously low. The attainment of any particular level or ratio of reserves is not by itself a guarantee against balance of payments crises; nevertheless, a more adequate cushion against balance of payments disturbances is clearly desirable so that more time may be available to make the necessary readjustments."

It should be noted that many of the countries to which reference was there made had not achieved a fundamental balance of payments equilibrium over a normal economic cycle. Each adequacy category used in this paper assumes that policies are always adequate to assure such a balance.

In determining the adequacy category into which any country falls, account should be taken of the availability of the resources of the Fund to extend temporary assistance to member countries which have achieved a fundamental payments balance. The provision of funds for the objectives indicated above—i.e., the avoidance of sharp declines in imports not required by a country's fundamental payments position, the maintenance of currency convertibility, and the avoidance of restrictions—is in accordance with the purposes of the Fund. Assistance from the Fund in carrying out these purposes should, therefore, enable member countries to meet their reserve needs more effectively than would be possible on the basis of their own reserves alone. The role of the Fund in times of depression presents special problems which will now be considered.

Reserves for combating the spread of depression

None of the adequacy categories just discussed implies that a country would be able to endure a prolonged period of world deflation without the imposition of exchange restrictions implying at least a severe limitation on convertibility. However, as has already been suggested, this would scarcely be a fair test of reserve adequacy. Just as, at one end of the spectrum, the subject of reserve adequacy does not become relevant unless the country itself is pursuing appropriate policies, so, at the other end, no country can be expected to maintain reserves sufficient to sustain free and nondiscriminatory multilateral trade in the face of world-wide deflation.

The experts' report, *Measures for International Economic Stability*, assumes that protracted depressions will be avoided by appropriate domestic measures, but that the U.S. economy, even on the assumption of a fairly rigorous anti-deflationary policy, is subject to short, sharp shocks, during which the rest of the world would need substantial reserves in order to maintain domestic anti-deflationary policies and a volume of imports from the United States corresponding to such policies, and thereby prevent the spread of the depression. The experts estimate that, in the event of a depression in the United States lasting for two years from its inception to its conclusion and involving a fall in industrial production of the same relative magnitude as that which occurred in the depression of 1937-38, the rest of the world would need to draw on its reserves to the extent of $8 billion to maintain its commodity imports from the United States at the level of those in the first half of 1951. To this, the experts add another $2 billion to cover anticipated accompanying declines in invisible current account payments by the United States and in private long-term capital outflow from the United States, and come up with an estimate that a total drain of $10 billion on reserves would be necessary to prevent the spread of a depression of the assumed magnitude. There is some reason to suppose that the assumptions of the experts may be unduly pessimistic. But they will not be investigated here, as no quantitative criticism of them would alter the conclusion of this paper that reserves are not, in general, adequate for combating the spread of a severe depression.

There are two essential questions implicit in the experts' report: (1) What actions in the field of monetary reserves should be taken *now* to prevent the spread of future depressions? (2) What actions should be taken when and if a depression starts?

In regard to the first, it would appear desirable for countries to increase their reserves to the extent that is possible and consistent with a progressive relaxation of trade and exchange restrictions and the maintenance of internal financial stability.

When analysis shows clearly that a depression is developing, it should be dealt with promptly by measures directed toward the maintenance of an adequate level of effective demand. Demand should, of course, be maintained on both the national and the international level. The measures taken to assure its maintenance should be primarily positive, and not merely defensive, in character. The essentially defensive character of supplementary reserves obtained with firm assurances of repayment in the short-term or medium-term future has already been pointed out. Defensive measures are important, however; and, in order to prevent small depressions from growing into large ones, such supplementary reserves should be supplied early, on liberal terms, and in adequate amounts. In the event of a severe depression, additional means for maintaining demand at the international level might be required, and it may be expected that the Fund would consult with its members on the desirability of additions to its resources and would consider possible changes in its modes of operations to meet the emergent situation. But primary reliance for the avoidance and cure of depressions must be placed upon appropriate measures at the national level, especially in industrial countries.[9]

APPENDIX

This Appendix reproduces in part an article by G. S. Dorrance and E. Hicks, "Gold and Foreign Exchange Statistics in IFS", in *International Financial Statistics*, June 1953, pp. vii-xii.

Problems of foreign exchange statistics

The statistics of foreign exchange are necessarily difficult to compile and difficult to use. Gold and foreign exchange statistics are intended to measure a country's international liquidity and hence its ability to finance temporary balance of payments reverses without recourse to either secondary deflation or quantitative restriction and to measure by their period-to-period changes the monetary effects of financing the balance of payments. The gold element of the total involves relatively few problems. In most countries gold is held entirely or predominantly by the monetary authorities, and measurement of their holdings provides an unambiguous statement of the gold holdings of the country. Gold is a single physical commodity whose quantity can be measured by weight and unambiguously valued in terms of U.S. dollars or in the currency of the holding country at its par rate of exchange. Lastly, the measurement of gold holdings does not ordinarily involve any problem of net or gross measurement.

The foreign exchange element of the total, on the contrary, involves many problems: Firstly,

---

[9] International Monetary Fund, *Annual Report, 1952*, pp. 45-46, states: "The Fund has also had under consideration the question of the part to be played by it in connection with the problems created by widespread recessions or depressions. The Articles of Agreement have entrusted to the Fund an important function in this field. The basic problem of depression cannot, however, be overcome by the availability of international short-term credit to be repaid in the next boom, whether this is credit from the Fund or from some other source. The cure for a depression will require national measures to maintain or stimulate effective demand, especially in the great industrial countries. It may take time, however, before these measures bring recovery. The Fund can assist members which in the meantime may be faced with serious balance of payments difficulties, and by so doing help to reduce the deflationary pressure on the world economy as a whole. A UN group of experts has recommended an enlargement of the Fund's resources so as to increase the effectiveness of its activities in such circumstances. The Fund has for some time had under consideration the question of increasing its members' quotas, having in mind such factors as the magnitude of possible balance of payments deficits in a depression and the fall in the purchasing power of money since 1946. It has, however, concluded that an increase in its resources is not a question for action at the present time. Its existing resources are by no means small as a source to finance a cyclical balance of payments deficits. The Fund's resources, moreover, are secondary reserves and the ability of countries to maintain important demand in a depression will depend also on the size of their own reserves. It is important, therefore, that countries follow financial policies that will enable them to build up reserves in periods of prosperity which would provide a first cushion to absorb the shock of a recession."

no completely satisfactory line can be drawn to separate foreign exchange from related items that also contribute to a country's international liquidity. Secondly, because foreign exchange is defined throughout *International Financial Statistics* as claims against foreigners rather than as claims in foreign currency, the foreign exchange holdings of one country are necessarily the foreign exchange liabilities of another, raising the problem of the extent to which foreign exchange liabilities are an offset to assets for a country, for an area, or for the world as a whole. Thirdly, the available international liquidity of a country is not limited to its holdings of foreign assets alone. International agencies, particularly the Fund and the EPU, provide additional sources of liquidity.

Foreign exchange and the similar items, other than gold, that make up a country's international liquidity might be grouped on at least three scales according to their usability. Foreign claims could be arrayed by *currency* from U.S. dollars at the top through the other convertible currencies and then through the inconvertible currencies in the order of their usefulness for meeting obligations in any country or in the country liable for the claim. The *holders* of foreign claims could be arrayed from the monetary authorities at the top through the other banks, other parts of the government, business, and individuals in the order in which their holdings might be thought to be available to the monetary authorities in times of need. Lastly, the *forms* that foreign claims take could be arrayed from currency and demand deposits at the top through other claims on banks, short-term claims on governments, commercial claims, long-term claims to money, equities, and so forth, in the order of their ability to be converted into currency or deposits rapidly and without risk of capital loss. The compilation of foreign exchange statistics involves selecting criteria for cutting these various scales, each at some point.

The statistics published in IFS result from cutting the three scales very unevenly, partly from choice, partly by following convention, and partly from the limitations of the available data. They include as foreign exchange claims in all *currencies*, whether convertible or inconvertible, and value each at its established parity. It would be very difficult to do otherwise since most reporting countries do not differentiate their holdings by currency. Moreover, sterling constitutes most of the inconvertible currency held as foreign exchange; and the nature of the restrictions imposed on sterling would make any classification into "available" and "non-available" most arbitrary. Nevertheless, the usefulness of the data is limited by the inclusion in a single total of currencies of all degrees of convertibility. The only *holders* included are the national monetary authorities. That is, the statistics include as foreign exchange only the holdings of central banks, stabilization funds, treasuries, and similar agencies, and exclude holdings of the other banks and of business and individuals. The choice of monetary policy or exchange restrictions as an alternative to the use of reserves lies with the monetary authorities, and it is their holdings that are primarily available for policy use. This restriction of the data may limit their usefulness since the larger the foreign exchange holdings of the other banks and of business and individuals throughout the world, the more the monetary authorities might be able to induce them to move in settlement of temporary imbalances through appropriate monetary policies. As regards the *form* of foreign claims, the statistics follow the traditional definition of foreign exchange except that they have been extended to include long-term foreign claims. If the holdings of the other banks or of business and individuals were included in the data, the inclusion of long-term foreign claims would not be reasonable. The monetary authorities, however, are not likely to hold long-term foreign securities solely for their income or solely for the prospect of their appreciation. It is mostly the sterling area countries whose central banks hold long-term foreign securities, and their holdings probably represent their decision to hold interest-bearing paper rather than non-interest-bearing deposits or low-interest-bearing treasury bills for some or all of their sterling which cannot be currently used. The inclusion of these investments is consistent with the inclusion of inconvertible currency holdings.

The second problem of foreign exchange statistics as a measure of a country's international liquidity involves the choice of net or gross statistics and the extent to which foreign exchange liabilities are an offset to foreign exchange assets. All of the foreign exchange data in IFS are reported gross insofar as possible, and liability statistics (also gross) are given for the United States and the United Kingdom only. One holder's foreign exchange asset, however, is necessarily another's foreign exchange liability. The world as a whole can have no net foreign exchange holdings.

It might seem, therefore, that data on foreign exchange should be reported net, with each country's foreign exchange liabilities deducted from its foreign exchange assets and with a world total of zero. A number of considerations, however, indicate that it is preferable to define foreign exchange for statistical purposes as gross.

Statistically, gross figures are more easily handled whenever more than one classification is required (e.g., by currency and by holder) for the same reasons that make gross national product a more useful measurement than national income. Conceptually, as in the analysis of banking data generally, the importance lies in the gross magnitudes of the different liabilities and assets, many of which are similar (a 30-day Treasury bill on the asset side and its counterpart of demand deposits on the liability side) and all of which would always net to zero.

Moreover, there are important nonparallelisms in foreign exchange assets and liabilities arising from (a) the fact that, while there are many classes of holders and obligors, the statistics measure only the assets and liabilities of the monetary authorities, and (b) the fact that, while it is intended to define foreign exchange assets and liabilities as claims on or to foreigners, records of some holders and debtors in some countries probably measure instead claims and obligations in foreign currency.

Statistics covering the net asset and liability accounts of the monetary authorities would not be the most useful net figure for the monetary authorities. Their gross assets are the only one of six items (the assets and liabilities of the monetary authorities, the assets and liabilities of the other banks, and the assets and liabilities of business and individuals) over which they have control, but it is they who, in the absence of exchange restrictions, are responsible to see that the economy meets all its foreign liabilities, including those of the banks and of business and individuals. Most of a country's foreign liabilities are obligations in national currency. For the obligor, whether official or private, meeting national currency obligations to foreigners is no more difficult than making payments to residents. But the problem of converting all such payments into foreign exchange must be met by the monetary authorities. The gross reserves of the monetary authorities are the principal means of assuring that their own and other obligations to foreigners can be met.

The net of all six accounts might provide a very useful figure, but information on private foreign exchange is insufficiently available to permit its calculation. Furthermore, the definition "claims against and obligations of foreigners" is probably not observed in the accounts of many of the private holders so that the true net figure would not be known even if all the accounts were consolidated.

A third problem in the compilation of foreign exchange statistics is that of accounting properly for the holdings and transactions of international agencies. Two of the international agencies (the Fund and the EPU) were established in part for the purpose of alleviating the reserve problems of their members. It would seem, therefore, that world reserve statistics should show an increase in the liquidity of members following the establishment of these agencies and should reflect their transactions in the accounts of the countries concerned in a clear and unambiguous manner. The complexities of the way the agencies operate and the differences in their methods of bookkeeping, however, make this impossible.

Members of the Fund make capital subscriptions to the Fund, partly in gold and partly in their national currencies. On this account the gold holdings of the members declined on the establishment of the Fund and the world's liquidity, measured as the sum of country statistics, declined. The Fund's holdings of gold and of the currencies of its members are, however, included in the world total. In this total the world's gold holdings remained unchanged on the establishment of the Fund, and the world's foreign exchange holdings rose by the sum of all members' subscriptions paid in member currencies. The members of the EPU, on the other hand, did not make subscription payments to the EPU, but agreed to finance through the EPU, and up to specified limits, their surpluses with other members. There are, therefore, no foreign exchange holdings (other than small amounts of dollars) to report as the holdings of the EPU, and the establishment of the EPU does not show an increase in the combined liquidity of its members. In fact, since pre-existing payments agreements balances were consolidated when the EPU was established, the figures would show a reduction in liquidity through the creation of the EPU.

The accounting of transactions is also different. Members of the EPU earning surpluses in their transactions with other members advance credits to the EPU and add the amount of the credit to their reported foreign exchange holdings. This is in some ways comparable to the manner in which the creditor would have kept his accounts if, in the absence of the EPU, the same transactions had occurred, financed by the debtor through reserves or foreign loans. The method of bookkeeping thus shows an increase in the liquidity of creditors, in the gross assets of Europe, and in the gross assets of the world which is larger the more the payments transactions of Europe are cumulatively unbalanced. The IFS table, based on accounts of members and reporting gross assets, shows the same increases for creditors, EPU countries as a whole, and the world when European payments transactions are unbalanced. In the case of Fund transactions, members whose currencies are drawn from the Fund obtain in effect a claim on the Fund in some respects similar to that which creditor countries of the EPU obtain on the EPU, but they do not add the item to their reported foreign exchange holdings. Hence, Fund transactions have no effect on the statistics of total foreign exchange holdings after the drawing country has spent the currency drawn from the Fund.

The reconciliation of reported data on foreign exchange holdings and foreign exchange liabilities

An attempt has been made to reconcile the foreign exchange data with the reported data on the foreign exchange liabilities of the United States, the United Kingdom, the European Payments Union, and the Bank for International Settlements. The results are presented in Table A, which shows the total gross foreign exchange assets of the world and of each of the monetary areas and compares with them the data on liabilities reported by the United States, the United Kingdom, EPU, and BIS. The difference is labeled "errors and omissions".

There are two principal disparities between the asset and liability data which, in addition to ordinary errors and omissions of many kinds, determine the size and sign of the "errors and omissions" line. Firstly, there are other currencies held and reported as foreign exchange but not reported in the liabilities section. Positive entries in the errors and omissions line may indicate the amounts of all such other currencies.

Secondly, the liability figures include some liabilities to other banks and to business and individuals, while the asset figures include official holdings only. All of the liability data published by the United Kingdom include liabilities to other banks and to business and individuals. Negative entries in the errors and omissions line may indicate the amounts of such liabilities.

The total of all U.S. liabilities to official agencies is available separately, so that this source of error is presumably excluded in the total world reconciliation. The figures as published by the United States, however, require two adjustments. For the year 1950 there is a large difference between the Bank of Canada's reported holdings of U.S. dollars and the U.S. reports of its liabilities to official agencies and banks in Canada.[10] Total U.S. liabilities were increased for 1950 by 619 million dollars to account for this difference. There is secondly a problem in the U.S. reports of liabilities to Japan. Japan publishes its official holdings of U.S. dollars. The amounts agree with U.S. reports of total liabilities to Japanese official agencies and banks, but apparently these amounts are included under liabilities to banks rather than under liabilities to official agencies in U.S. statistics.[11] Total U.S. liabilities to official agencies for all of the years shown have therefore been increased by the amount of Japanese reported official dollar holdings. This adjustment increases the reported U.S. liabilities to official agencies by 669 million dollars in 1952, or 15 per cent of the U.S. total.

In constructing the monetary area reconciliations, however, other problems arise in the data on U.S. liabilities. There are available from U.S. sources data by country for only the total of U.S. liabilities to official agencies and other banks for 1950 and later years, and only

---

[10] The difference presumably arose from Canadian purchases during 1950 of U.S. securities with original maturities slightly longer than one year. Cf. *Federal Reserve Bulletin*, March 1951, p. 232, in which Canadian holdings of U.S. securities with maturities up to 20 months are reported.

[11] "If reported private dollar balances are adjusted to exclude Japanese holdings (which are technically reported as private, though in reality of an official character). . . ." See *Federal Reserve Bulletin*, March 1952, p. 231.

Table A. Reconciliation of Gross Foreign Exchange Assets with
Foreign Exchange Liabilities
(In millions of U.S. dollars)

	1948	1949	1950	1951	1952
World Total[1]					
Total Gross Assets	13,300	10,250	12,900	12,350	12,350
Dollars[2]	2,917	3,071	4,507	4,062	5,133
Sterling[3]	1,478	7,856	8,163	7,870	6,506
Credit to EPU	—	—	402	665	1,077
Balances with BIS	52	108	250	192	364
Errors and omissions	−1,147	−785	−422	−439	−730
Canada					
Total Gross Assets	610	636	1,170	953	977
Dollars	596	631	1,162	937	975
Sterling	13	5	9	16	2
Errors and omissions	—	—	—	—	—
Latin America					
Dollar Countries					
Total Gross Assets	220	290	350	435	650
Dollars	285	359	360	405	607
Errors and omissions	−65	−69	−10	30	43
Non-Dollar Countries					
Total Gross Assets	1,229	820	825	595	525
Dollars	252	282	395	227	183
Sterling	544	224	126	160	17
Errors and omissions	433	314	304	208	325
Continental EPU Countries					
Total Gross Assets	1,905	2,045	2,720	3,030	3,450
Credit to EPU	—	—	177	665	1,077
Total Net Assets	1,905	2,045	2,543	2,365	2,373
Dollars	901	869	1,140	1,150	1,717
Sterling	1,491	1,229	1,106	1,145	899
Balances with BIS	52	108	250	192	364
Errors and omissions	−539	−161	47	−122	−607
United Kingdom					
Total Gross Assets	404	402	768	174	458
Dollars	251	338	400	135	346
Credit to EPU	—	—	225	—	—
Errors and omissions	153	64	143	39	112
Other Sterling Countries					
Total Gross Assets	6,404	4,138	4,747	4,428	3,800
Dollars	62	38	99	108	133
Sterling	7,290	4,959	5,544	5,110	4,488
Errors and omissions	−948	−859	−896	−790	−821
Rest of the World					
Total Gross Assets	2,540	1,910	2,335	2,720	2,455
Dollars	570	554	951	1,100	1,172
Sterling	2,140	1,439	1,378	1,439	1,100
Errors and omissions	−170	−83	6	181	183

[1] The monetary authorities of the United States hold no foreign exchange assets.
[2] Adjusted for Canadian and Japanese discrepancies. See text for details.
[3] Excluding U.K. liabilities to dependent areas and dollar countries other than to Bank of Canada.

the total of all U.S. liabilities including liabilities to business and individuals for earlier years. However, for five of the countries whose dollar holdings are especially important (Canada, Cuba, Japan, the Philippines, and the United Kingdom [12]), national figures on official holdings of U.S. dollars are available and were used. U.S. liabilities to the official agencies of other countries were therefore estimated by multiplying the liabilities to official agencies and banks of these countries (all liabilities prior to 1950) by an adjustment factor C/F calculated in the following way:

U.S. reported liabilities to all official holders plus adjustments for Canada and Japan	= A
Official holdings of dollars reported by Canada, Cuba, Japan, the Philippines, and the United Kingdom	= B
Estimated official holdings of dollars by other countries (A − B)	= C
U.S. reported liabilities to all official holders and banks (total holdings prior to 1950) plus adjustment for Canada in 1950	= D
U.S. reported liabilities to official holders and banks (total holdings prior to 1950) in Canada, Cuba, Japan, the Philippines, and the United Kingdom	= E
Liabilities to official holders and banks (total holdings prior to 1950) in other countries (D − E)	= F
Adjustment factor for estimation of official holdings of other countries	C/F

It is recognized that the table is not strictly a reconciliation table since in the cases discussed the same figures have been used on both sides of the reconciliation.

The reconciliation indicates that the basic data on foreign exchange are reasonably satisfactory and that most of the world's holdings of foreign exchange represent, as would be expected, the liabilities of either the United States or the United Kingdom. For the world as a whole, reported liabilities exceed reported assets by some 750 million dollars. This excess of liabilities over assets results from the inclusion in the liabilities data of sterling liabilities to banks, business, and individuals, and to the inclusion of both sterling and dollar liabilities to the Soviet bloc and a few small countries for which no assets data are reported. These amounts are offset in part by the inclusion in the assets data of holdings of currencies other than dollars and sterling. Some measure of the importance of sterling liabilities to nonofficial holders is given in the errors and omissions line for Other Sterling Countries. Since this entry alone exceeds the errors and omissions for the world total, it is apparent that holdings of other currencies play a small but significant role. Holdings of other currencies apparently play their largest role in the non-dollar countries of Latin America. The error arising from the inclusion in the liability data of liabilities to the Soviet bloc and other unreported countries is reflected largely in the Rest of the World figures insofar as sterling is concerned. The corresponding error for the dollar figures is distributed between most of the areas owing to the method of their calculation.

The reconciliation table also indicates that the problem of gross and net assets is not as serious as it might be since most of the foreign exchange holdings of the world represent the liabilities of only two countries, the United States and the United Kingdom, and these are almost entirely denominated in dollars or sterling (i.e., foreign currency from the holder's point of view). It follows from these facts that the net assets of the monetary authorities of most countries cannot be appreciably different from their gross assets, since if the monetary authorities of most countries had appreciable foreign liabilities the foreign assets of other countries would reflect them and lead to plus errors in the reconciliation table. And it follows directly from the facts that foreign exchange liabilities are largely claims against the United States and the United Kingdom and that these are largely denominated in dollars or sterling, that the statistics of foreign exchange of the monetary authorities must be approximately consistent with the definition "claims against foreigners" regardless of whether some countries use the definition "claims in foreign currency".

---

[12] The U.S. dollar holdings of the monetary authorities of the United Kingdom can be estimated by deducting the U.S. Federal Reserve Board's estimate of the U.K. gold holdings from the U.K. figure for gold and U.S. and Canadian dollar assets, on the assumption that Canadian dollar holdings are small.

International Reserves and Liquidity

In May 1957 South Africa requested that the staff should undertake a study of "the factors affecting the present state of international liquidity, including the world supply of monetary gold." References to a possible inadequacy of monetary reserves were made by a number of Governors during the Annual Meetings, 1957. A staff working party subsequently wrote a report on the subject, which was published on September 16, 1958. This was a staff document, prepared under the personal supervision of the Managing Director. It is reproduced below.

International Reserves and Liquidity
A Study by the Staff of the International Monetary Fund
(September 16, 1958)

CONTENTS

		PAGE
Chapter One:	Introduction	350
Chapter Two:	The Level and Composition of Reserves	357
Chapter Three:	The Adequacy of Individual Country Reserves	374
Chapter Four:	Prospective Reserves and Requirements	391
Chapter Five:	Summary and Conclusions	404

FOREWORD

In the course of 1957, and especially at the Annual Meeting in September of that year, several governments requested that the staff of the Fund prepare a study on international liquidity. This study has now been completed and is herewith published as a staff document; it does not necessarily represent the views of the Executive Directors.

An attempt has been made to review present problems in the light of past experience. The study takes account of very recent developments, and it has therefore fortunately been possible to consider the implications for international liquidity both of the extreme boom conditions of 1956–57 and of the subsequent recession. The consideration of the problems for the future has thus benefited from very recent experience in contrasting economic conditions.

PER JACOBSSON

Washington, D. C.
August 15, 1958

CHAPTER ONE: INTRODUCTION

The opportunity to examine afresh the question of international reserves and liquidity brings again to the attention of the staff of the Fund a number of problems which have, in varying degrees, attracted attention over many years. In one form or another, these problems have been discussed throughout the postwar period. In 1953, at the request of the Economic and Social Council of the United Nations, the Fund prepared an extensive report, "The Adequacy of Monetary Reserves."[1] Since 1956, as a number of countries have had to draw extensively on their reserves and to supplement their reserves by borrowing, even more demanding questions have been raised about the state of international liquidity. The most convenient introduction to these questions is through a consideration of the role of reserves and credit in international trade and payments.

Imports of goods and services are ultimately paid for with exports of goods and services, and any difference between imports and exports may be balanced by a movement of long-term or short-term capital. If a balance still remains, it is then paid with the country's own reserves or other cash holdings. The definition of international reserves must therefore be wide enough to include any kind of money which is acceptable in payment of foreign obligations. Reserves may consist of gold, dollars, and other convertible currencies, or of sterling, deutsche mark, and other currencies which are practically convertible. They may include inconvertible currencies when these are acceptable to particular trading partners. They may include balances due under payments agreements. In many cases, reserve assets are held not only by the official authorities but also by banks, business enterprises, and private individuals. Not infrequently, foreign obligations are met from private rather than from official holdings.

There is thus no unique definition of international reserves which is satisfactory for all purposes and for all countries. This makes the measurement of international reserves, and of changes in reserves from one period to another, peculiarly difficult. In fact, the measurement of reserves necessarily has qualitative as well as quantitative aspects.

Modern economic systems, moreover, operate on credit. Domestically, this takes the form of bank loans and overdrafts, consumer credit, and trade credit. Internationally, private credits may be obtained to finance imports and exports, and public credits may be obtained by one country from banks in, or governments of, other countries as well as from international organizations, such as the International Monetary Fund. As with individuals and business enterprises, the ability of a country (or of individuals in a country) to make payments depends not only upon the amount of cash in hand and the expected receipts of cash in the near future but also to some extent upon the ability to borrow on either short term or long term.

Thus, in appraising the adequacy of international reserves and the degree of international liquidity, account must be taken not only of all kinds of reserve holdings, public and private, but also of the credit-worthiness of countries and the ability of the international financial mechanism to extend credit under proper safeguards in good times and bad. In addition, the adequacy of reserves and the degree of liquidity depend upon the international environment, including, for example, the appropriateness of the structure of exchange rates, the extent to which balance prevails in international trade, and the presence or absence of that intangible, "confidence." There is nothing unique or new in this recital of the elements that combine and recombine to create any given

---
[1] See above, p. 311.

degree of international liquidity. For this reason, it is useful to approach the current problem of international reserves and liquidity in the perspective of the past.

During the heyday of the gold standard, immediately before the outbreak of World War I, monetary specialists were also concerned with the problems of the proper size, the distribution, and the rate of growth of international reserves. At that time, too, conflicting views were expressed. It would fall outside the scope of this inquiry to review those old controversies, which in many ways applied to conditions very different from those prevailing today. It is, however, certainly relevant to recall that at that time many countries, and particularly the United Kingdom, held reserves which seem to us now to have been astonishingly slender compared with the volume of trade and other transactions.

There are a number of reasons why this system operated as smoothly as it did in the generation preceding World War I. These reasons throw some light upon the present situation. In the first place, balance prevailed in international payments and economic relationships to a greater extent than has since been true for any extended period. The major use and need for reserves arise when balance is upset; the presence of economic balance and the feeling that balance will be maintained are perhaps more important than the actual size of reserves in creating a feeling that they are adequate. Moreover, day-to-day disturbances, and even seasonal movements, of international payments need make no great demands upon reserves when credits of various kinds can be arranged. There were widespread and effective facilities for granting credits in London and other centers. These facilities were available to governments and other official agencies as well as to overseas banks and foreign traders. London was responsible for the greater part of this financing, which not only supplemented international liquidity in a very important way but also gave London large sight claims on firms and banks in other countries. Changes in the amount of these claims, effected by means of changes in Bank Rate, buttressed with large long-term overseas investments, provided adequate supplements to London's slim gold reserves. There was widespread acceptance of the gold standard system, and of stable exchange rates within it, as the only desirable monetary system. This implied, as far as individual countries were concerned, clear and agreed objectives for monetary policy and for fiscal policy, and the latter was less important then than now because the role of government was much smaller. For these and other reasons, a large degree of confidence prevailed.

In the years immediately preceding the outbreak of World War I, London was the leading financial center. Other centers were secondary and of markedly less importance. After the war, this situation changed and New York emerged as an important international center alongside of London. This development had important implications for the financing of world trade and for the movement of funds. It may well be that a multicentered world can function as well as a one-centered world in periods of calm, but in periods of stress, it is subject to wide and sweeping movements. Such movements may create severe strains in the financial structure. Developments since 1946 have further increased the importance of New York as a financial center but have by no means given New York the same importance relative to London and other financial centers that London before 1914 had relative to all other centers.

The development of the institutions and arrangements that created operating smoothness and stability before 1914 required both time and a favorable environment. The last important war in Europe had taken place in 1870–71. In comparison with twentieth century experience, neither this war nor any of the subsequent smaller wars involved any large economic dislocation. There were some conflicts outside Europe but, again, these were short and relatively small. Looking backward, we can see that in this general environment the shocks to the economic system were much smaller than they have been since 1914.

It is, however, easy to overestimate the stability and the long duration of the international financial structure that existed immediately before World War I and, by contrast, to underestimate the characteristics of the system that has gradually developed in the postwar period. Though it is customary to refer to the second half of the nineteenth century as "the golden age of the gold standard," this overstates the case. The United Kingdom was on a gold standard as early as 1819, but the other countries of Western Europe and the United States were not until the 1870's. With a few exceptions, all other countries at that time had either a silver standard or an inconvertible currency. Since the price of silver was falling, the exchange value of all silver standard currencies was depreciating. The variations in the exchange rates of silver standard and inconvertible (flexible rate) currencies were astonishingly large, even when measured against recent developments.

Measured in terms of the number of countries involved, the last half of the nineteenth century was a period of considerable monetary change, with many devaluations, inconvertible currencies, and floating rates. Measured in terms of their importance to world trade, however, there was a solid core of countries on gold after the 1870's. These countries not only set the goal for monetary developments in all other countries, but they accounted for perhaps 70 per cent of the world's exports. Toward the end of the century, the gold standard was adopted by more and more countries: by Austria-Hungary in 1892; Russia and Japan in 1897; India in 1899; and Mexico in 1904.

Also of interest is the fact that, especially in the early years of the period, there was concern from time to time that the world's reserves of gold or silver or both were inadequate. There were also many criticisms (in the United Kingdom) that British reserves—that "thin film of gold"—were inadequate, and the reason often given for this state of affairs was that the Bank of England, as a private concern, was unwilling to tie up the necessary amount of assets in nonincome-earning form. To be sure, these criticisms decreased toward the end of the prewar period, as the United Kingdom acquired larger holdings of long-term and short-term investments, while the Bank of England developed increasingly effective techniques for dealing with monetary and exchange rate problems. It is not without interest, furthermore, that, from 1900 until 1913, in the face of large increases in trade, the gold holdings of the Bank of England increased by scarcely 10 per cent, so that the ratio of gold reserves to imports fell from 7 per cent to 5 per cent. For the world as a whole, the gold situation was greatly eased after 1890 by increases in gold output, especially in the Transvaal; and indeed, in some academic circles, the question was raised after the turn of the century whether gold production might not become too abundant.

Prices rose during World War I, and in the course of the 1920's they settled down to a level which, on a gold basis, was about 50 per cent higher than in prewar years. There was consequently an increase in the value of world trade, and the question soon arose whether the available reserves would be sufficient in view of these changed circumstances. Some feared the emergence of a gold shortage, and proposals were put forward to guard against it. This question was one of the main subjects of deliberation at the Genoa Conference in 1921, and it continued to be discussed in the 1920's. As a matter of fact, the ratio of reserves to the value of trade at the beginning of the

1920's was higher than it had been in 1913, in part because of the incorporation into official reserves of gold previously in circulation.

It will be remembered that the resolutions of the Genoa Conference recommended, on the one hand, wider use of the gold exchange standard and, on the other, establishment of central banks in all developed countries. Both of these recommendations were realized. Exchange holdings were increasingly used as official reserves in the 1920's. Though exchange holdings were reduced to very low levels in the 1930's, they became, during and after World War II, a reserves component on a scale never anticipated in 1921 (for further discussion of this point, see Chapter II). Central banks have also been established in the large majority of countries, developed as well as underdeveloped, though it must be admitted that their full potentialities for stability and development have not been achieved in all cases.

For some years after 1921, it seemed that the new system could be made to work effectively. Within a very few years, one country after another stabilized its currency under conditions of full convertibility. There were, however, many deep-seated elements of maladjustment. Some were a consequence of the war, and certain additional ones emerged in the postwar period. With the aid of hindsight, it is clear that these maladjustments were not solely or even largely of financial origin and that they could not have been solved by financial means. In some respects financial decisions were helpful, but in other respects they contributed new elements of disequilibrium. Exchange rates used in currency stabilizations were not always set at the most appropriate levels. Sterling was stabilized at an ambitiously high rate in relation to gold, and the French franc was later set at too low a rate. Reserves were generally increased in the European countries but, in many cases, they were borrowed instead of being acquired with national savings. They were sometimes borrowed on short term and pyramided from country to country, making the situation even more unstable. Unfortunately, at that time, these and other developments could not be effectively measured because of the inadequacy of the statistics then available.

The hopes entertained for the successful re-establishment of a stable and growing international financial system were frustrated by the maladjustments of the 1920's and finally shattered by the Great Depression and the devaluations of 1931–34. Three main conclusions can be drawn from this experience. The first is that considerable time and much effort are needed to restore a proper balance after a major war has caused widespread economic dislocation, inflation, and currency upheaval. The second is that when stabilization is attempted the exchange rate chosen must be appropriate and realistic, and if the rate is found to be incorrect prompt correction is necessary. The third is that once a crack starts in the exchange structure it is difficult to limit its effects. It may lead to the forced devaluation of major currencies—devaluations not dictated by the realities of foreign trade and competitive prices. Such a crack may start with a relatively minor currency, and yet gain such momentum that it ultimately sunders the whole international exchange structure. Thus, in the period between the two world wars, the failure of the Credit Anstalt in Vienna in 1931 led not only to considerable difficulties in the German banking structure but also to the devaluation of sterling and other currencies in the same year, and ultimately to the devaluation of the dollar in 1934 and of the gold bloc currencies in 1936.

After the devaluations of the 1930's, the world's financial system became increasingly fragmented. Although many countries maintained stable exchange rates in relation to the dollar, whose gold content was officially changed in 1934, and others maintained stable exchange rates through the sterling area, which was then more extensive than it is today, the dollar-sterling rate fluctuated. There was increased resort to trade restrictions, multiple currency practices, bilateral arrangements, and autarky. Closer examination of developments up to the outbreak of World War II suggests that there was a deterioration in the fundamental monetary position of parts of the sterling area, and that in general there were more difficulties in the day-to-day operations of foreign exchange markets than is often supposed. Growing political difficulties, in both Europe and the Far East, caused massive flights of capital, in large part to the United States. These took place on a scale much larger than before 1914, and from time to time they tended to gain a momentum of their own. Central banks and monetary authorities found it more difficult to know when and how to take a stand. Long-term capital movements dried up. Confidence decreased sharply—and there was good reason why this should have been the case. The basic conception of a *world* economy lost meaning, and the idea of separate, disconnected economies gained force.

World reserves increased sharply in the 1930's, and the ratio of reserves to trade reached all-time highs. A number of factors were responsible for this development. The value of all gold stocks was raised in 1934 when the price of gold was increased. The production of gold was stimulated by the falling prices and unemployment of the depression and further stimulated by the higher price of gold. On the other hand, both the value and the volume of trade decreased. Even in 1937, when there had been a substantial, though in no way complete, recovery from the depression, the ratio of gold and exchange reserves to trade for all countries other than the United States was 63 per cent, in comparison with 35 per cent in 1928 and 17 per cent in 1913. The world had very large reserves, but it was troubled by the inability of leading countries to restore balance in their internal economies and, for some of them, also in their foreign trade relations.

The ratio of reserves to trade is discussed in Chapter II of this report, where the data for the postwar years are analyzed and compared with those for 1937–38, as well as 1928 and 1913. One general conclusion that must be drawn from this discussion is that the adequacy of international reserves cannot be judged in a vacuum and that adequacy is not a simple matter of arithmetical relationship. The adequacy of reserves is always related to the degree of efficiency of the prevailing international credit system, and it is affected by the realism of the existing pattern of exchange rates and by the appropriateness of domestic monetary and fiscal policies.

To the creaking and disorganized international financial and economic mechanism of the 1930's, World War II added inflation, unparalleled destruction and economic dislocation, and sweeping changes in debtor-creditor positions.

While World War II was still being waged, ideas were put forward for a better monetary system. The principal objectives, once again, were to restore a properly working international monetary system with convertible currencies and with safeguards for the maintenance of exchange stability; to encourage a healthy and free flow of world trade; and to ensure financial assistance to individual countries to enable them to correct maladjustments without resorting to measures destructive of national or international prosperity. After much discussion, these main ideas were embodied in the Articles of Agreement of the International Monetary Fund. It was recognized, however, that special problems of adjustment would arise in what was called a "transitional period" and that certain existing restrictions would have to be permitted for part or all of this period.

Peace in 1945 brought problems of economic and financial reconstruction of unparalleled magnitude. There was actual inflation in practically all countries. There were accumulated shortages of consumer goods, of capital goods, and of working inventories at all levels of production. In most of Europe, there were the additional huge requirements growing out of wartime destruction and decapitalization. An enormous amount of investment was required to start an increase of production and then to raise it to high and efficient levels within a reasonable period of time. Domestic savings were generally not adequate to this task; consequently, there was an acute shortage of savings that tempted countries to rely excessively on credit creation, which contributed further to the inflationary pressure. As a matter of fact, the major part of the capital goods and working inventories required for these purposes could be obtained in large measure only from the United States. For Europe, these difficulties came to a head in 1947, when conditions were aggravated by widespread crop failures due to a very cold winter and a very dry summer. It was then that large-scale aid on a broad and imaginative scale was inaugurated by the announcement and implementation of the Marshall Plan.

Since the end of World War II, a large and growing supply of dollars, arising out of a steadily expanding volume of U.S. imports and payments for overseas services, capital exports, and aid, has been the dominant element in improving international liquidity. The European Payments Union (EPU) has provided additional liquidity by making it possible for intra-European payments to be settled partly in credits granted by the creditor members. The Fund made a substantial amount of resources available before the Marshall Plan went into effect. Subsequently, the countries that obtained Marshall Plan aid had no need to turn to the Fund, while the British Commonwealth countries were able to make use of the substantial sterling balances they had accumulated during the war, and many Latin American countries drew down dollar balances accumulated during the same period. At the beginning of the postwar period, the private credit system could not be relied upon to provide the required amount of commercial credit to finance international trade, but as time passed it began to play an increasingly important supplementary role. Gradually, and at times almost imperceptibly, there was a simplification of many exchange rate structures, and a reduction in restrictions and bilateralism.

In respect of international reserves and liquidity, there have been a number of developments. First, reserves of countries other than the United States increased from $22 billion at the end of 1948 to $30 billion at the end of 1957. The EPU countries as a group, which had had very low reserves at the end of 1948, substantially increased their holdings of gold and dollars, while a number of other countries that had accumulated large holdings of sterling or dollars during the war reduced their reserves. Most countries were able to show some improvement, but the improvement was distinctly uneven. The increases in reserves took place in those countries which invested part of their net savings in gold or exchange rather than in capital goods at home or in securities or businesses abroad. In fact, reserves can be increased only by applying to that end otherwise uncommitted savings, and the importance of having uncommitted savings is a matter to which further reference will be made in this study. Secondly, the methods whereby total reserves have been increased have been sound, and there has been no deterioration in the quality of reserves. As distinguished from the 1920's, reserves have, on the whole, not been borrowed, either on long term or (what is still more dangerous) on short term. On the contrary, the increase has resulted principally from saving part of the receipts arising from trade and from aid. There has been little if any of the international pyramiding of credit so characteristic of the 1920's. With the major exception of 1957, there have been few of the movements of "hot money" so feared in the 1930's, though changes in "leads and lags" have at times exerted strong speculative pressure, especially against sterling. Some countries have drawn down their sterling or dollar balances, but this was done largely to pay for imports. Thirdly, the gold holdings of the United States have been reduced by more than $3 billion since 1949, which meant the reversal of a trend that had gone on, with a few short exceptions, for at least two generations. In addition, there have been large increases in both private and official holdings of dollars by foreigners. The increases in official holdings are included in statistics on international reserves, but the increases in private holdings, which also add to international liquidity, are not. In fact, since 1948 there has been a distinct improvement in the distribution of the world's reserves of gold, and an even greater improvement in the distribution of the world's reserves of gold and foreign exchange. The scope and significance of this redistribution can be appreciated only by reference to the writings of the 1920's and 1930's, which treated any movement of reserves to the United States as sterilized and irreversible.

The healthy and balanced growth of world trade depends upon adequate and rising reserves and an efficient international credit system, both private and official.

The level of reserves influences the domestic volume of money and credit, while gains and losses of reserves are one of the most important indications of the state of balance of the domestic economy in relation to the economies of other countries. In the days of the gold standard, gold circulated as coin and, through cover percentages, determined the volume of credit money in a manner that was largely automatic. These links between gold and money are now much weaker, and monetary management plays a much larger role. This is true for two reasons. First, holdings of exchange, largely dollars and sterling, are a very important supplement to gold as a reserve against both the domestic money supply and fluctuations in the balance of payments. The growth of reserves now depends not only upon the additions to the stock of monetary gold from new production and dishoarding but also upon the additions to the world's holdings of dollars, sterling, and other currencies. These additions depend, in turn, upon the creation of domestic money by the United States and other countries, and upon the willingness of the rest of the world to hold reserve assets in this form. The ability of countries to create exchange liabilities, whether by reason of large gold reserves or other factors, has been, and will continue to be, very important in increasing world liquidity. Secondly, the relationship between reserves of gold and exchange and the volume of domestic money, although still influenced by the amount of international reserves, is within broad limits largely determined by monetary management. This management is less a question of the cover percentages, which still form part of the monetary legislation of many countries, than of a proper appreciation by the monetary authorities of the limits to the permissible supply of credit which are suggested by reserve movements. Changes in reserves are one of the factors which the monetary authorities must consider in judging the measures required to maintain the exchange rates and the international positions of their countries.

Total international reserves have grown, and the total has become more effective through redistribution since the percentage of total reserves held by the United States has fallen. The system of international credit has been strengthened unobtrusively but steadily during the postwar period. Private commercial credit is now more readily available to finance the movement of trade. The role of the Fund as a second line of monetary reserves has become increasingly important. On the other hand, from 1947 to 1957, the value of world trade increased by 110 per cent, and its volume by 90 per cent. The prices of goods traded internationally increased by 140 per cent between 1937 and 1957. There have been a number of monetary crises in the postwar period; sterling and other major European currencies are still not legally convertible; and many countries still employ multiple currency practices and exchange restrictions. For these and other reasons, there have been questions about the adequacy of reserves from the standpoint of both their total and their distribution, and about the appropriateness of the system of international credit, with account taken of the existing level of reserves.

CHAPTER TWO: THE LEVEL AND COMPOSITION OF RESERVES

Before examining the question of the amount of reserves that may be considered adequate for any individual country, it is of interest to review the level and composition of reserves as they are at present, together with comparable figures for previous years.

Changes in Total Reserves

International reserves are here taken to be a country's official holdings of gold, dollars, sterling, and other foreign exchange assets on a gross basis, i.e., without taking account of short-term liabilities that might be considered to be offsetting This is the most usual and at the same time the most practicable definition of international reserves, and the only one that can be used to deal with many countries over extended periods of time. Within its limits this definition makes possible greater precision in comparison than any other. For certain purposes, and for certain countries, a broader treatment of international assets and Liabilities is desirable and is therefore also used in this report. Private—or better, nonofficial—holdings of gold, dollars, sterling, and other currencies are a supplement to official holdings and in some cases are a substitute for them. Furthermore, the line between short-term and long-term assets is indistinct and shifting, and the conventional distinctions may not be appropriate in all cases. On the other hand, if account is to be taken of short-term liabilities, there is the difficulty of defining exactly what kind of short-term liabilities should properly be regarded as offsetting particular kinds of assets. The liabilities may be those of the central bank, the banking system, or the economy as a whole. Against some of these liabilities there are, in turn, short-term assets which are not included in official reserves, e.g., liabilities of foreigners on account of discounted acceptances. It is for these reasons that general and historical discussions of reserves use figures on a gross basis but introduce additional figures to deal with certain specific countries or problems.

At the end of 1957 the world's stock of monetary gold, as shown in Table 1, was valued at $38.6 billion, of which $37.0 billion was held by countries and $1.6 billion by international organizations—principally the International Monetary Fund. Country reserves in the form of official exchange were $15.9 billion, so that total country reserves of gold and foreign exchange came to $52.9 billion. As may be seen from the table, the figures for 1957 constituted all-time highs. Country reserves by themselves, excluding reserves held by international organizations, are at present twelve times as high as in 1913, four times as high as in 1928, and nearly twice as high as in 1937–38. The dollar value of reserves declined in 1949, largely because of the devaluation of sterling; it also declined slightly in 1950–51, during the Korean crisis. However, since 1951 there has again been an uninterrupted increase in total world reserves.

It is estimated that in 1913, in addition to official reserves shown in Table 1, there was about $3.6 billion of gold in circulation. This gold was very largely absorbed by monetary reserves during and after World War I. By 1928, monetary gold not included in reserves is estimated to have been less than 10 per cent of the amount held in reserves. In the period before World War I, gold held outside reserves served an important function as a medium of circulation and of hoarding, but it had little importance as a means of settling deficits in the balance of payments. Nevertheless, even if the amounts of gold held outside reserves were added to the reserve figures for 1913 and 1928, the present official reserves of gold and foreign exchange would be more than six times as large as those in 1913, and nearly four times as large as those in 1928. (On the other

Table 1. Gold and Exchange Reserves of Countries and International Organizations, Selected Years, 1913-57 [1]

(In billions of U.S. dollars)

Year	Countries			International Organizations			Total		
	Gold (1)	Exchange (2)	Total (1)+(2) (3)	Gold (4)	Exchange (5)	Total (4)+(5) (6)	Gold (1)+(4) (7)	Gold and country exchange reserves (7)+(2) (8)	Gold and all exchange reserves (3)+(6) (9)
1913	4.0	0.5[2]	4.5	—	—	—	4.0	4.5	4.5
1928	9.8	3.1	12.9	—	—	—	9.8	12.9	12.9
1937	25.3	2.4	27.7	—	—	—	25.3	27.7	27.7
1938	26.0	1.8	27.8	—	—	—	26.0	27.8	27.8
1948	32.8	13.4	46.2	1.5	5.5	7.0	34.3	47.7	53.2
1949	33.2	10.5	43.7	1.5	5.7	7.2	34.7	45.2	50.9
1950	33.6	13.6	47.2	1.7	6.1	7.8	35.3	48.9	55.0
1951	33.6	12.9	46.5	1.7	6.0	7.7	35.3	48.2	54.2
1952	33.6	13.2	46.8	2.0	6.1	8.1	35.6	48.8	54.9
1953	33.9	14.1	48.0	2.0	6.8	8.8	35.9	50.0	56.8
1954	34.4	15.1	49.5	2.1	6.9	9.0	36.5	51.6	58.5
1955	35.0	15.6	50.6	2.3	6.5	8.8	37.3	52.9	59.4
1956	35.6	16.2	51.8	2.1	6.8	8.9	37.7	53.9	60.7
1957	37.0	15.9	52.9	1.6	7.6	9.2	38.6	54.5	62.1

Sources: For 1937 and 1950-57, *International Financial Statistics (IFS)*, June 1958; for 1928, "The Adequacy of Monetary Reserves," *Staff Papers*, Vol. III, No. 2 (October 1953), pp. 181-227; for 1913, *Banking and Monetary Statistics* (Board of Governors of the Federal Reserve System, 1943), Table 160; for 1938, *IFS*, December 1954; for 1948, *IFS*, February 1958; for 1949, *IFS*, August 1955. Data exclude countries in the Soviet bloc.

[1] Gold is valued at $20.67 per ounce prior to 1934 and at $35 an ounce thereafter.

[2] Estimate. The Bank for International Settlements estimated exchange holdings as "at least $400 million and at most $600 million" (*The Gold Exchange Standard* [1932]). According to another estimate, exchange holdings prior to World War I were $300 million [Felix Mlynarski, *The Functioning of the Gold Standard* (League of Nations, A Memorandum Submitted to the Gold Delegation of the Financial Committee, 1931), p. 10].

hand, there are at the present time large holdings of gold and exchange outside of official reserves. Nonofficial holdings of gold are probably of the order of $10–12 billion, and nonofficial holdings of dollars and sterling may come to $7–8 billion. These are equal to at least one third of official country reserves of gold and exchange at the end of 1957. Moreover, all of those private holdings are owned outside the United States, so that it is more appropriate to compare them with the official reserves of those countries. For all countries excluding the United States, nonofficial holdings of gold, dollars, and sterling are equal to at least 60 per cent of their official reserves.)

All of these data on reserves are expressed in current dollars. For this reason, there was a substantial increase in gold reserves where the gold content of the dollar was reduced by 40 per cent in 1934. On the other hand, there have been decreases in the value of reserve holdings of sterling and other currencies because of devaluations against the dollar.

More attention will be given later in this chapter to the role of exchange holdings, when the question of the composition of reserves is examined. For the moment, it is sufficient to say that these holdings became more important in the 1920's, but that this development was not always sound, since the increases were to a large extent the counterpart of short-term borrowings. Reserve holdings of exchange fell sharply after 1929, but then recovered somewhat in the middle 1930's. After World War II, they reached an unprecedentedly high figure, reflecting the accumulation of net current earnings by many countries during the war. In contrast to the 1920's, they therefore were really "owned" by the countries holding them. By the end of 1957, these holdings represented nearly one third of total country reserves.

Under existing legislation in most countries, gold and foreign exchange reserves are held as cover for notes and other central bank liabilities. But at the same time, of course, they serve as a means of settling balances that arise in relation to other countries. Foreign trade is the largest item in the balance of payments of the various countries. It is therefore natural that in the first place reserves should be compared with a country's trade figures. Table 2 shows the ratio of gold and foreign exchange reserves to imports of all but the communist countries for the years 1913, 1928, 1937, 1938, 1948, and 1950 to 1957. Because of the large size of the U.S. gold holdings, both absolutely and in relation to U.S. imports, the table also shows the figures for all countries other than the United States (and other than the communist countries).

In the following paragraphs, the terms "all countries" and "the world as a whole" will be taken to exclude the communist bloc countries. It will be seen that for the world as a whole gold and exchange reserves in 1957 were equal to 49 per cent of imports, compared with 21 per cent in 1913 and 42 per cent in 1928. On the other hand, the high ratio of reserves to imports in 1937–38, when it averaged about 109 per cent, was due largely to the increase in the price of gold in 1934 and to the shrunken volume of world trade in those years. For the years after World War II, it may be noted that the amounts held by international organizations can be considered as increasing international liquidity. For the world as a whole, the addition of these amounts to official country reserves in 1957 would increase the ratio of reserves to imports in that year from 49 per cent to 51 per cent. This difference in ratios is, of course, very small, but it understates the importance of these organizations for international liquidity. No similar adjustment is required for the prewar figures, because such organizations either did not exist or played only a minor role.

When the United States is excluded, some significant differences emerge, although the relationship between the various years remains broadly the same. On this basis, the ratio of gold and foreign exchange to imports in 1957 was 32 per cent, compared with 17 per cent in 1913, 35 per cent in 1928, and 63 per cent in 1937–38. Again, if gold holdings of international organizations are included, the 1957 figure is raised to 34 per cent, while the others remain the same. The present ratio is therefore about twice as high as in 1913, about equal to that of 1928, and still significantly lower than in 1937–38. These are obviously key years, and insofar as historical comparison may be of value, they are the years which, together with the period since 1951, have to be examined in greater detail.

Reserves and Trade in 1913

Comparisons with a period as far back as 1913—more than two generations from the present time—must of course be made circumspectly because of the many fundamental changes that have taken place in the meantime. Even so, an understanding of

Table 2. Ratio of Reserves to Imports, All Countries Excluding the Communist Bloc, Selected Years, 1913-57

Year	Imports (billion dollars)	Countries		Countries and International Organizations	
		Gold as per cent of imports	Gold and exchange as per cent of imports[1]	Gold as per cent of imports	Gold and exchange as per cent of imports[1]
World					
1913	21.0	19	21	19	21
1928	30.6	32	42	32	42
1937	27.3	93	101	93	101
1938	23.6	110	117	110	117
1948	60.0	55	77	57	80
1950	59.3	57	80	60	82
1951	81.4	41	57	43	59
1952	80.2	42	58	44	61
1954	79.6	43	62	46	65
1955	89.0	39	57	42	59
1956	98.1	36	53	38	55
1957	107.0	35	49	35	51
World Excluding the United States					
1913	19.2	14	17	14	17
1928	26.2	23	35	23	35
1937	23.7	53	63	53	63
1938	21.1	54	63	54	63
1948	52.0	16	42	19	45
1950	49.7	22	49	25	52
1951	69.5	15	34	18	36
1952	68.5	15	34	18	37
1954	68.6	18	40	21	43
1955	76.6	17	38	20	41
1956	84.4	16	35	18	38
1957	92.8	15	32	16	34

Sources: For imports—1913, *Industrialization and Foreign Trade* (League of Nations, 1945), pp. 157-67; 1928, "The Adequacy of Monetary Reserves," *Staff Papers*, Vol. III, No. 2 October 1953), pp. 181-227; 1938, *International Financial Statistics (IFS)*, August 1955; 1948, *IFS*, February 1958; 1937 and 1950-57, *IFS*, June 1958. For reserves—1913, *Banking and Monetary Statistics* (Board of Governors of the Federal Reserve System, 1943); 1928, "The Adequacy of Monetary Reserves," *op. cit.*; 1938, *IFS*, December 1954; 1948, *IFS*, February 1958; 1937 and 1950-57, *IFS*, June 1958. Gold is valued in 1913 and 1928 at $20.67 per ounce.

[1] Exchange refers to exchange reserve holdings of countries and does not include those of international agencies.

the situation that prevailed during this period may be instructive in many respects. In 1913, for the world excluding the United States, gold reserves were equal to 14 per cent of imports, and gold and exchange reserves to 17 per cent of imports. Even if gold in circulation is included, the ratios are much lower than for the years 1928, 1937–38, or indeed for 1957.[1] By the standards of these more recent years, reserves were so low in 1913 that it now seems difficult to imagine how they were considered adequate at the time.

The figures for the United Kingdom are especially striking, the ratio of reserves to imports in 1913 amounting to only 5.3 per cent (Table 3). Before World War I, however, the United Kingdom had very substantial support for its reserves in the form of

Table 3. Ratio of Reserves to Imports, Eight European Countries, 1913 and 1928

Country	1913[1] Gold as per cent of imports	1928 Gold as per cent of imports	1928 Gold and exchange as per cent of imports
Denmark	9.4	10	17
France	41.7	60	12
Germany	10.8	19	23
Italy	37.7	23	50
Netherlands	3.8	16	24
Sweden	12.0	14	26
Switzerland	8.3	20	30
United Kingdom	5.3	13	13

Sources: For 1913, Felix Mlynarski, *Gold and Central Banks* (1929), p. 117; for 1928, "The Adequacy of Monetary Reserves," *Staff Papers*, Vol. III, No. 2 (October 1953), pp. 206-7.

[1] Total gold reserves of these countries were about $1.6 billion. All of them had exchange reserves except the United Kingdom. The world total of exchange reserves was perhaps $300-600 million. If these countries owned all of this—which is most unlikely—the percentage of reserves to imports for all of them could, at most, have been from one fifth to one third greater.

short-term bills discounted in London, payable by countries all over the world. For example, after the outbreak of hostilities in 1914 many of these bills were called in, with the result that even in the autumn of that difficult year the pound was particularly strong in relation to other currencies, including the dollar.[2]

---

[1] If the countries now in the communist bloc are excluded, gold reserves of all countries were $4.0 billion in 1913 and monetary gold not included in reserves was $3.6 billion. If the United States is also excluded, country gold reserves were $2.7 billion and monetary gold not included in reserves was $2.9 billion. By 1928, monetary gold not included in reserves was less than 10 per cent of the amount held in reserve. See League of Nations, *Interim Report of the Gold Delegation* (1930), Annex XIII, "Gold: Demand and Supply," by A. Loveday, Appendix II.

[2] Writing in 1931, the Committee on Finance and Industry (Macmillan Committee) explained the strong prewar situation of the United Kingdom as follows: (1) London was then by far the most powerful financial center in the world and had sight claims on the rest of the world much greater than those of the world on her and could thus by the operation of her Bank Rate immediately adjust her reserve position. (2) The liquid resources held by foreigners in London and in secondary financial centers were relatively small. In contrast they were large in the 1920's. *Report* (1931), pp. 124–26.

The ratio of gold and exchange reserves to imports was higher in 1928 than in 1913, not only for the United Kingdom but also for each of the seven other European countries shown in Table 3. Some of the reasons for the stability and relatively efficient working of the international monetary system before World War I were outlined in the introduction to this study, but it is useful to analyze them here in greater detail:

(1) The economies of the various countries, after a long period of peace, were in relatively good balance in relation to one another at the existing rates of exchange.

(2) If an imbalance occurred, the authorities and the public were prepared to apply strong monetary and fiscal measures to re-establish the appropriate equilibrium. Changes in official discount rates had undoubtedly a considerable effect when, as at that time, the public sector was relatively limited, rarely representing as much as 10 per cent of the economy, compared with 15 per cent to 25 per cent at present. In other ways, too, there were fewer obstacles in the pre-1914 system to making the changes required to restore equilibrium.

(3) The strain of seasonal and other imbalances rarely fell wholly on official reserves. A large part was carried by the international credit system. There was unquestioned confidence in sterling, whose gold convertibility dated back to 1819. There was great confidence in the stability of the other major currencies, which were almost all convertible at the existing rates of exchange. London was by far the most important money market in the world for both long-term and short-term capital. Particularly from the point of view of providing short-term credit, this was a one-centered world. As such, it was inherently more stable than the multicentered world that developed after World War I. Under these conditions, changes in interest rates could be counted upon to bring about equilibrating movements of funds fairly rapidly. In particular, an increase in the London rate could rapidly strengthen sterling by shifting financing to other centers and by stimulating repayment by foreigners of the large amount of outstanding current liabilities. Indeed, the stability of currencies was taken so much for granted that in the years 1919–22 it took a great deal to destroy confidence even in currencies that were affected by violent inflation.

(4) The leading monetary nation—the United Kingdom—was a free trade country. The commercial policies of other countries were generally stable, and many countries were tied together by commercial treaties containing most-favored-nation clauses. The result was that in a depression the deficit countries did not have to face the additional difficulty of increased barriers to trade.

(5) Gold production was large enough to provide the resources for a more or less regular increase in reserves and to give an impetus to an expansion in the volume of credit. This was particularly important at the time when, through the operation of cover percentages and in other ways, the internal credit policy of the various countries was largely tied to changes in the gold reserves. The general opinion was that the gold supply was abundant and that reserves were adequate.[3]

Reserves and Trade in 1928

While there had been a great deal of discussion in the 1920's about a possible gold shortage, and steps had been taken to economize gold, 1928 was still a year of great optimism. World trade was increasing, the gold standard was being re-established in more and more countries, efforts were being made to settle the reparations problem

---

[3] Cassel, *Theory of Social Economy* (1924), p. 453; Kitchin, in *Interim Report of the Gold Delegation* (1930), Appendix XI, p. 82.

permanently, and prices had remained relatively stable for several years. Indeed, there were many who held the view that the financial structure had been soundly re-established, and that the world could look forward to years of expanding production and trade under conditions of general prosperity and rising standards of living.

These hopes were soon disappointed. In retrospect, we are able to see more clearly the many maladjustments which before long made themselves felt. While it cannot be said that there is any general agreement about the causes of the Great Depression and their relative importance, there is much support for the view that the boom of 1927–29, which was not in itself exceptional, was followed in 1930 by what could well have been a more or less normal reaction. It was, however, when business activity began to decline that the existing maladjustments, together with the results of mistaken policies, made themselves felt and hampered the forces of recovery. As a result, the world was caught in a prolonged and severe depression.

These maladjustments were of various kinds. In some cases they were the result of adopting prewar parities for more or less conventional reasons. Other maladjustments were connected with much unwise lending and borrowing, especially on short-term account. There were, moreover, the massive flow of gold to France, which was related to the undervaluation of the French franc in 1926, and the attraction of funds to the short-term markets in New York. In addition, there remained the uncertainties regarding reparations and the payment of war debts, aggravated in many cases by high barriers to trade. It is interesting to record the view of the Gold Delegation of the League of Nations that the causes of the Great Depression did not have their origin in reserve positions; but that these causes combined to expose the international monetary and credit system to pressures which before long proved irresistible. It is consistent with this view that the weakness became concentrated in certain places. The Bank of England and the Reichsbank, especially, found it difficult to perform their useful functions as lenders of last resort and guardians of the exchange position. With larger reserves they might have held out longer, but even the sizable credits arranged in the summer of 1931 proved insufficient. It is indeed questionable in retrospect whether any amount of reserves would have been large enough to stave off the troubles in the existing exchange structure. To the extent that the difficulties stemmed from this source, the remedy was to adjust the exchange structure to reality, rather than to prop it up with additional reserves, particularly when these were borrowed. Indeed, it may be argued that, if countries had had from the first to earn the additional reserves they wanted, the difficulties in the exchange structure would have been exposed much more clearly and corrective action would have been taken much earlier. And, as later became clear, even the substantial reserves of the United States did not in the end protect that country from reducing the gold content of the dollar.

In fact, recent analysis has increasingly emphasized—in addition to the many maladjustments that developed outside the United States—the importance of the cyclical movements in that country. With the increasing importance of the economy of the United States in world affairs, the sudden stoppage of its capital exports and the sharp decline of its imports during the depression created a great many problems in other parts of the world.

It is now generally accepted that a high and rising level of world trade is impossible without a high and rising level of economic activity in the major industrial countries, and principally in the United States. In fact, as the contraction gathered momentum, the structure of reserves, the ways the reserves had been created, and to some extent the amount of reserves undoubtedly proved to be unstable factors in the situation, reinforcing the contraction.[4]

Reserves and Trade in 1937–38

Never have total reserves been more abundant in relation to trade than in 1937–38. The average ratio for those two years reached a high figure of 109 per cent for the world as a whole, and 63 per cent for the world excluding the United States. This high ratio was due to two main factors: (1) Falling costs after 1929 stimulated the output of gold, and the increase in the U.S. price of gold in 1934 stimulated it even more. The latter factor also led to a higher value for existing gold holdings. (2) World trade was depressed, being no greater in volume in 1937–38 than it had been in 1928.

Increased reserves failed to stimulate world trade. In fact, this was a period of economic disintegration, with a fluctuating rate between sterling and the dollar, and increasing bilateralism on the Continent of Europe. The movements of funds which took place were often not of an equilibrating character. Rather, they represented a flight of capital—reflecting political and monetary realities and fears—and had the effect of intensifying the disintegration. In the latter part of 1936 and at the beginning of 1937, the possibility of reducing the price of gold came to be widely discussed.[5] There was serious comment about excessive liquidity and of the difficulties and the increasing expense of sterilizing the large additions to gold reserves.[6] There were large amounts of "hot money"; and this in turn created a demand for gold reserves to handle the transfers of hot money.

Clearly it had not been the lack of international liquidity that had stood in the way of a larger volume of trade and an improvement in the level of employment. The situation provides a further illustration of the proposition that the environment in which a monetary mechanism operates is of greater importance than the level of available reserves.

Developments in 1951–57

It has already been noted that the ratio of reserves to trade is much lower now than in 1937–38. This reduction took place in two steps, the first during and immediately after World War II, and the second during the Korean War. Thus, for all countries other than the United States, the ratio of reserves to imports fell from 63 per cent in 1937–38 to 45 per cent in 1948. Though the value of reserves almost doubled in this period, the value of trade increased even more, the increase reflecting changes in prices and not growth in volume. From 1948 to 1950, the value of trade decreased slightly (the volume of trade increased by 20 per cent, but the decline in prices more than offset this), while the total of reserves increased. The ratio of reserves to imports therefore increased to 52 per cent in 1950. It is interesting to note that world reserves increased despite the fact that the dollar value of sterling exchange holdings was written down by 30 per cent in the devaluation of 1949, or by perhaps $4 billion. During the Korean War, the reserve ratio again fell sharply. World imports (excluding those of the United States) rose from $50 billion to $70 billion, or by 40 per cent; import prices rose

---

[4] League of Nations, *Report of the Gold Delegation* (1932), esp. pp. 16–23. Also, Cassel's "Memorandum of Dissent," p. 74, and Gregory's "The Causes of Gold Movements Into and Out of Great Britain, 1925 to 1930," League of Nations, *Selected Documents on the Distribution of Gold* (1931), esp. p. 28.

[5] League of Nations (R. Nurkse), *International Currency Experience* (1944), p. 133.

[6] Bank for International Settlements, *Annual Report for 1937*, p. 55.

by approximately 30 per cent; and the ratio of reserves to imports fell from 52 per cent in 1950 to 36 per cent in 1951.

Since 1951, liquidity has remained fairly constant and reserves have grown as rapidly as trade. For all countries other than the United States, imports increased from $70 billion in 1951 to $93 billion in 1957, or by one third, and the ratio of reserves to imports fell from 36 per cent to 34 per cent, having in the meantime reached a high of 43 per cent in 1954. There is considerable significance in the fact that the reserve level has remained fairly constant in the face of a growth of volume of trade of 5 per cent per year—a rate of growth that is high by historical standards and probably higher than can be maintained in the future.

So far in 1958 there has been a large flow of gold from the United States to the rest of the world, which has more than offset the flow to the United States in 1957. The value of trade has fallen somewhat, suggesting that in 1958 the ratio of reserves to imports for the world excluding the United States will undoubtedly be higher than in 1957.

A summary of the discussion up to this point would suggest that, for all countries except the United States, the ratio of reserves to imports has been fairly constant since 1951, and that the present ratio is much lower than in 1937–38, about the same as in 1928, and considerably higher than in 1913. It is clear that there is no one best year for comparison, and that in every case the level of reserves must be interpreted within the broad framework of many factors: the functioning of the international economic system, the extent of balance in individual national economies and in the relationship among them, the appropriateness of the structure of exchange rates, the operations of the international credit system, and other major factors. The statistical data do not by themselves suggest that the present level of reserves is inadequate. Any such conclusion, however, is essentially negative. It will be useful to go further and to consider whether the present situation is inherently unstable.

The question may be asked whether there are now, as in retrospect there were in 1928, actual and potential dislocating factors that may create pressures eventually leading to a disruption of the exchange system. This is always, of course, a most difficult question. Nevertheless, it is one that is particularly appropriate at this time considering, specifically, the present state of production and trade and, more generally, the question whether a recession today is likely to be overcome more easily than in the years after 1929.

In some important respects, the prospects now appear to be definitely more encouraging, even though in other respects there may be new difficulties.

Among the favorable circumstances in the present situation, the following may be mentioned:

(1) The economies of the majority of countries in the Western world are now in a state of fairly good balance, one with the other. Since the postwar devaluations of 1949, developments in credit and money volume in most of these countries have largely been of a nature to improve and consolidate a position of equilibrium. An important factor in this process has been the more general application of monetary measures, including the return to a flexible credit policy. One reflection of this improvement is to be seen in the fact that monetary reserves have been strengthened in many countries.

(2) While there have been periods since 1949 of acute exchange tension, with movements of funds taking the form to a large extent of changes in leads and lags,

granting international credit for commercial purposes appears to have been developing on a more normal basis. In contrast to the 1920's, there is no longer an excessive amount of short-term credit subject to sudden recall, at least not on the scale experienced in 1928. At the same time, international trade is increasingly being financed through normal commercial channels. Finally, intergovernmental debts do not present the problems that reparations and war debts posed in 1928 and the early 1930's. There is, therefore, no doubt that the international credit system is more firmly based than it was in 1928.

(3) Postwar recessions have been mild. This probably reflects not only the strengthening of the economic and financial structure in the more important countries, but also a better understanding of the problems involved, and a greater readiness to take corrective measures. It is, of course, dangerous to reason from the past to the future, but the present high degree of optimism is probably not wholly unfounded.

On the other hand, there are elements in the present situation which are less favorable than they were in 1928.

(1) The exchange holdings of the monetary authorities are now larger than ever before, and consist mainly of dollar and sterling balances. There is always the possibility—slight though it may be—that there may be a run to convert dollars into gold, and sterling into dollars or gold. The large gold reserves and the strong economic position of the United States are a protection against a run on the dollar. Dollar balances have grown even in the current recession. Such conversions into gold as have occurred have on the whole been in conformity with the postwar practices of the monetary authorities in dealing with their current net earnings of dollars. Sterling balances represent a more difficult problem in relation to the magnitude of the British gold and dollar reserves. But it is encouraging to note that recently these reserves have been increasing at the same time as sterling liabilities have been declining. Although pressures may again set in from many countries holding reserves in sterling, a considerable part of the balances now represents no more than is needed as working capital for the proper handling of settlements in sterling, together with (in some cases) the necessary cover against domestic money.

(2) The public sector has become more important in most countries, and this often makes economies less flexible. This is particularly apparent where ambitious development plans have been adopted and are being carried out. Low prices of primary products, or even fluctuating prices around a high point, may create situations which are extremely difficult for many countries.

(3) In many cases, foreign trade since 1945 has grown more rapidly than domestic gross national product. In such a situation, if monetary or other fears arise, changes in payments positions resulting from shifts in leads and lags (apart from speculative capital movements) may become very important.

(4) Finally, in a period of international tension, the possibility cannot be ignored that events of a nonmonetary nature may take place which adversely affect the payments situation. In such cases, it is important that remedial steps be able to be taken promptly in order to prevent any major crack in the exchange structure.

On balance, these elements do not suggest pessimism, but they inevitably demand caution in drawing overoptimistic conclusions. Whatever balance is struck, however, there is no doubt that individual countries cannot be expected to rely entirely on themselves to meet all adverse circumstances. In case of need they must have the assurance of recourse to a second line of reserves. This was one of the reasons why the

Fund was established. It has already been helpful in several difficult situations, and is now an integral part of the international financial structure. The financial assistance of the Fund is of course of a short-term character, mainly intended to bridge the gap while the countries themselves take whatever measures may be necessary to restore equilibrium. In view of the historical comparisons which have been drawn, and the assessment that has been made of the favorable and unfavorable elements in the present situation, any answer to the question whether present reserves are adequate must, necessarily, be conditional. If the need for flexible fiscal and credit policies continues to be accepted in many countries, if further steps are taken to strengthen the international credit system, if overambitious investment plans beyond the power of available financing are avoided, and if the international institutions are able to fulfill the role assigned to them, there is nothing in the over-all reserve position to indicate that present reserves are inadequate. Of course, dislocating factors may arise which are so overwhelming that even substantial reserves may suddenly appear insufficient. The environment in which monetary authorities operate is therefore as important a part of international liquidity as the size of their reserves.

One major change in relation to public policy has still to be noted. Since the Great Depression there has been a marked swing toward government policies aimed at securing and maintaining a high level of employment. To the extent that these efforts are successful in the United States and in other major countries with large reserves, trade cycles in these countries are likely to be shorter and shallower in the future than they were before World War II. Success in these countries will affect general business conditions in the world as a whole. This should make it easier for other countries to mitigate fluctuations in their business activity and level of employment without undue strain on their reserve positions. To this extent, any given ratio of reserves to imports in all other countries is likely to be more adequate now and in the future than it was in the past. This does not mean that difficult problems will not sometimes arise for countries whose reserves are slender. Countries will have to weigh the policies of maintaining external balance and defending their exchange rates, which may require a contractionary policy, against the repercussions of such a policy on the price and employment situation at home. There is no simple formula by which these problems can be solved, but the difficulties of coping with a recession are, of course, eased to the extent that countries are able to accumulate sufficient reserves during periods of expansion to bear some of the strains of contraction.

Composition of Reserves

In the disturbed period up to 1938, total exchange holdings fell to an amount of only $1.8 billion, equivalent to 6 per cent of the total gold and exchange reserves of all countries. During the war substantial purchases, especially by the United Kingdom— but to some extent also by the United States—led to the building up of sterling and dollar balances. While sterling balances were reduced in dollar value by the devaluation in 1949, dollar balances continued to increase. By the end of 1950 total exchange holdings were equal to about 30 per cent of total reserves, a proportion that remained almost unchanged up to and including 1957, when total exchange holdings were equal to $15.9 billion, compared with total reserves of $52.9 billion. However, the United States does not hold reserves in the form of exchange, so that the data for all other countries is perhaps of greater interest. Since 1949, the percentage of their reserves kept in the form of exchange has fluctuated within the narrow range of 53–56 per cent, and was 53 per cent at the end of 1957. This level was 10 per cent below that in 1948, largely because the devaluation of sterling reduced the dollar value of sterling exchange holdings in 1949. The percentage of reserves kept in the form of exchange in 1949–57 was more than 50 per cent larger than in 1928 and about three times as large as in 1937–38 and in 1913, as can be seen from Table 4.

At the close of World War II, sterling balances represented a very high proportion of the gross national product of the United Kingdom. The British authorities made it clear that they wished to avoid any further increase in these balances and that they

Table 4. Gross Reserves and Foreign Exchange Holdings of All Countries, Excluding the Communist Bloc, Selected Years, 1913-57

Year	All Countries		All Countries Except United States		
	Reserves (billion dollars)	Per cent in foreign exchange	Reserves (billion dollars)	Foreign exchange (billion dollars)	Per cent in foreign exchange
1913	4.5	11	2.7	0.5	18
1928	13.0	25	9.3	3.2	35
1937	27.7	9	14.9	2.4	16
1938	27.7	7	13.1	1.8	14
1948	46.4	29	22.1	13.7	62
1949	43.6	24	19.1	10.5	55
1950	47.0	29	24.2	13.6	56
1951	46.5	28	23.6	12.9	54
1952	46.7	28	23.4	13.2	56
1953	48.0	29	25.9	14.1	54
1954	49.5	30	27.7	15.1	54
1955	50.6	31	28.8	15.6	54
1956	51.8	31	29.7	16.2	55
1957	52.9	30	30.0	15.9	53

Sources: All years except 1913 are shown in Appendix Table 2. Data on gold reserves for 1913 are from *Banking and Monetary Statistics* (Board of Governors of the Federal Reserve System, 1943), Table 160.

hoped, if possible, to reduce them. In fact, sterling balances (official and private) as measured in sterling were not reduced between 1945 and 1951, remaining at £3.6 billion, though they were reduced almost 10 per cent between 1951 and 1957, when they stood at £3.3 billion. (There were, however, great changes, which will be discussed later, in the countries that held sterling.) In terms of dollars, the movement of sterling balances is indicated by the corresponding figures: 1945, $14.4 billion; 1951, $10.0 billion; and 1957, $9.1 billion. On the other hand, all dollar balances, official and private, doubled in the postwar period, and the data for the same years are as follows: 1945, $6.9 billion; 1951, $7.7 billion; and 1957, $13.6 billion.

From 1949 to the end of 1957, countries other than the United States increased their exchange holdings by $5.4 billion and their gold holdings by $5.5 billion. Increases of this magnitude over a period of several years must have offered many countries the opportunity to change the composition of their reserves substantially if they had wished to do so. The fact that as a group they added to their exchange holdings to such an extent that there was no change in the relative importance of exchange holdings in their total reserves shows that on the whole there was no such wish.

With the exception of the United States, nearly all areas maintained a larger percentage of their reserves in the form of exchange in 1957 than in either 1937 or 1928 (Table 5). The postwar developments in the period 1948–57 may be summarized by noting that Canada, Non-Dollar Latin America, and Sterling Area countries other than the United Kingdom decreased the percentage of reserves in the form of exchange;

Table 5. Percentage of Gross Reserves Held in Foreign Exchange, by Area, Selected Years, 1928-57

Area	1928	1937	1948	1956	1957
Canada	—	10	60	43	40
Latin America: Dollar Area	44	17	26	55	56
Latin America: Non-Dollar Area	12	17	59	39	33
Continental EPU Countries	45	12	40	47	45
United Kingdom	—	...	20	17	33
Other Sterling Area	49	65	92	85	83
Rest of the World [1]	24	33	77	79	75

Source: Appendix Table 2.
[1] Does not include the United States.

Dollar Latin America and Continental EPU increased their percentage; the Rest of the World remained practically unchanged. The position of the United Kingdom fluctuated irregularly, so that the percentage of its reserves in the form of exchange was lower in 1956, but higher in 1957, than in 1948.

A more detailed examination of these regional trends is instructive. Canada increased its reserves fivefold from 1937 to 1948, and at the same time increased the percentage of its reserves in foreign exchange from 10 to 60 (Table 6). From 1948 to 1957 it increased its reserves by 80 per cent, but reduced the percentage in exchange by one

Table 6. Gross Reserves and Percentage Held in Foreign Exchange, Canada and Latin America, Selected Years, 1928-57

	Canada		Latin America, Dollar Area		Latin America, Non-Dollar Area	
Year	Reserves (billion dollars)	Per cent in exchange	Reserves (billion dollars)	Per cent in exchange	Reserves (billion dollars)	Per cent in exchange
1928	0.1	—	0.1	44	1.0	12
1937	0.2	10	0.2	17	0.7	17
1938	0.2	15	0.2	29	0.6	12
1948	1.0	60	1.1	26	1.7	59
1949	1.1	57	1.2	27	1.6	52
1950	1.8	67	1.4	27	1.8	53
1951	1.8	54	1.5	31	1.4	36
1952	1.9	53	1.6	42	1.3	32
1953	1.8	46	1.6	45	1.6	35
1954	2.0	45	1.7	50	1.4	27
1955	1.9	41	1.8	53	1.3	25
1956	1.9	43	2.3	55	1.4	39
1957	1.8	40	2.7	56	1.0	33

Source: Appendix Table 2.

third, to 40 per cent. These changes reflect an increase in gold holdings, and a decrease in exchange reserves (largely U.S. dollars). The increases in total reserves in Dollar Latin America are strikingly similar to those in Canada, but the percentage in exchange, which decreased slightly from 1938 to 1948, doubled in the postwar period, and stood at 56 per cent in 1957. The countries in Non-Dollar Latin America [7] in 1948–57 decreased their gross reserves (from $1.7 billion to $1.0 billion), and, since they preferred to hold on to their gold reserves, which could be, and from time to time were, pledged as collateral against loans, they decreased the percentage of their reserves in the form of exchange from 59 to 33.

Continental EPU countries in 1928 held 46 per cent of their reserves in the form of exchange (Table 7). This percentage fell sharply in the 1930's but was restored during and after the war. It stood at 45 per cent in 1957. Reserves increased by almost 150 per cent from 1948 to 1957, but the proportions held in gold and in exchange were fairly constant.

Table 7. Gross Reserves and Percentage Held in Foreign Exchange, Sterling Area and Continental EPU, Selected Years, 1928-57

	United Kingdom		Other Sterling Area		Continental EPU Countries	
Year	Reserves (billion dollars)	Per cent in exchange	Reserves (billion dollars)	Per cent in exchange	Reserves (billion dollars)	Per cent in exchange
1928	0.7	—	0.8	49	5.1	46
1937	4.1	...	1.4	65	6.8	12
1938	2.9	...	1.2	54	6.5	8
1948	2.0	20	7.3	92	5.9	40
1949	1.8	23	4.7	88	6.2	38
1950	3.7	21	5.6	89	6.9	43
1951	2.4	7	5.2	88	7.5	45
1952	2.0	23	4.6	86	8.6	48
1953	2.5	10	5.0	88	10.1	50
1954	2.8	9	5.0	86	11.4	51
1955	2.2	5	4.7	85	12.9	49
1956	2.2	17	4.5	85	13.4	47
1957	2.4	33	4.0	83	14.6	45

Source: Appendix Table 2.

The United Kingdom's reserves, and the percentage of these kept in the form of exchange, have shown considerable fluctuation since the war. Its reserves were at a postwar high of $3.7 billion in 1950. Since then they have fallen irregularly. They were $2.4 billion at the end of 1957 (and more than $3 billion at the end of June 1958). The percentage in the form of exchange does not appear to be correlated with fluctuations in the total. In contrast, the Other Sterling Area countries show a slowly declining trend in the percentage of reserves held in the form of exchange since the war.[8] In 1948 it stood at 92. Since then it has been reduced gradually, and at the end of 1957 was 83. This percentage is much higher than that which prevailed before the war.

---

[7] Argentina, Brazil, Chile, Paraguay, Peru, and Uruguay.

[8] The results are largely influenced by India and Australia, which hold the greater part of the reserves of the area.

The Rest of the World [9] has, since 1949, steadily kept approximately three fourths of its reserves in the form of exchange holdings. This is three times as great as the percentage so kept in 1928, and more than double that in 1937–38. Of the countries in this group, Israel had all of its reserves in the form of exchange; Japan, 97 per cent; and the Philippines, 87 per cent.

Some countries, when drawing on their reserves, appear to follow the practice of using their exchange holdings first, leaving their gold holdings more or less intact. For the world as a whole, such reductions in exchange reserves as have from time to time been made in individual countries have, however, been more than made up by increases in others. Thus, the holding of foreign exchange has become an integral part of the system of international reserves and materially facilitates the problem of ensuring a volume of reserves adequate for the world's needs.

Table 8. Composition of Gross Foreign Exchange Assets, 1947-57
(In millions of U.S. dollars)

Year	Total	Dollars	Sterling	EPU Liabilities	BIS Deposits	Errors and Omissions
1947	13,900	1,850	12,147	—	8	− 105
1948	13,900	2,900	10,774	—	52	174
1949	10,850	3,050	7,414	—	108	278
1950	13,600	4,450	7,775	402	250	723
1951	13,000	4,050	7,646	665	192	447
1952	13,300	5,250	6,328	1,077	364	281
1953	14,250	6,050	6,825	1,272	352	− 249
1954	15,250	7,000	6,980	1,108	465	− 303
1955	15,750	7,900	6,591	994	412	− 147
1956	16,400	8,600	6,220	1,086	424	70
1957	16,050	8,300	5,833	1,269	409	239

Sources: For 1950-57, *International Financial Statistics (IFS)*, July 1958; for 1947-49, Fund estimates on the same basis.

The rapid growth of the dollar as a reserve currency, both absolutely and in relation to sterling, is a major development of the postwar period. Data recently made available by the U.K. Treasury classify area holdings of sterling for 1945, 1951, and 1957 as between central bank and other official funds, on the one hand, and nonofficial funds, on the other. Official holdings of sterling by all countries excluding the U.K. colonies (and for comparative purposes the Treasury data include Ghana and Malaya under this caption) stood at about $10.4 billion in 1945. By 1951 these holdings had been reduced to about $6.2 billion, and by 1957 to about $4.2 billion. If these data are compared with official dollar holdings they suggest—and the comparison must necessarily be rough—that in 1945 official sterling holdings were about four times as large as official dollar holdings. In 1951 they were 50 per cent larger than official dollar holdings. At the end of 1957, official sterling holdings by all independent countries, including Ghana and Malaya, may be estimated at $4.8 billion on the basis of the Treasury data and other information. This was equal to about 60 per cent of the reported official dollar holdings on that date, or $8.3 billion.

More detailed data on the composition of gross foreign exchange reserve holdings for 1947–57 by area, and by type of reserve holding, are shown in Table 8, which

---

[9] Includes Egypt, Finland, Indonesia, Iran, Israel, Japan, Lebanon, Philippines, Spain, Syria, and Thailand.

is based upon a reconciliation prepared by the Fund of reported foreign exchange assets and liabilities. Since, as already noted, the distribution between official and nonofficial holdings of sterling balances has been made available for only two of the years covered by this table, it has been necessary to use the published data on all sterling balances, official and nonofficial. In this table, therefore, official sterling holdings are overstated relative to all other types of exchange asset. (This and other errors are, of course, included in Errors and Omissions.) The official reserves represented by credits extended through EPU amounted to $1.3 billion at the end of 1957, and constituted more than 8 per cent of the exchange reserves of all countries. The amount of reserves kept in the form of deposits with the BIS increased from $8 million in 1947 to $465 million in 1954. Although it has decreased somewhat since that time, this amount has not fallen below $400 million.

The structure of the changing relationship between sterling and the dollar is clearly identifiable. Countries that have traditionally held exchange reserves in the form of dollars continue to do so, and when their total reserves increased their dollar holdings

Table 9. Sterling and Dollar Reserves in Selected Areas, Selected Years, 1948-57 [1]
(In billions of U.S. dollars)

Area	1948	1949	1950	1952	1956	1957
Continental EPU Countries						
Dollar holdings	0.8	0.8	1.1	1.7	3.9	3.7
Sterling holdings	1.5	1.2	0.9	0.7	0.5	0.7
Non-Dollar Latin America						
Dollar holdings	0.3	0.3	0.4	0.2	0.3	0.2
Sterling holdings	0.5	0.2	0.1	—[2]	0.1	0.1
Other Non-Dollar Non-Sterling[3]						
Dollar holdings	0.6	0.5	1.0	1.3	1.9	1.4
Sterling holdings	2.2	1.4	1.4	1.1	0.8	0.7
Total Non-Dollar Non-Sterling						
Dollar holdings	1.7	1.6	2.5	3.2	6.1	5.3
Sterling holdings	4.2	2.8	2.4	2.1	1.4	1.5

Sources: For 1948, *International Financial Statistics (IFS)*, February 1958; for 1949, *IFS*, February 1957; for other years, *IFS*, July 1958.

[1] In this table there may be some overstatement of sterling holdings, since the figures may include nonofficial holdings.

[2] $25 million.

[3] Sixteen countries: China (Taiwan), Egypt, Ethiopia, Finland, Indonesia, Iran, Israel, Japan, Korea, Lebanon, Philippines, Spain, Syria, Thailand, Viet-Nam, and Yugoslavia.

also increased. Canada and the Dollar Latin American countries which have held practically no sterling had $1 billion of dollar assets in 1948 and $2.1 billion in 1957. The countries in the sterling area held less sterling in 1957 than in 1948 because their total reserves had fallen. It is true that their dollar holdings increased from $50 million to $200 million, but even the latter figure was only 6 per cent of total reserves. The most striking change, as may be seen from Table 9, occurred in the non-dollar non-sterling countries. Their dollar holdings in 1957 were three times as large as in 1948, while their sterling holdings were about one third as large.

Private credits finance most of the world's international business; and private exchange holdings, together with private credits, play a role in settling international balances. Nonofficial exchange holdings are thus a complement to official holdings and in some cases may be a substitute for them. The total figures for all sterling and dollar balances, official and nonofficial, are compared in Table 10.

Dollar balances were reduced in the first years after the close of World War II, but have increased steadily since 1947. By 1957, they were almost three times as large as they had been a decade earlier. Sterling liabilities to the U.K. colonies grew steadily after 1945, and have doubled. (The decrease in 1949, as shown in Table 10, is the result of revaluation in terms of dollars.) Liabilities to the independent countries of the sterling area have decreased by about 15 per cent since 1951, and those to India, by about 60 per cent. Liabilities to the non-sterling countries have declined persistently since the war. From 1945 to 1957, they declined from £1,170 million to £568 million, i.e., from $4.7 billion to $1.6 billion.

It must be expected that the substantial balances held by the U.K. colonies will be drawn down in the future as these colonies expand their development expenditures. On the other hand, the amount of sterling held by various other countries using

Table 10. Comparison of All Dollar and All Sterling Liabilities, Selected Years, 1937-57
(In billions of U.S. dollars)

Year	Dollar Liabilities	Sterling Liabilities		
		Total	To colonies	To others
1937	1.9	4.0	0.4[1]	3.6
1945	6.9	14.4	1.7	12.7
1946	6.0	14.5	1.9	12.6
1947	4.8	14.1	1.9	12.2
1948	5.8	12.7	2.1	10.6
1949	6.0	8.8	1.5	7.3
1950	7.1	9.8	2.0	7.8
1951	7.7	10.0	2.6	7.4
1952	9.0	9.0	2.9	6.1
1953	10.0	9.8	3.1	6.7
1954	11.2	10.4	3.4	7.0
1955	11.7	10.0	3.6	6.4
1956	13.5	9.6	3.6	6.0
1957[2]	13.6	9.1	2.5	6.6

Sources: *International Financial Statistics (IFS)*, July 1958. Data for years not published there are from revised figures in *IFS* files.
[1] Estimated as 10 per cent of all sterling liabilities.
[2] The sterling holdings of Ghana and the Federation of Malaya are included under Liabilities to Other Sterling countries rather than Liabilities to U. K. colonies.

sterling as a trading currency may well increase with expanding world trade and a strengthening of the monetary position of sterling itself. If account is taken of the fact that the level of commodity prices in terms of dollars has increased by almost 150 per cent since 1937, it will be seen that the total of sterling liabilities by the end of 1956 was in real terms somewhat smaller than it had been in 1937.

It seems probable that a number of countries, which in recent years have suffered a reduction in their total reserves, to a greater or lesser extent in the form of a reduction in dollar balances, will wish to replenish their reserves, and presumably largely in the form of dollar balances. However, a number of countries have probably already been successful in increasing their reserves to a point which they consider adequate. A continued rapid increase in their reserves, including dollar balances, is therefore less likely in the years to come. It is perhaps vain to speculate what will be the net result of these conflicting tendencies, but it seems certain that exchange holdings, as a more readily usable form of asset than gold holdings, will continue to form an important part of any accumulation of reserves.

CHAPTER THREE: THE ADEQUACY OF INDIVIDUAL COUNTRY RESERVES

The preceding chapter reviewed the level and composition of reserves. It discussed the historical development of reserves, analyzed the relationship of reserves to trade on the basis of certain historical comparisons, and pointed out that the adequacy of reserves cannot be measured by a few percentage figures relating reserves to trade. International liquidity depends upon a combination of factors: country reserves, international borrowing and commercial credit operations, and the international financial structure. Two conclusions were reached: first, under certain fairly specific and broad conditions, the total amount of gold and foreign exchange reserves now held by the monetary authorities may prove to be adequate; and secondly, the existing composition of reserves permits the monetary authorities to hold the kind of reserves they wish.

This chapter considers more particularly the level and the adequacy of reserves of individual countries. Generalizations about individual country reserves are necessarily limited by the great variety of country reserve practices and policies, which in turn reflect differences between their economic situations, stages of development, and policy objectives.

The Meaning of Adequacy

The adequacy of reserves must be judged in relation to the aim that is envisaged. There is both a domestic aim and an international aim. The monetary legislation of most countries requires that the central bank or some other monetary authority maintain a given amount of gold, or of gold and foreign exchange, in support of the supply of domestic money. This reserve or cover may be a stated amount or, more usually, a percentage of the currency and deposit liabilities of the central bank. To be adequate, country reserves must therefore be at least large enough to meet these domestic legal minima, with some margin for operating purposes. These minima can be, and have been, adjusted by individual countries for their own purposes.

The domestic purpose of a monetary reserve is essentially to regulate or to limit the quantity of domestic money, and yet allow sufficient flexibility so that changing seasonal or regional needs may be met smoothly. Reserves for strictly domestic purposes were essential even when large amounts of gold coin and gold notes (backed 100 per cent by gold) circulated in the community, because provision had to be made for possible internal or regional drains. Since 1914, however, monetary authorities all over the world have called in practically all the gold coin and gold notes that had been in circulation, and added them to central reserves. Simultaneously, the strict and inelastic link between domestic money and gold has been weakened or, perhaps more accurately, replaced within broad limits by monetary and credit management. In practically all countries, the ratio of reserves to the domestic supply of money has been falling for many years. Stated in another way, the amount of reserves required to support a given expansion of the domestic money supply is much smaller now than it used to be. And in those countries which have large excess reserves, the money supply can be expanded without any increase in reserves. As will be noted in the next chapter, this has important implications for the development of world liquidity.

But even when the domestic purpose of reserves was more important than it now is, the main purpose of reserves was international—to provide the means for settling deficits in the balance of payments, and at the same time to inspire confidence that the foreign exchange position, including the foreign exchange rate, could be properly maintained. These external considerations have become more important, so that, increasingly, the purpose of reserves is to help individual countries maintain a smoothly functioning monetary and exchange system. But reserves are not the only thing that help a country do this. The ability to borrow, the use of an appropriate exchange rate, the adoption of monetary and fiscal policies which lead to development with stability, are also important. And since international balance is a matter of the relationship of one country with all others, the effects of the wisest policy in any one country are often limited by inflation, contraction, or inappropriate exchange rates in other countries.

An individual country will have to consider all of these factors in forming its reserve policy. This will rarely depend upon monetary considerations alone. Usually it is the result of various and often conflicting influences. Not infrequently its decision is influenced by unrealistic assumptions as to the real effects of policies adopted, e.g., that highly complex systems of exchange restrictions can be made to work rationally and even perfectly; that development can be financed partly or largely with credit creation without any danger of inflation; or that a predetermined amount of deficit financing will have only a minor effect upon the balance of payments. Distinctions must therefore be drawn between (1) the level of reserves a country thinks it "should" or "ought to" hold; (2) the level of reserves a country may expect to hold as a result of the policies it is following, the actual importance it attributes to reserves, and conditions in the world at large; and (3) the level of reserves it will actually hold as a result of the policies it follows.

It is the sum total of individual country decisions to increase, decrease, or maintain reserves which determines whether total reserves are adequate or inadequate. From an over-all point of view (such as was adopted in Chapter II), a reserve situation can be characterized as adequate when the total of reserves is sufficient, its composition is appropriate, and the distribution of reserves is in accordance with effective country demands for them. The presence or absence of these conditions cannot be determined a priori; it must be inferred from the results of country actions. If reserves are adequate, countries are able to make the adjustments they wish without seriously disturbing the system and without initiating a series of deflationary or countervailing actions. Whether a given reserve situation is adequate therefore depends upon whether countries are taking effective action to change their positions and whether their measures are unduly upsetting to other countries. Since conditions are constantly changing, this implies that the adequacy of reserves cannot be determined once and for all and that a good system of reserves must have elasticity. As already noted, the satisfactory operation of an international credit system—official, international, and private—is very important in this connection. In judging the adequacy of its reserves, every country will want to know whether it will be able in case of need to obtain resources from abroad.

Any decision to increase reserves is important because it requires, as a counterpart, an equivalent amount of uncommitted savings.

Unwillingness or inability to increase reserves means that none of a country's savings or of the proceeds of credits received from abroad has been applied to the kind of investment which results in an increase in reserves. It is of course obvious that below some minimum level an increase in reserves may become a major policy issue, while above some maximum level, reserves may serve to encourage a policy of expansion or they may play a more or less passive role. Within these limits, which will vary widely from country to country, the level of reserves generally has the character of a residual and is the net result of other policies. Thus a country may not be greatly concerned about raising its reserves from, say, 30 per cent of imports to 40 per cent, though it may attach considerable importance to raising them from 5 per cent to 25 or 30 per cent.

Admittedly, a policy designed to increase reserves or to maintain them at a certain level may be difficult or even impossible to carry out in a short period. Crop failures and declining prices resulting from gluts and other adverse circumstances may so severely reduce the flow of domestic savings that it becomes necessary to rely largely or even wholly on foreign credits to meet a balance of payments deficit. Errors and miscalculations in deciding economic policies or in carrying them out may have unanticipated effects upon reserves. It is therefore all the more important that the necessary steps be taken to set aside savings for restoring reserves in fairly prosperous years when foreign earnings are increasing.

Each country determines its reserve requirements in the light of its own situation, control policies, exchange rate, and alternative uses for the savings that would be used to acquire reserves. Generally, larger reserves are needed by countries with strong seasonal swings in their balance of payments, and of course also by countries with heavy short-term liabilities. Likewise, larger reserves will be needed by countries which are greatly dependent on international trade and which are thus likely to feel more keenly changes in foreign demand, often intensified by shifts in leads and lags. Countries with slender reserves have often relied on fluctuating exchange rates to balance their payments. Where the alternative to a fluctuating rate is likely to be the imposition of quantitative restrictions on imports or the proliferation of exchange rates, the adoption of a fluctuating rate system may well be the lesser evil, although it has grave disadvantages.

There have, of course, been countries which have sought to influence the reserve position by direct control of trade and payments instead of relying solely, or largely, on monetary and fiscal policies. Such attempts have not proved effective, for the imbalance which led to the imposition of controls is not overcome by the controls. Indeed, the consequent reduction in imports will usually tend to aggravate the imbalance, e.g., by ultimately reducing exports.

It is clear that there can be no one generally acceptable rule, valid in all cases, for the amount of reserves which can be considered adequate for an individual country. Account has to be taken of the particular circumstances, history, conventions, savings habits, and international banking position of each country. Indeed, the significance of all these particulars is that the term adequacy of reserves has a variety of meanings, different from country to country and from time to time. Reserves which are inadequate for one policy may be more than adequate for another; reserves which are inadequate in conjunction with one set of fiscal and monetary methods may be adequate with another set. Reserves which are insufficient when a country is facing a budgetary deficit and credit expansion may be sufficient when the government is running a surplus and credit is contracting. Reserves which are adequate where a country follows flexible policies may not be adequate when its policies are frozen or slow to adjust. Thus, in principle, it is difficult to determine the "real" adequacy of reserves in any one country, or to compare one country with another, without taking into account many factors other than reserves. To relate the reserve position to the volume of foreign trade is no doubt a useful method of approach, but it can give at best only a preliminary indication of adequacy. In all these matters, the element of convention in the determination of adequacy should not be overlooked. The level of reserves that a country has become accustomed to is often one that has gradually come to be considered adequate—partly, no doubt, because special credit arrangements have been concluded to provide relief for the reserves in periods of special strain.

It does not follow that a country whose reserves are inadequate in the judgment of outsiders—or even in its own judgment—is necessarily interested in trying to increase them. Many countries with inadequate reserves have, over a period of years, not carried out economic policies which are consistent with increasing them. It is not meaningful—and it may be misleading—to assume that a country with inadequate reserves is necessarily trying to add to them. This may be the case even though international circumstances are favorable and the volume and prices of its exports are high. In the last analysis, each country thus makes its own decision as to whether to retain or accumulate uncommitted savings in the form of reserves.

As to what assets should be considered as forming part of the reserves, it is now generally accepted (as already mentioned in Chapter II) that exchange holdings of convertible and widely transferable currencies should be included along with gold; indeed, these holdings are usually the most variable and therefore, to some extent, the most effective element of the total reserves. Practice varies as to whether net EFU creditor positions and surpluses in bilateral accounts are included in reserves. It is even more difficult to determine how much significance should be attached to total creditor positions. In the previous chapter, gross reserves have been used for the over-all comparisons of a mainly historical character, but where individual countries are concerned, account must often be taken also of the existence of short-term liabilities.

In some instances, as when gold holdings are pledged as collateral against foreign credits, exclusive attention to gross reserves would clearly give a distorted picture of the real situation. This is also the case where there are substantial short-term or medium-term commercial debts weighing on the exchange position, or large outstanding debit balances on bilateral accounts. Drawings from the Fund, since they are repayable within a few years, likewise affect the real exchange position. Furthermore, for the United Kingdom and the United States, there is the special question of the large amounts held by foreigners on deposit or in short-term securities in sterling and in dollars.

In view of these many qualifications, it is clearly impossible to lay down any simple rule in this matter. The particular conditions of a country or group of countries must be considered, and attention paid to past experience and behavior.

Analysis of the Level of Country Reserves

The basic statistical data on individual country reserves, imports, and the ratio of reserves to imports are shown in Appendix Table 1 for some 60 countries for 1928, 1937, 1948, and for each year from 1950 to 1957. It will be seen that the ratios vary widely from country to country, and that for some countries they vary widely from year to year. The table also reveals that the ownership of reserves is much more highly concentrated than trade. At the end of 1957, the United States alone held 43 per cent of the world's reserves of gold and exchange (Table 11), and the United States and the Federal Republic of Germany together held more than one half (54 per cent). Eleven countries held 80 per cent of the world's reserves.

The figure for the United Kingdom, the equivalent of $2.4 billion, reflects the reductions connected with the Suez events, the sterling-mark speculation in 1957, and short-term borrowings, including a drawing from the Fund. By the end of June 1958, the United Kingdom's reserves had risen to over $3 billion. The largest increases in 1957 were shown by Germany (an increase of $1.2 billion) and Venezuela ($500 million). Large decreases were shown by Japan, India, and France.

Reserves for all countries excluding those in the communist bloc in 1957 were equal to 49 per cent of imports, or excluding the United States, 32 per cent. Although over-all figures do not add much to our knowledge of the adequacy of reserves for

Table 11. Countries with Gold and Exchange Reserves Exceeding $1 Billion at End of 1957

Country	Reserves (billion dollars)	Per Cent
United States	22.9	43.3
Germany, Federal Republic of	5.6	10.6
United Kingdom	2.4	4.5
Switzerland	1.9	3.6
Canada	1.8	3.4
Italy	1.5	2.8
Venezuela	1.4	2.6
Australia	1.3	2.5
Belgium	1.1	2.1
Netherlands	1.1	2.1
Japan	1.0	1.9
All other	10.9	20.6
World	52.9	100.0

Source: Appendix Table 1.

individual countries, it is of some interest to distinguish between industrial and other countries, since they are often subject to different influences. In addition to the United States and the United Kingdom, which will be discussed individually, there are 12 countries which may be considered *industrial* on the basis of their exports. These are the continental members of the EPU, except Greece and Turkey, plus Japan. Their ratios of reserves to imports are presented in Table 12.

In the years studied, there were never fewer than three countries with a ratio of reserves to imports of less than 30 per cent, and never fewer than two with a ratio of over 50 per cent (Table 13). The number of countries in the middle range of

30 to 50 per cent was never less than one nor more than five; and, with a few exceptions (especially in 1937), it was the countries in this group which moved to below 30 per cent in some years and to above 50 per cent in others.

Throughout the postwar period the Scandinavian countries have had reserve ratios which are low by European standards, and low even by Latin American and Asian standards. These countries had low ratios even before World War I. At the other extreme, Switzerland and Portugal stand out with the highest reserve ratios, a particularly large increase having taken place in Portugal since 1928, while Switzerland,

Table 12. Ratio of Reserves to Imports, 12 Industrial Countries, Selected Years, 1928-57
(Arranged in order of size of ratio, expressed as a percentage, in 1957)

Country	1928	1937	1948	1950	1951	1952	1953	1954	1955	1956	1957
Denmark	17	19	12	11	12	15	17	12	11	10	13
France	121	165	...	44	20	23	24	32	44	24	13
Norway	19	41	19	18	17	17	16	14	15	15	14
Sweden	26	95	17	24	27	26	32	27	24	21	19
Japan	60	26	...	58	46	54	37	43	54	47	24
Netherlands	24	106	18	29	24	47	52	45	40	29	26
Belgium	39	89	46	38	40	42	44	41	40	35	33
Italy	50	29	35	59	46	39	39	43	46	41	42
Austria	28	27	13	19	16	23	59	63	41	42	45
Germany	23	...	...	10	15	31	52	58	53	65	75
Switzerland	30	187	143	150	120	138	150	141	124	107	98
Portugal	21	71	123	172	168	162	186	187	169	156	137

Source: Appendix Table 1.

Table 13. Industrial Countries (Excluding the United States and the United Kingdom)[1] Classified by Ratio of Reserves to Imports, Selected Years, 1928-57
(Ratio of reserves to imports, expressed as a percentage)

Year	Number of Countries	Average Ratio[2]	Number of Countries with Stated Percentage of Reserves to Imports		
			Less than 30	30-50	Over 50
1928	12	48	7	2	3
1937	11	70	4	1	6
1948	9	44	5	2	2
1950	12	42	6	2	4
1951	12	34	7	3	2
1952	12	41	5	4	3
1953	12	46	3	4	5
1954	12	48	3	5	4
1955	12	48	3	5	4
1956	12	43	5	4	3
1957	12	40	6	3	3

Source: Appendix Table 1.

[1] All continental members of EPU, except Greece and Turkey, plus Japan. Data for 1937 exclude Germany; data for 1948 exclude France, Germany, and Japan.

[2] Weighted average.

with large short-term liabilities to foreigners, in the form of deposits or investments, has felt it appropriate to hold large reserves, almost exclusively in gold.

The other countries in general appear to have tried to achieve ratios of between 30 and 50 per cent, or perhaps 40 and 50 per cent, in the sense that if reserves were below these levels they tried to increase reserves, and if reserves rose beyond some such level, they saw fit to adopt a more expansionist policy. Germany is a particular case. Its ratio of reserves to imports in 1928 was 23 per cent, which was not large; but it had at the same time contracted large amounts of short-term foreign debt so that its position was in reality much weaker than the reserve ratio would indicate. By the end of 1951, reserves were still dangerously low, but in the following years substantial additions were made, and by the end of 1957 the German ratio was higher than that of any other of these countries except Portugal and Switzerland. The uncommitted savings required to improve the German exchange position were very largely obtained by budget surpluses, accruing as a result both of revenue growing more rapidly than estimated and of certain delays in effecting expenditures.

In 1957, there were 49 countries classified as *nonindustrial* on the basis of their exports, and for which data on reserves and trade data were available. These ranged in size from countries with annual imports of less than $50 million, to Canada with imports of $6.3 billion. In 1957, 21 of these countries had a ratio of reserves to imports of less than 30 per cent, and 31 had a ratio of less than 40 per cent (Table 14).

Table 14. Nonindustrial Countries[1] Classified by Ratio of Reserves to Imports, Selected Years, 1928-57

(Ratio of reserves to imports, expressed as a percentage)

Year	Number of Countries	Number of Countries with Stated Percentage of Reserves to Imports				
		Less than 30	30-39	40-49	50-59	60 and more
1928	25	10	5	1	3	6
1937	38	17	4	5	4	8
1948	45	15	5	5	4	16
1950	45	13	3	3	9	17
1951	47	12	13	5	4	13
1952	47	18	8	6	4	11
1953	48	16	9	4	4	15
1954	48	16	8	7	5	12
1955	49	19	8	8	4	10
1956	49	20	7	6	3	13
1957	49	21	10	4	3	11

Source: Appendix Table 1.

[1] Nonindustrial countries are defined as all countries except the United States, the United Kingdom, Japan, and the continental members of EPU, with the exception of Greece and Turkey.

The reserve position of some individual countries changed substantially from one year to another in the postwar period, but the position of all of them together was comparatively stable. However, a comparison between the postwar years and the two prewar years, 1928 and 1937, reveals some interesting differences. Since there was a greater number of countries in the postwar period than previously, it is convenient to show the different situation of countries by means of percentages of the total number of countries (Table 15).

For the world as a whole the ratio of reserves to imports was much higher in 1937 than in the postwar years; it therefore seems strange at first sight that for the nonindustrial countries the tendency was rather the opposite. The explanation appears, at least partly, to be that the increase in the world's reserves after 1934 came largely from the revaluation of gold, so that these countries which had generally only a little gold to begin with (either because they had only low reserves or because they kept a large proportion of their reserves in foreign exchange) naturally had relatively low reserve ratios in 1937. Moreover, after 1933 these countries did not generally share in the recovery from the depression to the same extent as the industrial countries, and therefore had less opportunity to accumulate reserves.

There are persistent differences between the reserve levels and the reserve behavior of the nonindustrial countries similar to those already noted with regard to the

Table 15. Changes in Ratio of Reserves to Imports, Nonindustrial Countries, Selected Years, 1928-57

Year	Reserve Ratio Less Than 20 Per Cent		Reserve Ratio Less Than 30 Per Cent	
	Number of countries	Per cent of total	Number of countries	Per cent of total
1928	7	28	10	40
1937	8	21	17	45
1951	8	17	12	27
1953	4	8	16	33
1956	8	16	20	41
1957	13	27	21	43

industrial countries. In 1951, for example, 12 nonindustrial countries had reserves equal to less than 30 per cent of their imports, and six years later 10 of them were still in the same position. One other country which, on the basis of gross reserves, moved out of this group had not really improved its position for it had been able to increase its gross reserves only by increasing its liabilities. On the other hand, 13 countries in 1951 had reserves equal to more than 60 per cent of imports. In 1956, 10 of these countries, and in 1957, 7, were still in the same position. In some countries, such as India, the reduction in reserves represented heavy spending on development. This continuity in the relative position of various countries reflects the profound differences in their own situations, in their policies, and in their operating procedures, as the following examples suggest.

Israel and Yugoslavia have low reserves, and their other commitments are such that an accumulation of reserves has a low priority. Canada, having strong basic resources and close access to the New York money market, reportedly considered a reserve level of about 30 per cent as high enough in 1957.[1]

[1] As reported in *The Globe and Mail* (Toronto), October 24, 1957, and *The Journal of Commerce* (New York), October 29 and 31, 1957. Canada has a floating exchange rate. Whether the judgment would have been the same if it had a fixed rate is another question—the answer to which also depends upon the rate of capital imports and the balance of payments.

In 1956 South Africa had reserves of $370 million, equal to 24 per cent of imports. There is nothing to suggest that this country is anxious to increase the ratio to 30 per cent and still less to 40 per cent, though it would in all likelihood consider the 1957 ratio of 17 per cent (with reserves of $288 million) too low. It is a rapidly developing country, usually able to attract capital, and able to count on the ready disposal at a fixed price of its main export product, gold.

Malaya's ratio of reserves to imports was 23 per cent in 1957; it varied between 22 and 28 per cent in the years 1952 to 1957, compared with 27 per cent in 1937, and this seems to indicate that a ratio of this order has been found suitable for that country.

Most Latin American countries are anxious to develop their resources. Even in good years, when their products are selling at high prices, they do not substantially improve their reserve positions. If reserves increase one year, they will generally decline in a subsequent one.

On the other hand, there are countries that have maintained a high reserve level over a long period. Some of these countries, such as Egypt, accumulated substantial balances during the war. Others have benefited from the rapid development of oil and other natural resources, as did Iraq, Iran, and Venezuela.

The upward trend of world trade in the postwar period has provided opportunities for a large number of countries to improve their reserve positions. In fact, the countries which emerged from the war with practically no reserves have almost without exception been able to replenish them, although in some cases their reserves fluctuated widely during the period. This has been particularly evident in Europe. Aid from the United States and the operation of the European Payments Union have been of appreciable importance in these cases. On the other hand, other countries which accumulated reserves during the war spent heavily thereafter on supplies which had been unobtainable during the war and on goods required for development purposes. This spending, for example, in India and a number of Latin American countries, generally led to reductions in reserves. In some cases, these reductions have often gone farther than had been anticipated, and the decline has not yet been arrested.

As a group, all countries except the United States (and excluding the international agencies) increased their reserves from $22.1 billion in 1948 to $23.6 billion in 1951 and $29.7 billion in 1956. During the period 1948–56, reserves increased by $7.6 billion, or almost $1 billion per year. The rate of increase in this period was 4½ per cent per year, despite the reduction in reserves in 1949 which was caused by the devaluation of sterling. During the period 1951–56, which was one of comparative calm disturbed at the end by the Suez events, reserves increased by $6.1 billion, or $1.2 billion per year. The annual rate of increase in these five years was 5 per cent. These rates of increase are historically very large—and much larger than the rates of growth in the volume of trade over sustained periods. The situation in 1957 was disturbed by the inevitable liquidity stresses of the top of the boom, followed by the speculation in several key European currencies and the recession in the United States. There was in 1957 a considerable flow of gold to the United States. Even so, reserves of all countries except the United States increased by $300 million, though not without drawing on the Fund's resources. In the first six months of 1958, the outflow of gold from the United States ($1,445 million) was almost twice as great as the inflow in the whole of 1957 ($799 million). The prospect is for a substantial increase in 1958 in the reserves of all countries other than the United States.

The improvement in the reserve positions of many countries could not have taken place had they not restored balance in their positions, both internally and in relation to other economies. The foreign exchange markets provide further proof of this improvement. Quotations on free and black markets have moved closer to the official rates, and in some cases now almost coincide with them.

In several places, reference has been made to the fact that uncommitted savings are needed if gold and foreign exchange reserves are to be increased. An increase in reserves represents an investment which must be financed from savings in the same way as any other investment. In many cases, these savings accrue almost automatically. As production and trade grow, the needs of the economy for cash also grow. The increase in domestic cash holdings represents, in part, one source of savings which may form the counterpart of an increase in reserves. Banks and the rest of the private sector may also increase their exchange holdings in line with the increase in trade. However, for a more rapid increase in reserves, additional savings are required. Where pressure on reserves stems from inflationary tendencies, this involves either a decrease in the community's money income or a slowing down of the rate of its increase. Budget surpluses may be used to increase government deposits or (preferably) to repay government debt, particularly to the central bank. Part of the proceeds of foreign borrowing may be earmarked to increase reserves; and the proceeds of foreign aid may be sterilized for a similar purpose. In many cases, a reduction in private borrowing (or perhaps even the development of surpluses in the private sector) is required. The general theory, and even in some cases the specific measurements, of this mechanism are now well known and may be summarized very briefly. An inflationary increase in the money income of the community increases the demand for imports and it may also decrease exports; in any case, it leads to a decline of reserves. This increase in income may be the result of government borrowing, or private borrowing, or both. To stop the process requires a reduction in the rate of credit expansion; to reverse it requires a larger reduction. It is not necessary in most cases that credit not expand at all, for a growing and developing nation always needs some increase in its money supply.

It is in some respects instructive to examine what happened during the Korean crisis. As a result of the rise in prices, a number of countries, especially raw materials producing countries, were able rapidly to increase their earnings through larger exports. The immediate result was often a substantial increase in their foreign reserves. However, the increased earnings of the producers, traders, and others in these countries gave them a higher income which, when no special measures were taken, were gradually used for purchases of various kinds. After a certain lag, it was invariably found that imports rapidly increased, and often at a time when the export prices and receipts had begun to decline. As a result, the improvement in the reserve position was wiped out within a few years. When the increase in export incomes stimulated credit expansion to business or budget deficits by government the decline of reserves went even further. However, in some countries (especially some British colonies) steps were taken to pay the producers of the commodities exported only a part of the increased earnings resulting from the higher prices. The difference between the export price and the home price was accumulated in special reserves. In these cases there was no sudden increase in incomes leading to larger imports, and the exchange reserves which had been accumulated remained more or less intact.

There is now greater understanding of the conditions necessary for an improvement in the reserve position. For example, a recent statement by the Monetary Committee of the International Chamber of Commerce recommended that countries gradually reduce their debts to central banks, and thus strengthen not only their internal conditions but also their reserve holdings.

The Position of the United Kingdom

The role and the strength of sterling and the reserve position of the United Kingdom have been major financial concerns of the world in the postwar period and will continue to be such in the foreseeable future. This is a natural consequence of the importance of sterling in the world economy. A large part of the world's trade is financed in sterling; sterling assets constitute a substantial proportion (about 10 per cent) of the world's international reserves; the convertibility of sterling is a prerequisite for the convertibility of several other major currencies; and all these circumstances are involved in any assessment of the prospects for further moves toward the liberalization of trade.

In the postwar period, the United Kingdom has, with the exception of only a few years, had a surplus on the current account of its balance of payments. For the period 1948–56, the net surplus on current account amounted to a total of £1.2 billion, equivalent to almost $3.4 billion. The fact that the United Kingdom was nevertheless affected by several postwar financial crises has to be related to the following considerations:

(1) The United Kingdom emerged from the war with greatly reduced foreign assets and greatly increased foreign liabilities, mainly in the form of sterling balances which could easily be drawn upon and which could affect confidence in sterling. At the end of the war, sterling liabilities stood at $14.4 billion, compared with $4 billion in 1937. By 1948, these had been reduced to $12.7 billion, and after the devaluation of sterling, they amounted to $8.8 billion at the end of 1949. In 1957 they stood at $9.1 billion. But this stability covers important changes. In the meantime, a number of countries that had accumulated large sterling balances during the war (e.g., India) had drawn them down substantially, and a number of other countries that for various reasons wished to reduce their sterling balances had also done so. On the other hand, the British colonies (which for most of the postwar period included Malaya and Ghana) increased their balances substantially. Although a number of countries will undoubtedly wish to use their sterling balances for development in the next years, the total of all balances is certainly more stable than at any time since the war and, in real terms, no higher than in 1937. Nevertheless, the total of sterling liabilities is large in relation to reserves, so that the threat of any substantial movement is worrisome, especially when added to that of other elements.

(2) The foreign trade of the United Kingdom is large in relation to its national product and its reserves. Shifts in payment leads and lags may therefore cause important movements of reserves, and may well have involved movements of funds exceeding $500 million within periods as short as a few months.

(3) Such movements may, furthermore, be accentuated by changes in the extent to which use is made of sterling credits to finance trade not directly connected with the United Kingdom's own imports and exports.

(4) The surpluses arising on the current account of the balance of payments have been substantial, and they have not been used to increase reserves. Instead, they have had their counterpart mainly in the granting of foreign credits, investments abroad, and other foreign capital transactions, including repayment of debt.

Under these conditions, any adverse circumstances are likely to affect confidence in sterling and to lead to substantial changes in sterling reserves.

The fact that there has in most years been a surplus on the current account of the U.K. balance of payments would tend to show that sterling, at least since the devaluation of 1949, has not been overvalued. As to the use made of the balance of payments surpluses, the following figures are taken from a statement made by Sir Oliver Franks to the annual meeting of Lloyds Bank in January 1958.[2] In the five and a half years from January 1952 to June 1957, the total available from international transactions for foreign investment, repayment of debt, or addition to reserves was £1,051 million. This amount had its counterpart in the following transactions:

(1) Net capital investment in sterling countries to the amount of £359 million (representing a gross investment of £648 million, partly offset by an increase of £289 million in sterling balances);

(2) Repayment of sterling balances of non-sterling countries to the extent of £372 million;

(3) Other capital transactions with non-sterling countries to the amount of £304 million;

(4) As a net result, reserves in this period increased by only £16 million.

In considering these results, it is important to remember that the savings which were the counterpart of these surpluses on the current account of the balance of payments were made mainly by private firms and individuals. Frequently, they were in the form of profits ploughed back in the countries in which they were earned by U.K. firms operating abroad. The use to which the savings were put depended therefore to a great extent upon a large number of separate decisions, which in a period of expanding trade would naturally lead to expanded investments of various kinds. It would, of course, have been possible by direct controls to inhibit some of the transactions, and in 1957 some controls were in fact imposed on U.K. investment outside of the sterling area. On the other hand, the fact that the British financial system has been able to continue working without too many restrictions has been valuable in itself. The amounts used for these transactions in a large measure added to the earning capacity of the British economy, and they also benefited those areas in which investments were made.

The reserve problem of the United Kingdom is complex, and is the result of many developments over many years. After World War II, the United Kingdom had to adapt itself to a changed world and, compared with its situation before the war, it had to do this with lower reserves, much smaller overseas investments, much larger short-term liabilities, a great deal of wartime damage and obsolescence which had to be made up, and a pressing backlog of domestic demand for both capital and consumer goods. Although the course of the reserves problem reflects international developments, it also reflects the British decisions, implicit or explicit, about the priorities to be assigned to each of these complex demands upon its economy. As has been suggested, it would simplify the problem unduly to suggest that all, or even a much larger part, of the national saving on current account could have been turned into reserve holdings of gold and dollars. This might have unduly weakened the long-term position of the United Kingdom and it would in any case not have been easy to shift investment from

---

[2] As reported in *The Economist* (London), January 25, 1958.

overseas assets to reserves of gold and dollars. This might have required an extensive reorientation of trade, with perhaps a lower over-all level of employment and national income for a time. It would have had serious implications for the cohesiveness of the sterling area. On the other hand, in the longer run this investment in overseas assets would bolster future export markets for capital goods, provide future income, and perhaps (directly or indirectly) enable the sterling area to increase its exports to the non-sterling area and/or reduce its imports from it.

But perhaps even this way of looking at the reserves problem of the United Kingdom is too narrow. The gross national product in the period 1950–57 was almost £140 billion, or roughly $400 billion. Redirection of this gross product to increase purchases of gold or dollars by $2 billion in eight years would be equivalent to a change of ½ per cent in final product composition. Such redirection might not have been easy, considering the large number of competing alternatives (including the rise in defense expenditure as international tension increased), but it cannot be considered outside of practical possibilities.

In evaluating the total of, and the changes in, the reserves of the United Kingdom, account must always be taken of the movements in short-term sterling liabilities. An increase of reserves that accompanies, or results from, an increase in sterling balances may not signify any real improvement in reserve position. This has been the case on a number of occasions in the postwar period, and particularly in 1950 when at the height of the Korean boom reserves rose to $3.7 billion. The improvement in sterling reserves since the third quarter of 1957 has a different significance. It is to be regarded as the result of higher priority given to strengthening the international position of sterling. At the end of September 1957, in which month Bank Rate was increased from 5 per cent to 7 per cent, and a series of other important financial measures were taken, reserves stood at $1,850 million; by June 1958 they had increased to $3,180 million.[3] On the other hand, sterling liabilities at the end of the third quarter of 1957 stood at $9,433 million; by March 1958 (the latest date for which data are available), they had been reduced to $9,055 million.

These recent developments in reserve holdings and in sterling liabilities have undoubtedly improved the monetary position of the United Kingdom significantly, especially as they have not been accompanied by a reduction in raw materials and other inventories. It would appear, in addition, that this position improved gradually in the postwar period, even though this was not reflected in an increase in reserve holdings. The competitive position of British export industries has been strengthened as domestic backlogs have been worked off and the pressure of domestic demands moderated. The large foreign investments that have been made inside and outside the sterling area have improved the position of the United Kingdom, while their costs in terms both of goods and of their effects on reserves have largely been paid. Nevertheless, there is always the possibility that some countries will begin or continue to draw on their sterling balances for development and other purposes. If these drawings are sudden and large, and particularly if they are of a speculative character, they can cause financial inconvenience or even crisis. On the other hand, if they are moderate and for development purposes—and British export industries remain competitive—they should up to a point support the British balance of payments.

---

[3] To the extent of $250 million the increase was due to a drawing from the Export-Import Bank. This drawing was additional to the earlier drawing of $561 million from the International Monetary Fund in December 1956 at the time of the Suez tension.

Part of the present sterling balances do not represent savings which have been made with the prospect of eventually financing future development, or backing for various national currencies, but rather working balances for the conduct of international trade. If world trade continues to increase and confidence in sterling is maintained, it is not unlikely that a number of countries will need to add to their sterling holdings. The net result of these various movements on the position of sterling cannot be foreseen. Even less is it possible to foresee political or international crises which may have an equally important impact on sterling. With the improvement in the British position which has already taken place and which can be expected from a further net accumulation of reserves, the prospects for a continued relaxation of exchange controls are better than they have been in previous years. Sterling is, however, subject to large influences from all over the world, and it has therefore not been surprising that in the United Kingdom stress has been laid upon the importance of having a secondary line of defense available in case of need.

The Position of the United States

The gold holdings of the United States increased during and immediately after World War I, but were then comparatively stable for about ten years. From 1934 onward (when they were $8.3 billion) they again grew rapidly, and they continued to grow during World War II. By 1945 gold reserves were equal to $20.1 billion. By 1949, the all-time high point, gold holdings totaled $24.6 billion, or 74 per cent of the world's stock of monetary gold. In the following years there were variations in the level of gold reserves, but on balance there was a decline, so that by the end of June 1958 the amount of gold held by the United States was $21.4 billion, equal to 55 per cent of the world's monetary gold stock. If gold and foreign exchange reserves are taken together, the United States at the end of 1956 held about 40 per cent of the world's reserves, or approximately the same proportion that U.S. industrial output bears to the industrial output of the world (excluding here, as elsewhere, the communist countries).

The Federal Reserve System is required to maintain a gold reserve of 25 per cent against its deposit liabilities and paper currency issues (Federal Reserve Notes). This requirement has been in effect since 1945, and represents a reduction of about one third from the previous legal requirements of 35 per cent against deposits and 40 per cent against Federal Reserve Notes.

The Federal Reserve System has had large gold holdings in excess of legal requirements for many years. In the 1920's, for example, slightly more than half of its gold holdings were in excess of its reserve requirements, and this percentage increased sharply in the next decade, particularly after the price of gold was increased in 1934. In the period 1950–57, "free" gold in excess of requirements averaged $10.7 billion, or about 48 per cent of total gold holdings.

There is thus a large margin, according to present reserve requirements, for expanding the money supply of the United States or, alternatively, for reducing gold holdings. In addition, the money supply can be expanded in relation to gold if the reserve ratios of commercial banks are reduced, since these reserves consist of deposits in the Federal Reserve Banks. The combined effect of the reserve requirements of the Federal Reserve and the commercial banks was such that in 1957 gold was equal to 17 per cent of the money supply of $139 billion. This percentage may be compared with 20 per cent in 1947 and 43 per cent in 1937. Given the magnitude of the present margin of excess reserves, it is unlikely that the United States would exercise its power further to reduce the reserve requirements of the Federal Reserve System. The System also has authority temporarily to suspend reserve requirements,[4] but, for the same reasons, it is unlikely that it would do this.

The state of the gold reserves of the United States must also be considered in the light of its short-term liabilities. These have grown rapidly in recent years: they were $1.9 billion in 1937, $7.2 billion in 1948, and $14.8 billion at the end of 1957. Although these balances are not legally convertible into gold, the United States for many years has followed the practice of converting all official balances (almost two thirds of the total) upon request, and, as a practical matter, all dollar balances may be treated as convertible. This situation has led to questions in some quarters whether the United States has enough gold to meet its domestic reserve requirements as well as possible drains upon its gold supply that might follow from conversion of dollar balances. The data on gold holdings, gold in excess of reserve requirements, and dollar liabilities are given in Table 16.

There is, of course, always the possibility of a "run" on the dollar, in the same way as there is the possibility of a "run" on any other currency. If this were to take place, the pressure on the dollar could come from many sources other than the sale or conversion of short-term dollar holdings, a large part of which must represent working balances. Foreign holdings of stocks, bonds, and other securities which could be sold or pledged were valued at almost $9 billion in 1956. The pressure resulting from a change in "leads and lags" of foreign trade amounting to $25 billion a year, and the speculation against the dollar which might be financed with borrowed funds by both foreigners and U.S. citizens, must also be considered. In fact, as has already been noted in connection with the level of reserves in general and the reserves of individual countries in particular, the financial strength of a country depends upon many other factors besides its reserves. That the United States has huge gold holdings, equal to 55 per cent of the world's gold stock, and that it has large gold holdings in excess of its domestic reserve requirements, do not change this basic fact. Large reserves, of course, give the United States great opportunity for maneuver and for the exercise of monetary policy in dealing with speculative and other adverse developments. But the ultimate financial strength of the United States rests on its strong international position and the fact that it is an extremely important market, a dominant supplier of economic and other kinds of aid, and a major source of long-term and short-term capital. It would therefore be natural for the rest of the world to maintain large holdings of dollars for working balances, investment, and other purposes.

It is interesting to note that in each of the postwar periods of recession the level of dollar liabilities has remained very stable. The large outflow of gold in 1958, for example, did not reflect the conversion of dollar balances, but rather the normal reserve practices of countries with surpluses on the current account of their balances of payments.

Under the rules of the gold standard, it was the general practice to wait for an influx of gold before easing credit conditions. Today the U.S. authorities, thanks to the substantial gold holdings at their disposal, are able to relax credit even where there is an outflow of gold. It has been an element of strength that the United States has been able to face the task of preventing excessive fluctuations in business activity without being hampered by an insufficiency of monetary reserves. From the point of view of

---

[4] Federal Reserve Act, Sec. 11, para. 4. Requirements may be suspended for 30 days, and the suspension may be renewed for periods not exceeding 15 days.

world liquidity, too, the expansion of credit and the decline of interest rates in U.S. markets, in the face of a recession, have been of importance. This has made it increasingly possible for other countries to ease their own credit conditions, for account has to be taken not only of the absolute interest level in any one country but also of that interest level in relation to those in other economies and, especially, in the international financial centers.

Table 16. U.S. Gold Reserves, Domestic Reserve Requirements, and Short-Term Foreign Liabilities, Selected Years, 1922-57

(In billions of U.S. dollars)

Year	Gold Reserves	Domestic Reserve Requirements	"Free" Gold: In Excess of Reserve Requirements	Foreign Short-Term Dollar Balances	Per Cent of All Gold to Foreign Balances	Per Cent of 'Free" Gold to Foreign Balances
1922	3.5	1.7	1.8	1.0	350	180
1925	4.0	1.6	2.4	1.2	333	200
1926	4.1	1.6	2.5	1.6	256	156
1927	4.0	1.6	2.4	2.6	154	92
1928	3.7	1.6	2.1	2.5	148	84
1929	3.9	1.6	2.3	2.7	144	85
1930	4.2	1.6	2.6	2.3	183	113
1933	4.0	2.2	1.8	.4	1,000	450
1934	8.3	2.7	5.6	.7	1,038	700
1935	10.1	3.6	6.5	1.3	777	500
1936	11.4	4.1	7.3	1.6	712	456
1937	12.8	4.2	8.6	1.9	674	453
1938	14.6	5.1	9.5	2.2	664	432
1940	22.0	7.9	14.1	3.9	564	362
1945	20.1	10.9	9.2	7.1	283	130
1946	20.7	10.7	10.0	6.5	318	154
1947	22.9	11.3	11.6	7.1	323	163
1948	24.4	11.9	12.5	7.2	339	174
1949	24.6	10.8	13.8	7.6	324	182
1950	22.8	11.0	11.8	8.4	271	140
1951	22.9	11.7	11.2	8.3	276	135
1952	23.3	12.1	11.2	9.9	235	113
1953	22.1	12.0	10.1	10.8	205	94
1954	21.8	11.7	10.1	11.9	183	85
1955	21.8	11.9	9.9	13.0	168	76
1956	22.1	11.9	10.2	14.6	151	70
1957	22.9	11.9	11.0	14.8	155	74

Sources: Data on gold reserves, domestic requirements, and dollar balances for 1922-52 are from *Annual Report of the Secretary of the Treasury*, 1954, Exhibit 47; later data on gold reserves are from *Federal Reserve Bulletin*. Domestic reserve requirements were calculated from data published in *Federal Reserve Bulletin* table on "Statement of Condition of the Federal Reserve Banks." Short-term dollar balances are from *International Financial Statistics* and include holdings of government bonds and notes.

The Distribution of Monetary Reserves

Some countries habitually hold comparatively low reserves, while others over the years have held more ample reserves. If, by and large, these differences continue, there is little significance in any discussion of the redistribution of reserves. On the other hand, it is probable that the countries with very large reserves will not think it necessary to set aside substantial savings for the purpose of increasing their reserves, and it is desirable that countries with low reserves should improve their positions. It is, therefore, of some interest to outline what additional amounts of gold and foreign exchange would be required to raise reserves to, say, 30 per cent of imports for all countries that are below this level.

After exclusion of the United Kingdom, which is in many respects a special case, the additional amount required to raise to 30 per cent the reserve ratios of all countries that were below it in 1956 would be $1.8 billion of reserves. To reach a minimum of 40 per cent, $4.9 billion would be required.

These figures do no more than indicate the magnitude of the reserves that would have to be acquired if all countries which at present have low reserves were to try to acquire more over a reasonable period. But it is hardly likely that all these countries, whatever their wishes may be, will be prepared to take the steps necessary to improve their reserve positions to this extent. For the United Kingdom, as already mentioned, the amount of reserves has to be judged in relation to the movement of sterling balances. But if this country were to add another billion to its present reserves of $3 billion, and also all countries with low reserves were to try to reach a ratio of 40 per cent, the amount required over a number of years would be of the order of, say, $6 billion. To judge from developments in the postwar period, this would not seem out of the question. In the period 1949–57 reserves grew at the rate of almost $1.2 billion per year, and in the period 1951–57, at the rate of $1.0 billion per year. For the future, the addition to international reserves from current gold production at the present price of gold is likely to be $700 million per year, and, at a minimum, should be at least as large as the average addition in 1951–57, or about $550 million per year. There is no reason to assume that there could not be further additions to foreign-held dollar balances. Since it is perhaps also fair to assume that countries which now hold fairly large reserves see no urgent reason to add substantially to them, this annual flow of gold and other resources would largely be available to other countries prepared to take the necessary steps to improve their reserve positions.

Moreover, it is pertinent to recall that the amount of newly mined gold that has gone into private holdings since 1946, largely by reason of the lack of monetary confidence, has attained a total of between $3 billion and $4 billion. The amount of gold in private hoards is now estimated to be of the order of $10 billion to $12 billion, of which almost one half is held in Western Europe, and almost one third in France alone. If only one half of the newly mined gold that went into private hoards in the postwar period had been available for monetary reserves and had been acquired by the countries with the lowest reserves, it would have been enough to assure that every country had a ratio of reserves to imports equal to at least 25 per cent. A small amount of dishoarding was recently reported in France in connection with an issue of gold-indexed bonds. If dishoarding there and elsewhere should increase so that, on balance, there were no additions to gold hoards in the world at large, well over $700 million a year could be added to monetary reserves from current gold production, which has been increasing even with the present price of gold.

Thus the problem is not so much one of finding the resources in gold and foreign exchange which would be available for an improvement in the reserve position, but rather of the willingness of countries to take the necessary steps in the fiscal and credit fields to restore a proper balance within and among their various economies. It has often been emphasized that devaluation, useful as it may be in certain circumstances to attain a realistic rate of exchange, can lead to an effective solution of a country's difficulties only if it is combined with proper fiscal and credit policies. Since the prevailing exchange rates of a very large number of countries are much more realistic than they were in the immediate postwar period, the emphasis must necessarily be placed on the maintenance of internal balance if further monetary progress is to be made. There is no way of escaping these basic efforts. If they are made, there seems to be no evidence that the solution of the problems relating to an all-round improvement in the reserve position of individual countries will be hampered by an over-all scarcity of reserves. This conclusion remains, however, conditioned upon the continuance of constructive efforts to strengthen the international economic and credit system.

CHAPTER FOUR: PROSPECTIVE RESERVES AND REQUIREMENTS

As already mentioned in previous chapters, official reserves of gold, and of dollars, sterling, and other forms of exchange, have two functions. In the purely domestic sense, these reserves may be a prerequisite for an increase in the volume of domestic money—currency and bank deposits. In the international sense, they may be used to finance swings in the balance of payments. These two functions are interrelated. An excessive increase in the domestic money supply will make the balance of payments unfavorable and lead to declining reserves; a gain in reserves may ease credit policy and encourage an increase in the supply of domestic money.

Under the orthodox operation of the gold standard (which was never so strict in practice as it was often defined in theory), increases in the gold holdings of the banks of issue were, in general, a prerequisite for an increase in the volume of currency and deposits. Since an expansion in production and trade would need more credit, it was not unnatural to regard it as essential that gold output should keep pace with potential economic growth in the world at large. It is still true that changes in monetary reserves influence credit developments, both by their direct effects on the volume of money and by their influence on credit policy. But it is also true that for a fairly large number of countries, changes in monetary reserves no longer have the paramount importance that they previously did.

There are several reasons for this. First, many countries have weakened the link between the amount of reserves and the amount of domestic money in order to obtain more flexibility in their monetary operations. There has been a pronounced trend for reserves of gold and exchange to become a smaller and smaller percentage of the domestic money supply. In some cases this is the result of reducing the cover percentages of the central bank; in others, of reducing the reserve ratios of commercial banks or of permitting the growth of financial intermediaries whose effective reserve ratios are lower than those of commercial banks. In addition to these longer term developments, many countries, both developed and underdeveloped, are using changes in commercial bank reserve requirements as a supplement to the traditional weapons of discount rates and open market operations. Secondly, the link between the amount of reserves and the amount of domestic money has been weakened in all countries that have not made a stable fixed rate of exchange an overriding objective of monetary policy. An increase in the supply of domestic money may not lead to a loss of reserves if the exchange rate is allowed to depreciate but the declining value of the currency is, of course, a source of weakness in itself, which cannot be tolerated for long. Thirdly, as has already been pointed out above, a number of countries, and particularly those with large monetary reserves, can carry out credit policies relatively independently of changes in their reserve position. Indeed, the credit systems of several countries are now able to generate their own liquidity with a fairly high degree of freedom. These countries can adopt policies which may lead to a decline of gold reserves or to the growth of foreign holdings of their money. The liquidity of these countries is thus of outstanding importance for the liquidity position of the world. To a considerable extent, international liquidity can now be produced without the limiting factor of the gold base. Thus, the liquidity position of the world was greatly eased by the credit expansion in the United States in 1957–58 at a time when its gold reserve was declining.

In short, the growth of the domestic money supply in most countries is no longer so closely tied to the growth of international reserves as it was in the days of the gold standard. The required increase in the domestic money supply of individual countries no longer creates as large a proportional demand for gold cover as it did in the days of the gold standard. In addition, a number of countries are able to create additional liquidity on the basis of their existing reserves, and this adds to world liquidity.

The Growth of Reserves and Reserve Requirements

The preceding chapters have discussed the amount and the distribution of reserves and have related the level of reserves to the level of trade in various years. To the extent that this was possible, the amount of reserves was interpreted in terms of the adequacy or the inadequacy of reserve levels, and the qualifications that must surround any such judgment were made clear. In this section, the analysis will be pushed forward to take account of the probable development of reserve levels on the assumption—or perhaps, better, the requirement—of a continued growth of world trade. Here again it is necessary to emphasize the basic consideration that the adequacy of reserves depends very much on the environment in which the monetary system operates—the balance attained in the relationship of the various economies with one another, the readiness to take corrective measures when an imbalance occurs, the effectiveness of the private credit system, tariff policies, etc. Since developments in these fields play such a decisive role, there can be no fixed mathematical relationship between the growth of reserves and the expansion of production and foreign trade. It should not be assumed that an increase in reserves will more or less automatically induce an increase in the volume of trade—and indeed, there have been periods, as in the 1930's, when very substantial increases in reserves were accompanied by restrictionism and stagnant trade. Neither should it be assumed that the potential increase in the volume of trade can necessarily be no greater than the increase in the volume of international reserves.

It is of interest to consider what increase in production, and more particularly in foreign trade, is in prospect in, for example, the next decade, and how the world's reserve position is likely to develop. For this purpose, Table 17 shows the rates of increase of world trade and manufacturing production for various periods from 1876–80 to 1957.

A number of economic investigators—Cassel, Kitchin, and others—calculated that the rate of growth in the world economy was about 3 per cent per annum in the fifty years before 1914. It will be seen from the table, which is based upon the most recent data for the period, that the increase in manufacturing activity (which may have risen more rapidly than gross national product) was 4.1 per cent per year, while the increase in trade was somewhat less than 3.4 per cent per year.

The largest rates of growth occurred in the immediate postwar years after World Wars I and II. For the periods from 1921–25 to 1926–29, or roughly four and a half years, manufacturing activity grew 6.8 per cent per year; trade grew at a slightly lower rate. For the years from 1948 to 1956, manufacturing grew 6.1 per cent, and trade 7.5 per cent per year. For longer periods, which include the years of war and

Table 17. Average Annual Rates of Growth of Trade and Manufacturing, Selected Periods
(In per cent; compound basis)

Period	Trade [1]		Manufacturing Activity [2]
	Primary products	Manufactured products	
From 1876-80 to:			
1901-05	3.3	2.8	4.1
1913	3.4	3.3	4.1
1926-29	2.6	2.4	3.5
1930	2.6	2.2	3.3
1936-38	2.3	1.8	3.5
From 1901-05 to:			
1913	3.5	4.7	4.2
1926-29	2.0	2.1	3.1
1930	2.0	1.7	2.7
1936-38	1.5	1.1	3.1
From 1921-25 to:			
1926-29	6.3	7.1	6.8
1930	4.9	3.8	4.1
1936-38	2.2	1.3	4.4
From 1938 to 1948	0.0		3.7
From 1948 to 1956	7.5		6.1
From 1950 to 1956	6.5		5.7
From 1950 to 1957	6.3		5.1
From 1951 to 1957	5.4		5.0

[1] These rates of growth were calculated from the following basic data: (1) Data for 1876-80 to 1936-38 are from League of Nations, *Industrialization and Foreign Trade* (1945), and include the U.S.S.R. Trade covers exports and imports. There is no combined index of trade of primary products and manufactured articles, though trade in the latter was about 60 per cent as great as that in the former. (2) Data beginning with 1938 are from Special Table A in United Nations, *Monthly Bulletin of Statistics*, November 1957, January 1958, and June 1958. These data refer to total exports and exclude the countries in the communist bloc.

[2] These rates of growth were calculated from the following basic data: (1) Data for 1876-80 to 1936-38 are from League of Nations, *Industrialization and Foreign Trade* (1945), and include the U.S.S.R. (2) Data beginning with 1938 are from Special Table A in United Nations, *Monthly Bulletin of Statistics*, January 1958 and June 1958, and exclude countries in the communist bloc.

depression, the rates of growth are naturally much smaller. Thus, from the years 1876–80 to 1936–38, manufacturing activity grew at the rate of 3.5 per cent per year, while trade grew at about 2 per cent per year. Correspondingly, from 1938 to 1957 the annual rates of growth were 4.6 per cent for manufacturing and 3.3 per cent for trade.

A particular characteristic of the period after World War II has been the fact that trade has increased at a faster rate than industrial production, while in earlier periods it grew no faster than industrial production, as in the 1920's, or increased less than production, as was the case before 1914. There have been many special factors after World War II which have made for a rapid increase in trade. Certain countries had substantial reserves accumulated during the war which they were able to spend; special efforts were made to provide aid and credits, and this was reflected in an increased volume of trade; moreover, the rapid expansion in the output and use of oil led to a large increase in foreign trade of an unprecedented character.

Past experiences seem to show that periods of very rapid expansion are generally followed by periods of more moderate growth. It is of course impossible to forecast what the rate of growth will be in the years immediately ahead, but it would probably not be overoptimistic to retain the conventional "normal" annual rate of about 3 per cent for the growth of world trade. This would in itself assume some improvement over the rate of growth in the sixty years before World War II.

If reserves are also to grow at the rate of 3 per cent per year and maintain the ratio of reserves to imports that applied at the end of 1956, they would have to increase by $19 billion by 1966. Such an addition would assume, however, that even the countries which already have very substantial reserves, such as the United States, the Federal Republic of Germany, Venezuela, and Switzerland, would want to increase their reserves by more than one third. In fact, if these four countries were to increase their reserves at the rate of 3 per cent per year, they would absorb about $11 billion of the computed world requirement of $19 billion for the next decade. This is most unlikely. If the problem of increasing international reserves is therefore reduced to the dimensions of increasing the reserves of all other countries, the requirement for additional reserves is reduced to about $8 billion. It may be doubted whether all other countries would in fact wish to increase their reserves so much.

It is estimated that the increase of gold reserves from current gold production is likely at the present price of gold to be at least $700 million per year for the next decade, even after allowing for an increase in the present large gold hoards.[1] Thus, gold production alone would go very far toward meeting the requirements for additional reserves. In addition, reserve holdings of foreign exchange are likely to rise if there is full employment in the industrial countries and the requirements for overseas spending by the United States in the form of imports, capital investments, defense, and aid of various kinds are maintained. All foreign short-term dollar balances increased from $7.1 billion in 1947 to $14.8 billion in 1957, and official holdings of dollars increased from $1.8 billion to $8.3 billion. All short-term dollar balances in the last decade therefore increased on the average by $770 million per year, and official balances alone increased by $650 million per year. Sterling balances in the past decade have naturally been reduced from the swollen heights they attained by the end of World War II. In terms of sterling, they have come down by 10 per cent, or from £3.6 billion at the end of 1945 to £3.3 billion at the end of 1957. In terms of dollars, the reduction was much greater because of the devaluation of sterling in 1949. Sterling holdings at the end of the first quarter of 1958 were about the same as they had been at the end of 1949. When all kinds of exchange holdings are taken together, the

---

[1] O. L. Altman, "A Note on Gold Production and Additions to International Gold Reserves," *Staff Papers*, Vol. VI, No. 2 (April 1958).

available data suggest that these reserves increased by a net total of about $2 billion in the past decade, or by $200 million per year.

The reserves problem that the world will face in the next decade does not, therefore, appear to be insoluble. This conclusion accords with the results arrived at in the preceding chapters, and it of course assumes the same comments that were made there about the relationship of reserves to international liquidity and the international environment.

The question may, however, be asked whether it is likely that the countries with relatively slender reserves will be in a position to increase them in the next decade by more than one third, or by approximately $8 billion. Clearly, some countries will add to their reserves. Others undoubtedly believe that they can safely draw down their reserves for development purposes, and this group includes countries whose reserves are already substantially lower than they were at the end of World War II. Even if these latter countries will not reduce their reserves further in the next years, they are not all likely to give priority to increasing them. Some countries have reserves which they have no reason to regard as insufficient, and they would probably not want to increase them as rapidly as their trade. Other countries have for a number of years operated with very small reserves, and in 1956 had ratios of reserves to imports much below the average for all countries. They will have good reasons to increase their reserves as trade grows, and probably up to a point will do so, but perhaps not in the same proportion as the growth of trade. There is also the most important question whether the United Kingdom, and all the countries of the sterling area, will wish to increase their reserves by more than one third in the next ten years. As far as the United Kingdom is concerned, the improvement of its reserve position can come not only from increasing its reserves but also from reducing its short-term liabilities, increasing the strength of London as a center for long-term and short-term capital, and (over the long term) by increasing its income from overseas investments. The priority that the United Kingdom will accord to increasing reserves thus depends upon many factors, and not least among them is the possibility of borrowing in periods of strain.

The likelihood is thus that some of the gold from current production will not be absorbed by those countries which now have slender reserves, but will be sold to countries which already have relatively large reserves.

Some central banks will wish to add part of their additional reserves in the form of exchange holdings rather than gold. To achieve this result, part of the current supply of gold will very likely be sold to the monetary authorities in the main financial centers. By this and other means, including the normal operations of the sterling area, these countries will make their own currencies available for increasing the reserves of other countries. While it is always difficult to foretell what will happen in the future, there is reason to believe that current gold production, plus the continued increase in exchange holdings, will provide opportunities for a substantial addition to the monetary reserves of those countries that wish to acquire larger reserves.

World gold production, at the current fixed price of $35 per fine ounce, has been increasing year by year, particularly since 1951. There is no reason to expect a reversal of this trend in the foreseeable future. With a continued strengthening of monetary confidence through appropriate fiscal and credit policies, it should be possible to ensure that most of the newly produced gold becomes available for normal industrial uses and monetary reserves. Considerable progress in this direction has already been made.

In these circumstances, it cannot be argued that the current supply is inadequate for the requirements which can now be foreseen. There is no proven need for any abrupt increase in the volume of current gold production or in its monetary value by an increase in the price of gold. A measure of that kind might even detract attention from the real monetary problems of restoring and maintaining a proper balance in the individual economies, and in their relations with one another, and of strengthening the international credit system.

Monetary reserves are drawn upon for settlement of a country's deficits on foreign account, but the actual financing of foreign trade is, of course, effected primarily by the commercial banks. These as a rule hold working balances in foreign currencies. If trade grows, these balances, especially those held in the main financial centers, may likewise be expected to increase. These balances are held not only by commercial banks, but also by private firms and individuals. In part they represent commercial borrowing in these same centers; in part they represent the accumulation of net foreign earnings and the proceeds of securities transactions. The total of these privately held balances is large. Of the outstanding dollar balances at the end of 1957, about 40 per cent, or about $5.3 billion, was privately held. The percentage of sterling balances held on private account is much smaller than this. It has recently been reported that at the end of 1957 private holdings came to £759 million ($2.1 billion), or about 23 per cent of all sterling liabilities of £3.3 billion (excluding the £645 million due to international organizations). Especially as regards dollars, it is fair to assume that a portion of the amount held privately is to some extent hoarded by individuals and firms, i.e., the turnover of these holdings is relatively small. But the major portion, even for dollars—and certainly for sterling—represents working balances which are required in the course of financing current business.

With an increase in monetary confidence and a relaxation of exchange controls (which have imposed severe limits on private holdings of foreign exchange), it is likely that there will be increasing movements of privately held balances and that, as was the case before 1914, equilibrating movements of funds will thereby be facilitated. This should, up to a point, reduce the strain on official reserves. For such a development to take place it is, however, necessary that the monetary authorities in the individual countries pursue flexible credit policies. This has been the tendency in recent years, and it seems to be increasingly agreed that the results obtained have been good.

Strengthening of the World's Monetary Situation by International Organizations

The breakdown and subsequent disintegration of the world's monetary system in the interwar period has shown that the over-all reserve position was not in itself of decisive importance. In 1928 the ratio of reserves to imports for countries other than the United States was 35 per cent, compared with 17 per cent in 1913. But high as it was, it could not stave off the monetary disruptions in the following years. Still less did the very high ratio of 63 per cent in 1937–38 act as a cure for stagnant trade. In the same way, the opportunities that are likely to exist for an over-all improvement in reserve positions in the years to come in themselves afford no guarantee of healthy monetary developments. These can be assured only by simultaneous constructive efforts in many fields. It may perhaps seem trite to remark that general political developments will be of decisive importance, and not only to the extent that a major war is avoided. But the world will never be altogether calm, and periods of financial tension will recur. It is, therefore, wise always to have available safeguards of a financial character.

International cooperation in financial matters is not new. Even before 1914 there were many instances of contact and assistance between central banks. In the interwar period the need for cooperation between monetary authorities became more fully recognized. This recognition first developed in connection with stabilization loans to various countries in the 1920's, in many cases under the auspices of the League of Nations. In 1930, the Bank for International Settlements (BIS) was established, formally as a by-product of efforts to solve the German reparations problem, but essentially to foster international monetary cooperation. In addition to performing rather extensive banking and trustee functions, the BIS has continued to serve as a meeting place for the central bankers of the European countries. In 1936, the Tripartite Agreement was signed by the United States, the United Kingdom, and France; and later Belgium, the Netherlands, and Switzerland became associated with it.

During World War II, major efforts were made to establish monetary cooperation on a world-wide basis. These resulted in the formation of the Bretton Woods institutions —the International Monetary Fund and the International Bank for Reconstruction and Development. The International Bank for Reconstruction and Development provides long-term capital, under government guarantee, for specific projects. This type of financing provides an essential complement to the short-term credit facilities of the International Monetary Fund, and in effect helps prevent long-term capital problems from turning into short-term liquidity problems. The purposes of the Fund are set out in Article I of its Articles of Agreement as follows:

(i) To promote international monetary cooperation through a permanent institution which provides the machinery for consultation and collaboration on international monetary problems.

(ii) To facilitate the expansion and balanced growth of international trade, and to contribute thereby to the promotion and maintenance of high levels of employment and real income and to the development of the productive resources of all members as primary objectives of economic policy.

(iii) To promote exchange stability, to maintain orderly exchange arrangements among members, and to avoid competitive exchange depreciation.

(iv) To assist in the establishment of a multilateral system of payments in respect of current transactions between members and in the elimination of foreign exchange restrictions which hamper the growth of world trade.

(v) To give confidence to members by making the Fund's resources available to them under adequate safeguards, thus providing them with opportunity to correct maladjustments in their balance of payments without resorting to measures destructive of national or international prosperity.

(vi) In accordance with the above, to shorten the duration and lessen the degree of disequilibrium in the international balances of payments of members.

The Fund was provided with resources in gold and in the currencies of its members, with each member contributing in proportion to its quota. Quotas also regulated the rights of members to draw on these resources for short-term financing. On April 30, 1947, the Fund held $1.3 billion in gold and the equivalent of $2.1 billion in U.S. dollars and other convertible currencies. The first Fund transactions were made after this date (the Fund had declared itself ready for transactions on March 1, 1947), and by the end of 1948 there had been a substantial number of transactions totaling $676 million.

In a number of European countries, however, the general economic and financial situation became critical, and in April 1948 special assistance was provided for these countries by the Marshall Plan. As part of the Marshall Plan arrangements, the Organization for European Economic Cooperation (OEEC) was set up in Paris, and, after some initial experiments with compensation plans, the European Payments Union (EPU) came into operation for the settlement of intra-European balances. At first, the settlement of these EPU balances was graduated to a maximum rate of 50 per cent in gold or dollars and 50 per cent in credit; in 1955, this was changed to 75 per cent in gold and dollars and 25 per cent in credit. The reduction in the credit element coincided with an improvement of the working of the private credit system and a general strengthening of the reserves of the member countries. Through the mechanism of the EPU, credit was extended to a maximum of $1.5 billion. Substantial swings within this total have from time to time greatly eased the liquidity of members. It is pertinent to note that a number of countries outside of Europe belonging to currency areas centering in Europe (e.g., countries in the sterling area, French franc area, Belgian franc area, and Dutch guilder area) have largely settled their European payments, and their payments with one another, via the EPU.

The sterling balances accumulated during World War II by almost every country in the British Commonwealth had provided these countries with considerable monetary reserves. Moreover, a number of Latin American countries had also been able, during the war, to add appreciably to their monetary reserves, mainly in the form of increases in their dollar holdings.

In this situation, characterized by special assistance to Europe and the possession of relatively large monetary reserves in other parts of the world, there was little reason for members to draw on the resources of the Fund. From the point of view of business activity, the years from 1949 to 1955 were lean years for the Fund. Total transactions in this six-year period came to only $542 million, or 20 per cent less than in the two years 1947–48. In 1950, there were no transactions; and in a number of years drawings were very small—$35 million in 1951, $62 million in 1954, and $28 million in 1955. However, these years were important in other respects. In this period the Fund's working methods became fully organized, annual consultations were carried out under Article XIV with countries maintaining exchange restrictions, forms of technical assistance to member countries were developed, and policies and principles for the use of the Fund's resources were agreed upon.

Through consultations and technical assistance, the Fund became intimately acquainted with the financial problems and the economic structure of the great majority of member countries, and it has been gratifying to find the readiness with which the member countries concerned have wholeheartedly participated in this work.

One of the provisions that safeguards use of the Fund's resources by all members is the limitation that, unless there is a waiver by the Fund under Article V, drawings by any one member in any one year shall not exceed 25 per cent of its quota. As trade has grown and swings in the balance of payments have therefore widened, the Fund has increasingly used the waiver privilege in order to meet the realistic needs of its members for drawings. In fact, the granting of waivers has recently been more the rule than the exception (Table 18). The use of waivers on this scale may be taken as indicating that members' quotas are now on the low side in relation to the intentions of the signatories of the Articles of Agreement at Bretton Woods in 1944, which in turn were based upon trade data relating to the 1930's. This fact has been recognized in a number of individual cases, and increases in the quotas of nine smaller countries have been authorized in recent years.

Under the Articles of Agreement, members have automatic repurchase obligations which are broadly dependent upon the movements of their monetary reserves. In addition, however, the Fund has adopted principles under which members requesting a drawing or a stand-by arrangement are expected to undertake to repurchase within three to five years. Through these provisions the revolving nature of the Fund's resources has been emphasized and strengthened, and it is interesting to note that, of the assistance granted by the Fund up to the end of May 1958, an amount of $1.2 billion has been repurchased.

The Fund can be of maximum financial assurance to its members by developing a coherent body of precedents and principles that govern drawings by members and by adopting practices that meet their needs. The development of principles relating to drawings in different "tranches" and the creation of the stand-by were important steps in this direction. In 1952 the Fund laid down the principle that governs drawings within the gold tranche, i.e., that portion of a member's quota which can be regarded as the equivalent of its gold subscription. Within the gold tranche, members can expect to receive the overwhelming benefit of any doubt that may arise in connection with

Table 18. Use of Waiver in Fund Transactions, 1953-58

Calendar Year	All Transactions		Transactions with Waivers	
	Number	Amount (million dollars)	Number	Amount (million dollars)
1953	8	$ 203	2	$ 48
1954	3	62	2	48
1955	3	28	2	19
1956	14	693	12	665
1957	35	977	31	820
1958 [1]	12	265	11	240
Total	75	$2,228	60	$1,840

[1] Through July 31.

a request for a drawing. Subsequently, in connection with drawings in the first credit tranche, i.e., those drawings that raised the Fund's holdings of a member's currency above 100 per cent, but not beyond 125 per cent of quota, the Fund established the principle that members can confidently expect a favorable response to their applications provided they are making reasonable efforts to solve their problems. The criteria for larger drawings are still stricter, and include well-balanced and adequate programs to restore balance, to establish or maintain the enduring stability of the currency at a realistic rate of exchange, and to prepare the conditions for repayment of the drawing.

In 1952, for the first time, the Fund also approved an arrangement for a stand-by, i.e., an agreement that permits a member to draw up to a stated amount during a limited period of time, usually 6–12 months. Stand-bys are usually renewable unless either the Fund or the member determines that conditions have been basically altered so that the arrangement should be terminated. Since 1952 Fund members have made increasing use of stand-by arrangements. In the fiscal year ended April 30, 1958, stand-by arrangements were agreed or extended for 11 members, and since 1952 a total of 19 members have participated in one or more stand-bys.

The practices and principles which had been gradually formulated by the Fund proved of great value when, in the latter half of 1956, a new and more active phase began with regard to the transactions of the Fund. For the two years up to the end of April 1958, these transactions reached the total of $2.3 billion (including unused amounts under stand-by arrangements), an amount equal to nearly two thirds of all the transactions of the Fund since its inception. In comparative terms, this is equal to one quarter of the increase in all dollar balances during the postwar period, and to more than four years' increase in gold reserves from new gold production. In all, from March 1, 1947, when the Fund declared itself ready for operations, to April 30, 1958, total transactions amounted to the equivalent of $3,016 million. The Fund sold currency to 35 members, of whom 28 used the Fund's resources more than once. About 92 per cent of the currency sales was made in U.S. dollars, but there were also sales of sterling, Belgian francs, deutsche mark, Canadian dollars, and Netherlands guilders. In the same period, 37 members repurchased their currencies to the amount of $1,120 million. This total includes not only repurchases made by members in repayment of drawings, but also purchases by members who originally did not subscribe 25 per cent of their quotas in gold. In all, 18 members that originally paid in less than 25 per cent of their quotas in gold (out of a total of 32) purchased $136 million of their currency; and these purchases, added to their original gold subscriptions, put them in a position comparable to those members whose original gold subscriptions were equivalent to 25 per cent of quotas. This development is a significant commentary on the way the automatic repurchase provisions of the Fund Agreement help to ensure the revolving and liquid character of the Fund's assets.

The extent to which members of the Fund have used its resources may be compared by relating the total of their drawings and unused stand-bys (if any) to their quotas. By this measurement, the five members that made the greatest use of the Fund in relation to quota were (in order) Brazil, Chile, Iran, the United Kingdom, and Turkey. Brazil's drawings were equal to 137 per cent of quota, and Turkey's to 113 per cent of quota. In all, there were 13 members whose drawings and/or stand-bys are equivalent to 99 per cent of quota and more.

It is of particular interest to distinguish the characteristics of the transactions undertaken by the Fund during the years 1956–58.

(1) The most conspicuous transaction was the granting of financial assistance to the United Kingdom in connection with the Suez events, involving a drawing of $561 million and a stand-by of $739 million. This assistance was given on the basis of a declaration by the British Government that strict financial and credit policies would be pursued, that quantitative restrictions would not be reimposed, and that the value of sterling would be maintained. Thanks to this prompt action by the Fund, which was supplemented by a loan of $500 million from the Export-Import Bank of Washington, the position of this key currency was reinforced at a crucial moment, and a crack was avoided in the international exchange structure.

(2) In the course of 1957, the world-wide boom was accompanied by a general pressure on liquidity (internal as well as international), and a number of countries made requests for the use of the Fund's resources. The transactions included stand-by arrangements with Denmark, the Netherlands, Japan, and India. The drawings by these countries came to $428 million; the total, including stand-by arrangements granted but

not drawn upon, was $570 million. In India, the strains on the reserve position reflected to a great extent the volume of expenditure under the Five Year Plan, but the boom conditions also played their part, and private investment and imports increased at a more rapid rate than had been estimated when the Plan was drawn up. In all these cases, at the time that the requests for drawings were considered, in accordance with the principles mentioned above, the governments made statements to the Fund concerning the monetary and other relevant policies they intended to follow: in the case of stand-by arrangements, these "declarations of intent" were incorporated into the provisions of the agreements themselves.

(3) The decline in the volume of business activity which began to make itself felt in the third quarter of 1957, especially in the United States and Canada, had an effect on conditions elsewhere, and particularly on the raw material producing countries, mainly through the continued decline in the prices of primary products. Imports into the United States, and the gross supply of dollars made available to the rest of the world by trade, aid, and capital movements, however, remained at a high level. As far as the industrial countries in Europe were concerned, business activity was well sustained. In France, in particular, the rate of expansion continued to be very high and, with other expenditures increasing, a substantial deficit had to be met in the balance of payments, causing a further decline in the monetary reserves. Early in 1958, the French Government presented to the Fund a rehabilitation program and obtained, on the basis of this program, Fund assistance to the extent of $131 million, in the range of the third credit tranche. Simultaneously, France obtained $250 million through the EPU and $274 million from various U.S. agencies (largely in the form of postponements of debt service).

(4) There were many drawings by Latin American countries in the years before the most recent period. Several of these involved stabilization programs and looked forward to some simplification of the exchange system. Thus financial assistance was granted to Mexico and Colombia in 1954. Under the impact of continuing difficulties, since 1956 new transactions have been entered into with several countries in this part of the world, including Argentina, Bolivia, Brazil, Chile, Colombia, Cuba, Ecuador, El Salvador, Haiti, Honduras, Nicaragua, and Paraguay. Conditions within this group naturally varied considerably from country to country. Some of the countries (Cuba, Haiti, and Honduras) have been able to maintain convertible currencies—a result which has been facilitated by the assistance from the Fund, largely for seasonal needs. In regard to these countries, too, the policies which the governments intended to follow in the fiscal, credit, and exchange fields were outlined either as part of the stand-by agreements or in the form of special declarations. For several of these countries, assistance from other sources (including the U.S. Treasury, other U.S. agencies, and U.S. banks) has been arranged simultaneously with assistance from the Fund. In most of these cases, the Fund's assistance has been within the first credit tranche. For Brazil, however, a stand-by arrangement of June 1958 covered the third credit tranche; the Brazilian Government had presented with its request a general rehabilitation program aimed especially at the containment of inflationary pressures in the fiscal and credit spheres. From 1956 to the middle of 1958, Latin American countries have drawn more than $200 million from the Fund, and had undrawn amounts available under stand-bys of more than $50 million.

Thus the Fund has been concerned with the problems arising both in the recent boom and in the following recession. It has been expected for many years that the greatest need for the use of the Fund's resources would arise during periods of recession in the United States, leading to a drain on the monetary reserves of other countries, especially in Europe. These views were, of course, largely influenced by the difficulties that developed in the 1930's. As a matter of fact, by far the largest total of Fund transactions to date arose in the boom period of 1956–57. It is true that this period included the emergency of the Suez events, but the currencies of the two countries in Europe most immediately affected—the United Kingdom and France—were already exposed to other strains and stresses. The stresses arising from the boom were particularly evident in the period of tension in the European exchange markets in the summer of 1957, intensified by rumors about the possible revaluation of the deutsche mark. At the height of the tension in September, a number of measures were taken in the United Kingdom, including an increase in Bank Rate from 5 per cent to 7 per cent, while the Bundesbank reduced its discount rate from 4½ per cent to 4 per cent. These measures, together with strong declarations made at the Twelfth Annual Meeting of the Fund that the parities of both sterling and the deutsche mark would be maintained, proved sufficient to restore calm.

It is perhaps too early to say anything very definite about the recession of 1957–58, but one outstanding feature has been that in the first six months of 1958 there was an outflow of gold from the U.S. monetary gold stock to the extent of $1.5 billion, which more than reversed the inflow of 1957. This, taken together with the fact that the two previous postwar recessions have both been shallow and have not caused any considerable movement of funds to the United States, indicates the need for reappraising opinions with regard to the effects of a recession in the United States. At this stage it appears that a recession need not necessarily lead to a reduction in the supply of dollars. Whatever the conclusions of such a reappraisal, however, apprehensions will probably not be fully discarded, for much depends upon spending, fiscal, and credit policies in the United States and U.S. willingness not to increase tariffs in a recession. It would, indeed, be rash to conclude on the basis of postwar experience to date that there will be no drain on other countries' reserves in the event of a U.S. recession. Furthermore, it is clear that there are many ways in which disturbing movements of funds may arise, apart from a recession in the United States, and some of these may be difficult to handle.

The conclusion can only be that the Fund must remain prepared for diverse contingencies, many of which cannot clearly be defined in advance.

The Fund was able, when the Suez events occurred late in 1956, to extend financial assistance on a very considerable scale. This was due to the fact that the Fund had previously been inactive and the bulk of its resources in gold and U.S. and Canadian dollars was intact. The present situation is different. It may be that no similar grave situation needs to be envisaged, but it is desirable to see what resources the Fund would have available for an emergency today.

The Fund's available resources of gold and U.S. dollars are now about $2.2 billion, or, including Canadian dollars and deutsche mark, about $2.6 billion. From these should be deducted $880 million callable under existing stand-by arrangements. Net available gold and U.S. dollars are, therefore, about $1.3 billion, or, including its holdings of the other two currencies, about $1.7 billion. Potential drawings against these holdings cannot, of course, be known, but comparison can be made with the experience of 1956–57, when gross drawings came to $1.8 billion (allowing for repurchases, net drawings came to $1.5 billion) and the amounts callable under stand-by arrangements also increased by $800 million.

The size of Fund resources available to members may also be looked at from the point of view of their drawing rights. The unutilized drawing rights of all countries—with the exception of the United States, Canada, Germany, and China—in the gold tranche and the first and second credit tranches, and in the third credit tranche to the extent that this is provided for by existing stand-bys, amounted to $2.5 billion in June 1958. These unutilized drawing rights are relatively modest and, as a matter of fact, are equal to only 4 per cent of the imports of the countries concerned. Yet they are larger than the Fund's holdings of gold and U.S. dollars, and almost equal to these assets plus Canadian dollars and deutsche mark.

It is clear that there is no longer any great margin for the Fund to grant fully that financial assistance which, under its present practices and policies, should be available to its members.

It is also pertinent to note that the resources of the Fund constitute a much smaller proportion of international trade now than when the Fund was established. Exports in 1956 were four times as great as in 1937–38, and the size of quotas in relation to trade has fallen correspondingly. Only two countries had initial quotas equal to less than 10 per cent of trade in 1937–38, whereas in 1956, even after increases in a number of small quotas, there were 36 countries with quotas equal to or less than 10 per cent of exports (Table 19).

It may perhaps be argued that those responsible for the calculation of quotas at Bretton Woods expected that trade would expand and took this factor into account. It is quite unreasonable, however, to think that they could have envisaged a fourfold

Table 19. Fund Quotas as Per Cent of Exports, By Area, 1956[1]

	Median Per Cent	Number of Countries			
		Less than 5 per cent	5 to 9.9 per cent	10 per cent and more	Total
Latin America	8	3	9	8	20
Europe	7	2	7	4	13
Other Sterling Area	10	3	4	4	11
Rest of World	10	2	6	6	14
Total		10	26	22	58

Source: Based on data from *International Financial Statistics*, February 1958.
[1] Excluding United States, Canada, United Kingdom, and China.

increase of trade in 20 years. On the contrary, an examination of the views then generally held shows great fear of a postwar depression, which would be inconsistent with actual developments. In particular, it is unlikely that they could have foreseen that world export prices in 1957 (measured in U.S. dollars) would be almost 150 per cent higher than in 1937, and that wholesale prices in the United States would be 110 per cent higher. It is, therefore, probably fair to say that the Fund at the present time has less real resources than was contemplated at the time of Bretton Woods.

When the Fund was set up, the criticism was heard from some quarters that it might make its resources available to members too easily, and thus weaken the monetary discipline which was essential if its assets were to be truly revolving—and if countries were to make the necessary efforts to restore a balanced position internally and externally. Although thirteen years in the life of an institution such as the Fund is a short time, there would seem to be little doubt that this kind of argument would today be regarded as invalid. Instead, there is evidence suggesting that the possibility of having access to the Fund's resources may make countries more confident in their attempts to restore balance. Countries may be willing to take stricter measures than if they had to rely solely on their own resources. They seem to be encouraged by the knowledge that a second line of defense is available. In practice, they may therefore exert more discipline than if there were no Fund to draw from and consult with.

From an even broader point of view, one may say that public opinion, which still has not forgotten the hardships of the 1930's, will support the necessary disciplinary measures only if it can be assured that they are reasonable and that they will be effective. In this context, it is important that the Fund is not merely an additional source of reserve credit. It is coming to be recognized more and more as a source of credit which is available only to those member governments that have satisfied the Fund of their intention and their capacity to restore balance in their monetary affairs. The Fund thus helps to restore some measure of that international consensus and monetary discipline by which the gold standard maintained balance before World War I, and it can supply the credit to facilitate the adjustments that are required. The adjustments must still be made, but they can be made with less harshness and more rationality. If that were not the case, the granting of aid might prolong and worsen the unhealthy developments. The records are there to show that in practice the opposite has happened. Countries assisted by the Fund have shown a readiness to take corrective measures, often as part of a general program for restoring balance to their economies. The Fund thus affords an economical means of reinforcing the stability of international economic relationships in general, and of the exchange rate structure in particular.

The extent to which the Fund can discharge these most important responsibilities depends upon the consent of its members, the wisdom of its policies, and the amount of its resources.

CHAPTER FIVE: SUMMARY AND CONCLUSIONS

International liquidity is a concept with many facets. In assessing liquidity from the point of view of any individual country, account has to be taken of the various ways in which it may be able to meet, without great embarrassment, a strain on its balance of payments. This will depend not only on the degree of the strain and its available cash reserves, but also on the possibilities of mobilizing additional resources and on the effectiveness of the international credit system. The degree of strain will depend in part on general developments, such as world-wide fluctuations in business, and in part on the country's own inherent balance and its readiness to take corrective measures, if for any reason that balance is upset. For such measures to take effect, time is needed, and therefore the amount of monetary or international reserves at the country's disposal during the period of adjustment is a most important factor. Without neglecting these general considerations, a study of liquidity must therefore first direct its attention to the size of monetary reserves. While in the final analysis the reserves position of each individual country is important for the management of its affairs, it is useful to obtain an over-all picture by outlining the total of reserves available to all countries and relating them to the volume of world trade.

For all countries, except those in the communist area, the ratio of official gold and exchange reserves to imports in 1957 was 51 per cent. This is distinctly higher than in 1913, when the ratio was 21 per cent, or in 1928, when it was 42 per cent, but lower than in 1937–38, when it was as high as 100 per cent.

The effectiveness of reserves at these various dates is not necessarily indicated by the reserve percentages themselves, because conditions changed greatly during the period. Thus, reserves in 1913 were generally found to be adequate, even though they were very small in comparison with those in later periods. That was a time when there was a fair degree of balance among the various economies, when under the gold standard rules corrective measures were taken speedily, and when the international credit system was working with great effectiveness. In 1928, despite substantially higher reserves, the world economy was headed for a disaster: there were still many uncorrected maladjustments following World War I; dangerous credit policies had been pursued throughout the 1920's, not least in the international field; and individual countries had a tendency to resort too readily to tariff measures and other hindrances to trade when difficulties confronted them. On the other hand, reserves in the late 1930's, which stood at an unprecedentedly high level, were not in themselves able to give an impetus to production or trade. The world economy had been disintegrating in monetary and other respects, movements of funds were determined largely by political and monetary fears, and in many countries little scope was given to the dynamic forces of the economy.

The conclusion that can be drawn from a comparison with the past is, therefore, that the contribution of reserves to the achievement of full employment, to the increase of world trade, and to the genesis of both inflation and deflation is not a dominant one. Major world trends of production and trade are not determined solely by liquidity. The developments of the last forty years or so have been dominated not by changing liquidity ratios but rather by two major wars, several minor wars, vast expenditures preparing for wars, and large expenditures to repair the damages of wars.

In those periods, on the other hand, when war or warlike considerations are not the major factor, the broad cyclical or longer-run determinants of demand in the economically most important countries tend to dominate the world economy. If these factors are expansionary, production will rise and the value of world trade will also rise, whether world liquidity increases at the same rate or not. Therefore, the position of these larger countries is of outstanding importance, not least because the credit or fiscal policies they pursue and the role they play in the international credit system are vital factors for the trend of world liquidity in general. If their position is impaired, as it was in large measure in the 1930's, even an historically unprecedented increase in the world's stock of gold could not by itself reverse the situation.

The conditions prevailing in the late 1930's can therefore not be regarded as a useful basis for comparison with present conditions, since too many adverse factors of a non-reserve character then dominated the situation. In regard to the other years with which comparisons have been made, it must be said that, so far as the over-all picture is concerned and on a purely statistical basis, the ratio of reserves to trade in recent years cannot be considered low in itself.

The effectiveness of reserves depends, moreover, not only upon the total for all countries, but also upon their distribution among countries. After the one-sided flow of gold to the United States in the interwar period (due largely to political fears) the reserves of that country rose to such an extent that by the end of 1949 it held 74 per cent of the world's gold stock and 56 per cent of total gold and foreign exchange reserves. Since 1949 the trend has, however, run in the opposite direction. U.S. gold holdings have fallen and holdings of U.S. dollar exchange by the rest of the world have risen. This strengthening of the reserves of other countries, taken together with the fact that U.S. gold holdings are still sufficiently large to permit that country to pursue credit and fiscal policies in a large measure independently of the flow of gold, has clearly helped to improve world liquidity.

Another large country—the Federal Republic of Germany—has in recent years so strengthened its reserve position that it, too, now has great latitude in pursuing its fiscal and monetary policies. Recent statements of authoritative persons suggest that Germany has no particular interest in further increasing its monetary reserves.

For the United Kingdom, the effects of the war, and especially the accumulation by many countries of large sterling balances, have made the country's monetary position in many respects more vulnerable to sudden movements of funds. Its balance of payments on current account has, with few exceptions, shown surpluses in the postwar years. While the funds thus becoming available did not lead to a net increase in the reserves, they nevertheless helped the work of the credit machinery centering in London, and they added to the long-term foreign assets of the United Kingdom. In 1957–58, however, stricter fiscal and credit policies, together with favorable terms of trade, led to a substantial increase in reserves, coinciding with some decline in sterling balances, so that the net position was appreciably improved. While balance of payments considerations still remain a major factor in the formation of British policies, there would now seem to be less danger of any acute exchange crisis. Nevertheless, it must be remembered that the credit system centering in London is by its very nature affected by major upsets of an economic and political character in all parts of the world, and that the strengthening of international liquidity is of interest to all who use sterling in their international transactions.

Many countries have been able to strengthen their reserve positions in recent years, though there are important exceptions. By and large, it may be said that it is the industrial countries which have either maintained or improved their reserve positions. On the other hand, many nonindustrialized countries have decreased their reserves. In some countries, these decreases were planned, and used to finance development—though some of the decreases were perhaps greater or more rapid than had been anticipated. In some countries, the decreases in reserves followed the declines in recent years in the prices of primary products or were the natural consequence of sharp or prolonged inflation. The types of change may be outlined with a few illustrations. Thus, between 1948 and 1957, the ratio of reserves to imports was reduced in Ceylon from 84 per cent to 48 per cent, and in India, from 195 per cent to 43 per cent; in fact, most sterling area countries drew upon the sterling savings which had been accumulated during the war. In Latin America, the reserve ratio percentage was reduced in Bolivia from 37 to about 1; in Peru, from 26 to 9; and in Uruguay, from 120 to 69.

While the nonindustrialized countries have the urgent problem of obtaining international financial assistance, they realize, of course, that internal balance cannot be restored without further domestic measures.

Given this situation, it is necessary to reckon with a demand for monetary reserves from countries that now have insufficient reserves. Moreover, it is likely that with the growth of their foreign trade a number of other countries will also wish to strengthen their reserve positions. Sometimes it seems to be assumed that in order not to hinder the growth of foreign trade the aggregate reserves of all countries must be increased in the same proportion as the average annual growth of foreign trade, say, something like 3 per cent per year. Examination of past experience suggests, however, that there is no such fixed mathematical relation between the growth of foreign trade and the increase in reserves. It seems more realistic to assume that countries with really large reserves will not find it imperative to increase their holdings—and it may unfortunately also prove to be the case that some countries which ought to augment their reserves will not carry out the policies that would make such an increase possible.

Since the amount becoming available for monetary purposes from current gold production, without allowing for any receipts from dishoarding, is likely at the present price of gold to be about $700 million a year, it would seem that gold output alone can make a very substantial contribution to satisfying the need for increased reserves. Since it is, moreover, likely that there will be some increase in exchange holdings, the reserve problem with which the world will be faced over the next decade does not seem to be too difficult, provided that further progress is made, by sensible policies, in restoring and maintaining balance in the individual economies, in avoiding increased obstacles to trade, and in strengthening the international credit system.

These provisos are important, since the adequacy of reserves, both for the world as a whole and for individual countries, can be judged only in a broad international context. For example, a given level of reserves will have one degree of adequacy when economic conditions between countries are in reasonable balance and when exchange rates are appropriate. If these conditions are not satisfied, the same reserves will have a different degree of adequacy. Similarly, from the point of view of any one country, reserves that may be adequate if the country is following a program of development with stability may appear totally inadequate when it has an unbalanced budget or active credit inflation. No amount of reserves is adequate to finance a continuous deficit in the balance of payments resulting from excessive spending or insufficient revenue. In these cases, the immediate task is clearly to adopt fiscal and monetary policies that will restore external and internal equilibrium.

Over fairly long periods, some countries have had relatively large reserves (e.g., the United States, Switzerland, Portugal, and Venezuela), while others (e.g., the Scandinavian countries) have traditionally held rather low reserves in relation to their foreign trade. One cannot escape the conclusion that in this matter tradition and convention play a considerable role. Several of the countries with slender reserves have, even in the generally favorable economic environment of the postwar period, been beset by difficulties which those with larger reserves could take in their stride. Many countries may state that their reserves are too low or wish that they might be larger, without being prepared to take the steps necessary to strengthen them. An increase in reserves is part of a country's investments. It requires, like other investments, a counterpart in the form of uncommitted savings of one sort or another, as happens, for instance, when debts to the central bank are repaid from genuine budget surpluses.

At the end of 1957, the official reserves of all countries (outside the communist area) consisted of $37.0 billion in gold and $15.9 billion in foreign exchange, making together $52.9 billion. The quality of reserves is now undoubtedly sounder than it was in the late 1920's. At that time, a large part of the foreign exchange holdings was the counterpart of short-term foreign credits; now, for the most part, countries holding reserves are also their beneficial owners.

The short-term lending mechanism, which is an indispensable element in the liquidity of any international monetary system, may not yet be as efficient as it was in the days of supreme monetary confidence before World War I, but it is certainly better than in the period between the two World Wars. Private holdings of foreign currencies, needed as working capital for the financing of trade and other international payments, have in a fair degree been reconstituted. About 40 per cent of the foreign-owned dollar balances in the United States are privately owned and, after some rather violent fluctuations in the course of 1956–57, sterling balances were very largely replenished in the first six months of 1958. With an increase in monetary confidence and a relaxation of exchange controls, it is likely that, as was the case before 1914, equilibrating movements of funds will be facilitated. These, up to a point, should reduce the strain on official reserves. The fact that the monetary authorities in most countries have again begun to pursue flexible credit policies, including fairly frequent changes in interest rates, should be very helpful in encouraging such a development. It is certainly too early to conclude that the shifts in leads and lags, which from time to time during the postwar period have given rise to such disturbing movements of funds, will not occur again. Nevertheless, the way in which appropriate credit policies in the last few years have been able to reverse those movements is a hopeful sign for the future. Financial assistance from international institutions, including both the European Payments Union and the International Monetary Fund, have been helpful in this connection.

The important contribution of international institutions to liquidity has been a new development in the period after World War II. The financial activities of the International Monetary Fund were at a low ebb for several years. During these years, many countries in Europe met their needs with the help of funds provided by the Marshall Plan, and many countries outside Europe were able to use the liquid resources they had accumulated during the war (sterling balances in the British Commonwealth, and dollar balances in the Latin American countries). In connection with Marshall Aid, a system of intra-European settlements gradually evolved into the European Payments Union, which made an important contribution to liquidity, especially at the time when the private credit system had not yet been restored to working order.

For the Fund, the years of little business activity, stretching from 1948 to 1955, were used to get its working methods fully organized; to start the system of consultations with countries maintaining exchange restrictions required under Article XIV; to develop forms of technical assistance to member countries; and, what has proved very important, to agree on the policies and principles to be applied to requests for the use of the Fund's resources.

While requests for drawings of 25 per cent of a country's quota, normally corresponding to its own gold subscription, are almost automatically approved, the principle has been established that for the next 25 per cent members are required to show that they are making a reasonable effort to solve their own problems. For drawings beyond these limits, more substantial justification is required: namely, that the drawings must be in support of a sound program likely to ensure enduring stability at realistic rates of exchange. These principles are also applicable to requests for stand-by arrangements, and they proved to be of great practical value when, in the autumn of 1956, there was a distinct upturn in the business activity of the Fund—beginning with the financial assistance granted to the United Kingdom in connection with the Suez events, and followed by drawings and stand-by arrangements with a great number of countries in various parts of the world. In all these cases, when requests for drawings and stand-by arrangements were considered, the governments made statements to the Fund concerning the monetary and other relevant policies they intended to follow.

It is important to remember that the Fund is not merely an additional source of reserve credit available to the monetary authorities of its members. It is recognized more and more as a source of credit which is available only to member governments that have satisfied the Fund of their intention and their capacity to restore balance in their monetary affairs. The Fund thus helps to restore some measure of that monetary discipline by which the gold standard in its way maintained balance before World War I, but it also supplies a measure of credit by which harshness may be mitigated.

Total drawings on the Fund from its inception to the end of July 1958 amounted to $3.1 billion; in addition, at the end of July 1958 undrawn balances under existing stand-by arrangements amounted to $800 million. But the Fund's significance for international liquidity is greater than the amounts drawn would suggest, for several reasons: first, the Fund's resources constitute a particularly efficient form of reserves, since their use can be pinpointed to particular areas of financial strain; second, as already mentioned, drawings are generally coupled with specific undertakings with respect to monetary and fiscal policy on the part of the countries concerned; and, third, the favorable technical judgment of a country's economic and financial program, implied in the approval of a drawing by the Fund, not infrequently simplifies that country's task in obtaining additional sums from other sources. Furthermore, the possibility of having access to the Fund's resources, even when no assistance is actually granted, may make countries more confident in their attempts to restore balance—making them willing to take stricter measures than if they had to rely on their own resources alone. They may be encouraged by the knowledge that a second line of defense is available to them. In practice, they may therefore exert more discipline than if these opportunities did not exist.

It seems sometimes to have been assumed that the Fund would be called upon to render assistance particularly in periods of recession in the United States which, in accordance with the experiences of the 1930's, were expected to put a strain on the balances of payments of other countries. As a matter of fact, by far the major part of the financial transactions of the Fund so far have occurred in the boom period of 1956–57. It is true that the largest of these transactions, the financial assistance to the United Kingdom at the time of the Suez events, was of an emergency nature not directly connected with the boom. Subsequently, some other important transactions were undertaken to bring temporary relief to countries with deficits in their balances of payments resulting from the strains of an exaggerated boom in their own domestic economies. There have recently been some transactions which can be associated with the recession that began in the latter half of 1957, but they have been for relatively limited amounts. While raw material producing countries have suffered from the decline in the prices of primary products, the fact that the 1957–58 recession in the United States has been accompanied by an outflow of gold from that country has helped many countries, especially in Europe, to strengthen their monetary reserves. It can, of course, not be concluded that a recession in the United States will always have similar results. Nevertheless, experience in the last two years clearly indicates that the need for assistance from the Fund may arise quite independently of any particular phase of the business cycle. Indeed, the Fund must be prepared for diverse contingencies, many of which cannot be defined in advance.

The Fund was able, at the time of the events of Suez, to extend financial assistance on a very considerable scale. This was due largely to the fact that in the previous years there had been very few transactions, so that the bulk of the Fund's resources in gold and convertible currencies was intact. Since then, the many transactions undertaken by the Fund have considerably reduced its uncommitted holdings of gold and convertible currencies, which at the end of July 1958 amounted to $1.4 billion. On the other hand, some drawings have already been made in currencies other than U.S. dollars, such as deutsche mark, guilders, and sterling, and perhaps more use will be made of these currencies in the future. The Fund has authorized drawings to meet the balance of payments effects of changing levels of production and trade, to support stabilization programs, and to meet short-term strains in the balance of payments. It was able at the time of the Suez events to prevent a disruption of the exchange structure. Past experiences have shown that when cracks occur, they may not be confined only to the currencies immediately affected. The consequences of allowing such cracks to widen and spread may indeed be serious.

The question has been raised, for good reasons, whether the resources of the Fund are adequate for present tasks. The resources available to the Fund were determined at the Bretton Woods Conference in 1944, and most of the data on international trade available to the Conference related to the period before the war. The physical volume of world exports fell by 7 per cent from 1937 to 1947, but in the next ten years increased by 90 per cent, a rate of expansion almost unknown in the past. The prices of goods moving in international trade increased by 140 per cent between 1937 and 1957. Fluctuations in the balance of payments which may require use of the Fund's resources are therefore potentially much larger now than when the Fund quotas were established. If any lack of confidence were to set in, the potential movements of funds connected with shifts in the financing of trade would likewise be larger. The Fund's ability to provide assurance to its members and to act quickly on a massive scale if emergencies arise depends upon its having adequate resources, which have been made available in advance of any specific emergency. It is doubtful whether, in the circumstances of the world today, with world trade greatly expanded in volume and value, the Fund's resources are sufficient to enable it fully to perform its duties under the Articles of Agreement.

STATISTICAL APPENDIX

Appendix Table 1. Gross Official Reserves (Gold and Exchange), Imports, and Reserves as Per Cent of Imports, by Country, Selected Years, 1928-57

(Value figures in millions of U.S. dollars)

Country and Area	1928 Reserves	1928 Imports	1928 Per Cent	1937 Reserves	1937 Imports	1937 Per Cent	1948 Reserves	1948 Imports	1948 Per Cent	1950 Reserves	1950 Imports	1950 Per Cent	1951 Reserves	1951 Imports	1951 Per Cent
United States	3,746	4,427	85	12,790	3,573	358	24,399	8,058	303	22,820	9,601	238	22,873	11,882	193
Canada	93	1,364	7	200	939	21	1,011	3,024	33	1,770	3,202	55	1,826	4,194	44
Latin America	1,160	2,453	47	875	1,717	51	2,750	6,224	44	3,125	5,630	56	2,925	7,831	37
Dollar Countries	125	862	15	150	665	23	1,075	2,836	38	1,425	2,700	53	1,525	3,411	45
Bolivia	9	23	39	7	24	29	28	79	37	29	64	45	34	99	34
Colombia	62	161	39	20	96	21	84	337	25	101	365	28	125	419	30
Costa Rica	...	...	...	1	12	8	5	42	12	4	46	8	8	56	14
Cuba	...	234	...	1[1]	146	1	316	591	53	418	608	69	495	754	66
Dominican Republic	...	30	...	3[1]	13	23	15	74	20	19	50	38	30	86	35
Ecuador	8	16	50	5	14	36	28	60	47	37	49	76	31	62	50
El Salvador	5	18	28	8	10	80	30	41	73	41	48	85	43	63	68
Guatemala	5	31	16	8	21	38	46	68	68	37	71	52	40	81	49
Haiti	...	...	...	2	9	22	8	31	26	10	38	26	13	44	30
Honduras	...	...	...	1[1]	12	8	2[1]	37	5	11	39	28	20	53	38
Mexico	10	185	5	30	175	17	78	561	14	291	556	52	254	822	31
Nicaragua	...	...	...	1	7	14	3	28	11	3	29	10	9	35	26
Panama[1]	...	...	...	5[1]	24	21	44	73	60	38	70	54	49	76	64
Venezuela	21	81	26	59[1]	102	58	378	814	46	373	667	56	761	761	49
Non-Dollar Countries	1,035	1,591	65	725	1,052	69	1,675	3,388	49	1,750	2,930	60	1,400	4,420	32
Argentina	607	807	75	539	493	109	579	1,590	36	655	1,187	55	520	1,480	35
Brazil	177	441	40	50	335	15	758	1,134	67	666	1,098	61	517	2,011	26
Chile	120	163	74	38	89	43	59	269	22	58	247	23	55	328	17
Paraguay	...	13	...	1	10	10	6	27	22	13	22	59	18	29	62
Peru	47	70	67	26	59	44	44	168	26	54	176	31	60	262	23
Uruguay[3]	83	97	86	75	66	114	241	200	120	312	200	156	223	310	72
Continental EPU Countries	5,140	11,103	46	6,600	8,680	78	5,875	14,519	40	6,900	16,473	42	7,500	22,033	34
Austria	126	456	28	73	269	27	62	490	13	91	477	19	106	653	16
Belgium	345	889	39	827	928	89	938	2,046	46	733	1,942	38	1,019	2,535	40
Denmark	77	441	17	70	369	19	84	714	12	97	853	11	118	1,013	12
France[4]	2,541	2,097	121	2,784	1,689	165	...	3,443	...	1,334	3,030	44	912	4,457	20
Germany	776	3,335	23	...	2,196	...	295	364	...	274	2,697	10	518	3,491	15
Greece	55	161	34	34	140	54	189	364	52	187	428	44	132	398	33
Italy	583	1,173	50	212	734	29	539	1,539	35	878	1,488	59	1,003	2,167	46
Netherlands	263	1,078	24	938	883	106	343	1,871	18	606	2,056	29	618	2,553	24
Norway	50	269	19	132	320	41	141	750	19	122	679	18	151	878	17
Portugal	25	120	21	75	106	71	509	414	123	471	274	172	555	330	168
Sweden	121	458	26	513	541	95	233	1,377	17	289	1,182	24	484	1,776	27
Switzerland	152	512	30	774	414	187	1,660	1,163	143	1,579	1,056	150	1,644	1,375	120
Turkey	21	114	18	49	91	54	192	348	55	214	311	69	217	407	53

INTERNATIONAL RESERVES AND LIQUIDITY

United Kingdom	748	5,795	13	4,141[6]	5,082	81	2,009		3,668	7,305	50	2,374	10,934	22
Other Sterling Area Countries	754	2,670	28	1,425	2,870	46	7,275	8,370	5,550	6,528	85	5,225	9,652	54
Australia	200	669	30	332	526	63	1,265	7,627	1,492	1,622	92	1,134	2,422	47
Burma		75		[5]	91		114	1,411	119	111	107	159	137	116
Ceylon	[5]	193		[5]	90		254	176	191	245	78	217	327	66
Iceland	1[6]	17	6	1	12	8	13	301	8	38	21	9	57	16
India	440	837	53	590	671	88	3,354	71	2,000	1,165	172	1,888	1,793	105
Iraq		34		26	48	54	139	1,716	117	105	111	114	143	80
Ireland		288		59	219	27	209	183	245	446	55	206	573	36
Malaya					388	27	227	549	229	952	24	262	1,554	36
New Zealand	35	218	16	102	253	36	236	842	172	455	38	217	596	17
Pakistan[9]				92	[5]		800	450	507	403	126	638	549	36
Union of South Africa	78	393	20	228	572	40	652	312	476	986	48	386	1,501	116
								1,616						26
Rest of World	1,400	2,813	50	1,525	2,273	67	3,175	4,273	3,200	4,312	74	3,800	6,854	55
China (Taiwan)									15	120	12	49	145	34
Egypt	178	249	71	218	197	111	1,408	674	979	583	168	957	678	141
Ethiopia							15	37	14	27	52	20	40	50
Finland	27	202	13	73	199	37	74	488	84	388	22	209	676	31
Indonesia		403		66	283	23	207	464	356	440	81	511	873	59
Iran		76		34	84	40	273	167	252	262	96	196	211	93
Israel[10]		33		56	79	71	134	164	62	200	21	33	300	9
Japan[12]	598	990	60	297	1,138	26		684	564	974	58	924	1,995	46
Korea									27			38		
Lebanon	[8]	[8]					74	[8]	38			40	133	30
Philippines	50[7]	149	34		125		400	655	296	384	77	247	550	45
Spain	512	580	88	525			118[4]	468	75	390	19	60	384	16
Syria		51					84	214				19	133	14
Thailand	43[7]	80	54	52	49	106	217	144	288	209	138	359	272	132
Viet-Nam														
Yugoslavia				61	119	43	38	314	17	236	7	21	384	6

Sources: For 1928, "The Adequacy of Monetary Reserves," *Staff Papers*, Vol. III, No. 2 (October 1953), pp. 181–227. For other years, *International Financial Statistics* (*IFS*), February 1958 and following issues; footnotes to the summary trade and reserves tables therein apply to this table.

[1] Reserves not held officially.
[2] *IFS* estimate.
[3] Reserves data are gold and net foreign exchange. The nature of liabilities deducted from gross assets is unknown. Prior to 1951, forward exchange liabilities are also deducted. For 1955, gold only, since net foreign exchange is negative.
[4] Reserves estimated by Fund staff.
[5] Included with India.
[6] Gold only.
[7] Foreign exchange only.
[8] Included with Syria.
[9] Beginning with 1952, includes holdings of Issue Department only.
[10] Official and banks.
[11] End of November 1957.
[12] Excludes gold under dispute.

Appendix Table 1, cont. Gross Official Reserves (Gold and Exchange), Imports, and Reserves as Per Cent of Imports, by Country, Selected Years, 1928-57

(Value figures in millions of U.S. dollars)

Country and Area	1952			1953			1954			1955			1956			1957		
	Re-serves	Im-ports	Per Cent	Re-serves	Im-ports	Per Cent	Re-serves	Im-ports	Per Cent	Re-serves	Im-ports	Per Cent	Re-serves	Im-ports	Per Cent	Re-serves	Im-ports	Per Cent
United States	23,252	11,662	199	22,091	11,792	187	21,793	11,047	197	21,752	12,369	176	22,058	13,751	160	22,857	14,174	161
Canada	1,864	4,480	42	1,827	4,824	38	1,954	4,551	43	1,910	5,156	37	1,945	6,270	31	1,836	6,346	29
Latin America																		
Dollar Countries	2,925	7,683	38	3,200	6,541	49	3,025	7,411	41	3,150	7,550	42	3,675	7,940	46	3,775	9,100	41
Bolivia	1,600	3,563	45	1,660	3,578	46	1,675	3,898	43	1,850	4,135	45	2,325	4,621	50	2,725	5,202	52
Colombia	29	107	27	24	78	31	11	73	15	6	81	7	4	84	5	1	70[a]	1
Costa Rica	155	415	37	190	547	35	257	672	38	136	669	20	131	657	20	145	477	30
Cuba	16	68	24	18	74	24	16	80	20	20	87	23	12	91	13	12	103	12
Dominican Republic	448	745	60	481	591	81	454	599	76	493	633	78	479	714	67	441	706	62
Ecuador	32	111	29	28	99	28	36	94	38	36	114	32	37	126	29	46	136	34
El Salvador	44	70	63	39	75	52	38	120	32	34	112	30	32	108	30	39	110	35
Guatemala	44	69	64	43	72	60	44	87	51	39	92	42	39	105	37	40	115	35
Haiti	43	76	57	41	80	51	39	86	45	54	104	52	39	138	51	74	149	50
Honduras	13	53	25	10	44	23	11	48	23	8	46	17	7	50	14	4	40	10
Mexico	21	66	32	22	62	35	24	59	41	19	62	31	18	67	27	15	76	20
Nicaragua	250	807	31	218	807	27	201	800	25	418	885	47	500	1,072	47	419[11]	1,155	36
Panama[1]	15	47	32	16	51	31	13	68	19	14	70	20	7	69	10	11	81	14
Venezuela	52	84	62	52	82	63	48	83	58	42	88	48	42	98	43	29	116	25
Non-Dollar Countries	434	845	51	477	916	52	475	1,029	46	526	1,092	48	939	1,249	75	1,440	1,868	77
Argentina	1,325	4,120	32	1,550	2,963	52	1,375	3,513	39	1,300	3,414	38	1,350	3,312	41	1,050	3,898	27
Brazil	420	1,179	36	532	795	67	524	979	54	457	1,173	40	381	1,128	34	311	1,310	24
Chile	529	2,010	26	605	1,319	46	483	1,630	30	491	1,306	38	612	1,234	50	474	1,489	32
Paraguay	69	370	19	68	335	20	39	343	11	83	376	22	76	354	21	46	441	10
Peru	8	36	22	6	28	21	4	37	11	6	34	18	8	29	28	13	32	41
Uruguay[3]	56	288	19	49	293	17	56	250	22	52	300	17	67	361	19	34	400	9
	238	237	100	291	193	151	257	274	94	216	225	96	203	206	99	157	226	69
Continental EPU Countries	8,625	21,819	40	10,100	21,287	48	11,425	23,701	48	12,875	27,200	47	13,400	31,126	43	14,575	34,384	42
Austria	152	652	23	320	546	59	412	653	63	361	887	41	406	974	42	510	1,128	45
Belgium	1,030	2,444	42	1,067	2,405	44	1,032	2,535	41	1,127	2,830	40	1,143	3,272	35	1,132	3,432	33
Denmark	142	962	15	167	1,000	17	143	1,170	12	133	1,178	11	131	1,311	10	172	1,359	13
France[1]	987	4,326	23	956	3,942	24	1,369	4,221	32	2,076	4,739	44	1,356	5,553	24	775	6,170	13
Germany	1,190	3,814	31	1,958	3,771	52	2,636	4,571	58	3,076	5,793	53	4,291	6,617	65	5,644	7,478	75
Greece	141	346	41	191	296	65	199	330	60	210	382	55	218	464	47	192	525	37
Italy	918	2,336	39	952	2,420	39	1,041	2,439	43	1,237	2,711	46	1,308	3,174	41	1,532	3,626	42
Netherlands	1,037	2,224	47	1,224	2,376	52	1,276	2,858	45	1,277	3,208	40	1,072	3,725	29	1,056	4,105	26
Norway	151	874	17	142	912	16	138	1,019	14	165	1,090	15	179	1,211	15	183	1,274	14
Portugal	563	347	162	616	332	186	655	351	187	671	398	169	693	443	156	687	502	137
Sweden	446	1,730	26	507	1,579	32	478	1,776	27	470	1,997	24	473	2,209	21	456	2,424	19
Switzerland	1,667	1,208	138	1,768	1,176	150	1,837	1,300	141	1,846	1,489	124	1,893	1,766	107	1,918	1,964	98
Turkey	191	556	34	213	532	40	205	478	43	211	498	42	230	407	57	315	397	79

INTERNATIONAL RESERVES AND LIQUIDITY

Country										
United Kingdom	1,958	9,738	20	2,546	9,361	27	2,798	9,447	30	2,172	10,881	20	2,374	11,412	21
Other Sterling Area Countries	4,625	8,954	52	5,025	7,298	69	5,000	7,924	63	4,525	9,093	50	4,050	9,969	41
Australia	1,032	1,979	52	1,362	1,471	93	1,133	1,869	61	953	1,964	49	1,321	1,931	68
Burma	198	192	103	211	178	119	124	204	61	121	198	61	93	297	31
Ceylon	163	358	46	114	338	34	169	293	58	221	342	65	183	379	48
Iceland	9	56	16	16	68	24	20	69	29	14	90	16	16	83	19
India	1,729	1,696	102	1,765	1,208	146	1,782	1,297	137	1,360	1,698	80	878	2,022	43
Iraq	129	173	75	181	192	94	233	204	114	354	321	110	261	343	76
Ireland	220	482	46	234	511	46	260	504	52	234	512	46	258	517	50
Malaya	273	1,265	22	270	1,058	26	291	1,026	28	324	1,357	24	328	1,431	23
New Zealand	183	773	24	271	538	50	239	688	35	194	751	26	138	830	17
Pakistan[9]	296	630	47	296	350	85	328	334	98	373	417	89	291	440	66
Union of South Africa	382	1,350	28	295	1,386	21	416	1,436	29	372	1,524	24	288	1,696	17
Rest of World	3,500	7,038	50	3,250	7,380	44	3,525	7,344	48	4,050	9,676	42	3,400	11,375	30
China (Taiwan)	44	187	24	54	192	28	34	211	16	79	194	41	108	212	51
Egypt	752	640	118	728	516	141	732	472	155	566	535	106	465	524	89
Ethiopia	25	43	58	42	53	79	50	61	82	57	63	90	64	78	82
Finland	133	792	17	145	530	27	211	656	32	174	885	20	171	900	19
Indonesia	314	948	33	212	765	28	248	629	39	254	856	30	221	797	28
Iran	177	124	143	185	156	119	186	230	81	230	335[2]	69	245	375[3]	65
Israel[10]	30	321	9	33	281	12	00	207	24	00	004	24	01	407	20
Japan[12]	1,101	2,028	54	895	2,410	37	1,022	2,399	43	1,507	3,230	47	1,019	4,284	24
Korea	00	...	...	100	047	31	108	241	46	00	360	27	116	132	27
Lebanon	42	138	30	55	144	38	76	174	44	88	237	37	99	252	39
Philippines	236	484	49	240	534	45	207	545	38	161	597	27	71	727	10
Spain	61	518	12	80	596	13	117	614	19	89	767	12	69	862	8
Syria	29	138	21	44	131	34	47	174	27	62	187	33	54	171	32
Thailand	352	304	116	302	330	92	273	312	88	311	365	85	329	404	81
Viet-Nam	...	...	...	...	...	...	...	...	...	132	218	61	137	289	47
Yugoslavia	16	373	4	18	395	5	24	339	7	43	474	9	39	661	6

Sources: For 1928, "The Adequacy of Monetary Reserves," *Staff Papers*, Vol. III, No. 2 (October 1953), pp. 181–227. For other years, *International Financial Statistics* (IFS), February 1958 and following issues; footnotes to the summary trade and reserves tables therein apply to this table.

[1] Reserves not held officially.
[2] IFS estimate.
[3] Reserves data are gold and net foreign exchange. The nature of liabilities deducted from gross assets is unknown. Prior to 1951, forward exchange liabilities are also deducted. For 1955, gold only, since net foreign exchange is negative.
[4] Reserves estimated by Fund staff.
[5] Included with India.
[6] Gold only.
[7] Foreign exchange only.
[8] Included with Syria.
[9] Beginning with 1952, includes holdings of Issue Department only.
[10] Official and banks.
[11] End of November 1957.
[12] Excludes gold under dispute.

Appendix Table 2. Reserve Holdings of Gold and Foreign Exchange, By Area, Selected Years, 1928-57
(In millions of U.S. dollars)

Area	1928 Gold	1928 Foreign Exchange	1928 Total	1928 % Foreign Exchange	1937 Gold	1937 Foreign Exchange	1937 Total	1937 % Foreign Exchange	1938 Gold	1938 Foreign Exchange	1938 Total	1938 % Foreign Exchange
World	9,800	3,250	13,050	25	25,300	2,400	27,700	9	25,950	1,800	27,700	7
World minus United States	6,054	3,250	9,300	35	12,510	2,400	14,910	16	11,358	1,800	13,108	14
Canada	93	—	93	—	180	20	200	10	186	34	220	15
Latin America	985	175	1,160	15	725	150	875	17	675	100	800	12
Dollar Area	70	55	125	44	125	25	150	17	125	50	175	29
Non-Dollar Area	915	120	1,035	12	600	125	725	17	550	75	625	12
Continental EPU Countries	2,785	2,355	5,140	46	5,950	800	6,750	12	6,125	525	6,625	8
United Kingdom	748	—	748	—	4,141	....	4,141	....	2,877	....	2,877	....
Other Sterling Area	385	369	754	49	500	925	1,425	65	534	625	1,170	54
All Other Countries	1,060	340	1,400	24	975	475	1,475	33	925	500	1,395	35

Area	1948 Gold	1948 Foreign Exchange	1948 Total	1948 % Foreign Exchange	1949 Gold	1949 Foreign Exchange	1949 Total	1949 % Foreign Exchange	1950 Gold	1950 Foreign Exchange	1950 Total	1950 % Foreign Exchange
World	32,750	13,700	46,450	29	33,150	10,500	43,650	24	33,550	13,550	47,000	29
World minus United States	8,351	13,700	22,051	62	8,587	10,500	19,087	55	10,730	13,550	24,180	56
Canada	401	610	1,011	60	486	636	1,122	57	580	1,190	1,770	67
Latin America	1,500	1,275	2,750	46	1,650	1,125	2,775	41	1,875	1,300	3,125	41
Dollar Area	800	275	1,075	26	875	325	1,200	27	1,025	375	1,425	27
Non-Dollar Area	700	1,000	1,700	59	775	825	1,600	52	825	925	1,750	53
Continental EPU Countries	3,550	2,325	5,875	40	3,850	2,325	6,175	38	3,950	2,975	6,900	43
United Kingdom	1,605	404	2,009	20	1,350	402	1,752	23	2,900	768	3,668	21
Other Sterling Area	575	6,675	7,275	92	550	4,125	4,657	88	600	4,950	5,550	89
All Other Countries	725	2,400	3,125	77	725	1,875	2,600	72	800	2,350	3,175	75

	1951				1952				1953			
World	33,650	12,900	46,500	28	33,550	13,200	46,700	28	33,900	14,100	48,000	29
World minus United States	10,777	12,900	23,627	54	10,298	13,200	23,448	56	11,809	14,100	25,909	54
Canada	842	984	1,826	54	885	979	1,864	53	986	841	1,827	46
Latin America	1,950	950	2,925	33	1,825	1,075	2,900	37	1,925	1,300	3,200	40
Dollar Area	1,050	475	1,525	31	925	675	1,600	42	925	750	1,650	45
Non-Dollar Area	900	500	1,400	36	900	425	1,300	32	1,000	550	1,550	35
Continental EPU Countries	4,150	3,350	7,500	45	4,525	4,125	8,625	48	5,125	5,000	10,100	50
United Kingdom	2,200	174	2,374	7	1,500	458	1,958	23	2,300	246	2,546	10
Other Sterling Area	625	4,600	5,225	88	625	4,000	4,625	86	625	4,400	5,025	88
All Other Countries	975	2,800	3,775	74	925	2,525	3,475	73	850	2,350	3,225	73

	1954				1955				1956			
World	34,450	15,100	49,500	30	34,950	15,650	50,550	31	35,550	16,250	51,800	31
World minus United States	12,657	15,100	27,707	54	13,198	15,650	28,798	54	13,492	16,250	29,742	55
Canada	1,073	882	1,954	45	1,134	776	1,910	41	1,103	841	1,945	43
Latin America	1,850	1,200	3,025	39	1,850	1,300	3,150	41	1,875	1,800	3,675	49
Dollar Area	850	850	1,675	50	875	975	1,850	53	1,050	1,276	2,325	55
Non-Dollar Area	1,000	375	1,375	27	1,000	325	1,300	25	825	525	1,350	39
Continental EPU Countries	5,650	5,800	11,425	51	6,350	6,550	12,875	49	7,175	6,250	13,400	47
United Kingdom	2,550	248	2,798	9	2,050	106	2,156	5	1,800	372	2,172	17
Other Sterling Area	675	4,325	5,000	86	700	4,000	4,700	85	700	3,825	4,525	85
All Other Countries	825	2,625	3,475	76	875	3,125	3,975	78	850	3,150	4,025	79

	1957			
World	37,000	15,900	52,900	30
World minus United States	14,143	15,900	30,043	53
Canada	1,100	736	1,836	40
Latin America	1,900	1,900	3,800	50
Dollar Area	1,200	1,550	2,725	56
Non-Dollar Area	700	350	1,050	33
Continental EPU Countries	7,975	6,625	14,575	45
United Kingdom	1,600	774	2,374	33
Other Sterling Area	700	3,350	4,050	83
All Other Countries	850	2,525	3,375	75

Sources: For 1928, "The Adequacy of Monetary Reserves," *Staff Papers*, Vol. III, No. 2 (October 1953), pp. 181-227; for 1938, *International Financial Statistics (IFS)*, December 1954; for 1949, *IFS*, August 1955; and for 1937 and 1950-57, *IFS*, June 1958. Data for 1948 were prepared but not published in revised form. Totals may not equal sum of items because of rounding.

Appendix Table 3. Reconciliation of Foreign Exchange Assets and Liabilities, 1947-57
(In millions of U.S. dollars)

	1947	1948	1949	1950	1951	1952	1953	1954	1955	1956	1957
World Total											
Total gross assets	13,900	13,900	10,850	13,600	13,000	13,300	14,250	15,250	15,750	16,400	16,050
Liabilities of U.S.	1,850	2,900	3,050	4,450	4,050	5,250	6,050	7,000	7,900	8,600	8,300
Liabilities of U.K.	12,147	10,774	7,414	7,775	7,646	6,328	6,825	6,980	6,591	6,220	5,833
EPU liabilities	—	—	—	402	665	1,077	1,272	1,108	994	1,086	1,269
BIS deposits	8	52	108	250	192	364	352	465	412	424	409
Excess of reported assets	−105	174	278	723	447	281	−249	−303	−147	70	239
Canada											
Total gross assets	232	610	636	1,190	984	979	841	882	776	841	736
Liabilities of U.S.	215	596	631	1,162	937	975	832	870	767	833	728
Liabilities of U.K.	17	13	5	28	47	4	9	12	9	8	8
Latin America											
Dollar Countries											
Total gross assets	275	275	325	375	475	675	725	825	975	1,275	1,550
Liabilities of U.S.	375	400	550	350	450	625	700	800	950	1,150	1,400
Excess of reported assets	−100	−125	−225	25	25	50	25	25	25	125	150
Non-Dollar Countries											
Total gross assets	1,275	1,125	725	925	500	425	550	375	325	525	350
Liabilities of U.S.	200	250	250	350	175	175	200	225	225	275	150
Liabilities of U.K.	947	544	224	126	160	17	112	22	25	90	87
Excess of reported assets	128	331	251	449	165	233	238	128	75	160	113

Continental EPU Countries										
Total gross assets	2,050	2,325	2,475	2,975	3,350	4,125	5,000	5,800	6,350	6,250	6,625
Liabilities of U.S.	650	700	675	1,100	1,100	1,675	2,450	3,350	4,025	3,900	3,725
Liabilities of U.K.	1,689	1,245	997	879	918	669	624	683	596	540	722
EPU liabilities	—	—	—	177	665	1,077	1,272	1,108	994	1,086	1,269
BIS deposits	8	52	108	250	192	364	352	465	412	424	409
Excess of reported assets	−297	328	695	569	475	340	302	197	323	300	500
United Kingdom										
Total gross assets	208	404	402	768	174	458	246	248	106	372	774
Liabilities of U.S.	59	251	338	400	135	346	218	212	70	333	673
EPU liabilities	—	—	—	225	—	—	—	—	—	—	—
Excess of reported assets	149	153	64	143	39	112	28	36	36	39	101
Other Sterling Area Countries										
Total gross assets	7,550	6,675	4,400	4,950	4,650	4,050	4,475	4,400	4,075	3,900	3,400
Liabilities of U.S.	75	50	75	100	75	150	200	200	225	200	200
Liabilities of U.K.	7,173	6,820	4,738	5,353	5,070	4,523	5,044	5,059	4,793	4,734	4,333
Excess of reported assets	302	−195	−413	−503	−495	−623	−769	−859	−943	−1,034	−1,133
Rest of the World										
Total gross assets	2,275	2,450	1,850	2,400	2,850	2,575	2,425	2,700	3,175	3,225	2,600
Liabilities of U.S.	500	625	500	1,000	1,125	1,325	1,400	1,300	1,650	1,875	1,375
Liabilities of U.K.	2,321	2,152	1,450	1,389	1,450	1,114	1,036	1,204	1,168	848	683
Excess of reported assets	−550	−327	−100	11	275	136	−11	196	357	502	542

Sources: Data for 1950-57 were published in *International Financial Statistics* (*IFS*), July 1958. Data for 1947-49 were compiled by the Fund staff on the same basis. These data were derived from the statistics on foreign assets given on the country pages of *IFS* and defined in the notes to these country pages. For a description of the construction of, and the problems related to, this table for the period beginning with 1952, see *IFS*, July 1956, pp. 16-17; for earlier years, see the June 1953 issue, pp. x-xi. This table reconciles the total of exchange reserves reported by the holders with the official holdings by countries of dollar balances, as reported by the United States, and the holdings by countries of all sterling balances (official and other) as reported by the United Kingdom. In some cases, the U.S. reports of official holdings have been adjusted by the Fund. The totals of EPU liabilities and BIS deposits are as reported by these institutions.

The figures for Errors and Omissions are the result of a number of factors, some positive and some negative: (1) Dollar liabilities as reported by the United States include assets held by the Soviet bloc. The dollar assets held by the Soviet bloc are neither reported by the Soviet countries nor included in the area totals of the table. This residual is therefore included in Errors and Omissions with a positive sign. (2) Sterling liabilities reported by the United Kingdom include those held by private holders, which therefore are represented by a negative sign. (3) Country holdings of assets other than dollars and sterling are included in the Total but are not reported as liabilities by their obligors; the result is a positive sign. There are other errors and omissions, the sign of which is undetermined.

Data on sterling exclude liabilities to dependent areas and to Ghana.

Appendix Table 4. Indices of World Trade and Manufacturing Activity, 1871-75 to 1936-38
(Annual averages: 1913 = 100)

Period	Volume of Trade[1]		Manufacturing Activity
	Manufactured articles	Primary products	
1871-75	—	—	22.4
1876-80	32.1	31.2	24.5
1881-85	40.0	38.0	30.4
1886-90	45.1	44.5	36.8
1891-95	45.9	51.4	42.6
1896-1900	48.0	60.2	53.6
1901-05	63.2	70.8	67.0
1906-10	77.9	83.1	79.9
1911-13	95.6	97.0	94.3
1913	100.0	100.0	100.0
1920	—	—	93.2
1921-25	76.6	85.8	103.2
1926-29	104.3	112.7	138.9
1930	99.7	119.8	136.9
1931-35	75.5	107.2	128.2
1936-38	92.1	116.6	185.0

Source: League of Nations, *Industrialization and Foreign Trade* (1945), pp. 130-31 and 157. Data include the U.S.S.R.

[1] These two volume indices are not combined into one index. The value of world trade in manufactured articles during the period was about 60 per cent of that in primary products, fluctuating only slightly above and below that percentage (*ibid.*, p. 14).

Enlargement of Fund Resources Through Increases in Quotas

At the Annual Meetings in 1958 the subject discussed in the preceding document was extensively canvassed by Governors. On the motion of the Governor for the United States, a resolution was passed requesting the Executive Directors to consider promptly the question of enlarging the resources of the Fund through increases in quotas. As a result, the Board adopted, on December 19, 1958, the following report to the Governors. This was accepted by the Governors, and took effect from September 9, 1959.

Enlargement of Fund Resources
Through Increases in Quotas
Report by
the Executive Directors
to the Board of Governors
of the
International Monetary Fund
(December 1958)

CONTENTS

	PAGE
Introduction	421
I. Increase in the Fund's Resources	422
II. Magnitude of the Increase in the Fund's Resources	427
III. Payment of Additional Subscriptions	430
IV. Procedure	431
Annex: Resolutions	433
Quotas and Fund Holdings of Currencies and Gold	436
Exchange Transactions: Drawings and Their Repayment	438
Stand-By Arrangements	440
Balance Sheet	441

INTRODUCTION

At the Thirteenth Annual Meeting at New Delhi, the Board of Governors adopted the following Resolution:

RESOLVED:

That the Executive Directors promptly consider the question of enlarging the resources of the Fund through increases in quotas and that, if, having regard to views expressed by Governors and considering all other aspects of the matter, they find that action to carry out such increases would be desirable, they submit an appropriate proposal to the Board of Governors for action either at a meeting of the Board or by vote without a meeting, as the Executive Directors may determine.

Pursuant to this Resolution the Executive Directors have studied the question of enlarging the resources of the Fund by quota increases, so as to enable the Fund to promote more effectively its purposes as set out in the Articles of Agreement. They have concluded that a substantial enlargement of the resources of the Fund is highly desirable. The grounds for this conclusion and the manner in which an appropriate increase in Fund quotas could best be brought about are discussed in the following sections of this report.

To accomplish the proposed increase in the Fund's resources, the annexed Resolutions have been prepared for adoption by the Board of Governors. Attention is drawn to the requirement that votes, to be valid, must be received at the seat of the Fund on or before February 2, 1959.

I. INCREASE IN THE FUND'S RESOURCES

The need for an increase in the Fund's resources arises from the tasks which, under its Articles of Agreement, the Fund has to perform in an expanding world economy. The role that the Fund is likely to play in the future and the resources it will need for this purpose can best be assessed in the light of the experience it has accumulated and the policies it has pursued in the twelve years of its existence.

The Fund has two main tasks which are clearly intertwined. It promotes international monetary cooperation and exchange stability as a basis for the balanced growth of world trade. It also provides financial assistance to members to help them stabilize their currencies, maintain or move toward convertibility, and overcome temporary balance of payments problems without resort to policies that would be harmful to national or international prosperity. While the first task is a continuing one, experience has shown that the granting of financial assistance tends to be concentrated in certain periods characterized by exceptional strains in the world's monetary system. Major economic and financial developments will often affect several countries more or less at the same time, so that the calls on the Fund's resources may be of substantial proportions in a relatively short period. There was one such period in the early years of the Fund's existence, namely, in 1947-49, when certain European countries suffered from extreme foreign exchange shortages; and another, leading to even larger drawings, which started late in 1956. Although the extreme tensions that gripped the major exchange markets in 1956 and 1957 have now abated, requests for financial assistance from members continue to be received almost every month. Countries whose economies are subject to wide seasonal swings have called on the Fund for short-term assistance to bridge the seasonal troughs in their reserves, and many other countries have also come to the Fund for assistance when, for particular reasons affecting their own economies, they have experienced difficulties in their balance of payments.

Since the beginning of its operation, the Fund has made available about $4.1 billion to 36 countries. Of this sum, $3.2 billion was drawn in some 150 transactions; over $800 million is still available for drawing under open stand-by facilities; and stand-by credits of over $100 million were allowed to expire as the members concerned no longer felt the need for them (see tables, pages 436-41). About two thirds of the total of $4.1 billion has been arranged in the last two years. The needs for assistance in this recent period have arisen from a wide variety of causes which have revealed the many-sided nature of the Fund's financial activities.

The largest single transaction in this period arose out of the Suez events which caused sterling to come under pressure. In December 1956, the United Kingdom drew $561 million from the Fund and entered into a stand-by arrangement for $739 million—a total of $1,300 million. The assistance was granted on the basis of a declaration by the British Government that strict financial and credit policies would be pursued, that quantitative import restrictions would not be reimposed, and that the value of sterling would be maintained. This was an emergency situation in which the massive use of the Fund's resources was required to prevent a major crisis in the international exchange structure.

In the latter part of 1956 and the first half of 1957, highly expansionary developments in many countries produced severe pressures in national and international money and capital markets. Large government deficits gave rise to serious declines of foreign exchange in a number of countries. In the third quarter of 1957, lack of confidence in the stability of the pattern of European exchange rates led to large international movements of funds. These and other causes gave rise to requests for assistance from all over the world. Among the countries that drew on the Fund were Argentina, Bolivia, Brazil, Chile, Cuba, Denmark, France, Japan, and the Netherlands. For some countries, stand-by agreements were renegotiated, often with new provisions adapted to changed circumstances. In this period of pronounced boom, the pursuit of cautious credit policies was more than ever required, a fact which was reflected in the declarations of intent which were made by the Governments then requesting assistance from the Fund and on the basis of which the Fund acted.

The recession which started in 1957 brought a new set of circumstances. A number of industrial countries were able to improve their reserve positions substantially, but many of the primary producing countries suffered from the decline in raw material prices. As a result of the inherent strength of the major economies and the financial and commercial policies followed, the recession proved to be short and did not lead to an extensive use of Fund resources. Indeed, most of the Fund's transactions in 1957–58 were related to difficulties that found their main origin in inflationary pressures.

The correction of inflationary conditions requires internal corrective measures, and one of the principal benefits of Fund assistance is that it gives time for these measures to take effect. In some cases the assistance of the Fund has been closely linked to the carrying out of comprehensive stabilization programs; examples of this in Latin America are Bolivia, Brazil, Chile, Colombia, Haiti, Paraguay, and Peru, and elsewhere, France and Turkey. The main lines of these programs have been indicated to the Fund in declarations made by the Governments, and in these cases the declarations have formed an essential part of the stand-by arrangements. A noteworthy feature of these stabilization efforts is that the Fund's assistance has frequently been supplemented by substantial credits from other sources. Countries embarking on stabilization programs are often in need of different kinds of foreign resources; indeed, one of the advantages of such parallel arrangements is that in some measure they provide assistance tailored to the particular needs of the countries concerned. For instance, the Fund's assistance is of a short-term character designed to strengthen reserve positions, while resources obtained from other agencies may be either related to special categories of payment (as when furnished by the European Payments Union) or of a more long-term character, appropriate for investment financing. The importance of the Fund's participation in these parallel arrangements has generally been a double one: the Fund has played a leading role in assisting countries to work out their stabilization programs, and the strengthening by the Fund of the country's reserves has been an essential part of these programs.

The Fund's transactions have been fully described in its Annual Reports, but enough has been said here to indicate that the assistance obtained from the Fund has been requested under a great variety of circumstances: in an emergency at the time of the Suez events, in conditions of boom and expanding world trade, and in periods of recession, as well as in a wider context when stabilization efforts have been undertaken. The only conclusion can be that the Fund must remain prepared for diverse contingencies, many of which cannot be clearly defined in advance.

The ability of the Fund to grant assistance so promptly and on such a considerable scale in the last two years was due to the fact that, since in the immediately preceding period there had been very few transactions and nearly all the earlier drawings had been repaid, most of its resources in gold and convertible currencies were intact. The many transactions with the Fund in this recent period have, of course, considerably decreased the amount of its uncommitted resources. At the end of November 1958, the Fund's holdings of gold and U.S. dollars amounted to $2.3 billion. If commitments under stand-by arrangements, totaling $0.8 billion, are deducted, the balance of gold and U.S. dollars was $1.5 billion, compared with $3.5 billion at the end of September 1956. Considering that the use of the Fund's resources in the form of drawings and stand-by arrangements came to over $2.7 billion in the two years from October 1956 to September 1958, the resources of about $1.5 billion presently available cannot be considered adequate in the light of past experience to meet such calls on the Fund as may suddenly be made. This is even more evident if it is borne in mind that the Fund must always maintain enough liquid resources to give its members confidence that they have a second line of reserves in the Fund.

At the Thirteenth Annual Meeting of the Board of Governors in New Delhi, a number of Governors suggested that consideration be given to the increased effectiveness of the Fund's present resources that might be achieved if greater use were made of the currencies of the main industrial countries other than the United States, even though those currencies are not fully convertible within the meaning of the Fund's Articles of Agreement. The Executive Directors have not yet fully explored this question, but they are hopeful that measures can be devised that would facilitate such drawings. In recent transactions, there has already been an encouraging increase in the demand for currencies other than the U.S. dollar, and it is expected that there will be continued progress in this direction. The acceptance of convertibility under Article VIII, or even the more limited step of external convertibility by the more important trading countries, would be most helpful in this connection. As convertibility is attained or approached, the question whether drawings in these currencies can or cannot be repaid in the same currencies will lose much of its practical importance. However, while developments along these lines are certainly greatly to be welcomed and will help the Fund in the future, the Fund must nevertheless be prepared for situations in which its holdings of gold and convertible currencies may be of decisive importance.

It has been mentioned above that countries which have received assistance from the Fund have, as a rule, made declarations of intent as to the policies they would follow. They have done so in accordance with the principles governing the use of the Fund's resources, which had been laid down by the Executive Directors and stated in Annual Reports well before the recent period of increased activity. Because the Fund's policy toward requests for drawings or stand-by arrangements must be applicable to large and small countries alike, it is expressed in terms not of the absolute amount involved, but of the proportion which this amount bears to the country's quota.

Countries are given the overwhelming benefit of the doubt with respect to requests for drawings within the "gold tranche," i.e., the portion of quota which can be regarded as equivalent to the member's gold subscription. The Fund's attitude to requests for drawings within the first credit tranche (equal to the first 25 per cent of the quota above the "gold tranche") is a liberal one, provided that a member wishing to make such a drawing is also itself making reasonable efforts to solve its problems. Members' requests for drawings or stand-by arrangements beyond the first credit tranche are likely to be favorably received when they are intended to support well-balanced and adequate programs which are aimed at establishing or maintaining the enduring stability of the currencies concerned at realistic rates of exchange.

Along with these principles governing access to its resources, the Fund has established certain principles covering repurchases, which emphasize the basic requirement for a drawing, namely, that it is required to meet temporary balance of payments difficulties and that the Fund should be repaid within a period appropriate to the problem for which Fund assistance is sought. Hence, members are expected to repurchase drawings within an outside range of three to five years, but in appropriate circumstances the Fund requires repurchase within an even shorter period. A member entering into a stand-by arrangement is generally required to repurchase within three years of any drawing under the arrangement, but again this period may be shorter in appropriate circumstances. Several members have in fact completed their repurchases in much shorter periods than had originally been specified. Indeed, all the resources made available by the Fund before 1956 have now been repaid with the exception of $36.5 million, and this has not been outstanding for a protracted period. These policies for repurchase assure the revolving character of the Fund's resources. They are intended to replenish these resources within a reasonable period; they also ensure that each country that draws on the Fund to handle a particular difficulty will put itself in a position, by repaying the Fund as soon as possible, where it can avail itself again of the Fund's assistance whenever a new need presents itself.

The experience of the last two years has shown that these principles and practices of the Fund are eminently applicable to its transactions. Not only do they serve to give coherence to the financial side of the Fund's work, but the fact that they have been made fully known in an authoritative way to the members leaves no room for uncertainty as to the principles which are applied in the Fund's decisions on financial assistance. Whether a member country will in fact be allowed to use the Fund's resources is, of course, a matter for judgment in each decision, according to the particular circumstances of the case, and it is here that the Fund must apply appropriate flexibility within the framework of the accepted principles and practices. By the close link that the application of these principles and practices establishes between the Fund's financial assistance and the maintenance or adoption of the necessary remedial measures in the countries concerned, the Fund supports the observance of that degree of financial self-discipline without which the international monetary system cannot function properly. One of the consequences of the breakdown of the gold standard in the 1930's was a large measure of uncertainty as to the proper rules for monetary management and a corresponding need for countries both to agree on a new set of rules and to work out cooperative ways of applying them. In these respects, the Fund has already made, and should be able to continue to make, a substantial contribution. It is able to do so in connection with the use of its resources, and also in other ways. A most important function is performed by the consultations which the Fund holds once a year with each of the countries that still maintain exchange restrictions under Article XIV of the Agreement. These annual consultations provide an opportunity to review with a country whether there is a continued need for these restrictions, as well as the measures that could be taken by the country to create conditions in which restrictions could be reduced or abolished. The Fund can also make a contribution by providing a forum for the crystallization of world opinion, and through its publications and technical assistance.

The Executive Directors are of the opinion that the policies and practices governing the use of the Fund's resources, which have now successfully stood the test of practical application, should not be changed as a consequence of the increases in quotas now envisaged. While the Fund must, of course, remain alert to the needs of changing circumstances, it will at all times have to ensure that its transactions with its members promote the purposes of the Articles of Agreement.

The power of the Fund to help its members over difficulties is not confined to the actual transfer of resources to the members. There are several cases, some of them of great importance, in which countries that have entered into stand-by arrangements with the Fund have not in fact made any drawings under them. In this way the financial assistance of the Fund, in the form of a line of credit, has been effective even without any new money being injected into the world economy. Naturally, from the point of view of its own liquidity, the Fund is affected by these stand-by arrangements even though there is no actual transfer of currencies, since it must regard the corresponding resources as subject to a contingent liability.

The possibility of access to the Fund's resources serves in itself as a second line of reserves, which gives members more confidence in undertaking efforts to restore balance, and may indeed encourage them to move faster toward achieving the purposes of the Fund than if they had to rely on their own resources alone. In this manner the Fund can be helpful to many of its members, whether they are in the initial stages of freeing their trade and payments from the shackles of restrictions or are well on the way toward making their currencies convertible.

It must also be stressed that the benefits which the Fund conveys by the use of its resources are by no means limited to those countries which have sought or may seek assistance from the Fund. Countries which are in such a strong position that they do not envisage making any request to the Fund also share in the benefits. Countries all over the world have a great interest in the financial rehabilitation of countries in difficulties, and more generally in the establishment of a properly functioning international monetary system. As far as recent Fund activities are concerned, it was clearly in the general interest that a crack in the world's exchange structure was avoided in 1956, that tension in the European exchange markets was eliminated in 1957, and that countries have been helped to push forward with their stabilization programs. It is in the general interest that by means of a strengthening of the Fund's position, together with continued observance of financial self-discipline, a sound monetary basis is created for the renewed expansion of world trade. It should never be forgotten that pressure on one currency may, under adverse circumstances, affect the position of other currencies. In 1931, at the time of world-wide depression, a financial breakdown which began in Austria spread so widely that in the end almost every country in the world had to alter its exchange rate or introduce restrictions on trade and payments harmful from every point of view. While no progress can be achieved without appropriate steps being taken in individual countries, the granting of financial assistance through the Fund reflects the idea that international assistance may be required to enable countries to take these steps.

It is therefore in the interest of all members of the Fund that the common pool constituting a secondary reserve should be adequate to meet the difficulties which may arise in the future. In considering the need for an increase in the Fund's resources, account must be taken of the fact that in the last decade the volume of world trade has nearly doubled. While reserves of gold and foreign exchange of countries outside the United States have increased by about 50 per cent in that period, Fund quotas have, with minor exceptions, remained at the amounts determined in 1944; and the rise in dollar prices by at least 50 per cent since that date has correspondingly reduced the real value of the Fund's resources. In fact, the Fund has found it increasingly necessary to waive the provision limiting drawings in any twelve months to 25 per cent of a country's quota. In recent years, the large majority of the Fund's drawings and stand-by arrangements have involved waivers of this provision.

The expansion of trade and the greater freedom of international payments, including capital movements, tend to increase the problems that may arise if there should be a sudden change in confidence in any major currency. The occurrence of such a change at some future time cannot altogether be excluded in a world in which monetary confidence has not yet been fully restored and where memories of devaluations and other difficulties still exert an influence in the markets. Countries must therefore be alert to the increased risks to which their reserves may be exposed as a result of the operation of leads and lags in payments and other movements of funds.

Fortunately, over the last year many countries have been able to strengthen their reserves. But the Fund cannot be concerned with only the present or the immediate future; its members must be assured that it is adequately equipped to meet the strains which may arise in emergencies or other adverse circumstances.

The Executive Directors have, therefore, concluded that it is highly desirable to enlarge the Fund's resources through increases in quotas.

II. MAGNITUDE OF THE INCREASE IN THE FUND'S RESOURCES

An increase of 50 per cent is considered a reasonable basis at this time for quota increases to enlarge the resources of the Fund. A general increase of this magnitude, together with special increases for certain countries described below, would increase the resources of the Fund by $5.1 billion, including gold payments of nearly $1.3 billion. This appears to be as much as members generally can be expected to contribute. If these new resources are made available, members will have increased confidence in the capacity of the Fund to perform its tasks in the coming period.

As shown in Table 1, the proposed increase in quotas would produce a larger relative rise in the Fund's holdings of gold, U.S. dollars, and other currencies that have been drawn in the past. Thus the Fund's holdings of gold and U.S. dollars would double, increasing from $2.3 billion to $4.6 billion, and the holdings of gold and of the six currencies that have been drawn would increase by 75 per cent.

Special Increases

In view of the position in world trade of Canada, the Federal Republic of Germany, and Japan, and their recent relative economic growth, increases in their quotas beyond 50 per cent would be appropriate and highly desirable, particularly because this would enlarge the Fund's resources of currencies likely to be required by other members. In the light of these considerations and on the basis of statements made on behalf of these three countries, the Executive Directors recommend to the Board of Governors a quota increase for Canada to $550 million, for the Federal Republic of Germany to $787.5 million, and for Japan to $500 million.

Table 1. Changes in Fund Holdings of Gold and Currencies As a Result of Quota Increases
(In millions of U.S. dollars)

	Holdings As of November 30, 1958	Holdings After Quota Increase [1]	Amount of Increase
Gold and U.S. dollars			
Gold	1,531	2,810	1,279
U.S. dollars	787	1,818	1,031
	2,318	4,628	2,310
Other currencies that have been drawn			
Belgian francs	169	253	84
Canadian dollars	210	397	187
Deutsche mark	183	526	343
Netherlands guilders	206	309	103
Sterling	1,618	2,106	488
	2,386	3,591	1,205
Other currencies [2]	4,507	6,106	1,599
Total	9,211	14,325	5,114

[1] On the assumption that all quotas are increased by 50 per cent, that the quotas of Canada, the Federal Republic of Germany, and Japan are increased as indicated below, and that all additional subscriptions are paid in full. No allowance made for increases under the Second Resolution.

[2] Includes subscriptions receivable.

Countries with Small Quotas

In the Second Quinquennial Review of Quotas, the quotas of a number of the smaller countries were found to be particularly inadequate. As a result of that review, it was understood that requests for increases in small quotas would be sympathetically considered, and since then it has been the practice of the Executive Directors to recommend, and the Board of Governors to agree to, increases in accordance with the following formula:

Quotas below $5 million could be raised to $7.5 million;

Quotas of $5 million and above but below $10 million could be raised to $10 million;

Quotas of $10 million and above but below $15 million could be raised to $15 million; and

Quotas of $15 million and above but below $20 million could be raised to $20 million.

Eight countries with small quotas have taken advantage of this understanding during the last two years. The old quotas for these countries, their present quotas, and their present quotas increased by 50 per cent are shown in Table 2. A special adjustment, from $15 million to $50 million, for the Philippines has also been approved by the Board of Governors.

The other 24 countries with small quotas have not so far requested quota increases under this formula. It is recommended that they now have the opportunity

(i) To increase their present quotas by 50 per cent, or

(ii) To obtain a quota equal to the amount available under the small quota formula increased by 50 per cent, or

(iii) To consent to a quota of an amount between (i) and (ii) as they may choose.

The 24 countries concerned, their present quotas, and the amounts to which they could be raised under (i) and (ii) above, are shown in Table 3.

Further Adjustment of Quotas

The directive given to the Executive Directors by the Board of Governors was to consider promptly the question of enlarging the Fund's resources through increases in

Table 2

	Old Quota	Present Quota	Present Quota Increased by 50 Per Cent
	←————————(million U.S. dollars)————————→		
Dominican Republic	5	10	15
Ecuador	5	10	15
El Salvador	2.5	7.5	11.25
Haiti	2	7.5	11.25
Honduras	2.5	7.5	11.25
Israel	4.5	7.5	11.25
Nicaragua	2	7.5	11.25
Paraguay	3.5	7.5	11.25

quotas, and the Resolutions now recommended (see Annex) are based on the general idea of increases of 50 per cent in quotas, with special increases for Canada, the Federal Republic of Germany, and Japan.

The Executive Directors have, however, received from a number of other countries requests for increases beyond 50 per cent of their present quotas. Some of these countries have present quotas of less than $20 million, and have requested increases beyond the amounts available under the small quota formula increased by 50 per cent. It has not been possible within the time available to give adequate consideration to these requests, but the Executive Directors are continuing their consideration of them.

The Executive Directors will, as expeditiously as possible, reach their decisions on these requests and on any other requests that are received early in 1959. The recommendations that they decide to make will be submitted to the Governors in the form of new resolutions. These recommendations will be made promptly and, it is hoped, early enough to permit the members concerned to give their consent before September 15, 1959. It is expected that any such new resolutions would be similar to the Third Resolution annexed to this report.

III. PAYMENT OF ADDITIONAL SUBSCRIPTIONS

When a quota is increased, the member must pay an additional subscription equal to the increase, 25 per cent in gold and the balance in the member's currency. Payment of both portions of the additional subscription must be made before the increase in the member's quota can become effective, even by those few members which, in accordance with the Articles of Agreement, have not yet been required to pay their original subscriptions.

The present proposals for increases in quotas are based on the idea of a cooperative effort by the members of the Fund to provide larger resources against contingencies that may affect any member. In order to preserve the general character of that effort, it has been thought preferable not to exercise the discretion to reduce gold payments under Article III, Section 4. However, since the prompt payment in gold of 25 per

Table 3

	Present Quota	Present Quota Increased by 50 Per Cent	Quota Under Formula Increased by 50 Per Cent
	←————————(million U.S. dollars)————————→		
Afghanistan	10	15	22.5
Bolivia	10	15	22.5
Burma	15	22.5	30
Ceylon	15	22.5	30
Costa Rica	5	7.5	15
Ethiopia	6	9	15
Ghana	15	22.5	30
Guatemala	5	7.5	15
Iceland	1	1.5	11.25
Iraq	8	12	15
Jordan	3	4.5	11.25
Korea	12.5	18.75	22.5
Lebanon	4.5	6.75	11.25
Libya	5	7.5	15
Luxembourg	10	15	22.5
Panama	0.5	0.75	11.25
Saudi Arabia	10	15	22.5
Sudan	10	15	22.5
Thailand	12.5	18.75	22.5
Tunisia	12	18	22.5
UAR: Syria	6.5	9.75	15
Uruguay	15	22.5	30
Venezuela	15	22.5	30
Viet-Nam	12.5	18.75	22.5

cent of the quota increase might cause hardship in some cases, the facilities described in the next two paragraphs will be available to members consenting to increases under the First or the Second Resolution.

Provision has been made for such of these members as represent, for reasons which they shall submit to the Fund, that their reserves should not be reduced by an immediate 25 per cent gold payment, to have their quotas increased in installments corresponding to each installment of gold and currency paid. These members will pay an original installment, and an installment in each period of twelve months thereafter. Each installment shall be one fifth of the increase. Members may accelerate payment under this installment schedule.

In exceptional cases, members may wish to have the full increase in their quotas take effect immediately, or members paying under the installment schedule may wish to expedite the full increase in their quotas, but in either case would encounter undue payments difficulties through the reduction of their reserves by the payment of the 25 per cent gold subscription or of the outstanding balance. In order to assist members to meet these payments difficulties, the Fund will sympathetically consider a request, made within two years after the effective date of a member's quota increase or the first installment of the increase, for an exchange transaction up to 25 per cent of the increase. The Fund will expect that a member requesting such an exchange transaction beyond the gold tranche will represent that it will make a repurchase corresponding to any drawing in equal annual installments, to commence one year after the drawing and to be completed not later than three years after the drawing.

IV PROCEDURE

1. *Voting*

The Resolutions presented in the Annex are designed to enable the Board of Governors to vote at one time on all matters connected with increases in quotas therein proposed. When adopted, they will make it possible for increases in quotas to become effective without need for further reference to the Board of Governors.

To be valid, votes must be received at the seat of the Fund on or before February 2, 1959.

Separate votes are required on the First, Second, and Third Resolutions. In voting on the Third Resolution, a Governor may vote on the whole of that Resolution or on each of the increases of quotas there proposed.

2. *Date for Consent*

If the Resolutions are adopted by the necessary majority of four fifths of the total voting power, a member may consent to the increase in its quota at any time on or before September 15, 1959. Therefore, unless this period is extended by the Fund, members will have until September 15, 1959 to take whatever legal action may be necessary in their countries to enable them to give their consent.

3. *Participation*

In view of the cooperative nature of the proposed increase in the Fund's resources, it is provided that, before increases become effective, the Fund must determine that members having 75 per cent of the total of present quotas have consented to increases in their quotas.

In determining whether this degree of participation has been reached, the Fund will take into account all consents to increases, whether they be increases in full or by installments, under the First or Second Resolutions, or increases under the Third Resolution.

4. *Relation of Quota Increases to Increased Capital of International Bank for Reconstruction and Development*

Under the Resolutions recommended by the Executive Directors of the International Bank for Reconstruction and Development to the Board of Governors of the International Bank for Reconstruction and Development, provision is made for the proposed increase in authorized capital to take effect only if a specified aggregate amount of subscriptions is taken up.

The Fund Resolutions provide that increases in Fund quotas shall take effect only if this condition is satisfied in the Bank. However, it is also provided in the Fund Resolutions that the Board of Governors of the Fund may eliminate this condition by a four-fifths majority if the required member participation is attained in the Fund but not in the Bank.

It is not a condition in the Fund Resolutions that the required percentage of participation in the Fund and Bank must consist of the same members. However, according to the established policy of the Fund, it has been the practice, where an increase in quota is sought in the Fund, for the member to request a corresponding increase in its subscription in the Bank. The Fund, therefore, expects that any member consenting to an increase in its quota will request a corresponding increase in its subscription to the capital of the Bank.

5. *Date for Payment of Additional Subscription*

After the Resolutions are adopted, a member may pay its increased subscription in respect of the increase in its quota at any time before it is due. If a member pays before the increase in its quota takes effect, the additional subscription will be kept in separate accounts of the Fund and returned if it should be established that the increase cannot take effect. A member is required to pay its additional subscription not later than thirty days after the latest of the following events: its consent to its quota increase (see 2 above); the determination by the Fund that the condition as to participation in quota increases has been satisfied (see 3 above); and the similar requirement has been satisfied in the Bank (see 4 above).

6. *Effective Date of Quota Increases*

Increases in members' quotas will take effect as follows:

(a) When a member pays its additional subscription before the latest of the three events referred to in 5 above, the increase in its quota will take effect on the happening of the latest of these events.

(b) If a member pays its additional subscription after the latest of these three events, the increase in its quota will take effect on the day of payment.

7. *Increase of Quotas by Installments*

Members consenting to increases in their quotas under the First or Second Resolutions may consent to increases by installments. The foregoing paragraphs in this section of the report will apply to such members, except that the first installment instead of the whole additional subscription will have to be paid as described in 5 above. It should be noted that the increases in quotas will be equal to the installments actually paid.

ANNEX

ENLARGEMENT OF FUND RESOURCES THROUGH INCREASES IN QUOTAS

RESOLUTIONS

WHEREAS the Executive Directors have considered the question referred to them by the Resolution of the Board of Governors of the International Monetary Fund at their Thirteenth Annual Meeting:

> That the Executive Directors promptly consider the question of enlarging the resources of the Fund through increases in quotas and that, if, having regard to views expressed by Governors and considering all other aspects of the matter, they find that action to carry out such increases would be desirable, they submit an appropriate proposal to the Board of Governors for action either at a meeting of the Board or by vote without a meeting, as the Executive Directors may determine;

And having found that action to carry out increases in quotas would be desirable, have set out their conclusions in a report, entitled *Enlargement of Fund Resources Through Increases in Quotas*, in which it is proposed that the present quota of each member of the Fund shall be increased by 50 per cent, with additional increases for certain members;

And having noted that there are various legal requirements in member countries for giving effect to this proposal, have submitted to the Board of Governors the following Resolutions for a vote without meeting pursuant to Section 13 of the By-Laws of the Fund, which Resolutions propose increases of quotas for all members of the Fund, make provision for consents by members, and establish the conditions upon which the increases consented to shall take effect;

Now THEREFORE the Board of Governors hereby RESOLVES that

First Resolution

1. The International Monetary Fund proposes that, subject to the provisions of this Resolution, the quotas of members of the International Monetary Fund as of January 31, 1959 shall be increased by 50 per cent for each member.

2. None of the increases in quotas proposed in paragraph 1 of this Resolution shall become effective unless:

   (i) The member concerned has notified the Fund in writing that it consents to the increase in its quota; and

   (ii) The Fund determines that members having not less than 75 per cent of the total of quotas on January 31, 1959 have consented to increases in their quotas; and

   (iii) The requirement is satisfied of a minimum aggregate increase in subscriptions, contained in the Resolution of the Board of Governors of the International Bank for Reconstruction and Development entitled *Increase of $10,000,000,000 in Authorized Capital Stock and Subscriptions Thereto*, recommended by the Executive Directors of the International Bank for Reconstruction and Development; and

   (iv) The member concerned has paid the full increase in its quota.

Subject to paragraph 7 (c) of this Resolution, each increase in quota shall become effective upon the date of the latest of these four events.

3. The written notices prescribed in paragraph 2 (i) shall be signed by a competent official whose authority and signature are duly authenticated.

4. Notices in accordance with paragraph 2 (i) shall be received in the Fund not later than September 15, 1959, provided that the Executive Directors may extend this period as they may determine.

5. At any time after the percentage of participation prescribed in paragraph 2 (ii) of this Resolution has been reached, the Board of Governors may, by a four-fifths majority of the total voting power, eliminate the requirements in paragraph 2 (iii) of this Resolution, and may make such modifications as to the date of the effectiveness of increases in quotas as may then be determined.

6. Subject to paragraph 7 (b) of this Resolution, each member shall pay to the Fund within thirty days after the latest of the three events in paragraph 2 (i), (ii), and (iii) of this Resolution, 25 per cent of the increase in gold and the balance in its own currency.

7 (a). In giving notice in accordance with paragraph 2 (i) of this Resolution, a member may represent that, for reasons which it shall submit to the Fund, its reserves should not be reduced by an immediate full gold payment in accordance with paragraph 6 of this Resolution, and that it therefore consents to the increase in its quota proposed in paragraph 1 of this Resolution, as an increase by installments.

(b). Notwithstanding paragraph 2 (iv) of this Resolution, a member increasing its quota by installments shall pay not less than one fifth of the gold and currency prescribed in paragraph 6 within thirty days after the latest of the three events in paragraph 2 (i), (ii), and (iii), and shall pay further installments of gold and currency of not less than one fifth of the increase in each twelve months after the first payment until the full amount prescribed in paragraph 6 has been paid.

(c). Subject to paragraph 2 of this Resolution, on the completion of the payment of each installment of the increase, the member's quota shall be increased by an amount equal to the installment.

8. Since it is in the interests of the Fund and its members that the contemplated increase in its resources be expedited, members are invited to comply as soon as possible with the procedures for notice and payments to the Fund under this Resolution. Any payment made by a member before the effective date of increase in its quota will be kept in separate accounts of the Fund. If it should be established that such increase cannot become effective under this Resolution, the payment will be returned to the member.

Second Resolution

1. The International Monetary Fund proposes that, subject to the provisions of this Second Resolution, if any member to which the small quota policy of the Second Quinquennial Review applies so elects, its quota shall be increased beyond the amount specified in the First Resolution to such an amount, not exceeding a 50 per cent increase in the maximum quota available under the said policy, as such member shall communicate to the Fund at the time that it consents to the increase in its quota.

2. Paragraphs 2 (i) and (iv), 3, 4, 6, 7, and 8 of the First Resolution shall apply to this Second Resolution.

Third Resolution

1. The International Monetary Fund proposes that, subject to the provisions of this Third Resolution, if increases in quotas take effect under the First Resolution, the quotas

of Canada, the Federal Republic of Germany, and Japan shall be increased to the amounts shown below:

Canada	$550 million
Federal Republic of Germany	$787.5 million
Japan	$500 million

2. Paragraphs 2 (i) and (iv), 3, 4, 6, and 8 of the First Resolution shall apply to this Third Resolution.

Quotas and Fund Holdings of Currencies and Gold

(As of November 30, 1958. Amounts expressed in millions of U.S. dollars, except where noted)

Member	Quota	Subscription: Gold	Subscription: Currency	Subscription Account Repurchases	Sales of Gold for Currency	Net Member Drawings	Income, Expenditure, Etc.	Fund Holdings of Currencies	% of Quota
Afghanistan	10	2.5	—	—	—	—	—	—	—
Argentina	150	37.5	112.5	—	—	75.0	—	187.5	125
Australia	200	8.4	191.6	—	—	—	-.1	191.5	96
Austria	50	5.0	45.0	-7.5	—	—	—	37.5	75
Belgium	225	56.2	168.8	—	—	—	—	168.7	75
Bolivia	10	2.5	7.5	—	—	8.5	—	16.0	160
Brazil	150	37.5	112.5	—	—	112.5	—	225.0	150
Burma	15	.5	14.5	-3.2	—	15.0	—	26.3	175
Canada	300	75.0	225.0	—	—	-15.0	—	210.0	70
Ceylon	15	.8	14.2	-3.0	—	—	—	11.2	75
Chile	50	8.8	41.2	-3.7	—	40.2	—	77.7	155
China	550	.1	—	—	—	—	—	—	—
Colombia	50	12.5	37.5	—	—	35.0	—	72.5	145
Costa Rica	5	.4	4.6	-.9	—	—	—	3.7	75
Cuba	50	12.5	37.5	—	—	25.0	—	62.5	125
Denmark	68	5.9	62.1	-2.6	—	8.5	—	68.0	100
Dominican Republic	10	2.5	7.5	—	—	—	—	7.5	75
Ecuador	10	2.5	7.5	—	—	—	—	7.5	75
El Salvador	7.5	1.9	5.6	—	—	—	—	5.6	75
Ethiopia	6	.1	5.9	-1.4	—	—	—	4.5	75
Finland	38	.8	37.2	-8.7	—	—	—	28.5	75
France	525	108.1	416.9	-22.9	—	393.8	-.4	787.4	150
Germany (Fed. Rep.)	330	33.0	297.0	-45.1	—	-68.9	—	183.0	55
Ghana	15	.5	14.5	—	—	—	—	14.5	97
Greece	40	—	—	—	—	—	—	—	—
Guatemala	5	1.2	3.8	—	—	—	—	3.7	75
Haiti	7.5	1.9	5.6	—	—	3.5	—	9.1	122
Honduras	7.5	1.9	5.6	—	—	—	—	5.6	75
Iceland	1	.2	.8	—	—	—	-.1	.7	75
India	400	27.5	372.5	—	—	200.0	4.6	577.1	144
Indonesia	110	15.5	94.5	-12.0	—	55.0	—	137.5	125
Iran	35	8.8	26.2	—	—	16.9	—	43.1	123
Iraq	8	—	8.0	-2.0	—	—	—	6.0	75
Ireland	30	4.5	25.5	—	—	—	—	25.5	85
Israel	7.5	1.9	5.6	—	—	3.8	—	9.4	125
Italy	180	45.0	—	—	—	—	—	—	—

ENLARGEMENT OF FUND RESOURCES THROUGH INCREASES IN QUOTAS

Japan	250	62.5	187.5	—	—	—	187.5	75
Jordan	3	.1	2.9	—	—	—	2.9	97
Korea, Republic of	12.5	3.1	—	—	—	—	—	—
Lebanon	4.5	.3	4.2	−.9	—	—	3.3	75
Libya	5	.2	—	—	—	—	—	—
Luxembourg	10	.5	9.5	—	—	—	9.5	95
Malaya	25	.9	—	—	—	—	—	—
Mexico	90	22.5	67.5	—	—	—	67.5	75
Morocco	35	1.2	—	—	—	—	—	—
Netherlands	275	68.8	206.2	—	—	—	206.2	75
Nicaragua	7.5	1.9	5.6	—	—	—	5.6	75
Norway	50	12.5	37.5	—	—	—	37.5	75
Pakistan	100	3.5	96.5	—	—	—	96.5	96
Panama	.5	.1	.4	—	—	—	.4	75
Paraguay	7.5	1.9	5.6	—	—	6.3	11.9	158
Peru	25	3.2	21.8	−3.1	—	5.0	23.7	95
Philippines	15	3.8	11.2	—	—	15.0	26.2	175
Saudi Arabia	10	2.5	—	—	—	—	—	—
Spain	100	10.0	—	—	—	—	—	—
Sudan	10	.4	9.6	—	—	5.0	14.6	146
Sweden	100	17.0	83.0	−8.0	—	—	75.0	75
Thailand	12.5	3.1	—	—	—	—	—	—
Tunisia	12	.4	—	—	—	—	—	—
Turkey	43	10.8	32.2	—	—	38.5	70.6	164
Union of South Africa	100	25.0	75.0	—	—	36.2	111.2	111
U Arab Rep: Egypt	60	9.5	50.5	−5.5	—	30.0	75.0	125
Syria	6.5	.2	6.3	−1.4	—	—	4.9	75
United Kingdom	1,300	236.3	1,063.7	−3.7	—	545.3	13.0	1,618.3	124
United States	2,750	687.5	2,062.5	92.0	600.0	−1,919.5	−46.9	788.1	29
Uruguay	15	3.8	—	—	—	—	—	—
Venezuela	15	3.8	11.2	—	—	—	11.2	75
Viet-Nam	12.5	3.1	—	—	—	—	—	—
Yugoslavia	60	7.9	52.1	—	—	22.9	.1	75.1	125
Currency			6,517.6	−43.7	600.0	{ 1,697.0 / −2,003.4 }	−30.0	6,737.4	
Convertible			2,420.9	92.0	600.0	−1,906.0	−46.9	1,160.0	
Non-Convertible			4,096.7	−135.7	—	1,599.5	16.9	5,577.4	
Gold		1,731.8		43.7	−600.0	304.5	51.0	1,531.0	
Subscript. Receivable		943.6				−2.0	21.0	943.6	
Total	9,193.0	9,193.0		0	0			9,212.0	

Exchange Transactions: Drawings and Their Repayment
(As of November 30, 1958. Amounts expressed in millions of U.S. dollars)

Member	1947	1948	1949	1950	1951	1952	1953	1954	1955	1956	1957	1958 to Date	Total to Date Gross	Total to Date Net
Argentina	...	...	...	...	...	...	...	...	...	...	75.0	...	75.0	75.0
Australia	11.0	{ 22.0 / −11.4 }	20.0	...	...	30.0	...	−24.0	−14.0	...	...	...	50.0	0
Belgium	...	...	−.9	−20.7	...	▲	−12.0 ▲	...	...	...	50.0	−50.0	83.0	0
Bolivia	...	...	...	...	...	...	...	...	...	3.0 ▲	1.0 ▲	2.0 ▲	8.5	8.5 ▲
Brazil	...	...	37.5	...	28.0	{ 37.5 / −65.5 }	{ 65.5 / −37.5 }	...	...	−28.0	37.5	{ 54.8 / −17.2 }	260.8	112.5 ▲
Burma	...	...	...	...	...	...	...	...	...	15.0	...	...	15.0	15.0
Chile	8.8	...	...	...	−3.4	−3.7	{ 12.5 / −1.7 }	...	...	−.2 ▲	...	9.1 ▲	61.5	40.2 ▲
Colombia	...	...	...	...	...	...	...	25.0	...	...	{ 31.1 / −12.3 } { 5.0 ▲ / −5.0 }	10.0 ▲	40.0 ▲	35.0 ▲
Costa Rica	...	1.2	−.9	...	...	...	...	...	...	...	...	...	1.2	0
Cuba	...	...	...	...	...	...	...	...	...	12.5 ▲	{ 35.0 / −22.5 }	−25.0 / −25.0	72.5	25.0
Czechoslovakia*	...	6.0	...	...	...	...	...	...	−2.0*	−.7*	−.7*	−.6*	6.0	2.0*
Denmark	3.4	6.8	...	...	...	...	...	...	−10.2	...	34.0	−25.5	44.2	8.5
Ecuador	...	...	...	...	...	...	...	...	...	...	5.0	−5.0	5.0	0
El Salvador	...	...	...	...	...	...	...	...	...	2.5	−2.5	▲	2.5	0 ▲
Ethiopia	...	.3	.3	−.3	−.3	...	...	...	...	...	...	...	.6	0
Finland	...	...	...	...	...	4.5 ▲	{ 5.0 / −2.0 }	−4.5 ▲	−3.0	...	...	...	9.5	0
France	125.0	...	...	...	...	...	...	−20.0	−60.0	−45.0	262.5	131.2	518.8	393.8
Haiti	...	...	...	...	...	...	...	...	...	...	1.0	2.5 ▲	3.5	3.5 ▲
Honduras	...	...	...	...	...	...	...	...	...	...	{ 6.2 / −2.5 }	−3.8	6.2	0
India	...	68.3	31.7	...	...	...	...	−46.7	−40.7	−12.5	200.0	...	300.0	200.0
Indonesia	...	...	...	...	...	...	...	15.0	{ −8.7 / 17.5 }	{ −15.0 / 55.0 / −11.9 / 19.7 }	...	...	70.0	55.0
Iran	...	...	...	...	6.6	2.2	...	...	...	...	...	−8.4	46.0	16.9
Israel	...	...	...	...	...	...	...	...	...	...	3.8	...	3.8	3.8
Japan	...	...	...	...	...	...	{ 124.0 / −61.6 }	...	−62.4	...	125.0	−125.0	249.0	0
Mexico	22.5	...	...	...	−22.6	...	...	22.5 ▲	−22.4	...	...	...	45.0	0
Netherlands	52.0	23.3	...	...	...	−27.3	−48.0	...	...	...	{ 68.8 / −1.9 } ▲	−68.8	144.1	0
Nicaragua	...	.5	−.5	...	...	...	...	...	...	1.9 ▲	{ −3.8 ▲ / 3.8 }	−3.8 ▲	6.1	0 ▲

ENLARGEMENT OF FUND RESOURCES THROUGH INCREASES IN QUOTAS

Norway	...	9.6	...	...	-9.6	...	...	...	...	9.6	9.6	0
Paraguay	...	...	...	...	...	...	.9	...	-.4	...	...	7.3	6.3 ▲
Peru	...	...	...	...	...	...	...	...	▲	1.5	▲	5.0	5.0 ▲
Philippines	...	...	...	...	...	...	...	...	10.0	...	5.0	5.0	15.0	15.0
Sudan	5.0	...	...	...	...	20.0	...	...	...	5.0	5.0	5.0
Turkey	...	10.0	...	...	...	-10.0	{ 10.0 -5.0 }	...	-9.0	...	{ 13.5 -7.0 }	{ 25.0 -8.0 }	73.5	38.5
U of S Africa	{ 240.0 -6.0 }	...	3.0	-3.0	...	...	...	-6.0	...	...	...	36.2 ▲	46.2	36.2 ▲
U Arab Rep: Egypt	...	60.0	...	...	-28.0	...	...	...	...	15.0	15.0	...	33.0	30.0
United Kingdom	...	...	9.0	...	...	-157.6	...	-108.3	...	561.5 ▲	▲	-16.2 ▲	861.5	545.3 ▲
Yugoslavia	...	...	...	...	...	...	...	...	...	...	-9.0	22.9	31.9	22.9
Drawings	468	208	101	...	35	85	2.30	62	28	693	977	329	3,216	1,699
Currency Bought														
Belgian francs	...	*11.4*	...	...	...	...	...	...	...	...	...	...	*11.4*	
Canadian dollars	...	...	...	...	...	...	...	...	...	*15.0*	...	...	*15.0*	
German marks	...	...	...	...	...	...	*4.4*	...	...	...	...	*64.5*	*68.9*	
Guilders	...	...	...	...	...	...	...	...	...	...	...	*5.0*	*5.0*	
Pounds sterling	*6.1*	...	...	...	*28.0*	...	*157.6*	...	...	...	...	*16.2*	*207.9*	
US dollars	*461.6*	*196.6*	*101.5*	...	*6.6*	*85.1*	*67.5*	*62.5*	*27.5*	*677.6*	*977.0*	*243.7*	*2,907.3*	
Repayments	-6	-11	-2	-24	-74	-102	-320	-210	-232	-113	-64	-357	-1,517
by Repurchases	...	...	*-2*	*-24*	*-46*	*-102*	*-163*	*-210*	*-232*	*-113*	*-64*	*-336*	*-1,292*	
by Others' Drawings	*-6*	*-11*	...	...	*-28*	...	*-158*	...	...	...	...	*-21*	*-224*	
Net Drawings	462	197	99	-24	-39	-16	-91	-148	-205	579	913	-28	1,699†
Drawings Outstanding	462	658	757	733	694	678	587	439	234	814	1,727	1,699	1,699†
Stand-bys Agreed						55	...	62	...	1,077	183	239	1,617
Drawn						...	5	22	...	21	426	206	680
Expired						...	...	...	28	1	4	89	122
Amounts Available at End of Period						55	50	90	62	1,117	870	815	815 ▲
Members' Repurchases on Subscription Account	-6.4	-.9	-11.5	-4.7	-57.2	-4.8	-41.1	-9.1	...	-135.7

*Former member. Payments made on settlement of Czechoslovakia's debt to the Fund are included as if they were a member's repurchase. ▲Stand-by in effect at end of period and not drawn or not fully drawn. See table on Stand-by Arrangements. † Net member drawings plus outstanding debt of Czechoslovakia.

Stand-By Arrangements
(As of November 30, 1958. Amounts expressed in millions of U.S. dollars)

Member	Date of Agreement	Expiration Date of Agreement or Renewal	Amount Agreed	Amount Available						
				Dec 31 1952	Dec 31 1953	Dec 31 1954	Dec 31 1955	Dec 31 1956	Dec 31 1957	Nov 30 1958
Agreements in effect										
Bolivia	Nov 1956	Dec 1958	7.5	—	—	—	—	4.5	3.5	1.5
Brazil	June 1958	June 1959	37.5	—	—	—	—	—	—	—
Chile	Apr 1956	Mar 1959	35.0	—	—	—	—	35.0	16.2	7.2
Colombia	June 1957	June 1959	25.0	—	—	—	—	—	25.0	15.0
El Salvador	Oct 1958	Mar 1959	7.5	—	—	—	—	—	—	7.5
France	Jan 1958	Jan 1959	131.25	—	—	—	—	—	—	—
Haiti	July 1958	July 1959	5.0	—	—	—	—	—	—	2.5
Nicaragua	Sept 1958	Mar 1959	7.5	—	—	—	—	—	—	7.5
Paraguay	July 1957	July 1959	5.5	—	—	—	—	—	—	1.2
Peru	Feb 1958	Feb 1959	25.0	—	—	—	—	—	2.0	20.0
Union of S. Africa	Apr 1958	Apr 1959	25.0	—	—	—	—	—	—	13.8
United Kingdom	Dec 1956	Dec 1958	738.53	—	—	—	—	738.5	738.5	738.5
Agreements expired or canceled										
Belgium	June 1952	June 1957	50.0	50.0	50.0	50.0	50.0	50.0	—	—
Cuba	Dec 1956	June 1957	12.5	—	—	—	—	12.5	—	—
Finland	Dec 1952	June 1953	5.0	5.0	—	—	—	—	—	—
France	Oct 1956	Oct 1957	262.5	—	—	—	—	262.5	—	—
Honduras	Nov 1957	May 1958	3.75	—	—	—	—	—	—	—
India	Mar 1957	Mar 1958	72.5	—	—	—	—	—	—	—
Iran	May 1956	Nov 1956	17.5	—	—	—	—	—	—	—
Mexico	Apr 1954	Oct 1955	50.0	—	—	27.5	—	—	—	—
Netherlands	Sept 1957	Mar 1958	68.75	—	—	—	—	—	68.8	—
Nicaragua	Nov 1956	May 1957	3.75	—	—	—	—	1.9	—	—
	Oct 1957	Apr 1958	7.5	—	—	—	—	—	3.8	—
Peru	Feb 1954	Feb 1958	12.5	—	—	12.5	12.5	12.5	12.5	—
Total			1,616.53	55.0	50.0	90.0	62.5	1,117.4	870.3	814.7

Balance Sheet
(Amounts expressed in millions of U.S. dollars)

	April 30 1950	April 30 1951	April 30 1952	April 30 1953	April 30 1954	April 30 1955	April 30 1956	April 30 1957	April 30 1958	Oct 31 1958
Gold (at 35 dollars per fine ounce)	1,459.5	1,495.0	1,531.6	1,692.6	1,718.5	1,744.4	1,761.4	1,439.3	1,237.7	1,306.9
Investments [a]	—	—	—	—	—	—	50.0	200.0	200.0	200.0
Convertible Currencies	1,395.2	1,409.7	1,582.0	1,638.3	1,774.0	1,974.3	2,119.9	1,333.9	1,069.1	1,088.6
Balances with Depositories	125.1	126.0	107.1	156.9	167.8	168.3	226.5	167.1	175.2	176.8
Demand Securities [b]	1,270.0	1,283.7	1,475.0	1,481.4	1,606.2	1,802.4	1,892.0	1,175.2	891.4	911.9
Currency Adj. Rec. or Pay. (−)	—	—	—	—	—	3.6	1.4	−8.4	2.5	−.1
Sub Total	2,854.6	2,904.7	3,113.6	3,330.9	3,492.5	3,718.7	3,931.3	2,973.2	2,506.8	2,595.5
Non-Convertible Currencies	4,153.5	4,219.1	4,161.2	4,340.2	4,458.5	4,325.4	3,986.1	5,129.6	5,686.5	5,653.3
Balances with Depositories	620.6	588.6	696.3	658.9	688.8	656.8	572.8	943.8	1,246.2	1,253.7
Demand Securities [b]	3,533.0	3,630.4	3,464.9	3,681.3	3,769.7	3,669.0	3,413.3	4,185.8	4,431.2	4,399.2
Currency Adj. Rec. or Pay. (−)	—	—	—	—	—	−.4			9.1	.4
Subscriptions Receivable	892.8	906.5	870.8	1,056.7	888.8	797.7	814.5	816.8	898.4	958.1
Withdrawing Member's Currency	—	—	—	—	—	—	3.6	3.0	2.3	2.0
Other Assets	0.7	0.7	1.0	1.1	1.0	0.9	1.1	4.6	5.5	6.8
Total Assets = Total Liabilities	7,918.0	8,031.0	8,146.6	8,728.9	8,840.8	8,842.7	8,736.6	8,927.2	9,099.6	9,215.7
Capital: Auth. Subscriptions: paid	7,028.7	7,130.0	7,282.7	7,679.8	7,959.8	7,930.3	7,936.0	8,114.7	8,189.6	8,234.9
unpaid	892.8	906.5	870.8	1,056.7	888.8	797.7	814.5	816.8	898.4	958.1
Cumulated Deficit (−)	−3.8	−5.7	−7.2	−8.0	−8.0	−10.5	−14.2	−6.3	—	—
Net Capital	7,917.7	8,030.8	8,146.3	8,728.5	8,840.5	8,717.5	8,736.3	8,925.2	9,088.0	9,193.0
Withdrawing Member's Subscription	—	—	—	—	—	125.0	—	—	—	—
Reserves and Liabilities	.3	.2	.3	.4	.3	.2	.3	2.0	11.6	22.7

[a] US Treasury Bills and funds awaiting investment.   [b] Nonnegotiable, noninterest-bearing securities payable at face value on demand.

Compensatory Financing: First Report

In March 1959 the UN Commission on International Commodity Trade agreed to consider at its next session, in May 1960, international measures designed to compensate for fluctuations in export receipts, and invited the Fund to inform the Commission about its policies in this respect. A report by the Fund in response to this invitation was followed by further discussions, during which a number of alternative plans were examined.

In May 1962 the Commission considered comments by a technical working group set up to report on these plans, and invited the Fund to consider whether it could not play a larger part in financing fluctuations in export receipts. A draft response to this invitation, prepared by the staff, was reviewed by the Board in November and December 1962, and a revised version of it in February 1963. The latter was approved with slight amendments on February 27, and was sent to the Commission. It is reproduced below.

Compensatory Financing of Export Fluctuations

(February 1963)

A Report by the International Monetary Fund on Compensatory Financing of the Fluctuations in Exports of Primary Exporting Countries

CONTENTS

	PAGE
Introduction	442
I. Previous Consideration of the Problem by the Fund	443
II. Suggestions for Increased Use of Fund Resources for Compensatory Financing	444
III. Automatism and the Use of Fund Resources	446
IV. Quantitative Adequacy of Drawing Facilities in the Fund	449
V. Conclusions: Fund Action in Connection with Export Fluctuations	454

Tables

1. Adequacy of External Liquidity to Finance Fluctuations in Exports of Some Fund Members	452
Annex: Net Fund Drawings of Some Fund Members, 1947–62	457

INTRODUCTION

The United Nations Commission on International Commodity Trade, at its tenth session held in Rome in May 1962, "invited the International Monetary Fund, in the light of the discussion during the tenth session, and after consideration of the questions involved, to present, as soon as possible, a report as to whether and in what way the Fund might play an increased part in the compensatory financing of export fluctuations of primary exporting countries, and to keep the Technical Working Group currently informed of the progress of its deliberations on the subject."[1]

The present report by the International Monetary Fund is presented in fulfillment of the invitation extended by the Commission.

I. PREVIOUS CONSIDERATION OF THE PROBLEM BY THE FUND

In 1960, in response to an earlier request by the Commission on International Commodity Trade, the Fund prepared a study explaining its policies and procedures bearing on the compensatory financing of fluctuations in foreign exchange receipts from the export of primary commodities.[2] The main points in this study may be briefly summarized as follows:

(1) The provision of foreign exchange to Fund members to assist in the compensation of short-term fluctuations in the balance of payments constitutes a legitimate use of Fund resources.[3] Among such fluctuations are some that arise primarily from variations in export prices and proceeds. However, in order that balance of payments deficits from this cause should be suitable for financing by the Fund, the member's policies must be such as to enable it, with the financial assistance it obtains from the Fund, to overcome its difficulties within a reasonably short period of time.

(2) It would be neither practicable nor desirable to make the amount of such assistance dependent on any automatic formula, or to provide any separate form of Fund assistance to deal with export fluctuations alone. The reasons for this are (a) that judgment is required to determine the extent to which export fluctuations require, and are suitable for, compensatory financing in the light of the balance of payments as a whole, and the extent to which any compensation required should be provided by international transfers rather than by national reserve movements, and (b) that, if the Fund should give too much of its assistance automatically, its ability to influence countries toward the adoption of appropriate policies would be seriously impaired. Requests for drawings for all purposes in accordance with the Articles of Agreement are, however, treated liberally if they are within the gold tranche or the first credit tranche.

(3) Fund quotas (at the end of 1959) were considered adequate to provide for its primary exporting members a supplement to liquidity which, in the majority of cases, should be sufficient, in conjunction with their own resources, to enable them to deal with payments problems created by short-term fluctuations in exports or in receipts from abroad of the order experienced since World War II, provided they did their best to keep their income and costs adjusted to the longer-run changes in their external purchasing power.

---

[1] United Nations, Commission on International Commodity Trade, Report on the Tenth Session (E/CN.13/55, May 31, 1962), p. 41.

[2] "Fund Policies and Procedures in Relation to the Compensatory Financing of Commodity Fluctuations," *Staff Papers*, Vol. VIII (1960–61), pp. 1–76.

[3] Since the presentation of this study in April 1960, Fund transactions with primary exporting countries have greatly increased. Outstanding drawings by low-income primary exporters have nearly doubled over the last 3 years. For details see Annex Table (p. 457).

(4) There appeared (as of the same date) to be no reason why a shortage of Fund resources should be a factor limiting the amount of assistance that the Fund would otherwise consider it desirable to extend to its members.

(5) Consequently, it was concluded that "members of the Fund that are taking appropriate steps to preserve internal financial stability and to maintain their balance of payments in equilibrium, taking good years with bad, and that are otherwise making satisfactory progress toward the fulfillment of the Fund's purposes can anticipate with confidence that financing will be available from the Fund which, in conjunction with a reasonable use of their own reserves, should be sufficient to enable them to overcome temporary payments difficulties arising from export fluctuations." [4]

II. SUGGESTIONS FOR INCREASED USE OF FUND RESOURCES FOR COMPENSATORY FINANCING

Since the study summarized above was submitted to the United Nations in April 1960, the subject of compensatory financing has been actively considered within the framework of the United Nations (UN) and of the Organization of American States (OAS), in particular by the UN Committee of Experts which reported in January 1961,[5] and by the OAS Group of Experts which reported in April 1962.[6]

In general, the international bodies in which the matter has been discussed have displayed understanding toward the Fund's policies on compensatory financing, as outlined above (including the restricted scope given to automatism in Fund transactions), and appreciation for the assistance which the Fund has been able to give under its present rules to primary exporting countries having export difficulties. However, certain suggestions have been made for changes in policy that would permit an enhancement of the Fund's role in compensatory financing. Moreover, it has been argued that, even if the Fund should make a reasonable degree of progress in the direction indicated, enough uncertainty would remain in the minds of governments as to their ability to draw on the Fund to justify the consideration of other possible international measures of compensatory financing. The suggestion has therefore been made that some new financial institution separate from, though possibly affiliated with, the Fund is needed to provide compensatory financing for export fluctuations, in amounts or of a kind or with a degree of automatism that is either not practicable or not desirable for the Fund. In pursuance of this line of thought, the above mentioned UN Committee of Experts worked out schemes for a Development Insurance Fund, which have subsequently been elaborated by the UN Secretariat, whereas the scheme of the OAS Expert Group is on a loan basis.

The following are the principal suggestions made by the UN and OAS Experts regarding the policies and practices of the Fund in the use of its own resources.

1. *Qualitative criteria for the use of Fund resources*

The UN Commission on International Commodity Trade, at its session of May 1961, "considered that it would be desirable if the Fund would study the question whether

---

[4] *Ibid.*, p. 4.

[5] United Nations, *International Compensation for Fluctuations in Commodity Trade* (Report by a Committee of Experts, E/CN.13/40, New York, 1961).

[6] Organization of American States, *Final Report of the Group of Experts on the Stabilization of Export Receipts* (Washington, D.C., 1962).

the present criteria for the use of its resources are fully adapted to circumstances in which payments difficulties arise mainly from fluctuations in primary product markets." [7]

2. *Stand-bys or near stand-bys for compensatory financing*

According to the Report of the UN Committee of Experts, "through the increased use of stand-by arrangements or consultative procedures, the Fund should aim to clarify with interested members the conditions which would assure that the full use of quota without waiver (Fund holding of 200 per cent of a member's currency) or even more will be readily granted if it appears justifiable according to forecasts of commodity markets and other relevant considerations." [8]

3. *Extension of gold-tranche criterion to later tranches*

The Report of the UN Committee of Experts suggests that "in so far as drawings on the Fund are automatic, a country whose export proceeds fall has reliable access to a source of compensatory financing. At present only 25 per cent of a member country's quota comes close to being automatically available. Any significant increase in this percentage which the Fund could institute would be a valuable step toward providing compensatory financing to meet the needs of primary producing countries when threatened with the adverse impact of a decline in export proceeds." [9]

4. *Automatic compensatory drawing rights in first credit tranche*

In Appendix II of the Report of the UN Committee of Experts, one of the Experts suggested that "to offset fluctuations in the export proceeds of primary producing countries, compensatory drawings and repayments should be determined automatically by a formula. The fluctuations should be measured as a deviation from a trend which can be estimated on the basis of a moving average of three preceding years. A shortfall in export proceeds in any year should entitle the country to draw from the Fund automatically up to, say, an amount which causes the Fund's holdings of the country's currency to equal 125 per cent of its quota. . . . Subsequently, when export proceeds are above the trend, the excess earnings should be used automatically to repay the earlier drawings." [10] From the context it appears that this Expert had in mind full compensation of shortfalls as defined, up to the 125 per cent point, and subsequent repayment of the whole of any excess of export proceeds over trend.

5. *Automatic compensatory drawing rights additional to normal facilities*

At the Special Meeting of the Organization of American States at Punta del Este in August 1961, Chile proposed that Fund members affected by declines in prices of important export commodities should be enabled to draw from the Fund in amounts determined by the magnitude of the price decline in question relative to the average price in the three preceding years and by the volume of exports affected. Drawings under these special arrangements would be repaid when prices rose above the average

---

[7] United Nations, Commission on International Commodity Trade, Report of the Ninth Session (E/CN.13/42, May 1961), p. 21.

[8] UN Committee of Experts, *op. cit.*, p. 29.

[9] *Ibid.*, p. 28.

[10] *Ibid.*, p. 81.

in the three preceding years. The ability of members to make ordinary drawings would not be affected by the amounts outstanding under these special arrangements.[11]

* * * * * *

The proposals advanced, whether for new compensatory financing institutions or for changes in the policies and practices of the Fund, are evidence that the assistance provided by the Fund under present policies is considered either insufficiently automatic in character or inadequate in amount to deal with the payments problems that arise from fluctuations in exports of primary exporting countries. The question of automatism of Fund operations is discussed in Section III; that of the quantitative adequacy of members' access to the Fund, in Section IV. These sections lead to the Conclusions (set out in Section V of this report) which deal with Fund action.

III. AUTOMATISM AND THE USE OF FUND RESOURCES

The type of automatism envisaged in the various proposals that have been put forward—automatism of the "export compensatory" rather than of the "all purpose" type—has two principal features:

(1) A mathematical formula would be used to determine whether, and to what extent, exports in a particular year are to be considered so abnormally low as to require compensation, or so abnormally high as to permit the repayment of compensation received previously. No judgment would be made by the lending agency, in the light of any other information that might be available, as to whether, in a particular situation, the formula yields a reasonable estimate of normal exports.

(2) The lending agency, whether the Fund or a new agency, would make credit available to a country without question whenever the formula pointed to a statistical justification on export grounds alone. No regard would be paid to the over-all balance of payments need for such credit, to the likelihood that the country would be able, in the light of the policies it was pursuing, to repay the credits that were being granted or, in some proposals, to the amount that the country has already borrowed. The country itself could, of course, refuse to take up credits to which it was entitled or could repay credits before maturity.

With regard to the first point, the proposals now under consideration have assumed, virtually without question, that when exports are below the average for, say, the three preceding years they can safely be assumed to be abnormally low so that compensation would be appropriate. Statistical experiments, covering the postwar period, recently made for a large number of primary exporting countries, suggest, however, that this is by no means generally the case. The fact that exports in any given year have been lower (or higher) than they were in preceding years is very often an indication of a downward (or upward) trend which may well persist for some years to come. Export proceeds that seem low in relation to those of preceding years may well appear in retrospect as rather favorable. It follows from this that automatic formulae based on past and current export data can, at best, yield only rather unsatisfactory estimates of the true trend of exports. In the absence of foreknowledge of future exports, the least inaccurate estimate of the normal level in any given year is likely to be one that

---

[11] Pan American Union, Inter-American Economic and Social Council, Special Meeting at the Ministerial Level, Punta del Este, Minutes and Documents (Washington, D.C., 1962): Draft Resolution by the Delegation of Chile, pp. 550 ff. (in Spanish).

attributes a great weight to the exports of the year itself. Even when this is done, however, the extent to which it is possible to adjust export proceeds by adding or subtracting compensatory receipts or repayments so as to bring them closer to their true norm or to reduce their instability is limited.[12]

While great uncertainty must always attach to any attempt to estimate the medium-term trend or norm of exports, it is reasonable to assume that a better estimate could be made by the exercise of judgment based on an analysis of the causal factors at work than by any mathematical formula, however skillfully contrived, which is based on the mere statistical magnitude of current and previous exports.

In regard to the second aspect of automatism—the granting of credit irrespective of the general balance of payments situation or of the policies of the country receiving assistance—it may be useful to set out existing Fund policies and their rationale.

Under present Fund policies "members are given the overwhelming benefit of the doubt in relation to requests for transactions within the 'gold tranche,' that is, for drawings which do not increase the Fund's holdings of the currency beyond an amount equal to the member's quota. The Fund's attitude to requests for transactions within the 'first credit tranche'—that is, transactions which bring the Fund's holdings of a member's currency above 100 per cent but not above 125 per cent of its quota—is a liberal one, provided that the member itself is making reasonable efforts to solve its problems. Requests for transactions beyond these limits require substantial justification. They are likely to be favorably received when the drawings or stand-by arrangements are intended to support a sound program aimed at establishing or maintaining the enduring stability of the member's currency at a realistic rate of exchange."[13]

In the higher tranches, the Fund has therefore wished to be satisfied that a sound set of policies is being followed. The Fund may have reached this conclusion before the question of a drawing arose—e.g., if it has a stand-by arrangement with the country in question. If such policies are being followed, no change in them would be needed to meet payments difficulties that are due solely to temporary situations in foreign markets, or to such factors as a temporary fluctuation in crops. The mere fact of a falling off in exports would not be taken as an indication that a corrective program was necessary or that the corrective program already envisaged should be intensified. On the other hand, a need for corrective policies might arise either because the decline in exports appeared to foreshadow a lasting weakening of the country's balance of payments or because (though the export decline itself might be purely temporary and self correcting) the country's monetary and financial policies were such as to provoke, sooner or later, balance of payments difficulties even under satisfactory export conditions. Recognition by the Fund of the need for corrective policies in either of the two circumstances outlined above does not mean that the Fund has seized the occasion of a member country's financial plight to press for immediate adoption of the full range of what might be construed as "ideal" policies; for example, the elimination of all payments restrictions, the adoption of full currency convertibility at an effective par value, the abolition of all multiple rates, etc. Reference to the policies followed in regard to these matters by the many countries that are using the Fund in the second or higher credit tranches or that have stand-by arrangements permitting such use would dispel

---

[12] See J. Marcus Fleming, Rudolf Rhomberg, and Lorette Boissonneault, "Export Norms and Their Role in Compensatory Financing," Part I, *Staff Papers*, Vol. X (1963), pp. 98–124.

[13] International Monetary Fund, *Annual Report, 1962*, p. 31.

at once the notion of such an approach by the Fund. In accordance, however, with the purposes set out in Article I of the Fund's Articles of Agreement, Fund assistance, at least beyond the gold tranche, is not made available to any country that makes no effort to move toward the elimination of those aspects of its exchange and monetary policies that are detrimental to the interests of the member itself or those of other members.

The general case against providing compensatory credit without inquiry into general balance of payments need or into the policies of the country concerned has been argued at length in "Fund Policies and Procedures in Relation to the Compensatory Financing of Commodity Fluctuations," [14] and these arguments have not, in general, been challenged. As suggested by the UN Committee of Experts, a country exposed to export fluctuations might feel more secure if it had access to resources on which it could draw without having to satisfy any international organization or lending government as to the type of domestic or international economic policy it was pursuing. Moreover, it is possible that the availability of international credit on an automatic basis at times when exports are low, and the necessity of repaying such credit at times when exports are high, would have some effect in inducing countries to attempt to keep their domestic expenditures and imports on an even keel, on the basis of reasonable expectations as to the medium-term trend of their exports and other receipts. These potential advantages, however, have to be weighed against the disadvantages of automatic credit geared to a single element in the balance of payments. In this connection it may be appropriate to mention two considerations in particular:

(1) Even a statistically accurate determination that exports in a particular year are below normal implies nothing at all as to the cause of the shortfall. The cause may be a decline in world demand or a crop failure brought about by a natural calamity. But the reason may also lie in domestic inflation, leading to increasingly overvalued exchange rates, government purchases for stockpile at prices above those prevailing in world markets, or other national policies. When declines in exports occur, a most careful consideration of their possible causes is needed in order to determine whether some of them may not be open to remedial action by the country itself, so as to prevent export declines in the future if similar circumstances recur.

Thus, while it is desirable that countries have access to financial means to compensate for fluctuations in exports, it is not particularly desirable, and may be against the genuine interest of the country concerned, that this finance should be provided automatically and without an exploration of the causes of the decline in exports and the measures that might be taken to improve exports in the future.

In this connection, it should be pointed out that the benefits which a country derives from reaching an understanding with the Fund as to the policies appropriate to its situation may extend beyond the financial assistance obtained from the Fund itself. In such circumstances, agreement with the Fund is likely to strengthen opinion abroad and at home regarding the country's creditworthiness, and thus to facilitate the attraction of capital from other sources, official as well as private.

(2) The total amount of short-term credit made available to a country by one agency or under one arrangement cannot be totally divorced from the amount made available on similar terms by another agency or under another arrangement by the same agency. It would be shortsighted to think that a country would be fully justified in borrowing

---

[14] *Staff Papers*, Vol. VIII (1960–61), pp. 1–76.

a relatively large amount on short term to compensate for an export shortfall while totally disregarding the amount that it had already borrowed on short term for other purposes. Prudent countries would themselves see to it that their total indebtedness did not exceed what they could reasonably expect to repay, and this would take into account all indebtedness of a similar character. It would seem to be dubious wisdom to set up the terms of lending of an international agency in such a manner as to put governments under internal pressure to borrow sums that they themselves might consider beyond the bounds of prudence. If there are sensible limitations on total short-term borrowing, these limitations should be taken into account not only by the borrowing country itself but also in the policies of the international agency extending the credit.

IV. QUANTITATIVE ADEQUACY OF DRAWING FACILITIES IN THE FUND

The UN Committee of Experts responsible for producing *International Compensation for Fluctuations in Commodity Trade* calculated that 14 out of 46 primary producing countries experienced, over the years 1953–59, cumulative shortfalls of exports, when compared with average annual exports over the three preceding years, of such magnitude that to compensate them fully would have compelled them, after using up 125 per cent of their Fund quotas, to dip into their own reserves to an extent exceeding 30 per cent of reserves at the end of 1959.[15]

The Experts did not offer an opinion as to whether these facilities, had they been available on an automatic basis, would have been adequate to meet, to a reasonable extent, the need for compensatory financing of export fluctuations. However, they pointed out that if only the 25 per cent of quota constituting the gold tranche had been made available by the Fund to meet the cumulative export shortfalls, 20 of the countries concerned would have had to draw down their reserves by more than 30 per cent to achieve full compensation. These near-automatic facilities, they implied, were insufficient; and even if a reasonable degree of progress were made by the Fund in extending the automatism of drawings in many cases, the uncertainty of drawings would, they considered, offer a serious handicap to the object of continuity in development expenditure.

In a UN Secretariat Study,[16] it was calculated

(a) that for the average primary exporting member of the Fund the average shortfall in export earnings (compared with the mean of the previous three years' exports) over the period 1953–60 was approximately equal to half of its (1961) quota; and that in only half of the countries would drawings of up to 50 per cent of quota have sufficed to offset the average annual shortfall for years in which shortfalls occurred;[17] and

(b) that if each primary exporting member had sought to compensate 100 per cent of its export shortfalls by drawing on the Fund and had used 60 per cent of export excesses for repayment, subject to a limit of cumulative net drawings

---

[15] UN Committee of Experts, *op. cit.* pp. 25–29.

[16] *Consideration of Compensatory Financial Measures to Offset Flunctuations in the Export Income of Primary Producing Countries: Stabilization of Export Proceeds Through a Development Insurance Fund* (E/CN.13/43, January 1962).

[17] *Ibid.*, pp. 46–48 (Table 10) and p. 49.

of 50 per cent of quota, primary exporting members could have compensated in this way about one third of their total shortfalls.[18]

The authors of the study made it clear that their calculations were not intended to reflect on, or measure, the adequacy of the Fund as a means of assisting member countries, since usually reserves and other sources of credit could also be drawn upon and since Fund drawings are not limited to 50 per cent of quota.

The question of the quantitative adequacy of drawing facilities in the Fund to meet the needs for compensatory financing of export fluctuations is a difficult one, and no answer can be made to it without the help of many arbitrary suppositions. In arriving at these suppositions the following considerations are relevant:

(1) In the first place, as is generally recognized, Fund facilities are intended to be used in conjunction with national reserves and other sources of finance.

(2) Again, account has to be taken of the fact that all these forms of international liquidity are required to meet payments deficits arising not only from export shortfalls but also from fluctuations in other items in the balance of payments, notably fluctuations in imports. These fluctuations in other items are, indeed, rather more important than export shortfalls in the causation of payments deficits. Moreover, reserves cannot safely be run down to zero even to meet the severest drains. On the other hand, the various possible causes of deficit are unlikely to exercise their maximum effect simultaneously.

(3) In seeking to measure the probable need for compensatory financing of export shortfalls, it is impracticable to measure such shortfalls from a five-year moving average centered on the middle year (as was done in "Fund Policies and Procedures in Relation to the Compensatory Financing of Commodity Fluctuations"), and misleading to measure them from a moving average of the preceding three years (as was done by the UN Experts and Secretariat and by the OAS Experts). As has been pointed out elsewhere,[19] the five-year moving average centered on the current year, while it may be considered an "ideal" norm from which to measure export deviations, is not usable in practice since foreknowledge of the exports of future years is necessarily lacking. It would seem desirable, however, that the "practical" norm from which export deviations are measured should be close to this "ideal" norm insofar as the latter can be predicted on the basis of existing knowledge. Such a prediction is perhaps best made by the exercise of judgment in the light of all relevant information. If, however, the practical norm is defined by an automatic formula involving the exports of current and previous years, statistical calculations show that the formula, if it is not to diverge unnecessarily from the ideal norm, must give considerable weight to the current year's exports. Moreover, as was argued in "Fund Policies and Procedures in Relation to the Compensatory Financing of Commodity Fluctuations," the compensation of fluctuations should, in principle, be partial only. This implies that a target level of export availabilities [20] that is somewhat closer to actual exports than is the ideal norm be chosen. The result will be to increase still further the weight that should be given to the current year's exports in the calculation of the practical norm, or alternatively—what amounts to the same thing—deviations of actual exports from the practical norm should themselves be compensated only in part.

---

[18] *Ibid.*, p. 54.

[19] Fleming, Rhomberg, and Boissonneault, *op. cit.*

[20] That is, export proceeds adjusted for compensatory receipts and payments.

In Table 1 it is assumed that drawings on the Fund or drafts on national reserves will be made to cover two thirds of the shortfalls of actual exports with respect to a practical export norm defined as an average of exports in the present and two preceding years, with weights of 50 per cent given to the present year and 25 per cent to each of the two preceding years. It is assumed that two thirds of export surpluses with respect to this norm are used to repay drawings or reconstitute reserves. In order to ensure that countries with a downward long-term trend in exports do not indefinitely increase their claims on compensatory financing, it is assumed that drawings are repaid, or drafts on reserves are made good, in the fourth and fifth years of the drawing. In column 1 of the table, the maximum net cumulative requirements for compensatory financing over the period 1951–61 on these assumptions [21] are shown for low-income primary exporting members of the Fund.

Columns 2, 3, and 4 present three alternative measurements of the means presently available to meet the requirements set forth in column 1. Column 2 shows one third of each country's potential external liquidity, defined as its unused potential drawing facilities with the Fund (through the fourth credit tranche) *plus* its gross reserves of gold and convertible currency, as of mid-1962. The assumption underlying this column is that one third of external liquidity is approximately what can be used to meet export fluctuations, the remainder being required for basic reserves and for other types of payments deficits insofar as these coincide with export shortfalls. Column 3 shows one half of the excess of each country's potential external liquidity, as of mid-1962, over a presumed minimum reserve equal to the value of one month's imports at the 1961 rate. Column 4 gives each member country's Fund quota as of mid-1962. The assumption underlying column 4 is that each member would be in a position to use up to one half of its quota for the purpose of financing export fluctuations and would match this amount by an equal use of its own reserves, so that the combined use of reserves and Fund resources would amount to 100 per cent of quota.

The problem of the adequacy of Fund resources (in conjunction with national reserves) in meeting needs for the compensatory financing of export fluctuations is approached differently in columns 2 and 3 on the one hand, and in column 4 on the other. A comparison of column 1 with column 2 or 3 affords a measure of the extent to which member countries might have been able to meet export fluctuations of a defined magnitude on the basis of their external liquidity as of a given moment of time (viz., mid-1962). A comparison of column 1 with column 4 affords a measure of the extent to which member countries could meet such fluctuations on the basis of their normal drawing power in the Fund, starting from a position in which drawings for the purpose of export compensation are zero and assuming that the member will have adequate independent reserves to use *pari passu* with drawings on the Fund. In all cases, the need for financing is measured in relation to the experience of a particular decade (1951–61) and on the basis of specific assumptions regarding the degree of compensation. The comparisons of column 1 with columns 2 and 3 would seem the more relevant when considering the need for adding to the resources available to countries for compensatory financing. The comparison with column 4 is the more relevant when considering the adequacy of the Fund quotas of individual members.

---

[21] The assumptions are the same as those underlying Scheme 24 in Table 5 in the study by Fleming, Rhomberg, and Boissonneault, *op. cit.*—a scheme which yields export availabilities considerably closer to target and considerably smoother over time than those of Scheme 1 (the OAS Scheme) in that table.

Table 1. Adequacy of External Liquidity to Finance Fluctuations in Exports of Some Fund Members
(In millions of U.S. dollars)

Member	Maximum Financial Requirements Indicated by 1951-61 Experience[1] (1)	Assumed Limits of Finance Available				Excesses or Deficiencies (—) in Available Financing			
		One third of external liquidity[2] (2)	One half of excess external liquidity[3] (3)	Fund quota[4] (4)	One half of Fund quota[4] (5)	Column 2 minus column 1 (6)	Column 3 minus column 1 (7)	Column 4 minus column 1 (8)	Column 5 minus column 1 (9)
Argentina	192.3	101.3	91.2	280.0	140.0	—91.0	—101.1	87.7	—52.3
Bolivia	18.8	9.1	10.4	22.5	11.2	—9.7	—8.4	3.7	—7.6
Brazil	130.8	206.6	249.2	280.0	140.0	75.8	118.4	149.2	9.2
Burma	20.5	56.5	75.7	30.0	15.0	36.0	55.2	9.5	—5.5
Ceylon	25.8	42.6	49.0	45.0	22.5	16.8	23.2	19.2	—3.3
Chile	54.8	35.0	28.0	100.0	50.0	—19.8	—26.8	45.2	—4.8
Colombia	79.5	66.7	76.8	100.0	50.0	—12.8	—2.7	20.5	—29.5
Costa Rica	5.8	10.0	10.6	15.0	7.5	4.2	4.8	9.2	1.7
Cyprus	4.5	22.9	29.6	11.2	5.6	18.4	25.1	6.7	1.1
Dominican Republic	8.3	11.9	14.5	15.0	7.5	3.6	6.2	6.7	—0.8
Ecuador	5.8	13.8	15.9	15.0	7.5	8.0	10.1	9.2	1.7
El Salvador	7.8	15.4	18.6	11.2	5.6	7.6	10.8	3.4	—2.2
Ethiopia	4.7	29.6	40.6	13.2[5]	6.6[5]	24.9	35.9	8.5	1.9
Ghana	21.8	75.4	96.8	35.0	17.5	53.6	75.0	13.2	—4.3
Greece	12.3	116.7	145.3	60.0	30.0	104.4	133.0	47.7	17.7
Guatemala	5.7	22.5	28.2	15.0	7.5	16.8	22.5	9.3	1.8
Haiti	7.3	5.3	6.6	11.2	5.6	—2.0	—0.7	3.9	—1.7
Honduras	7.0	7.9	8.8	11.2	5.6	0.9	1.8	4.2	—1.4
India	148.0	305.6	368.2	600.0	300.0	157.6	220.2	452.0	152.0
Indonesia	135.0	89.9	101.8	165.0	82.5	—45.1	—33.2	30.0	—52.5
Iran	289.7	96.4	119.6	70.0	35.0	—193.3	—170.1	—219.7	—254.7
Iraq	54.7	56.0	67.1	15.0	7.5	1.3	12.4	—39.7	—47.2
Jordan	2.7	20.8	26.4	8.0[5]	4.0[5]	18.1	23.7	5.3	1.3
Korea	8.1	72.5	96.2	18.8	9.4	64.4	88.1	10.7	1.3
Lebanon	3.3	64.1	81.8	6.8	3.4	60.8	78.5	3.5	0.1

COMPENSATORY FINANCING: FIRST REPORT

Libya	1.7	36.3	48.2	11.0[5]	5.5[5]	34.6	46.5	9.3	3.8
Malaya	246.0	290.1	404.8	32.5[5]	16.2[5]	44.1	158.8	−213.5	−229.8
Mexico	60.2	185.6	231.1	180.0	90.0	125.4	170.9	119.8	29.8
Morocco	2.8	81.2	103.2	52.5	26.2	78.4	100.4	49.7	23.4
Nicaragua	3.4	12.9	16.2	11.2	5.6	9.5	12.8	7.8	2.2
Nigeria	15.8	80.0	94.1	50.0	25.0	64.2	78.3	34.2	9.2
Pakistan	143.0	142.1	186.4	150.0	75.0	−0.9	43.4	7.0	−68.0
Panama	1.8	10.3	9.4	0.5	0.2	8.5	7.6	−1.3	−1.6
Paraguay	4.0	5.0	5.9	11.2	5.6	1.0	1.9	7.2	1.6
Peru	11.0	42.2	43.8	32.5[5]	16.2[5]	31.2	32.8	21.5	5.2
Philippines	15.2	46.7	40.1	75.0	37.5	31.5	24.9	59.8	22.3
Saudi Arabia	4.2	114.3	158.9	55.0	27.5	110.1	154.7	50.8	23.3
Sudan	32.8	63.9	86.1	15.0	7.5	31.1	53.3	−17.8	−25.3
Syrian Arab Republic	28.2	9.2	6.7	15.0	7.5	−19.0	−21.5	−13.2	−20.7
Thailand	24.8	175.7	243.4	45.0	22.5	150.9	210.6	20.2	−2.3
Tunisia	18.8	30.3	36.6	18.3[5]	9.2[5]	11.5	17.8	−0.5	−9.6
Turkey	51.3	85.9	107.6	86.0	43.0	34.6	56.3	34.7	−8.3
United Arab Republic	77.8	77.9	89.3	90.0	45.0	0.1	11.5	12.2	−32.8
Uruguay	60.3	82.8	115.6	30.0	15.0	22.5	55.3	−30.3	−45.3
Venezuela	0	229.5	295.9	150.0	75.0	229.5	295.9	150.0	75.0
Viet-Nam	34.7	60.4	80.0	18.5[5]	9.2[5]	25.7	45.3	−16.2	−25.5
Yugoslavia	9.0	36.3	16.6	120.0	60.0	27.3	7.6	111.0	51.0
Total	2,101.8	3,453.1	4,276.8	3,203.3	1,601.4	1,351.3	2,175.0	1,101.5	−500.4

[1] As described on page 451.

[2] A country's external liquidity is defined as its gross gold and convertible foreign exchange reserves *plus* its total tranche position with the Fund. Figures given are for mid-1962. A country's total tranche position with the Fund is the amount that it could still draw, as of a given date, if its justification were sufficient, without increasing the Fund's holdings of its currency above 200 per cent of its quota.

[3] Excess external liquidity (as of mid-1962) is defined as external liquidity (described in footnote 2) less average monthly imports (for 1961).

[4] Quotas given are for mid-1962.

[5] Quotas to be increased by annual installments, as follows: Ethiopia to $15 million by September 1963; Jordan to $11.25 million by July 1964; Libya to $15 million by September 1963; Malaya to $37.5 million by October 1963; Peru to $37.5 million by September 1963; Tunisia to $22.5 million by May 1964; and Viet-Nam to $22.5 million by November 1963.

It might be argued that parts of the reserves of some countries are virtually unusable, in that they are pledged against certain liabilities, or for other reasons. To some extent this factor is taken into account in the concept of minimum reserves underlying the calculations in columns 2 and 3. However, since no allowance has been made for this factor in column 4, column 5 has been added to show the extent to which the compensatory financing of export fluctuations would be limited if countries' use of external liquidity for this purpose were to be limited to 50 per cent of Fund quotas—a rather extreme assumption in most cases.

The differences between the alternative measures of the means available for compensatory financing of export fluctuations shown in columns 2, 3, 4, and 5, and the computed requirements for such financing shown in column 1, are set forth in columns 6, 7, 8, and 9, respectively. It is noteworthy that the incidence of "minus" signs in columns 6 and 7 is almost identical. One third of external liquidity as of mid-1962 would have been inadequate to cover maximum compensatory requirements of only 9 countries out of 47. One half of the excess of such liquidity over one month's imports would have been similarly inadequate in 8 of the same 9 countries. A limitation of financing to 100 per cent of quota as shown in column 8 would again have restricted export compensation in only 9 countries. Since these groups partially overlap, 16 member countries would have been limited by one or the other criterion. The more stringent limitation of financing to 50 per cent of quota, illustrated in columns 5 and 9, would result in "minus" signs in 9 countries in addition to those referred to above. In view of the necessarily somewhat arbitrary nature of the criteria employed in these calculations, and their uniform application to all countries regardless of special circumstances, the results for individual countries should not be taken too seriously. The calculations do, however, yield a general impression of the magnitude of the problem.

In a few countries with declining medium-term trends over the 1951–61 period, limitation of the finance available for automatic compensation over that period would probably have exercised a beneficial effect through limiting the need for repayment at times when exports were low in relation to trend.

V. CONCLUSIONS: FUND ACTION IN CONNECTION WITH EXPORT FLUCTUATIONS

(1) The financing of deficits arising out of export shortfalls, notably those of primary exporting member countries, has always been regarded as a legitimate reason for the use of Fund resources, which have been drawn on frequently for this purpose. The Fund believes that such financing helps these members to continue their efforts to adopt adequate measures toward the solution of their financial problems and to avoid the use of trade and exchange restrictions to deal with balance of payments problems, and that this enables these members to pursue their programs of economic development with greater effectiveness.

(2) The Fund noted in its 1962 Annual Report that trends in prices of basic commodities in the past few years have adversely affected the export earnings of many Fund members, which has increased the strain on their reserves. In view of this and in order to ensure the maximum effectiveness for its support to members—in particular, primary exporting members—that are faced with fluctuations in export proceeds, the Fund is taking the action set forth below.

A. Quotas

(3) The quotas of many primary exporting countries, taken in conjunction with a reasonable use of their own reserves, are at present adequate for dealing with export fluctuations such as have occurred during the past decade. In those instances, however, where adjustment of the quotas of certain primary exporting countries, and in particular of countries with relatively small quotas, would be appropriate to make them more adequate in the light of fluctuations in export proceeds and other relevant criteria, the Fund is willing to give sympathetic consideration to requests for such adjustment.

B. Drawing policies

(4) Under the present policies and practices on the use of Fund resources, any member is given the overwhelming benefit of the doubt in relation to requests for transactions within the gold tranche, and the Fund's attitude to requests for transactions within the first credit tranche is a liberal one provided the member itself is making reasonable efforts to solve its problems. In the higher credit tranches too, where a member's policies are consistent with Fund policies and practices on the use of Fund resources in these tranches, the Fund gives assistance, on a substantial scale, toward meeting temporary payments deficits, including deficits arising out of export shortfalls. The policies and practices of the Fund on drawings and stand-by arrangements have been developed in order to help members to meet more effectively their temporary balance of payments difficulties and to enable them, where necessary, to pursue policies aimed at restoring external and internal equilibrium. Fund assistance in accordance with these policies and practices has made an effective contribution to the solution of the difficulties of these members and the achievement of equilibrium. It has often led, moreover, to the provision of further resources from public and private sources for meeting immediate and longer-term needs. In the application of its policies and practices governing the use of its resources, the Fund's attitude has been a flexible one, and account has been taken of special difficulties facing members.

(5) The Fund has reviewed its policies to determine how it could more readily assist members, particularly primary exporters, encountering payments difficulties produced by temporary export shortfalls, and has decided that such members can expect that their requests for drawings will be met where the Fund is satisfied that

(a) the shortfall is of a short-term character and is largely attributable to circumstances beyond the control of the member; and

(b) the member will cooperate with the Fund in an effort to find, where required, appropriate solutions for its balance of payments difficulties.

The amount of drawings outstanding under this decision will not normally exceed 25 per cent of the member's quota, and the drawings will be subject to the Fund's established policies and practices on repurchase. When drawings are made under this decision, the Fund will so indicate in an appropriate manner.

(6) In order to implement the Fund's policies in connection with compensatory financing of export shortfalls, the Fund will be prepared to waive the limit on Fund holdings of 200 per cent of quota, where appropriate. In particular, the Fund will be prepared to waive this limit (i) where a waiver is necessary to permit compensatory drawings to be made under paragraphs (4) and (5) above, or (ii) to the extent that drawings in accordance with paragraph (5) are still outstanding.

Whenever the Fund's holdings of a member's currency resulting from an outstanding compensatory drawing under paragraph (5) are reduced, by the member's repurchase or otherwise, this will restore *pro tanto* the member's facility to make a further compensatory drawing under that paragraph, should the need arise.

(7) In order to identify more clearly what are to be regarded as export shortfalls of a short-term character, the Fund, in conjunction with the member concerned, will seek to establish reasonable estimates regarding the medium-term trend of the member's exports on the basis of appropriate statistical data in conjunction with qualitative information about its export prospects.

(8) The provision of credit to deal with the balance of payments effects of export fluctuations provides immediate relief for a country's short-term difficulties. In many cases, however, it will also be necessary to introduce measures of a policy character in order to attain a satisfactory and lasting solution to a country's balance of payments problems. Members generally have actively cooperated with the Fund to find and adopt the measures necessary to this end. Beyond immediate balance of payments difficulties, the primary exporting countries are, in many instances, facing unfavorable long-term export trends, and all are trying to meet the challenge of achieving more rapid and sustained development through a strengthening and broadening of their economies. The last mentioned problem will require action in many fields and over many years by both the primary exporting countries and the industrial countries, separately and in concert, including readier access to the markets of the developed countries for the products of the developing countries and an appropriate and sustained flow of technical and financial assistance to the developing countries. The Fund considers that its activities can provide valuable assistance in helping to establish a climate within which longer-term measures can be more effectively pursued.

Annex: Net Fund Drawings[1] of Some Fund Members,[2] 1947-62

	Cumulative, 1947-57	1958	1959	1960	1961	1962	Cumulative,[3] 1947-62	Available Under Stand-by Arrangement, End 1962
Argentina	75.0	—	72.5	48.5	31.0	−9.0	218.0	50.0
Bolivia	6.5	2.0	2.4	−1.5	−2.0	1.3	8.5	6.5
Brazil	75.0	37.6	−20.2	47.7	40.0	−17.5	162.5	—
Burma	15.0	−3.0	−4.0	−4.0	−4.0	—	—	—
Ceylon	—	—	—	—	11.2	11.2	22.5	—
Chile	31.1	10.6	—	−12.4	59.3	−12.7	76.0	—
Colombia	25.0	5.0	−15.0	−15.0	65.0	7.5	72.5	—
Costa Rica	—	—	—	—	7.5	−4.1	3.4	11.6
Dominican Republic	—	—	—	9.0	—	—	9.0	—
Ecuador	5.0	−5.0	—	—	14.0	−2.2	11.9	2.0
El Salvador	—	—	5.5	5.7	−3.2	−8.0	—	11.2
Ghana	—	—	—	—	—	14.2	14.2	—
Guatemala	—	—	—	—	—	5.0	5.0	—
Haiti	1.0	2.5	1.9	−1.3	−1.3	1.9	4.8	5.0
Honduras	3.8	−3.8	3.8	1.2	1.2	1.3	7.5	3.8
India	200.0	—	—	−72.5	122.5	25.0	275.1	75.0
Indonesia	55.0	—	−9.0	−18.5	33.7	21.2	82.5	—
Iran	25.3	−8.4	−11.9	45.0	−12.0	−37.9	—	—
Mexico	—	—	—	—	45.0	−45.0	—	—
Nicaragua	3.8	−1.9	−1.9	—	4.5	—	4.5	—
Pakistan	—	—	—	12.5	—	—	12.5	—
Paraguay	5.5	0.8	−1.5	0.1	−1.6	−1.8	1.5	5.0
Peru	—	10.0	−10.0	—	—	—	—	30.0
Philippines	15.0	—	−6.2	3.3	−2.9	25.4	34.6	40.4
Sudan	—	5.0	1.2	−0.4	−2.9	−2.9	—	—
Syrian Arab Republic	—	—	—	15.0	−0.7	3.4	17.7	—
Turkey	21.5	17.0	−3.0	−3.0	10.5	5.5	48.5	—
United Arab Republic	30.0	—	−2.7	25.2	−2.7	57.4	107.2	5.0
Uruguay	—	—	—	—	—	15.0	15.0	15.0
Yugoslavia	—	22.9	—	—	67.5	−7.5	82.9	—
Total	593.5	91.3	1.9	84.6	479.6	46.7	1,297.8	260.5

Source: International Monetary Fund, *International Financial Statistics*.
[1] Minus sign indicates net repayment.
[2] Countries in Table 1 which have drawn on the Fund.
[3] Totals may not equal sums of annual data because of rounding.

Increases in Quotas: Fourth Quinquennial Review

The Fund is required at intervals of five years to review the quotas of members and to propose any adjustments that it believes to be desirable. No changes were proposed in the course of the first and second quinquennial reviews (1950 and 1955). The third review was in effect replaced by the general increase proposed by the Directors in December 1958 in the report reproduced above (pp. 421–41). The fourth quinquennial review, due in 1965, evoked the following report to the Governors, submitted on February 26, 1965. The proposals were accepted by the Governors, and took effect from February 23, 1966.

Increases in Quotas of Members—Fourth Quinquennial Review Report of the Executive Directors to the Board of Governors
(February 26, 1965)

1. At its Nineteenth Annual Meeting in Tokyo, the Board of Governors adopted the following Resolution:

    RESOLVED:

    That the Executive Directors proceed to consider the question of adjusting the quotas of members of the Fund and at an early date submit an appropriate proposal to the Board of Governors.

2. Pursuant to this Resolution, the Executive Directors have considered the question of adjusting the quotas of members and have concluded that in a world in which income and trade have expanded rapidly and are expected to do so, the need for the type of liquidity provided by the Fund, like the need for international liquidity in general, may be expected to grow. A reasonable expansion in quotas would increase the Fund's resources relative to the calls that are likely to be made upon them and enhance confidence in the Fund's ability to meet all justifiable requests for drawings. Provision of adequate resources, enabling the Fund to meet needs with a greater margin of safety, may also reduce those needs by marshaling the resources and demonstrating the international cooperation that could deter speculation. Accordingly, the Executive Directors have decided that proposals for increases in present quotas of 25 per cent, subject to the appropriate rounding of the resulting figures, and for larger increases for certain members should be submitted to the Board of Governors. For the purposes of this Report, present quotas are quotas as of February 26, 1965 or the maximum amount to which quotas could be increased under Resolutions adopted by or submitted to the Board of Governors before that date. The general increases of 25 per cent are provided for by the First of two Resolutions submitted to the Board of Governors with this Report. The formula for rounding the increased quotas is as follows: amounts below $500 million are rounded to the next higher multiple of one million, and amounts of $500 million or more are rounded to the next higher multiple of five million. The quotas to which members can consent under the First Resolution are shown in the Annex to this Report. The Second Resolution submitted with this Report provides for the special (i.e., larger)

increases. If the Board of Governors agrees to propose a special increase for a member under the Second Resolution, the member will be able to consent to that increase or to the smaller increase under the First Resolution. When such a member consents, it should declare under which Resolution it is choosing to consent, and its choice will then be final.

3. The increases in quotas under the attached Resolutions are without prejudice to the adjustment of quotas that members can request under the Fund's Decision on "Compensatory Financing of Export Fluctuations" (E.B. Decision No. 1477-(63/8). February 27, 1963). In this connection, E.B. Decision No. 1529-(63/33), June 14, 1963 will continue to be applicable.

4. The attached Resolutions are designed to enable the Board of Governors to vote at one time on all matters connected with the increases in quotas under the two Resolutions. Governors are requested to vote on both Resolutions. The First Resolution is to be voted on as a whole. In the case of the Second Resolution, Governors may vote on all or each of the special increases. Under the Resolutions, it will be possible for increases in quotas to become effective without the need for further reference to the Board of Governors. Attention is drawn to the requirement that, to be valid, votes must be received at the seat of the Fund on or before March 31, 1965.

5. If the Resolutions are adopted by the necessary majority of four-fifths of the total voting power, as required by Article III, Section 2 of the Articles of Agreement, a member may consent to the increase in its quota at any time on or before September 25, 1965. Therefore, unless this period is extended by the Executive Directors, members will have until September 25, 1965 to take whatever action may be necessary under their laws to enable them to give their consent.

6. In view of the cooperative nature of the increase in quotas under the Resolutions, it is provided that increases will not become effective until the Fund has determined that members having two-thirds of the total of quotas on February 26, 1965 have consented to increases in their quotas. In determining whether this degree of participation has been reached, the Fund will take into account all consents to increases, whether they be under the First or Second Resolutions and whether they be increases in full or by installments.

7. In view of past practice, any member consenting to a special increase under the Second Resolution will be expected to request an increase in its subscription to the capital of the International Bank for Reconstruction and Development corresponding to the special part of the increase in quota.

8. Under the Resolutions, a member may pay its additional subscription in respect of the increase in its quota at any time before it is due. If a member pays before the increase in its quota takes effect, the additional subscription will be kept in separate accounts of the Fund and returned if it should be established that the increase cannot take effect. A member is required to pay its additional subscription not later than 30 days after the later of the following events: (i) its consent to its quota increase, and (ii) the determination by the Fund, referred to in paragraph 6 above, that the condition as to participation in quota increases has been satisfied.

9. Increases in members' quotas will take effect as follows:

(a) When a member pays its additional subscription before the later of the two events referred to in the preceding paragraph, the increase in its quota will take effect on the happening of the later of these events.

(b) If a member pays its additional subscription after the later of these two events, the increase in its quota will take effect on the day of payment.

10. Each member increasing its quota must pay an additional subscription equal to the increase, of which 25 per cent shall be in gold and the balance in its currency. Payment of both portions of the additional subscription must be made before the increase in the member's quota can become effective, even by those members which, in accordance with the Articles of Agreement or Membership Resolutions, have not yet been required to pay their original subscriptions.

11. The increase in quotas under the Resolutions is based on the idea of a cooperative effort by the members of the Fund to provide larger resources against contingencies that may affect any member. In order to preserve the general character of that effort, it has been thought preferable not to exercise the discretion given to the Executive Directors under Article III, Section 4 of the Articles of Agreement to reduce gold payments in connection with these Resolutions. However, the payment in gold of 25 per cent of the quota increase may cause hardship in some cases, and therefore the Executive Directors have decided that the policies and practices described in the following paragraphs of this Report will be applied.

12. Under the Resolutions any member consenting to an increase in its quota may consent to an increase by installments. Each installment of the increase would correspond to the amount of additional subscription in gold and currency paid by the member. Any member consenting to an increase by installments must pay an original installment of additional subscription, and an installment in each period of 12 months thereafter. Each installment shall be one-fifth of the increase. Members may accelerate payment under this installment schedule.

13. A member that wishes to have the full increase in its quota take effect immediately or to expedite the full increase in its quota if it is paying under the installment schedule may find it a hardship to make prompt payment in gold of 25 per cent of the increase in its quota. In order to alleviate this hardship the member may request an exchange transaction in accordance with paragraphs 14 through 19 below.

14. Where a member requests an exchange transaction within the gold tranche, the established gold tranche policy and procedure will apply.

15. A member consenting to an increase in its quota under the First Resolution may request an exchange transaction beyond the gold tranche in an amount not in excess of 25 per cent of the increase. This facility will be available where (a) the member represents that it would encounter undue payments difficulties through the reduction in its reserves by the payment of the 25 per cent gold subscription or of the outstanding balance of that subscription; and (b) the member requests the exchange transaction within six months after the date of the consent to the increase or the determination by the Fund that the condition as to participation in quota increases has been satisfied, whichever is later.

16. The Fund will expect that a member requesting an exchange transaction under paragraph 15 above will represent that it will make a repurchase corresponding to the exchange transaction in accordance with the principles of E.B. Decision No. 102-(52/11) of February 13, 1952 and the following sub-paragraphs:

(i) The member will be expected to represent that it will make a repurchase corresponding to the exchange transaction in equal annual installments, to commence one year after the transaction and to be completed not later than five years after the transaction.

(ii) If the member, when requesting the exchange transaction or at any time thereafter, represents that, because of other repurchase commitments or for such other reasons as it shall submit, the schedule referred to in (i) above would create undue payments difficulties, the Fund may accept a representation that the member will repurchase in accordance with the provisions of E.B. Decision No. 102-(52/11).

17. The representation of a member with respect to undue payments difficulties referred to in paragraphs 15 and 16 above would not be challenged by the Fund except where it was clearly evident that the representation was without basis.

18. In order to facilitate the exchange transactions referred to in paragraph 15 above, the Fund will be prepared, where necessary, to grant a waiver of the quantitative limits prescribed in Article V, Section 3 (a) (iii) of the Articles of Agreement. The Fund will also be prepared to grant such a waiver, in appropriate cases, to the extent that an exchange transaction in accordance with the preceding paragaphs is still outstanding.

19. A member requesting an exchange transaction in accordance with the preceding paragraphs will be expected to consult the Managing Director on the currency to be drawn under E.B. Decision No. 1371-(62/36) of July 20, 1962. Many such members are likely to use the currency drawn to purchase gold from the monetary authorities of the member whose currency was drawn either to pay their additional gold subscription or to restore the level of their gold holdings if they have already paid the additional subscription. Normally, these members would purchase the gold from a reserve currency member. With a view to alleviating the impact on the gold holdings of the reserve currency members that would result from such purchases, the Fund, in the course of the consultation on the currency to be drawn, will suggest that certain of these exchange transactions, up to the equivalent of $150 million, be made in currencies which the Fund would then replenish by the sale of gold under Article VII, Section 2 (ii) up to the amount of such transactions.

20. The exchange transactions and replenishment of currency referred to in the preceding paragraphs will partially alleviate the impact of the additional gold subscriptions of members on the gold holdings of the reserve currency members. However, it is expected that, notwithstanding this alleviation and the likelihood that many members will meet their additional gold subscription from their own gold holdings, other members will purchase a substantial amount of gold from the reserve currency members, and in particular the United States and the United Kingdom. In order to provide a measure of further alleviation solely in connection with the quota increases provided for by the Resolutions submitted with this Report, the Fund will make general deposits of gold with its gold depositories designated by the United States and the United Kingdom in a total amount not exceeding the equivalent of $350 million. Approximately $250 million in gold will be placed on general deposit with the Fund's depository in the United States and approximately $100 million with the Fund's depository in the United Kingdom. Within the limit of $350 million or the reduced amount under paragraph 21 below, adjustments may be made in the amounts held on general deposit in these two depositories on the basis of the actual impact on the gold holdings of each of the two members of the sales of gold by them in connection with the additional subscriptions of other members.

21. If the Fund determines that the total sales of gold by the United States and the United Kingdom in connection with the additional subscriptions of other members are less than the equivalent of $350 million, the Fund will reduce its general deposits accordingly.

22. The general deposits will be subject to the following principles:

(a) A general deposit of gold by the Fund shall be a demand deposit. Accordingly, the Fund shall be entitled, at its sole discretion and on its demand to the depository, to the immediate transfer to an earmarked account in the sole name of the Fund at the depository, free of any claims, liens or encumbrances in favor of any other party, of an amount of gold not in excess of the amount then held by the Fund on general deposit with the depository, which transfer shall be made without charge or cost to the Fund.

(b) Whenever a member that designated the depository with which a general deposit is held so requests, the Fund shall demand that the depository transfer gold in the amount requested to an earmarked account.

(c) On the occasion of any use of gold, the Fund would normally use, in appropriate proportions, earmarked gold and gold on general deposit in accordance with the good management of its assets.

(d) The Managing Director will report periodically to the Executive Directors on the Fund's general deposits, and the Executive Directors shall review the policy with respect to general deposits not later than five years after the first such deposit is made.

February 26, 1965

Annex to Report

	Present Quota[1]	Increased Quota Under First Resolution			Present Quota[1]	Increased Quota Under First Resolution
	(Million U.S. dollars)				(Million U.S. dollars)	
1. Afghanistan	22.50	29	52. Korea		18.75	24
2. Algeria	60.00	75	53. Kuwait		50.00	63
3. Argentina	280.00	350	54. Laos		7.50	10
4. Australia	400.00	500	55. Lebanon		6.75	9
5. Austria	75.00	94	56. Liberia		11.25	15
6. Belgium	337.50	422	57. Libya		15.00	19
7. Bolivia	22.50	29	58. Luxembourg		15.00	19
8. Brazil	280.00	350	59. Malagasy Republic		15.00	19
9. Burma	30.00	38	60. Malaysia		100.00	125
10. Burundi	11.25	15	61. Mali		13.00	17
11. Cameroon	15.00	19	62. Mauritania		7.50	10
12. Canada	550.00	690	63. Mexico		180.00	225
13. Central African Republic	7.50	10	64. Morocco		52.50	66
14. Ceylon	62.00	78	65. Nepal		7.50	10
15. Chad	7.50	10	66. Netherlands		412.50	520
16. Chile	100.00	125	67. New Zealand		125.00	157
17. China	550.00	690	68. Nicaragua		11.25	15
18. Colombia	100.00	125	69. Niger		7.50	10
19. Congo (Brazzaville)	7.50	10	70. Nigeria		50.00	63
20. Congo, Democratic Republic of	45.00	57	71. Norway		100.00	125
			72. Pakistan		150.00	188
21. Costa Rica	20.00	25	73. Panama		11.25	15
22. Cyprus	11.25	15	74. Paraguay		11.25	15
23. Dahomey	7.50	10	75. Peru		37.50	47
24. Denmark	130.00	163	76. Philippines		75.00	94
25. Dominican Republic	25.00	32	77. Portugal		60.00	75
26. Ecuador	20.00	25	78. Rwanda		11.25	15
27. El Salvador	20.00	25	79. Saudi Arabia		72.00	90
28. Ethiopia	15.00	19	80. Senegal		25.00	32
29. Finland	57.00	72	81. Sierra Leone		11.25	15
30. France	787.50	985	82. Somalia		11.25	15
31. Gabon	7.50	10	83. South Africa		150.00	188
32. Germany, Federal Republic of	787.50	985	84. Spain		150.00	188
			85. Sudan		45.00	57
33. Ghana	55.00	69	86. Sweden		150.00	188
34. Greece	60.00	75	87. Syrian Arab Republic		30.00	38
35. Guatemala	20.00	25	88. Tanzania		25.00	32
36. Guinea	15.00	19	89. Thailand		76.00	95
37. Haiti	11.25	15	90. Togo		11.25	15
38. Honduras	15.00	19	91. Trinidad and Tobago		20.00	25
39. Iceland	11.25	15				
40. India	600.00	750	92. Tunisia		22.50	29
41. Indonesia	165.00	207	93. Turkey		86.00	108
42. Iran	70.00	88	94. Uganda		25.00	32
43. Iraq	55.00	69	95. United Arab Republic		120.00	150
44. Ireland	45.00	57				
45. Israel	50.00	63	96. United Kingdom		1,950.00	2,440
46. Italy	500.00	625	97. United States		4,125.00	5,160
47. Ivory Coast	15.00	19	98. Upper Volta		7.50	10
48. Jamaica	20.00	25	99. Uruguay		30.00	38
49. Japan	500.00	625	100. Venezuela		150.00	188
50. Jordan	11.25	15	101. Viet-Nam		22.50	29
51. Kenya	25.00	32	102. Yugoslavia		120.00	150

[1] As defined in paragraph 2 of the Report and paragraph 1(a) of the First Resolution.

RESOLUTIONS SUBMITTED TO THE BOARD OF GOVERNORS

WHEREAS the Executive Directors have considered the question referred to them by the Resolution of the Board of Governors of the International Monetary Fund at its Nineteenth Annual Meeting:

> "That the Executive Directors proceed to consider the question of adjusting the quotas of members of the Fund and at an early date submit an appropriate proposal to the Board of Governors."

Have found that proposals to carry out increases in quotas should be submitted to the Board of Governors; and

Have submitted to the Board of Governors a Report entitled "Increases in Quotas of Members—Fourth Quinquennial Review" and the following Resolutions of the Board of Governors for a vote without meeting pursuant to Section 13 of the By-Laws of the Fund, which Resolutions propose increases in the quotas of all members of the Fund, make provision for consents by members, and establish the conditions upon which the increases shall take effect;

Now, THEREFORE, the Board of Governors, noting the said Report of the Executive Directors, hereby resolves that:

First Resolution

1. (a) The International Monetary Fund proposes that, subject to the provisions of this First Resolution, the quotas of all members of the International Monetary Fund in effect on February 26, 1965 or the maximum quotas to which members could consent under Resolutions adopted by or submitted to the Board of Governors before that date shall be increased by 25 per cent, with the resulting amounts rounded according to the following formula:

    amounts below $500 million shall be rounded to the next higher multiple of one million;

    amounts of $500 million or more shall be rounded to the next higher multiple of five million.

   (b) When an increase in quota proposed in this First Resolution is calculated on the basis of a quota that includes an increase to which a member can consent under another Resolution adopted by or submitted to the Board of Governors before February 26, 1965 and there is no consent to such increase, the increase proposed in this First Resolution shall be 25 per cent of the quota in effect on February 26, 1965, rounded in accordance with paragraph 1 (a).

2. None of the increases in quotas proposed in this First Resolution shall become effective unless:

   (i) The member concerned has notified the Fund that it consents to the increase in its quota; and

   (ii) The Fund determines that members having not less than two-thirds of the total of quotas on February 26, 1965 have consented to increases in their quotas under the First or Second Resolution; and

   (iii) The member concerned has paid the full increase in its quota.

   Subject to paragraph 6 (c), each increase in quota shall become effective upon the date of the latest of these three events.

3. Notices in accordance with paragraph 2 (i) shall be executed by a duly authorized official of the member.

4. Notices in accordance with paragraph 2 (i) shall be received in the Fund not later than September 25, 1965, provided that the Executive Directors may extend this period as they may determine.

5. Subject to paragraph 6 (b), each member shall pay to the Fund within 30 days after the later of the two events in paragraph 2 (i) and (ii), 25 per cent of the increase in gold and the balance in its own currency.

6. (a) In giving notice in accordance with paragraph 2 (i), any member may consent to the increase in its quota as an increase by installments.

   (b) Notwithstanding paragraph 2 (iii), a member increasing its quota by installments shall pay not less than one-fifth of the gold and currency prescribed in paragraph 5 within 30 days after the later of the two events in paragraph 2 (i) and (ii) and shall pay further installments of gold and currency of not less than one-fifth of the increase in each twelve months after the first payment until the full amount prescribed in paragraph 5 has been paid.

   (c) Subject to paragraph 2, on the completion of the payment of each installment of the increase, the member's quota shall be increased by an amount equal to the installment.

7. Since it is in the interests of the Fund and its members that the contemplated increase in its resources be expedited, members are invited to comply as soon as possible with the procedure for notice and payments to the Fund under this First Resolution. Any payment made by a member before the effective date of increase in its quota will be kept in separate accounts of the Fund. If the Fund decides that such increase cannot become effective under this First Resolution, the payment will be returned to the member.

Second Resolution

1. The International Monetary Fund proposes that, subject to the provisions of this Second Resolution, the quotas of the following members shall be increased to the amounts shown against their names:

	Million U.S. dollars		Million U.S. dollars
1. Austria	175	9. Japan	725
2. Canada	740	10. Mexico	270
3. Finland	125	11. Norway	150
4. Germany, Federal Republic of	1,200	12. Philippines	110
5. Greece	100	13. South Africa	200
6. Iran	125	14. Spain	250
7. Ireland	80	15. Sweden	225
8. Israel	90	16. Venezuela	250

2. Paragraphs 2 through 7 of the First Resolution shall apply to this Second Resolution.

3. Members named in paragraph 1 of this Second Resolution shall be entitled to consent under either the First or the Second Resolution but not under both. Any such member shall declare under which Resolution it is consenting, and such choice shall be final.

Board of Governors Resolutions Nos. 20–6 and 20–7
Adopted March 31, 1965

PART IV

After 1965

Compensatory Financing: Second Report

In 1964 the UN Conference on Trade and Development reviewed the procedure for the compensatory financing of export fluctuations established in 1963 (pp. 442–57 above) and made recommendations for its modification. Supporting speeches were made by a number of Governors at the Annual Meetings, 1965, and in September 1966 the Executive Directors decided to expand the facility. Their report follows.

Compensatory Financing of Export Fluctuations—Developments in the Fund's Facility

(September 1966)

A Second Report by the International Monetary Fund
on Compensatory Financing of the Fluctuations
in Exports of Primary Producing Countries

CONTENTS

	PAGE
I. Introduction: The 1963 Decision	470
II. Subsequent Developments	
1. Quota Adjustments and Export Fluctuations	470
2. The Fund's Compensatory Facility	471
III. Application and Development of the Facility	
1. Nature of Shortfall	472
2. Estimation of Trend and Shortfall	474
3. Proposals Regarding the Mode of Determining the Shortfall	
A. Weight to be given to past years	475
B. Degree of reliance on automatic formulae	477
C. Account to be taken of terms of trade	478
4. Period for Which Shortfall is Calculated	479
5. Problem of Double Compensation	480
6. Responsibility for Shortfall and Policy Conditions	481
7. Separation of the Compensatory Facility from Other Drawing Facilities	482
8. The Limit on Compensatory Drawings	483
9. Repurchase of Compensatory Drawing	485
10. Changes in the Compensatory Facility and Fund Liquidity	490
IV. Conclusions for Action	491
V. Decision	492

Appendices

I. UNCTAD Recommendation	494
II. Excerpts from Speeches of Governors at the 1965 Annual Meeting	495
III. Decisions on Compensatory Financing of Export Fluctuations	496

I. INTRODUCTION: THE 1963 DECISION

In February 1963, in response to an invitation extended by the United Nations Commission on International Commodity Trade at its tenth session in May 1962, the Fund issued a report entitled *Compensatory Financing of Export Fluctuations*. This report, after reviewing the problems involved in financing by the Fund of fluctuations in exports of primary exporting countries, set forth in its concluding chapter an Executive Board Decision [1] covering two points: (a) quotas and (b) drawing policies.

With respect to quotas, the Fund declared its willingness to give sympathetic consideration to requests for the adjustment of the quotas of certain primary exporting countries, particularly those with relatively small quotas, to make them more adequate in the light of fluctuations in export proceeds and other relevant criteria.

As regards drawing policies, the Fund introduced a new facility, of which the principal features are as follows:

(1) It is open to all member countries, but designed in particular for primary producing countries.

(2) It is designed to compensate for temporary shortfalls in export receipts, rather than in export prices or in the terms of trade, or in the importing power of exports.

(3) By temporary shortfalls are meant deviations from a medium-term trend in export receipts.

(4) Compensation is paid in the form of a drawing subject to the normal conditions of repayments for Fund drawings, including an outside limit of three to five years.

(5) Compensation is paid to the full extent of the calculated shortfall, subject to the proviso that the total of compensatory drawings outstanding should not normally exceed 25 per cent of quota.

(6) The policies of members drawing under the facility do not have to meet the tests that the Fund would apply in the case of a non-compensatory drawing in the same tranche. However, members do have to satisfy the Fund that they are encountering payments difficulties, that the shortfall is of a short-term character and is largely attributable to circumstances beyond the member's control, and that the member will cooperate with the Fund in an effort to find solutions, where required, for its payments difficulties.

II. SUBSEQUENT DEVELOPMENTS

1. *Quota Adjustments and Export Fluctuations*

The Decision on Compensatory Financing has now been in operation for over three years, and the time has arrived when certain of its aspects can appropriately be reviewed.

In paragraph (3) of that Decision, the Fund recognized that some quota adjustments might be required or desirable, as follows: "The quotas of many primary exporting countries, taken in conjunction with a reasonable use of their own reserves, are at present adequate for dealing with export fluctuations such as have occurred during the past decade. In those instances, however, where adjustment of the quotas of certain primary exporting countries, and in particular of countries with relatively small quotas, would be appropriate to make them more adequate in the light of fluctuations in export proceeds and other relevant criteria, the Fund is willing to give sympathetic consideration to requests for such adjustment."

---

[1] Decision No. 1477-(63/8), adopted February 27, 1963; see above, pp. 238–40.

Since February 1963 the Fund has taken steps—apart from the general quota increase which came into effect on February 23, 1966—to implement this paragraph in several ways.

In the first place, it has approved more than 20 quota increases under a special policy applied to developing countries with relatively small quotas; 15 other countries appear to be eligible for such quota increases under that policy.

Secondly, the Fund facilitates drawings by such countries to enable them to purchase the amount of gold that must be paid in connection with the quota increases referred to above. This gives them the benefit of a quota increase immediately, and makes it possible to spread the reserve cost of the increase over a number of years.

Finally, in considering applications for individual quota increases, even from countries other than those to which paragraph (3) directly applies, the Fund has modified the formula which is taken into account in calculating quotas in such a way as to improve the position of developing countries. Variability of trade, which was a component of the so-called Bretton Woods formula, has now been defined in terms of the standard deviation around a five-year moving average. This new definition provides a more accurate measure of variability and is more favorable to quota calculations for countries exporting raw materials. The Fund has also modified the formula to give greater weight to trade and variability of trade, and less weight to national income and international reserves.

2. The Fund's Compensatory Facility

It might have been expected that the drawing facility established by the Fund in February 1963 to provide compensatory financing for export fluctuations would by this time have been used often enough to provide ample illustration of the types of problems that were liable to arise in applying it, and possibly also to indicate ways in which it could be improved. In fact, however, few countries have had even a prima facie case for using it, and only three countries have actually drawn: (1) Brazil in June 1963, the equivalent of $60 million (21 per cent of quota); (2) the United Arab Republic in October 1963, the equivalent of $16 million (18 per cent of quota); and (3) Sudan in June 1965, the equivalent of $11.25 million (25 per cent of quota).[2] This infrequency of use is largely attributable to the fact, illustrated in Table 1, that price developments over the past three or four years have been such as to permit the export earnings of less developed primary producing countries to show a generally upward trend, though one that tended to flatten out in 1965. Even the substantial declines in prices of tropical foodstuffs (other than coffee), which began in the spring of 1964 and continued through the greater part of 1965, have not reacted sufficiently on earnings to evoke many opportunities for the use of the facility.

Despite the small number of instances of use, there has been enough experience and enough reflection on the variety of situations that might present themselves to permit a reconsideration of several of the features of the 1963 Decision. Moreover, a number of suggestions have been made, both inside the Fund—notably at the Annual Meeting of the Board of Governors in 1965—and outside the Fund, as to ways in which the Fund's compensatory financing facility might be amended or improved.

Most of these suggestions are summed up in the three recommendations made by the United Nations Conference on Trade and Development (UNCTAD), 1964, to

---

[2] The quotas referred to in these percentages are those applicable at the times the drawings were made.

Governments that are members of the Fund as to changes that might be made in the facility, and in the request which it addressed directly to the Fund. The UNCTAD resolution containing these recommendations and request is reproduced in Appendix I below. Passages dealing with compensatory financing excerpted from speeches of Governors at the 1965 Annual Meeting are reproduced in Appendix II. It will be seen that most of the points made by the Governors are covered in the UNCTAD Recommendation referred to above, except for the reference to automatism in the speech of the Governor for Argentina, and the reference to terms of trade and import prices in the speech of the Governor for Ceylon.

Table 1. Changes in Prices and Export Earnings for Primary Producers, 1962-1965

Commodity	Prices[1] Percentage increase or decrease (−) from previous year			Export Earnings			
	1963	1964	1965	Countries mainly dependent on specified commodities[2]	1963	1964	1965[3]
Metals and minerals[4]	3	21	13	Metals and minerals	9	24	13
Agricultural products	20	—	−12	Agricultural products	12	10	4
Food	31	—	−17	Coffee	12	8	7
Coffee	*4*	*30*	*−5*	Mixed tropical foodstuffs	11	11	3
Sugar	*185*	*−31*	*−64*				
Cocoa	*20*	*−8*	*−26*	Mainly temperate products	14	12	2
Wheat	*1*	*4*	*−5*	Fibers and rubber	10	2	9
Non-food	4	—	−5				
Cotton	*2*	*29*	*−6*	Mixed	7	11	5
Wool	*18*	—	*−13*	Mixed mineral and agricultural	8	7	2
Rubber	*−7*	*−5*	*−1*				
All exports[4]	18	2	−9	All countries	11	10	4

[1] Group price changes are derived from indices published by the National Institute of Economic and Social Research, London. Specified commodity price series relate to world market quotations for representative grades only, and thus exclude the influence of prices determined under contracts.
[2] Countries obtaining at least one half of export earnings from commodity groups indicated. Excludes countries dependent on petroleum. Data relate to 71 countries.
[3] Provisional.
[4] Excluding petroleum.

III. APPLICATION AND DEVELOPMENT OF THE FACILITY

1. *Nature of Shortfall*

Drawings under paragraph (5) of the Compensatory Financing Decision of 1963 may be made only when the requesting member experiences payments difficulties produced by a temporary export shortfall, i.e., by an export shortfall which is "of a short-term character." Such shortfalls, according to paragraph (7) of the Decision, are to be identified on the basis of "estimates regarding the medium-term trend of the member's exports." In the 1963 Decision itself, no definition of the medium-term trend is given. However, in the earlier Fund report, "Fund Policies and Procedures in Relation to the Compensatory Financing of Commodity Fluctuations,"[3] the trend or norm was defined

---
[3] *Staff Papers*, Vol. VIII (1960–61), p. 9.

for purposes of illustration as the average of actual exports for the five years beginning two years before and ending two years after the year for which the trend value was calculated. The same definition was adopted in the staff paper [4] cited [on page 447] of *Compensatory Financing of Export Fluctuations*, and it was on the basis of this definition of the "ideal" trend or norm that certain conclusions were drawn in that report as to the best statistical method of estimating it in the absence of complete information.[5] This is also the definition that has been adopted in all applications of the Compensatory Financing Decision to particular countries up to the present time.

In the absence of precise quantitative knowledge as to the nature of the economic forces at work in determining trends and fluctuations, a moving average seems the best and most flexible way—better, for example, than fitting a trend line of any a priori shape—to reflect what is meant by trend. Moving averages of 4 years, 5 years, or 6 years, respectively, might, any one of them, serve as a reasonable definition of a "medium-term" trend. However, a five-year period is preferable to the others in that it contains a middle year, the trend value of which can be defined as the average of the period. The trend value for any year in any time series must anticipate the figures for subsequent as well as reflect those of previous years in that series. If this is not done— e.g., if the trend values are determined solely as an average of past years—the trend line might lie persistently above, or below, the actual series to a substantial extent, which would be contrary to the normal meaning of the term "trend." Only if the moving average is centered in the manner illustrated above can one expect to find, over a reasonable period of time, a rough balancing of shortfalls and surpluses of actual exports with respect to trend.[6]

Once the best possible estimate has been made of the medium-term trend, and hence of the shortfall, if any, from that trend, in accordance with paragraph (7) of the Decision of 1963, no separate judgment is required as to whether the shortfall in question is "temporary" or of a "short-term" character. The definition of the trend itself is such as to make it likely—though one can never be certain—that shortfalls with respect to it will be of short duration.[7] Any attempt to make a separate determination as to whether a given shortfall would cease to exist within, say, two or three years would involve estimating for that period ahead not only actual exports—which, as is indicated in the following section, may be involved in the estimation of the current norm—but also the export trend itself. To forecast the latter would involve estimating exports for still further years ahead. This, in the present state of forecasting techniques, would appear to be impracticable, and a determination that a shortfall of a given magnitude exists should, therefore, be taken as satisfying the requirement that the shortfall is of a short-term character.

---

[4] J. Marcus Fleming, Rudolf Rhomberg, and Lorette Boissonneault, "Export Norms and Their Role in Compensatory Financing," *Staff Papers*, Vol. X (1963), pp. 97–149.

[5] *Compensatory Financing of Export Fluctuations* (above, pp. 450–51).

[6] The balancing of surpluses and deficits is far from perfect, however; in any five-year period there is likely to be either an excess of surpluses over deficits exceeding 50 per cent of gross surpluses, or an excess of shortfalls over surpluses exceeding 50 per cent of gross shortfalls. This, however, appears to be quite unavoidable. There is no way of defining a norm or trend consistently from year to year in such a way as to secure a perfect balance of surpluses and shortfalls over any given period.

[7] Calculations covering 48 countries show that almost 50 per cent of all shortfalls with respect to a norm defined as above last only one year, nearly 85 per cent no more than two years, and 96 per cent no more than three years.

2. Estimation of Trend and Shortfall

In paragraph (7) of the 1963 Decision it is laid down that the Fund will seek to establish reasonable estimates regarding the medium-term trend of the member's exports "on the basis of appropriate statistical data in conjunction with qualitative information about its export prospects." This phrase appears to foreshadow a two-sided approach—"statistical" and "qualitative"—to the problem of estimation. However, while statistical estimation can be carried out without qualitative appraisal, qualitative appraisal can scarcely be applied without the aid of some statistical information, and the true alternative approaches are those of statistical automatism and the exercise of judgment, respectively.

In the three instances in which the Decision has been applied thus far, the estimation of normal exports has represented a compromise between (a) a figure or figures arrived at through the application of automatic formulae to past statistical data, and (b) an estimate based on a combination of these data with a forecast for actual exports two years ahead, these forecasts in turn being arrived at by a process of market appraisal using all available information.

The combination of the two methods in one form or another is justified by the knowledge that the result of either method is to a considerable extent uncertain. Any formula admittedly gives a precise answer; but no formula can be devised that gives a good approximation of the medium-term trend, as here defined, solely on the basis of past statistical data. On the other hand, any forecasting exercise must to some extent be subjective and uncertain. Given these facts it is necessary to strike a reasonable balance between these two methods, each less than satisfactory, which at the same time assures countries as much uniformity of treatment as possible.

As regards the automatic statistical approach to the estimation of the norm, the Fund has, in the past, used two types of formula, a "general" formula and a "national" formula, in both of which the norm for any given year is estimated as a weighted average of actual exports for the year in question and the two preceding years. In both formulae, the weights assigned to the various years are those which experience shows to provide the best approximation to the "true" norm as defined above.[8]

The "general" formula used in calculations contained in *Compensatory Financing of Export Fluctuations*, which was used in all three applications of the Decision to date, attaches a weight of .50 to the exports of the year for which the shortfall is being estimated, .25 to the preceding year, and .25 to the second preceding year. These weights were arrived at on the basis of analysis of the experience of some 48 countries over a period of nine testable years (thirteen years of data). While not absolutely the best of the formulae tested, it was chosen as a good formula with rounded weights close to those of the optimal formula.

"National" formulae have differed from country to country, the formula for each country being arrived at on the basis of export data for that country alone. It is

---

[8] The "true norm" for exports, x, in any year t, i.e., $\bar{x}_t$, is defined as

$$\frac{x^*_{t-2} + x_{t-1} + x_t + x_{t+1} + x_{t+2}}{5}.$$

The problem is to find weights w_0, w_1, w_2, such that the estimated norm

$$x_t = w_2 x_{t-2} + w_1 x_{t-1} + w_0 x_t$$

provides the best approximation to $\bar{x}_t$ for all values of t. This is found by regression analysis for years in which the relevant export data are available.

intended to discontinue the use of "national" formulae on the ground that they are based on too small a number of observations, and complicate the statistical side of the shortfall determination.

As regards the more subjective estimate, primarily based on market analysis, it is in the nature of the case more difficult to describe the method used, which varies from country to country. The procedure is first to estimate the average of exports in the two years following the year for which the shortfall is being determined and then to take an average of the five years centered on the shortfall year. The forecast in question is constructed largely on the basis of commodity analysis, taking into account the prospective price movements for the commodity in question and the prospective volume movements in the country in question. For the great majority of Fund members which are primary exporting countries, 60 per cent to 90 per cent of total exports is accounted for by a small number (1 to 4) of commodities; a large proportion of most countries' trade can, therefore be estimated on the basis of commodity market analysis. But there remains a sizable residual for which no such analysis is possible, and it may well prove desirable in particular instances to make a more or less automatic statistical estimate for this part of the exports. In this event the partial results of market analysis for major commodities would be combined with a more mechanical result for the residual to arrive at a global estimate.

In the past, "statistical" and "qualitative" estimates have been given approximately equal weight in determining the final estimate of the trend value of exports. However, the "qualitative" estimates, involving a direct forecast of exports two years ahead, have been found in practice to yield better results than the formula. Experience has tended to bear out the judgment that a "better estimate could be made by the exercise of judgment based on an analysis of the causal factors at work than by any mathematical formula, however skillfully contrived, which is based on the mere statistical magnitude of current and previous exports."[9] In future, therefore, it would seem advisable to give a somewhat greater weight than in the past to the "qualitative" as against the "statistical" estimate.

It is important, however, to give members some assurance that estimates of the trend value of exports will remain within a certain predictable range. This can be achieved by providing that, in the calculation of the trend, the average level of exports predicted for the two years following the shortfall year will not be assumed to exceed by more than ten per cent the average level experienced in the two years preceding the shortfall year and will not be assumed to be less than the level of exports experienced in the shortfall year itself.

3. *Proposals Regarding the Mode of Determining the Shortfall*

A. *Weight to be given to past years*

In the Recommendation on the Study of Measures Related to the Compensatory Credit System of the International Monetary Fund, set forth in Annex A.IV.17 of its report, the UNCTAD made the following request:

The Conference
....
2. *Requests* that the International Monetary Fund, in its determination of the shortfall in export receipts, consider giving greater weight to the actual experience of the three preceding years.

---

[9] *Compensatory Financing of Export Fluctuations* (above, p. 447).

The issue here, though it appears to be purely technical, in fact touches on a point of principle. At present, as has been explained above, the Fund's compensatory financing facility is designed to compensate for shortfalls from the presumed current trend level of exports rather than from a previous trend level. It is designed to help countries to bring their export availabilities—export receipts *plus* compensatory drawings *less* repayments of such drawings—closer to the presumed trend level rather than to provide them with a financial buffer against declines in exports from their previous standards. While it might be entirely appropriate to provide countries with such a buffer, it would seem preferable to supply this through the ordinary drawing facilities of the Fund, use of which could be made conditional, where necessary, on the adoption of measures to adapt the economy to new export conditions, or to improve the trend of exports, than through the compensatory financing facility, the use of which is more automatic.

It is because the aim of compensatory financing is conceived in the manner described above, that in the assessment of the norm with reference to which the shortfall is calculated account is taken of the expected exports of the ensuing years, that a substantial weight in the determination of the norm is given to the current year's exports, and that no weight is given, for example, to exports three or more years anterior to the year with respect to which the shortfall is being calculated. The weights assigned to the current and preceding years in the estimation of the export norm—insofar as it is estimated by formula—were arrived at on the basis of experience as to which weights gave the closest estimate of the current trend and the best implied forecast of the two years subsequent to the shortfall year.

A formula in which no weight was given to the shortfall year would, for this reason, tend to lead to a higher estimate of the trend value, and hence a larger shortfall and a larger drawing entitlement. Because of the long-term upward trend of exports, however, this effect would generally be offset to some extent by the inclusion in the weighting formula of the third year preceding the shortfall, or of still earlier years. From Table 2 it can be seen that a formula for trend estimation giving equal weights to the three years preceding the shortfall would have led, over the period 1951 to 1964, to somewhat larger drawing entitlements than the present formula. The same table, however, shows that the "performance" of the scheme (as measured by the degree to which compensatory drawings and repurchases bring export availabilities closer to the true trend value, and the degree to which they tend to smooth out export availabilities) would not have been improved, but if anything, worsened by such a change in formula. It is not the object of the compensatory facility to aim at the largest possible amount of drawings, and, as will be shown below, there are ways in which it would be possible for an increase in drawings outstanding to improve the performance of the scheme significantly, or even for the scheme to be improved without a net increase in drawings outstanding.

Some further points deserve mention.

The element of forecasting involved in the determination of a current rather than a past trend value of exports, though irksome and subject to uncertainty, is a good discipline for country and Fund alike, and may help to counteract the natural tendency to delay adaptations to changing circumstances.

More important is the fact that measurement solely from a past level would frequently yield "shortfalls" which could not by any means be described as "temporary." While countries with a rising trend of exports, even when the rise was subject to serious interruption, would seldom if ever be deemed to have shortfalls, those with a generally falling trend of exports would experience persistent shortfalls. Such a change in formula would necessitate the introduction of a separate determination as to whether or not the shortfall was temporary—a determination which, as already indicated, would involve forecasting much further ahead and hence a higher degree of guesswork than that involved in the determination of the trend by present methods.

Table 2. Fund Compensatory Financing Facility: Comparison of Weighting Systems, 1951-64[1]

Limit: Per Cent of Quota	Coefficients Applied to Years				Drawing Entitlement[2]	Average Drawings Outstanding[3]	Approximation Ratio[4]	Smoothness Ratio[5]
	t	t-1	t-2	t-3				
.25	0	1/3	1/3	1/3	1.04	.31	.022	.028
.25	.50	.25	.25		.97	.29	.023	.029
.50	0	1/3	1/3	1/3	1.82	.54	.033	.046
.50	.50	.25	.25		1.61	.48	.034	.046

[1] Schemes applied to a sample of 48 countries. Drawings are assumed to be repaid one half in the fourth and one half in the fifth year after drawing, regardless of the level of exports in those years. The quotas on which the limits are based are not present quotas but those obtaining at the relevant dates during the period 1951-64.

[2] Cumulative total entitlements over the period in billions of U.S. dollars.

[3] Average for all years of total amounts outstanding in billions of U.S. dollars.

[4] Proportionate decline in root mean square percentage deviation of export availabilities from trend value of exports.

[5] Proportionate decline in root mean square percentage deviation of export availabilities from trend value of such availabilities.

The other alternative would be to drop the proviso that export shortfalls—or rather declines—should be temporary. But this would scarcely be compatible with the legal requirement of temporariness in the use of Fund resources.

For these reasons it seems on balance undesirable to alter the present concept of the export norm.

B. *Degree of reliance on automatic formulae*

The Governor for Argentina, speaking at the 1965 Annual Meeting of the Fund on behalf of 19 Latin American countries and the Philippines, mentioned as one of the fundamental aspects of the Fund's compensatory financing decision which it would be advisable to consider:

(3) In conclusion, we would emphasize the nonautomatic nature of the drawings permitted. In the decisions on individual cases submitted to the consideration of the Executive Board there has been some flexibility, although in all of them there has been no lack of a subjective assessment in the determination both of the amount to be compensated and of the circumstances in which the loss of income occurs.[10]

This question, so far as it concerns the determination of the shortfall, has already been considered at some length above.

---

[10] *Summary Proceedings, Annual Meeting, 1965*, pp. 153–54.

It has been the experience of the Fund, based not only on its own export forecasts but on those of outside bodies, that a closer estimate of the medium-term trend can be arrived at by the use of short-term forecasts based on commodity analysis than by reliance on the best statistical formula. While greater reliance on formulae might give countries a slightly higher degree of certainty as to the amount of compensation they could rely on, the proposed balance between the two methods of estimation would seem to give as much weight as is prudent to the "automatic" element in the estimation process.

C. *Account to be taken of terms of trade*

At the 1965 Annual Meeting of the Fund, the Governor for Ceylon made a suggestion in the following terms:

> I was encouraged by the reference by Mr. Schweitzer to the work that the Fund is now undertaking to improve the compensatory financing facility. Several speakers have urged that compensatory assistance should be provided for a decline in the terms of trade rather than for a fall in export earnings alone. My own country's experience in recent years vividly illustrates the importance of this reform. We suffered a decline in the terms of trade by 13 per cent in two years alone, but since this was almost entirely due to an increase in import prices we were unable to avail ourselves of the compensatory financing facility. I do sincerely hope that this particular improvement in the scheme will be made effective at an early date.[11]

The terms of trade refer to the ratio between a country's export prices and its import prices. Fluctuations in export prices are, of course, reflected, along with fluctuations in export quantities, in the fluctuations in export proceeds. It might be argued that price fluctuations are more properly compensable than quantity fluctuations in that they are less easily affected by the policies of the exporting countries. On the other hand, some of the commonest and most genuinely short-run fluctuations in export proceeds are those arising from crop failures. More harm than good would probably be done by attempting to distinguish the specific roles of price and quantity in the fluctuations in export proceeds.

The case is different with fluctuations in import prices. There are undoubtedly good economic reasons for compensating not the money value but the real value, or importing power, of exports. An estimate of the latter could be arrived at by deflating exports (for the purpose of arriving at the trend value of exports) by an import price index based on the shortfall year.

There are, however, a number of practical and other objections to this procedure. Most primary producing countries have no import price index. Of those import price indices that exist, many are unrepresentative or unreliable. Moreover, such indices usually become available several months later than the data on export proceeds, so that the lag in the granting of a compensatory drawing behind the occurrence of the export shortfall would necessarily be increased. It might be thought that, where the import price indices of developing countries are unavailable, unreliable, or late in appearing, estimates could be formed on the basis of the export and import price indices of industrial countries. Such data, however, would provide extremely uncertain and disputable estimates for the import prices of any individual developing country. It has to be borne in mind that the developing countries that experience the largest fluctuations in import prices do so because they are substantial importers of primary products, often

---

[11] *Ibid.*, p. 207.

from other developing countries. Apart from such cases, the import price indices of primary producing countries do not, as a rule, show very large movements within a short period of years. For all these reasons, it seems better, at this time, to continue to adhere to the principle of compensating for shortfalls in export proceeds rather than in the importing power of exports.

4. *Period for Which Shortfall Is Calculated*

Thus far it has been the practice of the Fund to require that any request for the use of the compensatory facility shall relate to an export shortfall over the latest twelve-month period for which, at the time of the request, a reliable estimate of actual exports can be made. There must, in any event, be some maximum lapse of time within which any claim for compensation with respect to the exports of a given period should be made, and if the compensatory facility is to fulfil its purpose of enabling countries to stabilize their external expenditures as much as possible in the face of fluctuations in receipts, it seems desirable that the time lag between shortfall and compensatory financing should be as short as possible. As indicated below, countries need not be deterred from applying for a compensatory drawing as soon as a shortfall appears by the fact that they will thereby preclude themselves from claiming a larger compensation a little later if the shortfall has by then increased.[12]

The present practice permits a request for a compensatory drawing at any time during the year with respect to the twelve-month period immediately preceding. The question arises whether the timing of requests should be restricted in any way. There would seem to be no advantage in a system under which such claims could be made only with respect, say, to calendar years. A more plausible case could be made for ruling that, where exports are marked by seasonality, claims for compensatory drawings should be made only with respect to twelve-month periods which include all those months over which the principal export crop is liable to be marketed abroad. Otherwise, it might be argued, countries which marketed their crops early one year and late the following season might show a shortfall over a twelve-month period that spanned two seasons, whereas no shortfall would appear from a comparison of crop years. Bearing in mind, however, that most countries have a number of export crops with different seasonalities, it is doubtful whether the variability of seasonality is sufficient to justify the introduction of a restriction which would both reduce the value of the facility to the country and complicate its administration. It would be no easy task to determine for each country with respect to which twelve-month periods applications for compensatory financing would not be entertained. It should also be borne in mind that any shortfall that appeared to be artificially induced by deliberate delay in the timing of exports would be unlikely to be regarded as "largely attributable to circumstances beyond the control of the member" and in this event would not qualify for a compensatory drawing.

The arrangement outlined in the first paragraph of this section can be criticized from another angle, namely, that even a time lag of a few months between the shortfall and the compensatory drawing is undesirable, and that it would be better if the drawing could coincide with the shortfall. This means that the drawing would have to take place at a time when the precise amount of the shortfall was unknown. In order to meet this point and to facilitate the use of the stand-by and ordinary drawing facilities for the compensation of export shortfalls, it is intended, subject to what is said below,

---

[12] See pp. 480–81.

to allow members, within a six-month period of any drawing, to reclassify all or part of it as a compensatory drawing under paragraph (5) of the Decision. The drawing, when first made, would have to satisfy the ordinary conditions for drawing in the tranche in question, or, if made under a stand-by arrangement, the requirements appropriate to drawing under that arrangement. The reclassification of the drawing would have to satisfy the conditions for a compensatory drawing under paragraph (5) of the Decision with respect to an export shortfall for the latest twelve months for which data were available prior to the reclassification. The amount reclassified could not exceed the amount of that shortfall. Such reclassification would confer on the drawings the privilege of additionality as defined in (ii) of paragraph (6) of the 1963 Decision (with any enhancement of that privilege that may result from the separation of the compensatory facility from other drawing facilities, discussed below). It would not, however, reconstitute rights to draw under stand-by arrangement. Policy undertakings made in connection with the original drawing would remain unaffected by the reclassification.

It is estimated that if both the compensatory facility and the privilege of reclassification had existed over the period 1959–64, and the latter had been exercised to the full—which might not in all instances have been to the country's advantage—some 20 to 25 per cent of all non-compensatory drawings could have been so reclassified.

5. Problem of Double Compensation

It would be neither equitable, nor in accordance with the intention of the Decision on Compensatory Financing, that any member should be compensated twice for the same shortfall, or, more precisely, that the sum of any drawings made with respect to any given shortfall should exceed the amount of the shortfall.

Under the Decision a member can draw from the Fund with respect to a payments deficit arising out of an export shortfall *either* in the form of a drawing under ordinary tranche policies (referred to in paragraph (4) of the 1963 Decision) *or* in the form of a drawing under the special policies outlined in paragraph (5) of the Decision. Moreover, it is intended, as indicated in the preceding section, that a drawing originally made under ordinary tranche policies could in certain circumstances be reclassified. The problem of double compensation may arise either with respect to two drawings under paragraph (5), or with respect to a pair of drawings, one under paragraph (5) and another under paragraph (4).

In the event of two drawings under paragraph (5), where the period with respect to which a second such drawing is requested to be made (or reclassified) overlaps with that for which a first such drawing has been made (or reclassified), the first drawing will be prorated over the twelve months with respect to which it was made, and such part of it as corresponds to the overlap between the two periods will be subtracted from the drawing entitlement with respect to the second period.

As regards the problem of avoiding double counting between a paragraph (5) drawing and an ordinary drawing which can be considered as at least partly undertaken for compensatory purposes, there is no real difficulty if the ordinary drawing follows the paragraph (5) drawing and is not made under a stand-by arrangement approved before the latter drawing. In that case, the paragraph (5) drawing will simply be "taken into account" as one of the many factors affecting the balance of payments situation of the drawing country on the occasion of any subsequent drawing or stand-by arrangement.

The real difficulty arises if a paragraph (5) drawing or reclassification is requested after a stand-by arrangement has been approved or an ordinary drawing made—other than the drawing that is to be reclassified. It must then be asked whether the payments situation with respect to which the drawing or stand-by arrangement was approved included any part of the export shortfall with respect to which the paragraph (5) drawing or reclassification is being requested. Such a question would be difficult to answer since an ordinary drawing or stand-by arrangement is not usually approved to meet the payments deficit of any precisely defined period, still less to meet fluctuations in any specific item in the balance of payments.

One approach would be for the Fund to make a specific statement at the time of the ordinary drawing or stand-by arrangement as to the proportion thereof, if any, that should be regarded as granted with respect to an export shortfall, and as to the period of the shortfall. When approving stand-by arrangements, however, account is more often taken of the possibility of future shortfalls than of the accomplished fact of past shortfalls, and it is impossible to be precise as regards either the amount or the timing of future shortfalls. Rules will, therefore, have to be adopted as to the period and magnitude of the export shortfall which will be deemed to be compensated by ordinary drawings or drawings under stand-by arrangements approved before the request for a drawing or reclassification under the compensatory facility.

6. Responsibility for Shortfall and Policy Conditions

According to paragraph (5) (a) of the Compensatory Financing Decision of 1963, one of the conditions of a compensatory drawing is that the export shortfall should be "largely attributable to circumstances beyond the control of the member." Where this condition is clearly not satisfied, it would be inappropriate for a drawing to be made under the compensatory facility. However, there may be ambiguous cases where difficulties of interpretation arise. A shortfall can sometimes be attributed with equal propriety to any one of a number of causes, some of which may be under the member's control and others not. For example, suppose a combination of the following:

(a) a *rise* in foreign demand for the country's exports;

(b) a short crop due to weather;

(c) a rise in home consumption of the export product due to inflation, subsidization, or some other factor for which the government is responsible.

Given the rise in prices resulting from (a), the shortfall in export value may be no greater than could be entirely accounted for by *either* (b) *or* (c). A similar question arises where a shortfall takes place in the exports of a given product due to "act of God," but where an increase in the export of other products, which would otherwise have offset the shortfall, fails to occur because of the policies of the member. Again, there may be instances where the shortfall would not have occurred except for certain policies of the member but these policies were reasonable in the light of all the circumstances, or where the shortfall could have been prevented by certain policies but abstention from these policies on the part of the member was reasonable in the light of all the circumstances.

In such ambiguous cases an interpretation favorable to the member requesting the compensatory drawing will generally be adopted, and whenever the shortfall can be largely attributed to "circumstances beyond the control of the member" it will be so attributed.

One of the conditions for drawing under paragraph (5) of the 1963 Decision is that "the member will cooperate with the Fund in an effort to find, where required, appropriate solutions for its balance of payments difficulties."

In the application of the Decision to individual cases, the Fund, in accordance with the intention of the Decision, has not attempted to reach agreement with the member on what the nature of these solutions would have to be. This has been left to subsequent discussions, and has not stood in the way of prompt action on requests for compensatory drawings. Nevertheless, in one instance in which a compensatory drawing was requested, the country concerned made, at the time of the request, a statement of the policies it intended to follow. In the two other compensatory drawings, the Fund subsequently reached agreements on appropriate policies with the countries in question.

7. Separation of the Compensatory Facility from Other Drawing Facilities

One of the measures which the UNCTAD proposed for consideration by Fund member Governments runs as follows:

> (2) To place compensatory credits entirely outside the structure of the gold and successive credit tranches, so that the drawing of compensatory credits would not directly or indirectly prejudice a member's ability to make an ordinary drawing.

Presumably the measure recommended is to be interpreted in the sense that the amount drawn under the compensatory financing facility would be ignored by the Fund in computing the amount of drawing facilities still available to members under the principles applicable to the gold tranche, the first credit tranche, etc., as well as in computing the practical maximum drawing facilities open to members. In other words, the Fund would treat a request by a member for a drawing as if its holdings of the member's currency were less than its actual holdings by the amount of any drawings outstanding under the compensatory financing facility.

At present the Fund is prepared to waive the 200 per cent limit to the extent that compensatory drawings are outstanding. If the UNCTAD recommendation were accepted, the limits for gold tranche and first credit tranche policies would be extended beyond 100 per cent and beyond 125 per cent of holdings, respectively, to the extent that compensatory drawings were outstanding. Most compensatory drawings are likely to occur after a country has used its gold tranche and probably also its first credit tranche. To ignore the compensatory drawings not only from the standpoint of the total drawing facilities of a member but also from the standpoint of tranche policies to be applied to the member would have the advantage of rendering the facility clearly additional in all respects. It would also eliminate certain possible inequities as between countries utilizing the facility.[13] On the other hand, at any given level of holdings it would somewhat reduce the Fund's ability to secure satisfactory corrective programs in connection with ordinary drawings. It would not affect the level of charges corresponding to any given level of Fund holdings, nor would it affect the applicability to compensatory drawings of the repurchase provisions of Article V, Section 7 (b). The Fund is prepared to separate the compensatory facility from other drawing facilities in the sense described above.

---

[13] At present, a member that draws on its compensatory facility after having drawn its gold tranche and first credit tranche may in effect draw up to 75 per cent of quota on relatively easy policy conditions, while a member drawing on its compensatory tranche at an earlier stage could draw only up to 50 per cent on such conditions.

8. The Limit on Compensatory Drawings

Another measure recommended by UNCTAD to Governments members of the Fund for study is:

(1) To increase, as soon as possible, the amount allocated by the Fund to compensatory financing, over and above its current transactions, from 25 per cent to 50 per cent of a member country's quota.

It should be noted that the limit of 25 per cent of quota on outstanding compensatory drawings under paragraph (5) of the 1963 Decision is not an absolute one, but applies only "normally." However, it would clearly be undesirable for compensatory drawings to be accorded frequently or as a general rule in excess of the "normal" maximum. This would raise issues of discrimination, with respect both to the compensatory drawing facility and to total drawing facilities accorded to different countries. It would also defeat one purpose of the compensatory facility, namely, that a country can, to a large extent, rely on obtaining compensatory financing in the circumstances for which it is designed, and should, therefore, not have to rely on "rallonges" of this facility.

It is also important to bear in mind that the limit on drawings under the facility is not the limit on the amount a country may draw as a result of a payments difficulty arising out of an export shortfall. It is always open to the country to request an additional drawing under the ordinary drawing policies applicable to its tranche position with the Fund. Admittedly, this would reduce the amount of drawing facilities available for other purposes.

If one disregards the foregoing considerations, there can be little doubt that over any extended period of years an expansion of the 25 per cent limit on outstanding compensatory drawings would add significantly to the value of the assistance provided. Calculations as to how the Fund's compensatory facility might have worked if it had been applied, on a pure formula basis,[14] to the export earnings of primary producing countries over the period from 1951 to 1964, and if it had been used to the full, indicate that an extension of the limit on outstanding drawings from 25 to 50 per cent of quota would have increased the effectiveness of assistance provided under the facility in a proportion roughly commensurate with the increased "cost" involved. The extent to which export availabilities are brought closer to the trend value of exports would have been increased by almost 50 per cent, the extent to which availabilities are smoothed out would have risen by some 50 per cent, while the average drawings outstanding would have risen by some 65 per cent. The data are set forth in Table 3.

In the rather favorable circumstances which have prevailed since the compensatory financing decision, only three compensatory drawings have taken place. It is noteworthy, however, that in one of them (that by Sudan) the amount of compensation which would prima facie have been paid under the facility was restricted by the existence of the 25 per cent maximum. In the other two drawings the amount of compensation paid was not so restricted but in each instance a single compensatory drawing absorbed, respectively, 86 per cent and 71 per cent of a quota tranche.

From a compensatory financing standpoint there is much to be said for extending the limit of the facility from 25 to 50 per cent. Since, however, it would involve an addition to the amount of liquidity which the Fund provides on liberal conditions, it might tend

---

[14] It is, of course, impossible to establish in retrospect precisely what compensation would have been payable over the period 1951–64 either under the present scheme or with a higher limit, inasmuch as estimates of trend and shortfall would have been affected by qualitative appraisal as well as by formula.

to reduce countries' willingness to have recourse to facilities of a more strictly conditional character. This increase of automaticity will be somewhat intensified by the separation of the compensatory facility from other drawing facilities which has been discussed in the preceding section.

Account should also be taken of the possible effect on the Fund's own liquidity, i.e., the effect on the probable level of drawings relative to resources provided by quotas in the Fund. (See Section 10, pp. 490–91).

Table 3. Compensatory Financing: Fund Scheme with Varied Limits Applied to Data for Years 1951-64 [1]

Limit	Approximation Ratio [2]	Smoothness Ratio [3]	Average Drawings Outstanding [4]
.25 of Quota	.023	.029	.29
.50 of Quota			
(a) Unqualified	.034	.046	.48
(b) Qualified as to rate of use [5]	.035	.047	.45
None	.100	.121	1.36

[1] Scheme applied to a sample of 48 countries. Coefficients of .50, .25 and .25 applied to years t, $t-1$, and $t-2$, respectively, to compute shortfalls. Drawings are assumed to be repaid one half in the fourth and one half in the fifth year after drawing, regardless of the level of exports in those years. The quotas on which the limits are based are not present quotas but those obtaining at the relevant dates during the period 1951-64.

[2] Proportionate decline in root mean square percentage deviation of export availabilities from trend value of exports.

[3] Proportionate decline in root mean square percentage deviation of export availabilities from trend value of such availabilities.

[4] Average for all years of total amounts outstanding, in billions of U.S. dollars.

[5] Drawings outstanding may not increase in any year by more than 25 per cent of quota.

Balancing the divergent considerations discussed in this section, it is intended that

(i) the limit on the use of the compensatory facility under paragraph (5) of the Compensatory Financing Decision of 1963 should be raised from 25 per cent to 50 per cent of quota; but

(ii) the 50 per cent limit should apply in all circumstances and not merely, as with the present limit, "normally"; [15]

(iii) except in the case of shortfalls resulting from disasters or major emergencies, the net expansion in drawings outstanding under paragraph (5) of the Decision should not exceed 25 per cent of quota in any twelve-month period; and

(iv) any drawings the effect of which would be to raise drawings outstanding under paragraph (5) of the Decision beyond 25 per cent of quota will be granted only if the member country, in addition to fulfilling the requirements of the Decision, is found to have been cooperating with the Fund in an effort to find, where required, appropriate solutions for its balance of payments difficulties.

---

[15] The relevant words of the 1963 Decision are: "The amount of drawings outstanding under this decision will not normally exceed 25 per cent of the member's quota."

The limitation suggested under (iii) above will impose a delaying effect in utilizing the compensatory facility to the full extent proposed under (i). The exception to this rule envisaged in the case of disasters and major emergencies is intended to provide some flexibility in very exceptional circumstances. As will be seen from Table 3, this arrangement would probably yield slightly better results with respect both to approximation to export trend and to smoothness of export availabilities than would an unqualified limit of 50 per cent of quota, and would be slightly less expensive to the Fund in terms of drawings outstanding.

In connection with the delaying effect of proposal (iii), it should be borne in mind that Article XIV or Article VIII consultations would provide an opportunity for testing the extent to which a member had implemented its undertakings under earlier compensatory drawings to "cooperate with the Fund in an effort to find, where required, appropriate solutions for its balance of payments difficulties," and thus the extent to which it is complying with the conditions set forth in (iv) above.

If the resources needed by a member to deal with a particular shortfall exceeded the amounts permitted under the limits indicated above and the member desired additional assistance from the Fund, it could enter into discussions with the Fund for a drawing on the terms normally applicable to the tranche in which the country found itself.[16] This would be a drawing under paragraph (4) of the 1963 Decision, and, as such, would not be limited in magnitude to any a priori percentage of the member's quota.

As was indicated on p. 479 above, any request for the use of the compensatory facility has to relate to an export shortfall during a specified period, viz., during the latest twelve-month period for which, at the time of the request, a reliable estimate of actual exports can be made. It follows from this that if, for any reason, such as the limit of 25 per cent of quota per annum on the net expansion of compensatory drawings under (iii) above, or the limit of 50 per cent of quota on the amount of compensatory drawings outstanding, the amount of a compensatory drawing is less than the amount of the shortfall on which it is based, the uncompensated part of the shortfall could not be carried forward and added to the amount of some later compensatory drawing to which a member may be entitled.

9. *Repurchase of Compensatory Drawing*

The Compensatory Financing Decision of 1963 does not contain specific provisions with respect to the repurchase of Fund holdings of a member's currency arising from a compensatory drawing. Such drawings were thus to be repurchased in accordance with the Fund's general policy on repurchases as laid down in the Decision of February 13, 1952.[17] Under that Decision, the period during which drawings may remain outstanding should not exceed an outside range of three to five years.

From the point of view of the purpose of the compensatory facility—which is intended to reduce the fluctuations in members' export availabilities—it would be desirable to provide for repurchases of outstanding compensatory drawings, not on a fixed time schedule, but in years in which exports exceed the estimated trend value.

---

[16] In accordance with the provision discussed on p. 482 above, the terms in question would, of course, be determined by the Fund's holdings of the member's currency, exclusive of those arising from drawings outstanding under paragraph (5) of the Compensatory Financing Decision.

[17] Decision No. 102-(52/11), adopted February 13, 1952 (above, pp. 228–30).

As can be seen from Table 4 below, schemes in which (a) repurchases were made exclusively out of export excesses and (b) the full amount of such excesses was directed to repurchases would probably, over the years 1951–64, have enhanced the degree of approximation to the export trend by over 20 per cent, and the smoothing effect of the facility on export availabilities by over 50 per cent as compared to schemes involving repurchase under the fixed-term system (the three-to-five-year rule).[18] This holds true whether the limit on outstanding drawings is 25 per cent or 50 per cent of quota. For

Table 4. Compensatory Financing: Fund Scheme
With Varied Forms of Repayment, 1951-64 [1]

Repayment System	Fixed-Term [2]	Fully Compensatory [3]	Half Compensatory [4]	Mixed [5]
	25 Per Cent of Quota Limit			
Approximation Ratio [6]	.023	.028	.031	.030
Smoothness Ratio [7]	.029	.045	.048	.047
Average Drawings Outstanding [8]	.29	.17	.21	.20
	50 Per Cent of Quota Limit (Unqualified)			
Approximation Ratio	.034	.042	.044	.042
Smoothness Ratio	.046	.072	.073	.071
Average Drawings Outstanding	.48	.36	.47	.38
	50 Per Cent of Quota Limit (Qualified)			
Approximation Ratio	.035	.043	.046	.043
Smoothness Ratio	.047	.071	.073	.071
Average Drawings Outstanding	.45	.28	.38	.32
	No Limit			
Approximation Ratio	.100	.155	.168	.120
Smoothness Ratio	.121	.216	.199	.166
Average Drawings Outstanding	1.36	1.49	2.05	1.17

[1] Weights of .50, .25 and .25 applied to years t, $t-1$, and $t-2$, respectively, for estimating calculated norm. One hundred per cent compensation of calculated shortfall.

[2] Amounts outstanding at end of three years are assumed to be repaid one half in the fourth and one half in the fifth year after drawing, regardless of level of exports.

[3] One hundred per cent of export excesses applied to repayment in all years.

[4] Fifty per cent of export excesses applied to repayment in all years.

[5] Fifty per cent of export excesses applied to repayment in the first three years. In the fourth year either half the amount outstanding at the end of the third year or half of the export excess (whichever is the greater) applied to repayment. In the fifth year any amount outstanding at the end of the fourth year repaid.

[6] Proportionate decline in root mean square percentage deviation of export availabilities from trend value of exports.

[7] Proportionate decline in root mean square percentage deviation of export availabilities from trend value of such availabilities.

[8] Average for all years of total amounts outstanding, in billions of U.S. dollars.

---

[18] Under the "fixed-term" system, as the expression is used in this report, it is assumed that drawings are repurchased one half in the fourth and one half in the fifth year after the drawing, regardless of the level of exports.

schemes without limits the superiority of compensatory repurchase would have been still greater.

Contrary to what might perhaps at first sight be assumed, the change in the timing of repurchases would also, save in the "no limit" case, have reduced the average length of time for which compensatory drawings remained outstanding and hence have reduced the average amount of compensatory drawings outstanding at any one time. It seems probable, therefore, that a system whereby compensatory drawings are repaid out of export excesses rather than under the three-to-five-year rule would do much to improve the performance of the facility without any additional "cost"—indeed with a reduction in cost—in terms of drawings outstanding.

Two difficulties arise with respect to this fully compensatory system of repurchases out of export excesses. In the first place, countries might occasionally find it difficult to repurchase compensatory drawings to the full extent of any excess of actual over trend value of exports, partly because an expansion in exports would probably entail some increase in import requirements, and partly because the obligation to repay would not be known with certainty until after the event. This difficulty could be met, in part, by a system according to which members would use in repurchase of outstanding compensatory drawings, not the entire amount, but only one half of any excess of exports over the medium-term trend value. From Table 4 it can be seen that such a "half-compensatory" system of repurchases would show slightly better smoothness and approximation ratios than would one with fully compensatory repurchase, at least where outstanding compensatory drawings are subject to a limit. This at first sight somewhat surprising result is attributable to the fact that the repurchases are spread over a number of "excess" years for which export availabilities would otherwise have remained in their original unadjusted state. The average amount of drawings outstanding is somewhat greater under the half-compensatory than under the fully compensatory system of repurchase but less than under the fixed-term system.

The second difficulty about systems of repurchase out of export excesses is that a proportion of the repurchases would probably remain outstanding for longer periods than is compatible with the temporary character of Fund assistance. This does not mean that repayment would normally be more delayed than under the three-to-five-year rule. Indeed, if, as indicated in Table 4, the average amount of compensatory drawings outstanding is generally likely to be less when repayments are on a compensatory basis than when they are made under the fixed-term rule, the average length of time for which a drawing remains outstanding will also probably be less under a compensatory repayment system than under the fixed-term system. More direct measurements of probable periods for which compensatory drawings would remain outstanding if repayments were on a compensatory basis are given in Table 5, which is based on the experience of the years 1951–64. With a half-compensatory repayment system, about three fifths of all drawings would have been repaid within three years under the 25 per cent of quota limit, and one half under the qualified 50 per cent of quota limit. In the fixed-term system, by contrast, repayments may not even begin before the fourth year after any drawing. However, whereas repayments are completed at the end of five years under the fixed-term system, one third of all drawings would have remained outstanding longer than five years under the half-compensatory system with the qualified 50 per cent of quota limit.

Although it must be borne in mind that the repurchase obligations under Article V, Section 7, would, of course, continue to apply—a fact which could not be taken into account in the calculations set forth in Table 5—it is evident that the requirement that Fund assistance be temporary would not be adequately met by a purely compensatory repurchase system.

The features of a desirable system of repurchase may now be recapitulated.

First, in order to ensure the short-term character of the use of Fund resources by individual members, it is necessary to observe an outside limit of five years for repurchases.

Second, it would be desirable if, to some extent, repurchases within this five-year period were to be made on the compensatory principle. Such repurchases out of export excesses are in accordance not only with the purpose of the policy on compensatory financing, but also with the principles of the Decision of February 13, 1952, which states

Table 5. Duration of Drawings Outstanding Under Compensatory Repayment Systems [1]
(Based on data for the period 1951-64)

	25% of Quota Limit		50% of Quota Limit (Unqualified)		50% of Quota Limit (Qualified)	
	Billions of U.S. dollars	Per cent of drawings	Billions of U.S. dollars	Per cent of drawings	Billions of U.S. dollars	Per cent of drawings
Fully Compensatory System [2]						
Total drawings	.89	100	1.45	100	1.24	100
Repaid within 3 years	.74	83	.97	67	.97	78
Outstanding after the fifth year	.09	10	.27	18	.15	12
Half-compensatory System [3]						
Total drawings	.69	100	1.20	100	1.01	100
Repaid within 3 years	.41	59	.54	45	.49	49
Outstanding after the fifth year	.12	17	.43	36	.33	33

[1] Weights of .50, .25 and .25 applied to years t, $t-1$, and $t-2$, respectively, for estimating calculated norm. One hundred per cent compensation of calculated shortfall.

[2] One hundred per cent of excesses applied to repayment.

[3] Fifty per cent of excesses applied to repayment.

that "exchange purchased from the Fund should not remain outstanding beyond the period reasonably related to the payments problem for which it was purchased from the Fund." In this connection, it should be remembered that, for reasons already stated, compensatory repurchases amounting to one half of the export excesses are likely to result in greater reduction of the fluctuations of export availabilities around the trend than would fully compensatory repurchases.

Third, although compensatory repurchases ordinarily benefit the member concerned by contributing to a smoothing of the fluctuations in its export availabilities and by restoring its access to the compensatory facility at an earlier date than would be the case under fixed-term repurchases in the fourth and fifth years after a drawing, circumstances may, in a particular year, make it difficult for a member to take advantage of these benefits. A member may, for instance, encounter temporary balance of payments difficulties even though it experiences an export excess, say, because of an unavoidable increase in import requirements or an unexpected reduction in the inflow of foreign capital or aid. The arrangements with respect to compensatory repurchases must be sufficiently flexible to make it possible for members to take account of such circumstances which may make it desirable to use less than one half of an export excess in repayment or even to omit the indicated compensatory repurchase entirely.

A repurchase system which would give effect to these desiderata would operate as follows:

(a) As in the case of ordinary drawings, a member will make repurchases with respect to amounts which remain outstanding from a drawing under paragraph (5) in installments in the fourth and fifth years after the drawing, and complete repurchase by the end of the fifth year.

(b) In addition, the Fund recommends that, as soon as possible after the end of each of the four years following such a drawing, the member use in repurchase an amount approximately equal to one half of its export excess, if any.

In order to implement the provision under (b) above, calculations will be made at twelve-month intervals to see whether or not export excesses have occurred. These calculations will be made on the basis of the statistical formula adopted as an element in the calculation of shortfalls, for each twelve-month period, beginning with the twelve months immediately following the shortfall period with respect to which the drawing had been approved. Since the recommended amount is only an approximate one, the statistical calculation will not, as in the case of a shortfall determination, be partly based on the results of market forecasts of the member's export receipts.

In order to give an indication of the performance under such a repurchase system, calculations have been made for the period 1951–64, as shown in the last column of Table 4, on the assumption that members always followed the recommendation under (b). As can be seen from that table, on that assumption the performance as measured by the approximation ratio and smoothness ratio would have been better than that of the fixed-term system of repurchase, equivalent to that of the fully compensatory system, and only slightly inferior to that of the half-compensatory system of repurchase out of export excesses. This finding holds irrespective of the severity of the limits on outstanding drawings.

The "cost" in terms of drawings outstanding is much lower than under the system of fixed-term repurchase, and almost as low as under fully compensatory repurchase.

It should be noted that under the repurchase system described above a drawing member would make the same type of representation as to repurchase as that made in cases of ordinary drawings, i.e., that the drawing member would comply with the principles of the Decision of February 13, 1952. Such representations do not, as such, create a legal obligation, although they are often made binding on members as terms of a waiver under Article V, Section 4. The recommendation to members, referred to in (b) above, to use in repurchase one half of their export excesses would not create a legal obligation for members even in such cases, i.e., where the member's representation that it will repurchase in accordance with the principles of the 1952 Decision would have been made legally binding under a waiver. The purpose of the clause is to express the hope of the Fund, based on what it would regard as an appropriate application of the principles of the 1952 Decision, that members would use export excesses to repurchase compensatory drawings still outstanding, but members which did not act in accordance with that recommendation would not be violating an obligation.

In connection with this discussion of arrangements regarding repurchases, it may be appropriate to take up the somewhat related matter of refinancing of obligations arising from compensatory drawings.

One measure recommended by UNCTAD for study by Fund member Governments is:

> (3) To explore ways to secure possible refinancing of compensatory financing obligations of the developing countries in the event of a persistent shortfall in export receipts beyond the control of the country affected.

While there is no specific provision in the Compensatory Financing Decision of 1963 for refinancing of compensatory drawings, refinancing on a short-term to medium-term basis would, in effect, be possible in the circumstances that appear to be envisaged in the UNCTAD Recommendation, viz., in the case where at the time when a repurchase falls due in the fourth or fifth year following a compensatory drawing there is a shortfall in export receipts beyond the control of the affected country. The repurchase would restore the compensatory financing facility *pro tanto*, and if at that time an export shortfall of the type described persisted, the member would be in a position to apply for a new drawing under this facility. Moreover, when a repurchase obligation contributes to a member's temporary balance of payments difficulties, it would be possible for the Fund, in appropriate circumstances, to agree to an ordinary drawing at the time of the compensatory repurchase.

It should also be noted that the case envisaged in the UNCTAD Recommendation could only arise if the member had no export excesses in the years following the drawing and had to repurchase during the fourth and fifth years (under the three-to-five-year rule). If the member experienced export excesses prior to the time it must repurchase under the three-to-five-year rule, it would, by making the recommended repurchases, fully or partly restore its access to the Fund's resources under the compensatory facility. The consideration developed in the portion of the UNCTAD Recommendation quoted above arises, therefore, only under circumstances where shortfalls persist for at least four years in a row or where a shortfall is followed by three years without export excesses and then by other shortfalls. Where such circumstances occur there may be need for basic and long-run measures to restore the exporting power of the country or to ensure satisfactory growth of the market value of its exports. Such measures fall, however, outside the scope of the compensatory financing facility of the Fund.

10. *Changes in the Compensatory Facility and Fund Liquidity*

It may be appropriate, at this point, to estimate the possible charge on Fund liquidity that might result from additional drawings with the adoption of the two principal measures suggested above, viz., (1) the extension of the limit from 25 per cent to 50 per cent with the qualification that the increase in outstanding drawings in any year should not exceed 25 per cent, and (2) the adoption of the system of repurchase discussed above. For the purpose of these calculations it has been assumed that drawing members always follow the recommendation on compensatory repurchases; to the extent that they do not, the charge on Fund liquidity under the new system will tend to be higher than is indicated in the calculation given below. Some additional claims on Fund resources might also arise from the proposed separation of the compensatory facility from the other drawing facilities of the Fund, but this cannot be quantified and is unlikely to be large.

As can be seen from Table 4, if the compensatory facility had existed over the period 1951–64, and if all the 48 countries covered by the table had made full use of the facility, the transition from fixed-term repurchase with a 25 per cent of quota limit to the repurchase system described above with a qualified 50 per cent of quota limit would have involved an increase in the average level of compensatory drawings outstanding over the period from $290 million to $320 million, i.e., an increase of $30 million. From the standpoint of Fund liquidity, however, what matters is not so much the average amount of compensatory drawings outstanding as the amount liable to be outstanding at peak periods. It is estimated that, on the assumption set forth above, the maximum level of compensatory drawings outstanding would likewise have risen from $400 million to $470 million, i.e., by $70 million. On the assumption that peak-year potential compensatory drawings outstanding have expanded since 1955–58 in proportion to quotas, the change in the limit and the variation that would result from the recommended repurchases out of export excesses might, under present conditions, raise maximum potential compensatory drawings from $1,100 million to $1,300 million, i.e., by $200 million. Since, however, countries with adequate reserves will often not use opportunities for compensatory drawings that are open to them, and since any use made of the compensatory facility is likely to reduce to some extent requests for ordinary drawings, it seems unlikely that the increase in peak-year drawings occasioned by the proposed changes would in practice exceed half the amount mentioned above, viz., $100 million.

IV. CONCLUSIONS FOR ACTION

More than three years have now elapsed since the creation of the compensatory financing facility, and though it has not yet been extensively used the Fund has had sufficient experience with it to review and reappraise its application and scope. As a result it has been deemed desirable both to clarify the circumstances under which the facility can be used and to introduce into it certain modifications designed to increase the effectiveness of the assistance which the Fund provides to members.

In determining the medium-term export trend for the purpose of calculating the export shortfall the practice hitherto has been to give approximately equal weight to statistical and qualitative estimates. Experience suggests that qualitative estimates based on commodity analysis give a closer estimate of the trend; consequently qualitative estimates will receive a greater weight in the future.

At present, the Fund is prepared to waive the requirement that the Fund's holdings of a member's currency may not exceed 200 per cent of quota either to accommodate compensatory drawings or, to the extent that compensatory drawings are outstanding, to accommodate other drawings. However, drawings under the compensatory facility are included in Fund holdings of the member's currency in applying the tranche policies of the Fund to subsequent drawings. Full recognition of the special circumstances which give rise to compensatory drawings make it desirable to separate this facility from normal drawing facilities of the Fund so that compensatory drawings outstanding will not in any way affect the tranche policies applicable to other drawings.

While the use of the compensatory facility is most needed when a shortfall appears, members may be deterred from requesting use of the facility at that time since the full amount of the shortfall can be known only after the interval of several months. To meet this problem, members may request a compensatory drawing before a period of twelve months has elapsed since the last such drawing (or since an ordinary drawing which has been made entirely or partly in view of an export shortfall). The shortfall calculated at the time of the second drawing will be adjusted by a prorated amount of the earlier drawing. Moreover, a member may within six months of an ordinary drawing reclassify all or part of it as a compensatory drawing and thus restore to that extent its normal drawing rights for future contingencies.

Under the 1963 Decision, outstanding drawings under the compensatory facility are limited normally to 25 per cent of quota. It is believed that an extension of the limit on outstanding drawings from 25 to 50 per cent of quota would add substantially to the value of the assistance provided. At the same time it is important to avoid such changes as would tend to weaken the ability of the Fund to exert its influence with members toward early adoption of sound corrective policies. The new Decision provides, therefore, that compensatory drawings outstanding may amount to a maximum of 50 per cent of quota, but that, except in the case of shortfalls resulting from disasters and major emergencies, the amount of such drawings outstanding may not increase by a net amount of more than 25 per cent of quota during any twelve-month period and that requests which would increase outstanding compensatory drawings beyond 25 per cent of quota will be met only if the Fund is satisfied that the member has been cooperating with the Fund in an effort to find, where required, appropriate solutions for its balance of payments difficulties.

The question of repurchases of compensatory drawings has also been reconsidered in light of the possibility that the course of export receipts may make it undesirable for members to concentrate repurchases within three to five years after the drawings. On the other hand, repurchase terms can not be so changed as to undermine the revolving nature of Fund resources. Balancing these considerations, the repurchase system of the Decision of February 13, 1952 is to be maintained, but in addition the Fund recommends that, as soon as possible after the end of each of the four years following such a drawing, the member use in repurchase an amount approximately equal to one half of any excess of exports over the medium-term trend value of exports.

V. DECISION [19]

In the light of the considerations set forth in the foregoing sections of this report, Executive Board Decision No. 1477-(63/8) of February 27, 1963, on Compensatory Financing of Export Fluctuations is hereby amended by the deletion of paragraphs (5) through (8) and the substitution of the following paragraphs:

(5) The Fund has reviewed its policies to determine how it could more readily assist members, particularly primary exporters, encountering payments difficulties produced by temporary export shortfalls, and has decided that such members can expect that their request for drawings will be met where the Fund is satisfied that

(a) the shortfall is of a short-term character and is largely attributable to circumstances beyond the control of the member; and

(b) the member will cooperate with the Fund in an effort to find, where required, appropriate solutions for its balance of payments difficulties.

Drawings outstanding under this paragraph (5) may amount to 50 per cent of the

---

[19] See above, pp. 238–40, for the text of the Decision on Compensatory Financing of Export Fluctuations, adopted February 27, 1963.

member's quota provided that (i) except in the case of shortfalls resulting from disasters or major emergencies, such drawings will not be increased by a net amount of more than 25 per cent of the member's quota in any 12-month period, and (ii) requests for drawings which would increase the drawings outstanding under this paragraph (5) beyond 25 per cent of the member's quota will be met only if the Fund is satisfied that the member has been cooperating with the Fund in an effort to find, where required, appropriate solutions for its balance of payments difficulties.

The existence and amount of an export shortfall for the purpose of any drawing under this paragraph (5) shall be determined with respect to the latest 12-month period preceding the drawing request for which the Fund has sufficient statistical data, and any excess of a shortfall over the drawing made under this paragraph (5) in respect to that shortfall cannot be carried forward and covered by a later drawing under this paragraph (5).

(6) In order to identify more clearly what are to be regarded as export shortfalls of a short-term character, the Fund, in conjunction with the member concerned, will seek to establish reasonable estimates regarding the medium-term trend of the member's exports based partly on statistical calculation and partly on appraisal of export prospects.

(7) A member requesting a drawing under paragraph (5) will be expected to represent that it will make a repurchase corresponding to the drawing in accordance with the principles of E.B. Decision No. 102-(52/11) of February 13, 1952, as renewed by E.B. Decision No. 270-(53/95) of December 23, 1953. With a view to an application of these principles appropriate to drawings under paragraph (5), the Fund recommends that, as soon as possible after the end of each of the four years following a drawing under paragraph (5), the member repurchase an amount of the Fund's holdings of the member's currency approximately equal to one half of the amount by which the member's exports exceed the medium-term trend of its exports. Calculations of export excesses for this purpose will be made with respect to successive 12-month periods following the period of the shortfall with respect to which the drawing was made and on the basis of statistical information only.

(8) Whenever the Fund's holdings of a member's currency resulting from an outstanding compensatory drawing under paragraph (5) are reduced, by the member's repurchase or otherwise, this will restore *pro tanto* the member's facility to make a further compensatory drawing under that paragraph, should the need arise.

(9) When drawings are made under paragraph (5), the Fund will so indicate in an appropriate manner. Within six months from the date of any drawing which is not under paragraph (5) and to the extent that it is still outstanding, a member may request that all or part of the drawing be reclassified and treated, for all purposes of this decision, as a drawing made under paragraph (5). The Fund will agree to such a request if at the time of the request the member meets the requirements for a drawing of an equal amount under paragraph (5).

(10) In order to implement the Fund's policies in connection with compensatory financing of export shortfalls, the Fund will be prepared to waive the limit on Fund holdings of 200 per cent of quota, where appropriate. In particular, the Fund will be prepared to waive this limit (i) where a waiver is necessary to permit compensatory drawings to be made under paragraphs (4) and (5) above, or (ii) to the extent that drawings in accordance with paragraph (5) are still outstanding.

Moreover, the Fund will apply its tranche policies to drawing requests by a member as if the Fund's holdings of the member's currency were less than its actual holdings of that currency by the amount of any drawings outstanding under paragraph (5).

(11) The provision of credit to deal with the balance of payments effects of export fluctuations provides immediate relief for a country's short-term difficulties. In many cases, however, it will also be necessary to introduce measures of a policy character in order to attain a satisfactory and lasting solution to a country's balance of payments problems. Members generally have actively cooperated with the Fund to find and adopt the measures necessary to this end. Beyond immediate balance of payments difficulties, the primary exporting countries are, in many instances, facing unfavorable long-term export trends, and all are trying to meet the challenge of achieving more rapid and sustained development through a strengthening and broadening of their economies. The last-mentioned problem will require action in many fields and over many years by both the primary exporting countries and the industrial countries, separately and in concert, including readier access to the markets of the developed countries for the products of the developing countries and an appropriate and sustained flow of technical and financial assistance to the developing countries. The Fund considers that its activities can provide valuable assistance in helping to establish a climate within which longer-term measures can be more effectively pursued.

(12) The Fund will review this decision in the light of experience and developing circumstances.

APPENDIX I

United Nations Conference on Trade and Development
Final Act and Report
Annex A.IV.17

STUDY OF MEASURES RELATED TO THE COMPENSATORY CREDIT SYSTEM OF THE INTERNATIONAL MONETARY FUND

The Conference,

Considering that the compensatory credit system put into operation by the International Monetary Fund since February 1963 constitutes a definite step towards the solution of short-term financing problems,

Considering that, in view of the short-term needs of developing countries derived from fluctuations in their export receipts, this system should be reviewed,

1. *Recommends* that Governments members of the International Monetary Fund study the following measures:

(1) To increase, as soon as possible, the amount allocated by the Fund to compensatory financing, over and above its current transactions, from 25 per cent to 50 per cent of a member country's quota;

(2) To place compensatory credits entirely outside the structure of the gold and successive credit tranches, so that the drawing of compensatory credits would not directly or indirectly prejudice a member's ability to make an ordinary drawing;

(3) To explore ways to secure possible refinancing of compensatory financing obligations of the developing countries in the event of a persistent shortfall in export receipts beyond the control of the country affected.

2. *Requests* that the International Monetary Fund, in its determination of the shortfall in export receipts, consider giving greater weight to the actual experience of the three preceding years.

Appendix II

EXCERPTS FROM SPEECHES OF GOVERNORS AT THE 1965 ANNUAL MEETING

AFGHANISTAN

The recent fall in basic commodity prices and difficulties in marketing total available food supplies will necessitate compensatory financing in the coming months. To meet these needs, the facilities of the Fund need improvement.

ARGENTINA (On behalf of 19 Latin American countries and the Philippines)

We should like once more to reiterate our opinion regarding the decision adopted in 1963 by the Executive Board of the Fund on the compensatory financing of losses in the export proceeds of primary-producing countries. We recognize that this represents a contribution toward the partial solution of this very important problem. However, it would be advisable to consider three fundamental aspects:

(1) The need for considering the compensatory tranche in addition to the normal credit facilities of the Monetary Fund. The decision of February 1963, indeed, permits the drawing without taking into consideration the position of the requesting country with regard to the credit tranches. Nevertheless, the drawing has been added to those already made and thus may affect the country's position in respect of future transactions with the Fund. In our opinion it is of the greatest importance that the compensatory drawing be allotted quite separately from the others and invested with the supplementary nature that the different schemes favored by our countries have always upheld.

(2) The amount available under this type of loan, limited to 25 per cent of each member's quota, is of insufficient size even in the case of very moderate depressions. If this ceiling were raised from 25 to 50 per cent, more significant resources would be made available to the countries exporting primary products, without this entailing a very heavy burden on the resources of the institution.

(3) In conclusion, we would emphasize the non-automatic nature of the drawings permitted. In the decisions on individual cases submitted to the consideration of the Executive Board there has been some flexibility, although in all of them there has been no lack of a subjective assessment in the determination both of the amount to be compensated and of the circumstances in which the loss of income occurs.

CEYLON

I was encouraged by the reference by Mr. Schweitzer to the work that the Fund is now undertaking to improve the compensatory financing facility. Several speakers have urged that compensatory assistance should be provided for a decline in the terms of trade rather than for a fall in export earnings alone. My own country's experience in recent years vividly illustrates the importance of this reform. We suffered a decline in the terms of trade by 13 per cent in two years alone, but since this was almost entirely due to an increase in import prices we were unable to avail ourselves of the compensatory financing facility. I do sincerely hope that this particular improvement in the scheme will be made effective at an early date.

CHINA

However, the scanty application that developing countries have made of the compensatory financing facility of the Fund would seem to indicate that the economic problems of developing countries cannot readily be solved through temporary accessibility to credit.

GREECE

. . . improved facilities for compensatory financing and more flexible conditions for drawings and repurchases should also be envisaged to provide for a direct contribution to the liquidity position of the developing countries.

IRAQ

May I point out in this connection that the compensatory financing scheme of the Fund, though admirable in itself, suffers from one drawback. The borrowing facility under this scheme is available to primary producing countries when the shortfall in their exports is due to factors beyond their control. Since the decline in exports in such cases would be temporary and self-correcting, the Fund should not make the facility conditional on the pursuit by the country concerned of particular policies about its general balance of payments position.

SUDAN

Appreciative as we are of the Fund's efforts in this respect, we strongly feel that the terms and conditions under which the Fund provides such compensatory assistance (and, indeed, any other assistance) should be reconsidered with the view of softening them. It is no secret that a very limited number of members have so far made use of these arrangements, in spite of the pressing need of many for such assistance.

UGANDA

While the Fund's operations are properly concerned with short-term balance of payments aspects, it may not be possible under conditions of fluctuating export earnings to differentiate between the short- and the long-term aspects. Such conditions tend to make public debt burdens unduly onerous on developing countries which base the servicing of their public debt burden on the expectation of a steady and reasonable growth in export earnings. It is therefore important in my view that both the Bank and the Fund should continue their efforts to find solutions to these problems. The Fund, on the one hand, should review the present compensatory financing arrangements to take account of the problems of fluctuating export earnings. The Bank, on the other hand, should continue to play a prominent role in evolving price stabilization machinery for primary products in association with UNCTAD.

UNITED ARAB REPUBLIC

Thus, the compensatory financing facility could be increased from one tranche to two tranches and the criteria for using this facility could be improved to take into account results to date and discussions in UNCTAD.

VIET-NAM

In particular, the nonliberal trade policy adopted by developed countries has obstructed the entry into these countries of primary manufactured products from the underdeveloped countries. To be sure, the action of the Bank and Fund in the form of compensatory financing granted to countries exporting primary products or in the form of assistance for the development and expansion of trade has been highly effective. However, the action necessary for the removal of discriminatory trade practices or other obstacles to the development of international trade should be hastened. This action should be supplemented by a complete revision of the present system of international payments. We also have high hopes that with the general increase in Fund quotas, the Fund will be able not only to grant compensatory financing facilities on a broader basis, for example, by increasing the percentage of this financing, but also to consider ways to aid countries which have experienced a temporary export shortfall as a result of crop losses caused by war, floods, or other natural calamities.

APPENDIX III

DECISIONS ON COMPENSATORY FINANCING OF EXPORT FLUCTUATIONS

[As the two Decisions on Compensatory Financing are reproduced elsewhere in this volume, they have been omitted here. For the text of the original Decision (No. 1477-(63/8), February 27, 1963), see above, pp. 238–40; for the text of the 1966 Amendment (Decision No. 2192-(66/81), September 20, 1966), see above, pp. 492–94.]

Proposed Amendment of the Articles of Agreement

On April 17, 1968, the Executive Directors submitted to the Governors detailed proposals for amendments to the Articles of Agreement of the Fund. These proposals provided for a Facility Based on Special Drawing Rights in the Fund, and for some other changes in the Articles by which, inter alia, gold tranche drawings will become legally automatic, the provisions for repurchases will be substantially altered, and certain revisions will be made in voting requirements.

The proposals were approved by the Governors on May 31, 1968, and entered into force on July 28, 1969, having been accepted by 60 per cent of the members and by members having 80 per cent of the total votes.

Establishment of a Facility Based on Special Drawing Rights in the International Monetary Fund and Modifications in the Rules and Practices of the Fund
(April 1968)

A Report by the Executive Directors to the
Board of Governors Proposing Amendment of
the Articles of Agreement

TABLE OF CONTENTS

	PAGE
Introduction	499

PART I

The New Facility	501
1. General Comments	501
2. The Special Drawing Account	501
3. Participation in the Special Drawing Account	501
4. Holders of Special Drawing Rights Other than Participants	502
5. Recording and Information	503
6. Principles Governing Allocations and Cancellations	503
7. First Decision to Allocate Special Drawing Rights	503
8. Allocation and Cancellation	504
9. Decisions on Allocations and Cancellations	504
10. Operations and Transactions in Special Drawing Rights	504
11. Receipt of Allocations	505
12. Character of Special Drawing Rights	505
13. Designation of Participants to Provide Currency	505
14. Transactions not Requiring Designation	506
15. Requirement of Need	507

16. Transactions without Requirement of Need	507
17. Reconstitution	508
18. Operations and Transactions through the General Account	508
19. Exchange Rates	508
20. Interest and Charges	509
21. Expenses of the Special Drawing Account	509
22. Administration of the Special Drawing Account	509
23. Suspension of Participants' Use of Special Drawing Rights	510
24. Definition of Currency Convertible in Fact for Transactions in Special Drawing Rights	510
25. Definition of Reserve Position in the Fund	510
26. Termination of Participation	511
27. Liquidation	511

PART II

Modifications in Rules and Practices of the Fund	511
28. General Comments	511
29. Quota Changes and Related Matters	512
30. Uniform Proportionate Changes in Par Values and Maintenance of Gold Value	513
31. Temporary Character of Use of the Fund's Resources	513
32. Legal Automaticity of Gold Tranche Purchases	513
33. Definition of Gold Tranche Purchases	514
34. Termination of Power to Establish New Unconditional Facilities in the General Account	515
35. Rules on Repurchase	515
36. Service Charge	517
37. Remuneration	517
38. Distribution of Net Income	517
39. Interpretation	518

PART III

Procedure	518
40. Applicable Legal Provisions	518
41. Resolution of Board of Governors	519
42. Acceptance of Proposed Amendment by Members	519
43. Entry into Force of Proposed Amendment	519
44. Notification to Depositary of Articles of Agreement	520

ANNEX A

Resolution	520

PROPOSED AMENDMENT TO THE ARTICLES OF AGREEMENT OF THE INTERNATIONAL MONETARY FUND, PREPARED PURSUANT TO BOARD OF GOVERNORS RESOLUTION No. 22–8

A.	Introductory Article		521
B.	Article	I. Purposes	521
C.	Article	III. Quotas and Subscriptions	521
D.	Article	IV. Par Values of Currencies	522
E.	Article	V. Transactions with the Fund	522
F.	Article	VI. Capital Transfers	523
G.	Article	XII. Organization and Management	523
H.	Article	XVIII. Interpretation	524
I.	Article	XIX. Explanation of Terms	524

J.	Article	XX.	Final Provisions 525
K.	Articles XXI through XXXII 525
	Article	XXI.	Special Drawing Rights 525
	Article	XXII.	General Account and Special Drawing Account 525
	Article	XXIII.	Participants and Other Holders of Special Drawing Rights 525
	Article	XXIV.	Allocation and Cancellation of Special Drawing Rights 526
	Article	XXV.	Operations and Transactions in Special Drawing Rights 527
	Article	XXVI.	Special Drawing Account Interest and Charges 530
	Article	XXVII.	Administration of the General Account and the Special Drawing Account 530
	Article	XXVIII.	General Obligations of Participants 531
	Article	XXIX.	Suspension of Transactions in Special Drawing Rights 531
	Article	XXX.	Termination of Participation 532
	Article	XXXI.	Liquidation of the Special Drawing Account 533
	Article	XXXII.	Explanation of Terms with respect to Special Drawing Rights ... 534
L.	Schedule B. Provisions with respect to Repurchase by a Member of its Currency Held by the Fund 534
M.	Schedules F through I 535
	Schedule F. Designation 535
	Schedule G. Reconstitution 535
	Schedule H. Termination of Participation 536
	Schedule I. Administration of Liquidation of the Special Drawing Account 537

ANNEX B

Outline of a Facility Based on Special Drawing Rights in the Fund 538
    Introduction 538
    I. Establishment of a Special Drawing Account in the Fund 538
    II. Participants and Other Holders 538
    III. Allocation of Special Drawing Rights 538
    IV. Cancellation of Special Drawing Rights 539
    V. Use of Special Drawing Rights 539
    VI. Interest and Maintenance of Gold Value 540
    VII. Functions of Fund Organs and Voting 541
    VIII. General Provisions 541
    IX. Entry into Force 541

INTRODUCTION

At its Twenty-Second Annual Meeting at Rio de Janeiro in September 1967, the Board of Governors adopted the following Resolution:

WHEREAS the functioning of the international monetary system and its improvement, including arrangements to meet the need, as and when it arises, for a supplement to existing reserve assets, have been the subject of extensive study and international discussion resulting in the Outline of a Facility Based on Special Drawing Rights in the International Monetary Fund, which Outline is attached to this Resolution; and

WHEREAS studies are currently under way on possible improvements in the present rules and practices of the Fund;

NOW, THEREFORE, the Board of Governors hereby RESOLVES:

That the Executive Directors are requested to

    1. Proceed with their work relating to both

(a) the establishment in the Fund of a new facility on the basis of the Outline in order to meet the need, as and when it arises, for a supplement to existing reserve assets, and

(b) improvements in the present rules and practices of the Fund based on developments in world economic conditions and the experience of the Fund since the adoption of the Articles of Agreement of the Fund; and

2. Submit to the Board of Governors as soon as possible but not later than March 31, 1968

  (a) a report proposing amendments to the Articles of Agreement and the By-Laws for the purpose of establishing a new facility on the basis of the Outline, and

  (b) a report proposing such amendments to the Articles of Agreement and the By-Laws as would be required to give effect to those modifications in the present rules and practices of the Fund that the Executive Directors will recommend.

As the Governors have been informed, it was not possible to complete by March 31, 1968 the work on the two subjects referred to in paragraph 1 of this Resolution. The Executive Directors are now submitting to the Board of Governors the present Report which combines the two reports envisaged in paragraph 2 of the Resolution. Part I constitutes the first and Part II the second of these two reports. The recommendations of the Executive Directors are presented together in Annex A to this Report.

Annex A submits for approval by the Board of Governors a Resolution proposing modifications in the Articles of Agreement of the International Monetary Fund for the purpose of (a) establishing in the Fund a facility for special drawing rights based on the Outline, and (b) giving effect to certain changes in the present rules and practices of the Fund that the Executive Directors have decided to recommend. They are not recommending modifications in the By-Laws at this time. It would not be possible for the Board of Governors to adopt By-Laws relating to the new facility until the participation requirement prescribed in Article XXIII, Section 1, has been met. Recommendations will be submitted in due course.

The modifications in the Articles of Agreement under both (a) and (b) above are set forth in the Proposed Amendment which appears in the attachment to the Resolution. The Executive Directors recommend to the Board of Governors the adoption of this Resolution.

The Outline referred to above is also annexed to this Report (Annex B).

While the modifications set forth in Annex A are for the most part self-explanatory, the Executive Directors believe that brief comments on various aspects of these modifications may be useful to Governors and to member governments. They are to be found in Parts I and II of the Report.

In addition, Part III of the Report describes the procedure to be followed in order to give effect to the proposed modifications.

The Executive Directors wish to take this opportunity to express their great appreciation of the outstanding contribution made by the Staff of the Fund at all levels in the implementation of the Governors' Resolution. Working under intense pressure, sustained for more than six months, they have at all times given the Executive Directors the benefit of their skill and experience.

PART I

The New Facility

1. *General Comments*

The Resolution adopted by the Board of Governors at its Rio de Janeiro Meeting envisaged the establishment in the Fund of a new facility based on special drawing rights to meet the need, as and when it arises, for a supplement to existing reserve assets. The changes in the Introductory Article and the addition of Articles XXI through XXXII and Schedules F, G, H, and I, which are included in the Proposed Amendment, will achieve this purpose, and under them the Fund will acquire an important new function in the international monetary system. The new provisions also deal with the relationship of the new facility to the present functions of the Fund. However, the provisions of the Articles of Agreement, as amended, will constitute a single legal document.

As requested by the Rio de Janeiro Resolution, the Executive Directors, in drafting the modifications in the Articles of Agreement that would establish the new facility, have worked on the basis of the Outline attached to that Resolution. The Outline sets forth the main features of the new facility and several of its more detailed characteristics. It was, however, intentionally less than a complete plan of the facility, and the Executive Directors have had to elaborate certain aspects of the facility that were treated in the Outline only in a very general way. This applied, for example, to the establishment of the General and the Special Drawing Accounts, the terms on which the General Account may hold and use special drawing rights, the provision relating to "other holders," the cancellation of special drawing rights, the payment of interest, the levying of charges, withdrawal from the facility, and its liquidation. It was also necessary to provide in detail for the effects on the organizational structure of the Fund that follow from the fact that, while all members are entitled to become participants in the new facility, they are not required to participate. However, it has not been felt necessary to include in the Proposed Amendment a provision corresponding to Paragraph III. 3 (d) of the Outline under which the Executive Directors are to review the operations of the Special Drawing Account and the adequacy of global reserves as part of their Annual Report to the Board of Governors. On the analogy of Article XII, Section 7, and Section 10 of the By-Laws, this requirement will be included in the By-Laws.

2. *The Special Drawing Account*

Under the Articles of Agreement as amended, there will be maintained in the Fund two separate Accounts, a General Account and a Special Drawing Account. The Fund will carry on its present operations and transactions, including those of an administrative character, through the General Account, and its functions relating to special drawing rights through the Special Drawing Account. There will be a corresponding separation of assets and property as well as liabilities and obligations.

Operations and transactions involving the acceptance or holding of special drawing rights by the Fund in the General Account or the use of special drawing rights thus held will be carried out through and recorded in both Accounts.

The separation of the two Accounts does not create a new legal entity. The Fund will continue to be the same institution with a single international personality.

3. *Participation in the Special Drawing Account*

Participation in the Special Drawing Account will be open to members of the Fund and only to them. Each member of the Fund will continue to be entitled to take part in

General Account operations and transactions, but in order to become a participant in the Special Drawing Account a member will have to deposit with the Fund an instrument setting forth that it undertakes all the obligations of a participant in the Special Drawing Account in accordance with its law and that it has taken all steps necessary to enable it to carry out all these obligations. No member will become a participant, however, before these instruments have been deposited by members that have at least 75 per cent of the total quotas in the Fund.

Participation in the Special Drawing Account will involve the assumption of both financial and nonfinancial obligations. The basic financial obligation that each participant will assume will be the obligation under Article XXV, Section 4, to provide currency convertible in fact, when the participant is designated by the Fund, to another participant using its special drawing rights, up to a total net amount equivalent to twice the net amount of special drawing rights allocated to the designated participant. The participant providing currency will receive an equivalent amount of special drawing rights. The circumstances in which a participant will be designated to provide currency are set forth in Article XXV, Section 5, and Schedule F.

A participant whose Governor did not vote in favor of a decision under which allocations of special drawing rights are being made will not have to receive allocations under that decision if it does not wish to do so. A participant will be required to receive special drawing rights allocated to it if its Governor voted in favor of the decision under which the allocations are made. Accordingly, a participant that wishes to receive special drawing rights to be allocated to it under a decision and that needs parliamentary or other legal authorization in order to be able to meet the financial obligation assumed under Article XXV, Section 4, should obtain, prior to the adoption of the relevant decision to make allocations, the necessary authorization.

The domestic legal steps that each member will need to take in order to enable it to carry out the obligations of a participant, both financial and nonfinancial, will have to be determined by the authorities of the member in accordance with its own constitutional and other legal requirements. One way in which a member will be able to put itself into a position to meet its obligations under Article XXV, Section 4, to provide currency will be to give its central bank the power to acquire and hold special drawing rights without limitation, thus obviating any need for further legal action from time to time. Central banks in many countries already have authority to acquire gold and some or all forms of foreign exchange.

An alternative course would be for a member to seek parliamentary or other legal authority, as may be necessary, for a specified amount, e.g., authority to receive allocations equal to not less than 50 per cent of quota with the consequent obligation to provide currency up to a total net amount at least equal to its quota.

4. *Holders of Special Drawing Rights Other than Participants*

Allocations of special drawing rights may be made only to participants, but the holding of such rights is not restricted to participants. Article XXIII, Section 2, authorizes the Fund itself to accept and hold special drawing rights in, and use them through, the General Account. Detailed provisions with respect to these operations and transactions are contained in Article XXV, Section 7.

Section 3 of Article XXIII foresees the possibility that the Fund may permit others to accept, hold, and use special drawing rights. Under this provision the Fund, by an 85 per cent majority of the total voting power, will be able to permit nonmembers and members that are not participants to engage in operations and transactions involving special drawing rights. Other holders that the Fund could authorize to engage in these operations and transactions would be institutions that perform one or more functions of a central bank for more than one member. Regional organizations in which members or their central banks pool some of their reserves and the Bank for International Settlements are considered to fall within this description. The expression "operations and transactions" in Article XXIII, Section 3, will cover the operations and transactions of a central banking character engaged in by the organizations referred to in this section.

The Fund has the power to prescribe, by an 85 per cent majority, the terms and conditions for the operations and transactions between participants and these other holders, but these terms and conditions must be consistent with the provisions of the Articles. In exercising this power the Fund will necessarily be guided by the nature of special drawing rights as a supplement to existing reserve assets and by the desirability of ensuring their proper use. Under this power the Fund will be able to prescribe, where it is found appropriate, that operations and transactions between participants and other holders will be subject to the requirement of need which is discussed in section 15 below. It is expected that normally the requirement of need will be prescribed as part of the terms and conditions for transactions in which participants use special drawing rights to obtain currency from other holders.

5. *Recording and Information*

Article XXII, Section 3, provides that all changes in holdings of special drawing rights, whether the result of allocations and cancellations or of operations and transactions, will become effective only when recorded by the Fund in the Special Drawing Account. This will apply not only to operations and transactions between participants but also to operations and transactions between other holders and participants. The Fund will record changes resulting from operations and transactions that are in conformity with the obligations of participants under the provisions of the Articles or any terms and conditions prescribed by the Fund under these provisions. To enable the Fund to carry out this task, participants are required to inform the Fund of any operation or transaction involving special drawing rights that they enter into and to indicate at the same time the provisions of the Articles under which the operation or transaction is entered into. The obligation falls on both parties to the operation or transaction if they are participants. It is expected that a similar requirement will be included in the terms and conditions for other holders.

6. *Principles Governing Allocations and Cancellations*

Article XXIV, Section 1 (a), states the basic principle which is to govern all decisions to allocate or cancel special drawing rights. This principle is that the Fund must seek to meet the long-term global need, as and when it arises, to supplement existing reserve assets, in a manner that will promote the attainment of the Fund's purposes as set forth in Article I, and will avoid economic stagnation and deflation as well as excess demand and inflation in the world.

7. *First Decision to Allocate Special Drawing Rights*

Article XXIV, Section 1 (b), provides that the first decision to allocate special drawing rights shall be based on the principles that guide all decisions to allocate special drawing rights, and in addition, that it shall take into account certain special considerations. The first of these special considerations is a collective judgment that there is a global need to supplement reserves. The term "collective judgment" reflects the requirement of an 85 per cent majority of the total voting power for the adoption by the Board of Governors of decisions to allocate special drawing rights. The other special considerations are the attainment of a better balance of payments equilibrium and the likelihood of a better working of the adjustment process in the future. While the situation of all members is relevant to a judgment with respect to the attainment of a better balance of payments equilibrium, the judgment to be made at the time will necessarily be influenced predominantly by the situation of members that have a large share in world trade and payments.

8. *Allocation and Cancellation*

Special drawing rights will be allocated or cancelled over periods, referred to in the Articles as "basic" periods, which normally will be five years in duration and which will run consecutively. Allocations to participants will be made at yearly intervals and on the basis of their quotas on the date of the relevant decision to allocate, unless the Fund decides that allocations are to be made at different intervals or are to be based on quotas at different dates.

The concept of consecutive basic periods has been introduced for technical reasons and does not prejudice the exercise by the Fund of its discretion to allocate special drawing rights, or to cancel special drawing rights, or to do neither. The Fund will exercise its discretion on the basis of the judgment it forms on the need to supplement existing reserve assets. It will be possible to have basic periods in which there are neither allocations nor cancellations. A basic period can be an "empty period," either because the Governors have approved a proposal by the Managing Director that no allocation or cancellation should be made, or because the Managing Director, having ascertained that there is no broad support for a proposal that would be consistent with the requirements of the Articles, has been unable to make a proposal, or because a proposal by the Managing Director to allocate or to cancel has failed to command the required majority.

A member that becomes a participant after a basic period has started will not receive allocations during that basic period, unless the Fund decides that the member will start to receive allocations beginning with the next allocation after it becomes a participant. It is expected that normally the Fund will so decide.

9. *Decisions on Allocations and Cancellations*

Under Article XXIV, Section 4 (a), and Article XXVII (a) (i), decisions to allocate or cancel special drawing rights may be made only by the Board of Governors and only by an 85 per cent majority of the total voting power. These decisions may be made by the Governors only on the basis of proposals of the Managing Director concurred in by a decision of the Executive Directors.

The Managing Director is required to make proposals at certain times and in certain circumstances. Whenever he is required to make proposals but he reaches a conclusion that there is no proposal that would be consistent with the principles and considerations governing allocation and cancellation that would have broad support among participants, he must submit a report to both the Board of Governors and the Executive Directors.

10. *Operations and Transactions in Special Drawing Rights*

As stated in Article XXV, Section 1, special drawing rights may be used only in the operations and transactions authorized by or under the provisions of the Articles.

The term "transactions," as used in Articles XXI through XXXII, refers to uses of special drawing rights to obtain currency. The main examples are transactions under Article XXV, Section 2. The term "operations" refers to all other uses of special drawing rights authorized by or under the Articles, such as the payment of interest, charges, and assessments under Article XXVI.

11. *Receipt of Allocations*

Article XXIV, Section 2 (e), requires each member that has become a participant to accept an allocation of special drawing rights unless its Governor voted against or did not vote on the decision under which the allocation is to be made and, prior to the first allocation under that decision, the participant has given the Fund notice that it does not wish to receive the allocation. In other words, a participant whose Governor did not vote affirmatively may "opt out" of allocations under a decision (i.e., may choose not to receive special drawing rights and incur the corresponding obligations) by giving notice to that effect.

A participant that has opted out with respect to a basic period may "opt back in" (i.e., resume receiving allocations) with the permission of the Fund, but the participant will receive only the allocations made after it has been permitted to opt back in. Opting back in is not possible with respect to allocations that were made previously during the basic period. It is expected that the Fund will give sympathetic consideration to a request by a participant to opt back in.

12. *Character of Special Drawing Rights*

Special drawing rights will be issued by the Fund but they will not confer on participants a claim against the Fund itself to provide currency, except as prescribed by provisions of Articles XXX and XXXI and Schedules G and H relating to the termination of participation and liquidation. Participants will be able to use special drawing rights to obtain currency from other participants in accordance with the provisions of Article XXV. The provisions of Article XXV require the Fund to designate participants to provide currency to other participants using their special drawing rights in accordance with Section 2 (a) of that Article, so that participants can be assured that at all times they will be able to use their special drawing rights in a manner consistent with the provisions of the Articles.

13. *Designation of Participants to Provide Currency*

The principles that will govern the designation of participants to provide currency to other participants using their special drawing rights in accordance with Article XXV, Section 2 (a), are indicated in the three subsections of Section 5 (a) of the same Article. However, this listing is not exhaustive; the Fund may supplement these principles with other principles.

As regards the order of priority between designations under subsections (a) (i) and (a) (ii) of Section 5 and among the three categories mentioned in subsection (a) (ii), subsection (a) (iii) prescribes that priority shall normally be given to those participants that need to acquire special drawing rights to meet the objectives of designation under subsection (a) (ii). Thus, it may be assumed that, as a general rule, the Fund will designate participants under subsection (a) (ii) if there are participants that need special drawing rights in order to comply with the reconstitution requirements of Schedule G, to reduce a negative balance (i.e., the amount of special drawing rights that the participant owes the Fund because, at the time of a cancellation, it did not hold an amount of rights equivalent to its share of the cancellation), or to offset the effect of a failure to fulfill the expectation referred to in Article XXV, Section 3 (a), on the requirement of need for the use of special drawing rights.

The Outline contained two possible criteria to guide designation among participants with a sufficiently strong balance of payments and reserve position: (i) the ratios of these participants' holdings of special drawing rights to their gross reserves, and (ii) the ratios of such holdings in excess of net cumulative allocations to gross reserves.

The Executive Directors have examined the relative merits of these two criteria. The excess holdings criterion is expected, on balance, to offer significant advantages in its application and to give the new facility a broad basis for designation consistent with the universal approach of the scheme, thereby contributing to the confidence of participants in the new instrument of special drawing rights. At the same time the Executive Directors considered a certain flexibility to be desirable for the future, and they have therefore provided in Article XXV, Section 5 (c), for a review of the rules for designation before the end of each basic period, in order to enable the Fund to adopt new rules if it deems this to be desirable. The Executive Directors have also considered that the results of a system of designation will depend not only on the choice of a criterion to determine the target distribution of holdings of special drawing rights among participants but also on the selection of the participants that should be subject to designation and on the particular formula used to aim over time at harmonization of individual ratios.

Accordingly, Schedule F envisages that participants shall be designated for such amounts as will promote over time equality in their ratios of excess holdings of special drawing rights to their holdings of gold and foreign exchange. Because initially these ratios will be zero for all participants, paragraph (b) (i) of the Schedule indicates that participants will be designated in amounts that are proportionate to their official holdings of gold and foreign exchange. With the passage of time situations are likely to arise in which such ratios for one or more participants subject to designation may be significantly below those of the majority of other participants in the group. Paragraph (b) (ii) therefore envisages a designation process which will tend to reduce gradually the difference between low and high ratios among participants subject to designation, in order to avoid sudden and massive designation of participants with relatively low ratios. The intention is that such participants, once their position permitted their being made subject to designation, would be designated, to the extent that the volume of designation permits, in amounts calculated to raise their ratios at a steady pace within approximately one year to the vicinity of the ratios that are relatively high. The formula for doing this will be determined from time to time by the Fund. Any amounts not designated in accordance with this formula would normally be assigned to the other participants subject to designation under subsection (a) (i) of Article XXV, Section 5, in a manner consistent with the objective of a harmonization of ratios.

The Fund will exercise its power of designation in a manner that will ensure that participants will be able to use their special drawing rights in order to obtain currency. Thus, if a designated participant were to fail to provide currency to a participant using its special drawing rights in accordance with Article XXV, Section 2 (a), the Fund would make any necessary additional designations.

14. *Transactions not Requiring Designation*

Under Article XXV, Section 2 (b) (ii), the Fund is given the power to prescribe transactions in which a participant may engage in agreement with any other participant whether designated or not. The provision contains a list of transactions that the Fund may prescribe. The prescription of these transactions may be made by a decision or by rules and regulations adopted by the Executive Directors. The Fund is given discretion to specify transactions from among those listed. It may specify all or none of the categories listed; or it may specify individual transactions in one or more of the categories. By an 85 per cent majority in the Board of Governors, additional transactions or categories of transactions outside the categories in the list may be prescribed. Under Article XXV, Section 2 (b) (ii), a principle is established for the adoption of decisions under that provision. These decisions of the Fund must be consistent with the provisions of the Agreement and with the proper use of special drawing rights under the Agreement; participants will be expected to observe this principle and avoid engaging in transactions without designation which might prejudice basic features of the scheme such as the requirement of need.

Article XXV, Section 2 (b) (i), expressly exempts certain transactions from designation. The Fund may prescribe any necessary rules and regulations under Article XII, Section 2 (g), in order to implement this provision.

15. *Requirement of Need*

As a general rule, a participant will be expected to use special drawing rights in transactions with other participants only if it has a need as defined in Article XXV, Section 3 (a). Section 4 of this Report deals with the requirement of need in operations and transactions in which participants obtain currency from other prescribed holders.

The definition of need given in Article XXV, Section 3 (a), covers all balance of payments needs, whether these arise from current or capital transactions. Because these needs can be defined in various ways, reference is also made to "developments in its [a participant's] official holdings of gold, foreign exchange, and special drawing rights, and its reserve position in the Fund," to indicate that these developments, even if attributable to conversions of balances of the member's currency and not to a balance of payments deficit, may give rise to a need to use special drawing rights. Use of special drawing rights merely to reduce holdings of such rights while the total of holdings of gold and foreign exchange and the reserve position in the Fund is increasing or would increase as a result of such use would not be regarded as meeting the requirement of need. However, the use of rights to meet a payments need may have the incidental effect of changing the relative proportions in which a participant holds different reserve assets.

16. *Transactions without Requirement of Need*

Under Article XXV, Section 3 (c), the Fund is authorized to prescribe transactions in which participants may use special drawing rights without fulfilling the requirement of need. The categories of transactions listed in that provision are the same as those listed in Article XXV, Section 2 (b) (ii), but, in contrast to the exemptions from the requirement of designation, the list is exhaustive and the Fund cannot prescribe transactions that go beyond its scope. As in the case of the prescription of transactions that are not subject to designation, prescriptions under Article XXV, Section 3 (c), may be made by a decision or by rules and regulations adopted by the Executive Directors, and may relate to individual transactions or categories of transactions falling within the listed categories. The transactions exempted by prescription from the requirement of need do not have to coincide at any given time with those that are exempted from the requirement of designation. In prescribing transactions or categories of transactions that are exempted from the requirement of need the Fund will take into account the extent to which a participant has to obtain special drawing rights for the purpose of meeting the objectives of Section 3 (c) of Article XXV.

17. *Reconstitution*

Under the reconstitution principles set forth in Article XXV, Section 6, and Schedule G, a participant's net use of its special drawing rights must be such that the average of its daily holdings of special drawing rights over a five-year period will not be less than 30 per cent of the average of its daily net cumulative allocations of special drawing rights over the same period. It is envisaged that the Fund will assist participants to comply with this requirement through designation under Article XXV, Section 5 (a) (ii), and rules to that effect will be adopted by the Fund. If a participant is unable to obtain sufficient special drawing rights through designation, it must obtain them from the General Account or from another participant specified by the Fund for this purpose to the extent that the General Account is unable to supply them.

The reconstitution rules set forth in Schedule G will be reviewed by the Fund before the end of each basic period. The Board of Governors by an 85 per cent majority of the total voting power may adopt, modify, or abrogate rules for reconstitution.

18. *Operations and Transactions through the General Account*

The principal provisions governing the acceptance and use of special drawing rights by the Fund in operations and transactions conducted through the General Account are set forth in Article XXV, Section 7. These provisions impose an obligation on the Fund to accept special drawing rights in two specified cases in which the provisions of the Articles require payments to be made to the Fund in special drawing rights. However, the Fund will have authority to accept, to the extent that it may decide, special drawing rights in the General Account in the cases indicated in subsection (c) of Section 7.

Subsections (d), (e), and (f) describe the circumstances in which the Fund will be authorized to use special drawing rights held in the General Account to obtain currencies from participants. Under subsection (d) the Fund may require a participant to provide its currency to the Fund for special drawing rights, if the Fund deems it appropriate to replenish its holdings of the participant's currency in the General Account and has consulted the participant on alternative ways of replenishment under Article VII, Section 2. Under subsection (f) the Fund may use special drawing rights only by agreement with the participant involved in the operation or transaction.

In order to assist a participant to meet its need for special drawing rights to carry out the objective of reconstitution, to eliminate any negative balance, or to reverse the effects of a transaction engaged in inconsistently with the rule of need, subsection (e) authorizes the Fund to provide this participant with special drawing rights from the General Account for gold or currency acceptable to the Fund.

19. *Exchange Rates*

Under Article XXV, Section 8, the exchange rates for operations and transactions are to be such as will ensure that a participant using its special drawing rights will receive the same value, on the basis of the exchange rates prevailing at the time the transaction takes place, whatever the currencies that might be provided and whichever the participant that provides the currency. The Fund will have to adopt regulations to give effect to this principle, and will consult a participant on the procedure for determining rates of exchange for its currency.

The rates prescribed under Article XXV, Section 8, will not apply to operations and transactions in special drawing rights with the General Account. Those operations and transactions will be executed at the rate at which the Fund holds the currency involved, which normally is the par value of the currency.

20. *Interest and Charges*

Under the provisions of Article XXVI, the rate of interest and the rate of charges will be the same. The net effect of these provisions will be the payment of interest by the Fund to a participant on the excess of its holdings of special drawing rights over its net cumulative allocation, and the payment of charges by a participant on the amount by which its holdings of special drawing rights are less than its net cumulative allocation. As a matter of accounting practice, the amount of interest to be paid to a participant and the amount of charges to be paid by that participant will be offset and only the balance will be paid or collected, as the case may be, by the Fund. Interest and charges will be payable in special drawing rights.

Section 3 of Article XXVI sets the rate at 1½ per cent per annum, but the Fund is given authority to apply a different rate within maximum and minimum levels. Under this authority, the Fund could set the rate at the same level as the remuneration to be paid to members under Article V, Section 9, but it will not be required to do so.

If a participant does not have sufficient special drawing rights to meet the payment of charges, it will be able to obtain special drawing rights from the General Account or from another participant specified by the Fund for this purpose to the extent that the General Account is unable to supply them.

21. *Expenses of the Special Drawing Account*

The expenses of conducting the business of the Special Drawing Account are to be met by the Fund from the resources held in the General Account. However, under Article XXII, Section 2, the Fund will be reimbursed periodically on the basis of a reasonable estimate of these expenses. For the purpose of such reimbursement, the Fund will levy assessments under Article XXVI, Section 4, on all participants in proportion to their net cumulative allocations. The amounts assessed will be paid directly into the General Account and, like interest and charges, will be payable in special drawing rights.

22. *Administration of the Special Drawing Account*

Because participation may not be coextensive with membership in the Fund, Article XXVII contains special rules for calling meetings, determining quorums, and voting majorities for the Board of Governors and the Executive Directors of the Fund when these organs consider matters pertaining to the Special Drawing Account. There is no change in the composition of these two organs of the Fund. All Governors and Directors remain entitled to attend and participate in all meetings and in the discussion of any item on the agenda. However, if a decision is to be taken on an item that pertains exclusively to the Special Drawing Account, for example, on a proposal by the Managing Director to allocate or cancel special drawing rights, only Governors for members that are participants may vote and each Director will be able to cast only the votes of the Fund members appointing or electing him that are participants. It is, therefore, possible that a Director will not have any votes to cast. Similarly, whether a

Governor or Director may cast votes on an item pertaining exclusively to the Special Drawing Account will determine whether he may put an item on the agenda, whether he may request that a meeting be called, and whether there is a quorum for any meeting.

There is no special provision in Article XXVII regarding the voting power of members that are participants for the purpose of decisions on matters relating to the Special Drawing Account. There is no need for such a provision because the voting power of these members will be determined for all purposes by the present provisions of Article XII, Section 5. Accordingly, for the purposes of the Special Drawing Account as well, each participating member will have 250 votes plus one vote for each part of its quota equivalent to one hundred thousand U.S. dollars.

Decisions on certain important issues that require an 85 per cent majority of the total voting power as well as a decision to liquidate the Special Drawing Account can be taken only by the Board of Governors. These issues are those relating to the prescription of other holders, the allocation and cancellation of special drawing rights, the prescription of additional transactions not requiring designation, and the amendment or abrogation of reconstitution rules.

23. *Suspension of Participants' Use of Special Drawing Rights*

Article XXIX, Section 2 (f), makes it clear that the suspension of a participant's use of special drawing rights pursuant to the provisions of that Article will not affect, in any way, its right as a member to make use of the resources of the Fund in the General Account, and conversely, any limitation of this right of a member that is a participant will not affect, in any way, the participant's right to use its special drawing rights.

24. *Definition of Currency Convertible in Fact for Transactions in Special Drawing Rights*

The provisions of Article XXXII (b) are designed to ensure that any participant using special drawing rights to obtain "currency convertible in fact" from a designated participant can obtain, directly or indirectly, any one of a number of convertible currencies that he may choose, in amounts determined by the exchange rates prescribed under Article XXV, Section 8, in accordance with the principle of equal value.

This objective is to be achieved by establishing a group of currencies which will be interconvertible at appropriate rates of exchange for balances arising in connection with the use of special drawing rights. Only currencies with respect to which there are procedures designed to ensure this interconvertibility to the satisfaction of the Fund and which in addition are convertible in the sense that they are the currencies of participants that freely buy and sell gold under Article IV, Section 4 (b), or have accepted the obligations of Article VIII, Sections 2, 3, and 4, will qualify for inclusion in this group.

In addition to the currencies mentioned in the preceding paragraph, currency convertible in fact will also include balances of any other currency for which suitable arrangements exist for conversion, at rates of exchange prescribed by the Fund, into any of the currencies in the group that are interconvertible. Through one or more conversions, such balances can in fact be converted into any of the currencies in the group.

25. *Definition of Reserve Position in the Fund*

Article XXXII (c) defines a participant's "reserve position in the Fund" as the sum of the gold tranche purchases that the participant could make and the amount of any Fund indebtedness to the participant which is "readily repayable" under a loan agreement. Examples of the latter are the indebtedness of the Fund to participants in the General Arrangements to Borrow and the indebtedness to Italy under the 1966 Loan Agreement, both of which have been entered into under Article VII, Section 2. Members that have made loans to the Fund under these agreements may obtain early repayment by representing to the Fund that there is a balance of payments need for repayment and requesting such repayment.

26. *Termination of Participation*

The principles governing termination of participation in the Special Drawing Account, which are set forth in Article XXX and Schedule H, are generally the same as those governing the settlement of accounts on withdrawal of a member from membership in the Fund. A participant may terminate its participation in the Special Drawing Account at any time without withdrawing from membership in the Fund. Withdrawal from the Fund automatically terminates participation in the Special Drawing Account.

27. *Liquidation*

The principal issue in devising any procedure for liquidation is the distribution of the burden of any default. Article XXXI and Schedule I distribute the burden of default among all participants on the basis of their net cumulative allocations. This is accomplished by a system of liquidation under which the Fund redeems special drawing rights first from the participant that holds the largest amount in proportion to its net cumulative allocation until this portion is reduced to that of the participant with the second highest proportion. The Fund then redeems special drawing rights held by these two participants until the proportion held by each is reduced to that of the participant with the third highest proportion and so on until all amounts paid in the Fund by participants have been distributed. Thus a participant's share of any possible default does not increase as its holdings of special drawing rights increase above its net cumulative allocation.

PART II

Modifications in Rules and Practices of the Fund

28. *General Comments*

Board of Governors Resolution No. 22-8, which called on the Executive Directors to propose amendments to the Articles and the By-Laws of the Fund for the purpose of establishing the new facility based on special drawing rights, also requested the Executive Directors to consider at the same time and report on possible improvements in the present rules and practices of the Fund based on developments in world economic conditions and the experience of the Fund since the adoption of its Articles of Agreement. The Executive Directors have considered various suggestions for improvements and have decided to recommend the introduction of certain changes in the present rules and practices of the Fund, all of which would be made by amending the Articles. These changes relate to: certain quota increases and associated matters; uniform proportionate changes in par values and the maintenance of the gold value of the Fund's assets in the event that such changes in par values are made; the use of the Fund's resources in the gold tranche, including use for capital transfers; a limitation on the Fund's power to introduce new facilities in the General Account for the unconditional use of the Fund's resources; the rules on repurchase under Article V, Section 7; the payment of a remuneration to members whose currencies are held by the Fund in amounts less than 75 per cent of quota; the distribution of net income; and the interpretation of the

Articles of Agreement. The modifications in Articles I, III, IV, V, VI, XII, XVIII, and XIX, and in Schedule B, which are included in the Proposed Amendment, are intended to give effect to these changes.

Three general points should be made in connection with these modifications. First, some of them represent no more than a clarification or codification of practices developed over the years and followed currently by the Fund on the basis of the Articles of Agreement in their present form. Secondly, some modifications are intended to adapt the Articles to the fact that there will be a facility which will make it possible to allocate special drawing rights of an unconditional character. Finally, while one of the effects of these modifications will be to prevent the establishment of new facilities for the unconditional use of the Fund's resources, they are not intended to make the rules and practices relating to the use of the Fund's resources more restrictive than they are at the present time.

29. Quota Changes and Related Matters

Under Article III, Section 2, in its present form, all changes in quotas require a four-fifths majority of the total voting power. Under the Proposed Amendment decisions on changes in quotas, including special increases and increases by installments, proposed as the result of a general review will require a new special majority, i.e., 85 per cent of the total voting power. The general reviews referred to in the amended provision are those that have as their purpose an examination of the appropriateness of the quotas of all members, and they will include not only the reviews of the quotas of all members which the Fund is required to conduct at intervals of five years but also any reviews of this kind conducted at other times. All other changes in quotas will continue to require a four-fifths majority of the total voting power.

The majority of 85 per cent will also apply to decisions specifying conditions precedent to the effectiveness of quota increases proposed as a result of a general review. The adoption of these conditions is subject at present to the four-fifths majority which is applicable to quota increases. Examples of such conditions drawn from past practice are the requirement of a minimum total participation in a general increase and the payment of the additional subscriptions before the increases become effective. As at present, the power to adopt these conditions will be exercised by the Board of Governors as a reserved power.

Under a new provision, Article III, Section 4 (c), an 85 per cent majority will be required for decisions on other matters that are related to quota increases proposed as the result of a general quota review even though they do not involve conditions precedent to the effectiveness of the increases. These decisions include any decision pursuant to Article III, Section 4 (a), under which a member may be permitted to pay less than 25 per cent of its additional subscription in gold. The new provision will also apply to any decision intended to mitigate the effects of the payment of additional subscriptions. At present, the Articles provide that all of these decisions are to be made by the Executive Directors by a majority of the votes cast. After the Proposed Amendment enters into force the power to make such decisions will be reserved to the Board of Governors.

The special majority of 85 per cent of the total voting which will be required as the result of various changes in the rules and practices of the Fund is analogous to the majority required for a number of important decisions under the new facility based on special drawing rights.

30. *Uniform Proportionate Changes in Par Values and Maintenance of Gold Value*

Under the modifications in Article IV, Section 7, a decision to make a uniform proportionate change in par values also will require an 85 per cent majority of the total voting power. This changes the present provision in two respects. It replaces the simple majority with a special majority and eliminates the requirement that the uniform proportionate change be approved by those members that have 10 per cent or more of the total of Fund quotas. The power to make a uniform proportionate change in par values will continue to be reserved to the Board of Governors.

Under the modifications in Article IV, Section 8 (d), and Article XII, Section 2 (b) (iii), a decision to waive the maintenance of the gold value of the Fund's assets in the event of a uniform proportionate change in par values will require an 85 per cent majority of the total voting power, and the power to make the decision will be reserved to the Board of Governors. At present the power to make a decision of this kind is not reserved to the Board of Governors and a special majority is not required.

31. *Temporary Character of Use of the Fund's Resources*

The modifications in Article I and the inclusion in Article V of a new Section 3 (c) state expressly what is regarded as implicit in the present Articles, i.e., that use of the Fund's resources must be of a temporary character and that the Fund must adopt policies intended to encourage members to take measures that will help them to avoid a use which is not of such a character. In this way the Fund safeguards the revolving character of its resources. Therefore, no changes in the established policies and practices of the Fund, as set forth in the Fund's decision of February 13, 1952, and in other decisions would be called for by the entry into force of the Proposed Amendment. The resources of the Fund referred to in Article I (v) and in other provisions of the Articles are those that will be held by the Fund in the General Account.

32. *Legal Automaticity of Gold Tranche Purchases*

Requests for gold tranche purchases now enjoy *de facto* automaticity. One of the effects of the modifications in Article V, Section 3, will be to make the use of the Fund's resources in the gold tranche legally automatic.

After the amendment, the use of the Fund's resources in the gold tranche will continue to be subject to the provisions of Article V, Section 3 (a). Accordingly, members making requests for purchases in the gold tranche will still be required to make the representation of need prescribed by Article V, Section 3 (a) (i). However, the Fund will not have the legal power to challenge this representation.

Article V, Section 3 (a) (iii), will be amended to eliminate the necessity for a waiver that might have been required for a gold tranche purchase in certain circumstances. Furthermore, Article VI, Sections 1 (a) and 2, as amended, will remove the present limitation on making gold tranche purchases for meeting capital transfers. A member will be able to make gold tranche purchases even though they are to meet what might be regarded as a large or sustained outflow of capital. The established legal position will be maintained in respect of requests for purchases other than gold tranche purchases. Accordingly, a member will be able, as at present, to use the Fund's resources to meet capital outflows subject to Article VI, Section 1.

The legal automaticity of gold tranche purchases will not prejudice the application of the Fund's policies on the currencies to be used in purchases. These policies are set forth in the Fund's Decision of July 20, 1962 and are applicable to all purchases including gold tranche purchases.

The legal automaticity of gold tranche purchases raises the question of possible misuse by a member of its right to make such purchases without challenge by failing to observe the principle of need set forth in Article V, Section 3 (a) (i). The Executive Directors believe that if the question should arise it could be met by an adjustment, in due time, of the Fund's policies with respect to the currencies to be used in purchases in order to bring about a correction of the effects of any misuse by a member of the kind referred to above.

The Fund will continue to have authority under the Articles of Agreement to declare a member ineligible to use the Fund's resources even in the gold tranche if the member makes gold tranche purchases without observing the principle of need.

33. Definition of Gold Tranche Purchases

The changes in the Articles commented upon in sections 32, 34, and 36 of this Report should be understood in the light of the definition of gold tranche purchases in a new provision, Article XIX (j). This definition is somewhat different from the definition of gold tranche purchases which prevailed in Fund practice until less than two years ago and according to which a gold tranche purchase was understood as a purchase which did not cause the Fund's holdings of a member's currency to exceed 100 per cent of its quota. By permitting the exclusion of purchases under the compensatory financing facility and the holdings of currency acquired by the Fund as a result of those purchases, the definition in Article XIX (j) will make it possible for the Fund to continue the present practice of treating the compensatory financing facility as separate for the purpose of applying the Fund's policies on the use of its resources. This practice was introduced by the amendments to the Decision on Compensatory Financing of Export Fluctuations adopted on September 20, 1966, under which the Fund applies "its tranche policies to drawing requests by a member as if the Fund's holdings of the member's currency were less than its actual holdings of that currency by the amount of any drawing outstanding under paragraph (5)" of that decision.

Under the definition in Article XIX (j), a purchase under paragraph (5) of the compensatory financing decision will not be regarded as a gold tranche purchase even if it does not raise the Fund's holdings of a member's currency above the level of the member's quota. Conversely, a purchase not under the compensatory financing facility which raises the Fund's holdings above that level will be regarded as a gold tranche purchase, provided that the amount by which the quota level is exceeded will not be larger than the amount of any purchases outstanding under the compensatory financing decision.

In view of the possibility that, under the definition of gold tranche purchases in Article XIX (j), a gold tranche purchase may increase the Fund's holdings above the quota level and in order to preserve the legal automaticity of requests to make gold tranche purchases under Article V, Section 3 (d), the text of Article V, Section 3 (a) (iii), is amended so that a waiver under Article V, Section 4, will not be necessary. Under the amended text of Section 3 (a) (iii), however, a purchase under the compensatory financing decision which, together with any other net increases in the Fund's holdings of the member's currency, causes these holdings to increase by more than 25 per cent of quota during the period of 12 months ending on the date of the purchase, will require a waiver under Article V, Section 4, even though it does not raise the Fund's holdings above the quota level. At present, any purchase below the quota level, including a purchase under the compensatory financing decision, does not require a waiver.

34. Termination of Power to Establish New Unconditional Facilities in the General Account

As a result of the adoption of Article V, Section 3 (d), the Fund will not have the power to create any new facility in the General Account for the unconditional use of its resources. This provision reflects the view that, with the establishment of the new facility based on special drawing rights, any need for additions to existing reserve assets will be met, as and when it arises, through allocations of special drawing rights. The provision makes it explicit that a member's representation under Article V, Section 3 (a), must be examined in order to determine that the requested purchase would be consistent with the provisions of the Articles and the policies on the use of the Fund's resources adopted under Article V, Section 3 (c). This means that the Fund will not grant *de facto* automaticity (i.e., "the overwhelming benefit of any doubt" or treatment having the same effect) to requests for purchases other than gold tranche purchases. The Fund will continue to be able to adapt its policies governing purchases other than gold tranche purchases in all other respects.

The changes in Article V, Section 3, will be without prejudice also to the Fund's compensatory financing facility and the adjustment of that policy if this should be considered desirable. In addition, as already indicated, these changes are not intended to make the rules and practices relating to the use of the Fund's resources more restrictive than they are at present.

35. Rules on Repurchase

The modifications in Article V, Section 7, Article XII, Section 2 (b), Article XIX (a) and (e), and Schedule B, will introduce the following changes in the present rules on repurchase:

(a) At present, the amounts of a member's currency that are held by the governmental agencies and other official institutions of other members, as well as by banks within the territories of the latter, are deducted from the member's official holdings of gold and convertible currencies under Article XIX (e). The deduction of these currency liabilities will be abolished, thereby introducing a gross concept of monetary reserves as the basis of the calculation of members' repurchase obligations and for certain other purposes. This change is effected through the modifications in Article XIX (a) and (e). The new paragraph 6 of Schedule B sets forth a transitional rule designed to prevent the accrual of repurchase obligations solely because of the elimination of the deduction of currency liabilities during a financial year of the Fund. It will apply only in the year in which the Proposed Amendment enters into force and, thereafter, no deductions will be made for currency liabilities.

(b) The abatement of repurchase obligations calculated in a member's currency, which the Fund may not accept because the acceptance would increase the Fund's holdings of that currency above 75 per cent of the member's quota, will be eliminated. Under paragraph 1 (d) of Schedule B the amounts that would be abated for this reason will have to be discharged in other convertible currencies as determined by the Fund.

(c) The present paragraph 2 of Schedule B, which will be retained as paragraph 2 (a), prohibits the Fund from acquiring the currency of any nonmember by way of repurchase but does not indicate how repurchase obligations that accrue in specified nonmember currencies are to be treated. The proposed paragraph 2 (b) of Schedule B provides that repurchase obligations that accrue in specified nonmember currencies will be paid in the convertible currencies of members as determined by the Fund. The Fund has never specified a nonmember currency for the purposes of repurchases but would be likely to do so if it found that members held appreciable amounts of a nonmember currency.

(d) The present Article V, Section 7 (c) (i), provides that a repurchase shall not be carried out to the extent that it would reduce the repurchasing member's monetary reserves, as presently defined on a net basis, below an amount equal to its quota. Under the amended Article V, Section 7 (c) (i), a level of monetary reserves, defined on a gross basis, equivalent to 150 percent of quota will be substituted for the quota level. If a repurchase obligation accrues which would exceed this limit, the excess will be abated.

(e) Under the proposed Article V, Section 7 (c) (iv), there will be an annual limit on repurchases under Article V, Section 7 (b), equal to 25 per cent of a member's quota. Under the new paragraph 1 (e) of Schedule B, if an obligation accrues which exceeds this amount, the excess will be postponed to the end of the subsequent financial year or years, but not more than 25 per cent of the member's quota will have to be repurchased in any one year under postponed and other repurchase obligations accruing under Article V, Section 7 (b). This new rule will not affect repurchases made outside Article V, Section 7 (b).

(f) A change will be introduced in the formula on the basis of which repurchase obligations are calculated. The present formula takes account of increases in the Fund's holdings of a member's currency and increases or decreases in its monetary reserves during a year. Under the modified formula in Article V, Section 7 (b) (i), account will also be taken of decreases in the Fund's holdings of the member's currency during the year. This change will reduce a member's repurchase obligation under Article V, Section 7 (b), at the end of a financial year by the full amount of other repurchases made during that year, whereas at present they reduce the obligation only by one half of the full amount. It should be noted that, in respect of repurchases outside Article V, Section 7 (a) or (b), the Fund has legal authority to specify the acceptable convertible currencies that the repurchasing member may use.

(g) In accordance with paragraph 5 of Schedule B, the Fund, in its discretion, will be able to accede to a member's request that in the calculation of its monetary reserves a deduction be made for its outstanding obligations resulting from swap transactions with other members.

(h) The Fund will have the power to revise the percentage of quota below which repurchases may not reduce a repurchasing member's monetary reserves and the annual limit on repurchases under Article V, Section 7 (b). In addition, the Fund will be able to revise and supplement, in a manner consistent with the other repurchase provisions of the Articles, the newly introduced rules in paragraph 1 (c), (d), and (e) and paragraph 2 (b) of Schedule B. The Fund is granted this power under Article V, Section 7 (d). Under this provision and Article XII, Section 2 (b) (ix), the power is reserved to the Board of Governors which can exercise it by an 85 per cent majority of the total voting power.

(i) Under Article XXV, Section 7 (a) and (b), special drawing rights are to be included in the monetary reserves of members for the purposes of the Articles. As a result of these provisions and of the modifications in the introductory parts of Article V, Section 7 (b), and in paragraph 1 of Schedule B, repurchase obligations may accrue in special drawing rights, and the Fund will accept special drawing rights in repurchase under Article V, Section 7 (b). However, the Fund may decide that no account be taken of any increase or decrease in monetary reserves during a financial year which is due to allocations or cancellations of special drawing rights during the same year.

36. *Service Charge*

Article V, Section 8(a), as amended, will maintain the existing maximum rate of the service charge that the Fund can levy on exchange transactions. The present minimum rate for exchange transactions will be unaffected, except that the Fund will be authorized to levy a lower charge or no charge on gold tranche purchases. The Executive Directors believe that initially no service charge should be levied on gold tranche purchases, subject to any change in this policy that would be appropriate in the light of subsequent developments.

37. *Remuneration*

A new provision, Article V, Section 9, will require the Fund to pay a return to members on the excess of 75 per cent of a member's quota over the average of the Fund's holdings of the member's currency, or, in other words, on the Fund's net use of a member's normal currency subscription. The rate of remuneration will be $1\frac{1}{2}$ per cent per annum. However, the Executive Directors would be able to specify other rates within the limits of 1 to 2 per cent per annum by a majority of the votes cast. The Executive Directors would be able to make changes beyond these limits by a three-fourths majority of the total voting power, but it is not expected that this would be done unless it were necessary in the light of developments in international money markets.

The remuneration will be payable in gold or in the member's own currency or partly in gold and partly in that currency. The Executive Directors believe that the Fund's policy should be to pay remuneration in gold to the extent that receipts of gold from members in payment of charges under Article V, Section 8, would permit, subject again to any change in this policy that would be appropriate in the light of subsequent developments.

38. *Distribution of Net Income*

Article XII, Section 6, in its present form, requires that, before any distribution of the net income of any year is made by the Fund to all members on the basis of quotas, a 2 per cent noncumulative payment be made to each member on the amount by which 75 per cent of its quota exceeded the Fund's average holdings of the member's currency during the year. Under the amended provision, instead of the 2 per cent preferential payment, the Fund will have to distribute first to members eligible to receive remuneration under Article V, Section 9, an amount of net income which will raise to 2 per cent the return paid to them as remuneration for the year for which net income is distributed.

Under Article XII, Section 6 (c), the Fund will be able to transfer to general reserve all or part of its special reserve to which the yield of its investment is placed. The yield of the investment is not net income in the sense of, and cannot be distributed under, Article XII, Section 6. Moreover, it can be used only for the limited purpose of meeting administrative deficits. Amounts transferred from special to general reserve, however, will be available to meet a deficit of any character, whether operational or administrative, including a deficit resulting from the payment of remuneration under Article V,

Section 9, but they will continue to be unavailable for distribution as net income under Article XII, Section 6.

The power to make transfers to general reserve from the existing or any other special reserve will be without prejudice to any future decisions on the maintenance or termination of the Fund's investment. The power to make transfers will be exercised by the Board of Governors, and a provision reserving it to the Board of Governors is inserted as Article XII, Section 2 (b) (x).

39. *Interpretation*

Article XVIII, as amended, will require the establishment of a standing Committee on Interpretation of the Board of Governors. A question of interpretation of the Articles, on which the Executive Directors have given a decision under Article XVIII and which, at the request of a member made within three months from the date of that decision, is referred to the Board of Governors, will have to be considered first by this Committee. The decision of this Committee will be regarded as the decision of the Board of Governors, and therefore final, unless the Board of Governors decides otherwise by an 85 per cent majority of the total voting power. Article XVIII (b) prescribes that each member of the Committee on Interpretation shall have one vote. Other matters, such as the membership, procedures, and voting majorities of the Committee, are left for later determination by the Board of Governors by means of a By-Law. In addition, under Article XXVII (c), the Board of Governors will have the power to determine whether all members of the Committee will be entitled to vote on a question of interpretation pertaining exclusively to the Special Drawing Account.

PART III

Procedure

40. *Applicable Legal Provisions*

The procedure for the adoption of modifications in the Articles of Agreement is set forth in Article XVII which reads:

(a) Any proposal to introduce modifications in this Agreement, whether emanating from a member, a governor or the Executive Directors, shall be communicated to the chairman of the Board of Governors who shall bring the proposal before the Board. If the proposed amendment is approved by the Board the Fund shall, by circular letter or telegram, ask all members whether they accept the proposed amendment. When three-fifths of the members, having four-fifths of the total voting power, have accepted the proposed amendment, the Fund shall certify the fact by a formal communication addressed to all members.

(b) Notwithstanding (a) above, acceptance by all members is required in the case of any amendment modifying

(i) the right to withdraw from the Fund (Article XV, Section 1);

(ii) the provision that no change in a member's quota shall be made without its consent (Article III, Section 2);

(iii) the provision that no change may be made in the par value of a member's currency except on the proposal of that member (Article IV, Section 5 (b)).

(c) Amendments shall enter into force for all members three months after the date of the formal communication unless a shorter period is specified in the circular letter or telegram.

41. Resolution of Board of Governors

Annex A contains the text of a Resolution, and there is attached to it a Proposed Amendment to the Articles of Agreement. The Chairman of the Board of Governors has requested that on his behalf the Secretary of the Fund bring the Resolution and Proposed Amendment before the Board of Governors for its approval. Pursuant to this request the Secretary is transmitting them to the Board with this Report.

In the judgment of the Executive Directors the action requested of the Board of Governors should not be postponed until the next regular meeting of the Board and does not warrant the calling of a special meeting of the Board. For this reason, the Executive Directors, pursuant to Section 13 of the By-Laws, request Governors to vote without meeting. In accordance with established practice, the Executive Directors have also decided to waive the requirement that no Governor shall vote until seven days after the dispatch of the motion. To be valid votes must be received at the seat of the Fund on or before May 31, 1968.

For the adoption of the Resolution it will be necessary that replies be received from a majority of the Governors exercising two-thirds of the total voting power and that a majority of the votes cast be in favor of the Resolution. The Resolution must be voted on as a whole.

42. Acceptance of Proposed Amendment by Members

By adopting the annexed Resolution the Board of Governors will grant its approval to the Proposed Amendment of the Articles of Agreement. Members will then be asked, by circular letter or telegram, to notify the Fund whether they accept the Proposed Amendment. The Proposed Amendment can be accepted only in its entirety. That is to say, members will not be able to accept part only of the Proposed Amendment.

In accordance with Article XVII (a) the Proposed Amendment must be accepted by three-fifths of the members, having four-fifths of the total voting power, before it can enter into force.

43. Entry into Force of Proposed Amendment

When the Proposed Amendment has been accepted by the necessary majority, the Fund will certify the fact by a formal communication to be sent by the Secretary of the Fund to all members. Pursuant to Article XVII (c), the Executive Directors recommend that the Proposed Amendment enter into force on the date of the formal communication instead of three months after that date. In accordance with that provision and paragraph 3 of the Resolution, the circular letter or telegram by which members will be asked whether they accept the Proposed Amendment will specify the date of the formal communication referred to above as the date of the entry into force of the Proposed Amendment.

The Proposed Amendment will enter into force for all members on the date of the formal communication, whether they accepted the Amendment or not. Presumably, members accepting the Proposed Amendment will have taken any legislative and other action that may be necessary to enable them to carry out their obligations under the Articles of Agreement as amended. Other members that have not accepted the Proposed

Amendment will need to consider whether any action is necessary in order to enable them to carry out their obligations under the Articles of Agreement as amended.

44. *Notification to Depositary of Articles of Agreement*

Upon certification of the entry into force of the Proposed Amendment it is intended to notify that fact to the Government of the United States, which is the depositary of the Articles of Agreement of the Fund, so that it may record the Amendment. It is also intended to ask the Government of the United States to register the Amendment with the Secretary-General of the United Nations, pursuant to Article 102 of the United Nations Charter.

Annex A

RESOLUTION

WHEREAS the Executive Directors have completed their work relating to the establishment in the International Monetary Fund of a new facility based on special drawing rights in order to meet the need, as and when it arises, for a supplement to existing reserve assets, and on improvements in the present rules and practices of the Fund, pursuant to Resolution No. 22-8 of the Board of Governors of the International Monetary Fund at its Twenty-Second Annual Meeting in Rio de Janeiro; and

WHEREAS the Executive Directors have prepared a Report setting forth proposals for modifications in the Articles of Agreement of the International Monetary Fund for the purpose of establishing the new facility and giving effect to certain modifications in the present rules and practices of the Fund; and

WHEREAS the Chairman of the Board of Governors has requested the Secretary of the Fund to bring the proposals of the Executive Directors before the Board of Governors; and

WHEREAS the Report of the Executive Directors setting forth their proposals has been submitted to the Board of Governors by the Secretary of the Fund; and

WHEREAS the Executive Directors have requested the Board of Governors to vote on the following Resolution without meeting, pursuant to Section 13 of the By-Laws of the Fund;

NOW, THEREFORE, the Board of Governors, noting the said Report of the Executive Directors, hereby RESOLVES that:

1. The Proposed Amendment to the Articles of Agreement of the International Monetary Fund set forth in the attachment to this Resolution is approved.

2. The Secretary of the Fund is directed to ask, by letter or telegram, all members of the Fund whether they accept, in accordance with the provisions of Article XVII, the Proposed Amendment to the Articles of Agreement as set forth in the attachment to this Resolution.

3. The circular letter or telegram to be sent to all members in accordance with 2 above shall specify that the Proposed Amendment to the Articles of Agreement set forth in the attachment to this Resolution shall enter into force for all members as of the date on which the Fund certifies, by formal communication addressed to all members, that three-fifths of the members, having four-fifths of the total voting power, have accepted the modifications.

Proposed Amendment to the Articles of Agreement
of the International Monetary Fund
Prepared Pursuant to Board of Governors Resolution No. 22-8

A

INTRODUCTORY ARTICLE

The Introductory Article shall read:

"(i) The International Monetary Fund is established and shall operate in accordance with the provisions of this Agreement as originally adopted, and as subsequently amended in order to institute a facility based on special drawing rights and to effect certain other changes.

(ii) To enable the Fund to conduct its operations and transactions, the Fund shall maintain a General Account and a Special Drawing Account. Membership in the Fund shall give the right to participation in the Special Drawing Account.

(iii) Operations and transactions authorized by this Agreement shall be conducted through the General Account except that operations and transactions involving special drawing rights shall be conducted through the Special Drawing Account."

B

ARTICLE I

Purposes

1. Article I (v) shall read:

"(v) To give confidence to members by making the Fund's resources temporarily available to them under adequate safeguards, thus providing them with opportunity to correct maladjustments in their balance of payments without resorting to measures destructive of national or international prosperity."

2. The last sentence of Article I shall read:

"The Fund shall be guided in all its policies and decisions by the purposes set forth in this Article."

C

ARTICLE III

Quotas and Subscriptions

1. Section 2 shall read:

"Section 2. *Adjustment of quotas*

The Fund shall at intervals of not more than five years conduct a general review, and if it deems it appropriate propose an adjustment, of the quotas of the members. It may also, if it thinks fit, consider at any other time the adjustment of any particular quota at the request of the member concerned. An eighty-five percent majority of the total voting power shall be required for any change in quotas proposed as the result of a general review and a four-fifths majority of the total voting power shall be required for any other change in quotas. No quota shall be changed without the consent of the member concerned."

2. The following subsection (c) shall be added to Section 4. *Payments when quotas are changed*:

"(c) A majority of eighty-five percent of the total voting power shall be required for any decisions dealing with the payment, or made with the sole purpose of mitigating the effects of the payment, of increases in quotas proposed as the result of a general review of quotas."

D

ARTICLE IV

Par Values of Currencies

1. Section 7 shall read:

    "*Section 7. Uniform changes in par values*

    Notwithstanding the provisions of Section 5 (b) of this Article, the Fund by an eighty-five percent majority of the total voting power may make uniform proportionate changes in the par values of the currencies of all members. The par value of a member's currency shall, however, not be changed under this provision if, within seventy-two hours of the Fund's action, the member informs the Fund that it does not wish the par value of its currency to be changed by such action."

2. In Section 8. *Maintenance of gold value of the Fund's assets*, subsection (d) shall read:

    "(d) The provisions of this Section shall apply to a uniform proportionate change in the par values of the currencies of all members, unless at the time when such a change is made the Fund decides otherwise by an eighty-five percent majority of the total voting power."

E

ARTICLE V

Transactions with the Fund

1. In Section 3. *Conditions governing use of the Fund's resources*, subsection (a) (iii) shall read:

    "(iii) The proposed purchase would be a gold tranche purchase, or would not cause the Fund's holdings of the purchasing member's currency to increase by more than twenty-five percent of its quota during the period of twelve months ending on the date of the purchase or to exceed two hundred percent of its quota;"

2. The following subsections (c) and (d) shall be added to Section 3:

    "(c) A member's use of the resources of the Fund shall be in accordance with the purposes of the Fund. The Fund shall adopt policies on the use of its resources that will assist members to solve their balance of payments problems in a manner consistent with the purposes of the Fund and that will establish adequate safeguards for the temporary use of its resources."

    "(d) A representation by a member under (a) above shall be examined by the Fund to determine whether the proposed purchase would be consistent with the provisions of this Agreement and with the policies adopted under them, with the exception that proposed gold tranche purchases shall not be subject to challenge."

3. In Section 7. *Repurchase by a member of its currency held by the Fund*, the first sentence of subsection (b) shall read:

    "(b) At the end of each financial year of the Fund, a member shall repurchase from the Fund with each type of monetary reserve, as determined in accordance with Schedule B, part of the Fund's holdings of its currency under the following conditions:

    (i) Each member shall use in repurchases of its own currency from the Fund an amount of its monetary reserves equal in value to the following changes that have occurred during the year: one-half of any increase in the Fund's holdings of the member's currency, plus one-half of any increase, or minus one-half of any decrease, in the member's monetary reserves, or, if the Fund's holdings of the member's currency have decreased, one-half of any increase in the member's monetary reserves minus one-half of the decrease in the Fund's holdings of the member's currency."

4. In Section 7, subsection (c) shall read:

    "(c) None of the adjustments described in (b) above shall be carried to a point at which

(i) the member's monetary reserves are below one hundred fifty percent of its quota, or

(ii) the Fund's holdings of its currency are below seventy-five percent of its quota, or

(iii) the Fund's holdings of any currency required to be used are above seventy-five percent of the quota of the member concerned, or

(iv) the amount repurchased exceeds twenty-five percent of the quota of the member concerned."

5. The following subsection (d) shall be added to Section 7:

"(d) The Fund by an eighty-five percent majority of the total voting power may revise the percentages in (c) (i) and (iv) above and revise and supplement the rules in paragraph 1 (c), (d), and (e) and paragraph 2 (b) of Schedule B."

6. In Section 8. *Charges*, subsection (a) shall read:

"(a) Any member buying the currency of another member from the Fund in exchange for its own currency shall pay, in addition to the parity price, a service charge uniform for all members of not less than one-half percent and not more than one percent, as determined by the Fund, provided that the Fund in its discretion may levy a service charge of less than one-half percent on gold tranche purchases."

7. The following Section shall be added to Article V:

"Section 9. *Remuneration*

(a) The Fund shall pay remuneration, at a rate uniform for all members, on the amount by which seventy-five percent of a member's quota exceeded the average of the Fund's holdings of the member's currency, provided that no account shall be taken of holdings in excess of seventy-five percent of quota. The rate shall be one and one-half percent per annum, but the Fund in its discretion may increase or reduce this rate, provided that a three-fourths majority of the total voting power shall be required for any increase above two percent per annum or reduction below one percent per annum.

(b) Remuneration shall be paid in gold or a member's own currency as determined by the Fund."

F

ARTICLE VI

Capital Transfers

1. In Section 1. *Use of Fund's resources for capital transfers*, subsection (a) shall read:

"(a) A member may not use the Fund's resources to meet a large or sustained outflow of capital except as provided in Section 2 of this Article, and the Fund may request a member to exercise controls to prevent such use of the resources of the Fund. If, after receiving such a request, a member fails to exercise appropriate controls, the Fund may declare the member ineligible to use the resources of the Fund."

2. Section 2 shall read:

"Section 2. *Special provisions for capital transfers*

A member shall be entitled to make gold tranche purchases to meet capital transfers."

G

ARTICLE XII

Organization and Management

1. In Section 2. *Board of Governors*, subsection (b) (ii) and (iii) shall read:

"(ii) Approve a revision of quotas, or to decide on the payment, or on the mitigation of the effects of payment, or increases in quotas proposed as the result of a general review of quotas."

"(iii) Approve a uniform change in the par values of the currencies of all members, or to decide when such a change is made that the provisions relating to the maintenance of gold value of the Fund's assets shall not apply."

2. The following shall be added to Section 2 (b):

"(ix) Revise the provisions on repurchase or to revise and supplement the rules for the distribution of repurchases among types of reserves."

"(x) Make transfers to general reserve from any special reserve."

3. The title of Section 6 shall read:

"Reserves and distribution of net income"

4. In Section 6, subsection (b) shall read:

"(b) If any distribution is made of the net income of any year, there shall first be distributed to members eligible to receive remuneration under Article V, Section 9, for that year an amount by which two percent per annum exceeded any remuneration that has been paid for that year. Any distribution of the net income of that year beyond that amount shall be made to all members in proportion to their quotas. Payments to each member shall be made in its own currency."

5. The following subsection (c) shall be added to Section 6:

"(c) The Fund may make transfers to general reserve from any special reserve."

H

ARTICLE XVIII

INTERPRETATION

Article XVIII (b) shall read:

"(b) In any case where the Executive Directors have given a decision under (a) above, any member may require, within three months from the date of the decision, that the question be referred to the Board of Governors, whose decision shall be final. Any question referred to the Board of Governors shall be considered by a Committee on Interpretation of the Board of Governors. Each Committee member shall have one vote. The Board of Governors shall establish the membership, procedures, and voting majorities of the Committee. A decision of the Committee shall be the decision of the Board of Governors unless the Board by an eighty-five percent majority of the total voting power decides otherwise. Pending the result of the reference to the Board the Fund may, so far as it deems necessary, act on the basis of the decision of the Executive Directors."

I

ARTICLE XIX

EXPLANATION OF TERMS

1. Article XIX (a) shall read:

"(a) A member's monetary reserves means its official holdings of gold, of convertible currencies of other members, and of the currencies of such non-members as the Fund may specify."

2. Article XIX (e) shall read:

"(e) The sums deemed to be official holdings of other official institutions and other banks under (c) above shall be included in the member's monetary reserves."

3. The following shall be added to Article XIX:

"(j) Gold tranche purchase means a purchase by a member of the currency of another member in exchange for its own currency which does not cause the Fund's holdings of the member's currency to exceed one hundred percent of its quota, provided that for the purposes of this definition the Fund may exclude purchases and holdings under policies on the use of its resources for compensatory financing of export fluctuations."

J
ARTICLE XX
Final Provisions

The title of Article XX shall read:
"Inaugural Provisions"

K

The following Articles XXI through XXXII shall be added after Article XX:

"ARTICLE XXI
Special Drawing Rights

Section 1. *Authority to allocate special drawing rights*

To meet the need, as and when it arises, for a supplement to existing reserve assets, the Fund is authorized to allocate special drawing rights to members that are participants in the Special Drawing Account.

Section 2. *Unit of value*

The unit of value of special drawing rights shall be equivalent to 0.888 671 gram of fine gold.

ARTICLE XXII
General Account and Special Drawing Account

Section 1. *Separation of operations and transactions*

All operations and transactions involving special drawing rights shall be conducted through the Special Drawing Account. All other operations and transactions of the Fund authorized by or under this Agreement shall be conducted through the General Account. Operations and transactions pursuant to Article XXIII, Section 2, shall be conducted through the General Account as well as the Special Drawing Account.

Section 2. *Separation of assets and property*

All assets and property of the Fund shall be held in the General Account, except that assets and property acquired under Article XXVI, Section 2, and Articles XXX and XXXI and Schedules H and I shall be held in the Special Drawing Account. Any assets or property held in one Account shall not be available to discharge or meet the liabilities, obligations, or losses of the Fund incurred in the conduct of the operations and transactions of the other Account, except that the expenses of conducting the business of the Special Drawing Account shall be paid by the Fund from the General Account which shall be reimbursed from time to time by assessments under Article XXVI, Section 4, made on the basis of a reasonable estimate of such expenses.

Section 3. *Recording and information*

All changes in holdings of special drawing rights shall take effect only when recorded by the Fund in the Special Drawing Account. Participants shall notify the Fund of the provisions of this Agreement under which special drawing rights are used. The Fund may require participants to furnish it with such other information as it deems necessary for its functions.

ARTICLE XXIII
Participants and Other Holders of Special Drawing Rights

Section 1. *Participants*

Each member of the Fund that deposits with the Fund an instrument setting forth that it undertakes all the obligations of a participant in the Special Drawing Account in accordance with its law and that it has taken all steps necessary to enable it to carry out all of these obligations shall become a participant in the Special Drawing Account as of the date the instrument is deposited, except that no member shall become a participant before Articles XXI through XXXII and Schedules F through I have entered into force and instruments have been deposited under this Section by members that have at least seventy-five percent of the total of quotas.

Section 2. *General Account as a holder*

The Fund may accept and hold special drawing rights in the General Account and use them, in accordance with the provisions of this Agreement.

Section 3. *Other holders*

The Fund by an eighty-five percent majority of the total voting power may prescribe:

(i) as holders, non-members, members that are non-participants, and institutions that perform functions of a central bank for more than one member;

(ii) the terms and conditions on which these holders may be permitted to accept, hold, and use special drawing rights, in operations and transactions with participants; and

(iii) the terms and conditions on which participants may enter into operations and transactions with these holders.

The terms and conditions prescribed by the Fund for the use of special drawing rights by prescribed holders and by participants in operations and transactions with them shall be consistent with the provisions of this Agreement.

ARTICLE XXIV

Allocation and Cancellation of Special Drawing Rights

Section 1. *Principles and considerations governing allocation and cancellation*

(a) In all its decisions with respect to the allocation and cancellation of special drawing rights the Fund shall seek to meet the long-term global need, as and when it arises, to supplement existing reserve assets in such manner as will promote the attainment of its purposes and will avoid economic stagnation and deflation as well as excess demand and inflation in the world.

(b) The first decision to allocate special drawing rights shall take into account, as special considerations, a collective judgment that there is a global need to supplement reserves, and the attainment of a better balance of payments equilibrium, as well as the likelihood of a better working of the adjustment process in the future.

Section 2. *Allocation and cancellation*

(a) Decisions of the Fund to allocate or cancel special drawing rights shall be made for basic periods which shall run consecutively and shall be five years in duration. The first basic period shall begin on the date of the first decision to allocate special drawing rights or such later date as may be specified in that decision. Any allocations or cancellations shall take place at yearly intervals.

(b) The rates at which allocations are to be made shall be expressed as percentages of quotas on the date of each decision to allocate. The rates at which special drawing rights are to be cancelled shall be expressed as percentages of net cumulative allocations of special drawing rights on the date of each decision to cancel. The percentages shall be the same for all participants.

(c) In its decision for any basic period the Fund may provide, notwithstanding (a) and (b) above, that:

(i) the duration of the basic period shall be other than five years; or

(ii) the allocations or cancellations shall take place at other than yearly intervals; or

(iii) the basis for allocations or cancellations shall be the quotas or net cumulative allocations on dates other than the dates of decisions to allocate or cancel.

(d) A member that becomes a participant after a basic period starts shall receive allocations beginning with the next basic period in which allocations are made after it becomes a participant unless the Fund decides that the new participant shall start to receive allocations beginning with the next allocation after it becomes a participant. If the Fund decides that a member that becomes a participant during a basic period shall receive allocations during the remainder of that basic period and the participant was not a member on the dates established under (b) or (c) above, the Fund shall determine the basis on which these allocations to the participant shall be made.

(e) A participant shall receive allocations of special drawing rights made pursuant to any decision to allocate unless:

    (i) the governor for the participant did not vote in favor of the decision; and

    (ii) the participant has notified the Fund in writing prior to the first allocation of special drawing rights under that decision that it does not wish special drawing rights to be allocated to it under the decision. On the request of a participant, the Fund may decide to terminate the effect of the notice with respect to allocations of special drawing rights subsequent to the termination.

(f) If on the effective date of any cancellation the amount of special drawing rights held by a participant is less than its share of the special drawing rights that are to be cancelled, the participant shall eliminate its negative balance as promptly as its gross reserve position permits and shall remain in consultation with the Fund for this purpose. Special drawing rights acquired by the participant after the effective date of the cancellation shall be applied against its negative balance and cancelled.

Section 3. *Unexpected major developments*

The Fund may change the rates or intervals of allocation or cancellation during the rest of a basic period or change the length of a basic period or start a new basic period, if at any time the Fund finds it desirable to do so because of unexpected major developments.

Section 4. *Decisions on allocations and cancellations*

(a) Decisions under Section 2 (a), (b), and (c) or Section 3 of this Article shall be made by the Board of Governors on the basis of proposals of the Managing Director concurred in by the Executive Directors.

(b) Before making any proposal, the Managing Director, after having satisfied himself that it will be consistent with the provisions of Section 1 (a) of this Article, shall conduct such consultations as will enable him to ascertain that there is broad support among participants for the proposal. In addition, before making a proposal for the first allocation, the Managing Director shall satisfy himself that the provisions of Section 1 (b) of this Article have been met and that there is broad support among participants to begin allocations; he shall make a proposal for the first allocation as soon after the establishment of the Special Drawing Account as he is so satisfied.

(c) The Managing Director shall make proposals:

    (i) not later than six months before the end of each basic period;

    (ii) if no decision has been taken with respect to allocation or cancellation for a basic period, whenever he is satisfied that the provisions of (b) above have been met;

    (iii) when, in accordance with Section 3 of this Article, he considers that it would be desirable to change the rate or intervals of allocation or cancellation or change the length of a basic period or start a new basic period; or

    (iv) within six months of a request by the Board of Governors or the Executive Directors;

provided that, if under (i), (iii), or (iv) above the Managing Director ascertains that there is no proposal which he considers to be consistent with the provisions of Section 1 of this Article that has broad support among participants in accordance with (b) above, he shall report to the Board of Governors and to the Executive Directors.

(d) A majority of eighty-five percent of the total voting power shall be required for decisions under Section 2 (a), (b), and (c) or Section 3 of this Article except for decisions under Section 3 with respect to a decrease in the rates of allocation.

ARTICLE XXV

Operations and Transactions in Special Drawing Rights

Section 1. *Use of special drawing rights*

Special drawing rights may be used in the operations and transactions authorized by or under this Agreement.

Section 2. *Transactions between participants*

(a) A participant shall be entitled to use its special drawing rights to obtain an equivalent amount of currency from a participant designated under Section 5 of this Article.

(b) A participant, in agreement with another participant, may use its special **drawing** rights:

> (i) to obtain an equivalent amount of its own currency held by the other participant; or
>
> (ii) to obtain an equivalent amount of currency from the other participant in any transactions, prescribed by the Fund, that would promote reconstitution by the other participant under Section 6 (a) of this Article; prevent or reduce a negative balance of the other participant; offset the effect of a failure by the other participant to fulfill the expectation in Section 3 (a) of this Article; or bring the holdings of special drawing rights by both participants closer to their net cumulative allocations. The Fund by an eighty-five percent majority of the total voting power may prescribe additional transactions or categories of transactions under this provision. Any transactions or categories of transactions prescribed by the Fund under this subsection (b) (ii) shall be consistent with the other provisions of this Agreement and with the proper use of special drawing rights in accordance with this Agreement.

(c) A participant that provides currency to a participant using special drawing rights shall receive an equivalent amount of special drawing rights.

Section 3. *Requirement of need*

(a) In transactions under Section 2 of this Article, except as otherwise provided in (c) below, a participant will be expected to use its special drawing rights only to meet balance of payments needs or in the light of developments in its official holdings of gold, foreign exchange, and special drawing rights, and its reserve position in the Fund, and not for the sole purpose of changing the composition of the foregoing as between special drawing rights and the total of gold, foreign exchange, and reserve position in the Fund.

(b) The use of special drawing rights shall not be subject to challenge on the basis of the expectation in (a) above, but the Fund may make representations to a participant that fails to fulfill this expectation. A participant that persists in failing to fulfill this expectation shall be subject to Article XXIX, Section 2 (b).

(c) Participants may use special drawing rights without fulfilling the expectation in (a) above to obtain an equivalent amount of currency from another participant in any transactions, prescribed by the Fund, that would promote reconstitution by the other participant under Section 6 (a) of this Article; prevent or reduce a negative balance of the other participant; offset the effect of a failure by the other participant to fulfill the expectation in (a) above; or bring the holdings of special drawing rights by both participants closer to their net cumulative allocations.

Section 4. *Obligation to provide currency*

A participant designated by the Fund under Section 5 of this Article shall provide on demand currency convertible in fact to a participant using special drawing rights under Section 2 (a) of this Article. A participant's obligation to provide currency shall not extend beyond the point at which its holdings of special drawing rights in excess of its net cumulative allocation are equal to twice its net cumulative allocation or such higher limit as may be agreed between a participant and the Fund. A participant may provide currency in excess of the obligatory limit or any agreed higher limit.

Section 5. *Designation of participants to provide currency*

(a) The Fund shall ensure that a participant will be able to use its special drawing rights by designating participants to provide currency for specified amounts of special drawing rights for the purposes of Sections 2 (a) and 4 of this Article. Designations shall be made in accordance with the following general principles supplemented by such other principles as the Fund may adopt from time to time:

> (i) A participant shall be subject to designation if its balance of payments and gross reserve position is sufficiently strong, but this will not preclude the possibility that a participant with a strong reserve position will be designated even though it has a moderate balance of payments deficit. Participants shall be designated in such

manner as will promote over time a balanced distribution of holdings of special drawing rights among them.

(ii) Participants shall be subject to designation in order to promote reconstitution under Section 6 (a) of this Article; to reduce negative balances in holdings of special drawing rights; or to offset the effect of failures to fulfill the expectation in Section 3 (a) of this Article.

(iii) In designating participants the Fund normally shall give priority to those that need to acquire special drawing rights to meet the objectives of designation under (ii) above.

(b) In order to promote over time a balanced distribution of holdings of special drawing rights under (a) (i) above, the Fund shall apply the rules for designation in Schedule F or such rules as may be adopted under (c) below.

(c) The rules for designation shall be reviewed before the end of the first and each subsequent basic period and the Fund may adopt new rules as the result of a review. Unless new rules are adopted, the rules in force at the time of the review shall continue to apply.

Section 6. *Reconstitution*

(a) Participants that use their special drawing rights shall reconstitute their holdings of them in accordance with the rules for reconstitution in Schedule G or such rules as may be adopted under (b) below.

(b) The rules for reconstitution shall be reviewed before the end of the first and each subsequent basic period and new rules shall be adopted if necessary. Unless new rules are adopted or a decision is made to abrogate rules for reconstitution, the rules in force at the time of the review shall continue to apply. An eighty-five percent majority of the total voting power shall be required for decisions to adopt, modify, or abrogate the rules for reconstitution.

Section 7. *Operations and transactions through the General Account*

(a) Special drawing rights shall be included in a member's monetary reserves under Article XIX for the purposes of Article III, Section 4 (a), Article V, Section 7 (b) and (c), Article V, Section 8 (f), and Schedule B, paragraph 1. The Fund may decide that in calculating monetary reserves and the increase in monetary reserves during any year for the purpose of Article V, Section 7 (b) and (c), no account shall be taken of any increase or decrease in those monetary reserves which is due to allocations or cancellations of special drawing rights during the year.

(b) The Fund shall accept special drawing rights:

(i) in repurchases accruing in special drawing rights under Article V, Section 7 (b); and

(ii) in reimbursement pursuant to Article XXVI, Section 4.

(c) The Fund may accept special drawing rights to the extent it may decide:

(i) in payment of charges; and

(ii) in repurchases other than those under Article V, Section 7 (b), in proportions which, as far as feasible, shall be the same for all members.

(d) The Fund, if it deems such action appropriate to replenish its holdings of a participant's currency and after consultation with that participant on alternative ways of replenishment under Article VII, Section 2, may require that participant to provide its currency for special drawing rights held in the General Account subject to Section 4 of this Article. In replenishing with special drawing rights, the Fund shall pay due regard to the principles of designation under Section 5 of this Article.

(e) To the extent that a participant may receive special drawing rights in a transaction prescribed by the Fund to promote reconstitution by it under Section 6 (a) of this Article, prevent or reduce a negative balance, or offset the effect of a failure by it to fulfill the expectation in Section 3 (a) of this Article, the Fund may provide the participant with special drawing rights held in the General Account for gold or currency acceptable to the Fund.

(f) In any of the other operations and transactions of the Fund with a participant conducted through the General Account the Fund may use special drawing rights by agreement with the participant.

(g) The Fund may levy reasonable charges uniform for all participants in connection with operations and transactions under this Section.

Section 8. *Exchange rates*

(a) The exchange rates for operations or transactions between participants shall be such that a participant using special drawing rights shall receive the same value whatever currencies might be provided and whichever participants provide those currencies, and the Fund shall adopt regulations to give effect to this principle.

(b) The Fund shall consult a participant on the procedure for determining rates of exchange for its currency.

(c) For the purpose of this provision the term participant includes a terminating participant.

ARTICLE XXVI

Special Drawing Account Interest and Charges

Section 1. *Interest*

Interest at the same rate for all holders shall be paid by the Fund to each holder on the amount of its holdings of special drawing rights. The Fund shall pay the amount due to each holder whether or not sufficient charges are received to meet the payment of interest.

Section 2. *Charges*

Charges at the same rate for all participants shall be paid to the Fund by each participant on the amount of its net cumulative allocation of special drawing rights plus any negative balance of the participant or unpaid charges.

Section 3. *Rate of interest and charges*

The rate of interest shall be equal to the rate of charges and shall be one and one-half percent per annum. The Fund in its discretion may increase or reduce this rate, but the rate shall not be greater than two percent or the rate of remuneration decided under Article V, Section 9, whichever is higher, or smaller than one percent or the rate of remuneration decided under Article V, Section 9, whichever is lower.

Section 4. *Assessments*

When it is decided under Article XXII, Section 2, that reimbursement shall be made, the Fund shall levy assessments for this purpose at the same rate for all participants on their net cumulative allocations.

Section 5. *Payment of interest, charges, and assessments*

Interest, charges, and assessments shall be paid in special drawing rights. A participant that needs special drawing rights to pay any charge or assessment shall be obligated and entitled to obtain them, at its option for gold or currency acceptable to the Fund, in a transaction with the Fund conducted through the General Account. If sufficient special drawing rights cannot be obtained in this way, the participant shall be obligated and entitled to obtain them with currency convertible in fact from a participant which the Fund shall specify. Special drawing rights acquired by a participant after the date for payment shall be applied against its unpaid charges and cancelled.

ARTICLE XXVII

Administration of the General Account and the Special Drawing Account

(a) The General Account and the Special Drawing Account shall be administered in accordance with the provisions of Article XII, subject to the following:

  (i) The Board of Governors may delegate to the Executive Directors authority to exercise any powers of the Board with respect to special drawing rights except those under Article XXIII, Section 3, Article XXIV, Section 2 (a), (b), and (c), and Section 3, the penultimate sentence of Article XXV, Section 2 (b), Article XXV, Section 6 (b), and Article XXXI (a).

  (ii) For meetings of or decisions by the Board of Governors on matters pertaining exclusively to the Special Drawing Account only requests by or the presence and the votes of governors appointed by members that are participants shall be counted for the purpose of calling meetings and determining whether a quorum exists or whether a decision is made by the required majority.

(iii) For decisions by the Executive Directors on matters pertaining exclusively to the Special Drawing Account only directors appointed or elected by at least one member that is a participant shall be entitled to vote. Each of these directors shall be entitled to cast the number of votes allotted to the member which is a participant that appointed him or to the members that are participants whose votes counted towards his election. Only the presence of directors appointed or elected by members that are participants and the votes allotted to members that are participants shall be counted for the purpose of determining whether a quorum exists or whether a decision is made by the required majority.

(iv) Questions of the general administration of the Fund, including reimbursement under Article XXII, Section 2, and any question whether a matter pertains to both Accounts or exclusively to the Special Drawing Account shall be decided as if they pertained exclusively to the General Account. Decisions with respect to the acceptance and holding of special drawing rights in the General Account and the use of them, and other decisions affecting the operations and transactions conducted through both the General Account and the Special Drawing Account shall be made by the majorities required for decisions on matters pertaining exclusively to each Account. A decision on a matter pertaining to the Special Drawing Account shall so indicate.

(b) In addition to the privileges and immunities that are accorded under Article IX of this Agreement, no tax of any kind shall be levied on special drawing rights or on operations or transactions in special drawing rights.

(c) A question of interpretation of the provisions of this Agreement on matters pertaining exclusively to the Special Drawing Account shall be submitted to the Executive Directors pursuant to Article XVIII (a) only on the request of a participant. In any case where the Executive Directors have given a decision on a question of interpretation pertaining exclusively to the Special Drawing Account only a participant may require that the question be referred to the Board of Governors under Article XVIII (b). The Board of Governors shall decide whether a governor appointed by a member that is not a participant shall be entitled to vote in the Committee on Interpretation on questions pertaining exclusively to the Special Drawing Account.

(d) Whenever a disagreement arises between the Fund and a participant that has terminated its participation in the Special Drawing Account or between the Fund and any participant during the liquidation of the Special Drawing Account with respect to any matter arising exclusively from participation in the Special Drawing Account, the disagreement shall be submitted to arbitration in accordance with the procedures in Article XVIII (c).

ARTICLE XXVIII

General Obligations of Participants

In addition to the obligations assumed with respect to special drawing rights under other Articles of this Agreement, each participant undertakes to collaborate with the Fund and with other participants in order to facilitate the effective functioning of the Special Drawing Account and the proper use of special drawing rights in accordance with this Agreement.

ARTICLE XXIX

Suspension of Transactions in Special Drawing Rights

Section 1. *Emergency provisions*

In the event of an emergency or the development of unforeseen circumstances threatening the operations of the Fund with respect to the Special Drawing Account, the Executive Directors by unanimous vote may suspend for a period of not more than one hundred twenty days the operation of any of the provisions relating to special drawing rights, and the provisions of Article XVI, Section 1 (b), (c), and (d), shall then apply.

Section 2. *Failure to fulfill obligations*

(a) If the Fund finds that a participant has failed to fulfill its obligations under Article XXV, Section 4, the right of the participant to use its special drawing rights shall be suspended unless the Fund otherwise determines.

(b) If the Fund finds that a participant has failed to fulfill any other obligation with respect to special drawing rights, the Fund may suspend the right of the participant to use special drawing rights it acquires after the suspension.

(c) Regulations shall be adopted to ensure that before action is taken against any participant under (a) or (b) above, the participant shall be informed immediately of the complaint against it and given an adequate opportunity for stating its case, both orally and in writing. Whenever the participant is thus informed of a complaint relating to (a) above, it shall not use special drawing rights pending the disposition of the complaint.

(d) Suspension under (a) or (b) above or limitation under (c) above shall not affect a participant's obligation to provide currency in accordance with Article XXV, Section 4.

(e) The Fund may at any time terminate a suspension under (a) or (b) above, provided that a suspension imposed on a participant under (b) above for failure to fulfill the obligation under Article XXV, Section 6 (a), shall not be terminated until one hundred eighty days after the end of the first calendar quarter during which the participant complies with the rules for reconstitution.

(f) The right of a participant to use its special drawing rights shall not be suspended because it has become ineligible to use the Fund's resources under Article IV, Section 6, Article V, Section 5, Article VI, Section 1, or Article XV, Section 2 (a). Article XV, Section 2, shall not apply because a participant has failed to fulfill any obligations with respect to special drawing rights.

ARTICLE XXX

Termination of Participation

Section 1. *Right to terminate participation*

(a) Any participant may terminate its participation in the Special Drawing Account at any time by transmitting a notice in writing to the Fund at its principal office. Termination shall become effective on the date the notice is received.

(b) A participant that withdraws from membership in the Fund shall be deemed to have simultaneously terminated its participation in the Special Drawing Account.

Section 2. *Settlement on termination*

(a) When a participant terminates its participation in the Special Drawing Account, all operations and transactions by the terminating participant in special drawing rights shall cease except as otherwise permitted under an agreement made pursuant to (c) below in order to facilitate a settlement or as provided in Sections 3, 5, and 6 of this Article or in Schedule H. Interest and charges that accrued to the date of termination and assessments levied before that date but not paid shall be paid in special drawing rights.

(b) The Fund shall be obligated to redeem all special drawing rights held by the terminating participant, and the terminating participant shall be obligated to pay to the Fund an amount equal to its net cumulative allocation and any other amounts that may be due and payable because of its participation in the Special Drawing Account. These obligations shall be set off against each other and the amount of special drawing rights held by the terminating participant that is used in the setoff to extinguish its obligation to the Fund shall be cancelled.

(c) A settlement shall be made with reasonable dispatch by agreement between the terminating participant and the Fund with respect to any obligation of the terminating participant or the Fund after the setoff in (b) above. If agreement on a settlement is not reached promptly the provisions of Schedule H shall apply.

Section 3. *Interest and charges*

After the date of termination the Fund shall pay interest on any outstanding balance of special drawing rights held by a terminating participant and the terminating participant shall pay charges on any outstanding obligation owed to the Fund at the times and rates prescribed under Article XXVI. Payment shall be made in special drawing rights. A terminating participant shall be entitled to obtain special drawing rights with currency convertible in fact to pay charges or assessments in a transaction with a participant specified by the Fund or by agreement from any other holder, or to dispose of special drawing rights received as interest in a transaction with any participant designated under Article XXV, Section 5, or by agreement with any other holder.

Section 4. *Settlement of obligation to the Fund*

Gold or currency received by the Fund from a terminating participant shall be used by the Fund to redeem special drawing rights held by participants in proportion to the amount by which each participant's holdings of special drawing rights exceed its net cumulative allocation at the time the gold or currency is received by the Fund. Special drawing rights so redeemed and special drawing rights obtained by a terminating participant under the provisions of this Agreement to meet any installment due under an agreement on settlement or under Schedule H and set off against that installment shall be cancelled.

Section 5. *Settlement of obligation to a terminating participant*

Whenever the Fund is required to redeem special drawing rights held by a terminating participant, redemption shall be made with currency or gold provided by participants specified by the Fund. These participants shall be specified in accordance with the principles in Article XXV, Section 5. Each specified participant shall provide at its option the currency of the terminating participant or currency convertible in fact or gold to the Fund and shall receive an equivalent amount of special drawing rights. However, a terminating participant may use its special drawing rights to obtain its own currency, currency convertible in fact, or gold from any holder, if the Fund so permits.

Section 6. *General Account transactions*

In order to facilitate settlement with a terminating participant the Fund may decide that a terminating participant shall:

(i) use any special drawing rights held by it after the setoff in Section 2 (b) of this Article, when they are to be redeemed, in a transaction with the Fund conducted through the General Account to obtain its own currency or currency convertible in fact at the option of the Fund; or

(ii) obtain special drawing rights in a transaction with the Fund conducted through the General Account for a currency acceptable to the Fund or gold to meet any charges or installment due under an agreement or the provisions of Schedule H.

ARTICLE XXXI

Liquidation of the Special Drawing Account

(a) The Special Drawing Account may not be liquidated except by decision of the Board of Governors. In an emergency, if the Executive Directors decide that liquidation of the Special Drawing Account may be necessary, they may temporarily suspend allocations or cancellations and all transactions in special drawing rights pending decision by the Board. A decision by the Board of Governors to liquidate the Fund shall be a decision to liquidate both the General Account and the Special Drawing Account.

(b) If the Board of Governors decides to liquidate the Special Drawing Account, all allocations or cancellations and all operations and transactions in special drawing rights and the activities of the Fund with respect to the Special Drawing Account shall cease except those incidental to the orderly discharge of the obligations of participants and of the Fund with respect to special drawing rights, and all obligations of the Fund and of participants under this Agreement with respect to special drawing rights shall cease except those set out in this Article, Article XVIII (c), Article XXVI, Article XXVII (d), Article XXX and Schedule H, or any agreement reached under Article XXX subject to paragraph 4 of Schedule H, Article XXXII, and Schedule I.

(c) Upon liquidation of the Special Drawing Account, interest and charges that accrued to the date of liquidation and assessments levied before that date but not paid shall be paid in special drawing rights. The Fund shall be obligated to redeem all special drawing rights held by holders and each participant shall be obligated to pay the Fund an amount equal to its net cumulative allocation of special drawing rights and such other amounts as may be due and payable because of its participation in the Special Drawing Account.

(d) Liquidation of the Special Drawing Account shall be administered in accordance with the provisions of Schedule I.

ARTICLE XXXII

Explanation of Terms with Respect to Special Drawing Rights

In interpreting the provisions of this Agreement with respect to special drawing rights the Fund and its members shall be guided by the following:

(a) Net cumulative allocation of special drawing rights means the total amount of special drawing rights allocated to a participant less its share of special drawing rights that have been cancelled under Article XXIV, Section 2 (a).

(b) Currency convertible in fact means:

   (1) a participant's currency for which a procedure exists for the conversion of balances of the currency obtained in transactions involving special drawing rights into each other currency for which such procedure exists, at rates of exchange prescribed under Article XXV, Section 8, and which is the currency of a participant that

   (i) has accepted the obligations of Article VIII, Sections 2, 3, and 4, or

   (ii) for the settlement of international transactions in fact freely buys and sells gold within the limits prescribed by the Fund under Section 2 of Article IV; or

   (2) currency convertible into a currency described in paragraph (1) above at rates of exchange prescribed under Article XXV, Section 8.

(c) A participant's reserve position in the Fund means the sum of the gold tranche purchases it could make and the amount of any indebtedness of the Fund which is readily repayable to the participant under a loan agreement."

L

SCHEDULE B

Provisions with Respect to Repurchase by a Member of its Currency Held by the Fund

1. Paragraph 1 shall read:

   "1. In determining the extent to which repurchase of a member's currency from the Fund under Article V, Section 7 (b), shall be made with each convertible currency and each of the other types of monetary reserve, the following rule, subject to 2 below, shall apply:

   (a) If the member's monetary reserves have not increased during the year, the amount payable to the Fund shall be distributed among all types of reserves in proportion to the member's holdings thereof at the end of the year.

   (b) If the member's monetary reserves have increased during the year, a part of the amount payable to the Fund equal to one-half of the increase, minus one-half of any decrease in the Fund's holdings of the member's currency that has occurred during the year, shall be distributed among those types of reserves which have increased in proportion to the amount by which each of them has increased. The remainder of the sum payable to the Fund shall be distributed among all types of reserves in proportion to the member's remaining holdings thereof.

   (c) If after the repurchases required under Article V, Section 7 (b), had been made, the result would exceed either of the limits specified in Article V, Section 7 (c) (i) or (ii), the Fund shall require such repurchases to be made by the member proportionately in such manner that these limits will not be exceeded.

   (d) If after all the repurchases required under Article V, Section 7 (b), had been made, the result would exceed the limit specified in Article V, Section 7 (c) (iii), the amount by which the limit would be exceeded shall be discharged in convertible currencies as determined by the Fund without exceeding that limit.

(e) If a repurchase required under Article V, Section 7 (b), would exceed the limit specified in Article V, Section 7 (c) (iv), the amount by which the limit would be exceeded shall be repurchased at the end of the subsequent financial year or years in such a way that total repurchases under Article V, Section 7 (b), in any year would not exceed the limit specified in Article V, Section 7 (c) (iv)."

2. Paragraph 2 shall read:

"2. (a) The Fund shall not require the currency of any non-member under Article V, Section 7 (b) and (c).

(b) Any amount payable in the currency of a non-member under 1 (a) or 1 (b) above shall be paid in the convertible currencies of members as determined by the Fund."

3. The following paragraphs 5 and 6 shall be added to Schedule B:

"5. In calculating monetary reserves and the increase in monetary reserves during any year for the purpose of Article V, Section 7 (b) and (c), the Fund may decide in its discretion, on the request of a member, that deductions shall be made for obligations outstanding as the result of transactions between members under a reciprocal facility by which a member agrees to exchange on demand its currency for the currency of the other member up to a maximum amount and on terms requiring that each such transaction be reversed within a specified period not in excess of nine months."

"6. In calculating monetary reserves and the increase in monetary reserves for the purpose of Article V, Section 7 (b) and (c), Article XIX (e) shall apply except that the following provision shall apply at the end of a financial year if it was in effect at the beginning of that year:

'A member's monetary reserves shall be calculated by deducting from its central holdings the currency liabilities to the Treasuries, central banks, stabilization funds, or similar fiscal agencies of other members or non-members specified under (d) above, together with similar liabilities to other official institutions and other banks in the territories of members, or non-members specified under (d) above. To these net holdings shall be added the sums deemed to be official holdings of other official institutions and other banks under (c) above.' "

M

The following Schedules shall be added after Schedule E:

"SCHEDULE F

Designation

During the first basic period the rules for designation shall be as follows:

(a) Participants subject to designation under Article XXV, Section 5 (a) (i), shall be designated for such amounts as will promote over time equality in the ratios of the participants' holdings of special drawing rights in excess of their net cumulative allocations to their official holdings of gold and foreign exchange.

(b) The formula to give effect to (a) above shall be such that participants subject to designation shall be designated:

(i) in proportion to their official holdings of gold and foreign exchange when the ratios described in (a) above are equal; and

(ii) in such manner as gradually to reduce the difference between the ratios described in (a) above that are low and the ratios that are high.

SCHEDULE G

Reconstitution

1. During the first basic period the rules for reconstitution shall be as follows:

(a) (i) A participant shall so use and reconstitute its holdings of special drawing rights that, five years after the first allocation and at the end of each calendar quarter thereafter, the average of its total daily holdings of special drawing rights over the most recent five-year period will be not less than thirty percent of the average of its daily net cumulative allocation of special drawing rights over the same period.

(ii) Two years after the first allocation and at the end of each calendar month thereafter the Fund shall make calculations for each participant so as to ascertain whether and to what extent the participant would need to acquire special drawing rights between the date of the calculation and the end of any five-year period in order to comply with the requirement in (a) (i) above. The Fund shall adopt regulations with respect to the bases on which these calculations shall be made and with respect to the timing of the designation of participants under Article XXV, Section 5 (a) (ii), in order to assist them to comply with the requirement in (a) (i) above.

(iii) The Fund shall give special notice to a participant when the calculations under (a) (ii) above indicate that it is unlikely that the participant will be able to comply with the requirement in (a) (i) above unless it ceases to use special drawing rights for the rest of the period for which the calculation was made under (a) (ii) above.

(iv) A participant that needs to acquire special drawing rights to fulfill this obligation shall be obligated and entitled to obtain them, at its option for gold or currency acceptable to the Fund, in a transaction with the Fund conducted through the General Account. If sufficient special drawing rights to fulfill this obligation cannot be obtained in this way, the participant shall be obligated and entitled to obtain them with currency convertible in fact from a participant which the Fund shall specify.

(b) Participants shall also pay due regard to the desirability of pursuing over time a balanced relationship between their holdings of special drawing rights and their holdings of gold and foreign exchange and their reserve positions in the Fund.

2. If a participant fails to comply with the rules for reconstitution, the Fund shall determine whether or not the circumstances justify suspension under Article XXIX, Section 2 (b).

SCHEDULE H

Termination of Participation

1. If the obligation remaining after the setoff under Article XXX, Section 2 (b), is to the terminating participant and agreement on settlement between the Fund and the terminating participant is not reached within six months of the date of termination, the Fund shall redeem this balance of special drawing rights in equal half-yearly installments within a maximum of five years of the date of termination. The Fund shall redeem this balance as it may determine, either (a) by the payment to the terminating participant of the amounts provided by the remaining participants to the Fund in accordance with Article XXX, Section 5, or (b) by permitting the terminating participant to use its special drawing rights to obtain its own currency or currency convertible in fact from a participant specified by the Fund, the General Account, or any other holder.

2. If the obligation remaining after the setoff under Article XXX, Section 2 (b), is to the Fund and agreement on settlement is not reached within six months of the date of termination, the terminating participant shall discharge this obligation in equal half-yearly installments within three years of the date of termination or within such longer period as may be fixed by the Fund. The terminating participant shall discharge this obligation, as the Fund may determine, either (a) by the payment to the Fund of currency convertible in fact or gold at the option of the terminating participant, or (b) by obtaining special drawing rights, in accordance with Article XXX, Section 6, from the General Account or in agreement with a participant specified by the Fund or from any other holder, and the setoff of these special drawing rights against the installment due.

3. Installments under either 1 or 2 above shall fall due six months after the date of termination and at intervals of six months thereafter.

4. In the event of the Special Drawing Account going into liquidation under Article XXXI within six months of the date a participant terminates its participation, the settlement between the Fund and that government shall be made in accordance with Article XXXI and Schedule I.

SCHEDULE I

Administration of Liquidation of the Special Drawing Account

1. In the event of liquidation of the Special Drawing Account, participants shall discharge their obligations to the Fund in ten half-yearly installments, or in such longer periods as the Fund may decide is needed, in currency convertible in fact and the currencies of participants holding special drawing rights to be redeemed in any installment to the extent of such redemption, as determined by the Fund. The first half-yearly payment shall be made six months after the decision to liquidate the Special Drawing Account.

2. If it is decided to liquidate the Fund within six months of the date of the decision to liquidate the Special Drawing Account, the liquidation of the Special Drawing Account shall not proceed until special drawing rights held in the General Account have been distributed in accordance with the following rule:

> After the distribution made under 2 (a) of Schedule E, the Fund shall apportion its special drawing rights held in the General Account among all members that are participants in proportion to the amounts due to each participant after the distribution under 2 (a). To determine the amount due to each member for the purpose of apportioning the remainder of its holdings of each currency under 2 (c) of Schedule E, the Fund shall deduct the distribution of special drawing rights made under this rule.

3. With the amounts received under 1 above, the Fund shall redeem special drawing rights held by holders in the following manner and order:

   (a) Special drawing rights held by governments that have terminated their participation more than six months before the date the Board of Governors decides to liquidate the Special Drawing Account shall be redeemed in accordance with the terms of any agreement under Article XXX or Schedule H.

   (b) Special drawing rights held by holders that are not participants shall be redeemed before those held by participants, and shall be redeemed in proportion to the amount held by each holder.

   (c) The Fund shall determine the proportion of special drawing rights held by each participant in relation to its net cumulative allocation. The Fund shall first redeem special drawing rights from the participants with the highest proportion until this proportion is reduced to that of the second highest proportion; the Fund shall then redeem the special drawing rights held by these participants in accordance with their net cumulative allocations until the proportions are reduced to that of the third highest proportion; and this process shall be continued until the amount available for redemption is exhausted.

4. Any amount that a participant will be entitled to receive in redemption under 3 above shall be set off against any amount to be paid under 1 above.

5. During liquidation the Fund shall pay interest on the amount of special drawing rights held by holders, and each participant shall pay charges on the net cumulative allocation of special drawing rights to it less the amount of any payments made in accordance with 1 above. The rates of interest and charges and the time of payment shall be determined by the Fund. Payments of interest and charges shall be made in special drawing rights to the extent possible. A participant that does not hold sufficient special drawing rights to meet any charges shall make the payment with gold or a currency specified by the Fund. Special drawing rights received as charges in amounts needed for administrative expenses shall not be used for the payment of interest, but shall be transferred to the Fund and shall be redeemed first and with the currencies used by the Fund to meet its expenses.

6. While a participant is in default with respect to any payment required by 1 or 5 above, no amounts shall be paid to it in accordance with 2 or 5 above.

7. If after the final payments have been made to participants each participant not in default does not hold special drawing rights in the same proportion to its net cumulative allocation, those participants holding a lower proportion shall purchase from those holding a higher proportion such amounts in accordance with arrangements made by the Fund as will make the proportion of their holdings of special drawing rights the same. Each participant in default shall pay to the Fund its own currency in an amount equal to its default. The Fund shall apportion this currency and any residual claims among participants in proportion to the amount of special drawing rights held by each and these special drawing rights shall be cancelled. The Fund shall then close the books of the Special Drawing Account and all of the Fund's liabilities arising from the allocations of special drawing rights and the administration of the Special Drawing Account shall cease.

8. Each participant whose currency is distributed to other participants under this Schedule guarantees the unrestricted use of such currency at all times for the purchase of goods or for payments of sums due to it or to persons in its territories. Each participant so obligated agrees to compensate other participants for any loss resulting from the difference between the value at which the Fund distributed its currency under this Schedule and the value realized by such participants on disposal of its currency."

Annex B

OUTLINE OF A FACILITY BASED ON SPECIAL DRAWING RIGHTS IN THE FUND

Introduction

The facility described in this Outline is intended to meet the need, as and when it arises, for a supplement to existing reserve assets. It is to be established within the framework of the Fund and, therefore, by an Amendment of the Fund's Articles. Provisions relating to some of the topics in this Outline could be included in By-Laws adopted by the Board of Governors or Rules and Regulations adopted by the Executive Directors rather than in the Amendment.

I. Establishment of a Special Drawing Account in the Fund

(a) An Amendment to the Articles will establish a Special Drawing Account through which all the operations relating to special drawing rights will be carried out. The purposes of the facility will be set forth in the introductory section of the Amendment.

(b) The operations of and resources available under the Special Drawing Account will be separate from the operations of the present Fund which will be referred to as the General Account.

(c) Separate provisions will be included in the Amendment for withdrawal from or liquidation of the Special Drawing Account; Article XVI, Section 2 and Schedules D and E on withdrawal and liquidation will continue to apply as they do at present to the General Account of the Fund.

II. Participants and Other Holders

1. *Participants.* Participation in the Special Drawing Account will be open to any member of the Fund that undertakes the obligations of the Amendment. A member's quota in the Fund will be the same for the purposes of both the General and the Special Drawing Accounts of the Fund.

2. *Holding by General Account.* The General Account will be authorized to hold and use special drawing rights.

III. Allocation of Special Drawing Rights

1. *Principles for decisions.* The Special Drawing Account will allocate special drawing rights in accordance with the provisions of the Amendment. Special considerations applicable to the first decision to allocate special drawing rights, as well as the principles on which all decisions to allocate special drawing rights will be based, will be included in the introductory section of the Amendment and, to the extent necessary, in a Report explaining the Amendment.

2. *Basic period and rate of allocation.* The following provisions will apply to any decision to allocate special drawing rights:

(i) The decision will prescribe a basic period during which special drawing rights will be allocated at specified intervals. The period will normally be five years in length, but the Fund may decide that any basic period will be of different duration. The first basic period will begin on the effective date of the first decision to allocate special drawing rights.

(ii) The decision will also prescribe the rate or rates at which special drawing rights will be allocated during the basic period. Rates will be expressed as a percentage, uniform for all participants, of quotas on the date specified in the decision.

3. *Procedure for decisions.*

(a) Any decision on the basic period for, timing of, or rate of allocation of special drawing rights will be taken by the Board of Governors on the basis of a proposal by the Managing Director concurred in by the Executive Directors.

(b) Before formulating any proposal, the Managing Director after having satisfied himself that the considerations referred to in III.1 have been met, will conduct such consultations as will enable him to ascertain that there is broad support among participants for the allocation of special drawing rights at the proposed rate and for the proposed basic period.

(c) The Managing Director will make proposals with respect to the allocation of special drawing rights: (i) within sufficient time before the end of a basic period; (ii) in the circumstances of III.4; (iii) within six months after the Board of Governors or the Executive Directors request that he make a proposal. The Managing Director will make a proposal for the first basic period when he is of the opinion that there is broad support among the participants to start the allocation of special drawing rights.

(d) The Executive Directors will review both the operations of the Special Drawing Account and the adequacy of global reserves as part of their annual report to the Board of Governors.

4. *Change in rate of allocation or basic period.* If there are unexpected major developments which make it desirable to change the rate at which further special drawing rights are to be allocated for a basic period, (i) the rate may be increased or decreased, or (ii) the basic period may be terminated and a different rate of allocation adopted for a new basic period. Paragraph III.3 will apply to such changes.

5. *Voting majority.*

(a) For decisions on the basic period for, timing of, amount and rate of allocation of special drawing rights, an 85 per cent majority of the voting power of participants shall be required.

(b) Notwithstanding (a) above, the decisions to decrease the rate of allocation of special drawing rights for the remainder of the basic period will be taken by a simple majority of the voting power of participants.

6. *Opting out.* The Amendment will include provisions that will prescribe to what extent a participant will be required initially to receive special drawing rights, but will stipulate that beyond any such amount a participant that does not vote in favor of a decision to allocate special drawing rights may elect not to receive them under that decision.

IV. Cancellation of Special Drawing Rights

The principles set forth in III relating to the procedure and voting for the allocation of special drawing rights will be applicable, with appropriate modifications, to the cancellation of such rights.

V. Use of Special Drawing Rights

1. *Right to use special drawing rights.*

(a) A participant will be entitled, in accordance with the provisions of V, to use special drawing rights to acquire an equivalent amount of a currency convertible in fact. A participant which thus provides currency will receive an equivalent amount of special drawing rights.

(b) Within the framework of such rules and regulations as the Fund may adopt, a participant may obtain the currencies referred to in (a) either directly from another participant or through the Special Drawing Account.

(c) Except as indicated in V.3 (c), a participant will be expected to use its special drawing rights only for balance of payments needs or in the light of developments in its total reserves and not for the sole purpose of changing the composition of its reserves.

(d) The use of special drawing rights will not be subject to prior challenge on the basis of this expectation, but the Fund may make representations to any participant which, in the Fund's judgment, has failed to observe the expectation, and may direct drawings to such participant to the extent of such failure.

2. *Provision of currency.* A participant's obligation to provide currency will not extend beyond a point at which its holdings of special drawing rights in excess of the net cumulative amount of such rights allocated to it are equal to twice that amount. However, a participant may provide currency, or agree with the Fund to provide currency, in excess of this limit.

3. *Selection of participants to be drawn upon.* The Fund's rules and instructions relating to the participants from which currencies should be acquired by users of special drawing rights will be based on the following main general principles, supplemented by such principles as the Fund may find desirable from time to time:

(a) Normally, currencies will be acquired from participants that have a sufficiently strong balance of payments and reserve position, but this will not preclude the possibility that currency will be acquired from participants with strong reserve positions even though they have moderate balance of payments deficits.

(b) The Fund's primary criterion will be to seek to approach over time equality, among the participants indicated from time to time by the criteria in (a) above, in the ratios of their holdings of special drawing rights, or such holdings in excess of net cumulative allocations thereof, to total reserves.

(c) In addition, the Fund will, in its rules and instructions, provide for such use of special drawing rights, either directly between participants or through the intermediary of the Special Drawing Account, as will promote voluntary reconstitution and reconstitution under V.4.

(d) Subject to the provisions of V.1 (c), a participant may use its special drawing rights to purchase balances of its currency held by another participant, with the agreement of the latter.

4. *Reconstitution.*

(a) Members that use their special drawing rights will incur an obligation to reconstitute their position in accordance with principles which will take account of the amount and the duration of the use. These principles will be laid down in rules and regulations of the Fund.

(b) The rules for reconstitution of drawings made during the first basic period will be based on the following principles:

(i) The average net use, taking into account both use below and holdings above its net cumulative allocation, made by a participant of its special drawing rights calculated on the basis of the preceding five years, shall not exceed 70 per cent of its average net cumulative allocation during this period. Reconstitution under this subparagraph (i) will be brought about through the mechanism of transfers, by the Fund directing drawings correspondingly.

(ii) Participants will pay due regard to the desirability of pursuing over time a balanced relationship between their holdings of special drawing rights and other reserves.

(c) Reconstitution rules will be reviewed before the end of the first and of each subsequent period and new rules will be adopted, if necessary. If new rules are not adopted for a basic period, the rules for the preceding period shall apply unles it is decided to abrogate reconstitution rules. The same majority as is required for decisions on the basic period, timing of, or rate of allocation of special drawing rights will be required for decisions to adopt, amend, or abrogate reconstitution rules. Any amendment in the rules will govern the reconstitution of drawings made after the effective date of the amendment, unless otherwise decided.

VI. Interest and Maintenance of Gold Value

(a) *Interest.* A moderate rate of interest will be paid in special drawing rights on holdings of special drawing rights. The cost of this interest will be assessed against all participants in proportion to net cumulative allocations of special drawing rights to them.

(b) *Maintenance of gold value.* The unit of value for expressing special drawing rights will be equal to 0.888 671 grams of fine gold. The rights and obligations of participants and of the

Special Drawing Account will be subject to an absolute maintenance of gold value or to provisions similar to Article IV, Section 8 of the Fund's Articles.

VII. Functions of Fund Organs and Voting

1. *Exercise of powers.* The decisions taken with respect to the Special Drawing Account, and the supervision of its operations, will be carried out by the Board of Governors, the Executive Directors, the Managing Director, and the staff of the Fund. Certain powers, and in particular those relating to the adoption of decisions concerning the allocation, cancellation, and certain aspects of the use of special drawing rights, will be reserved to the Board of Governors. All other powers, except those specifically granted to other organs, will be vested in the Board of Governors which will be able to delegate them to the Executive Directors.

2. *Voting.* Except as otherwise provided in the Amendment, all decisions pertaining to the Special Drawing Account will be taken by a majority of votes cast. The precise formula for the voting power of participants, which will include basic and weighted votes, and possibly the adjustment of voting power in relation to the use of special drawing rights, will be the subject of later consideration.

VIII. General Provisions

1. *Collaboration.* Participants will undertake to collaborate with the Fund in order to facilitate the proper functioning and effective use of special drawing rights within the international monetary system.

2. *Nonfulfillment of obligations.*

(a) If the Fund finds that a participant has failed to fulfill its obligations to provide currency in accordance with the Amendment, the Fund may suspend the right of the participant to use its special drawing rights.

(b) If the Fund finds that a participant has failed to fulfill any other obligation under the Amendment, the Fund may suspend the participant's right to use any special drawing rights allocated to, or acquired by, it after the suspension.

(c) Suspension under (a) or (b) above will not affect a participant's obligation to provide currency in accordance with the Amendment.

(d) The Fund may at any time terminate a suspension under (a) or (b) above.

3. *Accounts.* All changes in holdings of special drawing rights will take effect when recorded in the accounts of the Special Drawing Account.

IX. Entry into Force

The Amendment would enter into force in accordance with the terms of Article XVII of the Fund's Articles.

PART V

Publications

Publications of the Fund

The following is a complete listing of the reports, documents, books, periodicals, pamphlets, and leaflets that have been made available to the general public from the Fund's inception to December 31, 1968. Except where otherwise stated, all were published by the Fund at Washington, D.C.

Agreement Between the United Nations and the International Monetary Fund. Accord entre les Nations Unies et le Fonds Monétaire International. 1956. 12 pp. Bilingual.

Annual Report of the Executive Directors . . . 1946 to date. Selected portions published also in French (1947, 1950, 1953, and 1962–67), German (1962 to date), and Spanish (1947 and 1962–67). Full Report (except index) published in French and Spanish beginning 1968.

Annual Report on Exchange Restrictions. 1950 to date. Supplement to Second Report concerning nonmembers of Fund published separately under title *Surveys of Exchange Controls and Restrictions in Argentina, Burma, Federal Republic of Germany, Hashemite Kingdom of the Jordan, Indonesia, Japan, New Zealand, Portugal, Spain, Sweden, Switzerland.*

Articles of Agreement of the International Monetary Fund. Adopted at the United Nations Monetary and Financial Conference, Bretton Woods, New Hampshire, July 22, 1944. Effective December 27, 1945. 1st printing, 1946; 7th printing, 1967. v + 65 pp. Published also in French and Spanish, without index. 1st printing issued under title *Articles of Agreement, International Monetary Fund, United Nations Monetary and Financial Conference, Bretton Woods, N.H., July 1 to 22, 1944.*

Articles of Agreement of the International Monetary Fund . . . As Modified by the Proposed Amendment Recommended by the Executive Directors April 16, 1968 and Approved by the Board of Governors May 31, 1968. [1968]. ix + 102 pp. Published also in French and Spanish.

Balance of Payments: Concepts and Definitions. 1968. iv + 47 pp. Published also in French and Spanish. (Pamphlet Series, No. 10.)

Balance of Payments: Its Meaning and Uses, by Poul Høst-Madsen. 1967. iv + 24 pp. Published also in French, German, and Spanish. (Pamphlet Series, No. 9.)

Balance of Payments Manual. 1948. 57 pp.; preliminary Spanish edition (mimeographed). 2nd ed., 1950. iii + 111 pp.; preliminary Spanish edition (mimeographed). 3rd ed., 1961. vii + 182 pp.; published also in French and Spanish.

Balance of Payments Yearbook.

Vol. 1: 1938, 1946, 1947	Vol. 8: 1950–54	Vol. 15: 1958–62
Vol. 2: 1948, preliminary 1949	Vol. 9: 1955–56	Vol. 16: 1959–63
Vol. 3: 1949–50	Vol. 10: 1956–57	Vol. 17: 1960–64
Vol. 4: 1950–51	Vol. 11: 1957–58	Vol. 18: 1961–65
Vol. 5: 1947–53	Vol. 12: 1955–59	Vol. 19: 1962–66
Vol. 6: 1953–54	Vol. 13: 1956–60	Vol. 20: 1963–67
Vol. 7: 1954–55	Vol. 14: 1957–61	

Vols. 1–4, bound; Vol. 5 to date in loose-leaf form; Vol. 19 to date available both loose-leaf and bound.

By-Laws, Rules and Regulations. Irregular. 1st issue, Mar. 1, 1947; 26th issue, Aug. 10, 1966.

Central Banking Legislation: A Collection of Central Bank, Monetary and Banking Laws. Statutes and related materials selected and annotated by Hans Aufricht. Vol. I, 1961. xxi + 1012 pp. (Monograph Series, No. 1.) Vol. II, Europe. 1967. xxiv + 921 pp. (Monograph Series, No. 4.)

Compensatory Financing of Export Fluctuations: A Report by the International Monetary Fund on Compensatory Financing of the Fluctuations in Exports of Primary Exporting Countries. 1963. 27 pp. Published also in French and Spanish.

Compensatory Financing of Export Fluctuations; Developments in the Fund's Facility: A Second Report by the International Monetary Fund on Compensatory Financing of the Fluctuations in Exports of Primary Producing Countries. 1966. 42 pp. Second printing, with minor editorial corrections, 1967. Published also in French and Spanish.

The Cuban Insurance Cases and the Articles of the Fund, by Joseph Gold. 1966. vii + 53 pp. Published also in Spanish. (Pamphlet Series, No. 8.)

Current Problems of Credit and Fiscal Policy: An Informal Discussion. Twelfth Annual Meeting of the Boards of Governors, International Bank for Reconstruction and Development, International Monetary Fund. 1957. 24 pp.

Direction of International Trade. Monthly, with annual issue. Vol. 1, No. 1 (Jan.–Mar. 1950)–Vol. 13, No. 1 (Jan. 1963); no issues published in 1961. Joint publication of Statistical Office of United Nations, International Monetary Fund, and International Bank for Reconstruction and Development, published by United Nations (New York). Annual issues, 1953 and 1955–60.

Direction of Trade: A Supplement to International Financial Statistics. Monthly, with annual issue. Jan.–Apr. 1964 to date. Published jointly by International Monetary Fund and International Bank for Reconstruction and Development.

Directory: Members, Quotas, Governors, Voting Power, Executive Board, Officers. Irregular. June 1947 to date. June 1947 and Feb. 3, 1948 issues published under title *Schedule of Quotas and Voting Power.*

Economic Development with Stability: A Report to the Government of India by a Mission of the International Monetary Fund. 1953. 77 pp.

Enlargement of Fund Resources Through Increases in Quotas: A Report by the Executive Directors to the Board of Governors of the International Monetary Fund. 1958. 28 pp.

Establishment of a Facility Based on Special Drawing Rights in the International Monetary Fund and Modifications in the Rules and Practices of the Fund: A Report by the Executive Directors to the Board of Governors Proposing Amendment of the Articles of Agreement. 1968. vi + 80 pp. (Cover title: Proposed Amendment of Articles of Agreement: New Facility Based on Special Drawing Rights, Changes in Fund Rules and Practices: A Report by the Executive Directors to the Board of Governors.) Published also in French and Spanish.

Finance and Development. Quarterly. Vol. 1, No. 1 (June 1964) to date. Vols. 1–4 carried subtitle The Fund and Bank Review. Published jointly by International Monetary Fund and International Bank for Reconstruction and Development. French and Spanish editions under titles Finances et développement and Finanzas y desarrollo, respectively. Annual issue, beginning 1966, of selected articles in Portuguese under title Finanças e desenvolvimento (Rio de Janeiro).

Financial Statement: Issued in Accordance with Article XII, Section 7 (a), of the Articles of Agreement. Quarterly. May 31, 1947 to date.

The Financial Structure of the Fund, by Rudolf Kroc. 1st ed., 1965. 2nd ed., 1967. iv + 41 pp. Published also in French and Spanish. (Pamphlet Series, No. 5.)

The First Ten Years of the International Monetary Fund. 1956. 49 pp.

The Fund Agreement in the Courts, by Joseph Gold. 1962. 159 pp. (Monograph Series, No. 2.)

The Fund and Non-Member States: Some Legal Effects, by Joseph Gold. 1966. vii + 55 pp. Published also in French and Spanish. (Pamphlet Series, No. 7.)

The Fund's Unknown Function, by Camille Gutt. 1949. 5 pp. Text of an article published in a slightly revised form and under a different title by United Nations World, December 1948.

Une grande espérance: conférence prononcée à l'Université Libre de Bruxelles, le 25 Avril 1947, by Camille Gutt. [1947]. 20 pp.

Information on Silver as Submitted by Member Countries. 1948. 58 pp. Tables and blank forms.

International Financial News Survey. Weekly. Vol. I, No. 1 (July 1, 1948) to date. Quarterly summary indexes covering first three quarters of year (1961 to date) and annual index. Supplements published irregularly.

International Financial Statistics. Monthly. Vol. I, No. 1 (Jan. 1948) to date. Trilingual edition (English, French, and Spanish) published also, Jan. 1966 to date. Annual supplements, 1961/62 to date.

An Introduction to IFS. n.d. 19 pp. Reprint of introductory articles from Jan.–May 1960 issues. Issued also in French (mimeographed).

Supplement on Money: Monthly Data and Seasonal Adjustments. 1964. 68 pp.

See also Direction of Trade.

IMF Institute. Program for 1965–66. 1965. 9 pp. In English and French. Program for 1966–1967. 1966. In English (11 pp.) and French (12 pp.). Program for 1967-1968. 1966. In English (18 pp.), French (18 pp.), and Spanish (19 pp.). Program for 1968–1969. 1967. In English (21 pp.), French (21 pp.), and Spanish (22 pp.). Program for 1969–1970. 1968. In English (25 pp.), French (25 pp.), and Spanish (25 pp.).

International Monetary Fund Activities in Relation to Latin America, 1946–1954; Prepared at the Request of the Inter-American Economic and Social Council for its Fourth Extraordinary Meeting, Rio de Janeiro, Brazil—1954. 1954. 17 pp.

The International Monetary Fund and International Law: An Introduction, by Joseph Gold. 1965. iv + 26 pp. Published also in French and Spanish. (Pamphlet Series, No. 4.)

The International Monetary Fund and Private Business Transactions: Some Legal Effects of the Articles of Agreement, by Joseph Gold. 1965. iv + 31 pp. Published also in French and Spanish. (Pamphlet Series, No. 3.)

The International Monetary Fund and the Trade Organization, Partners for International Trade: An Address Before the United Nations Conference on Trade and Employment, Havana, Cuba, November 21, 1947, by Camille Gutt. [1947]. 7 pp.

The International Monetary Fund: Its Form and Functions, by J. Marcus Fleming. 1964. v + 57 pp. (Pamphlet Series, No. 2.)

The International Monetary Fund: What It Is, What It Does. Leaflet. Irregular. Nov. 1948 to date. Variously published in English, French, German, Japanese, Portuguese, and Spanish. Nov. 1948–Aug. 1968 published under title *The International Monetary Fund: What It Is, What It Does, How It Works;* Sept. 1959 published under title *The International Monetary Fund: Purposes and Activities.*

International Monetary Problems, 1957–1963: Selected Speeches of Per Jacobsson. 1964. xiii + 368 pp. (Monograph Series, No. 3.)

International Reserves and Liquidity: A Study by the Staff of the International Monetary Fund. [1958]. 104 pp.

Interpretation by the Fund, by Joseph Gold. 1968. vii + 68 pp. Published also in French and Spanish. (Pamphlet Series, No. 11.)

Introduction to the Fund, by J. Keith Horsefield. 1st ed., 1964. 2nd ed., 1965. v + 36 pp. Published also in French, German, and Spanish. (Pamphlet Series, No. 1.)

Maintenance of the Gold Value of the Fund's Assets, by Joseph Gold. 1965. vii + 51 pp. Published also in French and Spanish. (Pamphlet Series, No. 6.)

The Practical Problem of Exchange Rates: An Address Before the Littauer School of Public Administration, Harvard University, Cambridge, Mass., February 13, 1948, by Camille Gutt. [1948]. 18 pp.

Report of the Executive Board of the International Monetary Fund on External Transactions in Gold at Premium Prices. 1950. 6 pp.

The Revival of Monetary Policy: Text and Charts of an Informal Discussion at the Eighth Annual Meeting of the Board of Governors of the International Monetary Fund, September 11, 1953. [1953]. 16 pp. Text issued also in Spanish (mimeographed).

Schedule of Par Values. Irregular. 1st issue, Dec. 18, 1946; 46th issue, Aug. 15, 1968.

Selected Decisions of the Executive Directors and Selected Documents. 3rd issue, 1965. 1st issue, 1962, and 2nd issue, 1963, issued under title *Selected Decisions of the Executive Directors.* 2nd and 3rd issues published also in French.

Selected Documents, Board of Governors Inaugural Meeting, Savannah, Ga., March 8 to 18, 1946. 1946. 60 pp.

Staff Papers. Three numbers constitute a volume. Vol. I, No. 1 (Feb. 1950)–Vol. VIII, No. 3 (Dec. 1961) issued twice a year. Beginning Vol. IX, No. 1 (Mar. 1962), issued three times a year. Index to Vols. I–X (1950–63).

Summary Proceedings of the . . . Annual Meeting of the Board of Governors. 1946 to date. Proceedings of the First Meeting published under title *First Annual Meeting* of the Board of Governors: Report of the Executive Directors and Summary Proceedings, September 27 to October 3, 1946.

Surveys of African Economies. Vol. I: Cameroon, Central African Republic, Chad, Congo (Brazzaville), and Gabon. 1968. xxiv + 365 pp. Published also in French under title Etudes générales sur les économies africaines. Tome 1: Cameroun, République Centrafricaine, Tchad, Congo (Brazzaville) et Gabon. 1968. xxiv + 393 pp.

Transactions of the International Monetary Fund. Leaflet. Aug. 1958, Aug. 1959, Apr. 1960, Sept. 1961, and Jan. 1962.

The World Payments Situation: A Series of Charts with Commentary Presented to the Seventh Annual Meeting of the Board of Governors of the International Monetary Fund at Mexico City, September 8, 1952. [1952]. 54 pp.